Reed's OCEAN NAVIGATOR

Third Edition

Edited by   JOHN F. KEMP, Ph.D., Extra Master, F.R.I.N.

Thomas Reed Publications Limited

LONDON : SUNDERLAND : GLASGOW

First Edition July 1968

Second Edition July 1970

Third Edition October 1977

Book designed by Ronald Ingles FSIA

Filmset in 'Univers' throughout

Made and printed in Great Britain

by Thomas Reed and Company Limited

Sunderland - London - Glasgow

ISBN O 900335 47 5

FOREWORD by

Mr. G. A. B. King

Managing Director

BP Tanker Company Ltd.

G. A. B. KING

TELEPHONE
01-920 6321

(SWITCHBOARD 01-920 8000)

BRITANNIC HOUSE,
MOOR LANE,
LONDON, EC2Y 9BU

It is a privilege to introduce a new edition of
Reed's Ocean Navigator.

Reed's is recognised as a standard reference book
on the bridge or in the cockpit. It is comprehensive,
accurate and sensibly laid out – a credit to the
editor and publisher and a blessing to the navigator
whether professional or amateur.

The Ocean Navigator's reputation is enhanced by this
excellent new edition.

G. A. B. King

SEA SENSE with Sperry

Shorter and simpler time on task equals profitable ship operation.

Ask Sperry about the short route to better ship and crew utilization with an emphasis on safety in operation, it's just plain sea sense.

- ☐ **INTEGRATED/SATELLITE NAVIGATION SYSTEMS**
- ☐ **COLLISION AVOIDANCE SYSTEMS**
- ☐ **STABILIZER SYSTEM** ☐ **RADARS**
- ☐ **GYROPILOTS** ☐ **GYROCOMPASSES**
- ☐ **STEERING SYSTEMS**
- ☐ **DOPPLER DOCKING**
- ☐ **DOPPLER SPEED LOGS** ☐ **OMEGA**

SPERRY
MARINE SYSTEMS
A WORLD OF EXPERIENCE
A DIVISION OF SPERRY RAND LTD

EUROPEAN HEADQUARTERS,
CORY HOUSE, THE RING, BRACKNELL, BERKSHIRE.
TEL : (0344) 51811. TELEX: 847044.

EDITOR'S PREFACE

Third Edition

The Ocean Navigator is intended as a working reference book for navigators of craft of all sizes, but particularly for those whose work takes them on international or offshore voyages.

In this Third Edition, the successful general format of previous editions has been retained but the opportunity has been taken to amend some of the content to keep abreast of changing requirements. Also, some items have been deleted and others added in order that the Ocean Navigator shall become complementary to, rather than overlapping with, Nautical Almanacs and particularly with Reed's Nautical Almanac. Unlike the Almanacs which are issued annually, the new edition of the Ocean Navigator is expected to remain current for several years.

Compared with the Second Edition, an important change has been the adoption of metric units throughout, although imperial units have, in most sections, also been included.

The short method sight reduction tables have been deleted and are replaced by instructions for using hand held calculators for the solution of both astronomical and great circle problems. Tables of natural sines, cosines and tangents, arranged so that all three functions of an angle can be obtained from a single entry, are included especially to facilitate the use of simple four function calculators for navigational applications.

The distance tables, previously limited to Australasia, have now been replaced by world-wide tables.

My thanks are due, not only to the many people who have helped with the preparation of this Third Edition, but also to all those associated with the previous editions whose work laid such excellent foundations.

John F. Kemp

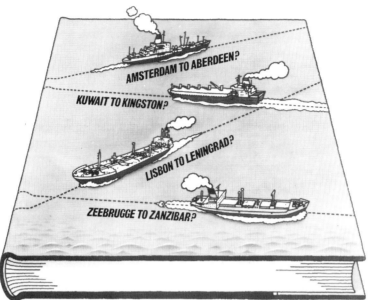

There's a great deal of mileage in this new publication.

This new completely revised set of marine distance tables from BP Tanker Company gives the distance in nautical miles between a range of ports throughout the world, including oil loading and discharging terminals.

It is one of the most comprehensive works of its kind ever published and is issued in two clearly printed and convenient volumes.

If you are concerned with freight forwarding, the planning of sea routes, marine insurance or sea transport problems of any kind, it is an indispensable and time-saving work of reference.

What the tables give you.

Divided into six main areas around the world, the distance tables give you over 640,000 separate calculations covering more than 1650 different ports and terminals.

The contents of the 2 books are as follows.

Volume 1

Table A – Contains distances between ports in the British Isles, English Channel, the Faroes, Iceland and Greenland.

Table B – Contains distances between ports on coasts of the North Sea, Skagerrak, Kattegat, Baltic Sea, White Sea, the Faroes, Iceland and Greenland.

Table C – Contains distances between ports in North Atlantic Ocean (including Greenland, Iceland and Norway from Aalesund to North Cape), South Atlantic Ocean and Gulf of Mexico.

Volume 2

Table D – Contains distances between ports in the Mediterranean Sea, Black Sea and Seas adjacent thereto.

Table E – Contains distances between ports in the Red Sea, Persian Gulf, Indian Ocean, Bay of Bengal, South and East Africa, the West and North Coast of Australia and parts of Indonesia.

Table F – Contains distances between ports in parts of Indonesia, India, China, Japan, Australia, New Zealand and North and South Pacific Oceans.

If you would like to purchase the new BPTC World-Wide Marine Distance Tables at the remarkably low cost of £40 per volume, simply complete and return the coupon with your cheque for the appropriate amount.

Contents

(for details refer to title page of each section)

Section A

A short glossary of navigational terms

ACTUAL TIME OF ARRIVAL (A.T.A.): The time at which a vessel arrives at a given point or destination.

ACTUAL TIME OF DEPARTURE (A.T.D.): The time at which a vessel leaves a given point or place.

ALTITUDE OF A HEAVENLY BODY:

True altitude: The angle at the centre of the celestial sphere between the direction of the body and the plane of the observers rational horizon.
Sextant Altitude: The uncorrected reading on the sextant.
Observed Altitude: Sextant altitude corrected for Index Error.
Apparent Altitude: Observed altitude corrected for Dip.

AMPLITUDE of a heavenly body: An arc of the rational horizon, or corresponding angle at the observer's zenith, contained between the prime vertical and the body when its centre is on the rational horizon. Amplitude is measured to the North or South (according to the body's declination) from the East Point when the body is rising, and the West Point when setting.

ANTIMERIDIAN: The meridian which is 180° of longitude from any particular meridian. A meridian and its antimeridian together form one great circle (e.g. The Greenwich Antimeridian is the Meridian of Longitude 180°).

APHELION: The point on a planet's orbit which is furthest from the Sun. The Earth is at Aphelion on about 1st-3rd July. The orbital point nearest to the Sun is called *Perihelion.*

APOGEE: The point on the Moon's orbit (or on the Sun's *apparent* orbit) which is furthest from the Earth.

APPARENT MOTION of a heavenly body is its movement as observed from the Earth. Thus the Sun appears to have a daily movement from east to west. (See Celestial Sphere.)

APPARENT TIME: See "Greenwich 'Apparent Time'" and "Local 'Apparent Time'".

APSIDES, Line of: The points on the orbit of a planet nearest to and furthest from the Sun are called "perihelion" and "aphelion" respectively. The Line of Apsides is the straight line joining perihelion and aphelion.

ARIES, First Point of: A point on the equinoctial where it is cut by the ecliptic and through which the Sun passes when changing its declination from South to North about 21st March. The diametrically opposite point in the heavens is called *the First Point of Libra*.

AUGMENTATION of the Moon's Semi-Diameter: Values of the Moon's Semi-Diameter given in the Nautical Almanac are calculated for an observer at the Earth's centre and are accurate only if the altitude is zero. Augmentation is an additive correction to the tabulated value of Semi-Diameter, and is maximum when the altitude is 90°.

AUTUMN: In the northern hemisphere, Autumn commences (astronomically) at the Autumnal Equinox (about 23rd September) and ends at the Winter Solstice (about 22nd December). In the southern hemisphere it begins at the Vernal Equinox (about 21st March) and ends at the Summer Solstice (about 21st June). The meteorological limits are not the same as the astronomical limits.

AZIMUTH OF A HEAVENLY BODY: An arc of the rational horizon, or corresponding angle at the observer's zenith, contained between the observer's meridian, and the vertical circle passing through the body.
Altitude-Azimuth: An azimuth determined by solution of the fundamental astronomical (PZX) triangle, given altitude, latitude and declination.
Time-Azimuth: An azimuth determined by solution of the fundamental astronomical (PZX) triangle, given hour angle, latitude and declination.

BAND OF POSITION: An area on either side of a position line of imperfect accuracy, within which the observer or a ship is considered to be located with a specified degree of confidence.

BELOW THE POLE: A term used to denote the position of a circumpolar body at lower meridian transit, that is when the altitude of the body is less than the altitude of the pole.

CABLE: One tenth of a nautical mile equal to approximately 185 metres or 608 feet.

CALENDAR, GREGORIAN: See "Year".

CALENDAR LINE: See "Date Line".

CELESTIAL EQUATOR: See "Equinoctial".

CELESTIAL MERIDIAN (or Hour Circle): A semi-great circle joining the celestial poles. The corresponding terrestial meridian lies in the same plane.

CELESTIAL SPHERE: (Commonly referred to as "The Heavens"). An imaginary, hollow, transparent sphere of infinite radius, and such magnitude that the Earth may be represented as a "point" at its centre. Its axis coincides with the Earth's axis. In general, for the purpose of astronomical navigation, it may be assumed that:
  (a) The terrestial graticule is projected from the common centre onto the celestial sphere.
  (b) The Earth remains stationary whilst the celestial sphere rotates on its axis from east to west.
  (c) All heavenly bodies, except the Earth, are located on the surface of the celestial sphere.
  (d) The stars are in fixed positions on this surface, but the Sun, Moon, and planets move amongst the stars on their own separate paths.

CIRCLE OF EQUIVALENT PROBABILITY (C.E.P.): A circle within which an observers position may be expected to lie on 50 per cent of occasions.

CIRCULAR POSITION LINE: The term generally refers to a position line obtained by vertical or horizontal sextant angle, range by range-finder, radar range, etc. (See also "Position Circle".)

CIRCUMPOLAR BODY: A heavenly body which is above the horizon at lower meridian passage, i.e., when its polar distance is less than the observer's latitude, or—when latitude and declination have the same name, and their sum exceeds 90°.

COCKED HAT: The triangle formed on a chart by three position lines which do not intersect at a point.

CO-LATITUDE: The arc of the observers meridian between his position and the nearer pole. (90°-Latitude)

COMPASS ERROR: The angle between the compass needle and the True Meridian. It is named East or West according to whichever side of the meridian the north end of the needle is deflected. Thus, using 360° compass notation, an easterly error is an additive correction when converting compass readings to True.

COMPOSITE TRACK: A modified great circle track having a limiting latitude beyond which navigation is considered unsafe. It is formed by the arcs of two great circles joined by an arc of the limiting parallel. The great circle arcs, one from departure point, and one to point of destination, are each tangential to the limiting parallel of latitude.

COMPRESSION (OR ELLIPTICITY) of the Earth is found by the formula $c = \dfrac{a-b}{a}$ where a = equatorial radius, and b = polar radius.

CONJUNCTION: Two heavenly bodies are in conjunction when they have the same sidereal hour angle. When the Sun lies between the Earth and a planet, the latter is in *superior conjunction.* When a planet lies between the Earth and the Sun it is in *inferior conjuction.*

CONSOL: A long range navigational aid. The Consol beacon transmits a radiation pattern of morse characters the count of which, when referred to either a consol chart or tables, provide the vessel with a position line. The signals can be received by any vessel equipped with a standard M.F. radio receiver. It is suitable for ocean navigation only.

CONVERGENCY of the meridians between two points is equal to the angular difference between the initial and final great circle courses between the points.
Half-Convergency is approximately equal to the angular difference between the rhumb line and the great circle bearings between two points. An approximate formula:
½ Convergency = ½ d.long × sin mean lat.
is used to convert great circle bearings into Mercatorial bearings, Half-Convergency being applied always towards the equator.

COURSE:
Compass Course: The angle between the compass needle and the ship's fore-and-aft line.
Magnetic Course: The angle between the magnetic meridian and the ship's fore-and-aft line.
True Course: The angle between the true meridian and the ship's fore-and-aft line.
Course Made Good: The angle between the true meridian and the ship's track over the ground.
Leeway Course (Wake Course): The angle between the true meridian and the ship's line of movement *through the water.*

CRITICAL TABLE: A table in which values for the required data are tabulated for limiting values of the entering argument, thus no interpolation is necessary.

CROSS BEARINGS: Two or more bearings used as intersecting position lines for fixing a ships position.

CULMINATION: of a heavenly body: Term used for meridian passage.

CURVE OF EQUAL BEARING (or Curve of Constant Bearing): A curve on the earth's surface joining all points from which the true great circle bearings of a given point are equal. The curve of equal bearing always lies on the equatorial side of the rhumb line bearing. Its direction differs from an observed bearing taken from the ship, by the value of the covergency.

CUSP: One of the horns of the crescent Moon or other heavenly body.

CUT: The angle of intersection of position lines constituting a fix.

DAY:
Apparent Solar Day: The time interval between two successive transits of the True Sun across the same meridian. It varies in length, due to the irregular speed of the Earth along its orbit, and averages 24 hours of mean solar time.
Mean Solar Day: The time interval between two successive transits of the Astronomical Mean Sun across the same meridian. Its length is equal to the average length of an apparent solar day, and is divided into 24 hours.
Civil Day: The civil day commences at midnight, when the Mean Sun makes its lower meridian passage, and ends at the following midnight, an interval of 24 mean solar hours. The first half, from midnight to noon, is counted up to 12 hours and denoted by Ante Meridiem (A.M.). The second half, from noon to midnight, is also counted up to 12 hours and denoted by Post Meridiem (P.M.).
Lunar Day: The time interval between two successive transits of the moon across the same meridian. It varies in length due to the irregular speed of the Moon along its orbit, and averages approximately 24h. 50m. of mean solar units.
Sidereal Day (Theoretical): The time interval between two successive transits of a fixed star across the same meridian. Its length is equal to 23h. 56m. 04.1s. of mean solar units. It is the duration of one 360° revolution of the Earth on its axis.
Sidereal Day (Practical): The time interval between two successive transits of the First Point of Aries across the same meridian. Its length is equal to 23h. 56m. 04.091s. of mean solar units— shorter than the theoretical sidereal day because of the westerly precession of the First Point of Aries.

DANGER ANGLE: The limiting horizontal angle (maximum or minimum) between two shore objects observed from the ship which confirms whether or not the vessel is at a safe distance from an off-lying danger; or a limiting vertical sextant angle of an object of known height achieves the same purpose.

DATE LINE (or Calendar Line): The 180th meridian, distorted so that islands belonging to any one group will be on the same side of the line. When crossing the date line, a vessel on a westerly course advances the date by one day, but a vessel on an easterly course puts the date back a day.

DATUM: A point, plane, level, line or value of reference from which any quantity is measured.

DECCA: An electronic position-fixing system whereby pairs of stations ashore transmit continuous synchronised radio waves. The ship's equipment measures the phase difference between the signals from a pair of stations. The reading is then referred to a navigational chart, which is overprinted with a family of hyperbolae. Each lattice line on the chart is numbered with its appropriate phase difference; thus simultaneous readings from two pairs of stations provide the ship with a fix.

DECLINATION of a heavenly body: An arc of the body's celestial meridian, or corresponding angle at the Earth's centre, contained between the equinoctial and the body. It is measured (0° to 90°) north or south from the equinoctial.

DEPARTURE between two points on the Earth's surface is their distance apart in nautical miles measured in an east-west direction.

DEPRESSED POLE: The celestial pole which is below the observer's rational horizon. It is in the hemisphere opposite to the observer's latitude.

DIAMOND OF ERROR: A diamond-shaped area, formed by the intersection of two bands of position, within which a ship is considered to be located at a specified level of probability.

DIFFERENCE OF LATITUDE between two places: An arc of a meridian, or corresponding angle at the Earth's centre, contained between the parallels of latitude passing through the places.

DIFFERENCE OF LONGITUDE between two places: The smaller arc of the equator, or corresponding angle at the pole contained between the meridians passing through the places.

DIFFERENCE OF MERIDIONAL PARTS (Meridional Difference of Latitude) between two parallels of latitude on a Mercator chart is the chart length of any meridian contained between those parallels, and is expressed in units of one minute of longitude from the longitude scale on the chart.

DIP of the horizon: The vertical angle at the observer's eye between the visible horizon and the sensible horizon. Its value depends on the height of eye above sea level, and is a subtractive correction from the observed altitude of a heavenly body when the sea horizon is used as a reference.

DIRECTIONAL BEACON: A beacon which beams its signal in one or more prescribed directions. Its main use in marine navigation is to provide an approach or leading line to an anchorage or harbour in poor visibility.

DOG LEG: An indirect approach to a destination point made by two true courses or tracks.

DRIFT of current: The distance which a vessel has been carried by current alone in a given time.

DUTCHMAN'S LOG: A piece of wood or other buoyant object thrown overboard to determine a vessel's speed. The passage of the object is timed between two points of known distance apart on the ship, and the speed calculated from these measurements.

ECLIPSE:
Solar Eclipse: Occurs when the Moon intervenes between the Earth and the Sun. A *total eclipse* of the Sun takes place within the area covered by the Moon's shadow. For some distance all round this area a *partial eclipse* is experienced. An *annular eclipse* occurs when the distance between the Earth and Moon is such that the Moon's umbra does not reach the Earth; in this case the apparent diameter of the Sun is greater than that of the Moon which, in the small central area of the eclipse, appears as a black disc surrounded by an annular ring of direct light from the Sun.
Lunar Eclipse: Occurs when the Moon passes through the Earth's umbra or penumbra, the latter is the partial shadow surrounding the umbra. The conditions necessary for an umbral eclipse are that the Moon must be on the Sun's antimeridian, and its declination must be the same value but opposite in name to that of the Sun.

ECLIPTIC: A great circle on the celestial sphere representing the True Sun's apparent yearly path over the surface of the celestial sphere. Its plane is in the same plane as the Earth's orbit and is inclined at approximately 23½° to the plane of the equinoctial.

ELEVATED POLE: See "Poles".

ELLIPTICITY: See "Compression".

ELONGATION of a planet is the angle at the Earth's centre between the planet and the Sun. It is named easterly or westerly according to whether the planet lies to the east or west of the Sun at the time of upper meridian passage. The maximum elongation of Venus is approximately 47°.

EPHEMERIS: A table giving the predicted positions of heavenly bodies at regular intervals.

EQUATION OF TIME: The excess of mean time over apparent time, i.e.
L.H.A. Mean Sun — L.H.A. True Sun = Eqn. T. Note that when L.H.A.T.S. is greater than L.H.A.M.S., the Equation of Time is a negative quantity.

EQUINOCTIAL (or Celestial Equator): A great circle on the celestial sphere whose plane is in the same plane as the terrestial equator and at 90° to the celestial axis.

EQUINOX:
Spring or Vernal Equinox: The time of the year (about 21st March) when the Apparent Sun crosses the equinoctial on its passage from south to north.

Autumnal Equinox: The time of the year (about 23rd September) when the Apparent Sun crosses the equinoctial on its passage from north to south.

EQUINOCTIAL POINTS: The two points at which the equinoctial and the ecliptic intersect. Also called the *equinoxes.* See "First Point of Aries" and "First Point of Libra".

ESTIMATED TIME OF ARRIVAL (E.T.A.): The predicted time of reaching a particular point or destination.

ESTIMATED TIME OF DEPARTURE (E.T.D.): The predicted time of leaving a particular point or place.

EX-MERIDIAN ALTITUDE: An altitude of a celestial body near the meridian, to which a correction can be added to determine the altitude at meridian passage. The latitude obtained from such an altitude is the latitude at the *time of observation.*

FIRST POINT OF ARIES: See "Aries".

FIRST POINT OF LIBRA: See "Libra".

FIX: A position determined by observation—visual, radio, celestial, radar, loran, etc. The term "observed position" is often used instead, particularly when the position is determined by celestial observations.

FIRST QUARTER: See "Moon's Phases".

FULL MOON: See "Moon's Phases".

GEOGRAPHICAL POSITION OF A HEAVENLY BODY: A point on the earth's surface vertically beneath the body.
Its latitude is equal to and named the same as the body's declination; its longitude (if measured, 0° to 360°, westwards from the Greenwich meridian) is equal to the Greenwich Hour Angle of the body. See "Sub-Point".

GIBBOUS MOON: Description when the visible portion is more than half a disc. It occurs between First Quarter and Full Moon, and again between Full Moon and Last Quarter.

GNOMONIC CHART: A chart on the gnomonic projection. Used principally for great circle sailing, but also for charts having a natural scale greater than 1:50,000 and some polar charts. A harbour plan is a form of gnomonic chart, the very small area of the Earth covered by the plan is assumed to be flat.

GNOMONIC PROJECTION: *Principle* — A source of light at the centre of a sphere (reduced to scale) projects the graticule onto a plane surface, which is placed tangential to the sphere at a point in the centre of the area to be charted. *Navigational properties*—(a) It is not orthomorphic; (b) Great circles appear as straight lines on the chart; (c) Rhumb lines appear as curves; (d) Angles are correctly represented *only* at the point of tangency.

GRATICULE: The network of lines formed by meridians and parallels on a globe, chart or map.

GREAT CIRCLE: A circle on the surface of a sphere, whose plane passes through the centre and divides the sphere into two halves.

GREAT CIRCLE DISTANCE: The shortest distance between two points on the Earth's surface. The length of the shorter great circle arc joining the points, usually expressed in nautical miles.

GREENWICH APPARENT TIME: An arc of the equinoctial, or corresponding angle at the celestial pole, contained between the Greenwich anti-meridian and the meridian of the True Sun. It is measured (0 to 24 hours) westwards from the Greenwich antimeridian.

GREENWICH MEAN TIME: An arc of the equinoctial, or corresponding angle at the celestial pole, contained between the Greenwich Anti-meridian and the meridian of the Mean Sun. It is measured (0 to 24 hours) westwards from the Greenwich Antimeridian.

GREENWICH SIDEREAL TIME: The Right Ascension of the Greenwich meridian or the Greenwich Hour Angle of Aries expressed in time units.

GYRO COMPASS: An instrument which seeks the direction of true north by sensing the rotation of the Earth.

HACHURING: A method of representing hills and slope of the ground on a map or chart, by shading with short disconnected lines *(hachures)* radiating from peaks and high ground in the direction of the slopes.

HARVEST MOON: The Full Moon nearest the Autumnal Equinox (about 23rd September).

HEADING: The direction in which a vessel is pointing. The term concerns only the fore-and-aft line of the vessel, and is unrelated to movement through the water or over the sea bed. Heading is designated as *Compass, Magnetic* or *True,* according to the meridian of reference.

HORIZON:
Rational Horizon (Celestial Horizon)—A great circle on the celestial sphere, whose plane is parallel to the plane of the sensible horizon.
Sensible Horizon—The horizontal plane through the observer's eye.
Visible Horizon (Sea Horizon)—A small circle on the Earth's surface which bounds the observer's view at sea.

HOUR ANGLE OF A HEAVENLY BODY:
Easterly Hour Angle—An arc of the equinoctial or corresponding angle at the celestial pole, contained between the observer's meridian and the meridian of the body. It is measured (0° to 360°) *eastwards* from the observer's meridian.
Greenwich Hour Angle—An arc of the equinoctial, or corresponding angle at the celestial pole, contained between the Greenwich meridian and the meridian of the body. It is measured (0° to 360°) *westwards* from the Greenwich meridian.
Local Hour Angle—An arc of the equinoctial, or corresponding angle at the celestial pole, contained between the observer's meridian and the meridian of the body. It is measured (0° to 360°) *westwards* from the observer's meridian.
Sidereal Hour Angle—An arc of the equinoctial, or corresponding angle at the celestial pole, contained between the meridian of Aries and the meridian of the body. It is measured (0° to 360°) *westwards* from the meridian of Aries.
Westerly Hour Angle—See "Local Hour Angle".

HOUR CIRCLE: See "Celestial Meridian".

HYPERBOLA: A curve, all points on which have a constant difference in distance from two fixed points called foci.

HYPERBOLIC NAVIGATION: Navigation by the use of hyperbolic position lines. The distance difference which defines a hyperbolic position line is generally found either by observing the phase difference between two radio signals radiated coherently from a pair of stations or by observing the time difference between the arrival of radio pulses emitted from such a pair of stations.

INCREMENT: An increase in a variable quantity.

INFERIOR PLANETS: Planets whose orbits are smaller than that of the Earth—Mercury and Venus.

INFERIOR CONJUNCTION: The conjunction of an inferior planet when it is between the Earth and the Sun. When the Sun lies between the planet and the Earth, the conjunction is designated *superior.*

INTEGER: A whole number.

INTERCARDINAL POINT: Any of the four compass points which lie midway between two cardinal points — NE, SE, SW and NW.

INTERCEPT: The difference in minutes of arc between the True and Computed Altitudes of a heavenly body. It is named "Towards" when the True Altitude is the greater of the two, and "Away" when it is the lesser. The **Intercept Terminal Point** is the point, at the end of the plotted intercept, through which the astronomical position line is drawn.

INERTIAL NAVIGATION: An automatic technique giving a continuous presentation of a ship's position and attitude based on the maintenance of a directional datum and the measurement of the accelerations of the craft within that datum.

ISOGONIC LINE (Isogonal): A line on a chart joining all points of equal magnetic variation.

KEPLER'S LAWS OF PLANETARY MOTION: (1) The orbits of planets are ellipses with the Sun at a common focus. (2) As a planet travels along its orbit, the line joining the centre of the planet to the centre of the Sun *(radius vector)* sweeps over equal areas in equal intervals of time. (3) The square of the time taken by a planet to complete one orbit is proportional to the cube of the major semi-axis.
Note: It follows from Laws (1) and (2) that the orbital speed of a planet is not constant, being maximum at perihelion and minimum at aphelion.

LAND MILE: See "Mile".

LAST QUARTER: See "Moon's Phases".

LATITUDE:
The Astronomical Latitude of a point is the angle between the vertical at that point and the plane of the equator. This is the latitude measured by astronomical observations. An observer's astronomical latitude is equal to the declination of his zenith and has the same value as the true altitude of the elevated pole.
The Geocentric Latitude of a point is the angle at the centre of the earth subtended by an arc of the meridian between the point and the equator. This latitude is not of direct use to navigators.
Celestial Latitude of a heavenly body: The angular distance north or south of the ecliptic, measured along the great circle passing through the body and the poles of the ecliptic. It is of interest to astronomers rather than navigators.

LATTICE: A network of lines on a chart formed by the intersection of two families of hyperbolae as, for example, on a Loran, Decca or Consol chart.

LEADING LINE: A straight line on a chart or harbour plan drawn through two leading marks which, when kept in transit, ensure the ship is in the proper channel or clear of danger.

LEADING MARKS: Natural or artificial shore objects which, when kept in transit, provide the ship with a leading line.

LEEWAY: The angle between the ship's fore-and-aft line and her line of movement through the water.

LIBRA, First Point of: A point on the equinoctial where it is cut by the ecliptic and through which the Sun passes when changing its declination from North to South, about 23rd September. The diametrically opposite point in the heavens is called the *First Point of Aries.*

LIBRATION, Moon's:
(1) The Moon's axis is inclined to the plane of its orbit by about 83½°, so that each lunar pole is alternatively visible and invisible as it is inclined towards or away from the Earth, respectively. This apparent oscillation is called *libration in latitude.* (2) The Moon rotates on its axis at a uniform rate. One 360° rotation takes exactly the same time as one complete orbit, thus the same side of the Moon is always turned towards the Earth, but because the orbital speed varies, a little more than a complete hemisphere is seen during the whole month. This apparent side to side oscillation is called *libration in longitude.*

LOCAL APPARENT TIME (Ship's Apparent Time): An arc of the equinoctial, or corresponding angle at the celestial pole, contained between the observer's antimeridian and the meridian of the True Sun. It is measured (0 to 24 hours) *westwards* from the observer's antimeridian.

LOCAL MEAN TIME (Ship's Mean Time): An arc of the equinoctial, or corresponding angle at the celestial pole, contained between the observer's antimeridian and the meridian of the Mean Sun. It is measured (0 to 24 hours) *westwards* from the observer's antimeridian.

LOCAL SIDEREAL TIME (Sidereal Time): The Local Hour Angle of Aries expressed in time units. An arc of the equinoctial, or corresponding angle at the celestial pole, contained between the observer's meridian and the meridian of Aries. It is measured (0 to 24 hours) *westwards* from the observer's meridian.

LONGITUDE OF A PLACE: An arc of the equator, or corresponding angle at the pole, contained between the Prime Meridian and the meridian of the place. It is measured (0° to 180°) east or west from the Prime Meridian.

LOOM of a light: The diffused glow from a light which is below the horizon.

LOOMING: Term used when land or objects are seen indistinctly through poor visibility, darkness or distance.

LORAN (LOng **R**ange **A**id to **N**avigation):
Loran A: *Principle*—A "pair" of shore stations consisting of Master and Slave, transmit synchronised radio pulses. The ship's equipment measures the time interval between reception of the Master and Slave pulses by means of a cathode ray tube. The reading is then referred to a navigational chart which is over-printed with a family of hyperbolae, each lattice line being numbered with its appropriate time difference. Thus the hyperbola on which the ship lies constitutes a position line. Two or more "pairs" of stations are required for a fix.
Loran C: A development of the Loran A principle but operating on a lower frequency to give longer range and employing cycle matching within the pulses to give increased accuracy.

LOWER TRANSIT: (Lower Meridian Passage). The transit of the antimeridian by a heavenly body.

LOXODROME: (Rhumb Line). A curved line on the Earth's surface cutting all meridians at the same angle. It is represented by a straight line on a Mercator Chart.

LUMINOUS VISIBILITY of a light: The maximum range of visibility when the line of sight is not broken by the curvature of the Earth.

LUNATION OR LUNAR MONTH *(Synodic Period* or *Synodical Month)*: The time interval between two successive New Moons, i.e. One revolution of the Moon with reference to the Sun. It takes about 29½ days.

MAGNETIC DIP at any place is the angle in the vertical plane between the horizontal and the line taken up by a freely suspended magnetic needle when influenced only by the Earth's magnetic force. It is designated plus or minus according to whether the north end of the needle is depressed or elevated, respectively.

MAGNETIC EQUATOR (Aclinic Line): A line on the Earth's surface joining all points where the magnetic dip is zero, and hence the Earth's total magnetic force is horizontal.

MAGNETIC MERIDIAN: The horizontal line taken up by a compass needle when under the influence of the Earth's magnetic field only.

MAGNETIC POLES: Two places on the Earth's surface where magnetic dip is 90°. The North magnetic pole is located at about 74° N latitude and 101° W longitude; and the South magnetic pole at about 67° S latitude and 143° E longitude; but they are not fixed, and their future positions have not been accurately predicted.

MAGNETIC VARIATION at any place is the angle in the horizontal plane between the True and Magnetic meridians. It is named *East* when Magnetic North lies to the east of True North, and *West* when Magnetic North is to the west of True North.

MAGNITUDE: See "Stellar Magnitudes".

MANTISSA: The decimal part of a logarithm; that part which lies to the left of the decimal point is called the *characteristic*.

MEAN LATITUDE: between two places is the arithmetic mean of their latitudes, and is exactly midway between the parallels of latitude passing through the places. This is not the same as middle-latitude.

MEAN SUN: See "Sun".

MEAN TIME: See "Local Mean Time" and "Greenwich Mean Time".

MEASURED MILE: Two pairs of transit beacons set up on shore, so that the transit lines are parallel to one another and separated by a known distance, usually one nautical mile. Thus a vessel on a course at 90° to the transit lines can determine her speed by timing the distance run between them with a stop watch.

MERIDIAN ALTITUDE: The altitude of a heavenly body at its meridian transit.

MERIDIAN OF LONGITUDE: Half a great circle on the Earth's surface joining the poles.

MERIDIONAL PARTS for any latitude: The chart length of any meridian on a Mercator chart, contained between the equator and the given latitude parallel, expressed in units of one minute of longitude from the longitude scale of that chart.

MIDDLE LATITUDE between two places is an intermediate parallel such that, for a vessel following a rhumbline track between the two places, the departure is equal to the product of the difference of longitude and the cosine of the middle latitude. It is obtained by applying a correction to the mean latitude.

MILE:
Geographical Mile: The length of an arc of the equator, subtending an angle of one minute (1') at the Earth's centre. (Approx. 1855 metres or 6087 feet.)
Nautical Mile: The length of an arc of a meridian subtending an angle of one minute (1') at the centre of curvature of the place. Due to the oblateness of the Earth, its length varies from approximately 1843 metres (6046 feet) at the equator to 1862 metres (6108 feet) at the poles.
International Nautical Mile: In order to provide a convenient standard for practical purposes, a length of 1852 metres (approx. 1876 feet) is adopted. This is the mean length of a nautical mile, rounded off to the nearest metre.
Statute Mile (Land mile): Decreed as 5280 feet by statute of Queen Elizabeth I. It is equivalent to approximately 1609 metres.

MILKY WAY: Seen at night as a broad band of misty light stretching right across the heavens, roughly in a great circle. It consists of many irregularly spaced star clouds.

MOON'S AGE: The number of mean solar days which have elapsed since the last New Moon.

MOON'S PHASES: Changes in the appearance of the Moon's disc due to variations in its position with reference to the Earth and Sun.
New Moon occurs when the Moon and Sun are on the same meridian, i.e. *in conjunction*. It is not visible from the Earth because the hemisphere nearest to the Earth is in darkness.
First Quarter occurs about seven days after New Moon. The Moon in then about 90° east of the Sun (East Quadrature) and its upper meridian passage takes place at about 1800 hours, when it is visible as a half-disc with its bow towards the west.
Full Moon occurs when the Moon is on the Sun's antimeridian, i.e. *in opposition,* about 15 days after New Moon. Upper meridian passage takes place at about midnight, and the Moon is then seen as a complete disc.
Last Quarter occurs about 22 days after New Moon. The Moon is then about 90° west of the Sun (West Quadrature) and its upper meridian passage takes place at about 0600 hours, when it is visible as a half-disc with its bow towards the east.

NADIR: The point on the celestial sphere vertically below the observer, and diametrically opposite to his zenith.

NAUTICAL MILE: see "Mile".

NEW MOON: See "Moon's Phases".

NODES (Nodal Points): The Moon's Nodes are two points on the ecliptic where it is cut by the Moon's apparent path on the celestial sphere. They move westwards along the ecliptic, completing one cycle in about 18½ years.
Ascending Node: The point on the ecliptic through which the Moon passes on its passage from south to north.
Descending Node: The point on the ecliptic through which the Moon passes on its passage from north to south.

NOON CONSTANT: A predetermined value to be added algebraically to an observed meridian altitude to obtain the latitude.

NORMAL (Normal line): Perpendicular.

NUTATION: Small variations in the precessional movement of the equinoxes due to the gravitational effect of the Moon.

OBLIQUITY OF THE ECLIPTIC: The angle at which the plane of the ecliptic is inclined to the plane of the equinoctial. Its value, approximately 23° 27′, is equal to the Sun's maximum declination.

OBSERVER'S MERIDIAN: The term refers, not only to the observer's terrestrial meridian, but also to the observer's celestial meridian.
Observer's Celestial Meridian: The vertical circle which passes through the North and South Points of the rational horizon. Its plane is in the same plane as the observer's terrestrial meridian.

OCCULTATION: The cutting-off from view of a heavenly body by another heavenly body passing between it and the Earth. When the Sun is occulted by the Moon the term "solar eclipse" is used.

OMEGA: A long range radio position fixing system using very low frequency (VLF) transmissions. Hyperbolic position lines are defined by phase comparison of signals from pairs of stations.

OMNIDIRECTIONAL: In all directions.

OPPOSITION: A heavenly body is in opposition to the Sun when their Sidereal Hour Angles differ by 180°.

ORTHODROME: Great circle.

ORTHOMORPHIC (Conformal): An orthomorphic chart projection is one in which the scale at any point on the chart is the same in all directions over small distances, and the parallel and meridian intersect at 90°. On such a chart— (a) Angles are correctly represented; (b) Scale of distance is correctly represented, irrespective of whether or not the scale is constant; (c) Shapes of *small* areas correctly represented. A Mercator chart is orthomorphic, whereas a gnomonic chart is not.

PARALLEL OF DECLINATION: A small circle on the celestial sphere, whose plane is parallel to the plane of the equinoctial.

PARALLEL OF LATITUDE: A small circle on the Earth's surface, whose plane is parallel to the plane of the equator.

PARALLAX:
Parallax-in-Altitude: The angle at the centre of a heavenly body subtended by the observer and the Earth's centre when the body is in altitude. It is equal in value to the altitude above the rational horizon minus the altitude above the sensible horizon.

Horizontal Parallax: The angle at the centre of a heavenly body subtended by the observer and the Earth's centre when the body is on the sensible horizon. It is the maximum value of parallax for any given date and time.

PERIGEE: The point on the Moon's orbit (or the Sun's apparent orbit) nearest to the Earth.

PERIHELION: The point on a planet's orbit nearest to the Sun.

PENUMBRA: See "Eclipse".

PERSONAL ERROR: A systematic error in instrumental observations due to the observer's characteristics.

PHASES OF THE MOON: See "Moon's Phases".

POLAR DISTANCE of a heavenly body: An arc of the celestial meridian passing through the body or corresponding angle at the Earth's centre, contained between the *elevated* pole and the body. Its value is (90° ± declination), minus when the latitude and declination have the same name.

POLES:
Poles of a Great Circle: Two points on the surface of the sphere relevant to that great circle, and which are 90° from all points on that great circle.
Celestial Poles: (The poles of the equinoctial). Two points on the celestial sphere which are the projections of the Earth's axis.
Poles of the Ecliptic: Two points on the celestial sphere through which all great circles which are secondary to the ecliptic must pass.
Elevated Pole: The celestial pole which is nearest to the observer's zenith.
Depressed Pole: The celestial pole which is nearest to the observer's nadir.
Terrestrial Poles: The extremities of the Earth's axis.

POSITION:
Assumed Position: The position at which an observer is assumed to be for purposes of computation.
Chosen Position: See "Assumed Position".
Dead Reckoning (D.R.) Position: A position based on speed, elapsed time and direction from a previously known position.
Observed Position: A position obtained by observations. The term applies more often to a position determined by celestial observations, whereas "fix" is more generally used for observations of terrestrial objects—radio fix, radar fix, etc.

POSITION CIRCLE: A small circle on the Earth's surface passing through the observer's position. Its centre is the geographical position of a heavenly body, and its radius is equal to the body's true zenith distance. An azimuth of the geographical position determines on which *part* of the position circle the observer is located.

PRECESSION OF THE EQUINOXES: The westerly movement of the equinoctial points along the ecliptic. It averages approximately 50 seconds of arc per year.

PRECOMPUTED ALTITUDE: The altitude of a heavenly body computed for a time ahead at which it is intended to make the observation, and with corrections to sextant altitude applied in reverse. When the observation is made, the intercept is found immediately by comparison with the sextant altitude. A correction is made to the precomputed altitude whenever the observation is not made at the exact time used for the calculation.

PRIME MERIDIAN: The meridian of Greenwich, which is the datum meridian from which longitude is measured.

PRIME VERTICAL: The vertical circle which passes through the East and West Points of the rational horizon. A heavenly body, when on the prime vertical, has a true bearing of 090° or 270°.

QUADRANTAL ERROR: An error in a loop or goniometer reading caused by interaction between the D/F aerial and vertical metal in the ship. It normally attains maximum value when the transmitter lies in a direction 45° from the fore-and-aft line, and changes its sign in each quadrant.

QUADRATURE: See "Moon's Phases".

RADAR:
Primary Radar: The use of radio waves reflected to obtain the range and bearing of distant objects.
Secondary Radar: The use of radio waves automatically retransmitted to gain information, such as identity, as well as the range and bearing of distant ships or navigation marks.

RACON (Responder Beacon): A radar beacon which transmits a pulse whenever it is triggered by a ship's radar pulse. The racon's signal appears on the ship's radar screen, and provides range, bearing and identification.

RADIOBEACON: A radio transmitter whose characteristic signals enable any vessel equipped with a radio direction finder to obtain radio bearings. See also "Directional Beacon".

RAMARK: A radar beacon which transmits its signal quite independently of a ship's radar. The ramark's signal shows on the ship's radar screen, and provides bearing and identification, but no range.

RECIPROCAL BEARING: Reverse bearing.

REDUCTION TO THE MERIDIAN: The process of applying a correction (called the *reduction*) to an ex-meridian altitude to obtain the altitude at meridian passage.

REDUCTION OF MOON'S HORIZONTAL PARALLAX: The latitude correction to be applied to the tabulated value of horizontal parallax. Values for H.P. given in the Nautical Almanac are calculated for an observer on the equator. In any other latitude the Earth's radius is reduced, and the H.P. is less than the tabulated value.

REDUCTION TABLES: Tables used for "reduction of sights". Generally refers to tables used for computation of altitude and azimuth.

REFRACTION: The bending of a light ray when passing through media of different densities. A light ray from a star, when entering the Earth's atmosphere, is refracted towards the vertical, hence the apparent altitude of a heavenly body is greater than the true altitude except when it is 90°, in which case the value of refraction is zero.

RHUMB LINE: See "Loxodrome".

RIGHT ASCENSION of a heavenly body: an arc of the equinoctial, or corresponding angle at the celestial pole, contained between the meridian of Aries and the meridian of the body. It is measured (0° to 360°) eastwards from the meridian of Aries.

SATELLITE: A natural or artificial body revolving round a planet, as the Moon orbiting the Earth.

SECONDARY GREAT CIRCLE: Any great circle whose plane is at right angles to the plane of the primary great circle, e.g., terrestrial meridians are secondary great circles to the equator.

SEMI-DIAMETER of a heavenly body is the angle at the observer subtended by the body's centre and its upper or lower limb.

SENSIBLE HORIZON: See "Horizon".

SET of Current: The direction *towards* which the current flows.

SHIP'S APPARENT TIME (Apparent Time at Ship): See "Local Apparent Time".

SHIP'S MEAN TIME (Mean Time at Ship): See "Local Mean Time".

SIDEREAL DAY: See "Day".

SIDEREAL HOUR ANGLE: See "Hour Angle".

SIDEREAL MONTH: The average time taken by the

Moon to complete one orbit with reference to a star, a period of approximately $27\frac{1}{3}$ Mean Solar Days.

SIDEREAL TIME: The Local Hour Angle of Aries expressed in time units. An arc of the equinoctial, or corresponding angle at the celestial pole, contained between the observer's meridian and the meridian of the First Point of Aries. It is measured (0 to 24 hours) westwards from the observer's meridian. 24 hours of Sidereal Time is equivalent to 23h. 56m. 04.091s. of Mean Solar Time.

SIX-HOUR CIRCLE: The celestial meridian which passes through the East and West points of the rational horizon. Its plane is at 90° to the plane of the observer's meridian. The Apparent Sun is located on the six-hour circle at Local Apparent Time 0600 hours and 1800 hours.

SMALL CIRCLE: Any circle on the surface of a sphere, whose plane does not pass through the centre of that sphere.

SOLAR ECLIPSE: See "Eclipse".

SOLSTICE:
Summer Solstice: The time of the year at which the Apparent Sun attains its maximum northerly declination, about 21st June.
Winter Solstice: The time of the year at which the Apparent Sun attains its maximum southerly declination, about 22nd December.

SOLSTITIAL POINTS (Also called Solstices): Two points on the ecliptic at which the Apparent Sun attains its maximum declination.

SPHERE: A solid body bounded by a surface every part of which is equidistant from a point within called the centre.

SPHEROID: A solid body the shape of which is described by the revolution of an ellipse about its axis. Revolution about the minor axis describes the shape of an *oblate spheroid.*

SPRING: In the northern hemisphere, spring commences (astronomically) at the Spring Equinox (about 21st March) and ends at the Summer Solstice (about 21st June). In the southern hemisphere it begins at the Autumn Equinox (about 23rd September) and ends at the Winter Solstice (about 22nd December). The meteorological limits are different to the astronomical limits.

STATUTE MILE: See "Mile".

STELLAR MAGNITUDE: A measure of the relative brightness of a heavenly body. A sixth-magnitude star is only just visible to the naked eye, and a star of the first magnitude is one hundred times brighter than a sixth-magnitude star. On this basis, a second-magnitude star is one hundred times brighter than a seventh-magnitude star, and a star of magnitude 0 is one hundred times brighter than a fifth-magnitude star; thus the smaller (algebraically) the number

indicating magnitude the brighter the body. A star of magnitude —1.0 is one hundred times brighter than a star of magnitude 4.0. **Sirius** is the brightest star in the heavens, and has a magnitude of —1.6. In practice, the term "first magnitude" star, or stars of the "first magnitude" generally refer to those stars brighter than magnitude 1.0.

SUB-LUNAR POINT: The geographical position of the Moon.

SUB-SOLAR POINT: The geographical position of the Sun.

SUB-STELLAR POINT: The geographical position of a star.

SUMMER: In the northern hemisphere summer commences (astronomically) at the Summer Solstice (about 21st June) and ends at the Autumn Equinox (about 23rd September). In the southern hemisphere it begins at the Winter Solstice (about 22nd December) and ends at the Spring Equinox (about 21st March). The meteorological limits are not the same as the astronomical limits.

SUMMER SOLSTICE: See "Solstice".

SUN:
Apparent Sun; The True Sun as it appears to revolve round the Earth (apparent motion). It is assumed to travel along the ecliptic at an irregular speed.
Astronomical Mean Sun (usually referred to as "Mean Sun"): An imaginary Sun assumed to travel eastwards along the *equinoctial* at a constant speed and to complete one revolution round the Earth in the same time as that taken by the Apparent Sun. The Astronomical Mean Sun and the Dynamical Mean Sun are on the same meridian only at the times of the equinoxes and solstices.
The Dynamical Mean Sun: An imaginary Sun which is assumed to travel eastwards along the *ecliptic* at a constant speed, and to complete one revolution round the Earth in the same time as that taken by the Apparent Sun. The Dynamical Mean Sun and the Apparent Sun coincide at Perigee and Apogee.
True Sun: The heavenly body around which the Earth (and other planets in the solar system) orbit.

SUNRISE AND SUNSET:
Theoretical Sunrise and Sunset: The instant when the Sun's centre is on the rational horizon. Due to the effect of refraction, the Sun's lower limb would appear to be about 0° 18' above the visible horizon, assuming the observer's eye to be at sea level.
Visible Sunrise and Sunset: The instant when the true depression of the Sun's centre is 0° 50' below the rational horizon. It is the optical phenomena when the Sun's upper limb makes contact with the visible horizon, assuming the observer's eye to be at sea level. Thus, in practice, the upper limb is *seen* on the sea horizon. The times of visible sunrise and sunset are tabulated in the Nautical Almanac.
Note: Amplitude tables are computed with a true zenith distance of 90°. Amplitude observations for

determination of compass error, therefore, should be made at *theoretical* sunrise or sunset, and not at the instant of the visible phenomena.

SUPERIOR CONJUNCTION: See "Conjunction".

SUPERIOR PLANETS: Planets whose orbits are larger than that of the Earth.

SUPERIOR TRANSIT: Upper meridian passage.

SYNODICAL MONTH: See "Lunation".

TERRESTRIAL: Pertaining to the Earth.

TRANSIT (U.S. Navy Satellite System): A world wide position fixing system based on the measurement of the Doppler shift in radio signals from low orbit artificial satellites.

TROPICAL YEAR: See "Year".

TRUE MERIDIAN: The meridian passing through the observer and the Earth's geographical poles.

TWILIGHT: The periods of the day when, although the Sun is below the visible horizon, the observer does not experience complete darkness, because indirect light from the Sun is received through reflection and scattering by the upper atmosphere.
Civil Twilight begins or ends when the Sun's centre is 6° below the rational horizon, at which time the sea horizon is clear, the brightest stars are visible, and there is sufficient illumination to permit normal outdoor work without artificial light. The times of civil twilight are tabulated in the Nautical Almanac.
Nautical Twilight begins or ends when the Sun's centre is 12° below the rational horizon, at which time the sea horizon is not clear enough to enable stellar observations to be taken with a marine sextant. The times of nautical twilight are tabulated in the Nautical Almanac.
Astronomical Twilight begins or ends when the Sun's centre is 18° below the rational horizon, at which time complete darkness ends or begins, respectively.

UMBRA: That part of a shadow in which all light is completely cut off by an intervening body. See "Eclipse".

UNIVERSAL TIME: Greenwich Mean Time.

VARIATION: See "Magnetic Variation".

VERNAL EQUINOX: Spring Equinox.

VERTICAL CIRCLE: Any great circle on the celestial sphere which passes through the observer's zenith. Its plane is at right angles to the plane of the rational horizon.

VISIBLE HORIZON: See "Horizon".

WANING MOON: The Moon between Full Moon and New Moon, during which time the visible area is decreasing.

WAXING MOON: The Moon between New Moon and Full Moon, during which time the visible area is increasing.

WINTER: In the northern hemisphere Winter commences (astronomically) at the Winter Solstice (about 22nd December) and ends at the Spring Equinox (about 21st March). In the southern hemisphere it begins at the Summer Solstice (about 21st June) and ends at the Autumnal Equinox (about 23rd September). The meteorological limits are not the same as the astronomical limits.

WINTER SOLSTICE: See "Solstice".

YEAR: The time interval between two successive transits of the Sun with a conventional datum relative to the Earth.
Sidereal Year; The datum is a star, and the interval is equal to 365.256 mean solar days. It is the period of one complete orbit of the Earth round the Sun with reference to a star.
Tropical Year: The datum is the First Point of Aries, and the interval is equal to 365.2422 mean solar days, shorter than a sidereal year by about 20 minutes due to the westerly precession of Aries.
Civil Year: Based on the Tropical year, and averages 365.2425 mean solar days in one 400-year cycle of the Gregorian Calendar.
Gregorian Calendar:
365 Days in each year.
366 Days in each *fourth* year (Leap Year).
365 Days in each *hundredth* year.
366 Days in each *four hundredth* year (Leap Year).
In 400 Years there are:

97 Leap Years	= 35,502 days
303 Years of 365 days	= 110,595 days
Total Number of days	= 146,097 days

$$\text{Average length of Civil Year} = \frac{146,097}{400}$$
$$= 365.2425 \text{ mean solar days.}$$

ZENITH: The point on the celestial sphere vertically above the observer.

ZENITH DISTANCE of a heavenly body: An arc of the vertical circle through the body, or corresponding angle at the centre of the Earth, contained between the observer's zenith and the body. Its value is equal to 90° minus the body's true altitude.

ZONE TIME: The Earth is divided into time zones, each covering 15° of longitude and so located that the longitude of its central meridian is an exact number of whole hours from the Greenwich meridian. The time kept in each zone is the *Local Mean Time of its central meridian.*

Section B

The Stars

APPARENT MOTION OF HEAVENLY BODIES

General: The Earth rotates on its axis from West to East, thus all heavenly bodies appear to move across the sky from East to West. Circumpolar bodies appear to travel on small circle paths, anticlockwise round the north celestial pole (the position of which is roughly indicated by POLARIS) and clockwise round the south celestial pole.

The stars cross the observer's meridian approximately four minutes earlier each day and they remain "fixed" in relation to one another. The Sun, Moon and planets appear to move about amongst the stars.

Rules governing motion of heavenly bodies:

(a) When latitude and declination have the same name, and their sum exceeds 90°, the body is circumpolar, i.e. it does not set.

(b) Bodies with northerly declination will rise to the North of East, and set to the North of West, irrespective of the observer's latitude.

(c) Bodies with southerly declination will rise to the South of East, and set to the South of West, irrespective of the observer's latitude.

(d) When latitude and declination have opposite names, the body does not cross the Prime Vertical.

(e) A body can cross the Prime Vertical *only when its declination has the same name and is less than the latitude.*

STELLAR MAGNITUDES

Stars are classified according to the amount of light received from them. The **magnitude** of a star is a measure of its *relative* brilliance; the actual grading is based on the definition that *"a star of magnitude 1 is one from which the Earth receives 100 times as much light as it receives from a star of magnitude 6".*

Thus, a star of magnitude 2 is 100 times brighter than a star of magnitude 7; a star of magnitude 3 is 100 times brighter than a star of magnitude 8. It follows, therefore, that a star of magnitude 0 is 100 times brighter than a star of magnitude 5, and a star which is 100 times brighter than a star of magnitude 4 must have a magnitude of –1.

Sirius, the brightest star in the heavens, has a magnitude of –1.6.

In practice, the term "stars of the first magnitude" refers to all those whose magnitude is greater than 1.0, of which there are 12.

Note that a sixth magnitude star is only just visible to the naked eye.

THE CONSTELLATIONS

The ancients divided the stars into groups called constellations. Each star was named with the constellation to which it belonged and prefixed with a Greek letter. The brightest star in a constellation is prefixed with α (Alpha), the second brightest β (Beta), and so on in descending order of brilliance. For example, α Crucis, β Crucis, and γ Crucis.

Proper names have also been given to the brightest stars, as for example, *Vega (α Lyrae), Hadar (β Centauri),* etc.

The bright stars are usually easily identifiable from their positions in their constellations, or positions relative to other stars. The constellations themselves often bear little or no resemblance to their names.

Star Charts Nos. 1, 2 and 3 show how the constellations are positioned in relation to one another; they also name those of the "Selected Stars" which are considered to be of greatest navigational importance, the remainder being identified by their *Nautical Almanac number.*

Auxiliary Star Charts, A to J, show the positioning of important stars within or in relation to the principal constellations.

IDENTIFICATION OF IMPORTANT STARS

Achernar (Mag. 0.6): Lies about 70° West of *Canopus,* midway between *Canopus* and *Fomalhaut,* and just off a line joining them. See Chart No. 2.

Acrux (Mag. 1.1): The brightest and most southerly star in the *Southern Cross.* See Chart 1.

Aldebaran (Mag. 1.1): Lies to the N.W. of *Orion* just north of a line through the belt produced. It has a reddish tint, and is at the extremity of one of the arms of a V-shaped cluster of small stars. See Charts 3 and G.

Alpheratz (Mag. 2.2): A straight line from *Polaris* passing about 3° east of *Schedar* (3) and continuing on for the same distance meets *Alpheratz,* which marks the N.E. corner of the *Square of Pegasus.* See Charts 1, 3, C and D.

Altair (Mag. 0.9): Easily identified—lies between two less bright stars in line with *Vega,* and is about 30° South of *Vega.* It is at the Southern apex of a triangle formed by *Deneb, Vega* and *Altair.* See Charts 1, 3 and F.

Antares (Mag. 1.2): A line from *Regulus* through *Spica* to about the same distance beyond meets *Antares*—a reddish star. Once identified, easily recognised again. See Charts 3 and J.

Arcturus (Mag. 0.2): A yellowish tinted star, and the second brightest in the northern heavens. It lies about 30° South of *Alkaid.* The curve of the tail of the *Plough,* if produced southwards, will lead to *Arcturus.* See Charts 1, 3 and B.

Betelgeuse (Mag. 0.1 to 1.2): A line from *Rigel* to *Alnilam* (15), the centre star of *Orion's* belt, produced for about the same distance meets *Betelgeuse,* which is easily identified by its reddish tint. See Charts G and H.

Canopus (Mag. –0.9): The second brightest star in the heavens, and pale blue in colour. It lies about 35° due south of *Sirius;* midway between *Sirius* and the south celestial pole. See Chart 2.

Capella (Mag. 0.2): A very bright yellow star, about 45° from *Polaris,* and located at the northern apex of a triangle formed by *Pollux, Betelgeuse,* and *Capella.* See Charts 1 and H.

Deneb (Mag. 1.3): The brightest star in the constellation of *The Swan.* It lies about 25° E.N.E. of *Vega.* See Charts 1, 3 and F.

Dubhe (Mag. 2.0): The northern of the two "Pointers" of the *Plough.* See Charts 1, 3 and A.

Fomalhaut (Mag. 1.3): One side of the *Square of Pegasus* produced about 45° southward from *Markab* (57) meets *Fomalhaut.* See Charts 3 and D.

Hadar (Mag. 0.9): Two very bright stars, *Rigil Kentaurus* and *Hadar* lie close eastward of the *Southern Cross,* and are called the "Southern Cross Pointers". *Hadar* is the nearer of the two to *Crux.* See Chart 3.

Peacock (Mag. 2.1): Lies alone about halfway between *Achernar* and *Rigil Kentaurus* (west from *Achernar)* on the same parallel of declination. It lies S.E. of *Antares* and S.W. of *Fomalhaut.* See Charts 2 and 3.

Polaris (Mag. 2.1): The "Pole Star". See Charts 1, 2 and A.

Pollux (Mag. 1.2): Lies 23° due north from *Procyon.* See Charts 3 and H.

Procyon (Mag. 0.5): Lies about midway between *Sirius* and *Pollux,* a little to the east of a line joining them. See Charts 3, G and H.

Regulus (Mag. 1.3): A line from *Bellatrix* through *Betelgeuse* meets *Regulus* which is about 60° east of *Betelgeuse* and 25° west of *Denebola* (28). Easily identifiable, as it is located at the end of the handle of the *Sickle.* See Charts 3 and E.

Rigel (Mag. 0.3): A line from *Betelgeuse* through *Alnilam* (15), the centre star in *Orion's* belt, meets *Rigel.* See Charts 3, G and H.

Rigil Kentaurus (Mag. 0.1): The brighter of two stars which lie close eastward of the *Southern Cross,* and form the "Pointers". It is farther from the Cross than the other pointer *(Hadar).* See Chart 3.

Sirius (Mag. –1.6): The brightest star in the heavens. It lies about 25° S.E. of *Orion's* belt and approximately in line with it. See Charts 3, G and H.

Spica (Mag. 1.2): If the curve of the tail of the *Plough* is continued through *Arcturus* and about 30° beyond it meets *Spica.* See Charts 1, 3 and B. Just S.W. of *Spica* are four stars in the form of a spanker sail (known as *"Spica's Spanker")* the gaff of which points to *Spica.*

Vega (Mag. 0.1): Lies about 25° W.S.W. from *Deneb,* and about 30° N.N.W. from *Altair.* See Charts 1, 3 and F.

WHAT STARS WILL BE AVAILABLE FOR OBSERVATION AT TWILIGHT?

The Rude Star Finder:
This device was originally designed for use in aircraft. It gives the positions of all the "Selected Stars" in the *Nautical Almanac* and is one of the most useful, quick-and-easy-to-use of navigational instruments. It takes up practically no space, and should be a part of every navigator's equipment. The complete instrument is contained in a flat circular leather envelope.

It consists of a plastic disc (called a star base) of about 8½ inches diameter, with the northern sky on one side and the southern on the other. There are a number of transparent templates (one for each 10° of latitude—5°, 15°, 25°, etc.), each being marked with a grid formed by azimuth curves intersecting circles of equal altitude.

To use the star finder: First deduce the L.H.A. Aries for the time at which it is intended to take star observations. Choose the template nearest to the D.R. latitude, and place the hole over the central peg of the star base. Rotate the template until the arrow on the 0°–180° line coincides with the appropriate L.H.A. Aries graduation mark on the circumference of the disc. The approximate altitudes and bearings of all important stars which are 10° or more above the horizon can be read off at a glance.

The instrument can also be used for star identification when the altitude and bearing are known.

It is obtainable from most of the well-known makers and sellers of nautical instruments.

The Star Globe:
Though somewhat expensive to buy as personal equipment, it is a very useful navigational asset in the chart room of any ocean going vessel. Unfortunately, too few ships are provided with this fine instrument. It is quick, accurate and probably offers the best means of identifying a star under normal conditions.

It consists of a globe, representing the celestial sphere, on which each star is clearly marked and correctly positioned. The Equinoctial, parallels of declination, ecliptic and celestial meridians are also shown, with the latter usually at 15° intervals and marked in both time and arc, thus providing a scale of Right Ascensions.

The globe is supported in a brass graduated meridian ring, and is rotatable by hand. The whole rests in a box, so that the upper hemisphere is exposed to view and the lower half is hidden in the box. The top side of the box defines the plane of the horizon, in which a ring surrounding the globe is graduated in degrees for bearings. A hemispherical cage, the vertical members of which are graduated in degrees and represent vertical circles intersecting at the observer's zenith is fitted over the globe. When the instrument is correctly set up, the upper exposed hemisphere shows the sky above the observer's horizon, as viewed from outside the celestial sphere.

To identify a star after having observed the altitude and bearing:

(1) *Set the meridian* ring to the ship's latitude by making the altitude of the pole equal to the latitude;

(2) *Rotate the globe* until the meridian marked with the L.H.A. Aries is under the meridian ring;

(3) *Turn the cage* until one of the vertical circles is aligned with the star's true bearing—then slide the small *brass pointer* along this vertical circle until it indicates the appropriate altitude;

(4) The pointer will now indicate which star has been observed;

(5) If no star is indicated, the body observed will be a **planet**—in which case read off the Right Ascension and declination, then consult the *Nautical Almanac* to determine which one has been observed.*

Note: It is often convenient to plot the planet positions on the globe with a soft pencil in advance. Venus should be plotted weekly, but it is normally necessary to plot Mars only once a fortnight, and Jupiter and Saturn every month.

To find what stars are available for observations: Proceed as in (1) and (2) above, select suitable stars, and take off the bearing and altitude of each by means of a vertical circle and brass pointer.

*R.A. = 360° – S.H.A.

THE EQUATORIAL STEREOGRAPHIC PROJECTION

It is possible to use an equatorial stereographic projection, as reproduced on page 28, for star identification. The procedure is as follows:

(1) Place a sheet of tracing paper over the projection and locate with a pin or the point of a pair of compasses through the centre.

(2) On the tracing paper, mark the position of the observer over point P on the projection and label this point Z. Mark the position of the star at a point corresponding to the observed azimuth and altitude with respect to the printed graticule and label this point X.

(3) Rotate the tracing paper until the point Z is at the observers latitude on the circumference of the printed graticule, making sure that the pin remains firmly in position. Use a clockwise rotation if the star is to the west of the observer or an anti-clockwise rotation if the star is to the east of the observer.

(4) Read off the declination and local hour angle of the star against the printed graticule.

(5) Apply the observer's longitude and the Greenwich hour angle of Aries for the time of observation to obtain the Siderial Hour Angle of the star.

(6) Compare the declination and siderial hour angle of the star with the table on page 17 to identify the star.

STAR CHARTS

No. 1 NORTHERN HEMISPHERE

No. 2 SOUTHERN HEMISPHERE

All stars shown are tabulated in the Nautical Almanac—Numbers 1 to 57.

Stars which are of special importance because of their brightness and disposition are shown RED.

★ **Stars of the first magnitude (names shown in capital letters).**

★ ★ **Stars of magnitude 2.0 to 1.0.**

★ **Stars which are less bright than mag. 2.0 but are listed and numbered as SELECTED STARS in the Nautical Almanac.**

● **Stars of lesser magnitude which have been included only to help in identification of some constellations.**

INDEX TO SELECTED STARS

Name	No.	Mag.	S.H.A.	Dec.
			°	°
Acamar	7	3·1	316	S. 40
Achernar	5	0·6	336	S. 57
Acrux	30	1·1	174	S. 63
Adhara	19	1·6	256	S. 29
Aldebaran	10	1·1	291	N. 16
Alioth	32	1·7	167	N. 56
Alkaid	34	1·9	153	N. 49
Al Na'ir	55	2·2	28	S. 47
Alnilam	15	1·8	276	S. 1
Alphard	25	2·2	218	S. 9
Alphecca	41	2·3	127	N. 27
Alpheratz	1	2·2	358	N. 29
Altair	51	0·9	63	N. 9
Ankaa	2	2·4	354	S. 42
Antares	42	1·2	113	S. 26
Arcturus	37	0·2	146	N. 19
Atria	43	1·9	109	S. 69
Avior	22	1·7	234	S. 59
Bellatrix	13	1·7	279	N. 6
Betelgeuse	16	Var.*	272	N. 7
Canopus	17	−0·9	264	S. 53
Capella	12	0·2	281	N. 46
Deneb	53	1·3	50	N. 45
Denebola	28	2·2	183	N. 15
Diphda	4	2·2	349	S. 18
Dubhe	27	2·0	194	N. 62
Elnath	14	1·8	279	N. 29
Eltanin	47	2·4	91	N. 51
Enif	54	2·5	34	N. 10
Fomalhaut	56	1·3	16	S. 30
Gacrux	31	1·6	173	S. 57
Gienah	29	2·8	176	S. 17
Hadar	35	0·9	149	S. 60
Hamal	6	2·2	329	N. 23
Kaus Australis	48	2·0	84	S. 34
Kochab	40	2·2	137	N. 74
Markab	57	2·6	14	N. 15
Menkar	8	2·8	315	N. 4
Menkent	36	2·3	149	S. 36
Miaplacidus	24	1·8	222	S. 70
Mirfak	9	1·9	309	N. 50
Nunki	50	2·1	77	S. 26
Peacock	52	2·1	54	S. 57
Pollux	21	1·2	244	N. 28
Procyon	20	0·5	245	N. 5
Rasalhague	46	2·1	97	N. 13
Regulus	26	1·3	208	N. 12
Rigel	11	0·3	282	S. 8
Rigil Kentaurus	38	0·1	140	S. 61
Sabik	44	2·6	103	S. 16
Schedar	3	2·5	350	N. 56
Shaula	45	1·7	97	S. 37
Sirius	18	−1·6	259	S. 17
Spica	33	1·2	159	S. 11
Suhail	23	2·2	223	S. 43
Vega	49	0·1	81	N. 39
Zubenelgenubi	39	2·9	138	S. 16

No.	Name	Mag.	S.H.A.	Dec.
			°	°
1	Alpheratz	2·2	358	N. 29
2	Ankaa	2·4	354	S. 42
3	Schedar	2·5	350	N. 56
4	Diphda	2·2	349	S. 18
5	Achernar	0·6	336	S. 57
6	Hamal	2·2	329	N. 23
7	Acamar	3·1	316	S. 40
8	Menkar	2·8	315	N. 4
9	Mirfak	1·9	309	N. 50
10	Aldebaran	1·1	291	N. 16
11	Rigel	0·3	282	S. 8
12	Capella	0·2	281	N. 46
13	Bellatrix	1·7	279	N. 6
14	Elnath	1·8	279	N. 29
15	Alnilam	1·8	276	S. 1
16	Betelgeuse	Var.*	272	N. 7
17	Canopus	−0·9	264	S. 53
18	Sirius	−1·6	259	S. 17
19	Adhara	1·6	256	S. 29
20	Procyon	0·5	245	N. 5
21	Pollux	1·2	244	N. 28
22	Avior	1·7	234	S. 59
23	Suhail	2·2	223	S. 43
24	Miaplacidus	1·8	222	S. 70
25	Alphard	2·2	218	S. 9
26	Regulus	1·3	208	N. 12
27	Dubhe	2·0	194	N. 62
28	Denebola	2·2	183	N. 15
29	Gienah	2·8	176	S. 17
30	Acrux	1·1	174	S. 63
31	Gacrux	1·6	173	S. 57
32	Alioth	1·7	167	N. 56
33	Spica	1·2	159	S. 11
34	Alkaid	1·9	153	N. 49
35	Hadar	0·9	149	S. 60
36	Menkent	2·3	149	S. 36
37	Arcturus	0·2	146	N. 19
38	Rigil Kentaurus	0·1	140	S. 61
39	Zubenelgenubi	2·9	138	S. 16
40	Kochab	2·2	137	N. 74
41	Alphecca	2·3	127	N. 27
42	Antares	1·2	113	S. 26
43	Atria	1·9	109	S. 69
44	Sabik	2·6	103	S. 16
45	Shaula	1·7	97	S. 37
46	Rasalhague	2·1	97	N. 13
47	Eltanin	2·4	91	N. 51
48	Kaus Australis	2·0	84	S. 34
49	Vega	0·1	81	N. 39
50	Nunki	2·1	77	S. 26
51	Altair	0·9	63	N. 9
52	Peacock	2·1	54	S. 57
53	Deneb	1·3	50	N. 45
54	Enif	2·5	34	N. 10
55	Al Na'ir	2·2	28	S. 47
56	Fomalhaut	1·3	16	S. 30
57	Markab	2·6	14	N. 15

* 0·1—1·2

Ⓐ THE PLOUGH

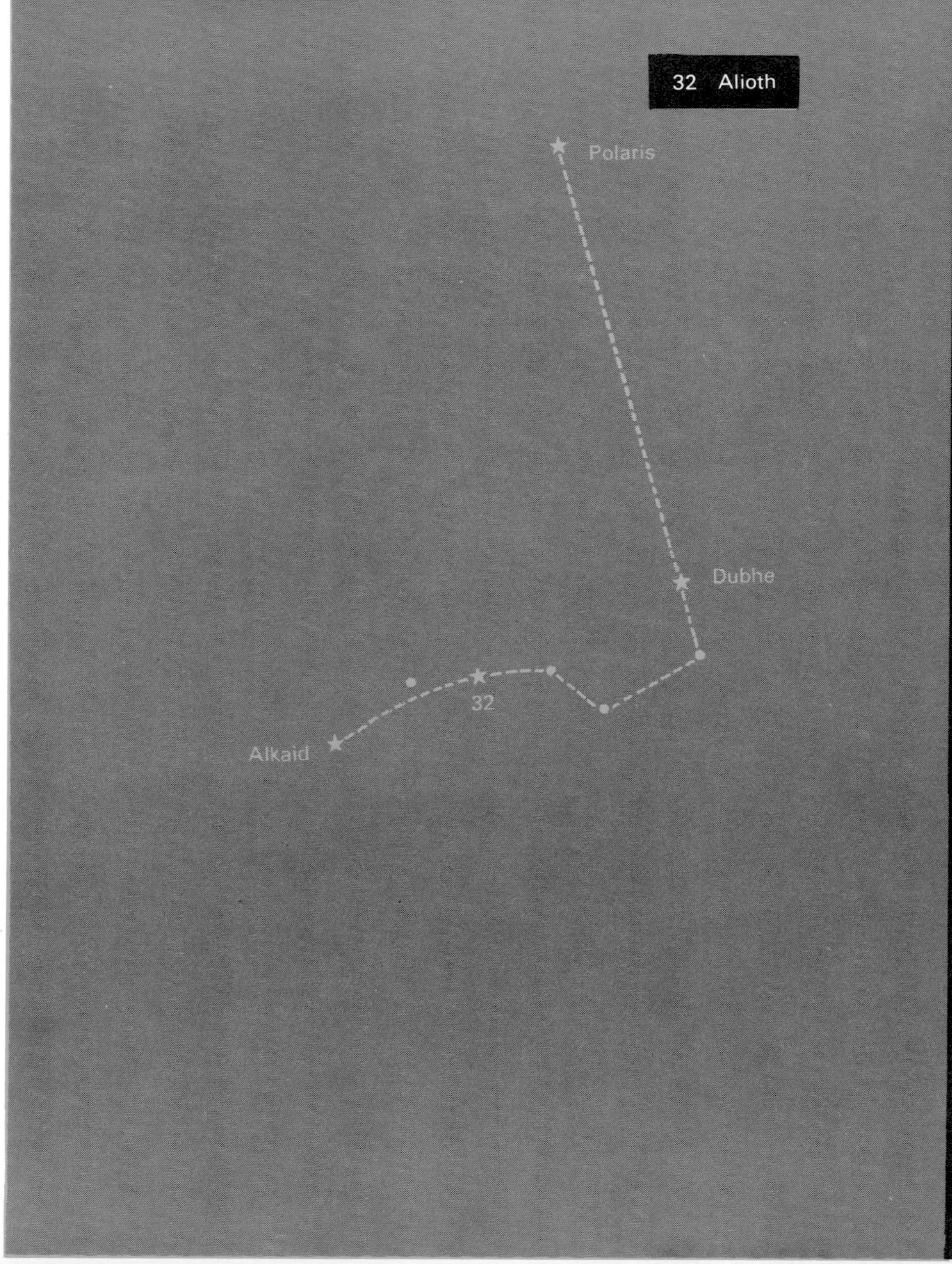

32 Alioth
Polaris
Dubhe
32
Alkaid

THE PLOUGH Ⓑ

28 Denebola
32 Alioth
41 Alphecca
Dubhe
32
Alkaid
41
ARCTURUS
28
Spica

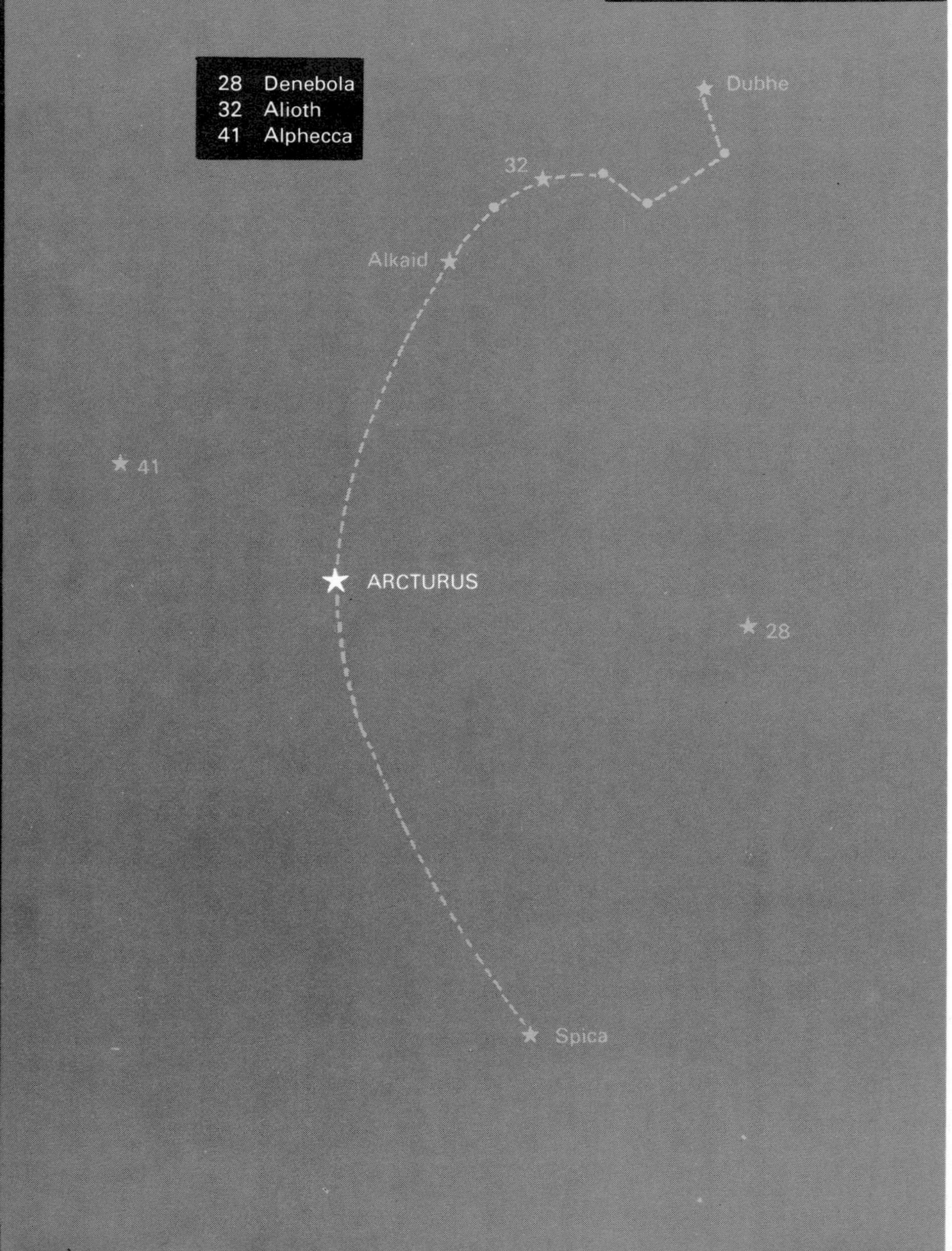

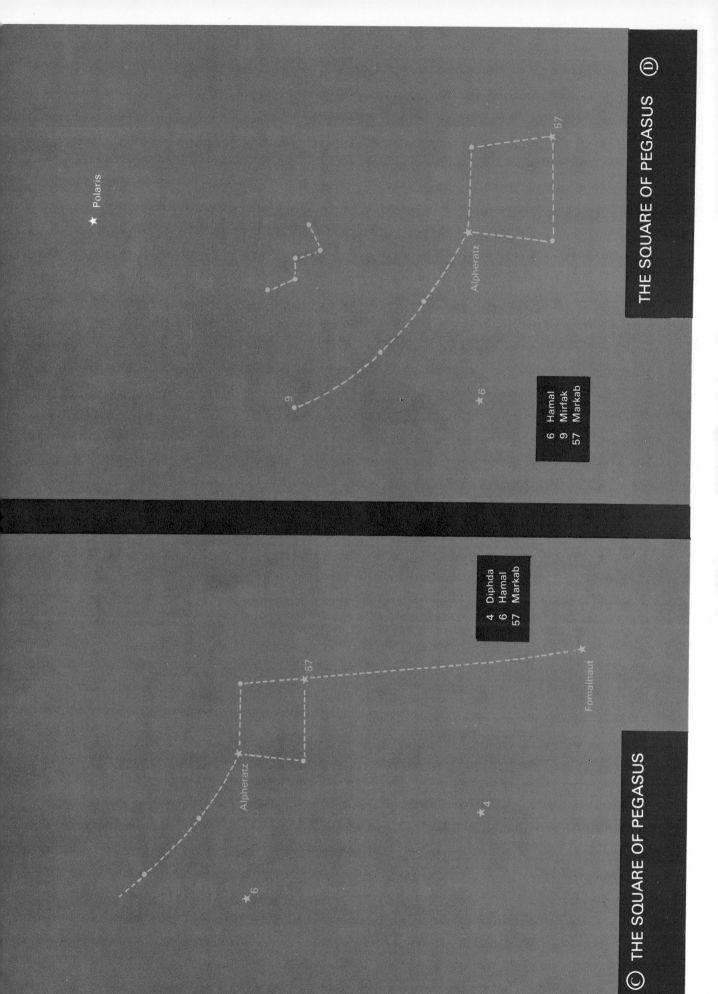

6   Hamal
9   Mirfak
57 Markab

Alpheratz

57

Polaris

9

6

4   Diphda
6   Hamal
57 Markab

Alpheratz

57

6

4

Fomalhaut

Ⓒ THE SQUARE OF PEGASUS

Ⓔ THE SWAN

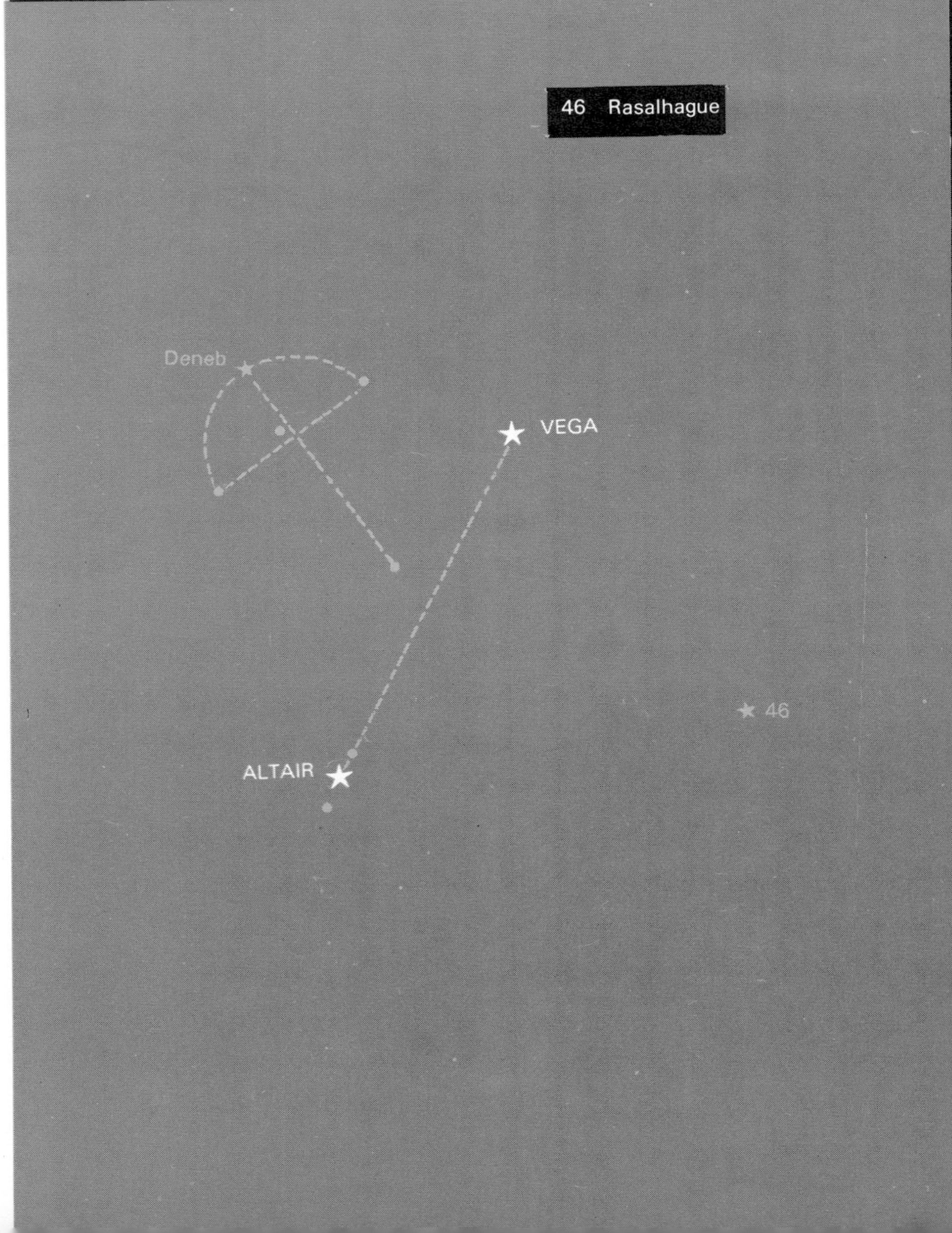
46 Rasalhague
Deneb
VEGA
ALTAIR
46

THE SICKLE Ⓕ

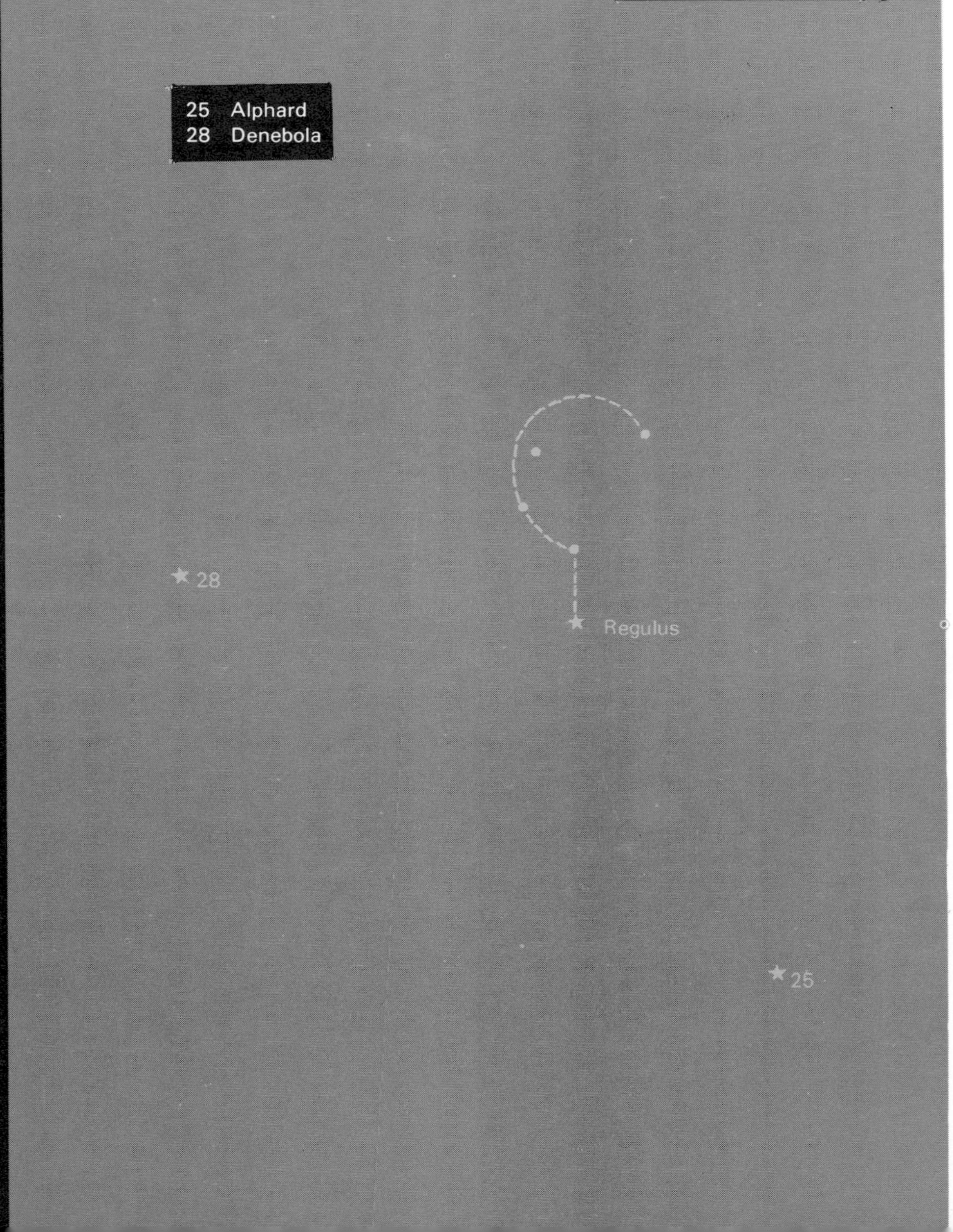
25 Alphard
28 Denebola
28
Regulus
25

CAPELLA

14

Pollux

BETELGUESE

13

15

RIGEL

PROCYON

SIRIUS

13	Bellatrix
14	Elnath
15	Alnilam

13	Bellatrix
14	Elnath
15	Alnilam
19	Adhara

Aldebaran

14

13

15

Pollux

BETELGUESE

RIGEL

SIRIUS

19

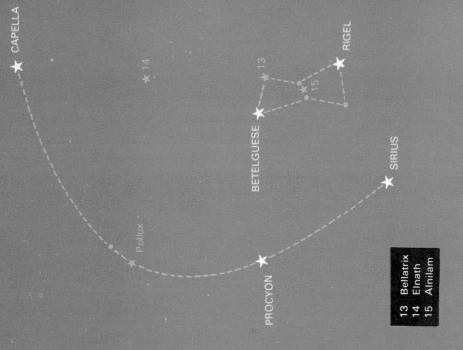

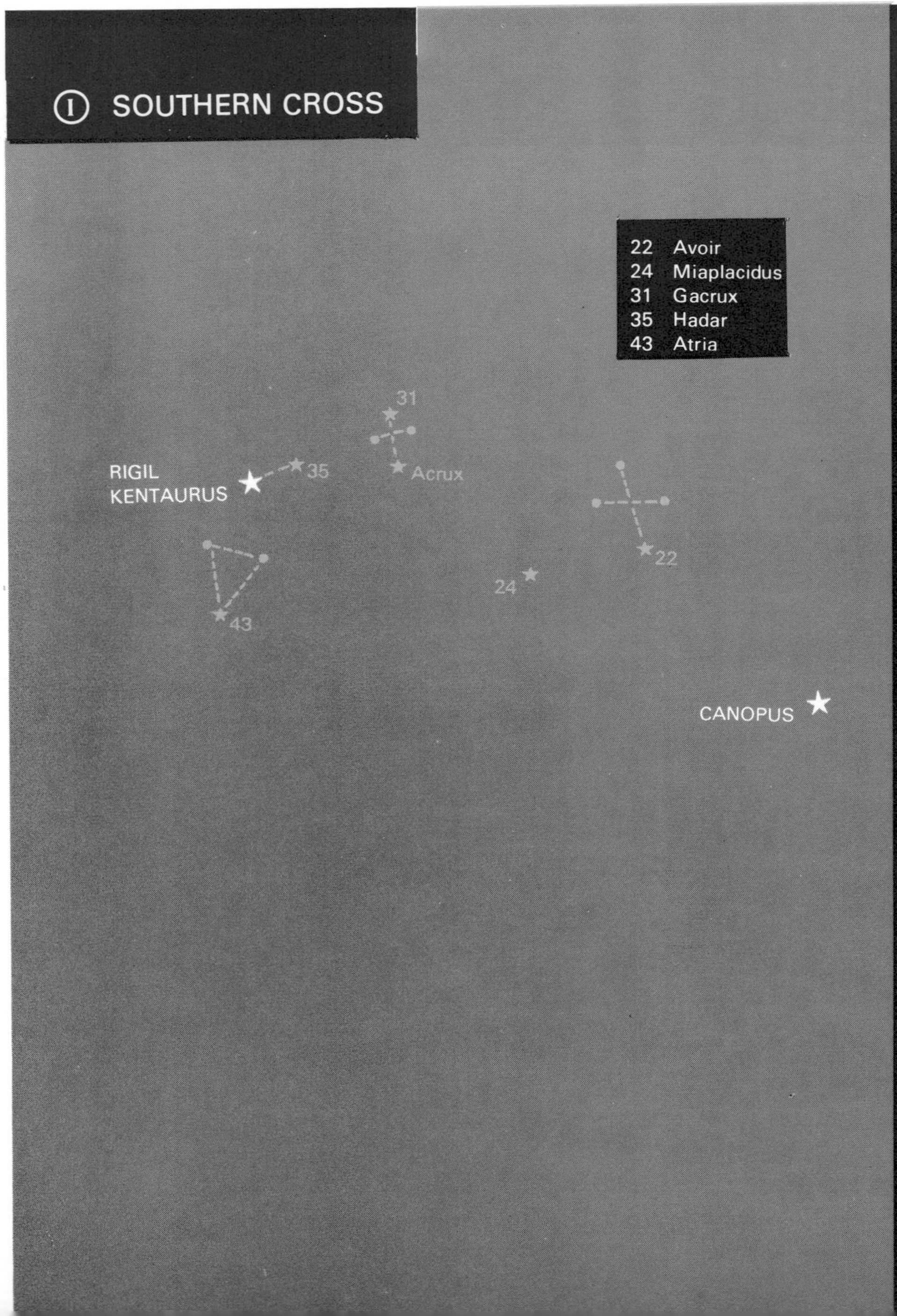

45 Shaula

Antares

45

22	Avoir
24	Miaplacidus
31	Gacrux
35	Hadar
43	Atria

CANOPUS

22

24

Acrux

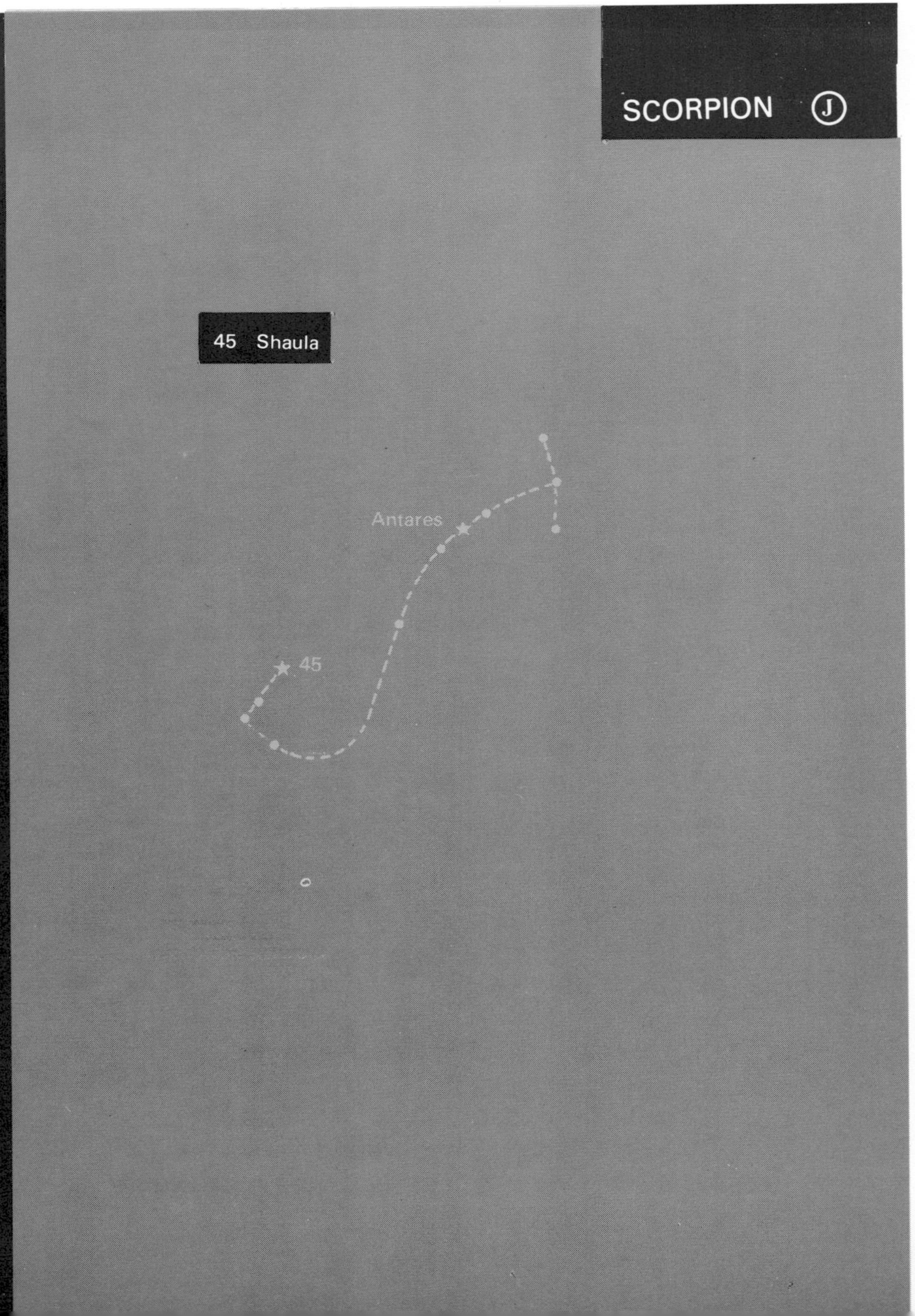

31

35

RIGIL
KENTAURUS

43

INSTRUCTIONS FOR USING STARS' MERIDIAN PASSAGE TABLE

(Table on pages 26 and 27)

1. TO FIND THE APPROXIMATE L.M.T. OF A STAR'S MERIDIAN PASSAGE:

(a) **At Upper Transit:** Enter the table with the star's name on the left and the month at the top. Write down the time given, and then SUBTRACT the date correction (which is given in a separate column, adjacent to the June column). This result is accurate enough for most practical purposes; but if further accuracy is desired, the longitude correction (found in the same column as the correction for date) should be applied according to its sign, i.e. add for E. longitudes and subtract for W. longitudes. See Examples 1 and 3 below. Finally, apply correction for the year (page 27) if necessary.

(b) **At Lower Transit:** Add or subtract (as appropriate to the date for which the time of transit is required) **11h. 58m.** to the time of upper transit. See Example 2, below.

2. TO FIND WHICH SELECTED STARS WILL BE ON OR NEAR THE OBSERVER'S MERIDIAN AT ANY GIVEN L.M.T. AND DATE:

Suppose that on the 10th day of the month (date correction 36 minutes) a star crossed a particular meridian at L.M.T. 1900 hrs., then, on the 1st day of that month, it would have crossed the same meridian at 1936 hours. On this basis, the procedure is as follows:

(1) To the given L.M.T. apply the corrections for date and longitude **(with signs reversed)**. Write down the result.

(2) Look down the appropriate "First day of the month" column, and make note of any times which are within a few minutes of that found by step (1), together with the name of the star relevant to each time noted.

(3) To each of the times found by step (2) apply the corrections for date and longitude, according to the signs given in the table. The results will give the L.M.T.s of meridian transits on the day in question.

3. WORKED EXAMPLES

Example 1: Find the approximate L.M.T. at which SIRIUS will cross the meridian of 175°E. on 21st March, 1977, 1981 or 1985, etc. (at ship).

	Mer. Pass.
SIRIUS	
1st March. L.M.T. from Table	2007 hrs.
Correction for Date (21st)	– 0119
	1848
Correction for longitude 175°E.	+ 2
Required L.M.T.	**1850 hrs.**

Example 2: At what L.M.T. (approx.) will DUBHE be on the meridian at **Lower Transit** on 6th July, 1977, 1981 or 1985, etc. (at ship)? Observer's longitude 29°W.

DUBHE	*Mer. Pass.*
1st July. L.M.T. from Table	1625 hrs.
Correction for Date (6th)	– 0020
Correction for longitude 29°W.	0000
	———
6th July. L.M.T.	1605
For Lower Mer. Pass. *Subtract	1158
	———
Required L.M.T.	**0407 hrs.**

Subtraction gives lower transit on 6th July, which is the time required. Adding, in this case, would give time of lower transit on the 7th.

Example 3: Required the approximate L.M.T. at which FOMALHAUT will cross the meridian of 16°E. on 18th September, 1977, 1981 or 1985, etc.

FOMALHAUT	*Mer. Pass.*
1st Sept. L.M.T. from Table	0020 hrs.
Correction for Date (**19th in this case**)	– 0111 §
	———
Required L.M.T. on 18th Sept.	**2309 hrs.**

§*Note that, in this case, had the correction for the 18th been applied, the answer would have been time of mer. pass. for the previous day (17th). The longitude correction for 16°E. is zero.*

Example 4: Find which of the selected stars (if any) will be within ± 7 minutes of the time of Civil Twilight (L.M.T. 1744 hrs.) on the evening of 13th February, 1977, 1981 or 1985, etc. Observer's longitude 26°W.

13th February given L.M.T.	1744 hrs.
Date Correction (with sign reversed)	+ 47
	———
Corresponding Mer. Pass. time for 1st Feb.	1831 hrs.

± 7 minutes gives 1824 to 1838 hrs. Look in February column for times within these limits; MIRFAK is the only one.

	Mer. Pass.
MIRFAK 1st February	1835 hrs.
Correction for Date	– 0047
	———
MIRFAK 14th February L.M.T. (approx.)	**1748 hrs.**

Example 5: Required to find which selected stars (if any) will be on the meridian within ±
5 minutes of Civil Twilight on the morning of 17th August, 1977, 1981 or 1985, etc. The
Ship's D.R. Position for that time is 14° 55′N. 152° 14′E.

Reed's Nautical Almanac, 17th August		
Lat. 12°N. gives Civil Twilight		0527 hrs.
Corr. for Date (sign reversed) +55 ⎫		
Corr. for Long. (sign reversed)– 2 ⎭	+	53
		————
Corresponding Mer. Pass. time for 1st Aug.		0620 hrs.

± 5 minutes gives limiting times 0615 to 0625. Table for 1st
August shows:

	ACAMAR	MENKAR
Mer. Pass.	0618 hrs.	0622 hrs.
Corr. for Date and Long.	– 53	– 53
	————	————
Mer. Pass. on 17th Aug.	**0525 hrs.**	**0529 hrs.**

Uses of table explained on pages 23-25

STAR	No.	Upper Meridian Passage on the First day of the month					
		JAN.	FEB.	MAR.	APR.	MAY	JUNE
Acamar	7	2012	1810	1620	1418	1220	1018
Achernar	5	1852	1650	1500	1258	1100	0858
Acrux	30	0544	0342	0152	2346	2148	1946
Adhara	19	0016	2210	2020	1818	1620	1418
Aldebaran	10	2149	1947	1757	1555	1357	1155
Alioth	32	0612	0410	0220	0018	2216	2014
Alkaid	34	0705	0503	0313	0111	2309	2107
Al Na'ir	55	1526	1324	1134	0932	0734	0532
Alnilam	15	2250	2048	1858	1656	1458	1256
Alphard	25	0245	0043	2249	2047	1849	1647
Alphecca	41	0852	0650	0500	0258	0100	2254
Alpheratz	1	1722	1520	1330	1128	0930	0728
Altair	51	1308	1106	0916	0714	0516	0314
Ankaa	2	1740	1538	1348	1146	0948	0746
Antares	42	0947	0745	0555	0353	0155	2349
Arcturus	37	0733	0531	0341	0139	2337	2135
Atria	43	1005	0803	0613	0411	0213	0011
Avoir	22	0141	2335	2145	1943	1745	1543
Bellatrix	13	2239	2037	1847	1645	1447	1245
Betelgeuse	16	2309	2107	1917	1715	1517	1315
Canopus	17	2338	2136	1946	1744	1546	1344
Capella	12	2230	2028	1838	1636	1438	1236
Deneb	53	1359	1157	1007	0805	0607	0405
Denebola	28	0507	0305	0115	2309	2111	1909
Diphda	4	1757	1555	1405	1203	1005	0803
Dubhe	27	0421	0219	0029	2223	2025	1823
Elnath	14	2240	2038	1848	1646	1448	1246
Eltanin	47	1115	0913	0723	0521	0323	0121
Enif	54	1502	1300	1110	0908	0710	0508
Fomalhaut	56	1615	1413	1223	1021	0823	0621
Gacrux	31	0549	0347	0157	2351	2153	1951
Gienah	29	0533	0331	0141	2335	2137	1935
Hadar	35	0721	0519	0329	0127	2325	2123
Hamal	6	1921	1719	1529	1327	1129	0927
Kaus Australis	48	1141	0939	0749	0547	0349	0147
Kochab	40	0810	0608	0418	0216	0018	2212
Markab	57	1622	1420	1230	1028	0830	0628
Menkar	8	2016	1814	1624	1422	1224	1022
Menkent	36	0724	0522	0332	0130	2328	2126
Miaplacidus	24	0232	0030	2236	2034	1836	1634
Mirfak	9	2037	1835	1645	1443	1245	1043
Nunki	50	1212	1010	0820	0618	0420	0218
Peacock	52	1342	1140	0950	0748	0550	0348
Pollux	21	0103	2257	2107	1905	1707	1505
Procyon	20	0057	2251	2101	1859	1701	1459
Rasalhague	46	1053	0851	0701	0459	0301	0059
Regulus	26	0326	0124	2330	2128	1930	1728
Rigel	11	2228	2026	1836	1634	1436	1234
Rigil Kentaurus	38	0757	0555	0405	0203	0005	2159
Sabik	44	1028	0826	0636	0434	0236	0034
Schedar	3	1754	1552	1402	1200	1002	0800
Shaula	45	1051	0849	0659	0457	0259	0057
Sirius	18	0003	2157	2007	1805	1607	1405
Spica	33	0643	0441	0251	0049	2247	2045
Suhail	23	0226	0024	2230	2028	1830	1628
Vega	49	1155	0953	0803	0601	0403	0201
Zuben'ubi	39	0808	0606	0416	0214	0016	2210

CORRECTION FOR DATE

Greenwich Date	SUBTRACT from time given on the first day	
	h.	m.
1st	0	00
2nd	0	04
3rd	0	08
4th	0	12
5th	0	16
6th	0	20
7th	0	24
8th	0	28
9th	0	32
10th	0	36
11th	0	39
12th	0	43
13th	0	47
14th	0	51
15th	0	55
16th	0	59
17th	1	03
18th	1	07
19th	1	11
20th	1	15
21st	1	19
22nd	1	23
23rd	1	26
24th	1	30
25th	1	34
26th	1	38
27th	1	42
28th	1	46
29th	1	50
30th	1	54
31st	1	58

CORRECTION FOR LONGITUDE

Long.	Cor.
	min.
0°	0
45¾°E	+1
137¼°E	+2
180°	−2
137¼°W	−1
45¾°W	0
0°	

Uses of table explained on pages 23-25

APPROXIMATE CORRECTION FOR THE YEAR	
Year	Corr. Min.
1977	0
1978	—3
1979	—2
1980	—1
1981	0
1982	—3
1983	—2
1984	—1
1985	0
1986	—3
1987	—2
1988	—1
1989	0

STAR	No.	Upper Meridian Passage on the First day of the month					
		JULY	AUG.	SEPT.	OCT.	NOV.	DEC.
Acamar	7	0820	0618	0417	0219	0017	2215
Achernar	5	0700	0458	0257	0059	2253	2055
Acrux	30	1748	1546	1345	1147	0945	0747
Adhara	19	1220	1018	0817	0619	0417	0219
Aldebaran	10	0957	0755	0554	0356	0154	2352
Alioth	32	1816	1614	1413	1215	1013	0815
Alkaid	34	0909	1707	1506	1308	1106	0908
Al Na'ir	55	0334	0132	2327	2129	1927	1729
Alnilam	15	1058	0856	0655	0457	0255	0057
Alphard	25	1449	1247	1046	0848	0646	0448
Alphecca	41	2056	1854	1653	1455	1253	1055
Alpheratz	1	0530	0328	0127	2325	2123	1925
Altair	51	0116	2310	2109	1911	1709	1511
Ankaa	2	0548	0346	0145	2343	2141	1943
Antares	42	2151	1949	1748	1550	1348	1150
Arcturus	37	1937	1735	1534	1336	1134	0936
Atria	43	2209	2007	1806	1608	1406	1208
Avoir	22	1345	1143	0942	0744	0542	0344
Bellatrix	13	1047	0845	0644	0446	0244	0046
Betelgeuse	16	1117	0915	0714	0516	0314	0116
Canopus	17	1146	0944	0743	0545	0343	0145
Capella	12	1038	0836	0635	0437	0235	0037
Deneb	53	0207	0005	2200	2002	1800	1602
Denebola	28	1711	1509	1308	1110	0908	0710
Diphda	4	0605	0403	0202	0004	2158	2000
Dubhe	27	1625	1423	1222	1024	0822	0624
Elnath	14	1048	0846	0645	0447	0245	0047
Eltanin	47	2319	2117	1916	1718	1516	1319
Enif	54	0310	0108	2303	2105	1903	1705
Fomalhaut	56	0423	0221	0020	2218	2016	1818
Gacrux	31	1753	1551	1350	1152	0950	0752
Gienah	29	1737	1535	1334	1136	0934	0736
Hadar	35	1925	1723	1522	1324	1122	0924
Hamal	6	0729	0527	0326	0128	2322	2124
Kaus Australis	48	2345	2143	1942	1744	1542	1344
Kochab	40	2014	1812	1611	1413	1211	1013
Markab	57	0430	0228	0027	2225	2023	1825
Menkar	8	0824	0622	0421	0223	0021	2219
Menkent	36	1928	1726	1525	1327	1125	0927
Miaplacidus	24	1436	1234	1033	0835	0633	0435
Mirfak	9	0845	0643	0442	0244	0042	2240
Nunki	50	0020	2214	2013	1815	1613	1415
Peacock	52	0150	2344	2143	1945	1743	1545
Pollux	21	1307	1105	0904	0706	0504	0306
Procyon	20	1301	1059	0858	0700	0458	0300
Rasalhague	46	2257	2055	1854	1656	1454	1256
Regulus	26	1530	1328	1127	0929	0727	0529
Rigel	11	1036	0834	0633	0435	0233	0035
Rigil Kentaurus	38	2001	1759	1558	1400	1158	1000
Sabik	44	2232	2030	1829	1631	1429	1231
Schedar	3	0602	0400	0159	2357	2155	1957
Shaula	45	2255	2053	1852	1654	1452	1254
Sirius	18	1207	1005	0804	0606	0404	0206
Spica	33	1847	1645	1444	1246	1044	0846
Suhail	23	1430	1228	1027	0829	0627	0429
Vega	49	0003	2157	1956	1758	1556	1358
Zuben'ubi	39	2012	1810	1609	1411	1209	1011

EQUATORIAL STEREOGRAPHIC
PROJECTION DIAGRAM

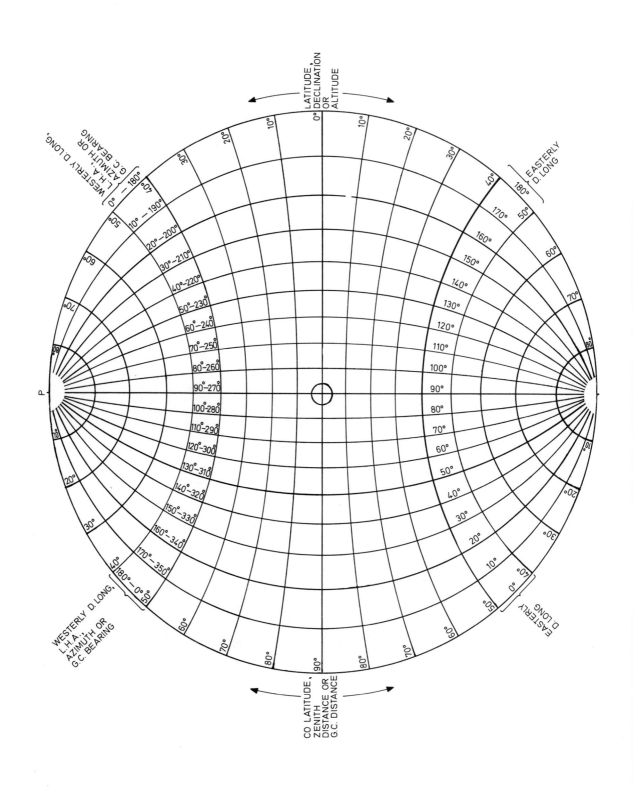

Section C

Selected Nautical Tables

TIME, SPEED and DISTANCE TABLE

Min.	Knots															Min.
	3·0	3·2	3·4	3·6	3·8	4·0	4·2	4·4	4·6	4·8	5·0	5·2	5·4	5·6	5·8	
	Miles	Miles	Miles	Miles	Miles	Miles	Miles	Miles	Miles	Miles	Miles	Miles	Miles	Miles	Miles	
1	0·1	0·1	0·1	0·1	0·1	0·1	0·1	0·1	0·1	0·1	0·1	0·1	0·1	0·1	0·1	1
2	0·1	0·1	0·1	0·1	0·1	0·1	0·1	0·1	0·2	0·2	0·2	0·2	0·2	0·2	0·2	2
3	0·2	0·2	0·2	0·2	0·2	0·2	0·2	0·2	0·2	0·2	0·3	0·3	0·3	0·3	0·3	3
4	0·2	0·2	0·2	0·2	0·3	0·3	0·3	0·3	0·3	0·3	0·3	0·3	0·4	0·4	0·4	4
5	0·3	0·3	0·3	0·3	0·3	0·3	0·4	0·4	0·4	0·4	0·4	0·4	0·5	0·5	0·5	5
6	0·3	0·3	0·3	0·4	0·4	0·4	0·4	0·4	0·5	0·5	0·5	0·5	0·5	0·6	0·6	6
7	0·4	0·4	0·4	0·4	0·4	0·5	0·5	0·5	0·5	0·6	0·6	0·6	0·6	0·7	0·7	7
8	0·4	0·4	0·5	0·5	0·5	0·5	0·6	0·6	0·6	0·6	0·7	0·7	0·7	0·7	0·8	8
9	0·5	0·5	0·5	0·5	0·6	0·6	0·6	0·7	0·7	0·7	0·8	0·8	0·8	0·8	0·9	9
10	0·5	0·5	0·6	0·6	0·6	0·7	0·7	0·7	0·8	0·8	0·8	0·9	0·9	0·9	1·0	10
11	0·6	0·6	0·6	0·7	0·7	0·7	0·8	0·8	0·8	0·9	0·9	1·0	1·0	1·0	1·1	11
12	0·6	0·6	0·7	0·7	0·8	0·8	0·8	0·9	0·9	1·0	1·0	1·0	1·1	1·1	1·2	12
13	0·7	0·7	0·7	0·8	0·8	0·9	0·9	1·0	1·0	1·0	1·1	1·1	1·2	1·2	1·3	13
14	0·7	0·7	0·8	0·8	0·9	0·9	1·0	1·0	1·1	1·1	1·2	1·2	1·3	1·3	1·4	14
15	0·8	0·8	0·9	0·9	1·0	1·0	1·1	1·1	1·2	1·2	1·3	1·3	1·4	1·4	1·5	15
16	0·8	0·9	0·9	1·0	1·0	1·1	1·1	1·2	1·2	1·3	1·3	1·4	1·4	1·5	1·5	16
17	0·9	0·9	1·0	1·0	1·1	1·1	1·2	1·2	1·3	1·4	1·4	1·5	1·5	1·6	1·6	17
18	0·9	1·0	1·0	1·1	1·1	1·2	1·3	1·3	1·4	1·4	1·5	1·6	1·6	1·7	1·7	18
19	1·0	1·0	1·1	1·1	1·2	1·3	1·4	1·4	1·5	1·5	1·6	1·6	1·7	1·8	1·8	19
20	1·0	1·1	1·1	1·2	1·3	1·3	1·4	1·5	1·5	1·6	1·7	1·7	1·8	1·9	1·9	20
21	1·1	1·1	1·2	1·3	1·3	1·4	1·5	1·5	1·6	1·7	1·8	1·8	1·9	2·0	2·0	21
22	1·1	1·2	1·2	1·3	1·4	1·5	1·5	1·6	1·7	1·8	1·8	1·9	2·0	2·0	2·1	22
23	1·2	1·2	1·3	1·4	1·5	1·5	1·6	1·7	1·8	1·8	1·9	2·0	2·1	2·1	2·2	23
24	1·2	1·3	1·4	1·4	1·5	1·6	1·7	1·8	1·8	1·9	2·0	2·1	2·2	2·2	2·3	24
25	1·3	1·3	1·4	1·5	1·6	1·7	1·8	1·8	1·9	2·0	2·1	2·2	2·3	2·3	2·4	25
26	1·3	1·4	1·5	1·6	1·6	1·7	1·8	1·9	2·0	2·1	2·2	2·3	2·3	2·4	2·5	26
27	1·4	1·4	1·5	1·6	1·7	1·8	1·9	2·0	2·1	2·2	2·3	2·3	2·4	2·5	2·6	27
28	1·4	1·5	1·6	1·7	1·8	1·9	2·0	2·1	2·1	2·2	2·3	2·4	2·5	2·6	2·7	28
29	1·5	1·5	1·6	1·7	1·8	1·9	2·0	2·1	2·2	2·3	2·4	2·5	2·6	2·7	2·8	29
30	1·5	1·6	1·7	1·8	1·9	2·0	2·1	2·2	2·3	2·4	2·5	2·6	2·7	2·8	2·9	30
31	1·6	1·7	1·8	1·9	2·0	2·1	2·2	2·3	2·4	2·5	2·6	2·7	2·8	2·9	3·0	31
32	1·6	1·7	1·8	1·9	2·0	2·1	2·2	2·3	2·5	2·6	2·7	2·8	2·9	3·0	3·1	32
33	1·7	1·8	1·9	2·0	2·1	2·2	2·3	2·4	2·5	2·6	2·8	2·9	3·0	3·1	3·2	33
34	1·7	1·8	1·9	2·0	2·2	2·3	2·4	2·5	2·6	2·7	2·8	2·9	3·1	3·2	3·3	34
35	1·8	1·9	2·0	2·1	2·2	2·3	2·5	2·6	2·7	2·8	3·0	3·0	3·2	3·3	3·4	35
36	1·8	1·9	2·0	2·2	2·3	2·4	2·5	2·6	2·8	2·9	3·0	3·1	3·2	3·4	3·5	36
37	1·9	2·0	2·1	2·2	2·3	2·5	2·6	2·7	2·8	3·0	3·1	3·2	3·3	3·5	3·6	37
38	1·9	2·0	2·2	2·3	2·4	2·6	2·7	2·8	2·9	3·0	3·2	3·3	3·4	3·5	3·7	38
39	2·0	2·1	2·2	2·3	2·5	2·6	2·7	2·9	3·0	3·1	3·3	3·4	3·5	3·6	3·8	39
40	2·0	2·1	2·3	2·4	2·5	2·7	2·8	2·9	3·1	3·2	3·3	3·5	3·6	3·7	3·9	40
41	2·1	2·2	2·3	2·5	2·6	2·7	2·9	3·0	3·1	3·3	3·4	3·6	3·7	3·8	4·0	41
42	2·1	2·2	2·4	2·5	2·7	2·8	2·9	3·1	3·2	3·4	3·5	3·6	3·7	3·9	4·1	42
43	2·2	2·3	2·4	2·6	2·7	2·9	3·0	3·2	3·3	3·4	3·6	3·7	3·9	4·0	4·2	43
44	2·2	2·3	2·5	2·6	2·8	3·0	3·1	3·2	3·4	3·5	3·7	3·8	4·0	4·1	4·3	44
45	2·3	2·4	2·6	2·7	2·9	3·0	3·2	3·3	3·5	3·6	3·8	3·9	4·1	4·2	4·4	45
46	2·3	2·5	2·6	2·8	2·9	3·1	3·2	3·4	3·5	3·7	3·8	4·0	4·1	4·3	4·4	46
47	2·4	2·5	2·7	2·8	3·0	3·1	3·3	3·4	3·6	3·8	3·9	4·1	4·2	4·4	4·5	47
48	2·4	2·6	2·7	2·9	3·0	3·2	3·4	3·5	3·7	3·8	4·0	4·2	4·3	4·5	4·6	48
49	2·5	2·6	2·8	2·9	3·1	3·3	3·4	3·6	3·8	3·9	4·1	4·2	4·4	4·6	4·7	49
50	2·5	2·7	2·8	3·0	3·2	3·3	3·5	3·7	3·8	4·0	4·2	4·3	4·5	4·7	4·8	50
51	2·6	2·7	2·9	3·1	3·2	3·4	3·6	3·7	3·9	4·1	4·3	4·4	4·6	4·8	4·9	51
52	2·6	2·8	3·0	3·1	3·3	3·5	3·6	3·8	4·0	4·2	4·3	4·5	4·7	4·9	5·0	52
53	2·7	2·8	3·0	3·2	3·4	3·5	3·7	3·9	4·1	4·2	4·4	4·6	4·8	4·9	5·1	53
54	2·7	2·9	3·1	3·2	3·4	3·6	3·8	4·0	4·1	4·3	4·5	4·7	4·9	5·0	5·2	54
55	2·8	2·9	3·1	3·3	3·5	3·7	3·9	4·0	4·2	4·4	4·6	4·8	5·0	5·1	5·3	55
56	2·8	3·0	3·2	3·4	3·5	3·7	3·9	4·1	4·3	4·5	4·7	4·9	5·0	5·2	5·4	56
57	2·9	3·0	3·2	3·4	3·6	3·8	4·0	4·2	4·4	4·6	4·8	4·9	5·1	5·3	5·5	57
58	2·9	3·1	3·3	3·5	3·7	3·9	4·1	4·3	4·4	4·6	4·8	5·0	5·2	5·4	5·6	58
59	3·0	3·1	3·3	3·5	3·7	3·9	4·1	4·3	4·5	4·7	4·9	5·1	5·3	5·5	5·7	59
60	3·0	3·2	3·4	3·6	3·8	4·0	4·2	4·4	4·6	4·8	5·0	5·2	5·4	5·6	5·8	60

TIME, SPEED and DISTANCE TABLE

Min.	6·0	6·2	6·4	6·6	6·8	7·0	7·2	7·4	7·6	7·8	8·0	8·2	8·4	8·6	8·8	Min.
	Knots															
	Miles	Miles	Miles	Miles	Miles	Miles	Miles	Miles	Miles	Miles	Miles	Miles	Miles	Miles	Miles	
1	0·1	0·1	0·1	0·1	0·1	0·1	0·1	0·1	0·1	0·1	0·1	0·1	0·1	0·1	0·1	1
2	0·2	0·2	0·2	0·2	0·2	0·2	0·2	0·2	0·3	0·3	0·3	0·3	0·3	0·3	0·3	2
3	0·3	0·3	0·3	0·3	0·3	0·4	0·4	0·4	0·4	0·4	0·4	0·4	0·4	0·4	0·4	3
4	0·4	0·4	0·4	0·4	0·5	0·5	0·5	0·5	0·5	0·5	0·5	0·5	0·6	0·6	0·6	4
5	0·5	0·5	0·5	0·6	0·6	0·6	0·6	0·6	0·6	0·7	0·7	0·7	0·7	0·7	0·7	5
6	0·6	0·6	0·6	0·7	0·7	0·7	0·7	0·7	0·8	0·8	0·8	0·8	0·8	0·9	0·9	6
7	0·7	0·7	0·7	0·8	0·8	0·8	0·9	0·9	0·9	0·9	0·9	1·0	1·0	1·0	1·0	7
8	0·8	0·8	0·9	0·9	0·9	0·9	1·0	1·0	1·0	1·0	1·1	1·1	1·1	1·1	1·2	8
9	0·9	0·9	1·0	1·0	1·0	1·1	1·1	1·1	1·1	1·2	1·2	1·2	1·3	1·3	1·3	9
10	1·0	1·0	1·1	1·1	1·1	1·2	1·2	1·2	1·3	1·3	1·3	1·4	1·4	1·4	1·5	10
11	1·1	1·1	1·2	1·2	1·2	1·3	1·3	1·4	1·4	1·4	1·5	1·5	1·5	1·6	1·6	11
12	1·2	1·2	1·3	1·3	1·4	1·4	1·4	1·5	1·5	1·6	1·6	1·6	1·7	1·7	1·8	12
13	1·3	1·3	1·4	1·4	1·5	1·5	1·6	1·6	1·6	1·7	1·7	1·8	1·8	1·9	1·9	13
14	1·4	1·5	1·5	1·5	1·6	1·6	1·7	1·7	1·8	1·8	1·9	1·9	2·0	2·0	2·1	14
15	1·5	1·6	1·6	1·7	1·7	1·8	1·8	1·9	1·9	2·0	2·0	2·1	2·1	2·2	2·2	15
16	1·6	1·7	1·7	1·8	1·8	1·9	1·9	2·0	2·0	2·1	2·1	2·2	2·2	2·3	2·3	16
17	1·7	1·8	1·8	1·9	1·9	2·0	2·0	2·1	2·2	2·2	2·3	2·3	2·4	2·4	2·5	17
18	1·8	1·9	1·9	2·0	2·0	2·1	2·2	2·2	2·3	2·3	2·4	2·5	2·5	2·6	2·6	18
19	1·9	2·0	2·0	2·1	2·2	2·2	2·3	2·3	2·4	2·5	2·6	2·6	2·7	2·7	2·8	19
20	2·0	2·1	2·1	2·2	2·3	2·3	2·4	2·5	2·5	2·6	2·7	2·7	2·8	2·9	2·9	20
21	2·1	2·2	2·2	2·3	2·4	2·5	2·5	2·6	2·7	2·7	2·8	2·9	2·9	3·0	3·1	21
22	2·2	2·3	2·3	2·4	2·5	2·6	2·6	2·7	2·8	2·9	2·9	3·0	3·1	3·2	3·2	22
23	2·3	2·4	2·5	2·5	2·6	2·7	2·8	2·8	2·9	3·0	3·1	3·1	3·2	3·3	3·4	23
24	2·4	2·5	2·6	2·6	2·7	2·8	2·9	3·0	3·0	3·1	3·2	3·3	3·4	3·4	3·5	24
25	2·5	2·6	2·7	2·8	2·8	2·9	3·0	3·1	3·2	3·3	3·3	3·4	3·5	3·6	3·7	25
26	2·6	2·7	2·8	2·9	2·9	3·0	3·1	3·2	3·3	3·4	3·5	3·6	3·6	3·7	3·8	26
27	2·7	2·8	2·9	3·0	3·1	3·2	3·2	3·3	3·4	3·5	3·6	3·7	3·8	3·9	4·0	27
28	2·8	2·9	3·0	3·1	3·2	3·3	3·4	3·5	3·5	3·6	3·7	3·8	3·9	4·0	4·1	28
29	2·9	3·0	3·1	3·2	3·3	3·4	3·5	3·6	3·7	3·8	3·9	4·0	4·1	4·2	4·3	29
30	3·0	3·1	3·2	3·3	3·4	3·5	3·6	3·7	3·8	3·9	4·0	4·1	4·2	4·3	4·4	30
31	3·1	3·2	3·3	3·4	3·5	3·6	3·7	3·8	3·9	4·0	4·1	4·2	4·3	4·4	4·6	31
32	3·2	3·3	3·4	3·5	3·6	3·7	3·8	3·9	4·1	4·2	4·3	4·4	4·5	4·6	4·7	32
33	3·3	3·4	3·5	3·6	3·7	3·9	4·0	4·1	4·2	4·3	4·4	4·5	4·6	4·7	4·8	33
34	3·4	3·5	3·6	3·7	3·9	4·0	4·1	4·2	4·3	4·4	4·5	4·6	4·8	4·9	5·0	34
35	3·5	3·6	3·7	3·9	4·0	4·1	4·2	4·3	4·4	4·6	4·7	4·8	4·9	5·0	5·1	35
36	3·6	3·7	3·8	4·0	4·1	4·2	4·3	4·4	4·6	4·7	4·8	4·9	5·0	5·2	5·3	36
37	3·7	3·8	3·9	4·1	4·2	4·3	4·4	4·6	4·7	4·8	4·9	5·1	5·2	5·3	5·4	37
38	3·8	3·9	4·1	4·2	4·3	4·4	4·6	4·7	4·8	4·9	5·1	5·2	5·3	5·4	5·6	38
39	3·9	4·0	4·2	4·3	4·4	4·6	4·7	4·8	4·9	5·1	5·2	5·3	5·5	5·6	5·7	39
40	4·0	4·1	4·3	4·4	4·5	4·7	4·8	4·9	5·1	5·2	5·3	5·5	5·6	5·7	5·9	40
41	4·1	4·2	4·4	4·5	4·6	4·8	4·9	5·1	5·2	5·3	5·5	5·6	5·7	5·9	6·0	41
42	4·2	4·3	4·5	4·6	4·8	4·9	5·0	5·2	5·3	5·5	5·6	5·7	5·9	6·0	6·2	42
43	4·3	4·4	4·6	4·7	4·9	5·0	5·2	5·3	5·4	5·6	5·7	5·9	6·0	6·2	6·3	43
44	4·4	4·5	4·7	4·8	5·0	5·1	5·3	5·4	5·6	5·7	5·9	6·0	6·2	6·3	6·5	44
45	4·5	4·7	4·8	5·0	5·1	5·3	5·4	5·6	5·7	5·9	6·0	6·2	6·3	6·5	6·6	45
46	4·6	4·8	4·9	5·1	5·2	5·4	5·5	5·7	5·8	6·0	6·1	6·3	6·4	6·6	6·7	46
47	4·7	4·9	5·0	5·2	5·3	5·5	5·6	5·8	6·0	6·1	6·3	6·4	6·6	6·7	6·9	47
48	4·8	5·0	5·1	5·3	5·4	5·6	5·8	5·9	6·1	6·2	6·4	6·6	6·7	6·9	7·0	48
49	4·9	5·1	5·2	5·4	5·6	5·7	5·9	6·0	6·2	6·4	6·5	6·7	6·9	7·0	7·2	49
50	5·0	5·2	5·3	5·5	5·7	5·8	6·0	6·2	6·3	6·5	6·7	6·8	7·0	7·2	7·3	50
51	5·1	5·3	5·4	5·6	5·8	6·0	6·1	6·3	6·5	6·6	6·8	7·0	7·1	7·3	7·5	51
52	5·2	5·4	5·5	5·7	5·9	6·1	6·2	6·4	6·6	6·8	6·9	7·1	7·3	7·5	7·6	52
53	5·3	5·5	5·7	5·8	6·0	6·2	6·4	6·5	6·7	6·9	7·1	7·2	7·4	7·6	7·8	53
54	5·4	5·6	5·8	5·9	6·1	6·3	6·5	6·7	6·8	7·0	7·2	7·4	7·6	7·7	7·9	54
55	5·5	5·7	5·9	6·0	6·2	6·4	6·6	6·8	7·0	7·2	7·3	7·5	7·7	7·9	8·1	55
56	5·6	5·8	6·0	6·2	6·3	6·5	6·7	6·9	7·1	7·3	7·5	7·7	7·8	8·0	8·2	56
57	5·7	5·9	6·1	6·3	6·5	6·7	6·8	7·0	7·2	7·4	7·6	7·8	8·0	8·2	8·4	57
58	5·8	6·0	6·2	6·4	6·6	6·8	7·0	7·2	7·3	7·5	7·7	7·9	8·1	8·3	8·5	58
59	5·9	6·1	6·3	6·5	6·7	6·9	7·1	7·3	7·5	7·7	7·9	8·1	8·3	8·5	8·7	59
60	6·0	6·2	6·4	6·6	6·8	7·0	7·2	7·4	7·6	7·8	8·0	8·2	8·4	8·6	8·8	60

TIME, SPEED and DISTANCE TABLE

Min.	Knots															Min.
	9·0	9·2	9·4	9·6	9·8	10·0	10·2	10·4	10·6	10·8	11·0	11·2	11·4	11·6	11·8	
	Miles	Miles	Miles	Miles	Miles	Miles	Miles	Miles	Miles	Miles	Miles	Miles	Miles	Miles	Miles	
1	0·2	0·2	0·2	0·2	0·2	0·2	0·2	0·2	0·2	0·2	0·2	0·2	0·2	0·2	0·2	1
2	0·3	0·3	0·3	0·3	0·3	0·3	0·3	0·3	0·4	0·4	0·4	0·4	0·4	0·4	0·4	2
3	0·5	0·5	0·5	0·5	0·5	0·5	0·5	0·5	0·5	0·5	0·6	0·6	0·6	0·6	0·6	3
4	0·6	0·6	0·6	0·6	0·7	0·7	0·7	0·7	0·7	0·7	0·7	0·7	0·8	0·8	0·8	4
5	0·8	0·8	0·8	0·8	0·8	0·8	0·9	0·9	0·9	0·9	0·9	0·9	1·0	1·0	1·0	5
6	0·9	0·9	0·9	1·0	1·0	1·0	1·0	1·0	1·1	1·1	1·1	1·1	1·1	1·2	1·2	6
7	1·1	1·1	1·1	1·1	1·1	1·2	1·2	1·2	1·2	1·3	1·3	1·3	1·3	1·4	1·4	7
8	1·2	1·2	1·3	1·3	1·3	1·3	1·4	1·4	1·4	1·4	1·5	1·5	1·5	1·5	1·6	8
9	1·4	1·4	1·4	1·4	1·5	1·5	1·5	1·6	1·6	1·6	1·7	1·7	1·7	1·7	1·8	9
10	1·5	1·5	1·6	1·6	1·6	1·7	1·7	1·7	1·8	1·8	1·8	1·9	1·9	1·9	2·0	10
11	1·7	1·7	1·7	1·8	1·8	1·8	1·9	1·9	1·9	2·0	2·0	2·1	2·1	2·1	2·2	11
12	1·8	1·8	1·9	1·9	2·0	2·0	2·0	2·1	2·1	2·2	2·2	2·2	2·3	2·3	2·4	12
13	2·0	2·0	2·0	2·1	2·1	2·2	2·2	2·3	2·3	2·3	2·4	2·4	2·5	2·5	2·6	13
14	2·1	2·2	2·2	2·2	2·3	2·3	2·4	2·4	2·5	2·5	2·6	2·6	2·7	2·7	2·8	14
15	2·3	2·3	2·4	2·4	2·5	2·5	2·6	2·6	2·7	2·7	2·8	2·8	2·9	2·9	3·0	15
16	2·4	2·5	2·5	2·5	2·6	2·7	2·7	2·7	2·8	2·9	2·9	3·0	3·0	3·1	3·1	16
17	2·6	2·6	2·7	2·7	2·8	2·8	2·9	3·0	3·0	3·1	3·1	3·2	3·2	3·3	3·3	17
18	2·7	2·8	2·8	2·9	2·9	3·0	3·1	3·1	3·2	3·2	3·3	3·4	3·4	3·5	3·5	18
19	2·9	2·9	3·0	3·0	3·1	3·2	3·2	3·3	3·4	3·4	3·5	3·5	3·6	3·7	3·7	19
20	3·0	3·1	3·1	3·2	3·3	3·3	3·4	3·5	3·5	3·6	3·7	3·7	3·8	3·9	3·9	20
21	3·2	3·2	3·3	3·4	3·4	3·5	3·6	3·6	3·7	3·8	3·9	3·9	4·0	4·1	4·1	21
22	3·3	3·4	3·4	3·5	3·6	3·7	3·7	3·8	3·9	4·0	4·0	4·1	4·2	4·3	4·3	22
23	3·5	3·5	3·6	3·7	3·8	3·8	3·9	4·0	4·1	4·1	4·2	4·3	4·4	4·4	4·5	23
24	3·6	3·7	3·8	3·8	3·9	4·0	4·1	4·2	4·2	4·3	4·4	4·5	4·6	4·6	4·7	24
25	3·8	3·8	3·9	4·0	4·1	4·2	4·3	4·3	4·4	4·5	4·6	4·7	4·8	4·8	4·9	25
26	3·9	4·0	4·1	4·2	4·2	4·3	4·4	4·5	4·6	4·7	4·8	4·9	4·9	5·0	5·1	26
27	4·1	4·1	4·2	4·3	4·4	4·5	4·6	4·7	4·8	4·9	5·0	5·0	5·1	5·2	5·3	27
28	4·2	4·3	4·4	4·5	4·6	4·7	4·8	4·9	4·9	5·0	5·1	5·2	5·3	5·4	5·5	28
29	4·4	4·4	4·5	4·6	4·7	4·8	4·9	5·0	5·1	5·2	5·3	5·4	5·5	5·6	5·7	29
30	4·5	4·6	4·7	4·8	4·9	5·0	5·1	5·2	5·3	5·4	5·5	5·6	5·7	5·8	5·9	30
31	4·7	4·8	4·9	5·0	5·1	5·2	5·2	5·4	5·5	5·6	5·7	5·8	5·9	6·0	6·1	31
32	4·8	4·9	5·0	5·1	5·2	5·3	5·4	5·5	5·7	5·8	5·9	6·0	6·1	6·2	6·3	32
33	5·0	5·1	5·2	5·3	5·4	5·5	5·6	5·7	5·8	5·9	6·1	6·2	6·3	6·4	6·5	33
34	5·1	5·2	5·3	5·4	5·6	5·7	5·8	5·9	6·0	6·1	6·2	6·3	6·5	6·6	6·7	34
35	5·3	5·4	5·5	5·6	5·7	5·8	6·0	6·1	6·2	6·3	6·4	6·5	6·7	6·8	6·9	35
36	5·4	5·5	5·6	5·8	5·9	6·0	6·1	6·2	6·4	6·5	6·6	6·7	6·8	7·0	7·1	36
37	5·6	5·7	5·8	5·9	6·0	6·2	6·3	6·4	6·5	6·7	6·8	6·9	7·0	7·2	7·3	37
38	5·7	5·8	6·0	6·1	6·2	6·3	6·5	6·6	6·7	6·8	7·0	7·1	7·2	7·4	7·5	38
39	5·9	6·0	6·1	6·2	6·4	6·5	6·6	6·8	6·9	7·0	7·2	7·3	7·4	7·5	7·7	39
40	6·0	6·1	6·3	6·4	6·5	6·7	6·8	6·9	7·1	7·2	7·3	7·5	7·6	7·7	7·9	40
41	6·2	6·3	6·4	6·6	6·7	6·8	7·0	7·1	7·2	7·4	7·5	7·7	7·8	7·9	8·1	41
42	6·3	6·4	6·6	6·7	6·9	7·0	7·1	7·3	7·4	7·6	7·7	7·8	8·0	8·1	8·3	42
43	6·5	6·6	6·7	6·9	7·0	7·2	7·3	7·5	7·6	7·7	7·9	8·0	8·2	8·3	8·5	43
44	6·6	6·7	6·9	7·0	7·2	7·3	7·5	7·6	7·8	7·9	8·1	8·2	8·4	8·5	8·7	44
45	6·8	6·9	7·1	7·2	7·4	7·5	7·7	7·8	8·0	8·1	8·3	8·4	8·6	8·7	8·9	45
46	6·9	7·1	7·2	7·4	7·5	7·7	7·8	8·0	8·1	8·3	8·4	8·6	8·7	8·9	9·0	46
47	7·1	7·2	7·4	7·5	7·7	7·8	8·0	8·1	8·3	8·5	8·6	8·8	8·9	9·1	9·2	47
48	7·2	7·4	7·5	7·7	7·8	8·0	8·2	8·3	8·5	8·6	8·8	9·0	9·1	9·3	9·4	48
49	7·4	7·5	7·7	7·8	8·0	8·2	8·3	8·5	8·7	8·8	9·0	9·1	9·3	9·5	9·6	49
50	7·5	7·7	7·8	8·0	8·2	8·3	8·5	8·7	8·8	9·0	9·2	9·3	9·5	9·7	9·8	50
51	7·7	7·8	8·0	8·2	8·3	8·5	8·7	8·8	9·0	9·2	9·4	9·5	9·7	9·9	10·0	51
52	7·8	8·0	8·1	8·3	8·5	8·7	8·8	9·0	9·2	9·4	9·5	9·7	9·9	10·1	10·2	52
53	8·0	8·1	8·3	8·5	8·7	8·8	9·0	9·2	9·4	9·5	9·7	9·9	10·1	10·2	10·4	53
54	8·1	8·3	8·5	8·6	8·8	9·0	9·2	9·4	9·5	9·7	9·9	10·1	10·3	10·4	10·6	54
55	8·3	8·4	8·6	8·8	9·0	9·2	9·4	9·5	9·7	9·9	10·1	10·3	10·5	10·6	10·8	55
56	8·4	8·6	8·8	9·0	9·1	9·3	9·5	9·7	9·9	10·1	10·3	10·5	10·6	10·8	11·0	56
57	8·6	8·7	8·9	9·1	9·3	9·5	9·7	9·9	10·1	10·3	10·5	10·6	10·8	11·0	11·2	57
58	8·7	8·9	9·1	9·3	9·5	9·7	9·9	10·1	10·2	10·4	10·6	10·8	11·0	11·2	11·4	58
59	8·9	9·0	9·2	9·4	9·6	9·8	10·0	10·2	10·4	10·6	10·8	11·0	11·2	11·4	11·6	59
60	9·0	9·2	9·4	9·6	9·8	10·0	10·2	10·4	10·6	10·8	11·0	11·2	11·4	11·6	11·8	60

TIME, SPEED and DISTANCE TABLE

Min.	12·0	12·2	12·4	12·6	12·8	13·0	13·2	13·4	13·6	13·8	14·0	14·2	14·4	14·6	14·8	Min.
	Miles	Miles	Miles	Miles	Miles	Miles	Miles	Miles	Miles	Miles	Miles	Miles	Miles	Miles	Miles	
1	0·2	0·2	0·2	0·2	0·2	0·2	0·2	0·2	0·2	0·2	0·2	0·2	0·2	0·2	0·2	1
2	0·4	0·4	0·4	0·4	0·4	0·4	0·4	0·4	0·5	0·5	0·5	0·5	0·5	0·5	0·5	2
3	0·6	0·6	0·6	0·6	0·6	0·7	0·7	0·7	0·7	0·7	0·7	0·7	0·7	0·7	0·7	3
4	0·8	0·8	0·8	0·8	0·9	0·9	0·9	0·9	0·9	0·9	0·9	0·9	1·0	1·0	1·0	4
5	1·0	1·0	1·0	1·1	1·1	1·1	1·1	1·1	1·1	1·2	1·2	1·2	1·2	1·2	1·2	5
6	1·2	1·2	1·2	1·3	1·3	1·3	1·3	1·3	1·4	1·4	1·4	1·4	1·4	1·5	1·5	6
7	1·4	1·4	1·4	1·5	1·5	1·5	1·5	1·6	1·6	1·6	1·6	1·7	1·7	1·7	1·7	7
8	1·6	1·6	1·7	1·7	1·7	1·7	1·8	1·8	1·8	1·8	1·9	1·9	1·9	1·9	2·0	8
9	1·8	1·8	1·9	1·9	1·9	2·0	2·0	2·0	2·0	2·1	2·1	2·1	2·2	2·2	2·2	9
10	2·0	2·0	2·1	2·1	2·1	2·2	2·2	2·2	2·3	2·3	2·3	2·4	2·4	2·4	2·5	10
11	2·2	2·2	2·3	2·3	2·3	2·4	2·4	2·5	2·5	2·5	2·6	2·6	2·6	2·7	2·7	11
12	2·4	2·4	2·5	2·5	2·6	2·6	2·6	2·7	2·7	2·8	2·8	2·8	2·9	2·9	3·0	12
13	2·6	2·6	2·7	2·7	2·8	2·8	2·9	2·9	2·9	3·0	3·0	3·1	3·1	3·2	3·2	13
14	2·8	2·8	2·9	2·9	3·0	3·0	3·1	3·1	3·2	3·2	3·3	3·3	3·4	3·4	3·5	14
15	3·0	3·1	3·1	3·2	3·2	3·3	3·3	3·4	3·4	3·5	3·5	3·6	3·6	3·7	3·7	15
16	3·2	3·3	3·3	3·4	3·4	3·5	3·5	3·6	3·6	3·7	3·7	3·8	3·8	3·9	3·9	16
17	3·4	3·5	3·5	3·6	3·6	3·7	3·7	3·8	3·9	3·9	4·0	4·0	4·1	4·1	4·2	17
18	3·6	3·7	3·7	3·8	3·8	3·9	4·0	4·0	4·1	4·1	4·2	4·3	4·3	4·4	4·4	18
19	3·8	3·9	3·9	4·0	4·1	4·1	4·2	4·2	4·3	4·4	4·4	4·5	4·6	4·6	4·7	19
20	4·0	4·1	4·1	4·2	4·3	4·3	4·4	4·5	4·5	4·6	4·7	4·7	4·8	4·9	4·9	20
21	4·2	4·3	4·3	4·4	4·5	4·6	4·6	4·7	4·8	4·8	4·9	5·0	5·0	5·1	5·2	21
22	4·4	4·5	4·5	4·6	4·7	4·8	4·8	4·9	5·0	5·1	5·1	5·2	5·3	5·4	5·4	22
23	4·6	4·7	4·8	4·8	4·9	5·0	5·1	5·1	5·2	5·3	5·4	5·4	5·5	5·6	5·7	23
24	4·8	4·9	5·0	5·0	5·1	5·2	5·3	5·4	5·4	5·5	5·6	5·7	5·8	5·8	5·9	24
25	5·0	5·1	5·2	5·3	5·3	5·4	5·5	5·6	5·7	5·8	5·8	5·9	6·0	6·1	6·2	25
26	5·2	5·3	5·4	5·5	5·5	5·6	5·7	5·8	5·9	6·0	6·1	6·2	6·2	6·3	6·4	26
27	5·4	5·5	5·6	5·7	5·8	5·9	5·9	6·0	6·1	6·2	6·3	6·4	6·5	6·6	6·7	27
28	5·6	5·7	5·8	5·9	6·0	6·1	6·2	6·3	6·3	6·4	6·5	6·6	6·7	6·8	6·9	28
29	5·8	5·9	6·0	6·1	6·2	6·3	6·4	6·5	6·6	6·7	6·8	6·9	7·0	7·1	7·2	29
30	6·0	6·1	6·2	6·3	6·4	6·5	6·6	6·7	6·8	6·9	7·0	7·1	7·2	7·3	7·4	30
31	6·2	6·3	6·4	6·5	6·6	6·7	6·8	6·9	7·0	7·1	7·2	7·3	7·4	7·5	7·6	31
32	6·4	6·5	6·6	6·7	6·8	6·9	7·0	7·1	7·3	7·4	7·5	7·6	7·7	7·8	7·9	32
33	6·6	6·7	6·8	6·9	7·0	7·2	7·3	7·4	7·5	7·6	7·7	7·8	7·9	8·0	8·1	33
34	6·8	6·9	7·0	7·1	7·3	7·4	7·5	7·6	7·7	7·8	7·9	8·0	8·2	8·3	8·4	34
35	7·0	7·1	7·2	7·4	7·5	7·6	7·7	7·8	7·9	8·1	8·2	8·3	8·4	8·5	8·6	35
36	7·2	7·3	7·4	7·6	7·7	7·8	7·9	8·0	8·2	8·3	8·4	8·5	8·6	8·8	8·9	36
37	7·4	7·5	7·6	7·8	7·9	8·0	8·1	8·3	8·4	8·5	8·6	8·8	8·9	9·0	9·1	37
38	7·6	7·7	7·9	8·0	8·1	8·2	8·4	8·5	8·6	8·7	8·9	9·0	9·1	9·2	9·4	38
39	7·8	7·9	8·1	8·2	8·3	8·5	8·6	8·7	8·8	9·0	9·1	9·2	9·4	9·5	9·6	39
40	8·0	8·1	8·3	8·4	8·5	8·7	8·8	8·9	9·1	9·2	9·3	9·5	9·6	9·7	9·9	40
41	8·2	8·3	8·5	8·6	8·7	8·9	9·0	9·2	9·3	9·4	9·6	9·7	9·8	10·0	10·1	41
42	8·4	8·5	8·7	8·8	9·0	9·1	9·2	9·4	9·5	9·7	9·8	9·9	10·1	10·2	10·4	42
43	8·6	8·7	8·9	9·0	9·2	9·3	9·5	9·6	9·7	9·9	10·0	10·2	10·3	10·5	10·6	43
44	8·8	8·9	9·1	9·2	9·4	9·5	9·7	9·8	10·0	10·1	10·3	10·4	10·6	10·7	10·9	44
45	9·0	9·2	9·3	9·5	9·6	9·8	9·9	10·1	10·2	10·4	10·5	10·7	10·8	11·0	11·1	45
46	9·2	9·4	9·5	9·7	9·8	10·0	10·1	10·3	10·4	10·6	10·7	10·9	11·0	11·2	11·3	46
47	9·4	9·6	9·7	9·9	10·0	10·2	10·3	10·5	10·7	10·8	11·0	11·1	11·3	11·4	11·6	47
48	9·6	9·8	9·9	10·1	10·2	10·4	10·6	10·7	10·9	11·0	11·2	11·4	11·5	11·7	11·8	48
49	9·8	10·0	10·1	10·3	10·5	10·6	10·8	10·9	11·1	11·3	11·4	11·6	11·8	11·9	12·1	49
50	10·0	10·2	10·3	10·5	10·7	10·8	11·0	11·2	11·3	11·5	11·7	11·8	12·0	12·2	12·3	50
51	10·2	10·4	10·5	10·7	10·9	11·0	11·2	11·4	11·6	11·7	11·9	12·1	12·2	12·4	12·6	51
52	10·4	10·6	10·7	10·9	11·1	11·3	11·4	11·6	11·8	12·0	12·1	12·3	12·5	12·7	12·8	52
53	10·6	10·8	11·0	11·1	11·3	11·5	11·7	11·8	12·0	12·2	12·4	12·5	12·7	12·9	13·1	53
54	10·8	11·0	11·2	11·3	11·5	11·7	11·9	12·1	12·2	12·4	12·6	12·8	13·0	13·1	13·3	54
55	11·0	11·2	11·4	11·6	11·7	11·9	12·1	12·3	12·5	12·7	12·8	13·0	13·2	13·4	13·6	55
56	11·2	11·4	11·6	11·8	11·9	12·1	12·3	12·5	12·7	12·9	13·1	13·3	13·4	13·6	13·8	56
57	11·4	11·6	11·8	12·0	12·2	12·4	12·5	12·7	12·9	13·1	13·3	13·5	13·7	13·9	14·1	57
58	11·6	11·8	12·0	12·2	12·4	12·6	12·8	13·0	13·1	13·3	13·5	13·7	13·9	14·1	14·3	58
59	11·8	12·0	12·2	12·4	12·6	12·8	13·0	13·2	13·4	13·6	13·8	14·0	14·2	14·4	14·6	59
60	12·0	12·2	12·4	12·6	12·8	13·0	13·2	13·4	13·6	13·8	14·0	14·2	14·4	14·6	14·8	60

TIME, SPEED and DISTANCE TABLE

Min.	Knots															Min.
	15·0	15·2	15·4	15·6	15·8	16·0	16·2	16·4	16·6	16·8	17·0	17·2	17·4	17·6	17·8	
	Miles	Miles	Miles	Miles	Miles	Miles	Miles	Miles	Miles	Miles	Miles	Miles	Miles	Miles	Miles	
1	0·3	0·3	0·3	0·3	0·3	0·3	0·3	0·3	0·3	0·3	0·3	0·3	0·3	0·3	0·3	1
2	0·5	0·5	0·5	0·5	0·5	0·5	0·5	0·5	0·6	0·6	0·6	0·6	0·6	0·6	0·6	2
3	0·8	0·8	0·8	0·8	0·8	0·8	0·8	0·8	0·8	0·8	0·9	0·9	0·9	0·9	0·9	3
4	1·0	1·0	1·0	1·0	1·0	1·1	1·1	1·1	1·1	1·1	1·1	1·1	1·2	1·2	1·2	4
5	1·3	1·3	1·3	1·3	1·3	1·3	1·4	1·4	1·4	1·4	1·4	1·4	1·5	1·5	1·5	5
6	1·5	1·5	1·5	1·6	1·6	1·6	1·6	1·6	1·7	1·7	1·7	1·7	1·7	1·8	1·8	6
7	1·8	1·8	1·8	1·8	1·8	1·9	1·9	1·9	1·9	2·0	2·0	2·0	2·0	2·1	2·1	7
8	2·0	2·0	2·1	2·1	2·1	2·1	2·2	2·2	2·2	2·2	2·3	2·3	2·3	2·3	2·4	8
9	2·3	2·3	2·3	2·3	2·4	2·4	2·4	2·5	2·5	2·5	2·6	2·6	2·6	2·6	2·7	9
10	2·5	2·5	2·6	2·6	2·6	2·7	2·7	2·7	2·8	2·8	2·8	2·9	2·9	2·9	3·0	10
11	2·8	2·8	2·8	2·9	2·9	2·9	3·0	3·0	3·0	3·1	3·1	3·2	3·2	3·2	3·3	11
12	3·0	3·0	3·1	3·1	3·2	3·2	3·2	3·3	3·3	3·4	3·4	3·4	3·5	3·5	3·6	12
13	3·3	3·3	3·3	3·4	3·4	3·5	3·5	3·6	3·6	3·6	3·7	3·7	3·8	3·8	3·9	13
14	3·5	3·5	3·6	3·6	3·7	3·7	3·8	3·8	3·9	3·9	4·0	4·0	4·1	4·1	4·2	14
15	3·8	3·8	3·9	3·9	4·0	4·0	4·1	4·1	4·2	4·2	4·3	4·3	4·4	4·4	4·5	15
16	4·0	4·1	4·1	4·2	4·2	4·3	4·3	4·4	4·4	4·5	4·5	4·6	4·6	4·7	4·7	16
17	4·3	4·3	4·4	4·4	4·5	4·5	4·6	4·6	4·7	4·8	4·8	4·9	4·9	5·0	5·0	17
18	4·5	4·6	4·6	4·7	4·7	4·8	4·9	4·9	5·0	5·0	5·1	5·2	5·2	5·3	5·3	18
19	4·8	4·8	4·9	4·9	5·0	5·1	5·1	5·2	5·3	5·3	5·4	5·4	5·5	5·6	5·6	19
20	5·0	5·1	5·1	5·2	5·3	5·3	5·4	5·5	5·5	5·6	5·7	5·7	5·8	5·9	5·9	20
21	5·3	5·3	5·4	5·5	5·5	5·6	5·7	5·7	5·8	5·9	6·0	6·0	6·1	6·2	6·2	21
22	5·5	5·6	5·6	5·7	5·8	5·9	5·9	6·0	6·1	6·2	6·2	6·3	6·4	6·5	6·5	22
23	5·8	5·8	5·9	6·0	6·1	6·1	6·2	6·3	6·4	6·4	6·5	6·6	6·7	6·7	6·8	23
24	6·0	6·1	6·2	6·2	6·3	6·4	6·5	6·6	6·6	6·7	6·8	6·9	7·0	7·0	7·1	24
25	6·3	6·3	6·4	6·5	6·6	6·7	6·8	6·8	6·9	7·0	7·1	7·2	7·3	7·3	7·4	25
26	6·5	6·6	6·7	6·8	6·8	6·9	7·0	7·1	7·2	7·3	7·4	7·5	7·5	7·6	7·7	26
27	6·8	6·8	6·9	7·0	7·1	7·2	7·3	7·4	7·5	7·6	7·7	7·7	7·8	7·9	8·0	27
28	7·0	7·1	7·2	7·3	7·4	7·5	7·6	7·7	7·7	7·8	7·9	8·0	8·1	8·2	8·3	28
29	7·3	7·3	7·4	7·5	7·6	7·7	7·8	7·9	8·0	8·1	8·2	8·3	8·4	8·5	8·6	29
30	7·5	7·6	7·7	7·8	7·9	8·0	8·1	8·2	8·3	8·4	8·5	8·6	8·7	8·8	8·9	30
31	7·8	7·9	8·0	8·1	8·2	8·3	8·4	8·5	8·6	8·7	8·8	8·9	9·0	9·1	9·2	31
32	8·0	8·1	8·2	8·3	8·4	8·5	8·6	8·7	8·9	9·0	9·1	9·2	9·3	9·4	9·5	32
33	8·3	8·4	8·5	8·6	8·7	8·8	8·9	9·0	9·1	9·2	9·4	9·5	9·6	9·7	9·8	33
34	8·5	8·6	8·7	8·8	9·0	9·1	9·2	9·3	9·4	9·5	9·6	9·7	9·9	10·0	10·1	34
35	8·8	8·9	9·0	9·1	9·2	9·3	9·5	9·6	9·7	9·8	9·9	10·0	10·2	10·3	10·4	35
36	9·0	9·1	9·2	9·4	9·5	9·6	9·7	9·8	10·0	10·1	10·2	10·3	10·4	10·6	10·7	36
37	9·3	9·4	9·5	9·6	9·7	9·9	10·0	10·1	10·2	10·4	10·5	10·6	10·7	10·9	11·0	37
38	9·5	9·6	9·8	9·9	10·0	10·1	10·3	10·4	10·5	10·6	10·8	10·9	11·0	11·1	11·3	38
39	9·8	9·9	10·0	10·1	10·3	10·4	10·5	10·7	10·8	10·9	11·1	11·2	11·3	11·4	11·6	39
40	10·0	10·1	10·3	10·4	10·5	10·7	10·8	10·9	11·1	11·2	11·3	11·5	11·6	11·7	11·9	40
41	10·3	10·4	10·5	10·7	10·8	10·9	11·1	11·2	11·3	11·5	11·6	11·8	11·9	12·0	12·2	41
42	10·5	10·6	10·8	10·9	11·1	11·2	11·3	11·5	11·6	11·8	11·9	12·0	12·2	12·3	12·5	42
43	10·8	10·9	11·0	11·2	11·3	11·5	11·6	11·8	11·9	12·0	12·2	12·3	12·5	12·6	12·8	43
44	11·0	11·1	11·3	11·4	11·6	11·7	11·9	12·0	12·2	12·3	12·5	12·6	12·8	12·9	13·1	44
45	11·3	11·4	11·6	11·7	11·9	12·0	12·2	12·3	12·5	12·6	12·8	12·9	13·1	13·2	13·4	45
46	11·5	11·7	11·8	12·0	12·1	12·3	12·4	12·6	12·7	12·9	13·0	13·2	13·3	13·5	13·6	46
47	11·8	11·9	12·1	12·2	12·4	12·5	12·7	12·8	13·0	13·2	13·3	13·5	13·6	13·8	13·9	47
48	12·0	12·2	12·3	12·5	12·6	12·8	13·0	13·1	13·3	13·4	13·6	13·8	13·9	14·1	14·2	48
49	12·3	12·4	12·6	12·7	12·9	13·1	13·2	13·4	13·6	13·7	13·9	14·0	14·2	14·4	14·5	49
50	12·5	12·7	12·8	13·0	13·2	13·3	13·5	13·7	13·8	14·0	14·2	14·3	14·5	14·7	14·8	50
51	12·8	12·9	13·1	13·3	13·4	13·6	13·8	13·9	14·1	14·3	14·5	14·6	14·8	15·0	15·1	51
52	13·0	13·2	13·3	13·5	13·7	13·9	14·0	14·2	14·4	14·6	14·7	14·9	15·1	15·3	15·4	52
53	13·3	13·4	13·6	13·8	14·0	14·1	14·3	14·5	14·7	14·8	15·0	15·2	15·4	15·5	15·7	53
54	13·5	13·7	13·9	14·0	14·2	14·4	14·6	14·8	14·9	15·1	15·3	15·5	15·7	15·8	16·0	54
55	13·8	13·9	14·1	14·3	14·5	14·7	14·9	15·0	15·2	15·4	15·6	15·8	16·0	16·1	16·3	55
56	14·0	14·2	14·4	14·6	14·7	14·9	15·1	15·3	15·5	15·7	15·9	16·1	16·2	16·4	16·6	56
57	14·3	14·4	14·6	14·8	15·0	15·2	15·4	15·6	15·8	16·0	16·2	16·3	16·5	16·7	16·9	57
58	14·5	14·7	14·9	15·1	15·3	15·5	15·7	15·9	16·0	16·2	16·4	16·6	16·8	17·0	17·2	58
59	14·8	14·9	15·1	15·3	15·5	15·7	15·9	16·1	16·3	16·5	16·7	16·9	17·1	17·3	17·5	59
60	15·0	15·2	15·4	15·6	15·8	16·0	16·2	16·4	16·6	16·8	17·0	17·2	17·4	17·6	17·8	60

TIME, SPEED and DISTANCE TABLE

Min.	Knots															Min.
	18·0	18·2	18·4	18·6	18·8	19·0	19·2	19·4	19·6	19·8	20·0	20·2	20·4	20·6	20·8	
	Miles	Miles	Miles	Miles	Miles	Miles	Miles	Miles	Miles	Miles	Miles	Miles	Miles	Miles	Miles	
1	0·3	0·3	0·3	0·3	0·3	0·3	0·3	0·3	0·3	0·3	0·3	0·3	0·3	0·3	0·3	1
2	0·6	0·6	0·6	0·6	0·6	0·6	0·6	0·6	0·7	0·7	0·7	0·7	0·7	0·7	0·7	2
3	0·9	0·9	0·9	0·9	0·9	1·0	1·0	1·0	1·0	1·0	1·0	1·0	1·0	1·0	1·0	3
4	1·2	1·2	1·2	1·2	1·3	1·3	1·3	1·3	1·3	1·3	1·3	1·3	1·4	1·4	1·4	4
5	1·5	1·5	1·5	1·6	1·6	1·6	1·6	1·6	1·6	1·7	1·7	1·7	1·7	1·7	1·7	5
6	1·8	1·8	1·8	1·9	1·9	1·9	1·9	1·9	2·0	2·0	2·0	2·0	2·0	2·1	2·1	6
7	2·1	2·1	2·1	2·2	2·2	2·2	2·2	2·3	2·3	2·3	2·3	2·4	2·4	2·4	2·4	7
8	2·4	2·4	2·5	2·5	2·5	2·5	2·6	2·6	2·6	2·6	2·7	2·7	2·7	2·7	2·8	8
9	2·7	2·7	2·8	2·8	2·8	2·9	2·9	2·9	2·9	3·0	3·0	3·0	3·1	3·1	3·1	9
10	3·0	3·0	3·1	3·1	3·1	3·2	3·2	3·2	3·3	3·3	3·3	3·4	3·4	3·4	3·5	10
11	3·3	3·3	3·4	3·4	3·4	3·5	3·5	3·6	3·6	3·6	3·7	3·7	3·7	3·8	3·8	11
12	3·6	3·6	3·7	3·7	3·8	3·8	3·8	3·9	3·9	4·0	4·0	4·0	4·1	4·1	4·2	12
13	3·9	3·9	4·0	4·0	4·1	4·1	4·2	4·2	4·2	4·3	4·3	4·4	4·4	4·5	4·5	13
14	4·2	4·2	4·3	4·3	4·4	4·4	4·5	4·5	4·6	4·6	4·7	4·7	4·8	4·8	4·9	14
15	4·5	4·6	4·6	4·7	4·7	4·8	4·8	4·9	4·9	5·0	5·0	5·1	5·1	5·2	5·2	15
16	4·8	4·9	4·9	5·0	5·1	5·1	5·1	5·2	5·2	5·3	5·3	5·4	5·4	5·5	5·6	16
17	5·1	5·2	5·2	5·3	5·3	5·4	5·4	5·5	5·6	5·6	5·7	5·7	5·8	5·8	5·9	17
18	5·4	5·5	5·5	5·6	5·6	5·7	5·8	5·8	5·9	5·9	6·0	6·1	6·1	6·2	6·2	18
19	5·7	5·8	5·8	5·9	6·0	6·0	6·1	6·1	6·2	6·3	6·3	6·4	6·5	6·5	6·6	19
20	6·0	6·1	6·1	6·2	6·3	6·3	6·4	6·5	6·5	6·6	6·7	6·7	6·8	6·9	6·9	20
21	6·3	6·4	6·4	6·5	6·6	6·7	6·7	6·8	6·9	6·9	7·0	7·1	7·1	7·2	7·3	21
22	6·6	6·7	6·7	6·8	6·9	7·0	7·0	7·1	7·2	7·3	7·3	7·4	7·5	7·6	7·6	22
23	6·9	7·0	7·1	7·1	7·2	7·3	7·4	7·4	7·5	7·6	7·7	7·7	7·8	7·9	8·0	23
24	7·2	7·3	7·4	7·4	7·5	7·6	7·7	7·8	7·8	7·9	8·0	8·1	8·2	8·2	8·3	24
25	7·5	7·6	7·7	7·8	7·8	7·9	8·0	8·1	8·2	8·3	8·3	8·4	8·5	8·6	8·7	25
26	7·8	7·9	8·0	8·1	8·1	8·2	8·3	8·4	8·5	8·6	8·7	8·8	8·8	8·9	9·0	26
27	8·1	8·2	8·3	8·4	8·5	8·6	8·6	8·7	8·8	8·9	9·0	9·1	9·2	9·3	9·4	27
28	8·4	8·5	8·6	8·7	8·8	8·9	9·0	9·1	9·1	9·2	9·3	9·4	9·5	9·6	9·7	28
29	8·7	8·8	8·9	9·0	9·1	9·2	9·3	9·4	9·5	9·6	9·7	9·8	9·9	10·0	10·1	29
30	9·0	9·1	9·2	9·3	9·4	9·5	9·6	9·7	9·8	9·9	10·0	10·1	10·2	10·3	10·4	30
31	9·3	9·4	9·5	9·6	9·7	9·8	9·9	10·0	10·1	10·2	10·3	10·4	10·5	10·6	10·7	31
32	9·6	9·7	9·8	9·9	10·0	10·1	10·2	10·3	10·5	10·6	10·7	10·8	10·9	11·0	11·1	32
33	9·9	10·0	10·1	10·2	10·3	10·5	10·6	10·7	10·8	10·9	11·0	11·1	11·2	11·3	11·4	33
34	10·2	10·3	10·4	10·5	10·7	10·8	10·9	11·0	11·1	11·2	11·3	11·4	11·6	11·7	11·8	34
35	10·5	10·6	10·7	10·9	11·0	11·1	11·2	11·3	11·4	11·6	11·7	11·8	11·9	12·0	12·1	35
36	10·8	10·9	11·0	11·2	11·3	11·4	11·5	11·6	11·8	11·9	12·0	12·1	12·2	12·4	12·5	36
37	11·1	11·2	11·3	11·5	11·6	11·7	11·8	12·0	12·1	12·2	12·3	12·5	12·6	12·7	12·8	37
38	11·4	11·5	11·7	11·8	11·9	12·0	12·2	12·3	12·4	12·5	12·7	12·8	12·9	13·0	13·2	38
39	11·7	11·8	12·0	12·1	12·2	12·4	12·5	12·6	12·7	12·9	13·0	13·1	13·3	13·4	13·5	39
40	12·0	12·1	12·3	12·4	12·5	12·7	12·8	12·9	13·1	13·2	13·3	13·5	13·6	13·7	13·9	40
41	12·3	12·4	12·6	12·7	12·8	13·0	13·1	13·3	13·4	13·5	13·7	13·8	13·9	14·1	14·2	41
42	12·6	12·7	12·9	13·0	13·2	13·3	13·4	13·6	13·7	13·9	14·0	14·1	14·3	14·4	14·6	42
43	12·9	13·0	13·2	13·3	13·5	13·6	13·8	13·9	14·0	14·2	14·3	14·5	14·6	14·7	14·9	43
44	13·2	13·3	13·5	13·6	13·8	13·9	14·1	14·2	14·4	14·5	14·7	14·8	15·0	15·1	15·3	44
45	13·5	13·7	13·8	14·0	14·1	14·3	14·4	14·6	14·7	14·9	15·0	15·2	15·3	15·5	15·6	45
46	13·8	14·0	14·1	14·3	14·4	14·6	14·7	14·9	15·0	15·2	15·3	15·5	15·6	15·8	15·9	46
47	14·1	14·3	14·4	14·6	14·7	14·9	15·0	15·2	15·4	15·5	15·7	15·8	16·0	16·1	16·3	47
48	14·4	14·6	14·7	14·9	15·0	15·2	15·4	15·5	15·7	15·8	16·0	16·2	16·3	16·5	16·6	48
49	14·7	14·9	15·0	15·2	15·4	15·5	15·7	15·8	16·0	16·2	16·3	16·5	16·7	16·8	17·0	49
50	15·0	15·2	15·3	15·5	15·7	15·8	16·0	16·2	16·3	16·5	16·7	16·8	17·0	17·2	17·3	50
51	15·3	15·5	15·6	15·8	16·0	16·2	16·3	16·5	16·7	16·8	17·0	17·2	17·3	17·5	17·7	51
52	15·6	15·8	15·9	16·1	16·3	16·5	16·6	16·8	17·0	17·2	17·3	17·5	17·7	17·9	18·0	52
53	15·9	16·1	16·3	16·4	16·6	16·8	17·0	17·1	17·3	17·5	17·7	17·8	18·0	18·2	18·4	53
54	16·2	16·4	16·6	16·7	16·9	17·1	17·3	17·5	17·6	17·8	18·0	18·2	18·4	18·5	18·7	54
55	16·5	16·7	16·9	17·1	17·2	17·4	17·6	17·8	18·0	18·2	18·3	18·5	18·7	18·9	19·1	55
56	16·8	17·0	17·2	17·4	17·5	17·7	17·9	18·1	18·3	18·5	18·7	18·9	19·0	19·2	19·4	56
57	17·1	17·3	17·5	17·7	17·9	18·0	18·2	18·4	18·6	18·8	19·0	19·2	19·4	19·6	19·7	57
58	17·4	17·6	17·8	18·0	18·2	18·4	18·6	18·8	18·9	19·1	19·3	19·5	19·7	19·9	20·1	58
59	17·7	17·9	18·1	18·3	18·5	18·7	18·9	19·1	19·3	19·5	19·7	19·9	20·1	20·3	20·5	59
60	18·0	18·2	18·4	18·6	18·8	19·0	19·2	19·4	19·6	19·8	20·0	20·2	20·4	20·6	20·8	60

TIME, SPEED and DISTANCE TABLE

Min.	|						Knots									Min.
	21·0	21·2	21·4	21·6	21·8	22·0	22·2	22·4	22·6	22·8	23·0	23·2	23·4	23·6	23·8	
	Miles	Miles	Miles	Miles	Miles	Miles	Miles	Miles	Miles	Miles	Miles	Miles	Miles	Miles	Miles	
1	0·4	0·4	0·4	0·4	0·4	0·4	0·4	0·4	0·4	0·4	0·4	0·4	0·4	0·4	0·4	1
2	0·7	0·7	0·7	0·7	0·7	0·7	0·7	0·7	0·8	0·8	0·8	0·8	0·8	0·8	0·8	2
3	1·1	1·1	1·1	1·1	1·1	1·1	1·1	1·1	1·1	1·1	1·2	1·2	1·2	1·2	1·2	3
4	1·4	1·4	1·4	1·4	1·5	1·5	1·5	1·5	1·5	1·5	1·5	1·5	1·6	1·6	1·6	4
5	1·8	1·8	1·8	1·8	1·8	1·8	1·9	1·9	1·9	1·9	1·9	1·9	2·0	2·0	2·0	5
6	2·1	2·1	2·1	2·2	2·2	2·2	2·2	2·2	2·3	2·3	2·3	2·3	2·3	2·4	2·4	6
7	2·5	2·5	2·5	2·5	2·5	2·6	2·6	2·6	2·6	2·7	2·7	2·7	2·7	2·8	2·8	7
8	2·8	2·8	2·9	2·9	2·9	2·9	3·0	3·0	3·0	3·0	3·1	3·1	3·1	3·1	3·2	8
9	3·2	3·2	3·2	3·2	3·3	3·3	3·3	3·4	3·4	3·4	3·5	3·5	3·5	3·5	3·6	9
10	3·5	3·5	3·6	3·6	3·6	3·7	3·7	3·7	3·8	3·8	3·8	3·9	3·9	3·9	4·0	10
11	3·9	3·9	3·9	4·0	4·0	4·0	4·1	4·1	4·1	4·2	4·2	4·3	4·3	4·3	4·4	11
12	4·2	4·2	4·3	4·3	4·4	4·4	4·4	4·5	4·5	4·6	4·6	4·6	4·7	4·7	4·8	12
13	4·6	4·6	4·6	4·7	4·7	4·8	4·8	4·9	4·9	4·9	5·0	5·0	5·1	5·1	5·2	13
14	4·9	4·9	5·0	5·0	5·1	5·1	5·2	5·2	5·3	5·3	5·4	5·4	5·5	5·5	5·6	14
15	5·3	5·3	5·4	5·4	5·5	5·5	5·6	5·6	5·7	5·7	5·8	5·8	5·9	5·9	6·0	15
16	5·6	5·7	5·7	5·8	5·8	5·9	5·9	6·0	6·0	6·1	6·1	6·2	6·2	6·3	6·3	16
17	6·0	6·0	6·1	6·1	6·2	6·2	6·3	6·3	6·4	6·5	6·5	6·6	6·6	6·7	6·7	17
18	6·3	6·4	6·4	6·5	6·5	6·6	6·7	6·7	6·8	6·8	6·9	7·0	7·0	7·1	7·1	18
19	6·7	6·7	6·8	6·8	6·9	7·0	7·0	7·1	7·2	7·2	7·3	7·4	7·4	7·5	7·5	19
20	7·0	7·1	7·1	7·2	7·3	7·3	7·4	7·5	7·5	7·6	7·7	7·7	7·8	7·9	7·9	20
21	7·4	7·4	7·5	7·6	7·6	7·7	7·8	7·8	7·9	8·0	8·1	8·1	8·2	8·3	8·3	21
22	7·7	7·8	7·8	7·9	8·0	8·1	8·1	8·2	8·3	8·4	8·4	8·5	8·6	8·7	8·7	22
23	8·1	8·1	8·2	8·3	8·4	8·4	8·5	8·6	8·7	8·7	8·8	8·9	9·0	9·0	9·1	23
24	8·4	8·5	8·6	8·6	8·7	8·8	8·9	9·0	9·0	9·1	9·2	9·3	9·4	9·4	9·5	24
25	8·8	8·8	8·9	9·0	9·1	9·2	9·3	9·3	9·4	9·5	9·6	9·7	9·8	9·8	9·9	25
26	9·1	9·2	9·3	9·4	9·4	9·5	9·6	9·7	9·8	9·9	10·0	10·1	10·1	10·2	10·3	26
27	9·5	9·5	9·6	9·7	9·8	9·9	10·0	10·1	10·2	10·3	10·4	10·4	10·5	10·6	10·7	27
28	9·8	9·9	10·0	10·1	10·2	10·3	10·4	10·5	10·6	10·6	10·7	10·8	10·9	11·0	11·1	28
29	10·2	10·2	10·3	10·4	10·5	10·6	10·7	10·8	10·9	11·0	11·1	11·2	11·3	11·4	11·5	29
30	10·5	10·6	10·7	10·8	10·9	11·0	11·1	11·2	11·3	11·4	11·5	11·6	11·7	11·8	11·9	30
31	10·9	11·0	11·1	11·2	11·3	11·4	11·5	11·6	11·7	11·8	11·9	12·0	12·1	12·2	12·3	31
32	11·2	11·3	11·4	11·5	11·6	11·7	11·8	11·9	12·1	12·2	12·3	12·4	12·5	12·6	12·7	32
33	11·6	11·7	11·8	11·9	12·0	12·1	12·2	12·3	12·4	12·5	12·7	12·8	12·9	13·0	13·1	33
34	11·9	12·0	12·1	12·2	12·4	12·5	12·6	12·7	12·8	12·9	13·0	13·1	13·3	13·4	13·5	34
35	12·3	12·4	12·5	12·6	12·7	12·8	13·0	13·1	13·2	13·3	13·4	13·5	13·7	13·8	13·9	35
36	12·6	12·7	12·8	13·0	13·1	13·2	13·3	13·4	13·6	13·7	13·8	13·9	14·0	14·2	14·3	36
37	13·0	13·1	13·2	13·3	13·4	13·6	13·7	13·8	13·9	14·1	14·2	14·3	14·4	14·6	14·7	37
38	13·3	13·4	13·6	13·7	13·8	13·9	14·1	14·2	14·3	14·4	14·6	14·7	14·8	14·9	15·1	38
39	13·7	13·8	13·9	14·0	14·2	14·3	14·4	14·6	14·7	14·8	15·0	15·1	15·2	15·3	15·5	39
40	14·0	14·1	14·2	14·4	14·5	14·7	14·8	14·9	15·1	15·2	15·3	15·5	15·6	15·7	15·9	40
41	14·4	14·5	14·6	14·8	14·9	15·0	15·2	15·3	15·4	15·6	15·7	15·8	16·0	16·1	16·3	41
42	14·7	14·8	15·0	15·1	15·3	15·4	15·5	15·7	15·8	16·0	16·1	16·2	16·4	16·5	16·7	42
43	15·1	15·2	15·3	15·5	15·6	15·8	15·9	16·1	16·2	16·3	16·5	16·6	16·8	16·9	17·1	43
44	15·4	15·6	15·7	15·8	16·0	16·1	16·3	16·4	16·6	16·7	16·9	17·0	17·2	17·3	17·5	44
45	15·8	15·9	16·1	16·2	16·4	16·5	16·7	16·8	17·0	17·1	17·3	17·4	17·6	17·7	17·9	45
46	16·1	16·3	16·4	16·6	16·7	16·9	17·0	17·2	17·3	17·5	17·6	17·8	17·9	18·1	18·2	46
47	16·5	16·6	16·8	16·9	17·1	17·2	17·4	17·5	17·7	17·9	18·0	18·2	18·3	18·5	18·6	47
48	16·8	17·0	17·1	17·3	17·4	17·6	17·8	17·9	18·1	18·2	18·4	18·6	18·7	18·9	19·0	48
49	17·2	17·3	17·5	17·6	17·8	18·0	18·1	18·3	18·5	18·6	18·8	18·9	19·1	19·3	19·4	49
50	17·5	17·7	17·8	18·0	18·2	18·3	18·5	18·7	18·8	19·0	19·2	19·3	19·5	19·7	19·8	50
51	17·9	18·0	18·2	18·4	18·5	18·7	18·9	19·0	19·2	19·4	19·6	19·7	19·9	20·1	20·2	51
52	18·2	18·4	18·5	18·7	18·9	19·1	19·2	19·4	19·6	19·8	19·9	20·1	20·3	20·5	20·6	52
53	18·6	18·7	18·9	19·1	19·3	19·4	19·6	19·8	20·0	20·1	20·3	20·5	20·7	20·8	21·0	53
54	18·9	19·1	19·2	19·4	19·6	19·8	20·0	20·2	20·3	20·5	20·7	20·9	21·1	21·2	21·4	54
55	19·3	19·4	19·6	19·8	20·0	20·2	20·4	20·5	20·7	20·9	21·1	21·3	21·5	21·6	21·8	55
56	19·6	19·8	20·0	20·2	20·3	20·5	20·7	20·9	21·1	21·3	21·5	21·6	21·8	22·0	22·2	56
57	20·0	20·1	20·3	20·5	20·7	20·9	21·1	21·3	21·5	21·7	21·9	22·0	22·2	22·4	22·6	57
58	20·3	20·5	20·7	20·9	21·1	21·3	21·5	21·7	21·8	22·0	22·2	22·4	22·6	22·8	23·0	58
59	20·7	20·8	21·0	21·2	21·4	21·6	21·8	22·0	22·2	22·4	22·6	22·8	23·0	23·2	23·4	59
60	21·0	21·2	21·4	21·6	21·8	22·0	22·2	22·4	22·6	22·8	23·0	23·2	23·4	23·6	23·8	60

TIME, SPEED and DISTANCE TABLE

Min.	Knots															Min.
	24.0	24.2	24.4	24.6	24.8	25.0	25.2	25.4	25.6	25.8	26.0	26.2	26.4	26.6	26.8	
	Miles	Miles	Miles	Miles	Miles	Miles	Miles	Miles	Miles	Miles	Miles	Miles	Miles	Miles	Miles	
1	0·4	0·4	0·4	0·4	0·4	0·4	0·4	0·4	0·4	0·4	0·4	0·4	0·4	0·4	0·4	1
2	0·8	0·8	0·8	0·8	0·8	0·8	0·8	0·8	0·9	0·9	0·9	0·9	0·9	0·9	0·9	2
3	1·2	1·2	1·2	1·2	1·2	1·3	1·3	1·3	1·3	1·3	1·3	1·3	1·3	1·3	1·3	3
4	1·6	1·6	1·6	1·6	1·7	1·7	1·7	1·7	1·7	1·7	1·7	1·7	1·8	1·8	1·8	4
5	2·0	2·0	2·0	2·1	2·1	2·1	2·1	2·1	2·1	2·2	2·2	2·2	2·2	2·2	2·2	5
6	2·4	2·4	2·4	2·5	2·5	2·5	2·5	2·5	2·6	2·6	2·6	2·6	2·6	2·7	2·7	6
7	2·8	2·8	2·8	2·9	2·9	2·9	2·9	3·0	3·0	3·0	3·0	3·1	3·1	3·1	3·1	7
8	3·2	3·2	3·3	3·3	3·3	3·3	3·4	3·4	3·4	3·4	3·5	3·5	3·5	3·5	3·6	8
9	3·6	3·6	3·7	3·7	3·7	3·8	3·8	3·8	3·8	3·9	3·9	3·9	4·0	4·0	4·0	9
10	4·0	4·0	4·1	4·1	4·1	4·2	4·2	4·2	4·3	4·3	4·3	4·4	4·4	4·4	4·5	10
11	4·4	4·4	4·5	4·5	4·5	4·6	4·6	4·7	4·7	4·7	4·8	4·8	4·8	4·9	4·9	11
12	4·8	4·8	4·9	4·9	5·0	5·0	5·0	5·1	5·1	5·2	5·2	5·2	5·3	5·3	5·4	12
13	5·2	5·2	5·3	5·3	5·4	5·4	5·5	5·5	5·5	5·6	5·6	5·7	5·7	5·8	5·8	13
14	5·6	5·6	5·7	5·7	5·8	5·8	5·9	5·9	6·0	6·0	6·1	6·1	6·2	6·2	6·3	14
15	6·0	6·1	6·1	6·2	6·2	6·3	6·3	6·4	6·4	6·5	6·5	6·6	6·6	6·7	6·7	15
16	6·4	6·5	6·5	6·6	6·6	6·7	6·7	6·8	6·8	6·9	6·9	7·0	7·0	7·1	7·1	16
17	6·8	6·9	6·9	7·0	7·0	7·1	7·1	7·2	7·3	7·3	7·4	7·4	7·5	7·5	7·6	17
18	7·2	7·3	7·3	7·4	7·4	7·5	7·6	7·6	7·7	7·8	7·8	7·9	7·9	8·0	8·0	18
19	7·6	7·7	7·7	7·8	7·9	7·9	8·0	8·0	8·1	8·2	8·2	8·3	8·4	8·4	8·5	19
20	8·0	8·1	8·1	8·2	8·3	8·3	8·4	8·5	8·5	8·6	8·7	8·7	8·8	8·9	8·9	20
21	8·4	8·5	8·5	8·6	8·7	8·8	8·9	8·9	9·0	9·0	9·1	9·2	9·2	9·3	9·4	21
22	8·8	8·9	8·9	9·0	9·1	9·2	9·2	9·3	9·4	9·5	9·5	9·6	9·7	9·8	9·8	22
23	9·2	9·3	9·4	9·4	9·5	9·6	9·7	9·7	9·8	9·9	10·0	10·0	10·1	10·2	10·3	23
24	9·6	9·7	9·8	9·8	9·9	10·0	10·1	10·2	10·2	10·3	10·4	10·5	10·6	10·6	10·7	24
25	10·0	10·1	10·2	10·3	10·3	10·4	10·5	10·6	10·7	10·8	10·8	10·9	11·0	11·1	11·2	25
26	10·4	10·5	10·6	10·7	10·7	10·8	10·9	11·0	11·1	11·2	11·3	11·4	11·4	11·5	11·6	26
27	10·8	10·9	11·0	11·1	11·2	11·3	11·3	11·4	11·5	11·6	11·7	11·8	11·9	12·0	12·1	27
28	11·2	11·3	11·4	11·5	11·6	11·7	11·8	11·9	11·9	12·0	12·1	12·2	12·3	12·4	12·5	28
29	11·6	11·7	11·8	11·9	12·0	12·1	12·2	12·3	12·4	12·5	12·6	12·7	12·8	12·9	13·0	29
30	12·0	12·1	12·2	12·3	12·4	12·5	12·6	12·7	12·8	12·9	13·0	13·1	13·2	13·3	13·4	30
31	12·4	12·5	12·6	12·7	12·8	12·9	13·0	13·1	13·2	13·3	13·4	13·5	13·6	13·7	13·9	31
32	12·8	12·9	13·0	13·1	13·2	13·3	13·4	13·5	13·7	13·8	13·9	14·0	14·1	14·2	14·3	32
33	13·2	13·3	13·4	13·5	13·6	13·8	13·9	14·0	14·1	14·2	14·3	14·4	14·5	14·6	14·7	33
34	13·6	13·7	13·8	13·9	14·1	14·2	14·3	14·4	14·5	14·6	14·7	14·8	15·0	15·1	15·2	34
35	14·0	14·1	14·2	14·4	14·5	14·6	14·7	14·8	14·9	15·1	15·2	15·3	15·4	15·5	15·6	35
36	14·4	14·5	14·6	14·8	14·9	15·0	15·1	15·2	15·4	15·5	15·6	15·7	15·8	16·0	16·1	36
37	14·8	14·9	15·0	15·2	15·3	15·4	15·5	15·7	15·8	15·9	16·0	16·2	16·3	16·4	16·5	37
38	15·2	15·3	15·5	15·6	15·7	15·8	16·0	16·1	16·2	16·3	16·5	16·6	16·7	16·8	17·0	38
39	15·6	15·7	15·9	16·0	16·1	16·3	16·4	16·5	16·6	16·8	16·9	17·0	17·2	17·3	17·4	39
40	16·0	16·1	16·3	16·4	16·5	16·7	16·8	16·9	17·1	17·2	17·3	17·5	17·6	17·7	17·9	40
41	16·4	16·5	16·7	16·8	16·9	17·1	17·2	17·4	17·5	17·6	17·8	17·9	18·0	18·2	18·3	41
42	16·8	16·9	17·1	17·2	17·4	17·5	17·6	17·8	17·9	18·1	18·2	18·3	18·5	18·6	18·8	42
43	17·2	17·3	17·5	17·6	17·8	17·9	18·1	18·2	18·3	18·5	18·6	18·8	18·9	19·1	19·2	43
44	17·6	17·7	17·9	18·0	18·2	18·3	18·5	18·6	18·7	18·9	19·1	19·2	19·4	19·5	19·7	44
45	18·0	18·2	18·3	18·5	18·6	18·8	18·9	19·1	19·2	19·4	19·5	19·7	19·8	20·0	20·1	45
46	18·4	18·6	18·7	18·9	19·0	19·2	19·3	19·5	19·6	19·8	19·9	20·1	20·2	20·4	20·5	46
47	18·8	19·0	19·1	19·3	19·4	19·6	19·7	19·9	20·0	20·2	20·4	20·5	20·7	20·8	21·0	47
48	19·2	19·4	19·5	19·7	19·8	20·0	20·2	20·3	20·5	20·6	20·8	21·0	21·1	21·3	21·4	48
49	19·6	19·8	19·9	20·1	20·3	20·4	20·6	20·7	20·9	21·1	21·2	21·4	21·6	21·7	21·9	49
50	20·0	20·2	20·3	20·5	20·7	20·8	21·0	21·2	21·3	21·5	21·7	21·8	22·0	22·2	22·3	50
51	20·4	20·6	20·7	20·9	21·1	21·3	21·4	21·6	21·8	21·9	22·1	22·3	22·4	22·6	22·8	51
52	20·8	21·0	21·1	21·3	21·5	21·7	21·8	22·0	22·2	22·4	22·5	22·7	22·9	23·1	23·2	52
53	21·2	21·4	21·6	21·7	21·9	22·1	22·3	22·4	22·6	22·8	23·0	23·1	23·3	23·5	23·7	53
54	21·6	21·8	22·0	22·1	22·3	22·5	22·7	22·9	23·0	23·2	23·4	23·6	23·8	23·9	24·1	54
55	22·0	22·2	22·4	22·6	22·7	22·9	23·1	23·3	23·5	23·7	23·8	24·0	24·2	24·4	24·6	55
56	22·4	22·6	22·8	23·0	23·1	23·3	23·5	23·7	23·9	24·1	24·3	24·4	24·5	24·8	25·0	56
57	22·8	23·0	23·2	23·4	23·6	23·8	23·9	24·1	24·3	24·5	24·7	24·9	25·1	25·3	25·5	57
58	23·2	23·4	23·6	23·8	24·0	24·2	24·4	24·6	24·7	24·9	25·1	25·3	25·5	25·7	25·9	58
59	23·6	23·8	24·0	24·2	24·4	24·6	24·8	25·0	25·2	25·4	25·6	25·8	26·0	26·2	26·4	59
60	24·0	24·2	24·4	24·6	24·8	25·0	25·2	25·4	25·6	25·8	26·0	26·2	26·4	26·6	26·8	60

TIME, SPEED and DISTANCE TABLE

Min.	Knots 27·0	27·2	27·4	27·6	27·8	28·0	28·2	28·4	28·6	28·8	29·0	29·2	29·4	29·6	29·8	Min.
	Miles	Miles	Miles	Miles	Miles	Miles	Miles	Miles	Miles	Miles	Miles	Miles	Miles	Miles	Miles	
1	0·5	0·5	0·5	0·5	0·5	0·5	0·5	0·5	0·5	0·5	0·5	0·5	0·5	0·5	0·5	1
2	0·9	0·9	0·9	0·9	0·9	0·9	0·9	0·9	1·0	1·0	1·0	1·0	1·0	1·0	1·0	2
3	1·4	1·4	1·4	1·4	1·4	1·4	1·4	1·4	1·4	1·4	1·5	1·5	1·5	1·5	1·5	3
4	1·8	1·8	1·8	1·8	1·9	1·9	1·9	1·9	1·9	1·9	1·9	1·9	2·0	2·0	2·0	4
5	2·3	2·3	2·3	2·3	2·3	2·3	2·4	2·4	2·4	2·4	2·4	2·4	2·5	2·5	2·5	5
6	2·7	2·7	2·7	2·8	2·8	2·8	2·8	2·8	2·9	2·9	2·9	2·9	2·9	3·0	3·0	6
7	3·2	3·2	3·2	3·2	3·2	3·3	3·3	3·3	3·3	3·4	3·4	3·4	3·4	3·5	3·5	7
8	3·6	3·6	3·7	3·7	3·7	3·7	3·8	3·8	3·8	3·8	3·9	3·9	3·9	3·9	4·0	8
9	4·1	4·1	4·1	4·1	4·2	4·2	4·2	4·3	4·3	4·3	4·4	4·4	4·4	4·4	4·5	9
10	4·5	4·5	4·6	4·6	4·6	4·7	4·7	4·7	4·8	4·8	4·8	4·9	4·9	4·9	5·0	10
11	5·0	5·0	5·0	5·1	5·1	5·1	5·2	5·2	5·2	5·3	5·3	5·4	5·4	5·4	5·5	11
12	5·4	5·4	5·5	5·5	5·6	5·6	5·6	5·7	5·7	5·8	5·8	5·8	5·9	5·9	6·0	12
13	5·9	5·9	5·9	6·0	6·0	6·1	6·1	6·2	6·2	6·2	6·3	6·3	6·4	6·4	6·5	13
14	6·3	6·3	6·4	6·4	6·5	6·5	6·6	6·6	6·7	6·7	6·8	6·8	6·9	6·9	7·0	14
15	6·8	6·8	6·9	6·9	7·0	7·0	7·1	7·1	7·2	7·2	7·3	7·3	7·4	7·4	7·5	15
16	7·2	7·3	7·3	7·4	7·4	7·5	7·5	7·6	7·6	7·7	7·7	7·8	7·8	7·9	7·9	16
17	7·7	7·7	7·8	7·8	7·9	7·9	8·0	8·0	8·1	8·2	8·2	8·3	8·3	8·4	8·4	17
18	8·1	8·2	8·2	8·3	8·3	8·4	8·5	8·5	8·6	8·6	8·7	8·8	8·8	8·9	8·9	18
19	8·6	8·6	8·7	8·7	8·8	8·9	8·9	9·0	9·1	9·1	9·2	9·2	9·3	9·4	9·4	19
20	9·0	9·1	9·1	9·2	9·3	9·3	9·4	9·5	9·5	9·6	9·7	9·7	9·8	9·9	9·9	20
21	9·5	9·5	9·6	9·7	9·7	9·8	9·9	9·9	10·0	10·1	10·2	10·2	10·3	10·4	10·4	21
22	9·9	10·0	10·0	10·1	10·2	10·3	10·3	10·4	10·5	10·6	10·6	10·7	10·8	10·9	10·9	22
23	10·4	10·4	10·5	10·6	10·7	10·7	10·8	10·9	11·0	11·0	11·1	11·2	11·3	11·3	11·4	23
24	10·8	10·9	11·0	11·0	11·1	11·2	11·3	11·4	11·4	11·5	11·6	11·7	11·8	11·8	11·9	24
25	11·3	11·3	11·4	11·5	11·6	11·7	11·8	11·8	11·9	12·0	12·1	12·2	12·3	12·3	12·4	25
26	11·7	11·8	11·9	12·0	12·0	12·1	12·2	12·3	12·4	12·5	12·6	12·7	12·7	12·8	12·9	26
27	12·2	12·2	12·3	12·4	12·5	12·6	12·7	12·8	12·9	13·0	13·1	13·1	13·2	13·3	13·4	27
28	12·6	12·7	12·8	12·9	13·0	13·1	13·2	13·3	13·3	13·4	13·5	13·6	13·7	13·8	13·9	28
29	13·1	13·1	13·2	13·3	13·4	13·5	13·6	13·7	13·8	13·9	14·0	14·1	14·2	14·3	14·4	29
30	13·5	13·6	13·7	13·8	13·9	14·0	14·1	14·2	14·3	14·4	14·5	14·6	14·7	14·8	14·9	30
31	14·0	14·1	14·2	14·3	14·4	14·5	14·6	14·7	14·8	14·9	15·0	15·1	15·2	15·3	15·4	31
32	14·4	14·5	14·6	14·7	14·8	14·9	15·0	15·1	15·3	15·4	15·5	15·6	15·7	15·8	15·9	32
33	14·9	15·0	15·1	15·2	15·3	15·4	15·5	15·6	15·7	15·8	16·0	16·1	16·2	16·3	16·4	33
34	15·3	15·4	15·5	15·6	15·7	15·9	16·0	16·1	16·2	16·3	16·4	16·5	16·7	16·8	16·9	34
35	15·8	15·9	16·0	16·1	16·2	16·3	16·5	16·6	16·7	16·8	16·9	17·0	17·2	17·3	17·4	35
36	16·2	16·3	16·4	16·6	16·7	16·8	16·9	17·0	17·2	17·3	17·4	17·5	17·6	17·8	17·9	36
37	16·7	16·8	16·9	17·0	17·1	17·3	17·4	17·5	17·6	17·8	17·9	18·0	18·1	18·3	18·4	37
38	17·1	17·2	17·4	17·5	17·6	17·7	17·9	18·0	18·1	18·2	18·4	18·5	18·6	18·7	18·9	38
39	17·6	17·7	17·8	17·9	18·1	18·2	18·3	18·5	18·6	18·7	18·9	19·0	19·1	19·2	19·4	39
40	18·0	18·1	18·3	18·4	18·5	18·7	18·8	18·9	19·1	19·2	19·3	19·5	19·6	19·7	19·9	40
41	18·5	18·6	18·7	18·9	19·0	19·1	19·3	19·4	19·5	19·7	19·8	20·0	20·1	20·2	20·4	41
42	18·9	19·0	19·2	19·3	19·5	19·6	19·7	19·9	20·0	20·2	20·3	20·4	20·6	20·7	20·9	42
43	19·4	19·5	19·6	19·8	19·9	20·1	20·2	20·4	20·5	20·6	20·8	20·9	21·1	21·2	21·4	43
44	19·8	20·0	20·1	20·2	20·4	20·5	20·7	20·8	21·0	21·1	21·3	21·4	21·6	21·7	21·9	44
45	20·3	20·4	20·6	20·7	20·9	21·0	21·2	21·3	21·5	21·6	21·8	21·9	22·1	22·2	22·4	45
46	20·7	20·9	21·0	21·2	21·3	21·5	21·6	21·8	21·9	22·1	22·2	22·4	22·5	22·7	22·8	46
47	21·2	21·3	21·5	21·6	21·8	21·9	22·1	22·2	22·4	22·6	22·7	22·9	23·0	23·2	23·3	47
48	21·6	21·8	21·9	22·1	22·2	22·4	22·6	22·7	22·9	23·0	23·2	23·4	23·5	23·7	23·8	48
49	22·1	22·2	22·4	22·5	22·7	22·9	23·0	23·2	23·4	23·5	23·7	23·9	24·0	24·2	24·3	49
50	22·5	22·7	22·8	23·0	23·2	23·3	23·5	23·7	23·8	24·0	24·2	24·3	24·5	24·7	24·8	50
51	23·0	23·1	23·3	23·5	23·6	23·8	24·0	24·1	24·3	24·5	24·7	24·8	25·0	25·2	25·3	51
52	23·4	23·6	23·7	23·9	24·1	24·3	24·4	24·6	24·8	25·0	25·1	25·3	25·5	25·7	25·8	52
53	23·9	24·0	24·2	24·4	24·6	24·7	24·9	25·1	25·3	25·4	25·6	25·8	26·0	26·1	26·3	53
54	24·3	24·5	24·7	24·8	25·0	25·2	25·4	25·6	25·7	25·9	26·1	26·3	26·5	26·6	26·8	54
55	24·8	24·9	25·1	25·3	25·5	25·7	25·9	26·0	26·2	26·4	26·6	26·8	27·0	27·1	27·3	55
56	25·2	25·4	25·6	25·8	25·9	26·1	26·3	26·5	26·7	26·9	27·1	27·3	27·4	27·6	27·8	56
57	25·7	25·8	26·0	26·2	26·4	26·6	26·8	27·0	27·2	27·4	27·6	27·7	27·9	28·1	28·3	57
58	26·1	26·3	26·5	26·7	26·9	27·1	27·3	27·5	27·6	27·8	28·0	28·2	28·4	28·6	28·8	58
59	26·6	26·7	26·9	27·1	27·3	27·5	27·7	27·9	28·1	28·3	28·5	28·7	28·9	29·1	29·3	59
60	27·0	27·2	27·4	27·6	27·8	28·0	28·2	28·4	28·6	28·8	29·0	29·2	29·4	29·6	29·8	60

DAY'S RUN, STEAMING TIME and AVERAGE SPEED

Dist.	Steaming Time—Hours											Dist.
	22	22·5	23	23·5	24	24·5	25	25·5	26	26·5	27	
100	4·55	4·44	4·35	4·26	4·17	4·08	4·00	3·92	3·85	3·77	3·70	100
101	4·59	4·49	4·39	4·30	4·21	4·12	4·04	3·96	3·88	3·81	3·74	101
102	4·64	4·53	4·43	4·34	4·25	4·16	4·08	4·00	3·92	3·85	3·78	102
103	4·68	4·58	4·48	4·38	4·29	4·20	4·12	4·04	3·96	3·89	3·81	103
104	4·73	4·62	4·52	4·43	4·33	4·24	4·16	4·08	4·00	3·92	3·85	104
105	4·77	4·67	4·57	4·47	4·38	4·29	4·20	4·12	4·04	3·96	3·89	105
106	4·82	4·71	4·61	4·51	4·42	4·33	4·24	4·16	4·08	4·00	3·93	106
107	4·86	4·76	4·65	4·55	4·46	4·37	4·28	4·20	4·12	4·04	3·96	107
108	4·91	4·80	4·70	4·60	4·50	4·41	4·32	4·24	4·15	4·08	4·00	108
109	4·95	4·84	4·74	4·64	4·54	4·45	4·36	4·27	4·19	4·11	4·04	109
110	5·00	4·89	4·78	4·68	4·58	4·49	4·40	4·31	4·23	4·15	4·07	110
111	5·05	4·93	4·83	4·72	4·63	4·53	4·44	4·35	4·27	4·19	4·11	111
112	5·09	4·98	4·87	4·77	4·67	4·57	4·48	4·39	4·31	4·23	4·15	112
113	5·14	5·02	4·91	4·81	4·71	4·61	4·52	4·43	4·35	4·26	4·19	113
114	5·18	5·07	4·96	4·85	4·75	4·65	4·56	4·47	4·38	4·30	4·22	114
115	5·23	5·11	5·00	4·89	4·79	4·69	4·60	4·51	4·42	4·34	4·26	115
116	5·27	5·16	5·04	4·94	4·83	4·73	4·64	4·55	4·46	4·38	4·30	116
117	5·32	5·20	5·09	4·98	4·88	4·78	4·68	4·59	4·50	4·42	4·33	117
118	5·36	5·24	5·13	5·02	4·92	4·82	4·72	4·63	4·54	4·45	4·37	118
119	5·41	5·29	5·17	5·06	4·96	4·86	4·76	4·67	4·58	4·49	4·41	119
120	5·45	5·33	5·22	5·11	5·00	4·90	4·80	4·71	4·62	4·53	4·44	120
121	5·50	5·38	5·26	5·15	5·04	4·94	4·84	4·75	4·65	4·57	4·48	121
122	5·55	5·42	5·30	5·19	5·08	4·98	4·88	4·78	4·69	4·60	4·52	122
123	5·59	5·47	5·35	5·23	5·13	5·02	4·92	4·82	4·73	4·64	4·56	123
124	5·64	5·51	5·39	5·28	5·17	5·06	4·96	4·86	4·77	4·68	4·59	124
125	5·68	5·56	5·43	5·32	5·21	5·10	5·00	4·90	4·81	4·72	4·63	125
126	5·73	5·60	5·48	5·36	5·25	5·14	5·04	4·94	4·85	4·75	4·67	126
127	5·77	5·64	5·52	5·40	5·29	5·18	5·08	4·98	4·88	4·79	4·70	127
128	5·82	5·69	5·57	5·45	5·33	5·22	5·12	5·02	4·92	4·83	4·74	128
129	5·86	5·73	5·61	5·49	5·38	5·27	5·16	5·06	4·96	4·87	4·78	129
130	5·91	5·78	5·65	5·53	5·42	5·31	5·20	5·10	5·00	4·91	4·81	130
131	5·95	5·82	5·70	5·57	5·46	5·35	5·24	5·14	5·04	4·94	4·85	131
132	6·00	5·87	5·74	5·62	5·50	5·39	5·28	5·18	5·08	4·98	4·89	132
133	6·05	5·91	5·78	5·66	5·54	5·43	5·32	5·22	5·12	5·02	4·93	133
134	6·09	5·96	5·83	5·70	5·58	5·47	5·36	5·25	5·15	5·06	4·96	134
135	6·14	6·00	5·87	5·74	5·63	5·51	5·40	5·29	5·19	5·09	5·00	135
136	6·18	6·04	5·91	5·79	5·67	5·55	5·44	5·33	5·23	5·13	5·04	136
137	6·23	6·09	5·96	5·83	5·71	5·59	5·48	5·37	5·27	5·17	5·07	137
138	6·27	6·13	6·00	5·87	5·75	5·63	5·52	5·41	5·31	5·21	5·11	138
139	6·32	6·18	6·04	5·91	5·79	5·67	5·56	5·45	5·35	5·25	5·15	139
140	6·36	6·22	6·09	5·96	5·83	5·71	5·60	5·49	5·38	5·28	5·19	140
141	6·41	6·27	6·13	6·00	5·88	5·76	5·64	5·53	5·42	5·32	5·22	141
142	6·45	6·31	6·17	6·04	5·92	5·80	5·68	5·57	5·46	5·36	5·26	142
143	6·50	6·36	6·22	6·09	5·96	5·84	5·72	5·61	5·50	5·40	5·30	143
144	6·55	6·40	6·26	6·13	6·00	5·88	5·76	5·65	5·54	5·43	5·33	144
145	6·59	6·44	6·30	6·17	6·04	5·92	5·80	5·69	5·58	5·47	5·37	145
146	6·64	6·49	6·35	6·21	6·08	5·96	5·84	5·73	5·62	5·51	5·41	146
147	6·68	6·53	6·39	6·26	6·13	6·00	5·88	5·76	5·65	5·55	5·44	147
148	6·73	6·58	6·43	6·30	6·17	6·04	5·92	5·80	5·69	5·58	5·48	148
149	6·77	6·62	6·48	6·34	6·21	6·08	5·96	5·84	5·73	5·62	5·52	149
150	6·82	6·67	6·52	6·38	6·25	6·12	6·00	5·88	5·77	5·66	5·56	150
151	6·86	6·71	6·57	6·43	6·29	6·16	6·04	5·92	5·81	5·70	5·59	151
152	6·91	6·76	6·61	6·47	6·33	6·20	6·08	5·96	5·85	5·74	5·63	152
153	6·95	6·80	6·65	6·51	6·38	6·24	6·12	6·00	5·88	5·77	5·67	153
154	7·00	6·84	6·70	6·55	6·42	6·29	6·16	6·04	5·92	5·81	5·70	154
155	7·05	6·89	6·74	6·60	6·46	6·33	6·20	6·08	5·96	5·85	5·74	155
156	7·09	6·93	6·78	6·64	6·50	6·37	6·24	6·12	6·00	5·89	5·78	156
157	7·14	6·98	6·83	6·68	6·54	6·41	6·28	6·16	6·04	5·92	5·81	157
158	7·18	7·02	6·87	6·72	6·58	6·45	6·32	6·20	6·08	5·96	5·85	158
159	7·23	7·07	6·91	6·77	6·63	6·49	6·36	6·24	6·12	6·00	5·89	159
160	7·27	7·11	6·96	6·81	6·67	6·53	6·40	6·27	6·15	6·04	5·93	160
Dist.	22	22·5	23	23·5	24	24·5	25	25·5	26	26·5	27	Dist.

DAY'S RUN, STEAMING TIME and AVERAGE SPEED

Dist.	Steaming Time—Hours											Dist.
	22	22·5	23	23·5	24	24·5	25	25·5	26	26·5	27	
161	7·32	7·16	7·00	6·85	6·71	6·57	6·44	6·31	6·19	6·08	5·96	161
162	7·36	7·20	7·04	6·89	6·75	6·61	6·48	6·35	6·23	6·11	6·00	162
163	7·41	7·24	7·09	6·94	6·79	6·65	6·52	6·39	6·27	6·15	6·04	163
164	7·45	7·29	7·13	6·98	6·83	6·69	6·56	6·43	6·31	6·19	6·07	164
165	7·50	7·33	7·17	7·02	6·88	6·73	6·60	6·47	6·35	6·23	6·11	165
166	7·55	7·38	7·22	7·06	6·92	6·78	6·64	6·51	6·38	6·26	6·15	166
167	7·59	7·42	7·26	7·11	6·96	6·82	6·68	6·55	6·42	6·30	6·19	167
168	7·64	7·47	7·30	7·15	7·00	6·86	6·72	6·59	6·46	6·34	6·22	168
169	7·68	7·51	7·35	7·19	7·04	6·90	6·76	6·63	6·50	6·38	6·26	169
170	7·73	7·56	7·39	7·23	7·08	6·94	6·80	6·67	6·54	6·42	6·30	170
171	7·77	7·60	7·43	7·28	7·13	6·98	6·84	6·71	6·58	6·45	6·33	171
172	7·82	7·64	7·48	7·32	7·17	7·02	6·88	6·75	6·62	6·49	6·37	172
173	7·86	7·69	7·52	7·36	7·21	7·06	6·92	6·78	6·65	6·53	6·41	173
174	7·91	7·73	7·57	7·40	7·25	7·10	6·96	6·82	6·69	6·57	6·44	174
175	7·95	7·78	7·61	7·45	7·29	7·14	7·00	6·86	6·73	6·60	6·48	175
176	8·00	7·82	7·65	7·49	7·33	7·18	7·04	6·90	6·77	6·64	6·52	176
177	8·05	7·87	7·70	7·53	7·38	7·22	7·08	6·94	6·81	6·68	6·56	177
178	8·09	7·91	7·74	7·57	7·42	7·27	7·12	6·98	6·85	6·72	6·59	178
179	8·14	7·96	7·78	7·62	7·46	7·31	7·16	7·02	6·88	6·75	6·63	179
180	8·18	8·00	7·83	7·66	7·50	7·35	7·20	7·06	6·92	6·79	6·67	180
181	8·23	8·04	7·87	7·70	7·54	7·39	7·24	7·10	6·96	6·83	6·70	181
182	8·27	8·09	7·91	7·74	7·58	7·43	7·28	7·14	7·00	6·87	6·74	182
183	8·32	8·13	7·96	7·79	7·63	7·47	7·32	7·18	7·04	6·91	6·78	183
184	8·36	8·18	8·00	7·83	7·67	7·51	7·36	7·22	7·08	6·94	6·81	184
185	8·41	8·22	8·04	7·87	7·71	7·55	7·40	7·25	7·12	6·98	6·85	185
186	8·45	8·27	8·09	7·91	7·75	7·59	7·44	7·29	7·15	7·02	6·89	186
187	8·50	8·31	8·13	7·96	7·79	7·63	7·48	7·33	7·19	7·06	6·93	187
188	8·55	8·36	8·17	8·00	7·83	7·67	7·52	7·37	7·23	7·09	6·96	188
189	8·59	8·40	8·22	8·04	7·88	7·71	7·56	7·41	7·27	7·13	7·00	189
190	8·64	8·44	8·26	8·09	7·92	7·76	7·60	7·45	7·31	7·17	7·04	190
191	8·68	8·49	8·30	8·13	7·96	7·80	7·64	7·49	7·35	7·21	7·07	191
192	8·73	8·53	8·35	8·17	8·00	7·84	7·68	7·53	7·38	7·25	7·11	192
193	8·77	8·58	8·39	8·21	8·04	7·88	7·72	7·57	7·42	7·28	7·15	193
194	8·82	8·62	8·43	8·26	8·08	7·92	7·76	7·61	7·46	7·32	7·19	194
195	8·86	8·67	8·48	8·30	8·13	7·96	7·80	7·65	7·50	7·36	7·22	195
196	8·91	8·71	8·52	8·34	8·17	8·00	7·84	7·69	7·54	7·40	7·26	196
197	8·95	8·76	8·57	8·38	8·21	8·04	7·88	7·73	7·58	7·43	7·30	197
198	9·00	8·80	8·61	8·43	8·25	8·08	7·92	7·76	7·62	7·47	7·33	198
199	9·05	8·84	8·65	8·47	8·29	8·12	7·96	7·80	7·65	7·51	7·37	199
200	9·09	8·89	8·70	8·51	8·33	8·16	8·00	7·84	7·69	7·55	7·41	200
201	9·14	8·93	8·74	8·55	8·38	8·20	8·04	7·88	7·73	7·58	7·44	201
202	9·18	8·98	8·78	8·60	8·42	8·24	8·08	7·92	7·77	7·62	7·48	202
203	9·23	9·02	8·83	8·64	8·46	8·29	8·12	7·96	7·81	7·66	7·52	203
204	9·27	9·07	8·87	8·68	8·50	8·33	8·16	8·00	7·85	7·70	7·56	204
205	9·32	9·11	8·91	8·72	8·54	8·37	8·20	8·04	7·88	7·74	7·59	205
206	9·36	9·16	8·96	8·77	8·58	8·41	8·24	8·08	7·92	7·77	7·63	206
207	9·41	9·20	9·00	8·81	8·63	8·45	8·28	8·12	7·96	7·81	7·67	207
208	9·45	9·24	9·04	8·85	8·67	8·49	8·32	8·16	8·00	7·85	7·70	208
209	9·50	9·29	9·09	8·89	8·71	8·53	8·36	8·20	8·04	7·89	7·74	209
210	9·55	9·33	9·13	8·94	8·75	8·57	8·40	8·24	8·08	7·92	7·78	210
211	9·59	9·38	9·17	8·98	8·79	8·61	8·44	8·27	8·12	7·96	7·81	211
212	9·64	9·42	9·22	9·02	8·83	8·65	8·48	8·31	8·15	8·00	7·85	212
213	9·68	9·47	9·26	9·06	8·88	8·69	8·52	8·35	8·19	8·04	7·89	213
214	9·73	9·51	9·30	9·11	8·92	8·73	8·56	8·39	8·23	8·08	7·93	214
215	9·77	9·56	9·35	9·15	8·96	8·78	8·60	8·43	8·27	8·11	7·96	215
216	9·82	9·60	9·39	9·19	9·00	8·82	8·64	8·47	8·31	8·15	8·00	216
217	9·86	9·64	9·43	9·23	9·04	8·86	8·68	8·51	8·35	8·19	8·04	217
218	9·91	9·69	9·48	9·28	9·08	8·90	8·72	8·55	8·38	8·23	8·07	218
219	9·95	9·73	9·52	9·32	9·13	8·94	8·76	8·59	8·42	8·26	8·11	219
220	10·00	9·78	9·57	9·36	9·17	8·98	8·80	8·63	8·46	8·30	8·15	220
Dist.	22	22·5	23	23·5	24	24·5	25	25·5	26	26·5	27	Dist.

DAY'S RUN, STEAMING TIME and AVERAGE SPEED

Dist.	Steaming Time—Hours											Dist.
	22	22·5	23	23·5	24	24·5	25	25·5	26	26·5	27	
221	10·05	9·82	9·61	9·40	9·21	9·02	8·84	8·67	8·50	8·34	8·19	221
222	10·09	9·87	9·65	9·45	9·25	9·06	8·88	8·71	8·54	8·38	8·22	222
223	10·14	9·91	9·70	9·49	9·29	9·10	8·92	8·75	8·58	8·42	8·26	223
224	10·18	9·96	9·74	9·53	9·33	9·14	8·96	8·78	8·62	8·45	8·30	224
225	10·23	10·00	9·78	9·57	9·38	9·18	9·00	8·82	8·65	8·49	8·33	225
226	10·27	10·04	9·83	9·62	9·42	9·22	9·04	8·86	8·69	8·53	8·37	226
227	10·32	10·09	9·87	9·66	9·46	9·27	9·08	8·90	8·73	8·57	8·41	227
228	10·36	10·13	9·91	9·70	9·50	9·31	9·12	8·94	8·77	8·60	8·44	228
229	10·41	10·18	9·96	9·74	9·54	9·35	9·16	8·98	8·81	8·64	8·48	229
230	10·45	10·22	10·00	9·79	9·58	9·39	9·20	9·02	8·85	8·68	8·52	230
231	10·50	10·27	10·04	9·83	9·63	9·43	9·24	9·06	8·88	8·72	8·56	231
232	10·55	10·31	10·09	9·87	9·67	9·47	9·28	9·10	8·92	8·75	8·59	232
233	10·59	10·36	10·13	9·91	9·71	9·51	9·32	9·14	8·96	8·79	8·63	233
234	10·64	10·40	10·17	9·96	9·75	9·55	9·36	9·18	9·00	8·83	8·67	234
235	10·68	10·44	10·22	10·00	9·79	9·59	9·40	9·22	9·04	8·87	8·70	235
236	10·73	10·49	10·26	10·04	9·83	9·63	9·44	9·25	9·08	8·91	8·74	236
237	10·77	10·53	10·30	10·09	9·88	9·67	9·48	9·29	9·12	8·94	8·78	237
238	10·82	10·58	10·35	10·13	9·92	9·71	9·52	9·33	9·15	8·98	8·81	238
239	10·86	10·62	10·39	10·17	9·96	9·76	9·56	9·37	9·19	9·02	8·85	239
240	10·91	10·67	10·43	10·21	10·00	9·80	9·60	9·41	9·23	9·06	8·89	240
241	10·95	10·71	10·48	10·26	10·04	9·84	9·64	8·45	9·27	9·09	8·93	241
242	11·00	10·76	10·52	10·30	10·08	9·88	9·68	9·49	9·31	9·13	8·96	242
243	11·05	10·80	10·57	10·34	10·13	9·92	9·72	9·53	9·35	9·17	9·00	243
244	11·09	10·84	10·61	10·38	10·17	9·96	9·76	9·57	9·38	9·21	9·04	244
245	11·14	10·89	10·65	10·43	10·21	10·00	9·80	9·61	9·42	9·25	9·07	245
246	11·18	10·93	10·70	10·47	10·25	10·04	9·84	9·65	9·46	9·28	9·11	246
247	11·23	10·98	10·74	10·51	10·29	10·08	9·88	9·69	9·50	9·32	9·15	247
248	11·27	11·02	10·78	10·55	10·33	10·12	9·92	9·73	9·54	9·36	9·19	248
249	11·32	11·07	10·83	10·60	10·38	10·16	9·96	9·76	9·58	9·40	9·22	249
250	11·36	11·11	10·87	10·64	10·42	10·20	10·00	9·80	9·62	9·43	9·26	250
251	11·41	11·16	10·91	10·68	10·46	10·24	10·04	9·84	9·65	9·47	9·30	251
252	11·45	11·20	10·96	10·72	10·50	10·29	10·08	9·88	9·69	9·51	9·33	252
253	11·50	11·24	11·00	10·77	10·54	10·33	10·12	9·92	9·73	9·55	9·37	253
254	11·55	11·29	11·04	10·81	10·58	10·37	10·16	9·96	9·77	9·58	9·41	254
255	11·59	11·33	11·09	10·85	10·63	10·41	10·20	10·00	9·81	9·62	9·44	255
256	11·64	11·38	11·13	10·89	10·67	10·45	10·24	10·04	9·85	9·66	9·48	256
257	11·68	11·42	11·17	10·94	10·71	10·49	10·28	10·08	9·88	9·70	9·52	257
258	11·73	11·47	11·22	10·98	10·75	10·53	10·32	10·12	9·92	9·74	9·56	258
259	11·77	11·51	11·26	11·02	10·79	10·57	10·36	10·16	9·96	9·77	9·59	259
260	11·82	11·56	11·30	11·06	10·83	10·61	10·40	10·20	10·00	9·81	9·63	260
261	11·86	11·60	11·35	11·11	10·88	10·65	10·44	10·24	10·04	9·85	9·67	261
262	11·91	11·64	11·39	11·15	10·92	10·69	10·48	10·27	10·08	9·89	9·70	262
263	11·95	11·69	11·43	11·19	10·96	10·73	10·52	10·31	10·12	9·92	9·74	263
264	12·00	11·73	11·48	11·23	11·00	10·78	10·56	10·35	10·15	9·96	9·78	264
265	12·05	11·78	11·52	11·28	11·04	10·82	10·60	10·39	10·19	10·00	9·81	265
266	12·09	11·82	11·57	11·32	11·08	10·86	10·64	10·43	10·23	10·04	9·85	266
267	12·14	11·87	11·61	11·36	11·13	10·90	10·68	10·47	10·27	10·08	9·89	267
268	12·18	11·91	11·65	11·40	11·17	10·94	10·72	10·51	10·31	10·11	9·93	268
269	12·23	11·96	11·70	11·45	11·21	10·98	10·76	10·55	10·35	10·15	9·96	269
270	12·27	12·00	11·74	11·49	11·25	11·02	10·80	10·59	10·38	10·19	10·00	270
271	12·32	12·04	11·78	11·53	11·29	11·06	10·84	10·63	10·42	10·23	10·04	271
272	12·36	12·09	11·83	11·57	11·33	11·10	10·88	10·67	10·46	10·26	10·07	272
273	12·41	12·13	11·87	11·62	11·38	11·14	10·92	10·71	10·50	10·30	10·11	273
274	12·45	12·18	11·91	11·66	11·42	11·18	10·96	10·75	10·54	10·34	10·15	274
275	12·50	12·22	11·96	11·70	11·46	11·22	11·00	10·78	10·58	10·38	10·19	275
276	12·55	12·27	12·00	11·74	11·50	11·27	11·04	10·82	10·62	10·42	10·22	276
277	12·59	12·31	12·04	11·79	11·54	11·31	11·08	10·86	10·65	10·45	10·26	277
278	12·64	12·36	12·09	11·83	11·58	11·35	11·12	10·90	10·69	10·49	10·30	278
279	12·68	12·40	12·13	11·87	11·63	11·39	11·16	10·94	10·73	10·53	10·33	279
280	12·73	12·44	12·17	11·91	11·67	11·43	11·20	10·98	10·77	10·57	10·37	280
Dist.	22	22·5	23	23·5	24	24·5	25	25·5	26	26·5	27	Dist.

DAY'S RUN, STEAMING TIME and AVERAGE SPEED

Dist.	Steaming Time—Hours											Dist.
	22	22·5	23	23·5	24	24·5	25	25·5	26	26·5	27	
281	12·77	12·49	12·22	11·96	11·71	11·47	11·24	11·02	10·81	10·60	10·41	281
282	12·82	12·53	12·26	12·00	11·75	11·51	11·28	11·06	10·85	10·64	10·44	282
283	12·86	12·58	12·30	12·04	11·79	11·55	11·32	11·10	10·88	10·68	10·48	283
284	12·91	12·62	12·35	12·09	11·83	11·59	11·36	11·14	10·92	10·72	10·52	284
285	12·95	12·67	12·39	12·13	11·88	11·63	11·40	11·18	10·96	10·75	10·56	285
286	13·00	12·71	12·43	12·17	11·92	11·67	11·44	11·22	11·00	10·79	10·59	286
287	13·05	12·76	12·48	12·21	11·96	11·71	11·48	11·25	11·04	10·83	10·63	287
288	13·09	12·80	12·52	12·26	12·00	11·76	11·52	11·29	11·08	10·87	10·67	288
289	13·14	12·84	12·57	12·30	12·04	11·80	11·56	11·33	11·12	10·91	10·70	289
290	13·18	12·89	12·61	12·34	12·08	11·84	11·60	11·37	11·15	10·94	10·74	290
291	13·23	12·93	12·65	12·38	12·13	11·88	11·64	11·41	11·19	10·98	10·78	291
292	13·27	12·98	12·70	12·43	12·17	11·92	11·68	11·45	11·23	11·02	10·81	292
293	13·32	13·02	12·74	12·47	12·21	11·96	11·72	11·49	11·27	11·06	10·85	293
294	13·36	13·07	12·78	12·51	12·25	12·00	11·76	11·53	11·31	11·09	10·89	294
295	13·41	13·11	12·83	12·55	12·29	12·04	11·80	11·57	11·35	11·13	10·93	295
296	13·45	13·16	12·87	12·60	12·33	12·08	11·84	11·61	11·38	11·17	10·96	296
297	13·50	13·20	12·91	12·64	12·38	12·12	11·88	11·65	11·42	11·21	11·00	297
298	13·55	13·24	12·96	12·68	12·42	12·16	11·92	11·69	11·46	11·25	11·04	298
299	13·59	13·29	13·00	12·72	12·46	12·20	11·96	11·73	11·50	11·28	11·07	299
300	13·64	13·33	13·04	12·77	12·50	12·24	12·00	11·76	11·54	11·32	11·11	300
301	13·68	13·38	13·09	12·81	12·54	12·29	12·04	11·80	11·58	11·36	11·15	301
302	13·73	13·42	13·13	12·85	12·58	12·33	12·08	11·84	11·62	11·40	11·19	302
303	13·77	13·47	13·17	12·89	12·63	12·37	12·12	11·88	11·65	11·43	11·22	303
304	13·82	13·51	13·22	12·94	12·67	12·41	12·16	11·92	11·69	11·47	11·26	304
305	13·86	13·56	13·26	12·98	12·71	12·45	12·20	11·96	11·73	11·51	11·30	305
306	13·91	13·60	13·30	13·02	12·75	12·49	12·24	12·00	11·77	11·55	11·33	306
307	13·95	13·64	13·35	13·06	12·79	12·53	12·28	12·04	11·81	11·58	11·37	307
308	14·00	13·69	13·39	13·11	12·83	12·57	12·32	12·08	11·85	11·62	11·41	308
309	14·05	13·73	13·43	13·15	12·88	12·61	12·36	12·12	11·88	11·66	11·44	309
310	14·09	13·78	13·48	13·19	12·92	12·65	12·40	12·16	11·92	11·70	11·48	310
311	14·14	13·82	13·52	13·23	12·96	12·69	12·44	12·20	11·96	11·74	11·52	311
312	14·18	13·87	13·57	13·28	13·00	12·73	12·48	12·24	12·00	11·77	11·56	312
313	14·23	13·91	13·61	13·32	13·04	12·78	12·52	12·27	12·04	11·81	11·59	313
314	14·27	13·96	13·65	13·36	13·08	12·82	12·56	12·31	12·08	11·85	11·63	314
315	14·32	14·00	13·70	13·40	13·13	12·86	12·60	12·35	12·12	11·89	11·67	315
316	14·36	14·04	13·74	13·45	13·17	12·90	12·64	12·39	12·15	11·92	11·70	316
317	14·41	14·09	13·78	13·49	13·21	12·94	12·68	12·43	12·19	11·96	11·74	317
318	14·45	14·13	13·83	13·53	13·25	12·98	12·72	12·47	12·23	12·00	11·78	318
319	14·50	14·18	13·87	13·57	13·29	13·02	12·76	12·51	12·27	12·04	11·81	319
320	14·55	14·22	13·91	13·62	13·33	13·06	12·80	12·55	12·31	12·08	11·85	320
321	14·59	14·27	13·96	13·66	13·38	13·10	12·84	12·59	12·35	12·11	11·89	321
322	14·64	14·31	14·00	13·70	13·42	13·14	12·88	12·63	12·38	12·15	11·93	322
323	14·68	14·36	14·04	13·74	13·46	13·18	12·92	12·67	12·42	12·19	11·96	323
324	14·73	14·40	14·09	13·79	13·50	13·22	12·96	12·71	12·46	12·23	12·00	324
325	14·77	14·44	14·13	13·83	13·54	13·27	13·00	12·75	12·50	12·26	12·04	325
326	14·82	14·49	14·17	13·87	13·58	13·31	13·04	12·78	12·54	12·30	12·07	326
327	14·86	14·53	14·22	13·91	13·63	13·35	13·08	12·82	12·58	12·34	12·11	327
328	14·91	14·58	14·26	13·96	13·67	13·39	13·12	12·86	12·62	12·38	12·15	328
329	14·95	14·62	14·30	14·00	13·71	13·43	13·16	12·90	12·65	12·42	12·19	329
330	15·00	14·67	14·35	14·04	13·75	13·47	13·20	12·94	12·69	12·45	12·22	330
331	15·05	14·71	14·39	14·09	13·79	13·51	13·24	12·98	12·73	12·49	12·26	331
332	15·09	14·76	14·43	14·13	13·83	13·55	13·28	13·02	12·77	12·53	12·30	332
333	15·14	14·80	14·48	14·17	13·88	13·59	13·32	13·06	12·81	12·57	12·33	333
334	15·18	14·84	14·52	14·21	13·92	13·63	13·36	13·10	12·85	12·60	12·37	334
335	15·23	14·89	14·57	14·26	13·96	13·67	13·40	13·14	12·88	12·64	12·41	335
336	15·27	14·93	14·61	14·30	14·00	13·71	13·44	13·18	12·92	12·68	12·44	336
337	15·32	14·98	14·65	14·34	14·04	13·76	13·48	13·22	12·96	12·72	12·48	337
338	15·36	15·02	14·70	14·38	14·08	13·80	13·52	13·25	13·00	12·75	12·52	338
339	15·41	15·07	14·74	14·43	14·13	13·84	13·56	13·29	13·04	12·79	12·56	339
340	15·45	15·11	14·78	14·47	14·17	13·88	13·60	13·33	13·08	12·83	12·59	340
Dist.	22	22·5	23	23·5	24	24·5	25	25·5	26	26·5	27	Dist.

DAY'S RUN, STEAMING TIME and AVERAGE SPEED

Dist.	Steaming Time—Hours											Dist.
	22	22·5	23	23·5	24	24·5	25	25·5	26	26·5	27	
341	15·50	15·16	14·83	14·51	14·21	13·92	13·64	13·37	13·12	12·87	12·63	341
342	15·55	15·20	14·87	14·55	14·25	13·96	13·68	13·41	13·15	12·91	12·67	342
343	15·59	15·24	14·91	14·60	14·29	14·00	13·72	13·45	13·19	12·94	12·70	343
344	15·64	15·29	14·96	14·64	14·33	14·04	13·76	13·49	13·23	12·98	12·74	344
345	15·68	15·33	15·00	14·68	14·38	14·08	13·80	13·53	13·27	13·02	12·78	345
346	15·73	15·38	15·04	14·72	14·42	14·12	13·84	13·57	13·31	13·06	12·81	346
347	15·77	15·42	15·09	14·77	14·46	14·16	13·88	13·61	13·35	13·09	12·85	347
348	15·82	15·47	15·13	14·81	14·50	14·20	13·92	13·65	13·38	13·13	12·89	348
349	15·86	15·51	15·17	14·85	14·54	14·24	13·96	13·69	13·42	13·17	12·93	349
350	15·91	15·56	15·22	14·89	14·58	14·29	14·00	13·73	13·46	13·21	12·96	350
351	15·95	15·60	15·26	14·94	14·63	14·33	14·04	13·76	13·50	13·25	13·00	351
352	16·00	15·64	15·30	14·98	14·67	14·37	14·08	13·80	13·54	13·28	13·04	352
353	16·05	15·69	15·35	15·02	14·71	14·41	14·12	13·84	13·58	13·32	13·07	353
354	16·09	15·73	15·39	15·06	14·75	14·45	14·16	13·88	13·62	13·36	13·11	354
355	16·14	15·78	15·43	15·11	14·79	14·49	14·20	13·92	13·65	13·40	13·15	355
356	16·18	15·82	15·48	15·15	14·83	14·53	14·24	13·96	13·69	13·43	13·19	356
357	16·23	15·87	15·52	15·19	14·88	14·57	14·28	14·00	13·73	13·47	13·22	357
358	16·27	15·91	15·57	15·23	14·92	14·61	14·32	14·04	13·77	13·51	13·26	358
359	16·32	15·96	15·61	15·28	14·96	14·65	14·36	14·08	13·81	13·55	13·30	359
360	16·36	16·00	15·65	15·32	15·00	14·69	14·40	14·12	13·85	13·58	13·33	360
361	16·41	16·04	15·70	15·36	15·04	14·73	14·44	14·16	13·88	13·62	13·37	361
362	16·45	16·09	15·74	15·40	15·08	14·78	14·48	14·20	13·92	13·66	13·41	362
363	16·50	16·13	15·78	15·45	15·13	14·82	14·52	14·24	13·96	13·70	13·44	363
364	16·55	16·18	15·83	15·49	15·17	14·86	14·56	14·27	14·00	13·74	13·48	364
365	16·59	16·22	15·87	15·53	15·21	14·90	14·60	14·31	14·04	13·77	13·52	365
366	16·64	16·27	15·91	15·57	15·25	14·94	14·64	14·35	14·08	13·81	13·56	366
367	16·68	16·31	15·96	15·62	15·29	14·98	14·68	14·39	14·12	13·85	13·59	367
368	16·73	16·36	16·00	15·66	15·33	15·02	14·72	14·43	14·15	13·89	13·63	368
369	16·77	16·40	16·04	15·70	15·38	15·06	14·76	14·47	14·19	13·92	13·67	369
370	16·82	16·44	16·09	15·74	15·42	15·10	14·80	14·51	14·23	13·96	13·70	370
371	16·86	16·49	16·13	15·79	15·46	15·14	14·84	14·55	14·27	14·00	13·74	371
372	16·91	16·53	16·17	15·83	15·50	15·18	14·88	14·59	14·31	14·04	13·78	372
373	16·95	16·58	16·22	15·87	15·54	15·22	14·92	14·63	14·35	14·08	13·81	373
374	17·00	16·62	16·26	15·91	15·58	15·27	14·96	14·67	14·38	14·11	13·85	374
375	17·05	16·67	16·30	15·96	15·63	15·31	15·00	14·71	14·42	14·15	13·89	375
376	17·09	16·71	16·35	16·00	15·67	15·35	15·04	14·75	14·46	14·19	13·93	376
377	17·14	16·76	16·39	16·04	15·71	15·39	15·08	14·78	14·50	14·23	13·96	377
378	17·18	16·80	16·43	16·09	15·75	15·43	15·12	14·82	14·54	14·26	14·00	378
379	17·23	16·84	16·48	16·13	15·79	15·47	15·16	14·86	14·58	14·30	14·04	379
380	17·27	16·89	16·52	16·17	15·83	15·51	15·20	14·90	14·62	14·34	14·07	380
381	17·32	16·93	16·57	16·21	15·88	15·55	15·24	14·94	14·65	14·38	14·11	381
382	17·36	16·98	16·61	16·26	15·92	15·59	15·28	14·98	14·69	14·42	14·15	382
383	17·41	17·02	16·65	16·30	15·96	15·63	15·32	15·02	14·73	14·45	14·19	383
384	17·45	17·07	16·70	16·34	16·00	15·67	15·36	15·06	14·77	14·49	14·22	384
385	17·50	17·11	16·74	16·38	16·04	15·71	15·40	15·10	14·81	14·53	14·26	385
386	17·55	17·16	16·78	16·43	16·08	15·76	15·44	15·14	14·85	14·57	14·30	386
387	17·59	17·20	16·83	16·47	16·13	15·80	15·48	15·18	14·88	14·60	14·33	387
388	17·64	17·24	16·87	16·51	16·17	15·84	15·52	15·22	14·92	14·64	14·37	388
389	17·68	17·29	16·91	16·55	16·21	15·88	15·56	15·25	14·96	14·68	14·41	389
390	17·73	17·33	16·96	16·60	16·25	15·92	15·60	15·29	15·00	14·72	14·44	390
391	17·77	17·38	17·00	16·64	16·29	15·96	15·64	15·33	15·04	14·75	14·48	391
392	17·82	17·42	17·04	16·68	16·33	16·00	15·68	15·37	15·08	14·79	14·52	392
393	17·86	17·47	17·09	16·72	16·38	16·04	15·72	15·41	15·12	14·83	14·56	393
394	17·91	17·51	17·13	16·77	16·42	16·08	15·76	15·45	15·15	14·87	14·59	394
395	17·95	17·56	17·17	16·81	16·46	16·12	15·80	15·49	15·19	14·91	14·63	395
396	18·00	17·60	17·22	16·85	16·50	16·16	15·84	15·53	15·23	14·94	14·67	396
397	18·05	17·64	17·26	16·89	16·54	16·20	15·88	15·57	15·27	14·98	14·70	397
398	18·09	17·69	17·30	16·94	16·58	16·24	15·92	15·61	15·31	15·02	14·74	398
399	18·14	17·73	17·35	16·98	16·63	16·29	15·96	15·65	15·35	15·06	14·78	399
400	18·18	17·78	17·39	17·02	16·67	16·33	16·00	15·69	15·38	15·09	14·81	400
Dist.	22	22·5	23	23·5	24	24·5	25	25·5	26	26·5	27	Dist.

DAY'S RUN, STEAMING TIME and AVERAGE SPEED

Dist.	22	22·5	23	23·5	24	24·5	25	25·5	26	26·5	27	Dist.
					Steaming Time—Hours							
401	18·23	17·82	17·43	17·06	16·71	16·37	16·04	15·73	15·42	15·13	14·85	401
402	18·27	17·87	17·48	17·11	16·75	16·41	16·08	15·76	15·46	15·17	14·89	402
403	18·32	17·91	17·52	17·15	16·79	16·45	16·12	15·80	15·50	15·21	14·93	403
404	18·36	17·96	17·57	17·19	16·83	16·49	16·16	15·84	15·54	15·25	14·96	404
405	18·41	18·00	17·61	17·23	16·88	16·53	16·20	15·88	15·58	15·28	15·00	405
406	18·45	18·04	17·65	17·28	16·92	16·57	16·24	15·92	15·62	15·32	15·04	406
407	18·50	18·09	17·70	17·32	16·96	16·61	16·28	15·96	15·65	15·36	15·07	407
408	18·55	18·13	17·74	17·36	17·00	16·65	16·32	16·00	15·69	15·40	15·11	408
409	18·59	18·18	17·78	17·40	17·04	16·69	16·36	16·04	15·73	15·43	15·15	409
410	18·64	18·22	17·83	17·45	17·08	16·73	16·40	16·08	15·77	15·47	15·19	410
411	18·68	18·27	17·87	17·49	17·13	16·78	16·44	16·12	15·81	15·51	15·22	411
412	18·73	18·31	17·91	17·53	17·17	16·82	16·48	16·16	15·85	15·55	15·26	412
413	18·77	18·36	17·96	17·57	17·21	16·86	16·52	16·20	15·88	15·58	15·30	413
414	18·82	18·40	18·00	17·62	17·25	16·90	16·56	16·24	15·92	15·62	15·33	414
415	18·86	18·44	18·04	17·66	17·29	16·94	16·60	16·27	15·96	15·66	15·37	415
416	18·91	18·49	18·09	17·70	17·33	16·98	16·64	16·31	16·00	15·70	15·41	416
417	18·95	18·53	18·13	17·74	17·38	17·02	16·68	16·35	16·04	15·74	15·44	417
418	19·00	18·58	18·17	17·79	17·42	17·06	16·72	16·39	16·08	15·77	15·48	418
419	19·05	18·62	18·22	17·83	17·46	17·10	16·76	16·43	16·12	15·81	15·52	419
420	19·09	18·67	18·26	17·87	17·50	17·14	16·80	16·47	16·15	15·85	15·56	420
421	19·14	18·71	18·30	17·91	17·54	17·18	16·84	16·51	16·19	15·89	15·59	421
422	19·18	18·76	18·35	17·96	17·58	17·22	16·88	16·55	16·23	15·92	15·63	422
423	19·23	18·80	18·39	18·00	17·63	17·27	16·92	16·59	16·27	15·96	16·67	423
424	19·27	18·84	18·43	18·04	17·67	17·31	16·96	16·63	16·31	16·00	15·70	424
425	19·32	18·89	18·48	18·09	17·71	17·35	17·00	16·67	16·35	16·04	15·74	425
426	19·36	18·93	18·52	18·13	17·75	17·39	17·04	16·71	16·38	16·08	15·78	426
427	19·41	18·98	18·57	18·17	17·79	17·43	17·08	16·75	16·42	16·11	15·81	427
428	19·45	19·02	18·61	18·21	17·83	17·47	17·12	16·78	16·46	16·15	15·85	428
429	19·50	19·07	18·65	18·26	17·88	17·51	17·16	16·82	16·50	16·19	15·89	429
430	19·55	19·11	18·70	18·30	17·92	17·55	17·20	16·86	16·54	16·23	15·93	430
431	19·59	19·16	18·74	18·34	17·96	17·59	17·24	16·90	16·58	16·26	15·96	431
432	19·64	19·20	18·78	18·38	18·00	17·63	17·28	16·94	16·62	16·30	16·00	432
433	19·68	19·24	18·83	18·43	18·04	17·67	17·32	16·98	16·65	16·34	16·04	433
434	19·73	19·29	18·87	18·47	18·08	17·71	17·36	17·02	16·69	16·38	16·07	434
435	19·77	19·33	18·91	18·51	18·13	17·76	17·40	17·06	16·73	16·42	16·11	435
436	19·82	19·38	18·96	18·55	18·17	17·80	17·44	17·10	16·77	16·45	16·15	436
437	19·86	19·42	19·00	18·60	18·21	17·84	17·48	17·14	16·81	16·49	16·19	437
438	19·91	19·47	19·04	18·64	18·25	17·88	17·52	17·18	16·85	16·53	16·22	438
439	19·95	19·51	19·09	18·68	18·29	17·92	17·56	17·22	16·88	16·57	16·26	439
440	20·00	19·56	19·13	18·72	18·33	17·96	17·60	17·25	16·92	16·60	16·30	440
441	20·05	19·60	19·17	18·77	18·38	18·00	17·64	17·29	16·96	16·64	16·33	441
442	20·09	19·64	19·22	18·81	18·42	18·04	17·68	17·33	17·00	16·68	16·37	442
443	20·14	19·69	19·26	18·85	18·46	18·08	17·72	17·37	17·04	16·72	16·41	443
444	20·18	19·73	19·30	18·89	18·50	18·12	17·76	17·41	17·08	16·75	16·44	444
445	20·23	19·78	19·35	18·94	18·54	18·16	17·80	17·45	17·12	16·79	16·48	445
446	20·27	19·82	19·39	18·98	18·58	18·20	17·84	17·49	17·15	16·83	16·52	446
447	20·32	19·87	19·43	19·02	18·63	18·24	17·88	17·53	17·19	16·87	16·56	447
448	20·36	19·91	19·48	19·06	18·67	18·29	17·92	17·57	17·23	16·91	16·59	448
449	20·41	19·96	19·52	19·11	18·71	18·33	17·96	17·61	17·27	16·94	16·63	449
450	20·45	20·00	19·57	19·15	18·75	18·37	18·00	17·65	17·31	16·98	16·67	450
451	20·50	20·04	19·61	19·19	18·79	18·41	18·04	17·69	17·35	17·02	16·70	451
452	20·55	20·09	19·65	19·23	18·83	18·45	18·08	17·73	17·38	17·06	16·74	452
453	20·59	20·13	19·70	19·28	18·88	18·49	18·12	17·76	17·42	17·09	16·78	453
454	20·64	20·18	19·74	19·32	18·92	18·53	18·16	17·80	17·46	17·13	16·81	454
455	20·68	20·22	19·78	19·36	18·96	18·57	18·20	17·84	17·50	17·17	16·85	455
456	20·73	20·27	19·83	19·40	19·00	18·61	18·24	17·88	17·54	17·21	16·89	456
457	20·77	20·31	19·87	19·45	19·04	18·65	18·28	17·92	17·58	17·25	16·93	457
458	20·82	20·36	19·91	19·49	19·08	18·69	18·32	17·96	17·62	17·28	16·96	458
459	20·86	20·40	19·96	19·53	19·13	18·73	18·36	18·00	17·65	17·32	17·00	459
460	20·91	20·44	20·00	19·57	19·17	18·78	18·40	18·04	17·69	17·36	17·04	460
Dist.	22	22·5	23	23·5	24	24·5	25	25·5	26	26·5	27	Dist.

DAY'S RUN, STEAMING TIME and AVERAGE SPEED

Dist.	22	22·5	23	23·5	24	24·5	25	25·5	26	26·5	27	Dist.
						Steaming Time—Hours						
461	20·95	20·49	20·04	19·62	19·21	18·82	18·44	18·08	17·73	17·40	17·07	461
462	21·00	20·53	20·09	19·66	19·25	18·86	18·48	18·12	17·77	17·43	17·11	462
463	21·05	20·58	20·13	19·70	19·29	18·90	18·52	18·16	17·81	17·47	17·15	463
464	21·09	20·62	20·17	19·74	19·33	18·94	18·56	18·20	17·85	17·51	17·19	464
465	21·14	20·67	20·22	19·79	19·38	18·98	18·60	18·24	17·88	17·55	17·22	465
466	21·18	20·71	20·26	19·83	19·42	19·02	18·64	18·27	17·92	17·58	17·26	466
467	21·23	20·76	20·30	19·87	19·46	19·06	18·68	18·31	17·96	17·62	17·30	467
468	21·27	20·80	20·35	19·91	19·50	19·10	18·72	18·35	18·00	17·66	17·33	468
469	21·32	20·84	20·39	19·96	19·54	19·14	18·76	18·39	18·04	17·70	17·37	469
470	21·36	20·89	20·43	20·00	19·58	19·18	18·80	18·43	18·08	17·74	17·41	470
471	21·41	20·93	20·48	20·04	19·63	19·22	18·84	18·47	18·12	17·77	17·44	471
472	21·45	20·98	20·52	20·09	19·67	19·27	18·88	18·51	18·15	17·81	17·48	472
473	21·50	21·02	20·57	20·13	19·71	19·31	18·92	18·55	18·19	17·85	17·52	473
474	21·55	21·07	20·61	20·17	19·75	19·35	18·96	18·59	18·23	17·89	17·56	474
475	21·59	21·11	20·65	20·21	19·79	19·39	19·00	18·63	18·27	17·92	17·59	475
476	21·64	21·16	20·70	20·26	19·83	19·43	19·04	18·67	18·31	17·96	17·63	476
477	21·68	21·20	20·74	20·30	19·88	19·47	19·08	18·71	18·35	18·00	17·67	477
478	21·73	21·24	20·78	20·34	19·92	19·51	19·12	18·75	18·38	18·04	17·70	478
479	21·77	21·29	20·83	20·38	19·96	19·55	19·16	18·78	18·42	18·08	17·74	479
480	21·82	21·33	20·87	20·43	20·00	19·59	19·20	18·82	18·46	18·11	17·78	480
481	21·86	21·38	20·91	20·47	20·04	19·63	19·24	18·86	18·50	18·15	17·81	481
482	21·91	21·42	20·96	20·51	20·08	19·67	19·28	18·90	18·54	18·19	17·85	482
483	21·95	21·47	21·00	20·55	20·13	19·71	19·32	18·94	18·58	18·23	17·89	483
484	22·00	21·51	21·04	20·60	20·17	19·76	19·36	18·98	18·62	18·26	17·93	484
485	22·05	21·56	21·09	20·64	20·21	19·80	19·40	19·02	18·65	18·30	17·96	485
486	22·09	21·60	21·13	20·68	20·25	19·84	19·44	19·06	18·69	18·34	18·00	486
487	22·14	21·64	21·17	20·72	20·29	19·88	19·48	19·10	18·73	18·38	18·04	487
488	22·18	21·69	21·22	20·77	20·33	19·92	19·52	19·14	18·77	18·42	18·07	488
489	22·23	21·73	21·26	20·81	20·38	19·96	19·56	19·18	18·81	18·45	18·11	489
490	22·27	21·78	21·30	20·85	20·42	20·00	19·60	19·22	18·85	18·49	18·15	490
491	22·32	21·82	21·35	20·89	20·46	20·04	19·64	19·25	18·88	18·53	18·19	491
492	22·36	21·87	21·39	20·94	20·50	20·08	19·68	19·29	18·92	18·57	18·22	492
493	22·41	21·91	21·43	20·98	20·54	20·12	19·72	19·33	18·96	18·60	18·26	493
494	22·45	21·96	21·48	21·02	20·58	20·16	19·76	19·37	19·00	18·64	18·30	494
495	22·50	22·00	21·52	21·06	20·63	20·20	19·80	19·41	19·04	18·68	18·33	495
496	22·55	22·04	21·57	21·11	20·67	20·24	19·84	19·45	19·08	18·72	18·37	496
497	22·59	22·09	21·61	21·15	20·71	20·29	19·88	19·49	19·12	18·75	18·41	497
498	22·64	22·13	21·65	21·19	20·75	20·33	19·92	19·53	19·15	18·79	18·44	498
499	22·68	22·18	21·70	21·23	20·79	20·37	19·96	19·57	19·19	18·83	18·48	499
500	22·73	22·22	21·74	21·28	20·83	20·41	20·00	19·61	19·23	18·87	18·52	500
501	22·77	22·27	21·78	21·32	20·88	20·45	20·04	19·65	19·27	18·91	18·56	501
502	22·82	22·31	21·83	21·36	20·92	20·49	20·08	19·69	19·31	18·94	18·59	502
503	22·86	22·36	21·87	21·40	20·96	20·53	20·12	19·73	19·35	18·98	18·63	503
504	22·91	22·40	21·91	21·45	21·00	20·57	20·16	19·76	19·38	19·02	18·67	504
505	22·95	22·44	21·96	21·49	21·04	20·61	20·20	19·80	19·42	19·06	18·70	505
506	23·00	22·49	22·00	21·53	21·08	20·65	20·24	19·84	19·46	19·09	18·74	506
507	23·05	22·53	22·04	21·57	21·13	20·69	20·28	19·88	19·50	19·13	18·78	507
508	23·09	22·58	22·09	21·62	21·17	20·73	20·32	19·92	19·54	19·17	18·81	508
509	23·14	22·62	22·13	21·66	21·21	20·78	20·36	19·96	19·58	19·21	18·85	509
510	23·18	22·67	22·17	21·70	21·25	20·82	20·40	20·00	19·62	19·25	18·89	510
511	23·23	22·71	22·22	21·74	21·29	20·86	20·44	20·04	19·65	19·28	18·93	511
512	23·27	22·76	22·26	21·79	21·33	20·90	20·48	20·08	19·69	19·32	18·96	512
513	23·32	22·80	22·30	21·83	21·38	20·94	20·52	20·12	19·73	19·36	19·00	513
514	23·36	22·84	22·35	21·87	21·42	20·98	20·56	20·16	19·77	19·40	19·04	514
515	23·41	22·89	22·39	21·91	21·46	21·02	20·60	20·20	19·81	19·43	19·07	515
516	23·45	22·93	22·43	21·96	21·50	21·06	20·64	20·24	19·85	19·47	19·11	516
517	23·50	22·98	22·48	22·00	21·54	21·10	20·68	20·27	19·88	19·51	19·15	517
518	23·55	23·02	22·52	22·04	21·58	21·14	20·72	20·31	19·92	19·55	19·19	518
519	23·59	23·07	22·57	22·09	21·63	21·18	20·76	20·35	19·96	19·58	19·22	519
520	23·64	23·11	22·61	22·13	21·67	21·22	20·80	20·39	20·00	19·62	19·26	520
Dist.	22	22·5	23	23·5	24	24·5	25	25·5	26	26·5	27	Dist.

DAY'S RUN, STEAMING TIME and AVERAGE SPEED

Dist.	Steaming Time—Hours											Dist.
	22	22·5	23	23·5	24	24·5	25	25·5	26	26·5	27	
521	23·68	23·16	22·65	22·17	21·71	21·27	20·84	20·43	20·04	19·66	19·30	521
522	23·73	23·20	22·70	22·21	21·75	21·31	20·88	20·47	20·08	19·70	19·33	522
523	23·77	23·24	22·74	22·26	21·79	21·35	20·92	20·51	20·12	19·74	19·37	523
524	23·82	23·29	22·78	22·30	21·83	21·39	20·96	20·55	20·15	19·77	19·41	524
525	23·86	23·33	22·83	22·34	21·88	21·43	21·00	20·59	20·19	19·81	19·44	525
526	23·91	23·38	22·87	22·38	21·92	21·47	21·04	20·63	20·23	19·85	19·48	526
527	23·95	23·42	22·91	22·43	21·96	21·51	21·08	20·67	20·27	19·89	19·52	527
528	24·00	23·47	22·96	22·47	22·00	21·55	21·12	20·71	20·31	19·92	19·56	528
529	24·05	23·51	23·00	22·51	22·04	21·59	21·16	20·75	20·35	19·96	19·59	529
530	24·09	23·56	23·04	22·55	22·08	21·63	21·20	20·78	20·38	20·00	19·63	530
531	24·14	23·60	23·09	22·60	22·13	21·67	21·24	20·82	20·42	20·04	19·67	531
532	24·18	23·64	23·13	22·64	22·17	21·71	21·28	20·86	20·46	20·08	19·70	532
533	24·23	23·69	23·17	22·68	22·21	21·76	21·32	20·90	20·50	20·11	19·74	533
534	24·27	23·73	23·22	22·72	22·25	21·80	21·36	20·94	20·54	20·15	19·78	534
535	24·32	23·78	23·26	22·77	22·29	21·84	21·40	20·98	20·58	20·19	19·81	535
536	24·36	23·82	23·30	22·81	22·33	21·88	21·44	21·02	20·62	20·23	19·85	536
537	24·41	23·87	23·35	22·85	22·38	21·92	21·48	21·06	20·65	20·26	19·89	537
538	24·45	23·91	23·39	22·89	22·42	21·96	21·52	21·10	20·69	20·30	19·93	538
539	24·50	23·96	23·43	22·94	22·46	22·00	21·56	21·14	20·73	20·34	19·96	539
540	24·55	24·00	23·48	22·98	22·50	22·04	21·60	21·18	20·77	20·38	20·00	540
541	24·59	24·04	23·52	23·02	22·54	22·08	21·64	21·22	20·81	20·42	20·04	541
542	24·64	24·09	23·57	23·06	22·58	22·12	21·68	21·25	20·85	20·45	20·07	542
543	24·68	24·13	23·61	23·11	22·63	22·16	21·72	21·29	20·88	20·49	20·11	543
544	24·73	24·18	23·65	23·15	22·67	22·20	21·76	21·33	20·92	20·53	20·15	544
545	24·77	24·22	23·70	23·19	22·71	22·24	21·80	21·37	20·96	20·57	20·19	545
546	24·82	24·27	23·74	23·23	22·75	22·29	21·84	21·41	21·00	20·60	20·22	546
547	24·86	24·31	23·78	23·28	22·79	22·33	21·88	21·45	21·04	20·64	20·26	547
548	24·91	24·36	23·83	23·32	22·83	22·37	21·92	21·49	21·08	20·68	20·30	548
549	24·95	24·40	23·87	23·36	22·88	22·41	21·96	21·53	21·12	20·72	20·33	549
550	25·00	24·44	23·91	23·40	22·92	22·45	22·00	21·57	21·15	20·75	20·37	550
551	25·05	24·49	23·96	23·45	22·96	22·49	22·04	21·61	21·19	20·79	20·41	551
552	25·09	24·53	24·00	23·49	23·00	22·53	22·08	21·65	21·23	20·83	20·44	552
553	25·14	24·58	24·04	23·53	23·04	22·57	22·12	21·69	21·27	20·87	20·48	553
554	25·18	24·62	24·09	23·57	23·08	22·61	22·16	21·73	21·31	20·91	20·52	554
555	25·23	24·67	24·13	23·62	23·13	22·65	22·20	21·76	21·35	20·94	20·56	555
556	25·27	24·71	24·17	23·66	23·17	22·69	22·24	21·80	21·38	20·98	20·59	556
557	25·32	24·76	24·22	23·70	23·21	22·73	22·28	21·84	21·42	21·02	20·63	557
558	25·36	24·80	24·26	23·74	23·25	22·78	22·32	21·88	21·46	21·06	20·67	558
559	25·41	24·84	24·30	23·79	23·29	22·82	22·36	21·92	21·50	21·09	20·70	559
560	25·45	24·89	24·35	23·83	23·33	22·86	22·40	21·96	21·54	21·13	20·74	560
561	25·50	24·93	24·39	23·87	23·38	22·90	22·44	22·00	21·58	21·17	20·78	561
562	25·55	24·98	24·43	23·91	23·42	22·94	22·48	22·04	21·62	21·21	20·81	562
563	25·59	25·02	24·48	23·96	23·46	22·98	22·52	22·08	21·65	21·25	20·85	563
564	25·64	25·07	24·52	24·00	23·50	23·02	22·56	22·12	21·69	21·28	20·89	564
565	25·68	25·11	24·57	24·04	23·54	23·06	22·60	22·16	21·73	21·32	20·93	565
566	25·73	25·16	24·61	24·09	23·58	23·10	22·64	22·20	21·77	21·36	20·96	566
567	25·77	25·20	24·65	24·13	23·63	23·14	22·68	22·24	21·81	21·40	21·00	567
568	25·82	25·24	24·70	24·17	23·67	23·18	22·72	22·27	21·85	21·43	21·04	568
569	25·86	25·29	24·74	24·21	23·71	23·22	22·76	22·31	21·88	21·47	21·07	569
570	25·91	25·33	24·78	24·26	23·75	23·27	22·80	22·35	21·92	21·51	21·11	570
571	25·95	25·38	24·83	24·30	23·79	23·31	22·84	22·39	21·96	21·55	21·15	571
572	26·00	25·42	24·87	24·34	23·83	23·35	22·88	22·43	22·00	21·58	21·19	572
573	26·05	25·47	24·91	24·38	23·88	23·39	22·92	22·47	22·04	21·62	21·22	573
574	26·09	25·51	24·96	24·43	23·92	23·43	22·96	22·51	22·08	21·66	21·26	574
575	26·14	25·56	25·00	24·47	23·96	23·47	23·00	22·55	22·12	21·70	21·30	575
576	26·18	25·60	25·04	24·51	24·00	23·51	23·04	22·59	22·15	21·74	21·33	576
577	26·23	25·64	25·09	24·55	24·04	23·55	23·08	22·63	22·19	21·77	21·37	577
578	26·27	25·69	25·13	24·60	24·08	23·59	23·12	22·67	22·23	21·81	21·41	578
579	26·32	25·73	25·17	24·64	24·13	23·63	23·16	22·71	22·27	21·85	21·44	579
580	26·36	25·78	25·22	24·68	24·17	23·67	23·20	22·75	22·31	21·89	21·48	580
Dist.	22	22·5	23	23·5	24	24·5	25	25·5	26	26·5	27	Dist.

DAY'S RUN, STEAMING TIME and AVERAGE SPEED

Dist.	Steaming Time—Hours											Dist.
	22	22.5	23	23.5	24	24.5	25	25.5	26	26.5	27	
581	26.41	25.82	25.26	24.72	24.21	23.71	23.24	22.78	22.35	21.92	21.52	581
582	26.45	25.87	25.30	24.77	24.25	23.76	23.28	22.82	22.38	21.96	21.56	582
583	26.50	25.91	25.35	24.81	24.29	23.80	23.32	22.86	22.42	22.00	21.59	583
584	26.55	25.96	25.39	24.85	24.33	23.84	23.36	22.90	22.46	22.04	21.63	584
585	26.59	26.00	25.43	24.89	24.38	23.88	23.40	22.94	22.50	22.08	21.67	585
586	26.64	26.04	25.48	24.94	24.42	23.92	23.44	22.98	22.54	22.11	21.70	586
587	26.68	26.09	25.52	24.98	24.46	23.96	23.48	23.02	22.58	22.15	21.74	587
588	26.73	26.13	25.57	25.02	24.50	24.00	23.52	23.06	22.62	22.19	21.78	588
589	26.77	26.18	25.61	25.06	24.54	24.04	23.56	23.10	22.65	22.23	21.81	589
590	26.82	26.22	25.65	25.11	24.58	24.08	23.60	23.14	22.69	22.26	21.85	590
591	26.86	26.27	25.70	25.15	24.63	24.12	23.64	23.18	22.73	22.30	21.89	591
592	26.91	26.31	25.74	25.19	24.67	24.16	23.68	23.22	22.77	22.34	21.93	592
593	26.95	26.36	25.78	25.23	24.71	24.20	23.72	23.25	22.81	22.38	21.96	593
594	27.00	26.40	25.83	25.28	24.75	24.24	23.76	23.29	22.85	22.42	22.00	594
595	27.05	26.44	25.87	25.32	24.79	24.29	23.80	23.33	22.88	22.45	22.04	595
596	27.09	26.49	25.91	25.36	24.83	24.33	23.84	23.37	22.92	22.49	22.07	596
597	27.14	26.53	25.96	25.40	24.88	24.37	23.88	23.41	22.96	22.53	22.11	597
598	27.18	26.58	26.00	25.45	24.92	24.41	23.92	23.45	23.00	22.57	22.15	598
599	27.23	26.62	26.04	25.49	24.96	24.45	23.96	23.49	23.04	22.60	22.19	599
600	27.27	26.67	26.09	25.53	25.00	24.49	24.00	23.53	23.08	22.64	22.22	600
601	27.32	26.71	26.13	25.57	25.04	24.53	24.04	23.57	23.12	22.68	22.26	601
602	27.36	26.76	26.17	25.62	25.08	24.57	24.08	23.61	23.15	22.72	22.30	602
603	27.41	26.80	26.22	25.66	25.13	24.61	24.12	23.65	23.19	22.75	22.33	603
604	27.45	26.84	26.26	25.70	25.17	24.65	24.16	23.69	23.23	22.79	22.37	604
605	27.50	26.89	26.30	25.74	25.21	24.69	24.20	23.73	23.27	22.83	22.41	605
606	27.55	26.93	26.35	25.79	25.25	24.73	24.24	23.76	23.31	22.87	22.44	606
607	27.59	26.98	26.39	25.83	25.29	24.78	24.28	23.80	23.35	22.91	22.48	607
608	27.64	27.02	26.43	25.87	25.33	24.82	24.32	23.84	23.38	22.94	22.52	608
609	27.68	27.07	26.48	25.91	25.38	24.86	24.36	23.88	23.42	22.98	22.56	609
610	27.73	27.11	26.52	25.96	25.42	24.90	24.40	23.92	23.46	23.02	22.59	610
611	27.77	27.16	26.57	26.00	25.46	24.94	24.44	23.96	23.50	23.06	22.63	611
612	27.82	27.20	26.61	26.04	25.50	24.98	24.48	24.00	23.54	23.09	22.67	612
613	27.86	27.24	26.65	26.09	25.54	25.02	24.52	24.04	23.58	23.13	22.70	613
614	27.91	27.29	26.70	26.13	25.58	25.06	24.56	24.08	23.62	23.17	22.74	614
615	27.95	27.33	26.74	26.17	25.63	25.10	24.60	24.12	23.65	23.21	22.78	615
616	28.00	27.38	26.78	26.21	25.67	25.14	24.64	24.16	23.69	23.25	22.81	616
617	28.05	27.42	26.83	26.26	25.71	25.18	24.68	24.20	23.73	23.28	22.85	617
618	28.09	27.47	26.87	26.30	25.75	25.22	24.72	24.24	23.77	23.32	22.89	618
619	28.14	27.51	26.91	26.34	25.79	25.27	24.76	24.27	23.81	23.36	22.93	619
620	28.18	27.56	26.96	26.38	25.83	25.31	24.80	24.31	23.85	23.40	22.96	620
621	28.23	27.60	27.00	26.43	25.88	25.35	24.84	24.35	23.88	23.43	23.00	621
622	28.27	27.64	27.04	26.47	25.92	25.39	24.88	24.39	23.92	23.47	23.04	622
623	28.32	27.69	27.09	26.51	25.96	25.43	24.92	24.43	23.96	23.51	23.07	623
624	28.36	27.73	27.13	26.55	26.00	25.47	24.96	24.47	24.00	23.55	23.11	624
625	28.41	27.78	27.17	26.60	26.04	25.51	25.00	24.51	24.04	23.58	23.15	625
626	28.45	27.82	27.22	26.64	26.08	25.55	25.04	24.55	24.08	23.62	23.19	626
627	28.50	27.87	27.26	26.68	26.13	25.59	25.08	24.59	24.12	23.66	23.22	627
628	28.55	27.91	27.30	26.72	26.17	25.63	25.12	24.63	24.15	23.70	23.26	628
629	28.59	27.96	27.35	26.77	26.21	25.67	25.16	24.67	24.19	23.74	23.30	629
630	28.64	28.00	27.39	26.81	26.25	25.71	25.20	24.71	24.23	23.77	23.33	630
631	28.68	28.04	27.43	26.85	26.29	25.76	25.24	24.75	24.27	23.81	23.37	631
632	28.73	28.09	27.48	26.89	26.33	25.80	25.28	24.78	24.31	23.85	23.41	632
633	28.77	28.13	27.52	26.94	26.38	25.84	25.32	24.82	24.35	23.89	23.44	633
634	28.82	28.18	27.57	26.98	26.42	25.88	25.36	24.86	24.38	23.92	23.48	634
635	28.86	28.22	27.61	27.02	26.46	25.92	25.40	24.90	24.42	23.96	23.52	635
636	28.91	28.27	27.65	27.06	26.50	25.96	25.44	24.94	24.46	24.00	23.56	636
637	28.95	28.31	27.70	27.11	26.54	26.00	25.48	24.98	24.50	24.04	23.59	637
638	29.00	28.36	27.74	27.15	26.58	26.04	25.52	25.02	24.54	24.08	23.63	638
639	29.05	28.40	27.78	27.19	26.63	26.08	25.56	25.06	24.58	24.11	23.67	639
640	29.09	28.44	27.83	27.23	26.67	26.12	25.60	25.10	24.62	24.15	23.70	640
Dist.	22	22.5	23	23.5	24	24.5	25	25.5	26	26.5	27	Dist

DAY'S RUN, STEAMING TIME and AVERAGE SPEED

Dist.	Steaming Time—Hours											Dist.
	22	22·5	23	23·5	24	24·5	25	25·5	26	26·5	27	
641	29·14	28·49	27·87	27·28	26·71	26·16	25·64	25·14	24·65	24·19	23·74	641
642	29·18	28·53	27·91	27·32	26·75	26·20	25·68	25·18	24·69	24·23	23·78	642
643	29·23	28·58	27·96	27·36	26·79	26·24	25·72	25·22	24·73	24·26	23·81	643
644	29·27	28·62	28·00	27·40	26·83	26·29	25·76	25·25	24·77	24·30	23·85	644
645	29·32	28·67	28·04	27·45	26·88	26·33	25·80	25·29	24·81	24·34	23·89	645
646	29·36	28·71	28·09	27·49	26·92	26·37	25·84	25·33	24·85	24·38	23·93	646
647	29·41	28·76	28·13	27·53	26·96	26·41	25·88	25·37	24·88	24·42	23·96	647
648	29·45	28·80	28·17	27·57	27·00	26·45	25·92	25·41	24·92	24·45	24·00	648
649	29·50	28·84	28·22	27·62	27·04	26·49	25·96	25·45	24·96	24·49	24·04	649
650	29·55	28·89	28·26	27·66	27·08	26·53	26·00	25·49	25·00	24·53	24·07	650
651	29·59	28·93	28·30	27·70	27·13	26·57	26·04	25·53	25·04	24·57	24·11	651
652	29·64	28·98	28·35	27·74	27·17	26·61	26·08	25·57	25·08	24·60	24·15	652
653	29·68	29·02	28·39	27·79	27·21	26·65	26·12	25·61	25·12	24·64	24·19	653
654	29·73	29·07	28·43	27·83	27·25	26·69	26·16	25·65	25·15	24·68	24·22	654
655	29·77	29·11	28·48	27·87	27·29	26·73	26·20	25·69	25·19	24·72	24·26	655
656	29·82	29·16	28·52	27·91	27·33	26·78	26·24	25·73	25·23	24·75	24·30	656
657	29·86	29·20	28·57	27·96	27·38	26·82	26·28	25·76	25·27	24·79	24·33	657
658	29·91	29·24	28·61	28·00	27·42	26·86	26·32	25·80	25·31	24·83	24·37	658
659	29·95	29·29	28·65	28·04	27·46	26·90	26·36	25·84	25·35	24·87	24·41	659
660	30·00	29·33	28·70	28·09	27·50	26·94	26·40	25·88	25·38	24·91	24·44	660
661	30·05	29·38	28·74	28·13	27·54	26·98	26·44	25·92	25·42	24·94	24·48	661
662	30·09	29·42	28·78	28·17	27·58	27·02	26·48	25·96	25·46	24·98	24·52	662
663	30·14	29·47	28·83	28·21	27·63	27·06	26·52	26·00	25·50	25·02	24·56	663
664	30·18	29·51	28·87	28·26	27·67	27·10	26·56	26·04	25·54	25·06	24·59	664
665	30·23	29·56	28·91	28·30	27·71	27·14	26·60	26·08	25·58	25·09	24·63	665
666	30·27	29·60	28·96	28·34	27·75	27·18	26·64	26·12	25·62	25·13	24·67	666
667	30·32	29·64	29·00	28·38	27·79	27·22	26·68	26·16	25·65	25·17	24·70	667
668	30·36	29·69	29·04	28·43	27·83	27·27	26·72	26·20	25·69	25·21	24·74	668
669	30·41	29·73	29·09	28·47	27·88	27·31	26·76	26·24	25·73	25·25	24·78	669
670	30·45	29·78	29·13	28·51	27·92	27·35	26·80	26·27	25·77	25·28	24·81	670
671	30·50	29·82	29·17	28·55	27·96	27·39	26·84	26·31	25·81	25·32	24·85	671
672	30·55	29·87	29·22	28·60	28·00	27·43	26·88	26·35	25·85	25·36	24·89	672
673	30·59	29·91	29·26	28·64	28·04	27·47	26·92	26·39	25·88	25·40	24·93	673
674	30·64	29·96	29·30	28·68	28·08	27·51	26·96	26·43	25·92	25·43	24·96	674
675	30·68	30·00	29·35	28·72	28·13	27·55	27·00	26·47	25·96	25·47	25·00	675
676	30·73	30·04	29·39	28·77	28·17	27·59	27·04	26·51	26·00	25·51	25·04	676
677	30·77	30·09	29·43	28·81	28·21	27·63	27·08	26·55	26·04	25·55	25·07	677
678	30·82	30·13	29·48	28·85	28·25	27·67	27·12	26·59	26·08	25·58	25·11	678
679	30·86	30·18	29·52	28·89	28·29	27·71	27·16	26·63	26·12	25·62	25·15	679
680	30·91	30·22	29·57	28·94	28·33	27·76	27·20	26·67	26·15	25·66	25·19	680
681	30·95	30·27	29·61	29·98	28·38	27·80	27·24	26·71	26·19	25·70	25·22	681
682	31·00	30·31	29·65	29·02	28·42	27·84	27·28	26·75	26·23	25·74	25·26	682
683	31·05	30·36	29·70	29·06	28·46	27·88	27·32	26·78	26·27	25·77	25·30	683
684	31·09	30·40	29·74	29·11	28·50	27·92	27·36	26·82	26·31	25·81	25·33	684
685	31·14	30·44	29·78	29·15	28·54	27·96	27·40	26·86	26·35	25·85	25·37	685
686	31·18	30·49	29·83	29·19	28·58	28·00	27·44	26·90	26·38	25·89	25·41	686
687	31·23	30·53	29·87	29·23	28·63	28·04	27·48	26·94	26·42	25·92	25·44	687
688	31·27	30·58	29·91	29·28	28·67	28·08	27·52	26·98	26·46	25·96	25·48	688
689	31·32	30·62	29·96	29·32	28·71	28·12	27·56	27·02	26·50	26·00	25·52	689
690	31·36	30·67	30·00	29·36	28·75	28·16	27·60	27·06	26·54	26·04	25·56	690
691	31·41	30·71	30·04	29·40	28·79	28·20	27·64	27·10	26·58	26·08	25·59	691
692	31·45	30·76	30·09	29·45	28·83	28·24	27·68	27·14	26·62	26·11	25·63	692
693	31·50	30·80	30·13	29·49	28·88	28·29	27·72	27·18	26·65	26·15	25·67	693
694	31·55	30·84	30·17	29·53	28·92	28·33	27·76	27·22	26·69	26·19	25·70	694
695	31·59	30·89	30·22	29·57	28·96	28·37	27·80	27·25	26·73	26·23	25·74	695
696	31·64	30·93	30·26	29·62	29·00	28·41	27·84	27·29	26·77	26·26	25·78	696
697	31·68	30·98	30·30	29·66	29·04	28·45	27·88	27·33	26·81	26·30	25·81	697
698	31·73	31·02	30·35	29·70	29·08	28·49	27·92	27·37	26·85	26·34	25·85	698
699	31·77	31·07	30·39	29·74	29·13	28·53	27·96	27·41	26·88	26·38	25·89	699
700	31·82	31·11	30·43	29·79	29·17	28·57	28·00	27·45	26·92	26·42	25·93	700
Dist.	22	22·5	23	23·5	24	24·5	25	25·5	26	26·5	27	Dist.

DISTANCE OFF BY VERTICAL SEXTANT ANGLE

Distance off Miles	Height of Object in Metres												Distance off Miles
	14	16	18	20	22	24	26	28	30	32	34	36	
0·1	4°19′	4°56′	5°33′	6°10′	6°46′	7°23′	7°59′	8°36′	9°12′	9°48′	10°24′	11°00′	0·1
0·2	2°10′	2°28′	2°47′	3°05′	3°24′	3°42′	4°01′	4°19′	4°38′	4°56′	5°15′	5°33′	0·2
0·3	1°27′	1°39′	1°51′	2°04′	2°16′	2°28′	2°41′	2°53′	3°05′	3°18′	3°30′	3°42′	0·3
0·4	1°05′	1°14′	1°23′	1°33′	1°42′	1°51′	2°01′	2°10′	2°19′	2°28′	2°38′	2°47′	0·4
0·5	0°52′	0°59′	1°07′	1°14′	1°22′	1°29′	1°36′	1°44′	1°51′	1°59′	2°06′	2°14′	0·5
0·6	0°43′	0°49′	0°56′	1°02′	1°08′	1°14′	1°20′	1°27′	1°33′	1°39′	1°45′	1°51′	0·6
0·7	0°37′	0°42′	0°48′	0°53′	0°58′	1°04′	1°09′	1°14′	1°19′	1°25′	1°30′	1°35′	0·7
0·8	0°32′	0°37′	0°40′	0°46′	0°51′	0°56′	1°00′	1°05′	1°10′	1°14′	1°19′	1°23′	0·8
0·9	0°29′	0°33′	0°37′	0°41′	0°45′	0°49′	0°54′	0°58′	1°02′	1°06′	1°10′	1°14′	0·9
1·0	0°26′	0°30′	0°33′	0°37′	0°41′	0°45′	0°48′	0°52′	0°56′	0°59′	1°03′	1°07′	1·0
1·1	0°24′	0°27′	0°30′	0°34′	0°37′	0°40′	0°44′	0°47′	0°51′	0°54′	0°57′	1°01′	1·1
1·2	0°22′	0°25′	0°28′	0°31′	0°34′	0°37′	0°40′	0°43′	0°46′	0°49′	0°53′	0°56′	1·2
1·3	0°20′	0°23′	0°26′	0°29′	0°31′	0°34′	0°37′	0°40′	0°43′	0°46′	0°49′	0°51′	1·3
1·4	0°19′	0°21′	0°24′	0°27′	0°29′	0°32′	0°34′	0°37′	0°40′	0°42′	0°45′	0°48′	1·4
1·5	0°17′	0°20′	0°22′	0°25′	0°27′	0°30′	0°32′	0°35′	0°37′	0°40′	0°42′	0°45′	1·5
1·6	0°16′	0°19′	0°21′	0°23′	0°26′	0°28′	0°30′	0°32′	0°35′	0°37′	0°39′	0°42′	1·6
1·7	0°15′	0°17′	0°20′	0°22′	0°24′	0°26′	0°28′	0°31′	0°33′	0°35′	0°37′	0°39′	1·7
1·8	0°14′	0°16′	0°19′	0°21′	0°23′	0°25′	0°27′	0°29′	0°31′	0°33′	0°35′	0°37′	1·8
1·9	0°14′	0°16′	0°18′	0°20′	0°21′	0°23′	0°25′	0°27′	0°29′	0°31′	0°33′	0°35′	1·9
2·0	0°13′	0°15′	0°17′	0°19′	0°20′	0°22′	0°24′	0°26′	0°28′	0°30′	0°32′	0°33′	2·0
2·1	0°12′	0°14′	0°16′	0°18′	0°19′	0°21′	0°23′	0°25′	0°27′	0°28′	0°30′	0°32′	2·1
2·2	0°12′	0°13′	0°15′	0°17′	0°19′	0°20′	0°22′	0°24′	0°25′	0°27′	0°29′	0°30,	2·2
2·3	0°11′	0°13′	0°14′	0°16′	0°18′	0°19′	0°21′	0°23′	0°24′	0°26′	0°27′	0°29′	2·3
2·4	0°11′	0°12′	0°14′	0°15′	0°17′	0°19′	0°20′	0°22′	0°23′	0°25′	0°26′	0°28′	2·4
2·5	0°10′	0°12′	0°13′	0°15′	0°16′	0°18′	0°19′	0°21′	0°22′	0°24′	0°25′	0°27′	2·5
2·6	0°10′	0°11′	0°13	0°14′	0°16′	0°17′	0°19′	0°20′	0°21′	0°23′	0°24′	0°26′	2·6
2·7	0°10′	0°11′	0°12′	0°14′	0°15′	0°16′	0°18′	0°19′	0°21′	0°22′	0°23′	0°25′	2·7
2·8		0°11′	0°12′	0°13′	0°15′	0°16′	0°17′	0°19′	0°20′	0°21′	0°23′	0°24′	2·8
2·9		0°10′	0°11′	0°13′	0°14′	0°15′	0°17′	0°18′	0°19′	0°20′	0°22′	0°23′	2·9
3·0		0°10′	0°11′	0°12′	0°14′	0°15′	0°16′	0°17′	0°19′	0°20′	0°21′	0°22′	3·0
3·2			0°10′	0°12′	0°13′	0°14′	0°15′	0°16′	0°17′	0°19′	0°20′	0°21′	3·2
3·4			0°10′	0°11′	0°12′	0°13′	0°14′	0°15′	0°16′	0°17′	0°19′	0°20′	3·4
3·6				0°10′	0°11′	0°12′	0°13′	0°14′	0°15′	0°16′	0°18′	0°19′	3·6
3·8				0°10′	0°11′	0°12′	0°13′	0°14′	0°15′	0°16′	0°17′	0°18′	3·8
4·0					0°10′	0°11′	0°12′	0°13′	0°14′	0°15′	0°16′	0°17′	4·0
4·2					0°10′	0°11′	0°11′	0°12′	0°13′	0°14′	0°15′	0°16′	4·2
4·4						0°10′	0°11′	0°12′	0°13′	0°13′	0°14′	0°15′	4·4
4·6						0°10′	0°10′	0°11′	0°12′	0°13′	0°14′	0°15′	4·6
4·8							0°10′	0°11′	0°12′	0°12′	0°13′	0°14′	4·8
5·0							0°10′	0°10′	0°11′	0°12′	0°13′	0°13′	5·0
5·2								0°10′	0°11′	0°11′	0°12′	0°13′	5·2
5·4								0°10′	0°10′	0°11′	0°12′	0°12′	5·4
5·6									0°10′	0°11′	0°11′	0°12′	5·6
5·8									0°10′	0°10′	0°11′	0°12′	5·8
6·0										0°10′	0°11′	0°11′	6·0

D

Distance off Miles	Height of Object in Metres												Distance off Miles
	38	40	42	44	46	48	50	52	54	56	58	60	
0·1	11°35′	12°11′	12°46′	13°21′	13°56′	14°31′	15°06′	15°41′	16°15′	16°49′	17°23′	17°57′	0·1
0·2	5°51′	6°10′	6°28′	6°46′	7°05′	7°23′	7°41′	7°59′	8°17′	8°36′	8°54′	9°12′	0·2
0·3	3°55′	4°07′	4°19′	4°32′	4°44′	4°56′	5°08′	5°21′	5°33′	5°45′	5°57′	6°10′	0·3
0·4	2°56′	3°05′	3°15′	3°24′	3°33′	3°42′	3°52′	4°01′	4°10′	4°19′	4°28′	4°38′	0·4
0·5	2°21′	2°28′	2°36′	2°43′	2°51′	2°58′	3°05′	3°13′	3°20′	3°28′	3°35′	3°42′	0·5
0·6	1°57′	2°04′	2°10′	2°16′	2°22′	2°28′	2°34′	2°41′	2°47′	2°53′	2°59′	3°05′	0·6
0·7	1°41′	1°46′	1°51′	1°57′	2°02′	2°07′	2°12′	2°18′	2°23′	2°28′	2°34′	2°39′	0·7
0·8	1°28′	1°33′	1°37′	1°42′	1°47′	1°51′	1°56′	2°01′	2°05′	2°10′	2°14′	2°19′	0·8
0·9	1°18′	1°22′	1°27′	1°31′	1°35′	1°39′	1°43′	1°47′	1°51′	1°55′	2°00′	2°04′	0·9
1·0	1°10′	1°14′	1°18′	1°22′	1°25′	1°29′	1°33′	1°36′	1°40′	1°44′	1°48′	1°51′	1·0
1·1	1°04′	1°07′	1°11′	1°14′	1°18′	1°21′	1°24′	1°28′	1°31′	1°34′	1°38′	1°41′	1·1
1·2	0°59′	1°02′	1°05′	1°08′	1°11′	1°14′	1°17′	1°20′	1°23′	1°27′	1°30′	1°33′	1·2
1·3	0°54′	0°57′	1°00′	1°03′	1°06′	1°08′	1°11′	1°14′	1°17′	1°20′	1°23′	1°26′	1·3
1·4	0°50′	0°53′	0°56′	0°58′	1°01′	1°04′	1°06′	1°09′	1°12′	1°14′	1°17′	1°19′	1·4
1·5	0°47′	0°49′	0°52′	0°54′	0°57′	0°59′	1°02′	1°04′	1°07′	1°09′	1°12′	1°14′	1·5
1·6	0°44′	0°46′	0°49′	0°51′	0°53′	0°56′	0°58′	1°00′	1°03′	1°05′	1°07′	1°10′	1·6
1·7	0°41′	0°44′	0°46′	0°48′	0°50′	0°52′	0°55′	0°57′	0°59′	1°01′	1°03′	1°05′	1·7
1·8	0°39′	0°41′	0°43′	0°45′	0°47′	0°49′	0°52′	0°54′	0°56′	0°58′	1°00′	1°02′	1·8
1·9	0°37′	0°39′	0°41′	0°43′	0°45′	0°47′	0°49′	0°51′	0°53′	0°55′	0°57′	0°59′	1·9
2·0	0°35′	0°37′	0°39′	0°41′	0°43′	0°45′	0°46′	0°48′	0°50′	0°52′	0°54′	0°56′	2·0
2·1	0°34′	0°35′	0°37′	0°39′	0°41′	0°42′	0°44′	0°46′	0°48′	0°49′	0°51′	0°53′	2·1
2·2	0°32′	0°34′	0°35′	0°37′	0°39′	0°40′	0°42′	0°44′	0°46′	0°47′	0°49′	0°51′	2·2
2·3	0°31′	0°32′	0°34′	0°35′	0°37′	0°39′	0°40′	0°42′	0°44′	0°45′	0°47′	0°48′	2·3
2·4	0°29′	0°31′	0°32′	0°34′	0°36′	0°37′	0°39′	0°40′	0°42′	0°43′	0°45′	0°46′	2·4
2·5	0°28′	0°30′	0°31′	0°33′	0°34′	0°36′	0°37′	0°39′	0°40′	0°42′	0°43′	0°45′	2·5
2·6	0°27′	0°29′	0°30′	0°31′	0°33′	0°34′	0°36′	0°37′	0°39′	0°40′	0°41′	0°43′	2·6
2·7	0°26′	0°27′	0°29′	0°30′	0°32′	0°33′	0°34′	0°36′	0°37′	0°38′	0°40′	0°41′	2·7
2·8	0°25′	0°27′	0°28′	0°29′	0°30′	0°32′	0°33′	0°34′	0°36′	0°37′	0°38′	0°40′	2·8
2·9	0°24′	0°26′	0°27′	0°28′	0°29′	0°31′	0°32′	0°33′	0°35′	0°36′	0°37′	0°38′	2·9
3·0	0°23′	0°25′	0°26′	0°27′	0°28′	0°30′	0°31′	0°32′	0°33′	0°35′	0°36′	0°37′	3·0
3·2	0°22′	0°23′	0°24′	0°26′	0°27′	0°28′	0°29′	0°30′	0°31′	0°32′	0°34′	0°35′	3·2
3·4	0°21′	0°22′	0°23′	0°24′	0°25′	0°26′	0°27′	0°28′	0°29′	0°31′	0°32′	0°33′	3·4
3·6	0°20′	0°21′	0°22′	0°23′	0°24′	0°25′	0°26′	0°27′	0°28′	0°29′	0°30′	0°31′	3·6
3·8	0°19′	0°20′	0°21′	0°21′	0°22′	0°23′	0°24′	0°25′	0°26′	0°27′	0°28′	0°29′	3·8
4·0	0°18′	0°19′	0°19′	0°20′	0°21′	0°22′	0°23′	0°24′	0°25′	0°26′	0°27′	0°28′	4·0
4·2	0°17′	0°18′	0°19′	0°19′	0°20′	0°21′	0°22′	0°23′	0°24′	0°25′	0°26′	0°27′	4·2
4·4	0°16′	0°17′	0°18′	0°19′	0°19′	0°20′	0°21′	0°22′	0°23′	0°24′	0°24′	0°25′	4·4
4·6	0°15′	0°16′	0°17′	0°18′	0°19′	0°19′	0°20′	0°21′	0°22′	0°23′	0°23′	0°24′	4·6
4·8	0°15′	0°15′	0°16′	0°17′	0°18′	0°19′	0°19′	0°20′	0°21′	0°22′	0°22′	0°23′	4·8
5·0	0°14′	0°15′	0°16′	0°16′	0°17′	0°18′	0°19′	0°19′	0°20′	0°21′	0°22′	0°22′	5·0
5·2	0°14′	0°14′	0°15′	0°16′	0°16′	0°17′	0°18′	0°19′	0°19′	0°20′	0°21′	0°21′	5·2
5·4	0°13′	0°14′	0°14′	0°15′	0°16′	0°16′	0°17′	0°18′	0°19′	0°19′	0°20′	0°21′	5·4
5·6	0°13′	0°13′	0°14′	0°15′	0°15′	0°16′	0°17′	0°17′	0°18′	0°19′	0°19′	0°20′	5·6
5·8	0°12′	0°13′	0°13′	0°14′	0°15′	0°15′	0°16′	0°17′	0°17′	0°18′	0°19′	0°19′	5·8
6·0	0°12′	0°12′	0°13′	0°14′	0°14′	0°15′	0°15′	0°16′	0°17′	0°17′	0°18′	0°19′	6·0
6·2	0°11′	0°12′	0°13′	0°13′	0°14′	0°14′	0°15′	0°15′	0°16′	0°17′	0°17′	0°18′	6·2
6·4	0°11′	0°12′	0°12′	0°13′	0°13′	0°14′	0°14′	0°15′	0°16′	0°16′	0°17′	0°18′	6·4
6·6	0°11′	0°11′	0°12′	0°12′	0°13′	0°13′	0°14′	0°15′	0°15′	0°16′	0°16′	0°17,	6·6
6·8	0°10′	0°11′	0°11′	0°12′	0°13′	0°13′	0°14′	0°14′	0°15′	0°15′	0°16′	0°16′	6·8
7·0	0°10′	0°11′	0°11′	0°12′	0°12′	0°13′	0°13′	0°14′	0°15′	0°15′	0°15′	0°16′	7·0

Distance off Miles	Height of Object in Metres												Distance off Miles
	62	64	66	68	70	72	74	76	78	80	82	84	
0·1	18°30′	19°03′	19°36′	20°09′	20°42′	21°14′	21°46′	22°18′	22°50′	23°21′	23°52′	24°23′	0·1
0·2	9°30′	9°48′	10°06′	10°24′	10°42′	11°00′	11°18′	11°35′	11°53′	12°11′	12°29′	12°46′	0·2
0·3	6°22′	6°34′	6°46′	6°58′	7°11′	7°23′	7°35′	7°47′	7°59′	8°11′	8°23′	8°36′	0·3
0·4	4°47′	4°56′	5°05′	5°15′	5°24′	5°33′	5°42′	5°51′	6°00′	6°10′	6°19′	6°28′	0·4
0·5	3°50′	3°57′	4°04′	4°12′	4°19′	4°27′	4°34′	4°41′	4°49′	4°56′	5°03′	5°11′	0·5
0·6	3°12′	3°18′	3°24′	3°30′	3°36′	3°42′	3°48′	3°55′	4°01′	4°07′	4°13′	4°19′	0·6
0·7	2°44′	2°49′	2°55′	3°00′	3°05′	3°11′	3°16′	3°21′	3°26′	3°32′	3°37′	3°42′	0·7
0·8	2°24′	2°28′	2°33′	2°38′	2°42′	2°47′	2°51′	2°56′	3°01′	3°05′	3°10′	3°15′	0·8
0·9	2°08′	2°12′	2°16′	2°20′	2°24′	2°28′	2°32′	2°37′	2°41′	2°45′	2°49′	2°53′	0·9
1·0	1°55′	1°59′	2°02′	2°06′	2°10′	2°14′	2°17′	2°21′	2°25′	2°28′	2°32′	2°36′	1·0
1·1	1°45′	1°48′	1°51′	1°55′	1°58′	2°01′	2°05′	2°08′	2°11′	2°15′	2°18′	2°22′	1·1
1·2	1°36′	1°39′	1°42′	1°45′	1°48′	1°51′	1°54′	1°57′	2°01′	2°04′	2°07′	2°10′	1·2
1·3	1°28′	1°31′	1°34′	1°37′	1°40′	1°43′	1°46′	1°48′	1°51′	1°54′	1°57′	2°00′	1·3
1·4	1°22′	1°25′	1°27′	1°30′	1°33′	1°35′	1°38′	1°41′	1°43′	1°46′	1°49′	1°51′	1·4
1·5	1°17′	1°19′	1°22′	1°24′	1°27′	1°29′	1°32′	1°34′	1°36′	1°39′	1°41′	1°44′	1·5
1·6	1°12′	1°14′	1°17′	1°19′	1°21′	1°23′	1°26′	1°28′	1°30′	1°33′	1°35′	1°37′	1·6
1·7	1°08′	1°10′	1°12′	1°14′	1°16′	1°19′	1°21′	1°23′	1°25′	1°27′	1°29′	1°32′	1·7
1·8	1°04′	1°06′	1°08′	1°10′	1°12′	1°14′	1°16′	1°18′	1°20′	1°22′	1°24′	1°27′	1·8
1·9	1°01′	1°02′	1°04′	1°06′	1°08′	1°10′	1°12′	1°14′	1°16′	1°18′	1°20′	1°22′	1·9
2·0	0°58′	0°59′	1°01′	1°03′	1°05′	1°07′	1°09′	1°10′	1°12′	1°14′	1°16′	1°18′	2·0
2·1	0°55′	0°57′	0°58′	1°00′	1°02′	1°04′	1°05′	1°07′	1°09′	1°11′	1°12′	1°14′	2·1
2·2	0°52′	0°54′	0°56′	0°57′	0°59′	1°01′	1°02′	1°04′	1°06′	1°07′	1°09′	1°11′	2·2
2·3	0°50′	0°52′	0°53′	0°55′	0°56′	0°58′	1°00′	1°01′	1°03′	1°05′	1°06′	1°08′	2·3
2·4	0°48′	0°49′	0°51′	0°53′	0°54′	0°56′	0°57′	0°59′	1°00′	1°02′	1°03′	1°05′	2·4
2·5	0°46′	0°47′	0°49′	0°50′	0°52′	0°53′	0°55′	0°56′	0°58′	0°59′	1°01′	1°02′	2·5
2·6	0°44′	0°46′	0°47′	0°49′	0°50′	0°51′	0°53′	0°54′	0°56′	0°57′	0°59′	1°00′	2·6
2·7	0°43′	0°44′	0°45′	0°47′	0°48′	0°49′	0°51′	0°52′	0°54′	0°55′	0°56′	0°58′	2·7
2·8	0°41′	0°42′	0°44′	0°45′	0°46′	0°48′	0°49′	0°50′	0°52′	0°53′	0°54′	0°56′	2·8
2·9	0°40′	0°41′	0°42′	0°43′	0°45′	0°46′	0°47′	0°49′	0°50′	0°51′	0°52′	0°54′	2·9
3·0	0°38′	0°40′	0°41′	0°42′	0°43′	0°45′	0°46′	0°47′	0°48′	0°49′	0°51′	0°52′	3·0
3·2	0°36′	0°37′	0°38′	0°39′	0°41′	0°42′	0°43′	0°44′	0°45′	0°46′	0°48′	0°49′	3·2
3·4	0°34′	0°35′	0°36′	0°37′	0°38′	0°39′	0°40′	0°41′	0°43′	0°44′	0°45′	0°46′	3·4
3·6	0°32′	0°33′	0°34′	0°35′	0°36′	0°37′	0°38′	0°39′	0°40′	0°41′	0°42′	0°43′	3·6
3·8	0°30′	0°31′	0°32′	0°33′	0°34′	0°35′	0°36′	0°37′	0°38′	0°39′	0°40′	0°41′	3·8
4·0	0°29′	0°30′	0°31′	0°32′	0°32′	0°33′	0°34′	0°35′	0°36′	0°37′	0°38′	0°39′	4·0
4·2	0°27′	0°28′	0°29′	0°30′	0°31′	0°32′	0°33′	0°34′	0°34′	0°35′	0°36′	0°37′	4·2
4·4	0°26′	0°27′	0°28′	0°29′	0°30′	0°30′	0°31′	0°32′	0°33′	0°34′	0°35′	0°35′	4·4
4·6	0°25′	0°26′	0°27′	0°27′	0°28′	0°29′	0°30′	0°31′	0°31′	0°32′	0°33′	0°34′	4·6
4·8	0°24′	0°25′	0°26′	0°26′	0°27′	0°28′	0°29′	0°29′	0°30′	0°31′	0°32′	0°32′	4·8
5·0	0°23′	0°24′	0°24′	0°25′	0°26′	0°27′	0°27′	0°28′	0°29′	0°30′	0°30′	0°31′	5·0
5·2	0°22′	0°23′	0°24′	0°24′	0°25′	0°26′	0°26′	0°27′	0°28′	0°29′	0°29′	0°30′	5·2
5·4	0°21′	0°22′	0°23′	0°23′	0°24′	0°25′	0°25′	0°26′	0°27′	0°27′	0°28′	0°29′	5·4
5·6	0°21′	0°21′	0°22′	0°23′	0°23′	0°24′	0°25′	0°25′	0°26′	0°27′	0°27′	0°28′	5·6
5·8	0°20′	0°20′	0°21′	0°22′	0°22′	0°23′	0°24′	0°24′	0°25′	0°26′	0°26′	0°27′	5·8
6·0	0°19′	0°20′	0°20′	0°21′	0°22′	0°22′	0°23′	0°23′	0°24′	0°25′	0°25′	0°26′	6·0
6·2	0°19′	0°19′	0°20′	0°20′	0°21′	0°22′	0°22′	0°23′	0°23′	0°24′	0°24′	0°25′	6·2
6·4	0°18′	0°19′	0°19′	0°20′	0°20′	0°21′	0°21′	0°22′	0°23′	0°23′	0°24′	0°24′	6·4
6·6	0°17′	0°18′	0°19′	0°19′	0°20′	0°20′	0°21′	0°21′	0°22′	0°22′	0°23′	0°24′	6·6
6·8	0°17′	0°17′	0°18′	0°19′	0°19′	0°20′	0°20′	0°21′	0°21′	0°22′	0°22′	0°23′	6·8
7·0	0°16′	0°17′	0°17′	0°18′	0°19′	0°19′	0°20′	0°20′	0°21′	0°21′	0°22′	0°22′	7·0

Distance off Miles	86	88	90	92	94	96	98	100	102	104	106	108	Distance off Miles
					Height of Object in Metres								
0·1	24°54′	25°24′	25°54′	26°24′	26°54′	27°23′	27°52′	28°21′	28°50′	29°18′	29°46′	30°14′	0·1
0·2	13°04′	13°21′	13°39′	13°56′	14°14′	14°31′	14°49′	15°06′	15°23′	15°41′	15°58′	16°15′	0·2
0·3	8°48′	9°00′	9°12′	9°24′	9°36′	9°48′	10°00′	10°12′	10°24′	10°36′	10°48′	11°00′	0·3
0·4	6°37′	6°46′	6°55′	7°05′	7°14′	7°23′	7°32′	7°41′	7°50′	7°59′	8°08′	8°17′	0·4
0·5	5°18′	5°26′	5°33′	5°40′	5°48′	5°55′	6°02′	6°10′	6°17′	6°24′	6°32′	6°39′	0·5
0·6	4°25′	4°32′	4°38′	4°44′	4°50′	4°56′	5°02′	5°08′	5°15′	5°21′	5°27′	5°33′	0·6
0·7	3°48′	3°53′	3°58′	4°03′	4°09′	4°14′	4°19′	4°25′	4°30′	4°35′	4°40′	4°46′	0·7
0·8	3°19′	3°24′	3°28′	3°33′	3°38′	3°42′	3°47′	3°52′	3°56′	4°01′	4°05′	4°10′	0·8
0·9	2°57′	3°01′	3°05′	3°09′	3°14′	3°18′	3°22′	3°26′	3°30′	3°34′	3°38′	3°42′	0·9
1·0	2°39′	2°43′	2°47′	2°51′	2°54′	2°58′	3°02′	3°05′	3°09′	3°13′	3°16′	3°20′	1·0
1·1	2°25′	2°28′	2°32′	2°35′	2°38′	2°42′	2°45′	2°49′	2°52′	2°55′	2°59′	3°02′	1·1
1·2	2°13′	2°16′	2°19′	2°22′	2°25′	2°28′	2°31′	2°34′	2°38′	2°41′	2°44′	2°47′	1·2
1·3	2°03′	2°06′	2°08′	2°11′	2°14′	2°17′	2°20′	2°23′	2°25′	2°28′	2°31′	2°34′	1·3
1·4	1°54′	1°57′	1°59′	2°02′	2°05′	2°07′	2°10′	2°12′	2°15′	2°18′	2°20′	2°23′	1·4
1·5	1°46′	1°49′	1°51′	1°54′	1°56′	1°59′	2°01′	2°04′	2°06′	2°09′	2°11′	2°14′	1·5
1·6	1°40′	1°42′	1°44′	1°47′	1°49′	1°51′	1°54′	1°56′	1°58′	2°01′	2°03′	2°05′	1·6
1·7	1°34′	1°36′	1°38′	1°40′	1°43′	1°45′	1°47′	1°49′	1°51′	1°53′	1°56′	1°58′	1·7
1·8	1°29′	1°31′	1°33′	1°35′	1°37′	1°39′	1°41′	1°43′	1°45′	1°47′	1°49′	1°51′	1·8
1·9	1°24′	1°26′	1°28′	1°30′	1°32′	1°34′	1°36′	1°38′	1°40′	1°42′	1°43′	1°45′	1·9
2·0	1°20′	1°22′	1°23′	1°25′	1°27′	1°29′	1°31′	1°33′	1°35′	1°36′	1°38′	1°40′	2·0
2·1	1°16′	1°18′	1°19′	1°21′	1°23′	1°25′	1°27′	1°28′	1°30′	1°32′	1°34′	1°35′	2·1
2·2	1°13′	1°14′	1°16′	1°18′	1°19′	1°21′	1°23′	1°24′	1°26′	1°28′	1°29′	1°31′	2·2
2·3	1°09′	1°11′	1°13′	1°14′	1°16′	1°17′	1°19′	1°21′	1°22′	1°24′	1°25′	1°27′	2·3
2·4	1°06′	1°08′	1°10′	1°11′	1°13′	1°14′	1°16′	1°17′	1°19′	1°20′	1°22′	1°23′	2·4
2·5	1°04′	1°05′	1°07′	1°08′	1°10′	1°11′	1°13′	1°14′	1°16′	1°17′	1°19′	1°20′	2·5
2·6	1°01′	1°03′	1°04′	1°06′	1°07′	1°08′	1°10′	1°11′	1°13′	1°14′	1°16′	1°17′	2·6
2·7	0°59′	1°00′	1°02′	1°03′	1°05′	1°06′	1°07′	1°09′	1°10′	1°11′	1°13′	1°14′	2·7
2·8	0°57′	0°58′	1°00′	1°01′	1°02′	1°04′	1°05′	1°06′	1°08′	1°09′	1°10′	1°12′	2·8
2·9	0°55′	0°56′	0°58′	0°59′	1°00′	1°01′	1°03′	1°04′	1°05′	1°07′	1°08′	1°09′	2·9
3·0	0°53′	0°54′	0°56′	0°57′	0°58′	0°59′	1°01′	1°02′	1°03′	1°04′	1°06′	1°07′	3·0
3·2	0°50′	0°51′	0°52′	0°53′	0°54′	0°56′	0°57′	0°58′	0°59′	1°00′	1°01′	1°03′	3·2
3·4	0°47′	0°48′	0°49′	0°50′	0°51′	0°52′	0°53′	0°55′	0°56′	0°57′	0°58′	0°59′	3·4
3·6	0°44′	0°45′	0°46′	0°47′	0°48′	0°49′	0°50′	0°52′	0°53′	0°54′	0°55′	0°56′	3·6
3·8	0°42′	0°43′	0°44′	0°45′	0°46′	0°47′	0°48′	0°49′	0°50′	0°51′	0°52′	0°53′	3·8
4·0	0°40′	0°41′	0°42′	0°43′	0°44′	0°45′	0°45′	0°46′	0°47′	0°48′	0°49′	0°50′	4·0
4·2	0°38′	0°39′	0°40′	0°41′	0°42′	0°42′	0°43′	0°44′	0°45′	0°46′	0°47′	0°48′	4·2
4·4	0°36′	0°37′	0°38′	0°39′	0°40′	0°40′	0°41′	0°42′	0°43′	0°44′	0°45′	0°46′	4·4
4·6	0°35′	0°35′	0°36′	0°37′	0°38′	0°39′	0°40′	0°40′	0°41′	0°42′	0°43′	0°44′	4·6
4·8	0°33′	0°34′	0°35′	0°36′	0°36′	0°37′	0°38′	0°39′	0°39′	0°40′	0°41′	0°42′	4·8
5·0	0°32′	0°33′	0°33′	0°34′	0°35′	0°36′	0°36′	0°37′	0°38′	0°39′	0°39′	0°40′	5·0
5·2	0°31′	0°31′	0°32′	0°33′	0°34′	0°34′	0°35′	0°36′	0°36′	0°37′	0°38′	0°39′	5·2
5·4	0°30′	0°30′	0°31′	0°32′	0°32′	0°33′	0°34′	0°34′	0°35′	0°36′	0°36′	0°37′	5·4
5·6	0°28′	0°29′	0°30′	0°30′	0°31′	0°32′	0°32′	0°33′	0°34′	0°34′	0°35′	0°36′	5·6
5·8	0°27′	0°28′	0°29′	0°29′	0°30′	0°31′	0°31′	0°32′	0°33′	0°33′	0°34′	0°35′	5·8
6·0	0°27′	0°27′	0°28′	0°28′	0°29′	0°30′	0°30′	0°31′	0°32′	0°32′	0°33′	0°33′	6·0
6·2	0°26′	0°26′	0°27′	0°28′	0°28′	0°29′	0°29′	0°30′	0°31′	0°31′	0°32′	0°32′	6·2
6·4	0°25′	0°25′	0°26′	0°27′	0°27′	0°28′	0°28′	0°29′	0°30′	0°30′	0°31′	0°31′	6·4
6·6	0°24′	0°25′	0°25′	0°26′	0°26′	0°27′	0°28′	0°28′	0°29′	0°29′	0°30′	0°30′	6·6
6·8	0°23′	0°24′	0°25′	0°25′	0°26′	0°26′	0°27′	0°27′	0°28′	0°28′	0°29′	0°29′	6·8
7·0	0°23′	0°23′	0°24′	0°24′	0°25′	0°25′	0°26′	0°27′	0°27′	0°28′	0°28′	0°29′	7·0

Distance off Miles		Height of Object in Metres												Distance off Miles
	110	112	114	116	118	120	122	124	126	128	130	135	
0·1	30°42′	31°09′	31°36′	32°03′	32°29′	32°56′	33°22′	33°47′	34°13′	34°38′	35°03′	36°05′	0·1
0·2	16°32′	16°49′	17°06′	17°23′	17°40′	17°57′	18°13′	18°30′	18°47′	19°03′	19°20′	20°01′	0·2
0·3	11°12′	11°23′	11°35′	11°47′	11°59′	12°11′	12°23′	12°34′	12°46′	12°58′	13°10′	13°39′	0·3
0·4	8°26′	8°36′	8°45′	8°54′	9°03′	9°12′	9°21′	9°30′	9°39′	9°48′	9°57′	10°19′	0·4
0·5	6°46′	6°54′	7°01′	7°08′	7°15′	7°23′	7°30′	7°37′	7°45′	7°52′	7°59′	8°17′	0·5
0·6	5°39′	5°45′	5°51′	5°57′	6°04′	6°10′	6°16′	6°22′	6°28′	6°34′	6°40′	6°55′	0·6
0·7	4°51′	4°56′	5°01′	5°07′	5°12′	5°17′	5°22′	5°28′	5°33′	5°38′	5°43′	5°57′	0·7
0·8	4°15′	4°19′	4°24′	4°28′	4°33′	4°38′	4°42′	4°47′	4°51′	4°56′	5°01′	5°12′	0·8
0·9	3°46′	3°51′	3°55′	3°59′	4°03′	4°07′	4°11′	4°15′	4°19′	4°23′	4°27′	4°38′	0·9
1·0	3°24′	3°28′	3°31′	3°35′	3°39′	3°42′	3°46′	3°50′	3°53′	3°57′	4°01′	4°10′	1·0
1·1	3°05′	3°09′	3°12′	3°15′	3°19′	3°22′	3°26′	3°29′	3°32′	3°36′	3°39′	3°47′	1·1
1·2	2°50′	2°53′	2°56′	2°59′	3°02′	3°05′	3°08′	3°12′	3°15′	3°18′	3°21′	3°28′	1·2
1·3	2°37′	2°40′	2°43′	2°45′	2°48′	2°51′	2°54′	2°57′	3°00′	3°02′	3°05′	3°12′	1·3
1·4	2°26′	2°28′	2°31′	2°34′	2°36′	2°39′	2°42′	2°44′	2°47′	2°49′	2°52′	2°59′	1·4
1·5	2°16′	2°18′	2°21′	2°23′	2°26′	2°28′	2°31′	2°33′	2°36′	2°38′	2°41′	2°47′	1·5
1·6	2°07′	2°10′	2°12′	2°14′	2°17′	2°19′	2°21′	2°24′	2°26′	2°28′	2°31′	2°36′	1·6
1·7	2°00′	2°02′	2°04′	2°07′	2°09′	2°11′	2°13′	2°15′	2°17′	2°20′	2°22′	2°27′	1·7
1·8	1°53′	1°55′	1°57′	2°00′	2°02′	2°04′	2°06′	2°08′	2°10′	2°12′	2°14′	2°19′	1·8
1·9	1°47′	1°49′	1°51′	1°53′	1°55′	1°57′	1°59′	2°01′	2°03′	2°05′	2°07′	2°12′	1·9
2·0	1°42′	1°44′	1°46′	1°48′	1°49′	1°51′	1°53′	1°55′	1°57′	1°59′	2°01′	2°05′	2·0
2·1	1°37′	1°39′	1°41′	1°42′	1°44′	1°46′	1°48′	1°50′	1°51′	1°53′	1°55′	1°59′	2·1
2·2	1°33′	1°34′	1°36′	1°38′	1°39′	1°41′	1°43′	1°45′	1°46′	1°48′	1°50′	1°54′	2·2
2·3	1°29′	1°30′	1°32′	1°34′	1°35′	1°37′	1°38′	1°40′	1°42′	1°43′	1°45′	1°49′	2·3
2·4	1°25′	1°27′	1°28′	1°30′	1°31′	1°33′	1°34′	1°36′	1°37′	1°39′	1°40′	1°44′	2·4
2·5	1°22′	1°23′	1°25′	1°26′	1°28′	1°29′	1°31′	1°32′	1°33′	1°35′	1°36′	1°40′	2·5
2·6	1°18′	1°20′	1°21′	1°23′	1°24′	1°26′	1°27′	1°28′	1°30′	1°31′	1°33′	1°36′	2·6
2·7	1°16′	1°17′	1°18′	1°20′	1°21′	1°22′	1°24′	1°25′	1°27′	1°28′	1°29′	1°33′	2·7
2·8	1°13′	1°14′	1°16′	1°17′	1°18′	1°19′	1°21′	1°22′	1°23′	1°25′	1°26′	1°29′	2·8
2·9	1°10′	1°12′	1°13′	1°14′	1°15′	1°17′	1°18′	1°19′	1°21′	1°22′	1°23′	1°26′	2·9
3·0	1°08′	1°09′	1°10′	1°12′	1°13′	1°14′	1°15′	1°17′	1°18′	1°19′	1°20′	1°23′	3·0
3·2	1°04′	1°05′	1°06′	1°07′	1°08′	1°10′	1°11′	1°12′	1°13′	1°14′	1°15′	1°18′	3·2
3·4	1°00′	1°01′	1°02′	1°03′	1°04′	1°05′	1°07′	1°08′	1°09′	1°10′	1°11′	1°14′	3·4
3·6	0°57′	0°58′	0°59′	1°00′	1°01′	1°02′	1°03′	1°04′	1°05′	1°06′	1°07′	1°10′	3·6
3·8	0°54′	0°55′	0°56′	0°57′	0°58′	0°59′	1°00′	1°01′	1°02′	1°02′	1°03′	1°06′	3·8
4·0	0°51′	0°52′	0°53′	0°54′	0°55′	0°56′	0°57′	0°58′	0°58′	0°59′	1°00′	1°03′	4·0
4·2	0°49′	0°49′	0°50′	0°51′	0°52′	0°53′	0°54′	0°55′	0°56′	0°57′	0°57′	1°00′	4·2
4·4	0°46′	0°47′	0°48′	0°49′	0°50′	0°51′	0°51′	0°52′	0°53′	0°54′	0°55′	0°57′	4·4
4·6	0°43′	0°45′	0°46′	0°47′	0°48′	0°48′	0°49′	0°50′	0°51′	0°52′	0°52′	0°54′	4·6
4·8	0°43′	0°43′	0°44′	0°45′	0°46′	0°46′	0°47′	0°48′	0°49′	0°49′	0°50′	0°52′	4·8
5·0	0°41′	0°42′	0°42′	0°43′	0°44′	0°45′	0°45′	0°46′	0°47′	0°47′	0°48′	0°50′	5·0
5·2	0°39′	0°40′	0°41′	0°41′	0°42′	0°43′	0°44′	0°44′	0°45′	0°46′	0°46′	0°48′	5·2
5·4	0°38′	0°38′	0°39′	0°40′	0°41′	0°41′	0°42′	0°43′	0°43′	0°44′	0°45′	0°46′	5·4
5·6	0°36′	0°37′	0°38′	0°38′	0°39′	0°40′	0°40′	0°41′	0°42′	0°42′	0°43′	0°45′	5·6
5·8	0°35′	0°36′	0°36′	0°37′	0°38′	0°38′	0°39′	0°40′	0°40′	0°41′	0°42′	0°43′	5·8
6·0	0°34′	0°35′	0°35′	0°36′	0°36′	0°37′	0°38′	0°38′	0°39′	0°40′	0°40′	0°42′	6·0
6·2	0°33′	0°33′	0°34′	0°35′	0°35′	0°36′	0°36′	0°37′	0°38′	0°38′	0°39′	0°40′	6·2
6·4	0°32′	0°32′	0°33′	0°34′	0°34′	0°35′	0°35′	0°36′	0°37′	0°37′	0°38′	0°39′	6·4
6·6	0°31′	0°31′	0°32′	0°33′	0°33′	0°34′	0°34′	0°35′	0°35′	0°36′	0°37′	0°38′	6·6
6·8	0°30′	0°31′	0°31′	0°32′	0°32′	0°33′	0°33′	0°34′	0°34′	0°35′	0°35′	0°37′	6·8
7·0	0°29′	0°30′	0°30′	0°31′	0°31′	0°32′	0°32′	0°33′	0°33′	0°34′	0°34′	0°36′	7·0

Distance off Miles	Height of Object in Metres												Distance off Miles
	140	145	150	155	160	165	170	175	180	185	190	195	
0·1	37°04′	38°03′	38°59′	39°55′	40°49′	41°41′	42°32′	43°22′	44°10′	44°57′			0·1
0·2	20°42′	21°22′	22°02′	22°42′	23°21′	24°00′	24°39′	25°17′	25°54′	26°32′	27°09′	27°45′	0·2
0·3	14°08′	14°37′	15°06′	15°35′	16°03′	16°32′	17°00′	17°28′	17°57′	18°24′	18°52′	19°20′	0·3
0·4	10°42′	11°04′	11°26′	11°49′	12°11′	12°33′	12°55′	13°17′	13°39′	14°01′	14°23′	14°44′	0·4
0·5	8°36′	8°54′	9°12′	9°30′	9°48′	10°06′	10°24′	10°42′	11°00′	11°18′	11°35′	11°53′	0·5
0·6	7°11′	7°26′	7°41′	7°56′	8°11′	8°26′	8°42′	8°57′	9°12′	9°27′	9°42′	9°57′	0·6
0·7	6°10′	6°23′	6°36′	6°49′	7°02′	7°15′	7°28′	7°41′	7°54′	8°07′	8°20′	8°33′	0·7
0·8	5°24′	5°35′	5°47′	5°58′	6°10′	6°21′	6°33′	6°44′	6°55′	7°07′	7°18′	7°30′	0·8
0·9	4°48′	4°58′	5°08′	5°19′	5°29′	5°39′	5°49′	5°59′	6°10′	6°20′	6°30′	6°40′	0·9
1·0	4°19′	4°28′	4°38′	4°47′	4°56′	5°05′	5°15′	5°24′	5°33′	5°42′	5°51′	6°00′	1·0
1·1	3°56′	4°04′	4°13′	4°21′	4°29′	4°38′	4°46′	4°54′	5°03′	5°11′	5°20′	5°28′	1·1
1·2	3°36′	3°44′	3°52′	3°59′	4°07′	4°15′	4°22′	4°30′	4°38′	4°45′	4°53′	5°01′	1·2
1·3	3°20′	3°27′	3°34′	3°41′	3°48′	3°55′	4°02′	4°09′	4°16′	4°23′	4°31′	4°38′	1·3
1·4	3°05′	3°12′	3°19′	3°25′	3°32′	3°38′	3°45′	3°52′	3°58′	4°05′	4°11′	4°18′	1·4
1·5	2°53′	2°59′	3°05′	3°12′	3°18′	3°24′	3°30′	3°36′	3°42′	3°48′	3°55′	4°01′	1·5
1·6	2°42′	2°48′	2°54′	3°00′	3°05′	3°11′	3°17′	3°23′	3°28′	3°34′	3°40′	3°46′	1·6
1·7	2°33′	2°38′	2°44′	2°49′	2°54′	3°00′	3°05′	3°11′	3°16′	3°22′	3°27′	3°33′	1·7
1·8	2°24′	2°29′	2°34′	2°40′	2°45′	2°50′	2°55′	3°00′	3°05′	3°10′	3°16′	3°21′	1·8
1·9	2°17′	2°22′	2°26′	2°31′	2°36′	2°41′	2°46′	2°51′	2°56′	3°00′	3°05′	3°10′	1·9
2·0	2°10′	2°14′	2°19′	2°24′	2°28′	2°33′	2°38′	2°42′	2°47′	2°51′	2°56′	3°01′	2·0
2·1	2°04′	2°08′	2°12′	2°17′	2°21′	2°26′	2°30′	2°34′	2°39′	2°43′	2°48′	2°52′	2·1
2·2	1°58′	2°02′	2°06′	2°11′	2°15′	2°19′	2°23′	2°27′	2°32′	2°36′	2°40′	2°44′	2·2
2·3	1°53′	1°57′	2°01′	2°05′	2°09′	2°13′	2°17′	2°21′	2°25′	2°29′	2°33′	2°37′	2·3
2·4	1°48′	1°52′	1°56′	2°00′	2°04′	2°07′	2°11′	2°15′	2°19′	2°23′	2°27′	2°31′	2·4
2·5	1°44′	1°48′	1°51′	1°55′	1°59′	2°02′	2°06′	2°10′	2°14′	2°17′	2°21′	2°25′	2·5
2·6	1°40′	1°43′	1°47′	1°51′	1°54′	1°58′	2°01′	2°05′	2°08′	2°12′	2°16′	2°19′	2·6
2·7	1°36′	1°40′	1°43′	1°46′	1°50′	1°53′	1°57′	2°00′	2°04′	2°07′	2°10′	2°14′	2·7
2·8	1°33′	1°36′	1°39′	1°43′	1°46′	1°49′	1°53′	1°56′	1°59′	2°03′	2°06′	2°09′	2·8
2·9	1°30′	1°33′	1°36′	1°39′	1°42′	1°46′	1°49′	1°52′	1°55′	1°58′	2°01′	2°05′	2·9
3·0	1°27′	1°30′	1°33′	1°36′	1°39′	1°42′	1°45′	1°48′	1°51′	1°54′	1°57′	2°01′	3·0
3·2	1°21′	1°24′	1°27′	1°30′	1°33′	1°36′	1°39′	1°41′	1°44′	1°47′	1°50′	1°53′	3·2
3·4	1°16′	1°19′	1°22′	1°25′	1°27′	1°30′	1°33′	1°35′	1°38′	1°41′	1°44′	1°46′	3·4
3·6	1°12′	1°15′	1°17′	1°20′	1°22′	1°25′	1°28′	1°30′	1°33′	1°35′	1°38′	1°40′	3·6
3·8	1°08′	1°11′	1°13′	1°16′	1°18′	1°21′	1°23′	1°25′	1°28′	1°30′	1°33′	1°35′	3·8
4·0	1°05′	1°07′	1°10′	1°12′	1°14′	1°17′	1°19′	1°21′	1°23′	1°26′	1°28′	1°30′	4·0
4·2	1°02′	1°04′	1°06′	1°08′	1°11′	1°13′	1°15′	1°17′	1°19′	1°22′	1°24′	1°26′	4·2
4·4	0°59′	1°01′	1°03′	1°05′	1°07′	1°10′	1°12′	1°14′	1°16′	1°18′	1°20′	1°22′	4·4
4·6	0°56′	0°58′	1°00′	1°03′	1°05′	1°07′	1°09′	1°11′	1°13′	1°15′	1°17′	1°19′	4·6
4·8	0°54′	0°56′	0°58′	1°00′	1°02′	1°04′	1°06′	1°08′	1°10′	1°11′	1°13′	1°15′	4·8
5·0	0°52′	0°54′	0°56′	0°58′	0°59′	1°01′	1°03′	1°05′	1°07′	1°09′	1°10′	1°12′	5·0
5·2	0°50′	0°52′	0°54′	0°55′	0°57′	0°59′	1°01′	1°02′	1°04′	1°06′	1°08′	1°10′	5·2
5·4	0°48′	0°50′	0°52′	0°53′	0°55′	0°57′	0°58′	1°00′	1°02′	1°04′	1°05′	1°07′	5·4
5·6	0°46′	0°48′	0°50′	0°51′	0°53′	0°55′	0°56′	0°58′	1°00′	1°01′	1°03′	1°05′	5·6
5·8	0°45′	0°46′	0°48′	0°50′	0°51′	0°53′	0°54′	0°56′	0°58′	0°59′	1°01′	1°02′	5·8
6·0	0°43′	0°45′	0°46′	0°48′	0°49′	0°51′	0°53′	0°54′	0°56′	0°57′	0°59′	1°00′	6·0
6·2	0°42′	0°43′	0°45′	0°46′	0°48′	0°49′	0°51′	0°52′	0°54′	0°55′	0°57′	0°58′	6·2
6·4	0°41′	0°42′	0°43′	0°45′	0°46′	0°48′	0°49′	0°51′	0°52′	0°54′	0°55′	0°57′	6·4
6·6	0°39′	0°41′	0°42′	0°44′	0°45′	0°46′	0°48′	0°49′	0°51′	0°52′	0°53′	0°55′	6·6
6·8	0°38′	0°40′	0°41′	0°42′	0°44′	0°45′	0°46′	0°48′	0°49′	0°50′	0°52′	0°53′	6·8
7·0	0°37′	0°38′	0°40′	0°41′	0°42′	0°44′	0°45′	0°46′	0°48′	0°49′	0°50′	0°52′	7·0

Distance off Miles	200	210	220	230	240	250	260	270	280	290	300	310	Distance off Miles
					Height of Object in Metres								
0·1													0·1
0·2	28°21′	29°32′	30°42′	31°49′	32°56′	34°00′	35°03′	36°05′	37°04′	38°03′	38°59′	39°55′	0·2
0·3	19°47′	20°42′	21°35′	22°29′	23°21′	24°13′	25°04′	25°54′	26°44′	27°33′	28°21′	29°09′	0·3
0·4	15°06′	15°49′	16°32′	17°14′	17°57′	18°38′	19°20′	20°01′	20°42′	21°22′	22°02′	22°42′	0·4
0·5	12°11′	12°46′	13°21′	13°56′	14°31′	15°06′	15°41′	16°15′	16°49′	17°23′	17°57′	18°30′	0·5
0·6	10°12′	10°42′	11°12′	11°41′	12°11′	12°40′	13°10′	13°39′	14°08′	14°37′	15°06′	15°35′	0·6
0·7	8°46′	9°12′	9°38′	10°03′	10°29′	10°55′	11°20′	11°46′	12°11′	12°36′	13°01′	13°26′	0·7
0·8	7°41′	8°04′	8°26′	8°49′	9°12′	9°34′	9°57′	10°19′	10°42′	11°04′	11°26′	11°49′	0·8
0·9	6°50′	7°11′	7°31′	7°51′	8°11′	8°32′	8°52′	9°12′	9°32′	9°52′	10°12′	10°32′	0·9
1·0	6°10′	6°28′	6°46′	7°05′	7°23′	7°41′	7°59′	8°17′	8°36′	8°54′	9°12′	9°30′	1·0
1·1	5°36′	5°53′	6°10′	6°26′	6°43′	7°00′	7°16′	7°33′	7°49′	8°06′	8°22′	8°39′	1·1
1·2	5°08′	5°24′	5°39′	5°54′	6°10′	6°25′	6°40′	6°55′	7°11′	7°26′	7°41′	7°56′	1·2
1·3	4°45′	4°59′	5°13′	5°27′	5°41′	5°56′	6°10′	6°24′	6°38′	6°52′	7°06′	7°20′	1·3
1·4	4°25′	4°38′	4°51′	5°04′	5°17′	5°30′	5°43′	5°57′	6°10′	6°23′	6°36′	6°49′	1·4
1·5	4°07′	4°19′	4°32′	4°44′	4°56′	5°08′	5°21′	5°33′	5°45′	5°57′	6°10′	6°22′	1·5
1·6	3°52′	4°03′	4°15′	4°26′	4°38′	4°49′	5°01′	5°12′	5°24′	5°35′	5°47′	5°58′	1·6
1·7	3°38′	3°49′	4°00′	4°11′	4°21′	4°32′	4°43′	4°54′	5°05′	5°16′	5°26′	5°37′	1·7
1·8	3°26′	3°36′	3°46′	3°57′	4°07′	4°17′	4°27′	4°38′	4°48′	4°58′	5°08′	5°19′	1·8
1·9	3°15′	3°25′	3°35′	3°44′	3°54′	4°04′	4°13′	4°23′	4°33′	4°43′	4°52′	5°02′	1·9
2·0	3°05′	3°15′	3°24′	3°33′	3°42′	3°52′	4°01′	4°10′	4°19′	4°28′	4°38′	4°47′	2·0
2·1	2°57′	3°05′	3°14′	3°23′	3°32′	3°41′	3°49′	3°58′	4°07′	4°16′	4°25′	4°33′	2·1
2·2	2°49′	2°57′	3°05′	3°14′	3°22′	3°31′	3°39′	3°47′	3°56′	4°04′	4°13′	4°21′	2·2
2·3	2°41′	2°49′	2°57′	3°05′	3°13′	3°21′	3°29′	3°37′	3°46′	3°54′	4°02′	4°10′	2·3
2·4	2°34′	2°42′	2°50′	2°58′	3°05′	3°13′	3°21′	3°28′	3°36′	3°44′	3°52′	3°59′	2·4
2·5	2°28′	2°36′	2°43′	2°51′	2°58′	3°05′	3°13′	3°20′	3°28′	3°35′	3°42′	3°50′	2·5
2·6	2°23′	2°30′	2°37′	2°44′	2°51′	2°58′	3°05′	3°12′	3°20′	3°27′	3°34′	3°41′	2·6
2·7	2°17′	2°24′	2°31′	2°38′	2°45′	2°52′	2°58′	3°05′	3°12′	3°19′	3°26′	3°33′	2·7
2·8	2°12′	2°19′	2°26′	2°32′	2°39′	2°46′	2°52′	2°59′	3°05′	3°12′	3°19′	3°25′	2·8
2·9	2°08′	2°14′	2°21′	2°27′	2°33′	2°40′	2°46′	2°53′	2°59′	3°05′	3°12′	3°18′	2·9
3·0	2°04′	2°10′	2°16′	2°22′	2°28′	2°34′	2°41′	2°47′	2°53′	2°59′	3°05′	3°12′	3·0
3·2	1°56′	2°02′	2°07′	2°13′	2°19′	2°25′	2°31′	2°36′	2°42′	2°48′	2°54′	3°00′	3·2
3·4	1°49′	1°55′	2°00′	2°05′	2°11′	2°16′	2°22′	2°27′	2°33′	2°38′	2°44′	2°49′	3·4
3·6	1°43′	1°48′	1°53′	1°58′	2°04′	2°09′	2°14′	2°19′	2°24′	2°29′	2°34′	2°40′	3·6
3·8	1°38′	1°42′	1°47′	1°52′	1°57′	2°02′	2°07′	2°12′	2°17′	2°22′	2°26′	2°31′	3·8
4·0	1°33′	1°37′	1°42′	1°47′	1°51′	1°56′	2°01′	2°05′	2°10′	2°14′	2°19′	2°24′	4·0
4·2	1°28′	1°33′	1°37′	1°42′	1°46′	1°50′	1°55′	1°59′	2°04′	2°08′	2°12′	2°17′	4·2
4·4	1°24′	1°29′	1°33′	1°37′	1°41′	1°45′	1°50′	1°54′	1°58′	2°02′	2°06′	2°11′	4·4
4·6	1°21′	1°25′	1°29′	1°33′	1°37′	1°41′	1°45′	1°49′	1°53′	1°57′	2°01′	2°05′	4·6
4·8	1°17′	1°21′	1°25′	1°29′	1°33′	1°37′	1°40′	1°44′	1°48′	1°52′	1°56′	2°00′	4·8
5·0	1°14′	1°18′	1°22′	1°25′	1°29′	1°33′	1°36′	1°40′	1°44′	1°48′	1°51′	1°55′	5·0
5·2	1°11′	1°15′	1°18′	1°22′	1°26′	1°29′	1°33′	1°36′	1°40′	1°43′	1°47′	1°51′	5·2
5·4	1°09′	1°12′	1°16′	1°19′	1°22′	1°26′	1°29′	1°33′	1°36′	1°40′	1°43′	1°46′	5·4
5·6	1°06′	1°10′	1°13′	1°16′	1°19′	1°23′	1°26′	1°29′	1°33′	1°36′	1°39′	1°43′	5·6
5·8	1°04′	1°07′	1°10′	1°14′	1°17′	1°20′	1°23′	1°26′	1°30′	1°33′	1°36′	1°39′	5·8
6·0	1°02′	1°05′	1°08′	1°11′	1°14′	1°17′	1°20′	1°23′	1°27′	1°30′	1°33′	1°36′	6·0
6·2	1°00′	1°03′	1°06′	1°09′	1°12′	1°15′	1°18′	1°21′	1°24′	1°27′	1°30′	1°33′	6·2
6·4	0°58′	1°01′	1°04′	1°07′	1°10′	1°12′	1°15′	1°18′	1°21′	1°24′	1°27′	1°30′	6·4
6·6	0°56′	0°59′	1°02′	1°05′	1°07′	1°10′	1°13′	1°16′	1°19′	1°21′	1°24′	1°27′	6·6
6·8	0°55′	0°57′	1°00′	1°03′	1°05′	1°08′	1°11′	1°14′	1°16′	1°19′	1°22′	1°25′	6·8
7·0	0°53′	0°56′	0°58′	1°01′	1°04′	1°06′	1°09′	1°12′	1°14′	1°17′	1°19′	1°22′	7·0

Distance off Miles	Height of Object in Metres												Distance off Miles
	320	330	340	350	360	370	380	390	400	410	420	430	
0·1													0·1
0·2	40°49′	41°41′	42°32′	43°22′	44°10′								0·2
0·3	29°56′	30°42′	31°27′	32°12′	32°56′	33°39′	34°21′	35°03′	35°44′	36°25′	37°04′	37°43′	0·3
0·4	23°21′	24°00′	24°39′	25°17′	25°54′	26°32′	27°09′	27°45′	28°21′	28°57′	29°32′	30°07′	0·4
0·5	19°03′	19°36′	20°09′	20°42′	21°14′	21°46′	22°18′	22°50′	23°21′	23°52′	24°23′	24°54′	0·5
0·6	16°03′	16°32′	17°00′	17°28′	17°57′	18°24′	18°52′	19°20′	19°47′	20°15′	20°42′	21°09′	0·6
0·7	13°52′	14°16′	14°41′	15°06′	15°31′	15°55′	16°20′	16°44′	17°08′	17°32′	17°57′	18°20′	0·7
0·8	12°11′	12°33′	12°55′	13°17′	13°39′	14°01′	14°23′	14°44′	15°06′	15°28′	15°49′	16°11′	0·8
0·9	10°52′	11°12′	11°31′	11°51′	12°11′	12°31′	12°50′	13°10′	13°29′	13°49′	14°08′	14°27′	0·9
1·0	9°48′	10°06′	10°24′	10°42′	11°00′	11°18′	11°35′	11°53′	12°11′	12°29′	12°46′	13°04′	1·0
1·1	8°56′	9°12′	9°28′	9°45′	10°01′	10°17′	10°34′	10°50′	11°06′	11°22′	11°39′	11°55′	1·1
1·2	8°11′	8°26′	8°42′	8°57′	9°12′	9°27′	9°42′	9°57′	10°12′	10°27′	10°42′	10°57′	1·2
1·3	7°34′	7°48′	8°02′	8°16′	8°30′	8°44′	8°58′	9°12′	9°26′	9°40′	9°53′	10°07′	1·3
1·4	7°02′	7°15′	7°28′	7°41′	7°54′	8°07′	8°20′	8°33′	8°46′	8°59′	9°12′	9°25′	1·4
1·5	6°34′	6°46′	6°58′	7°11′	7°23′	7°35′	7°47′	7°59′	8°11′	8°23′	8°36′	8°48′	1·5
1·6	6°10′	6°21′	6°33′	6°44′	6°55′	7°07′	7°18′	7°30′	7°41′	7°52′	8°04′	8°15′	1·6
1·7	5°48′	5°59′	6°10′	6°20′	6°31′	6°42′	6°53′	7°03′	7°14′	7°25′	7°36′	7°46′	1·7
1·8	5°29′	5°39′	5°49′	5°59′	6°10′	6°20′	6°30′	6°40′	6°50′	7°00′	7°11′	7°21′	1·8
1·9	5°12′	5°21′	5°31′	5°41′	5°50′	6°00′	6°10′	6°19′	6°29′	6°39′	6°48′	6°58′	1·9
2·0	4°56′	5°05′	5°15′	5°24′	5°33′	5°42′	5°51′	6°00′	6°10′	6°19′	6°28′	6°37′	2·0
2·1	4°42′	4°51′	5°00′	5°08′	5°17′	5°26′	5°35′	5°43′	5°52′	6°01′	6°10′	6°18′	2·1
2·2	4°29′	4°38′	4°46′	4°54′	5°03′	5°11′	5°20′	5°28′	5°36′	5°45′	5°53′	6°01′	2·2
2·3	4°18′	4°26′	4°34′	4°42′	4°50′	4°58′	5°06′	5°14′	5°22′	5°30′	5°38′	5°46′	2·3
2·4	4°07′	4°15′	4°22′	4°30′	4°38′	4°45′	4°53′	5°01′	5°08′	5°16′	5°24′	5°31′	2·4
2·5	3°57′	4°04′	4°12′	4°19′	4°27′	4°34′	4°41′	4°49′	4°56′	5°03′	5°11′	5°18′	2·5
2·6	3°48′	3°55′	4°02′	4°09′	4°16′	4°23′	4°31′	4°38′	4°45′	4°52′	4°59′	5°06′	2·6
2·7	3°40′	3°46′	3°53′	4°00′	4°07′	4°14′	4°21′	4°27′	4°34′	4°41′	4°48′	4°55′	2·7
2·8	3°32′	3°38′	3°45′	3°52′	3°58′	4°05′	4°11′	4°18′	4°25′	4°31′	4°38′	4°44′	2·8
2·9	3°25′	3°31′	3°37′	3°44′	3°50′	3°56′	4°03′	4°09′	4°15′	4°22′	4°28′	4°35′	2·9
3·0	3°18′	3°24′	3°30′	3°36′	3°42′	3°48′	3°55′	4°01′	4°07′	4°13′	4°19′	4°25′	3·0
3·2	3°06′	3°11′	3°17′	3°23′	3°28′	3°34′	3°40′	3°46′	3°52′	3°57′	4°03′	4°09′	3·2
3·4	2°55′	3°00′	3°05′	3°11′	3°16′	3°22′	3°27′	3°33′	3°38′	3°43′	3°49′	3°54′	3·4
3·6	2°45′	2°50′	2°55′	3°00′	3°05′	3°10′	3°16′	3°21′	3°26′	3°31′	3°36′	3°41′	3·6
3·8	2°37′	2°41′	2°46′	2°51′	2°56′	3°00′	3°05′	3°10′	3°15′	3°20′	3°25′	3°30′	3·8
4·0	2°29′	2°33′	2°38′	2°42′	2°47′	2°51′	2°56′	3°01′	3°05′	3°10′	3°15′	3°19′	4·0
4·2	2°21′	2°26′	2°30′	2°34′	2°39′	2°43′	2°48′	2°52′	2°57′	3°01′	3°05′	3°10′	4·2
4·4	2°15′	2°19′	2°23′	2°27′	2°32′	2°36′	2°40′	2°44′	2°49′	2°53′	2°57′	3°01′	4·4
4·6	2°09′	2°13′	2°17′	2°21′	2°25′	2°29′	2°33′	2°37′	2°41′	2°45′	2°49′	2°53′	4·6
4·8	2°04′	2°07′	2°11′	2°15′	2°19′	2°23′	2°27′	2°31′	2°34′	2°38′	2°42′	2°46′	4·8
5·0	1°59′	2°03′	2°06′	2°10′	2°14′	2°17′	2°21′	2°25′	2°28′	2°32′	2°36′	2°39′	5·0
5·2	1°54′	1°58′	2°01′	2°05′	2°08′	2°12′	2°16′	2°19′	2°23′	2°26′	2°30′	2°33′	5·2
5·4	1°50′	1°53′	1°57′	2°00′	2°04′	2°07′	2°10′	2°14′	2°17′	2°21′	2°24′	2°28′	5·4
5·6	1°46′	1°49′	1°53′	1°56′	1°59′	2°03′	2°06′	2°09′	2°12′	2°16′	2°19′	2°22′	5·6
5·8	1°42′	1°46′	1°49′	1°52′	1°55′	1°58′	2°01′	2°05′	2°08′	2°11′	2°14′	2°17′	5·8
6·0	1°39′	1°42′	1°45′	1°48′	1°51′	1°54′	1°57′	2°01′	2°04′	2°07′	2°10′	2°13′	6·0
6·2	1°36′	1°39′	1°42′	1°45′	1°48′	1°51′	1°54′	1°57′	2°00′	2°03′	2°06′	2°09′	6·2
6·4	1°33′	1°36′	1°39′	1°41′	1°44′	1°47′	1°50′	1°53′	1°56′	1°59′	2°02′	2°05′	6·4
6·6	1°30′	1°33′	1°36′	1°38′	1°41′	1°44′	1°47′	1°50′	1°52′	1°55′	1°58′	2°01′	6·6
6·8	1°27′	1°30′	1°33′	1°35′	1°38′	1°41′	1°44′	1°46′	1°49′	1°52′	1°55′	1°57′	6·8
7·0	1°25′	1°27′	1°30′	1°33′	1°35′	1°38′	1°41′	1°43′	1°46′	1°49′	1°51′	1°54′	7·0

DISTANCE OFF BY VERTICAL SEXTANT ANGLE

Distance Miles	HEIGHT OF OBJECT IN FEET																Distance Miles
	40	50	60	70	80	90	100	110	120	130	140	150	160	170	180	190	
	° ′	° ′	° ′	° ′	° ′	° ′	° ′	° ′	° ′	° ′	° ′	° ′	° ′	° ′	° ′	° ′	
0·1	3 46	4 42	5 38	6 34	7 30	8 25	9 20	10 15	11 10	12 04	12 58	13 52	14 45	15 37	16 29	17 21	0·1
0·2	1 53	2 21	2 49	3 18	3 46	4 14	4 42	5 10	5 38	6 06	6 34	7 02	7 30	7 58	8 25	8 53	0·2
0·3	1 15	1 34	1 53	2 12	2 31	2 49	3 08	3 27	3 46	4 05	4 23	4 42	5 01	5 19	5 38	5 57	0·3
0·4	0 57	1 11	1 25	1 39	1 53	2 07	2 21	2 35	2 49	3 04	3 18	3 32	3 46	4 00	4 14	4 28	0·4
0·5	0 45	0 57	1 08	1 19	1 30	1 42	1 53	2 04	2 16	2 27	2 38	2 49	3 01	3 12	3 23	3 35	0·5
0·6	0 38	0 47	0 57	1 06	1 15	1 25	1 34	1 44	1 53	2 02	2 12	2 21	2 31	2 40	2 49	2 59	0·6
0·7	0 32	0 40	0 48	0 57	1 05	1 13	1 21	1 29	1 37	1 45	1 53	2 01	2 09	2 17	2 25	2 33	0·7
0·8	0 28	0 35	0 42	0 49	0 57	1 04	1 11	1 18	1 25	1 32	1 39	1 46	1 53	2 00	2 07	2 14	0·8
0·9	0 25	0 31	0 38	0 44	0 50	0 57	1 03	1 09	1 15	1 22	1 28	1 34	1 40	1 47	1 53	1 59	0·9
1·0	0 23	0 28	0 34	0 40	0 45	0 51	0 57	1 02	1 08	1 14	1 19	1 25	1 30	1 36	1 42	1 47	1·0
1·1	0 21	0 26	0 31	0 36	0 41	0 46	0 51	0 57	1 02	1 07	1 12	1 17	1 22	1 27	1 33	1 38	1·1
1·2	0 19	0 24	0 28	0 33	0 38	0 42	0 47	0 52	0 57	1 01	1 06	1 11	1 15	1 20	1 25	1 30	1·2
1·3	0 17	0 22	0 26	0 30	0 35	0 39	0 44	0 48	0 52	0 57	1 01	1 05	1 10	1 14	1 18	1 23	1·3
1·4	0 16	0 20	0 24	0 28	0 32	0 36	0 40	0 44	0 48	0 53	0 57	1 01	1 05	1 09	1 13	1 17	1·4
1·5	0 15	0 19	0 23	0 26	0 30	0 34	0 38	0 41	0 45	0 49	0 53	0 57	1 00	1 04	1 08	1 12	1·5
1·6	0 14	0 18	0 21	0 25	0 28	0 32	0 35	0 39	0 42	0 46	0 49	0 53	0 57	1 00	1 04	1 07	1·6
1·7	0 13	0 17	0 20	0 23	0 27	0 30	0 33	0 37	0 40	0 43	0 47	0 50	0 53	0 57	1 00	1 03	1·7
1·8	0 13	0 16	0 19	0 22	0 25	0 28	0 31	0 35	0 38	0 41	0 44	0 47	0 50	0 53	0 57	1 00	1·8
1·9	0 12	0 15	0 18	0 21	0 24	0 27	0 30	0 33	0 36	0 39	0 42	0 45	0 48	0 51	0 54	0 57	1·9
2·0	0 11	0 14	0 17	0 20	0 23	0 25	0 28	0 31	0 34	0 37	0 40	0 42	0 45	0 48	0 51	0 54	2·0
2·1	0 10	0 14	0 16	0 19	0 22	0 24	0 27	0 30	0 32	0 35	0 38	0 40	0 43	0 46	0 48	0 51	2·1
2·2	0 10	0 13	0 15	0 18	0 21	0 23	0 26	0 28	0 31	0 33	0 36	0 39	0 41	0 44	0 46	0 49	2·2
2·3	0 10	0 12	0 14	0 17	0 20	0 22	0 25	0 27	0 30	0 32	0 34	0 37	0 39	0 42	0 44	0 47	2·3
2·4	0 10	0 12	0 14	0 17	0 19	0 21	0 24	0 26	0 28	0 31	0 33	0 35	0 38	0 40	0 42	0 45	2·4
2·5	0 9	0 11	0 13	0 16	0 18	0 20	0 23	0 25	0 27	0 29	0 32	0 34	0 36	0 38	0 41	0 43	2·5
2·6	0 9	0 11	0 13	0 15	0 17	0 20	0 22	0 24	0 26	0 28	0 30	0 33	0 35	0 37	0 39	0 41	2·6
2·7	0 9	0 10	0 12	0 15	0 17	0 19	0 21	0 23	0 25	0 27	0 29	0 31	0 34	0 36	0 38	0 40	2·7
2·8	0 8	0 10	0 12	0 14	0 16	0 18	0 20	0 22	0 24	0 26	0 28	0 30	0 32	0 34	0 36	0 38	2·8
2·9	0 8	0 10	0 11	0 14	0 16	0 18	0 20	0 21	0 23	0 25	0 27	0 29	0 31	0 33	0 35	0 37	2·9
3·0	0 8	0 9	0 10	0 13	0 15	0 17	0 19	0 21	0 23	0 24	0 26	0 28	0 30	0 32	0 34	0 36	3·0
3·2				0 12	0 14	0 16	0 18	0 19	0 21	0 23	0 25	0 27	0 28	0 30	0 32	0 34	3·2
3·4				0 12	0 13	0 15	0 17	0 18	0 20	0 22	0 23	0 25	0 27	0 28	0 30	0 32	3·4
3·6				0 11	0 13	0 14	0 16	0 17	0 19	0 20	0 22	0 24	0 25	0 27	0 28	0 30	3·6
3·8				0 10	0 12	0 13	0 15	0 16	0 18	0 19	0 21	0 22	0 24	0 25	0 27	0 28	3·8
4·0				0 10	0 11	0 13	0 14	0 16	0 17	0 18	0 20	0 21	0 23	0 24	0 25	0 27	4·0
4·2						0 12	0 14	0 15	0 16	0 17	0 19	0 20	0 22	0 23	0 24	0 26	4·2
4·4						0 12	0 13	0 14	0 15	0 17	0 18	0 19	0 21	0 22	0 23	0 24	4·4
4·6						0 11	0 13	0 14	0 15	0 16	0 17	0 18	0 20	0 21	0 22	0 23	4·6
4·8						0 11	0 12	0 13	0 14	0 15	0 16	0 18	0 19	0 20	0 21	0 22	4·8
5·0						0 10	0 11	0 12	0 14	0 15	0 16	0 17	0 18	0 19	0 20	0 21	5·0
5·2								0 12	0 13	0 14	0 15	0 16	0 17	0 18	0 20	0 21	5·2
5·4								0 12	0 13	0 14	0 15	0 16	0 17	0 18	0 19	0 20	5·4
5·6								0 11	0 12	0 13	0 14	0 15	0 16	0 17	0 18	0 19	5·6
5·8								0 11	0 12	0 13	0 14	0 15	0 16	0 17	0 18	0 19	5·8
6·0								0 10	0 11	0 12	0 13	0 14	0 15	0 16	0 17	0 18	6·0
6·2								0 10	0 11	0 12	0 13	0 14	0 15	0 16	0 16	0 17	6·2
6·4									0 11	0 11	0 12	0 13	0 14	0 15	0 16	0 17	6·4
6·6									0 10	0 11	0 12	0 13	0 14	0 15	0 15	0 16	6·6
6·8									0 10	0 11	0 12	0 12	0 13	0 14	0 15	0 16	6·8
7·0										0 10	0 11	0 12	0 13	0 14	0 15	0 16	7·0
Distance	40	50	60	70	80	90	100	110	120	130	140	150	160	170	180	190	Distance

DISTANCE OFF BY VERTICAL SEXTANT ANGLE

Distance Miles	HEIGHT OF OBJECT IN FEET																Distance Miles
	200	210	220	230	240	250	260	270	280	290	300	310	320	330	340	350	
	° ′	° ′	° ′	° ′	° ′	° ′	° ′	° ′	° ′	° ′	° ′	° ′	° ′	° ′	° ′	° ′	
0·1	18 13	19 03	19 54	20 43	21 32	22 21	23 09	23 57	24 44	25 30	26 16	26 01	27 46	28 29	29 13	29 56	0·1
0·2	9 20	9 48	10 15	10 43	11 10	11 37	12 04	12 31	12 58	13 25	13 52	14 08	14 45	15 11	15 37	16 03	0·2
0·3	6 15	6 34	6 53	7 11	7 30	7 48	8 07	8 25	8 44	9 02	9 20	9 39	9 57	10 15	10 34	10 52	0·3
0·4	4 42	4 56	5 10	5 24	5 38	5 52	6 06	6 20	6 34	6 48	7 02	7 16	7 30	7 44	7 58	8 11	0·4
0·5	3 46	3 57	4 08	4 20	4 31	4 42	4 53	5 05	5 16	5 27	5 38	5·49	6 01	6 12	6 23	6 34	0·5
0·6	3 08	3 18	3 27	3 36	3 46	3 55	4 05	4 14	4 23	4 33	4 42	4 51	5 01	5 10	5 19	5 29	0·6
0·7	2 41	2 49	2 58	3 06	3 14	3 22	3 30	3 38	3 46	3 54	4 02	5 10	4 18	4 26	4 43	4 42	0·7
0·8	2 21	2 28	2 35	2 42	2 49	2 57	3 04	3 11	3 18	3 25	3 32	3 39	3 46	3 53	4 00	4 07	0·8
0·9	2 06	2 12	2 18	2 24	2 31	2 37	2 43	2 49	2 56	3 02	3 08	3 15	3 21	3 27	3 33	3 40	0·9
1·0	1 53	1 59	2 04	2 10	2 16	2 21	2 27	2 33	2 38	2 44	2 49	2 55	3 01	3 06	3 12	3 18	1·0
1·1	1 43	1 48	1 53	1 58	2 03	2 08	2 14	2 19	2 24	2 29	2 34	2 39	2 44	2 49	2 55	3 00	1·1
1·2	1 34	1 39	1 44	1 48	1 53	1 58	2 02	2 07	2 12	2 17	2 21	2 26	2 31	2 35	2 40	2 45	1·2
1·3	1 27	1 31	1 36	1 40	1 44	1 49	1 53	1 57	2 02	2 06	2 10	2 15	2 19	2 23	2 28	2 32	1·3
1·4	1 21	1 25	1 29	1 33	1 37	1 41	1 45	1 49	1 53	1 57	2 01	2 05	2 09	2 13	2 17	2 21	1·4
1·5	1 15	1 19	1 23	1 27	1 30	1 34	1 38	1 42	1 46	1 49	1 53	1 57	2 01	2 04	2 08	2 12	1·5
1·6	1 11	1 14	1 18	1 21	1 25	1 28	1 32	1 35	1 39	1 42	1 46	1 50	1 53	1 57	2 00	2 04	1·6
1·7	1 07	1 10	1 13	1 16	1 20	1 23	1 26	1 30	1 33	1 36	1 40	1 43	1 46	1 50	1 53	1 56	1·7
1·8	1 03	1 06	1 09	1 12	1 15	1 19	1 22	1 25	1 28	1 31	1 34	1 37	1 40	1 44	1 47	1 50	1·8
1·9	1 00	1 02	1 05	1 08	1 11	1 14	1 17	1 20	1 23	1 26	1 29	1 32	1 35	1 38	1 41	1 44	1·9
2·0	0 57	0 59	1 02	1 05	1 08	1 11	1 14	1 16	1 19	1 22	1 25	1 28	1 30	1 33	1 36	1 39	2·0
2·1	0 54	0 57	0 59	1 02	1 05	1 07	1 10	1 13	1 15	1 18	1 21	1 23	1 26	1 29	1 32	1 34	2·1
2·2	0 51	0 54	0 57	0 59	1 02	1 04	1 07	1 09	1 12	1 15	1 17	1 20	1 22	1 25	1 27	1 30	2·2
2·3	0 49	0 52	0 54	0 57	0 59	1 01	1 04	1 06	1 09	1 11	1 14	1 16	1 19	1 21	1 24	1 26	2·3
2·4	0 47	0 49	0 52	0 54	0 57	0 59	1 01	1 04	1 06	1 08	1 11	1 13	1 15	1 18	1 20	1 22	2·4
2·5	0 45	0 48	0 50	0 52	0 54	0 57	0 59	1 01	1 03	1 06	1 08	1 10	1 12	1 15	1 17	1 19	2·5
2·6	0 44	0 46	0 48	0 50	0 52	0 54	0 57	0 59	1 01	1 03	1 05	1 07	1 10	1 12	1 14	1 16	2·6
2·7	0 42	0 44	0 46	0 48	0 50	0 52	0 54	0 57	0 59	1 01	1 03	1 05	1 07	1 09	1 11	1 13	2·7
2·8	0 40	0 42	0 44	0 46	0 48	0 50	0 53	0 55	0 57	0 59	1 01	1 03	1 05	1 07	1 09	1 11	2·8
2·9	0 39	0 41	0 43	0 45	0 47	0 49	0 51	0 53	0 55	0 57	0 58	1 00	1 02	1 04	1 06	1 08	2·9
3·0	0 38	0 40	0 41	0 43	0 45	0 47	0 49	0 51	0 53	0 55	0 57	0 58	1 00	1 02	1 04	1 06	3·0
3·2	0 35	0 37	0 39	0 41	0 42	0 44	0 46	0 48	0 49	0 51	0 53	0 55	0 57	0 58	1 00	1 02	3·2
3·4	0 33	0 35	0 37	0 38	0 40	0 42	0 43	0 45	0 47	0 48	0 50	0 52	0 53	0 55	0 57	0 58	3·4
3·6	0 31	0 33	0 35	0 36	0 38	0 39	0 41	0 42	0 44	0 46	0 47	0 49	0 50	0 52	0 53	0 55	3·6
3·8	0 30	0 31	0 33	0 34	0 36	0 37	0 39	0 40	0 42	0 43	0 45	0 46	0 48	0 49	0 51	0 52	3·8
4·0	0 28	0 30	0 31	0 33	0 34	0 35	0 37	0 38	0 40	0 41	0 42	0 44	0 45	0 47	0 48	0 49	4·0
4·2	0 27	0 28	0 30	0 31	0 32	0 34	0 35	0 36	0 38	0 39	0 40	0 42	0 43	0 44	0 46	0 47	4·2
4·4	0 26	0 27	0 28	0 30	0 31	0 32	0 33	0 35	0 36	0 37	0 39	0 40	0 41	0 42	0 44	0 45	4·4
4·6	0 25	0 26	0 27	0 28	0 30	0 31	0 32	0 33	0 34	0 36	0 37	0 38	0 39	0 41	0 42	0 43	4·6
4·8	0 24	0 25	0 26	0 27	0 28	0 30	0 31	0 32	0 33	0 34	0 35	0 37	0 38	0 39	0 40	0 41	4·8
5·0	0 23	0 24	0 25	0 26	0 27	0 28	0 29	0 31	0 32	0 33	0 34	0 35	0 36	0 37	0 38	0 40	5·0
5·2	0 22	0 23	0 24	0 25	0 26	0 27	0 28	0 29	0 30	0 32	0 33	0 34	0 35	0 36	0 37	0 38	5·2
5·4	0 21	0 22	0 23	0 24	0 25	0 26	0 27	0 28	0 29	0 30	0 31	0 32	0 34	0 34	0 36	0 37	5·4
5·6	0 20	0 21	0 22	0 23	0 24	0 25	0 26	0 27	0 28	0 29	0 30	0 31	0 32	0 33	0 34	0 35	5·6
5·8	0 19	0 20	0 21	0 22	0 23	0 24	0 25	0 26	0 27	0 28	0 29	0 30	0 31	0 32	0 33	0 34	5·8
6·0	0 19	0 20	0 21	0 22	0 23	0 24	0 25	0 25	0 26	0 27	0 28	0 29	0 30	0 31	0 32	0 33	6·0
6·2	0 18	0 19	0 20	0 21	0 22	0 23	0 24	0 25	0 26	0 26	0 27	0 28	0 29	0 30	0 31	0 32	6·2
6·4	0 18	0 19	0 20	0 21	0 21	0 22	0 23	0 24	0 25	0 26	0 27	0 27	0 28	0 29	0 30	0 31	6·4
6·6	0 17	0 18	0 19	0 20	0 21	0 21	0 22	0 23	0 24	0 25	0 26	0 27	0 27	0 28	0 29	0 30	6·6
6·8	0 17	0 18	0 18	0 19	0 20	0 21	0 22	0 22	0 23	0 24	0 25	0 26	0 27	0 27	0 28	0 29	6·8
7·0	0 16	0 17	0 18	0 19	0 19	0 20	0 21	0 22	0 23	0 23	0 24	0 25	0 26	0 27	0 27	0 28	7·0
Distance	200	210	220	230	240	250	260	270	280	290	300	310	320	330	340	350	Distance

DISTANCE OFF BY VERTICAL SEXTANT ANGLE

Distance Miles	360	370	380	390	400	450	500	550	600	650	700	800	900	1000	1500	2000	Distance Miles
	° ′	° ′	° ′	° ′	° ′	° ′	° ′	° ′	° ′	° ′	° ′	° ′	° ′	° ′	° ′	° ′	
0·1	30 38	31 19	32 00	32 41	33 20	36 30	39 26	42 08	44 37								0·1
0·2	16 29	16 55	17 21	17 47	18 13	20 18	22 21	24 20	26 16	28 08	29 56	33 20	36 30	39 26			0·2
0·3	11 10	11 28	11 46	12 04	12 22	13 52	15 20	16 47	18 13	19 37	21 00	23 41	26 16	28 44			0·3
0·4	8 25	8 39	8 53	9 07	9 20	10 29	11 37	12 45	13 52	14 58	16 03	18 13	20 18	22 21			0·4
0·5	6 45	6 56	7 08	7 19	7 30	8 25	9 20	10 15	11 10	12 04	12 58	14 45	16 30	18 13	26 15		0·5
0·6	5 38	5 47	5 47	6 06	6 15	7 02	7 48	8 34	9 20	10 06	10 52	12 22	13 52	15 20	22 20	28 44	0·6
0·7	4 50	4 58	5 06	5 14	5 22	6 02	6 42	7 22	8 01	8 41	9 20	10 39	11 56	13 13	19 25	25 10	0·7
0·8	4 14	4 21	4 28	4 35	4 42	5 17	5 52	6 27	7 02	7 37	8 11	9 20	10 29	11 37	17 08	22 21	0·8
0·9	3 46	3 52	3 58	4 05	4 11	4 42	5 13	5 44	6 15	6 46	7 17	8 19	9 20	10 21	15 19	20 05	0·9
1·0	3 23	3 29	3 35	3 40	3 46	4 14	4 42	5 10	5 38	6 06	6 34	7 30	8 25	9 20	13 51	18 13	1·0
1·1	3 05	3 10	3 15	3 20	3 25	3 51	4 17	4 42	5 08	5 33	5 59	6 49	7 40	8 30	12 38	16 39	1·1
1·2	2 49	2 54	2 59	3 04	3 08	3 32	3 55	4 19	4 42	5 05	5 29	6 15	7 02	7 48	11 37	15 20	1·2
1·3	2 36	2 41	2 45	2 49	2 54	3 16	3 37	3 59	4 20	4 42	5 04	5 47	6 30	7 13	10 45	14 12	1·3
1·4	2 25	2 29	2 37	2 37	2 41	3 02	3 22	3 42	4 02	4 22	4 42	5 22	6 02	6 42	10 00	13 13	1·4
1·5	2 16	2 19	2 23	2 27	2 31	2 49	3 08	3 27	3 46	4 05	4 23	5 01	5 38	6 15	9 20	12 22	1·5
1·6	2 07	2 11	2 14	2 18	2 21	2 39	2 57	3 14	3 32	3 49	4 07	4 42	5 17	5 52	8 46	11 37	1·6
1·7	2 00	2 03	2 06	2 10	2 13	2 30	2 46	3 03	3 19	3 36	3 52	4 26	4 59	5 32	8 15	10 57	1·7
1·8	1 53	1 56	1 59	2 02	2 06	2 21	2 37	2 53	3 08	3 24	3 40	4 11	4 42	5 13	7 48	10 21	1·8
1·9	1 47	1 50	1 53	1 56	1 59	2 14	2 29	2 44	2 58	3 13	3 28	3 58	4 27	4 57	7 25	9 50	1·9
2·0	1 42	1 45	1 47	1 50	1 53	2 07	2 21	2 35	2 49	3 04	3 18	3 46	4 14	4 42	7 02	9 20	2·0
2·1	1 37	1 40	1 42	1 45	1 48	2 01	2 15	2 28	2 41	2 55	3 08	3 35	4 02	4 29	6 41	8 53	2·1
2·2	1 33	1 35	1 38	1 40	1 43	1 56	2 08	2 21	2 34	2 47	3 00	3 25	3 51	4 17	6 23	8 30	2·2
2·3	1 29	1 31	1 33	1 36	1 38	1 51	2 03	2 15	2 27	2 40	2 52	3 16	3 41	4 05	6 07	8 09	2·3
2·4	1 25	1 27	1 30	1 32	1 34	1 46	1 58	2 10	2 21	2 33	2 45	3 08	3 32	3 55	5 52	7 48	2·4
2·5	1 21	1 24	1 26	1 28	1 30	1 42	1 53	2 04	2 16	2 27	2 38	3 01	3 23	3 46	5 38	7 30	2·5
2·6	1 18	1 20	1 23	1 25	1 27	1 38	1 49	2 00	2 10	2 21	2 32	2 54	3 16	3 37	5 25	7 13	2·6
2·7	1 15	1 17	1 20	1 23	1 24	1 34	1 45	1 55	2 06	2 16	2 27	2 47	3 08	3 29	5 13	6 57	2·7
2·8	1 13	1 15	1 17	1 19	1 21	1 31	1 41	1 51	2 01	2 11	2 21	2 41	3 02	3 22	5 02	6 42	2·8
2·9	1 11	1 12	1 14	1 16	1 18	1 28	1 37	1 47	1 57	2 07	2 16	2 36	2 55	3 15	4 52	6 28	2·9
3·0	1 08	1 10	1 12	1 14	1 15	1 25	1 34	1 44	1 53	2 02	2 12	2 31	2 49	3 08	4 42	6 15	3·0
3·2	1 04	1 05	1 07	1 09	1 11	1 20	1 28	1 37	1 46	1 55	2 04	2 21	2 39	2 57	4 24	5 52	3·2
3·4	1 00	1 02	1 03	1 05	1 07	1 15	1 23	1 31	1 40	1 48	1 56	2 13	2 30	2 46	4 09	5 32	3·4
3·6	0 57	0 58	1 00	1 01	1 03	1 11	1 19	1 26	1 34	1 42	1 50	2 06	2 21	2 37	3 55	5 13	3·6
3·8	0 54	0 55	0 57	0 58	1 00	1 07	1 14	1 22	1 29	1 37	1 44	1 59	2 14	2 29	3 43	4 57	3·8
4·0	0 51	0 52	0 54	0 55	0 57	1 04	1 11	1 18	1 25	1 32	1 39	1 53	2 07	2 21	3 31	4 42	4·0
4·2	0 48	0 50	0 51	0 53	0 54	1 01	1 07	1 14	1 21	1 28	1 34	1 48	2 01	2 15	3 21	4 29	4·2
4·4	0 46	0 48	0 49	0 50	0 51	0 58	1 04	1 11	1 17	1 24	1 30	1 43	1 56	2 08	3 12	4 17	4·4
4·6	0 44	0 45	0 47	0 48	0 49	0 55	1 01	1 08	1 14	1 20	1 26	1 38	1 51	2 03	3 04	4 05	4·6
4·8	0 42	0 44	0 45	0 46	0 47	0 53	0 59	1 05	1 11	1 17	1 22	1 34	1 46	1 58	2 57	3 55	4·8
5·0	0 41	0 42	0 43	0 44	0 45	0 51	0 57	1 02	1 08	1 14	1 19	1 30	1 42	1 53	2 50	3 46	5·0
5·2	0 39	0 40	0 41	0 42	0 43	0 49	0 54	1 00	1 05	1 11	1 16	1 27	1 38	1 49	2 44	3 38	5·2
5·4	0 38	0 39	0 40	0 41	0 42	0 47	0 52	0 58	1 03	1 08	1 13	1 24	1 34	1 45	2 38	3 30	5·4
5·6	0 36	0 37	0 38	0 39	0 40	0 45	0 50	0 56	1 01	1 06	1 11	1 21	1 31	1 41	2 32	3 22	5·6
5·8	0 35	0 36	0 37	0 38	0 39	0 44	0 49	0 54	0 58	1 03	1 08	1 18	1 28	1 37	2 26	3 15	5·8
6·0	0 34	0 35	0 36	0 37	0 38	0 42	0 47	0 52	0 57	1 01	1 06	1 15	1 25	1 34	2 21	3 09	6·0
6·2	0 33	0 34	0 35	0 36	0 36	0 41	0 46	0 50	0 55	0 59	1 04	1 13	1 22	1 31	2 16	3 02	6·2
6·4	0 32	0 33	0 34	0 34	0 35	0 40	0 44	0 49	0 53	0 57	1 02	1 11	1 20	1 28	2 12	2 57	6·4
6·6	0 31	0 32	0 33	0 33	0 34	0 38	0 43	0 47	0 51	0 56	1 00	1 09	1 17	1 26	2 08	2 51	6·6
6·8	0 30	0 31	0 32	0 32	0 33	0 37	0 42	0 46	0 50	0 54	0 58	1 07	1 15	1 23	2 04	2 46	6·8
7·0	0 29	0 30	0 31	0 31	0 32	0 36	0 40	0 44	0 48	0 53	0 57	1 05	1 13	1 21	2 01	2 42	7·0
Distance	360	370	380	390	400	450	500	550	600	650	700	800	900	1000	1500	2000	Distance

DISTANCE TO SEA HORIZON

Ht.	Dist.	Ht.	Dist.	Ht.	Dist.	Ht.	Dist.	Ht.	Dist.	Ht.	Dist.	Ht.	Dist.
Feet	Miles	Feet	Miles	Feet	Miles	Feet	Miles	Feet	Miles	Feet	Miles	Feet	Miles
10	3·6	120	12·6	320	20·6	520	26·2	720	30·8	920	34·9	2,200	53·9
15	4·5	130	13·1	330	20·9	530	26·5	730	31·0	930	35·1	2,300	55·1
20	5·1	140	13·6	340	21·2	540	26·7	740	31·2	940	35·3	2,400	56·3
25	5·7	150	14·1	350	21·5	550	27·0	750	31·5	950	35·4	2,500	57·5
30	6·3	160	14·5	360	21·8	560	27·2	760	31·7	960	35·6	2,600	58·6
35	6·8	170	15·0	370	22·1	570	27·4	770	31·9	970	35·8	2,700	59·7
40	7·3	180	15·4	380	22·4	580	27·7	780	32·1	980	36·0	2,800	60·8
45	7·7	190	15·8	390	22·7	590	27·9	790	32·3	990	36·2	2,900	61·9
50	8·1	200	16·2	400	23·0	600	28·1	800	32·5	1,000	36·4	3,000	63·0
55	8·5	210	16·6	410	23·3	610	28·4	810	32·7	1,100	38·1	3,500	68·0
60	8·9	220	17·0	420	23·5	620	28·6	820	32·9	1,200	39·8	4,000	72·7
65	9·3	230	17·4	430	23·8	630	28·9	830	33·1	1,300	41·5	4,500	77·1
70	9·6	240	17·8	440	24·1	640	29·1	840	33·3	1,400	43·0	5,000	81·3
75	10·0	250	18·2	450	24·4	650	29·3	850	33·5	1,500	44·5	5,500	85·3
80	10·3	260	18·5	460	24·6	660	29·5	860	33·7	1,600	46·0	6,000	89·1
85	10·6	270	18·9	470	24·9	670	29·8	870	33·9	1,700	47·4	6,500	92·7
90	10·9	280	19·2	480	25·2	680	30·0	880	34·1	1,800	48·7	7,000	96·2
95	11·2	290	19·6	490	25·4	690	30·2	890	34·3	1,900	50·1	8,000	102·9
100	11·5	300	19·9	500	25·7	700	30·4	900	34·5	2,000	51·4	9,000	109·1
110	12.1	310	20·2	510	26·0	710	30·6	910	34·7	2,100	52·7	10,000	115·0

HALF CONVERGENCY CORRECTION TABLE

Mean Lat. °	Longitude Difference between Radio Station and Ship												
0	2°	4°	6°	8°	10°	12°	14°	16°	18°	20°	22°	24°	26°
3	0·1	0·1	0·2	0·2	0·3	0·3	0·4	0·4	0·5	0·5	0·6	0·6	0·7
6	0·1	0·2	0·3	0·4	0·5	0·6	0·7	0·8	0·9	1·0	1·1	1·2	1·3
9	0·2	0·3	0·5	0·6	0·9	0·9	1·1	1·2	1·4	1·5	1·7	1·8	2·0
12	0·2	0·4	0·6	0·8	1·1	1·2	1·5	1·6	1·9	2·0	2·3	2·5	2·7
15	0·3	0·5	0·8	1·0	1·3	1·6	1·9	2·0	2·3	2·5	2·8	3·1	3·3
18	0·3	0·6	1·0	1·2	1·6	1·9	2·2	2·4	2·8	3·0	3·4	3·7	4·0
21	0·3	0·7	1·1	1·4	1·9	2·2	2·5	2·8	3·2	3·5	3·9	4·3	4·6
24	0·4	0·8	1·2	1·6	2·1	2·5	2·9	3·2	3·6	4·0	4·4	4·8	5·2
27	0·4	0·9	1·3	1·8	2·3	2·8	3·2	3·6	4·0	4·5	5·0	5·4	5·9
30	0·5	1·0	1·4	2·0	2·5	3·0	3·5	4·0	4·5	5·0	5·5	6·0	6·5
33	0·5	1·1	1·5	2·2	2·7	3·3	3·8	4·4	4·9	5·4	6·0	6·5	7·1
36	0·6	1·2	1·7	2·4	2·9	3·5	4·1	4·7	5·3	5·9	6·5	7·0	7·6
39	0·6	1·3	1·8	2·6	3·1	3·8	4·4	5·0	5·6	6·3	7·0	7·5	8·1
42	0·7	1·4	1·9	2·8	3·3	4·0	4·7	5·3	6·0	6·7	7·5	8·0	8·7
45	0·7	1·5	2·0	2·9	3·5	4·2	5·0	5·6	6·3	7·1	7·9	8·5	9·2
48	0·7	1·5	2·1	3·0	3·7	4·5	5·3	5·9	6·7	7·4	8·2	8·9	9·6
51	0·8	1·6	2·3	3·2	3·9	4·7	5·5	6·2	7·0	7·8	8·5	9·3	10·0
54	0·8	1·6	2·4	3·4	4·1	4·9	5·7	6·5	7·3	8·1	8·9	9·7	10·5
57	0·8	1·7	2·5	3·5	4·3	5·1	5·9	6·8	7·6	8·4	9·2	10·0	10·9
60	0·9	1·8	2·6	3·6	4·4	5·2	6·1	7·0	7·9	8·7	9·5	10·3	11·2

To convert Great Circle bearings to Mercatorial bearings always apply
Half Convergency TOWARDS THE EQUATOR

CHANGE OF ALTITUDE IN ONE MINUTE OF TIME
Use of this Table is explained in Section E

Lat.	0°	1°	2°	3°	4°	5°	6°	7°	8°	9°	10°	11°	12°	13°	14°	15°	16°	17°	Lat.
0°	0·0	0·3	0·5	0·8	1·0	1·3	1·6	1·8	2·1	2·3	2·6	2·9	3·1	3·4	3·6	3·9	4·1	4·4	0°
4°	0·0	0·3	0·5	0·8	1·0	1·3	1·6	1·8	2·1	2·3	2·6	2·9	3·1	3·4	3·6	3·9	4·1	4·4	4°
8°	0·0	0·3	0·5	0·8	1·0	1·3	1·6	1·8	2·1	2·3	2·6	2·8	3·1	3·3	3·6	3·8	4·1	4·3	8°
12°	0·0	0·3	0·5	0·8	1·0	1·3	1·5	1·8	2·0	2·3	2·5	2·8	3·1	3·3	3·6	3·8	4·0	4·3	12°
14°	0·0	0·3	0·5	0·8	1·0	1·3	1·5	1·8	2·0	2·3	2·5	2·8	3·0	3·3	3·5	3·8	4·0	4·3	14°
16°	0·0	0·3	0·5	0·8	1·0	1·3	1·5	1·8	2·0	2·3	2·5	2·8	3·0	3·2	3·5	3·7	4·0	4·2	16°
18°	0·0	0·2	0·5	0·7	1·0	1·2	1·5	1·7	2·0	2·2	2·5	2·7	3·0	3·2	3·5	3·7	3·9	4·2	18°
20°	0·0	0·2	0·5	0·7	1·0	1·2	1·5	1·7	2·0	2·2	2·4	2·7	2·9	3·2	3·4	3·6	3·9	4·1	20°
22°	0·0	0·2	0·5	0·7	1·0	1·2	1·5	1·7	1·9	2·2	2·4	2·7	2·9	3·1	3·4	3·6	3·8	4·1	22°
23°	0·0	0·2	0·5	0·7	1·0	1·2	1·4	1·7	1·9	2·2	2·4	2·6	2·9	3·1	3·3	3·6	3·8	4·0	23°
24°	0·0	0·2	0·5	0·7	1·0	1·2	1·4	1·7	1·9	2·1	2·4	2·6	2·8	3·1	3·3	3·5	3·8	4·0	24°
25°	0·0	0·2	0·5	0·7	0·9	1·2	1·4	1·7	1·9	2·1	2·4	2·6	2·8	3·1	3·3	3·5	3·7	4·0	25°
26°	0·0	0·2	0·5	0·7	0·9	1·2	1·4	1·6	1·9	2·1	2·3	2·6	2·8	3·0	3·3	3·5	3·7	3·9	26°
27°	0·0	0·2	0·5	0·7	0·9	1·2	1·4	1·6	1·9	2·1	2·3	2·6	2·8	3·0	3·2	3·5	3·7	3·9	27°
28°	0·0	0·2	0·5	0·7	0·9	1·2	1·4	1·6	1·8	2·1	2·3	2·5	2·8	3·0	3·2	3·4	3·6	3·9	28°
29°	0·0	0·2	0·5	0·7	0·9	1·1	1·4	1·6	1·8	2·1	2·3	2·5	2·7	3·0	3·2	3·4	3·6	3·8	29°
30°	0·0	0·2	0·5	0·7	0·9	1·1	1·4	1·6	1·8	2·0	2·3	2·5	2·7	2·9	3·1	3·4	3·6	3·8	30°
31°	0·0	0·2	0·4	0·7	0·9	1·1	1·3	1·6	1·8	2·0	2·2	2·5	2·7	2·9	3·1	3·3	3·5	3·8	31°
32°	0·0	0·2	0·4	0·7	0·9	1·1	1·3	1·6	1·8	2·0	2·2	2·4	2·6	2·9	3·1	3·3	3·5	3·7	32°
33°	0·0	0·2	0·4	0·7	0·9	1·1	1·3	1·5	1·8	2·0	2·2	2·4	2·6	2·8	3·0	3·3	3·5	3·7	33°
34°	0·0	0·2	0·4	0·7	0·9	1·1	1·3	1·5	1·7	1·9	2·2	2·4	2·6	2·8	3·0	3·2	3·4	3·6	34°
35°	0·0	0·2	0·4	0·6	0·9	1·1	1·3	1·5	1·7	1·9	2·1	2·3	2·6	2·8	3·0	3·2	3·4	3·6	35°
36°	0·0	0·2	0·4	0·6	0·8	1·1	1·3	1·5	1·7	1·9	2·1	2·3	2·5	2·7	2·9	3·1	3·3	3·5	36°
37°	0·0	0·2	0·4	0·6	0·8	1·0	1·3	1·5	1·7	1·9	2·1	2·3	2·5	2·7	2·9	3·1	3·3	3·5	37°
38°	0·0	0·2	0·4	0·6	0·8	1·0	1·2	1·4	1·6	1·8	2·1	2·3	2·5	2·7	2·9	3·1	3·3	3·5	38°
39°	0·0	0·2	0·4	0·6	0·8	1·0	1·2	1·4	1·6	1·8	2·0	2·2	2·4	2·6	2·8	3·0	3·2	3·4	39°
40°	0·0	0·2	0·4	0·6	0·8	1·0	1·2	1·4	1·6	1·8	2·0	2·2	2·4	2·6	2·8	3·0	3·2	3·4	40°
41°	0·0	0·2	0·4	0·6	0·8	1·0	1·2	1·4	1·6	1·8	2·0	2·2	2·4	2·5	2·7	2·9	3·1	3·3	41°
42°	0·0	0·2	0·4	0·6	0·8	1·0	1·2	1·4	1·6	1·7	1·9	2·1	2·3	2·5	2·7	2·9	3·1	3·3	42°
43°	0·0	0·2	0·4	0·6	0·8	1·0	1·1	1·3	1·5	1·7	1·9	2·1	2·3	2·5	2·7	2·8	3·0	3·2	43°
44°	0·0	0·2	0·4	0·6	0·8	1·0	1·1	1·3	1·5	1·7	1·9	2·1	2·2	2·4	2·6	2·8	3·0	3·2	44°
45°	0·0	0·2	0·4	0·6	0·7	0·9	1·1	1·3	1·5	1·7	1·8	2·0	2·2	2·4	2·6	2·7	2·9	3·1	45°
46°	0·0	0·2	0·4	0·5	0·7	0·9	1·1	1·3	1·5	1·6	1·8	2·0	2·2	2·3	2·5	2·7	2·9	3·1	46°
47°	0·0	0·2	0·4	0·5	0·7	0·9	1·1	1·2	1·4	1·6	1·8	2·0	2·1	2·3	2·5	2·6	2·8	3·0	47°
48°	0·0	0·2	0·4	0·5	0·7	0·9	1·0	1·2	1·4	1·6	1·7	1·9	2·1	2·3	2·4	2·6	2·8	2·9	48°
49°	0·0	0·2	0·3	0·5	0·7	0·9	1·0	1·2	1·4	1·5	1·7	1·9	2·0	2·2	2·4	2·5	2·7	2·9	49°
50°	0·0	0·2	0·3	0·5	0·7	0·8	1·0	1·2	1·3	1·5	1·7	1·8	2·0	2·2	2·3	2·5	2·7	2·8	50°
51°	0·0	0·2	0·3	0·5	0·7	0·8	1·0	1·2	1·3	1·5	1·6	1·8	1·9	2·1	2·3	2·4	2·6	2·8	51°
52°	0·0	0·2	0·3	0·5	0·6	0·8	1·0	1·1	1·3	1·4	1·6	1·8	1·9	2·1	2·2	2·4	2·5	2·7	52°
53°	0·0	0·2	0·3	0·5	0·6	0·8	0·9	1·1	1·3	1·4	1·6	1·7	1·9	2·0	2·2	2·3	2·5	2·6	53°
54°	0·0	0·2	0·3	0·4	0·6	0·8	0·9	1·1	1·2	1·4	1·5	1·7	1·8	2·0	2·1	2·3	2·4	2·6	54°
55°	0·0	0·2	0·3	0·4	0·6	0·8	0·9	1·0	1·2	1·3	1·5	1·6	1·8	1·9	2·1	2·2	2·4	2·5	55°
56°	0·0	0·1	0·3	0·4	0·6	0·7	0·9	1·0	1·2	1·3	1·5	1·6	1·7	1·9	2·0	2·2	2·3	2·5	56°
57°	0·0	0·1	0·3	0·4	0·6	0·7	0·9	1·0	1·1	1·3	1·4	1·6	1·7	1·8	2·0	2·1	2·3	2·4	57°
58°	0·0	0·1	0·3	0·4	0·6	0·7	0·8	1·0	1·1	1·2	1·4	1·5	1·7	1·8	1·9	2·1	2·2	2·3	58°
59°	0·0	0·1	0·3	0·4	0·5	0·7	0·8	0·9	1·1	1·2	1·3	1·5	1·6	1·7	1·9	2·0	2·1	2·3	59°
60°	0·0	0·1	0·3	0·4	0·5	0·7	0·8	0·9	1·0	1·2	1·3	1·4	1·6	1·7	1·8	1·9	2·1	2·2	60°
61°	0·0	0·1	0·3	0·4	0·5	0·6	0·8	0·9	1·0	1·1	1·3	1·4	1·5	1·6	1·8	1·9	2·0	2·1	61°
62°	0·0	0·1	0·2	0·4	0·5	0·6	0·7	0·9	1·0	1·1	1·2	1·3	1·5	1·6	1·7	1·8	1·9	2·0	62°
63°	0·0	0·1	0·2	0·4	0·5	0·6	0·7	0·8	0·9	1·1	1·2	1·3	1·4	1·5	1·6	1·8	1·9	2·0	63°
64°	0·0	0·1	0·2	0·3	0·5	0·6	0·7	0·8	0·9	1·0	1·1	1·3	1·4	1·5	1·6	1·7	1·8	1·9	64°
65°	0·0	0·1	0·2	0·3	0·4	0·6	0·7	0·8	0·9	1·0	1·1	1·2	1·3	1·4	1·5	1·6	1·7	1·9	65°
Lat.	0°	1°	2°	3°	4°	5°	6°	7°	8°	9°	10°	11°	12°	13°	14°	15°	16°	17°	Lat.

AZIMUTH

CHANGE OF ALTITUDE IN ONE MINUTE OF TIME

Use of this Table is explained in Section E

Lat.	AZIMUTH																		Lat.
	18°	19°	20°	21°	22°	23°	24°	25°	26°	27°	28°	29°	30°	32°	34°	36°	38°	40°	
0°	4·6	4·9	5·1	5·4	5·6	5·9	6·1	6·3	6·6	6·8	7·0	7·3	7·5	7·9	8·4	8·8	9·2	9·6	0°
4°	4·6	4·9	5·1	5·4	5·6	5·8	6·1	6·3	6·6	6·8	7·0	7·3	7·5	7·9	8·4	8·8	9·2	9·6	4°
8°	4·6	4·8	5·1	5·3	5·6	5·8	6·0	6·3	6·5	6·7	7·0	7·2	7·4	7·9	8·3	8·7	9·2	9·6	8°
12°	4·5	4·8	5·0	5·3	5·5	5·7	6·0	6·2	6·4	6·7	6·9	7·1	7·3	7·8	8·2	8·6	9·0	9·4	12°
14°	4·5	4·7	5·0	5·2	5·4	5·7	5·9	6·2	6·4	6·6	6·8	7·1	7·3	7·7	8·1	8·6	9·0	9·4	14°
16°	4·5	4·7	4·9	5·2	5·4	5·6	5·9	6·1	6·3	6·5	6·8	7·0	7·2	7·6	8·1	8·5	8·9	9·3	16°
18°	4·4	4·6	4·9	5·1	5·3	5·6	5·8	6·0	6·3	6·5	6·7	6·9	7·1	7·6	8·0	8·4	8·8	9·2	18°
20°	4·4	4·6	4·8	5·1	5·3	5·5	5·7	6·0	6·2	6·4	6·6	6·8	7·0	7·5	7·9	8·3	8·7	9·1	20°
22°	4·3	4·5	4·8	5·0	5·2	5·4	5·7	5·9	6·1	6·3	6·5	6·7	7·0	7·4	7·8	8·2	8·6	8·9	22°
23°	4·3	4·5	4·7	4·9	5·2	5·4	5·6	5·8	6·1	6·3	6·5	6·7	6·9	7·3	7·7	8·1	8·5	8·9	23°
24°	4·2	4·5	4·7	4·9	5·1	5·4	5·6	5·8	6·0	6·2	6·4	6·6	6·9	7·3	7·7	8·1	8·4	8·8	24°
25°	4·2	4·4	4·6	4·9	5·1	5·3	5·5	5·7	6·0	6·2	6·4	6·6	6·8	7·3	7·6	8·0	8·4	8·7	25°
26°	4·2	4·4	4·6	4·8	5·1	5·3	5·5	5·7	5·9	6·1	6·3	6·5	6·7	7·2	7·5	7·9	8·3	8·7	26°
27°	4·1	4·4	4·6	4·8	5·0	5·2	5·4	5·6	5·9	6·1	6·3	6·5	6·7	7·1	7·5	7·9	8·2	8·6	27°
28°	4·1	4·3	4·5	4·7	5·0	5·2	5·4	5·6	5·8	6·0	6·2	6·4	6·6	7·0	7·4	7·8	8·2	8·5	28°
29°	4·1	4·3	4·5	4·7	4·9	5·1	5·3	5·5	5·8	6·0	6·2	6·4	6·6	7·0	7·3	7·7	8·1	8·4	29°
30°	4·0	4·2	4·4	4·7	4·9	5·1	5·3	5·5	5·7	5·9	6·1	6·3	6·5	6·9	7·3	7·6	8·0	8·3	30°
31°	4·0	4·2	4·4	4·6	4·8	5·0	5·2	5·4	5·6	5·8	6·0	6·2	6·4	6·8	7·2	7·6	7·9	8·3	31°
32°	3·9	4·1	4·4	4·6	4·8	5·0	5·2	5·4	5·6	5·8	6·0	6·2	6·4	6·7	7·1	7·5	7·8	8·2	32°
33°	3·9	4·1	4·3	4·5	4·7	4·9	5·1	5·3	5·5	5·7	5·9	6·1	6·3	6·7	7·0	7·4	7·7	8·1	33°
34°	3·8	4·0	4·3	4·5	4·7	4·9	5·1	5·3	5·5	5·6	5·8	6·0	6·2	6·6	7·0	7·3	7·7	8·0	34°
35°	3·8	4·0	4·2	4·4	4·6	4·8	5·0	5·2	5·4	5·6	5·8	6·0	6·1	6·5	6·9	7·2	7·6	7·9	35°
36°	3·8	4·0	4·2	4·3	4·5	4·7	4·9	5·1	5·3	5·5	5·7	5·9	6·1	6·4	6·8	7·1	7·5	7·8	36°
37°	3·7	3·9	4·1	4·3	4·5	4·7	4·9	5·1	5·3	5·4	5·6	5·8	6·0	6·3	6·7	7·0	7·4	7·7	37°
38°	3·7	3·8	4·0	4·2	4·4	4·6	4·8	5·0	5·2	5·4	5·5	5·7	5·9	6·3	6·6	6·9	7·3	7·6	38°
39°	3·6	3·8	4·0	4·2	4·4	4·6	4·7	4·9	5·1	5·3	5·5	5·7	5·8	6·2	6·5	6·9	7·2	7·5	39°
40°	3·6	3·7	3·9	4·1	4·3	4·5	4·7	4·9	5·0	5·2	5·4	5·6	5·7	6·1	6·4	6·8	7·1	7·4	40°
41°	3·5	3·7	3·9	4·1	4·2	4·4	4·6	4·8	5·0	5·1	5·3	5·5	5·7	6·0	6·3	6·7	7·0	7·1	41°
42°	3·4	3·6	3·8	4·0	4·2	4·4	4·5	4·7	4·9	5·1	5·2	5·4	5·6	5·9	6·2	6·6	6·9	7·2	42°
43°	3·4	3·6	3·8	3·9	4·1	4·3	4·5	4·6	4·8	5·0	5·2	5·3	5·5	5·8	6·1	6·5	6·8	7·1	43°
44°	3·3	3·5	3·7	3·9	4·0	4·2	4·4	4·6	4·7	4·9	5·1	5·2	5·4	5·7	6·0	6·3	6·6	6·9	44°
45°	3·3	3·5	3·6	3·8	4·0	4·1	4·3	4·5	4·6	4·8	5·0	5·1	5·3	5·6	5·9	6·2	6·5	6·8	45°
46°	3·2	3·4	3·6	3·7	3·9	4·1	4·2	4·4	4·6	4·7	4·9	5·1	5·2	5·5	5·8	6·1	6·4	6·7	46°
47°	3·2	3·3	3·5	3·7	3·8	4·0	4·2	4·3	4·5	4·6	4·8	5·0	5·1	5·4	5·7	6·0	6·3	6·6	47°
48°	3·1	3·3	3·4	3·6	3·8	3·9	4·1	4·2	4·4	4·6	4·7	4·9	5·0	5·3	5·6	5·9	6·2	6·5	48°
49°	3·0	3·2	3·4	3·5	3·7	3·8	4·0	4·2	4·3	4·5	4·6	4·8	4·9	5·2	5·5	5·8	6·1	6·3	49°
50°	3·0	3·1	3·3	3·5	3·6	3·8	3·9	4·1	4·2	4·4	4·5	4·7	4·8	5·1	5·4	5·7	5·9	6·2	50°
51°	2·9	3·1	3·2	3·4	3·5	3·7	3·8	4·0	4·1	4·3	4·4	4·6	4·7	5·0	5·3	5·5	5·8	6·1	51°
52°	2·9	3·0	3·2	3·3	3·5	3·6	3·8	3·9	4·1	4·2	4·3	4·5	4·6	4·9	5·2	5·4	5·7	5·9	52°
53°	2·8	2·9	3·1	3·2	3·4	3·5	3·7	3·8	4·0	4·1	4·2	4·4	4·5	4·8	5·0	5·3	5·6	5·8	53°
54°	2·7	2·9	3·0	3·2	3·3	3·4	3·6	3·7	3·9	4·0	4·1	4·3	4·4	4·7	4·9	5·2	5·4	5·7	54°
55°	2·7	2·8	2·9	3·1	3·2	3·4	3·5	3·6	3·8	3·9	4·0	4·2	4·3	4·6	4·8	5·1	5·3	5·5	55°
56°	2·6	2·7	2·9	3·0	3·1	3·3	3·4	3·5	3·7	3·8	3·9	4·1	4·2	4·4	4·7	4·9	5·2	5·4	56°
57°	2·5	2·7	2·8	2·9	3·1	3·2	3·3	3·5	3·6	3·7	3·8	4·0	4·1	4·3	4·6	4·8	5·0	5·3	57°
58°	2·5	2·6	2·7	2·8	3·0	3·1	3·2	3·4	3·5	3·6	3·7	3·9	4·0	4·2	4·4	4·7	4·9	5·1	58°
59°	2·4	2·5	2·6	2·8	2·9	3·0	3·1	3·3	3·4	3·5	3·6	3·7	3·9	4·1	4·3	4·5	4·8	5·0	59°
60°	2·3	2·4	2·6	2·7	2·8	2·9	3·1	3·2	3·3	3·4	3·5	3·6	3·8	4·0	4·2	4·4	4·6	4·8	60°
61°	2·2	2·4	2·5	2·6	2·7	2·8	3·0	3·1	3·2	3·3	3·4	3·5	3·6	3·9	4·1	4·3	4·5	4·7	61°
62°	2·2	2·3	2·4	2·5	2·6	2·8	2·9	3·0	3·1	3·2	3·3	3·4	3·5	3·7	3·9	4·1	4·3	4·5	62°
63°	2·1	2·2	2·3	2·4	2·6	2·7	2·8	2·9	3·0	3·1	3·2	3·3	3·4	3·6	3·8	4·0	4·2	4·4	63°
64°	2·0	2·1	2·2	2·4	2·5	2·6	2·7	2·8	2·9	3·0	3·1	3·2	3·3	3·5	3·7	3·9	4·1	4·2	64°
65°	2·0	2·1	2·2	2·3	2·4	2·5	2·6	2·7	2·8	2·9	3·0	3·1	3·2	3·4	3·5	3·7	3·9	4·1	65°
Lat.	18°	19°	20°	21°	22°	23°	24°	25°	26°	27°	28°	29°	30°	32°	34°	36°	38°	40°	Lat.
	AZIMUTH																		

CHANGE OF ALTITUDE IN ONE MINUTE OF TIME
Use of this Table is explained in Section E

Lat.	AZIMUTH																		Lat.
	42°	44°	46°	48°	50°	52°	54°	56°	58°	60°	62°	64°	66°	68°	70°	75°	80°	90°	
0°	10.0	10.4	10.8	11.1	11.5	11.8	12.1	12.4	12.7	13.0	13.2	13.5	13.7	13.9	14.1	14.5	14.8	15.0	0°
4°	10.0	10.4	10.8	11.1	11.5	11.8	12.1	12.4	12.7	13.0	13.2	13.5	13.7	13.9	14.1	14.5	14.7	15.0	4°
8°	9.9	10.3	10.7	11.0	11.4	11.7	12.0	12.3	12.6	12.9	13.1	13.4	13.6	13.8	14.0	14.3	14.6	14.9	8°
12°	9.8	10.2	10.6	10.9	11.2	11.6	11.9	12.2	12.4	12.7	13.0	13.2	13.4	13.6	13.8	14.2	14.5	14.7	12°
14°	9.7	10.1	10.5	10.8	11.1	11.5	11.8	12.1	12.3	12.6	12.9	13.1	13.3	13.5	13.7	14.0	14.3	14.6	14°
16°	9.6	10.0	10.4	10.7	11.0	11.4	11.7	12.0	12.2	12.5	12.7	13.0	13.2	13.4	13.5	13.9	14.2	14.4	16°
18°	9.5	9.9	10.3	10.6	10.9	11.2	11.5	11.8	12.1	12.4	12.6	12.8	13.0	13.2	13.4	13.7	14.0	14.3	18°
20°	9.4	9.8	10.1	10.5	10.8	11.1	11.4	11.7	12.0	12.2	12.4	12.7	12.9	13.1	13.2	13.6	13.9	14.1	20°
22°	9.3	9.7	10.0	10.3	10.7	11.0	11.3	11.5	11.8	12.0	12.3	12.5	12.7	12.9	13.1	13.4	13.7	13.9	22°
23°	9.2	9.6	9.9	10.3	10.6	10.9	11.2	11.4	11.7	12.0	12.2	12.4	12.6	12.8	13.0	13.3	13.6	13.8	23°
24°	9.2	9.5	9.9	10.2	10.5	10.8	11.1	11.4	11.6	11.9	12.1	12.3	12.5	12.7	12.9	13.2	13.5	13.7	24°
25°	9.1	9.4	9.8	10.1	10.4	10.7	11.0	11.3	11.5	11.8	12.0	12.2	12.4	12.6	12.8	13.1	13.4	13.6	25°
26°	9.0	9.4	9.7	10.0	10.3	10.6	10.9	11.2	11.4	11.7	11.9	12.1	12.3	12.5	12.7	13.0	13.3	13.5	26°
27°	8.9	9.3	9.6	9.9	10.2	10.5	10.8	11.1	11.3	11.6	11.8	12.0	12.2	12.4	12.6	12.9	13.2	13.4	27°
28°	8.9	9.2	9.5	9.8	10.1	10.4	10.7	11.0	11.2	11.5	11.7	11.9	12.1	12.3	12.4	12.8	13.1	13.2	28°
29°	8.8	9.1	9.4	9.7	10.0	10.3	10.6	10.9	11.1	11.4	11.6	11.8	12.0	12.2	12.3	12.6	12.9	13.1	29°
30°	8.7	9.0	9.3	9.7	9.9	10.2	10.5	10.8	11.0	11.2	11.5	11.7	11.9	12.0	12.2	12.5	12.8	13.0	30°
31°	8.6	8.9	9.2	9.6	9.8	10.1	10.4	10.7	10.9	11.1	11.4	11.6	11.7	11.9	12.1	12.4	12.7	12.9	31°
32°	8.5	8.8	9.1	9.5	9.7	10.0	10.3	10.5	10.8	11.0	11.2	11.4	11.6	11.8	12.0	12.3	12.5	12.7	32°
33°	8.4	8.7	9.0	9.3	9.6	9.9	10.2	10.4	10.7	10.9	11.1	11.3	11.5	11.7	11.8	12.1	12.4	12.6	33°
34°	8.3	8.6	8.9	9.2	9.5	9.8	10.1	10.3	10.5	10.8	11.0	11.2	11.4	11.5	11.7	12.0	12.2	12.4	34°
35°	8.2	8.5	8.8	9.1	9.4	9.7	9.9	10.2	10.4	10.6	10.8	11.0	11.2	11.4	11.5	11.8	12.1	12.3	35°
36°	8.1	8.4	8.7	9.0	9.3	9.6	9.8	10.1	10.3	10.5	10.7	10.9	11.1	11.3	11.4	11.7	12.0	12.1	36°
37°	8.0	8.3	8.6	8.9	9.2	9.4	9.7	9.9	10.2	10.4	10.6	10.7	10.9	11.1	11.3	11.6	11.8	12.0	37°
38°	7.9	8.2	8.5	8.8	9.1	9.3	9.6	9.8	10.0	10.2	10.4	10.6	10.8	11.0	11.1	11.4	11.6	11.8	38°
39°	7.8	8.1	8.4	8.7	8.9	9.2	9.4	9.7	9.9	10.1	10.3	10.5	10.6	10.8	11.0	11.3	11.5	11.7	39°
40°	7.7	8.0	8.3	8.5	8.8	9.1	9.3	9.5	9.7	9.9	10.1	10.3	10.5	10.7	10.8	11.1	11.3	11.5	40°
41°	7.6	7.9	8.1	8.4	8.7	8.9	9.2	9.4	9.6	9.8	10.0	10.2	10.3	10.5	10.6	10.9	11.1	11.3	41°
42°	7.5	7.7	8.0	8.3	8.5	8.8	9.0	9.2	9.5	9.7	9.8	10.0	10.2	10.3	10.5	10.8	11.0	11.1	42°
43°	7.3	7.6	7.9	8.2	8.4	8.6	8.9	9.1	9.3	9.5	9.7	9.9	10.0	10.2	10.3	10.6	10.8	11.0	43°
44°	7.2	7.5	7.8	8.0	8.3	8.5	8.7	8.9	9.1	9.3	9.5	9.7	9.9	10.0	10.1	10.4	10.6	10.8	44°
45°	7.1	7.4	7.6	7.9	8.1	8.4	8.6	8.8	9.0	9.2	9.4	9.5	9.7	9.8	10.0	10.2	10.4	10.6	45°
46°	7.0	7.2	7.5	7.7	8.0	8.2	8.4	8.6	8.8	9.0	9.2	9.4	9.5	9.7	9.8	10.1	10.3	10.4	46°
47°	6.8	7.1	7.4	7.6	7.8	8.1	8.3	8.5	8.7	8.9	9.0	9.2	9.3	9.5	9.6	9.9	10.1	10.2	47°
48°	6.7	7.0	7.2	7.5	7.7	7.9	8.1	8.3	8.5	8.7	8.9	9.0	9.2	9.3	9.4	9.7	9.9	10.0	48°
49°	6.6	6.8	7.1	7.3	7.5	7.8	8.0	8.2	8.3	8.5	8.7	8.8	9.0	9.1	9.2	9.5	9.7	9.8	49°
50°	6.5	6.7	6.9	7.2	7.4	7.6	7.8	8.0	8.2	8.3	8.5	8.7	8.8	8.9	9.1	9.3	9.5	9.6	50°
51°	6.3	6.6	6.8	7.0	7.2	7.4	7.6	7.8	8.0	8.2	8.3	8.5	8.6	8.8	8.9	9.1	9.3	9.4	51°
52°	6.2	6.4	6.6	6.9	7.1	7.3	7.5	7.7	7.8	8.0	8.2	8.3	8.4	8.6	8.7	8.9	9.1	9.2	52°
53°	6.0	6.3	6.5	6.7	6.9	7.1	7.3	7.5	7.7	7.8	8.0	8.1	8.2	8.4	8.5	8.7	8.9	9.0	53°
54°	5.9	6.1	6.3	6.6	6.8	6.9	7.1	7.3	7.5	7.6	7.8	7.9	8.1	8.2	8.3	8.5	8.7	8.8	54°
55°	5.8	6.0	6.2	6.4	6.6	6.8	7.0	7.1	7.3	7.5	7.6	7.7	7.9	8.0	8.1	8.3	8.5	8.6	55°
56°	5.6	5.8	6.0	6.2	6.4	6.6	6.8	7.0	7.1	7.3	7.4	7.5	7.7	7.8	7.9	8.1	8.3	8.4	56°
57°	5.5	5.7	5.9	6.1	6.3	6.4	6.6	6.8	6.9	7.1	7.2	7.3	7.5	7.6	7.7	7.9	8.0	8.2	57°
58°	5.3	5.5	5.7	5.9	6.1	6.3	6.4	6.6	6.7	6.9	7.0	7.2	7.3	7.4	7.5	7.7	7.8	7.9	58°
59°	5.2	5.4	5.6	5.7	5.9	6.1	6.2	6.4	6.6	6.7	6.8	6.9	7.1	7.2	7.3	7.5	7.6	7.7	59°
60°	5.0	5.2	5.4	5.6	5.7	5.9	6.1	6.2	6.4	6.5	6.6	6.7	6.9	7.0	7.0	7.2	7.4	7.5	60°
61°	4.9	5.1	5.2	5.4	5.6	5.7	5.9	6.0	6.2	6.3	6.4	6.5	6.6	6.7	6.8	7.0	7.2	7.3	61°
62°	4.7	4.9	5.1	5.2	5.4	5.5	5.7	5.8	6.0	6.1	6.2	6.3	6.4	6.5	6.6	6.8	6.9	7.0	62°
63°	4.6	4.7	4.9	5.1	5.2	5.4	5.5	5.6	5.8	5.9	6.0	6.1	6.2	6.3	6.4	6.6	6.7	6.8	63°
64°	4.4	4.6	4.7	4.9	5.0	5.2	5.3	5.5	5.6	5.7	5.8	5.9	6.0	6.1	6.2	6.4	6.5	6.6	64°
65°	4.2	4.4	4.6	4.7	4.9	5.0	5.1	5.3	5.4	5.5	5.6	5.7	5.8	5.9	6.0	6.1	6.2	6.3	65°
Lat.	42°	44°	46°	48°	50°	52°	54°	56°	58°	60°	62°	64°	66°	68°	70°	75°	80°	90°	Lat.
	AZIMUTH																		

TABLE OF NATURAL SINES, COSINES AND TANGENTS

′	**0°** Sin	Cos	Tan	**1°** Sin	Cos	Tan	**2°** Sin	Cos	Tan	′
0	0.00000	1.00000	0.00000	0.01745	0.99985	0.01746	0.03490	0.99939	0.03492	0
1	.00029	1.00000	.00029	.01774	.99984	.01775	.03519	.99938	.03521	1
2	.00058	1.00000	.00058	.01803	.99984	.01804	.03548	.99937	.03550	2
3	.00087	1.00000	.00087	.01833	.99983	.01832	.03577	.99936	.03579	3
4	.00116	1.00000	.00116	.01862	.99983	.01862	.03606	.99935	.03609	4
5	.00145	1.00000	.00145	.01891	.99982	.01891	.03635	.99934	.03638	5
6	.00175	1.00000	0.00175	.01920	.99982	0.01920	.03664	.99933	0.03667	6
7	.00204	1.00000	.00204	.01949	.99981	.01949	.03693	.99932	.03696	7
8	.00233	1.00000	.00233	.01978	.99980	.01978	.03723	.99931	.03725	8
9	.00262	1.00000	.00262	.02007	.99980	.02007	.03752	.99930	.03754	9
10	.00291	1.00000	.00291	.02036	.99979	.02037	.03781	.99929	.03783	10
11	0.00320	1.00000	0.00320	0.02065	0.99979	0.02066	0.03810	0.99927	0.03812	11
12	.00349	.99999	.00349	.02094	.99978	.02095	.03839	.99926	.03842	12
13	.00378	.99999	.00378	.02123	.99978	.02124	.03868	.99925	.03871	13
14	.00407	.99999	.00407	.02152	.99977	.02153	.03897	.99924	.03900	14
15	.00436	.99999	.00436	.02182	.99976	.02182	.03926	.99923	.03929	15
16	.00465	.99999	0.00465	.02211	.99976	0.02211	.03955	.99922	0.03958	16
17	.00495	.99999	.00495	.02240	.99975	.02240	.03984	.99921	.03987	17
18	.00524	.99999	.00524	.02269	.99974	.02269	.04013	.99919	.04016	18
19	.00553	.99999	.00553	.02298	.99974	.02298	.04042	.99918	.04046	19
20	.00582	.99998	.00582	.02327	.99973	.02328	.04071	.99917	.04075	20
21	0.00611	0.99998	0.00611	0.02356	0.99972	0.02357	0.04100	0.99916	0.04104	21
22	.00640	.99998	.00640	.02385	.99972	.02386	.04129	.99915	.04133	22
23	.00669	.99998	.00669	.02414	.99971	.02415	.04159	.99914	.04162	23
24	.00698	.99998	.00698	.02443	.99970	.02444	.04188	.99912	.04191	24
25	.00727	.99997	.00727	.02472	.99969	.02473	.04217	.99911	.04220	25
26	.00756	.99997	0.00756	.02501	.99969	0.02502	.04246	.99910	0.04250	26
27	.00785	.99997	.00785	.02531	.99968	.02531	.04275	.99909	.04279	27
28	.00815	.99997	.00815	.02560	.99967	.02560	.04304	.99907	.04308	28
29	.00844	.99996	.00844	.02589	.99967	.02589	.04333	.99906	.04337	29
30	.00873	.99996	.00873	.02618	.99966	.02619	.04362	.99905	.04366	30
31	0.00902	0.99996	0.00902	0.02647	0.99965	0.02648	0.04391	0.99904	0.04395	31
32	.00931	.99996	.00931	.02676	.99964	.02677	.04420	.99903	.04424	32
33	.00960	.99995	.00960	.02705	.99963	.02706	.04449	.99901	.04454	33
34	.00989	.99995	.00989	.02734	.99963	.02735	.04478	.99900	.04483	34
35	.01018	.99995	.01018	.02763	.99962	.02764	.04507	.99898	.04512	35
36	.01047	.99995	0.01047	.02792	.99961	0.02793	.04536	.99897	0.04541	36
37	.01076	.99994	.01076	.02821	.99960	.02822	.04565	.99896	.04570	37
38	.01105	.99994	.01105	.02850	.99959	.02851	.04594	.99894	.04599	38
39	.01134	.99994	.01135	.02879	.99959	.02881	.04624	.99893	.04628	39
40	.01164	.99993	.01164	.02909	.99958	.02910	.04653	.99892	.04658	40
41	0.01193	0.99993	0.01193	0.02938	0.99957	0.02939	0.04682	0.99890	0.04687	41
42	.01222	.99993	.01222	.02967	.99956	.02968	.04711	.99889	.04716	42
43	.01251	.99992	.01251	.02996	.99955	.02997	.04740	.99888	.04745	43
44	.01280	.99992	.01280	.03025	.99954	.03026	.04769	.99886	.04774	44
45	.01309	.99991	.01309	.03054	.99953	.03055	.04798	.99885	.04803	45
46	.01338	.99991	0.01338	.03083	.99953	0.03084	.04827	.99883	0.04833	46
47	.01367	.99991	.01367	.03112	.99952	.03114	.04856	.99882	.04862	47
48	.01396	.99990	.01396	.03141	.99951	.03143	.04885	.99881	.04891	48
49	.01425	.99990	.01425	.03170	.99950	.03172	.04914	.99879	.04920	49
50	.01454	.99989	.01455	.03199	.99949	.03201	.04943	.99878	.04949	50
51	0.01484	0.99989	0.0484	0.03228	0.99948	0.03230	0.04972	0.99876	0.04978	51
52	.01513	.99989	.01513	.03257	.99947	.03259	.05001	.99875	.05007	52
53	.01542	.99988	.01542	.03286	.99946	.03288	.05030	.99873	.05037	53
54	.01571	.99988	.01571	.03316	.99945	.03317	.05059	.99872	.05066	54
55	.01600	.99887	.01600	.03345	.99944	.03346	.05088	.99871	.05095	55
56	.01629	.99987	0.01629	.03374	.99943	0.03376	.05117	.99869	0.05124	56
57	.01658	.99986	.01658	.03403	.99942	.03405	.05146	.99868	.05153	57
58	.01687	.99986	.01687	.03432	.99941	.03434	.05176	.99866	.05182	58
59	.01716	.99985	.01716	.03461	.99940	.03463	.05205	.99865	.05212	59
60	0.01745	0.99985	01746	0.03490	0.99939	.03492	0.05324	0.99863	.05241	60

TABLE OF NATURAL SINES, COSINES AND TANGENTS

′	3° Sin	Cos	Tan	4° Sin	Cos	Tan	5° Sin	Cos	Tan	′
0	0.05234	0.99863	0.05241	0.06976	0.99756	0.06993	0.08716	0.99620	0.08749	0
1	.05263	.99861	.05270	.07005	.99754	.07022	.08745	.99617	.08778	1
2	.05292	.99860	.05299	.07034	.99752	.07051	.08774	.99614	.08807	2
3	.05321	.99858	.05328	.07063	.99750	.07080	.08803	.99612	.08837	3
4	.05350	.99857	.05357	.07092	.99748	.07110	.08832	.99609	.08866	4
5	.05379	.99855	.05387	.07121	.99746	.07139	.08861	.99607	.08895	5
6	.05408	.99854	0.05416	.07150	.99744	0.07168	.08889	.99604	0.08925	6
7	.05437	.99852	.05445	.07179	.99742	.07197	.08918	.99602	.08954	7
8	.05466	.99851	.05474	.07208	.99740	.07227	.08947	.99599	.08983	8
9	.05495	.99849	.05503	.07237	.99738	.07256	.08976	.99596	.09013	9
10	.05524	.99847	.05533	.07266	.99736	.07285	.09005	.99594	.09042	10
11	0.05553	0.99846	0.05562	0.07295	0.99734	0.07314	0.09034	0.99591	0.09071	11
12	.05582	.99844	.05591	.07324	.99731	.07344	.09063	.99588	.09101	12
13	.05611	.99843	.05620	.07353	.99729	.07373	.09092	.99586	.09130	13
14	.05640	.99841	.05649	.07382	.99727	.07402	.09121	.99583	.09159	14
15	.05669	.99839	.05678	.07411	.99725	.07431	.09150	.99581	.09189	15
16	.05698	.99838	0.05708	.07440	.99723	0.07461	.09179	.99578	0.09218	16
17	.05727	.99836	.05737	.07469	.99721	.07490	.09208	.99575	.09247	17
18	.05756	.99834	.05766	.07498	.99719	.07519	.09237	.99573	.09277	18
19	.05785	.99833	.05795	.07527	.99716	.07548	.09266	.99570	.09306	19
20	.05815	.99831	.05824	.07556	.99714	.07578	.09295	.99567	.09335	20
21	0.05844	0.99829	0.05854	0.07585	0.99712	0.07607	0.09324	0.99564	0.09365	21
22	.05873	.99827	.05883	.07614	.99710	.07636	.09353	.99562	.09394	22
23	.05902	.99826	.05912	.07643	.99708	.07665	.09382	.99559	.09423	23
24	.05931	.99824	.05941	.07672	.99705	.07695	.09411	.99556	.09453	24
25	.05960	.99822	.05970	.07701	.99703	.07724	.09440	.99554	.09482	25
26	.05989	.99821	0.05999	.07730	.99701	0.07753	.09469	.99551	0.09511	26
27	.06018	.99819	.06029	.07759	.99699	.07782	.09498	.99548	.09541	27
28	.06047	.99817	.06058	.07788	.99696	.07812	.09527	.99545	.09570	28
29	.06076	.99816	.06087	.07817	.99694	.07841	.09556	.99542	.09600	29
30	.06105	.99814	.06116	.07846	.99692	.07870	.09585	.99540	.09629	30
31	0.06134	0.99812	0.06145	0.07875	0.99689	0.07899	0.09614	0.99537	0.09658	31
32	.06163	.99810	.06175	.07904	.99687	.07929	.09643	.99534	.09688	32
33	.06192	.99808	.06204	.07933	.99685	.07958	.09671	.99531	.09717	33
34	.06221	.99806	.06233	.07962	.99683	.07987	.09700	.99528	.09746	34
35	.06250	.99805	.06262	.07991	.99680	.08017	.09729	.99526	.09776	35
36	.06279	.99803	0.06291	.08020	.99678	0.08046	.09758	.99523	0.09805	36
37	.06308	.99801	.06321	.08049	.99676	.08075	.09787	.99520	.09834	37
38	.06337	.99799	.06350	.08078	.99673	.08104	.09816	.99517	.09864	38
39	.06366	.99797	.06379	.08107	.99671	.08134	.09845	.99514	.09893	39
40	.06395	.99795	.06408	.08136	.99669	.08163	.09874	.99511	.09923	40
41	0.06424	0.99793	0.06438	0.08165	0.99666	0.08192	0.09903	0.99508	0.09952	41
42	.06453	.99792	.06467	.08194	.99664	.08222	.09932	.99506	.09981	42
43	.06482	.99790	.06496	.08223	.99661	.08251	.09961	.99503	.10011	43
44	.06511	.99788	.06525	.08252	.99659	.08280	.09990	.99500	.10040	44
45	.06540	.99786	.06554	.08281	.99657	.08309	.10019	.99497	.10069	45
46	.06569	.99784	0.06584	.08310	.99654	0.08339	.10048	.99494	0.10099	46
47	.06598	.99782	.06613	.08339	.99652	.08368	.10077	.99491	.10128	47
48	.06627	.99780	.06642	.08368	.99649	.08397	.10106	.99488	.10158	48
49	.06656	.99778	.06671	.08397	.99647	.08427	.10135	.99485	.10187	49
50	.06685	.99776	.06700	.08426	.99644	.08456	.10164	.99482	.10216	50
51	0.06715	0.99774	0.06730	0.08455	0.99642	0.08485	0.10192	0.99479	0.10246	51
52	.06744	.99772	.06759	.08484	.99640	.08514	.10221	.99476	.10275	52
53	.06773	.99770	.06788	.08513	.99637	.08544	.10250	.99473	.10305	53
54	.06802	.99768	.06817	.08542	.99635	.08573	.10279	.99470	.10334	54
55	.06831	.99766	.06847	.08571	.99632	.08602	.10308	.99467	.10363	55
56	.06860	.99765	0.06876	.08600	.99630	0.08632	.10337	.99464	0.10393	56
57	.06889	.99763	.06905	.08629	.99627	.08661	.10366	.99461	.10422	57
58	.06918	.99760	.06934	.08658	.99625	.08690	.10395	.99458	.10452	58
59	.06947	.99758	.06963	.08687	.99622	.08720	.10424	.99455	.10481	59
60	0.06976	0.99756	.06993	0.08716	0.99620	.08749	0.10453	0.99452	.10510	60

TABLE OF NATURAL SINES, COSINES AND TANGENTS

′	6° Sin	Cos	Tan	7° Sin	Cos	Tan	8° Sin	Cos	Tan	′
0	0.10453	0.99452	0.10510	0.12187	0.99255	0.12278	0.13917	0.99027	0.14054	0
1	.10482	.99449	.10540	.12216	.99251	.12308	.13946	.99023	.14084	1
2	.10511	.99446	.10569	.12245	.99248	.12338	.13975	.99019	.14113	2
3	.10540	.99443	.10599	.12274	.99244	.12367	.14004	.99015	.14143	3
4	.10569	.99440	.10628	.12302	.99240	.12397	.14033	.99011	.14173	4
5	.10598	.99437	.10658	.12331	.99237	.12426	.14061	.99007	.14202	5
6	.10626	.99434	0.10687	.12360	.99233	0.12456	.14090	.99002	0.14232	6
7	.10655	.99431	.10716	.12389	.99230	.12485	.14119	.98998	.14262	7
8	.10684	.99428	.10746	.12418	.99226	.12515	.14148	.98994	.14291	8
9	.10713	.99425	.10775	.12447	.99222	.12544	.14177	.98990	.14321	9
10	.10742	.99421	.10805	.12476	.99219	.12574	.14205	.98986	.14351	10
11	0.10771	0.99418	0.10834	0.12505	0.99215	0.12603	0.14234	0.98982	0.14381	11
12	.10800	.99415	.10863	.12533	.99212	.12633	.14263	.98978	.14410	12
13	.10829	.99412	.10893	.12562	.99208	.12662	.14292	.98974	.14440	13
14	.10858	.99409	.10922	.12591	.99204	.12692	.14321	.98969	.14470	14
15	.10887	.99406	.10952	.12620	.99201	.12722	.14349	.98965	.14499	15
16	.10916	.99403	0.10981	.12649	99197	0.12751	.14378	.98961	0.14529	16
17	.10945	.99399	.11011	.12678	.99193	.12781	.14407	.98957	.14559	17
18	.10973	.99396	.11040	.12707	.99189	.12810	.14436	.98953	.14588	18
19	.11002	.99393	.11070	.12735	.99186	.12840	.14464	.98948	.14618	19
20	.11031	.99390	.11099	.12764	.99182	.12869	.14493	.98944	.14648	20
21	0.11060	0.99387	0.11128	0.12793	0.99178	0.12899	0.14522	0.98940	0.14678	21
22	.11089	.99383	.11158	.12822	.99175	.12929	.14551	.98936	.14707	22
23	.11118	.99380	.11187	.12851	.99171	.12958	.14580	.98932	.14737	23
24	.11147	.99377	.11217	.12880	.99167	.12988	.14608	.98927	.14767	24
25	.11176	.99374	.11246	.12908	.99163	.13017	.14637	.98923	.14796	25
26	.11205	.99370	0.11276	.12937	.99160	0.13047	.14666	.98919	0.14826	26
27	.11234	.99367	.11305	.12966	.99156	.13076	.14695	.98915	.14856	27
28	.11263	.99364	.11335	.12995	.99152	.13106	.14723	.98910	.14886	28
29	.11291	.99361	.11364	.13024	.99148	.13136	.14752	.98906	.14915	29
30	.11320	.99357	.11394	.13053	.99145	.13165	.14781	.98902	.14945	30
31	0.11349	0.99354	0.11423	0.13082	0.99141	0.13195	0.14810	0.98897	0.14975	31
32	.11378	.99351	.11453	.13110	.99137	.13224	.14839	.98893	.15005	32
33	.11407	.99347	.11482	.13139	.99133	.13254	.14867	.98889	.15034	33
34	.11436	.99344	.11511	.13168	.99129	.13284	.14896	.98884	.15064	34
35	.11465	.99341	.11541	.13197	.99125	.13313	.14925	.98880	.15094	35
36	.11494	.99337	0.11570	.13226	.99122	0.13343	.14954	.98876	0.15124	36
37	.11523	.99334	.11600	.13255	.99118	.13372	.14982	.98871	.15153	37
38	.11552	.99331	.11629	.13283	.99114	.13402	.15011	.98867	.15183	38
39	.11580	.99327	.11659	.13312	.99110	.13432	.15040	.98863	.15213	39
40	.11609	.99324	.11688	.13341	.99106	.13461	.15069	.98858	.15243	40
41	0.11638	0.99321	0.11718	0.13370	0.99102	0.13491	0.15097	0.98854	0.15272	41
42	.11667	.99317	.11747	.13399	.99098	.13521	.15126	.98849	.15302	42
43	.11696	.99314	.11777	.13427	.99094	.13550	.15155	.98845	.15332	43
44	.11725	.99310	.11806	.13456	.99091	.13580	.15184	.98841	.15361	44
45	.11754	.99307	.11836	.13485	.99087	.13609	.15212	.98836	.15391	45
46	.11783	.99303	0.11865	.13514	.99083	0.13639	.15241	.98832	0.15421	46
47	.11812	.99300	.11895	.13543	.99079	.13669	.15270	.98827	.15451	47
48	.11840	.99297	.11924	.13572	.99075	.13698	.15299	.98823	.15481	48
49	.11869	.99293	.11954	.13600	.99071	.13728	.15327	.98818	.15511	49
50	.11898	.99290	.11983	.13629	.99067	.13756	.15356	.98814	.15540	50
51	0.11927	0.99286	0.12013	0.13658	0.99063	0.13787	0.15385	0.98809	0.15570	51
52	.11956	.99283	.12042	.13687	.99059	.13817	.15414	.98805	.15600	52
53	.11985	.99279	.12072	.13716	.99055	.13847	.15442	.98801	.15630	53
54	.12014	.99276	.12101	.13745	.99051	.13876	.15471	.98796	.15660	54
55	.12043	.99272	.12131	.13773	.99047	.13906	.15500	.98792	.15689	55
56	.12071	.99269	0.12160	.13802	.99043	0.13935	.15529	.98787	0.15719	56
57	.12100	.99265	.12190	.13831	.99039	.13965	.15557	.98782	.15749	57
58	.12129	.99262	.12219	.13860	.99035	.13995	.15586	.98778	.15779	58
59	.12158	.99258	.12249	.13889	.99031	.14024	.15615	.98773	.15809	59
60	0.12187	0.99255	.12278	0.13917	0.99027	.14054	0.15643	0.98769	.15838	60

TABLE OF NATURAL SINES, COSINES AND TANGENTS

,	9° Sin	9° Cos	9° Tan	10° Sin	10° Cos	10° Tan	11° Sin	11° Cos	11° Tan	,
0	0.15643	0.98769	0.15838	0.17365	0.98481	0.17633	0.19081	0.98163	0.19438	0
1	.15672	.98764	.15868	.17394	.98476	.17663	.19110	.98157	.19468	1
2	.15701	.98760	.15898	.17422	.98471	.17693	.19138	.98152	.19498	2
3	.15730	.98755	.15928	.17451	.98466	.17723	.19167	.98146	.19529	3
4	.15758	.89751	.15958	.17479	.98461	.17753	.19195	.98141	.19559	4
5	.15787	.98746	.15988	.17508	.98455	.17783	.19224	.98135	.19589	5
6	.15816	.98741	0.16017	.17537	.98450	0.17813	.19252	.98129	0.19619	6
7	.15845	.98737	.16047	.17565	.98445	.17843	.19281	.98124	.19649	7
8	.15873	.98732	.16077	.17594	.98440	.17873	.19309	.98118	.19680	8
9	.15902	.98728	.16107	.17623	.98435	.17903	.19338	.98112	.19710	9
10	.15931	.98723	.16137	.17651	.98430	.17933	.19366	.98107	.19740	10
11	0.15959	0.98718	0.16167	0.17680	0.98425	0.17963	0.19395	0.98101	0.19770	11
12	.15988	.98714	.16196	.17709	.98420	.17993	.19423	.98096	.19801	12
13	.16017	.98709	.16226	.17737	.98414	.18023	.19452	.98090	.19831	13
14	.16046	.98704	.16256	.17766	.98409	.18053	.19481	.98084	.19861	14
15	.16074	.98700	.16286	.17794	.98404	.18083	.19509	.98079	.19891	15
16	.16103	.98695	0.16316	.17823	.98400	0.18113	.19538	.98073	0.19921	16
17	.16132	.98690	.16346	.17852	.98394	.18143	.19566	.98067	.19952	17
18	.16160	.98686	.16376	.17880	.98389	.18173	.19595	.98062	.19982	18
19	.16189	.98681	.16405	.17909	.98383	.18203	.19623	.98056	.20012	19
20	.16218	.98676	.16435	.17938	.98378	.18233	.19652	.98050	.20042	20
21	0.16247	0.98671	0.16465	0.17966	0.98373	0.18263	0.19680	0.98044	0.20073	21
22	.16275	.98667	.16495	.17995	.98368	.18293	.19709	.98039	.20103	22
23	.16304	.98662	.16525	.18023	.98362	.18323	.19737	.98033	.20133	23
24	.16333	.98657	.16555	.18052	.98357	.18353	.19766	.98027	.20164	24
25	.16361	.98653	.16585	.18081	.98352	.18384	.19794	.98021	.20194	25
26	.16390	.98648	0.16615	.18109	.98347	0.18414	.19823	.98016	0.20224	26
27	.16419	.98643	.16645	.18138	.98341	.18444	.19851	.98010	.20254	27
28	.16447	.98639	.16674	.18166	.98336	.18474	.19880	.98004	.20285	28
29	.16476	.98634	.16704	.18195	.98331	.18504	.19908	.97998	.20315	29
30	.16505	.98629	.16734	.18224	.98326	.18534	.19937	.97993	.20345	30
31	0.16533	0.98624	0.16764	0.18252	0.98320	0.18564	0.19965	0.97987	0.20376	31
32	.16562	.98619	.16794	.18281	.98315	.18594	.19994	.97981	.20406	32
33	.16591	.98614	.16824	.18309	.98310	.18624	.20022	.97975	.20436	33
34	.16620	.98609	.16854	.18338	.98304	.18654	.20051	.97969	.20466	34
35	.16648	.98605	.16884	.18367	.98299	.18684	.20079	.97963	.20497	35
36	.16677	.98600	0.16914	.18395	.98294	0.18714	.20108	.97958	0.20527	36
37	.16706	.98595	.16944	.18424	.98288	.18745	.20136	.97952	.20557	37
38	.16734	.98590	.16974	.18452	.98283	.18775	.20165	.97946	.20588	38
39	.16763	.98585	.17004	.18481	.98277	.18805	.20193	.97940	.20618	39
40	.16792	.98580	.17033	.18510	.98272	.18835	.20222	.97934	.20648	40
41	0.16820	0.98575	0.17063	0.18538	0.98267	0.18865	0.20250	0.97928	0.20679	41
42	.16849	.98570	.17093	.18567	.98261	.18895	.20279	.97922	.20709	42
43	.16878	.98565	.17123	.18595	.98256	.18925	.20307	.97916	.20739	43
44	.16906	.98561	.17153	.18624	.98251	.18955	.20336	.97911	.20770	44
45	.16935	.98556	.17183	.18652	.98245	.18986	.20364	.97905	.20800	45
46	.16964	.98551	0.17213	.18681	.98240	0.19016	.20393	.97899	0.20830	46
47	.16992	.98546	.17243	.18710	.98234	.19046	.20421	.97893	.20861	47
48	.17021	.98541	.17273	.18738	.98229	.19076	.20450	.97887	.20891	48
49	.17050	.98536	.17303	.18767	.98223	.19106	.20478	.97881	.20921	49
50	.17078	.98531	.17333	.18795	.98218	.19136	.20507	.97875	.20952	50
51	0.17107	.98526	0.17363	0.18824	0.98212	0.19166	0.20535	0.97869	0.20982	51
52	.17136	.98521	.17393	.18852	.98207	.19197	.20564	.97863	.21013	52
53	.17164	.98516	.17423	.18881	.98201	.19227	.20592	.97857	.21043	53
54	.17193	.98511	.17453	.18910	.98196	.19257	.20620	.97851	.21073	54
55	.17222	.98506	.17483	.18938	.98190	.19287	.20649	.97845	.21104	55
56	.17250	.98501	0.17513	.18967	.98185	0.19317	.20677	.97839	0.21134	56
57	.17279	.98496	.17543	.18995	.98179	.19347	.20706	.97833	.21164	57
58	.17308	.98491	.17573	.19024	.98174	.19378	.20734	.97827	.21195	58
59	.17336	.98486	.17603	.19052	.98168	.19408	.20763	.97821	.21225	59
60	0.17365	0.98481	.17633	0.19081	0.98163	.19438	0.20791	0.97815	.21256	60

TABLE OF NATURAL SINES, COSINES AND TANGENTS

′	12° Sin	Cos	Tan	13° Sin	Cos	Tan	14° Sin	Cos	Tan	′
0	0.20791	0.97815	0.21256	0.22495	0.97437	0.23087	0.24192	0.97030	0.24933	0
1	.20820	.97809	.21286	.22523	.97431	.23117	.24220	.97023	.24964	1
2	.20848	.97803	.21316	.22552	.97424	.23148	.24249	.97016	.24995	2
3	.20877	.97797	.21347	.22580	.97417	.23179	.24277	.97008	.25026	3
4	.20905	.97791	.21377	.22609	.97411	.23209	.24305	.97001	.25056	4
5	.00933	.97784	.21408	.22637	.97404	.23240	.24333	.96994	.25087	5
6	.20962	.97778	0.21438	.22665	.97398	0.23271	.24362	.96987	0.25118	6
7	.20990	.97772	.21469	.22694	.97391	.23301	.24390	.96980	.25149	7
8	.21019	.97766	.21499	.22722	.97384	.23332	.24418	.96973	.25180	8
9	.21047	.97760	.21529	.22750	.97378	.23363	.24446	.96966	.25211	9
10	.21076	.97754	.21560	.22778	.97371	.23393	.24474	.96959	.25242	10
11	0.21104	0.97748	0.21590	0.22807	0.97365	0.23424	0.24503	0.96952	0.25273	11
12	.21133	.97742	.21621	.22835	.97358	.23455	.24531	.96945	.25304	12
13	.21161	.97735	.21651	.22863	.97351	.23485	.24559	.96937	.25335	13
14	.21189	.97729	.21682	.22892	.97345	.23516	.24587	.96930	.25366	14
15	.21218	.97723	.21712	.22920	.97338	.23547	.24615	.96923	.25397	15
16	.21246	.97717	0.21743	.22948	.97331	0.23577	.24644	.96916	0.25428	16
17	.21275	.97711	.21773	.22977	.97325	.23608	.24672	.96909	.25459	17
18	.21303	.97705	.21804	.23005	.97318	.23639	.24700	.96902	.25490	18
19	.21332	.97698	.21834	.23033	.97311	.23670	.24728	.96894	.25521	19
20	.21360	.97692	.21864	.23062	.97305	.23700	.24756	.96887	.25552	20
21	0.21388	0.97686	0.21895	0.23090	0.97298	0.23731	0.24785	0.96880	0.25583	21
22	.21417	.97680	.21925	.23118	.97291	.23762	.24813	.96873	.25614	22
23	.21445	.97674	.21956	.23147	.97284	.23793	.24841	.96866	.25645	23
24	.21474	.97667	.21986	.23175	.97278	.23823	.24869	.96858	.25676	24
25	.21502	.97661	.22017	.23203	.97271	.23854	.24897	.96851	.25707	25
26	.21530	.97655	0.22047	.23231	.97264	0.23885	.24925	.96844	0.25738	26
27	.21559	.97649	.22078	.23260	.97257	.23916	.24954	.96837	.25769	27
28	.21587	.97642	.22108	.23288	.97251	.23946	.24982	.96829	.25800	28
29	.21616	.97636	.22139	.23316	.97244	.23977	.25010	.96822	.25831	29
30	.21644	.97630	.22169	.23345	.97237	.24008	.25038	.96815	.25862	30
31	0.21672	0.97623	0.22200	0.23373	0.97230	0.24039	0.25066	0.96808	0.25893	31
32	.21701	.97617	.22230	.23401	.97223	.24069	.25094	.96800	.25924	32
33	.21729	.97611	.22261	.23429	.97217	.24100	.25123	.96793	.25955	33
34	.21758	.97604	.22292	.23458	.97210	.24131	.25151	.96786	.25986	34
35	.21786	.97598	.22322	.23486	.97203	.24162	.25179	.96778	.26017	35
36	.21814	.97592	0.22353	.23514	.97196	0.24193	.25207	.96771	0.26048	36
37	.21843	.97585	.22383	.23543	.97189	.24223	.25235	.96764	.26079	37
38	.21871	.97579	.22414	.23571	.97182	.24254	.25263	.96756	.26110	38
39	.21900	.97573	.22444	.23599	.97176	.24285	.25291	.96749	.26141	39
40	.21928	.97566	.22475	.23627	.97169	.24316	.25320	.96742	.26172	40
41	0.21956	0.97560	0.22505	0.23656	0.97162	0.24347	0.25348	0.96734	0.26203	41
42	.21985	.97554	.22536	.23684	.97155	.24377	.25376	.96727	.26235	42
43	.22013	.97547	.22567	.23712	.07148	.24408	.25404	.96720	.26266	43
44	.22041	.97541	.22597	.23740	.97141	.24439	.25432	.96712	.26297	44
45	.22070	.97534	.22628	.23769	.97134	.24470	.25460	.96705	.26328	45
46	.22098	.97528	0.22658	.23797	.97127	0.24501	.25488	.96697	0.26359	46
47	.22127	.97521	.22689	.23825	.97120	.24532	.25517	.96690	.26390	47
48	.22155	.97515	.22719	.23853	.97113	.24562	.25545	.96682	.26421	48
49	.22183	.97509	.22750	.23882	.97107	.24593	.25573	.96675	.26452	49
50	.22212	.97502	.22781	.23910	.97100	.24624	.25601	.96668	.26483	50
51	0.22240	0.97496	0.22811	0.23938	0.97093	0.24655	0.25629	0.96660	0.26515	51
52	.22268	.97489	.22842	.23966	.97086	.24686	.25657	.96653	.26546	52
53	.22297	.97483	.22872	.23995	.97079	.24717	.25685	.96645	.26577	53
54	.22325	.97476	.22903	.24023	.97072	.24748	.25713	.96638	.26608	54
55	.22353	.97470	.22934	.24051	.97065	.24778	.25741	.96630	.26639	55
56	.22382	.97463	0.22964	.24079	.97058	0.24809	.25770	.96623	0.26670	56
57	.22410	.97457	.22995	.24108	.97051	.24840	.25798	.96615	.26701	57
58	.22438	.97450	.23026	.24136	.97044	.24871	.25826	.96608	.26733	58
59	.22467	.97444	.23056	.24164	.97037	.24902	.25854	.96600	.26764	59
60	0.22495	0.97437	.23087	0.24192	0.97030	.24933	0.25882	0.96593	.26795	60

TABLE OF NATURAL SINES, COSINES AND TANGENTS

,	15° Sin	Cos	Tan	16° Sin	Cos	Tan	17° Sin	Cos	Tan	,
0	0.25882	0.96593	0.26795	0.27564	0.96126	0.28675	0.29237	0.95631	0.30573	0
1	.25910	.96585	.26826	.27592	.96118	.28706	.29265	.95622	.30605	1
2	.25938	.96578	.26857	.27620	.96110	.28738	.29293	.95613	.30637	2
3	.25966	.96570	.26888	.27648	.96102	.38769	.29321	.95605	.30669	3
4	.25994	.96562	.26920	.27676	.06094	.28801	.29348	.95596	.30700	4
5	.26022	.96555	.26951	.27704	.96086	.28832	.29376	.95588	.30732	5
6	.26051	.96547	0.26982	.27732	.96078	0.28864	.29404	.95579	0.30764	6
7	.26079	.96540	.27013	.27759	.96070	.28895	.29432	.95571	.30796	7
8	.26107	.96532	.27044	.27787	.96062	.28927	.29460	.95562	.30828	8
9	.26135	.96525	.27076	.27815	.96054	.28958	.29487	.95554	.30860	9
10	.26163	.96517	.27107	.27843	.96046	.28990	.29515	.95545	.30891	10
11	0.26191	0.96509	0.27138	0.27871	0.96038	0.29021	0.29543	0.95536	0.30923	11
12	.26219	.96502	.27169	.27899	.96029	.29053	.29571	.95528	.30955	12
13	.26247	.96494	.27201	.27927	.96021	.29084	.29599	.95519	.30987	13
14	.26275	.96486	.27232	.27955	.96013	.29116	.29626	.95511	.31019	14
15	.26303	.96479	.27263	.27983	.96005	.29147	.29654	.95502	.31051	15
16	.26331	.96471	0.27294	.28011	.95997	0.29179	.29682	.95493	0.31083	16
17	.26359	.96463	.27326	.28039	.95989	.29210	.29710	.95485	.31115	17
18	.26387	.96456	.27357	.28067	.95981	.29242	.29738	.95476	.31147	18
19	.26415	.96448	.27388	.28095	.95972	.29274	.29765	.95467	.31178	19
20	.26443	.96440	.27419	.28123	.95964	.29305	.29793	.95459	.31210	20
21	0.26472	0.96433	0.27451	0.28150	0.95956	0.29337	0.29821	0.95450	0.31242	21
22	.26500	.96425	.27482	.28178	.95948	.29368	.29849	.95441	.31274	22
23	.26528	.96417	.27513	.28206	.95940	.29400	.29876	.95433	.31306	23
24	.26556	.96410	.27545	.28234	.95931	.29432	.29904	.95424	.31338	24
25	.26584	.96402	.27576	.28262	.95923	.29463	.29932	.95415	.31370	25
26	.26612	.96394	0.27607	.28290	.95915	0.29495	.29960	.95407	0.31402	26
27	.26640	.96386	.27639	.28318	.95907	.29526	.29987	.95398	.31434	27
28	.26668	.96379	.27670	.28346	.95899	.29558	.30015	.95389	.31466	28
29	.26696	.96371	.27701	.28374	.95890	.29590	.30043	.95380	.31498	29
30	.26724	.96363	.27732	.28402	.95882	.29621	.30071	.95372	.31530	30
31	0.26752	0.96355	0.27764	0.28429	0.95874	0.29653	0.30098	0.95363	0.31562	31
32	.26780	.96348	.27795	.28457	.95865	.29685	.30126	.95354	.31594	32
33	.26808	.96340	.27826	.28485	.95857	.29716	.30154	.95345	.31626	33
34	.26836	.96332	.27858	.28513	.95849	.29748	.30182	.95337	.31658	34
35	.26864	.96324	.27889	.28541	.95841	.29780	.30209	.95328	.31690	35
36	.26892	.96316	0.27921	.28569	.95832	0.29811	.30237	.95319	0.31722	36
37	.26920	.96308	.27952	.28597	.95824	.29843	.30265	.95310	.31754	37
38	.26948	.96301	.27983	.28625	.95816	.29875	.30292	.95302	.31786	38
39	.26976	.96293	.28015	.28652	.95807	.29906	.30320	.95293	.31818	39
40	.27004	.96285	.28046	.28680	.95799	.29938	.30348	.95284	.31850	40
41	0.27032	0.96277	0.28077	0.28708	0.95791	0.29970	0.30376	0.95275	0.31882	41
42	.27060	.96269	.28109	.28736	.95782	.30001	.30403	.95266	.31914	42
43	.27088	.96261	.28140	.28764	.95774	.30033	.30431	.95257	.31946	43
44	.27116	.96253	.28172	.28792	.95766	.30065	.30459	.95248	.31978	44
45	.27144	.96246	.28203	.28820	.95757	.30097	.30486	.95240	.32010	45
46	.27172	.96238	0.28234	.28848	.95749	0.30128	.30514	.95231	0.32042	46
47	.27200	.96230	.28266	.28875	.95740	.30160	.30542	.95222	.32074	47
48	.27228	.96222	.28297	.28903	.95732	.30192	.30570	.95213	.32106	48
49	.27256	.96214	.28329	.28931	.95724	.30224	.30597	.95204	.32139	49
50	.27284	.96206	.28360	.28959	.95715	.30255	.30625	.95195	.32171	50
51	0.27312	0.96198	0.28391	0.28987	0.95707	0.30287	0.30653	0.95186	0.32203	51
52	.27340	.96190	.28423	.29015	.95698	.30319	.30680	.95177	.32235	52
53	.27368	.96182	.28454	.29042	.95690	.30351	.30708	.95168	.32267	53
54	.27396	.96174	.28486	.29070	.95681	.30382	.30736	.95159	.32299	54
55	.27424	.96166	.28517	.29098	.95673	.30414	.30763	.95151	.32331	55
56	.27452	.96158	0.28549	.29126	.95664	0.30446	.30791	.95142	0.32363	56
57	.27480	.96150	.28580	.29154	.95656	.30478	.30819	.95133	.32396	57
58	.27508	.96142	.28612	.29182	.95648	.30509	.30846	.95124	.32428	58
59	.27536	.96134	.28643	.29209	.95639	.30541	.30874	.95115	.32460	59
60	0.27564	0.96126	.28675	0.29237	0.95631	.30573	0.30902	0.95106	.32492	60

TABLE OF NATURAL SINES, COSINES AND TANGENTS

′	18° Sin	Cos	Tan	19° Sin	Cos	Tan	20° Sin	Cos	Tan	′
0	0.30902	0.95106	0.32492	0.32557	0.94552	0.34433	0.34202	0.93969	0.36397	0
1	.30929	.95097	.32524	.32584	.94542	.34465	.34229	.93959	.36430	1
2	.30957	.95088	.32556	.32612	.94533	.34498	.34257	.93949	.36463	2
3	.30985	.95079	.32588	.32639	.94523	.34530	.34284	.93939	.36496	3
4	.31012	.95070	.32621	.32667	.94514	.34563	.34311	.93929	.36529	4
5	.31040	.95061	.32653	.32694	.94504	.34596	.34339	.93919	.36562	5
6	.31068	.95052	0.32685	.32722	.94495	0.34628	.34366	.93909	0.36595	6
7	.31095	.95043	.32717	.32749	.94485	.34661	.34393	.93899	.36628	7
8	.31123	.95034	.32749	.32777	.94476	.34693	.34421	.93889	.36661	8
9	.31151	.95024	.32782	.32804	.94467	.34726	.34448	.93879	.36694	9
10	.31178	.95015	.32814	.32832	.94457	.34758	.34475	.93869	.36727	10
11	0.31206	0.95006	0.32846	0.32859	0.94447	0.34791	0.34503	0.93859	0.36760	11
12	.31234	.94997	.32878	.32887	.94438	.34824	.34530	.93849	.36793	12
13	.31261	.94988	.32911	.32914	.94428	.34856	.34557	.93839	.36826	13
14	.31289	.94979	.32943	.32942	.94419	.34889	.34584	.93829	.36859	14
15	.31316	.94970	.32975	.32969	.94409	.34922	.34612	.93819	.36892	15
16	.31344	.94961	0.33007	.32997	.94399	.34954	.34639	.93809	.36925	16
17	.31372	.94952	.33040	.33024	.94390	.34987	.34666	.93799	.36958	17
18	.31399	.94943	.33072	.33051	.94380	.35020	.34694	.93789	.36991	18
19	.31427	.94933	.33104	.33079	.94371	.35052	.34721	.93779	.37024	19
20	.31455	.94924	.33136	.33106	.94361	.35085	.34748	.93769	.37057	20
21	0.31482	0.94915	0.33169	0.33134	0.94351	0.35118	0.34775	0.93759	0.37090	21
22	.31510	.94906	.33201	.33161	.94342	.35150	.34803	.93749	.37123	22
23	.31537	.94897	.33233	.33189	.94332	.35183	.34830	.93738	.37157	23
24	.31565	.94888	.33266	.33216	.94322	.35216	.34857	.93728	.37190	24
25	.31593	.94878	.33298	.33244	.94313	.35248	.34885	.93718	.37223	25
26	.31620	.94869	0.33330	.33271	.94303	0.35281	.34912	.93708	0.37256	26
27	.31648	.94860	.33363	.33298	.94293	.35314	.34939	.93698	.37289	27
28	.31675	.94851	.33395	.33326	.94284	.35346	.34966	.93688	.37322	28
29	.31703	.94842	.33427	.33353	.94274	.35379	.34994	.93677	.37355	29
30	.31731	.94832	.33460	.33381	.94264	.35412	.35021	.93667	.37388	30
31	0.31758	0.94823	0.33492	0.33408	0.94254	0.35445	0.35048	0.93657	0.37422	31
32	.31786	.94814	.33524	.33436	.94245	.35477	.35075	.93647	.37455	32
33	.31813	.94805	.33557	.33463	.94235	.35510	.35103	.93637	.37488	33
34	.31841	.94795	.33589	.33490	.94225	.35543	.35130	.93626	.37521	34
35	.31868	.94786	.33621	.33518	.94216	.35576	.35157	.93616	.37554	35
36	.31896	.94777	0.33654	.33545	.94206	0.35608	.35184	.93606	0.37588	36
37	.31924	.94768	.33686	.33573	.94196	.35641	.35211	.93596	.37621	37
38	.31951	.94758	.33719	.33600	.94186	.35674	.35239	.93586	.37654	38
39	.31979	.94749	.33751	.33627	.94176	.35707	.35266	.93575	.37687	39
40	.32006	.94740	.33783	.33655	.94167	.35740	.35293	.93565	.37720	40
41	0.32034	0.94730	0.33816	0.33682	0.94157	0.35772	0.35320	0.93555	0.37754	41
42	.32061	.94721	.33848	.33710	.94147	.35805	.35348	.93544	.37787	42
43	.32089	.94712	.33881	.33737	.94137	.35838	.35375	.93534	.37820	43
44	.32116	.94702	.33913	.33764	.94127	.35871	.35402	.93524	.37853	44
45	.32144	.94693	.33945	.33792	.94118	.35904	.35429	.93514	.37887	45
46	.32172	.94684	0.33978	.33819	.94108	0.35937	.35456	.93503	0.37920	46
47	.32199	.94674	.34010	.33846	.94098	.35969	.35484	.93493	.37953	47
48	.32227	.94665	.34043	.33874	.94088	.36002	.35511	.93483	.37986	48
49	.32254	.94656	.34075	.33901	.94078	.36035	.35538	.93472	.38020	49
50	.32282	.94646	.34108	.33929	.94068	.36068	.35565	.93462	.38053	50
51	0.32309	0.94637	0.34140	0.33956	0.94059	0.36101	0.35592	0.93452	0.38086	51
52	.32337	.94627	.34173	.33983	.94049	.36134	.35619	.93441	.38120	52
53	.32364	.94618	.34205	.34011	.94039	.36167	.35647	.93431	.38153	53
54	.32392	.94609	.34238	.34038	.94029	.36199	.35674	.93420	.38186	54
55	.32419	.94599	.34270	.34065	.94019	.36232	.35701	.93410	.38220	55
56	.32447	.94590	0.34303	.34093	.94009	0.36265	.35728	.93400	0.38253	56
57	.32474	.94580	.34335	.34120	.93999	.36298	.35755	.93389	.38286	57
58	.32502	.94571	.34368	.34147	.93989	.36331	.35783	.93379	.38320	58
59	.32529	.94561	.34400	.34175	.93979	.36364	.35810	.93369	.38353	59
60	0.32557	0.94552	.34433	0.34202	0.93969	.36397	0.35837	0.93358	.38386	60

TABLE OF NATURAL SINES, COSINES AND TANGENTS

′	21° Sin	Cos	Tan	22° Sin	Cos	Tan	23° Sin	Cos	Tan	′
0	0.35837	0.93358	0.38386	0.37461	0.92718	0.40403	0.39073	0.92051	0.42447	0
1	.35864	.93348	.38420	.37488	.92708	.40436	.39100	.92039	.42482	1
2	.35891	.93337	.38453	.37515	.92697	.40470	.39127	.92028	.42516	2
3	.35918	.93327	.38487	.37542	.92686	.40504	.39153	.92016	.42551	3
4	.35945	.93316	.38520	.37569	.92675	.40538	.39180	.92005	.42585	4
5	.35973	.93306	.38553	.37596	.92664	.40572	.39207	.91994	.42619	5
6	.36000	.93295	0.38587	.37622	.92653	0.40606	.39234	.91982	0.42654	6
7	.36027	.93285	.38620	.37649	.92642	.40640	.39261	.91971	.42688	7
8	.36054	.93274	.38654	.37676	.92631	.40674	.39287	.91959	.42722	8
9	.36081	.93264	.38687	.37703	.92620	.40707	.39314	.91948	.42757	9
10	.36108	.93253	.38721	.37730	.92609	.40741	.39341	.91936	.42791	10
11	0.36135	0.93243	0.38754	0.37757	0.92598	0.40775	0.39368	0.91925	0.42826	11
12	.36163	.93232	.38787	.37784	.92587	.40809	.39394	.91914	.42860	12
13	.36190	.93222	.38821	.37811	.92576	.40843	.39421	.91902	.42894	13
14	.36217	.93211	.38854	.37838	.92565	.40877	.39448	.91891	.42929	14
15	.36244	.93201	.38888	.37865	.92554	.40911	.39474	.91879	.42963	15
16	.36271	.93190	0.38921	.37892	.92543	0.40945	.39501	.91868	0.42998	16
17	.36298	.93180	.38955	.37919	.92532	.40979	.39528	.91856	.43032	17
18	.36325	.93169	.38988	.37946	.92521	.41013	.39555	.91845	.43067	18
19	.36352	.93159	.39022	.37973	.92510	.41047	.39581	.91833	.43101	19
20	.36379	.93148	.39055	.37999	.92499	.41081	.39608	.91822	.43136	20
21	0.36406	0.93137	0.39089	0.38026	0.92487	0.41115	0.39635	0.91810	0.43170	21
22	.36434	.93127	.39122	.38053	.92477	.41149	.39661	.91799	.43205	22
23	.36461	.93116	.39156	.38080	.92466	.41183	.39688	.91787	.43239	23
24	.36488	.93106	.39190	.38107	.92455	.41217	.39715	.91776	.43274	24
25	.36515	.93095	.39223	.38134	.92444	.41251	.39742	.91764	.43308	25
26	.36542	.93084	0.39257	.38161	.92432	0.41285	.39768	.91752	0.43343	26
27	.36569	.93074	.39290	.38188	.92421	.41319	.39795	.91741	.43378	27
28	.36596	.93063	.39324	.38215	.92410	.41353	.39822	.91729	.43412	28
29	.36623	.93052	.39357	.38242	.92399	.41387	.39848	.91718	.43447	29
30	.36650	.93042	.39391	.38268	.92388	.41421	.39875	.91706	.43481	30
31	0.36677	0.93031	0.39425	0.38295	0.92377	0.41455	0.39902	0.91694	0.43516	31
32	.36704	.93020	.39458	.38322	.92366	.41490	.39928	.91683	.43550	32
33	.36731	.93010	.39492	.38349	.92355	.41524	.39955	.91671	.43585	33
34	.36758	.92999	.39526	.38376	.92343	.41558	.39982	.91660	.43620	34
35	.36785	.92988	.39559	.38403	.92332	.41592	.40008	.91648	.43654	35
36	.36813	.92978	0.39593	.38430	.92321	0.41626	.40035	.91636	0.43689	36
37	.36840	.92967	.39626	.38456	.92310	.41660	.40062	.91625	.43724	37
38	.36867	.92956	.39660	.38483	.92299	.41694	.40088	.91613	.43758	38
39	.36894	.92946	.39694	.38510	.92287	.41728	.40115	.91601	.43793	39
40	.36921	.92935	.39727	.38537	.92276	.41763	.40142	.91590	.43828	40
41	0.36948	0.92924	0.39761	0.38564	0.92265	0.41797	0.40168	0.91578	0.43862	41
42	.36975	.92913	.39795	.38591	.92254	.41831	.40195	.91566	.43897	42
43	.37002	.92903	.39829	.38617	.92243	.41865	.40221	.91555	.43932	43
44	.37029	.92892	.39862	.38644	.92231	.41899	.40248	.91543	.43966	44
45	.37056	.92881	.39896	.38671	.92220	.41933	.40275	.91531	.44001	45
46	.37083	.92870	0.39930	.38698	.92209	0.41968	.40301	.91519	0.44036	46
47	.37110	.92859	.39963	.38725	.92198	.42002	.40328	.91508	.44071	47
48	.37137	.92849	.39997	.38752	.92186	.42036	.40355	.91496	.44105	48
49	.37164	.92838	.40031	.38778	.92175	.42070	.40381	.91484	.44140	49
50	.37191	.92827	.40065	.38805	.92164	.42105	.40408	.91473	.44175	50
51	0.37218	0.92816	0.40098	0.38832	0.92153	0.42139	0.40434	0.91461	0.44210	51
52	.37245	.92805	.40132	.38859	.92141	.42173	.40461	.91449	.44244	52
53	.37272	.92795	.40166	.38886	.92130	.42207	.40488	.91437	.44279	53
54	.37299	.92784	.40200	.38912	.92119	.42242	.40514	.91425	.44314	54
55	.37326	.92773	.40234	.38939	.92107	.42276	.40541	.91414	.44349	55
56	.37353	.92762	0.40267	.38966	.92096	0.42310	.40567	.91402	0.44384	56
57	.37380	.92751	.40301	.38993	.92085	.42345	.40594	.91390	.44418	57
58	.37407	.92740	.40335	.39020	.92073	.42379	.40621	.91378	.44453	58
59	.37434	.92729	.40369	.39046	.92062	.42413	.40647	.91366	.44488	59
60	0.37461	0.92718	.40403	0.39073	0.92051	.42447	0.40674	0.91355	.44523	60

TABLE OF NATURAL SINES, COSINES AND TANGENTS

′	24° Sin	Cos	Tan	25° Sin	Cos	Tan	26° Sin	Cos	Tan	′
0	0.40674	0.91355	0.44523	0.42262	0.90631	0.46631	0.43837	0.89880	0.48773	0
1	.40700	.91343	.44558	.42288	.90619	.46666	.43863	.89867	.58809	1
2	.40727	.91331	.44593	.42315	.90606	.46702	.43889	.89854	.48845	2
3	.40753	.91319	.44627	.42341	.90594	.46737	.43916	.89841	.48881	3
4	.40780	.91307	.44662	.42367	.90582	.46773	.43942	.89828	.48917	4
5	.40807	.91295	.44697	.42394	.90569	.46808	.43968	.89816	.48953	5
6	.40833	.91283	0.44732	.42420	.90557	0.46843	.43994	.89803	0.48989	6
7	.40860	.91272	.44767	.42446	.90545	.46879	.44020	.89790	.49026	7
8	.40886	.91260	.44802	.42473	.90532	.46914	.44046	.89777	.49062	8
9	.40913	.91248	.44837	.42499	.90520	.46950	.44072	.89764	.49098	9
10	.40939	.91236	.44872	.42525	.90508	.46985	.44098	.89752	.49134	10
11	0.40966	0.91224	0.44907	0.42552	0.90495	0.47021	0.44125	0.89739	0.49170	11
12	.40992	.91212	.44942	.42578	.90483	.47056	.44151	.89726	.49206	12
13	.41019	.91200	.44977	.42604	.90470	.47092	.44177	.89713	.49242	13
14	.41045	.91188	.45012	.42631	.90458	.47128	.44203	.89700	.49278	14
15	.41072	.91176	.45047	.42657	.90446	.47163	.44229	.89687	.49315	15
16	.41098	.91164	0.45082	.42683	.90433	0.47199	.44255	.89674	0.49351	16
17	.41125	.91152	.45117	.42710	.90421	.47234	.44281	.89662	.49387	17
18	.41151	.91140	.45152	.42736	.90408	.47270	.44307	.89649	.49423	18
19	.41178	.91128	.45187	.42762	.90396	.47305	.44333	.89636	.49459	19
20	.41205	.91116	.45222	.42788	.90383	.47341	.44359	.89623	.49495	20
21	0.41231	0.91104	0.45257	0.42815	0.90371	0.47377	0.44385	0.89610	0.49532	21
22	.41258	.91092	.45292	.42841	.90359	.47412	.44411	.89597	.49568	22
23	.41284	.91080	.45327	.42867	.90346	.47448	.44438	.89584	.49604	23
24	.41310	.91068	.45362	.42894	.90334	.47483	.44464	.89571	.49640	24
25	.41337	.91056	.45397	.42920	.90321	.47519	.44490	.89558	.49677	25
26	.41363	.91044	0.45432	.42946	.90309	0.47555	.44516	.89545	0.49713	26
27	.41390	.91032	.45467	.42972	.90296	.47590	.44542	.89532	.49749	27
28	.41416	.91020	.45502	.42999	.90284	.47626	.44568	.89519	.49786	28
29	.41443	.91008	.45538	.43025	.90271	.47662	.44594	.89506	.49822	29
30	.41469	.90996	.45573	.43051	.90259	.47698	.44620	.89493	.49858	30
31	0.41496	0.90984	0.45608	0.43077	0.90246	0.47733	0.44646	0.89481	0.49894	31
32	.41522	.90972	.45643	.43104	.90234	.47769	.44672	.89468	.49931	32
33	.41549	.90960	.45678	.43130	.90221	.47805	.44698	.89455	.49967	33
34	.51575	.90948	.45713	.43156	.90208	.47840	.44724	.89442	.50004	34
35	.41602	.90936	.45748	.43182	.90196	.47876	.44750	.89428	.50040	35
36	.41628	.90924	0.45784	.43209	.90183	0.47912	.44776	.89415	0.50076	36
37	.41655	.90912	.45819	.43235	.90171	.47948	.44802	.89402	.50113	37
38	.41681	.90899	.45854	.43261	.90158	.47984	.44828	.89389	.50149	38
39	.41707	.90887	.45889	.43287	.90146	.48019	.44854	.89376	.50185	39
40	.41734	.90875	.45924	.43314	.90133	.48055	.44880	.89363	.50222	40
41	0.41760	0.90863	0.45960	0.43340	0.90120	0.48091	0.44906	0.89350	0.50258	41
42	.41787	.90851	.45995	.43366	.90108	.48127	.44932	.89337	.50295	42
43	.41813	.90839	.46030	.43392	.90095	.48163	.44958	.89324	.50331	43
44	.41840	.90827	.46065	.43418	.90083	.48198	.44984	.89311	.50368	44
45	.41866	.90814	.46101	.43445	.90070	.48234	.45010	.89298	.50404	45
46	.41892	.90802	0.46136	.43471	.90057	0.48270	.45036	.89285	0.50441	46
47	.41919	.90790	.46171	.43497	.90045	.48306	.45062	.89272	.50477	47
48	.41945	.90778	.46206	.43523	.90032	.48342	.45088	.89259	.50514	48
49	.41972	.90766	.46242	.43549	.90019	.48378	.45114	.89246	.50550	49
50	.41998	.90753	.46277	.43576	.90007	.48414	.45140	.89232	.50587	50
51	0.42024	0.90741	0.46312	0.43602	0.89994	0.48450	0.45166	0.89219	0.50623	51
52	.42051	.90729	.46348	.43628	.89981	.48486	.45192	.89206	.50660	52
53	.42077	.90717	.46383	.43654	.89969	.48521	.45218	.89193	.50696	53
54	.42104	.90704	.46418	.43680	.89956	.48557	.45244	.89180	.50733	54
55	.42130	.90692	.46454	.43706	.89943	.48593	.45269	.89167	.50769	55
56	.42156	.90680	0.46489	.43733	.89930	0.48629	.45295	.89153	0.50806	56
57	.42183	.90668	.46524	.43759	.89918	.48665	.45321	.89140	.50843	57
58	.42209	.90655	.46560	.43785	.89905	.48701	.45347	.89127	.50879	58
59	.42236	.90643	.46595	.43811	.89892	.48737	.45373	.89114	.50916	59
60	0.42262	0.90631	.46631	0.43837	0.89879	.48773	0.45399	0.89101	.50953	60

TABLE OF NATURAL SINES, COSINES AND TANGENTS

′	27° Sin	Cos	Tan	28° Sin	Cos	Tan	29° Sin	Cos	Tan	′
0	0.45399	0.89101	0.50953	0.46947	0.88295	0.53171	0.48481	0.87462	0.55431	0
1	.45425	.89087	.50989	.46973	.88281	.53208	.48506	.87448	.55469	1
2	.45451	.89074	.51026	.46999	.88267	.53246	.48532	.87434	.55507	2
3	.45477	.89061	.51063	.47024	.88254	.53283	.48557	.87420	.55545	3
4	.45503	.89048	.51099	.47050	.88240	.53320	.48583	.87406	.55583	4
5	.45529	.89035	.51136	.47076	.88226	.53358	.48608	.87391	.55621	5
6	.45555	.89021	0.51173	.47101	.88213	0.53395	.48634	.87377	0.55659	6
7	.45580	.89008	.51209	.47127	.88199	.53432	.48659	.87363	.55697	7
8	.45606	.88995	.51246	.47153	.88185	.53470	.48684	.87349	.55736	8
9	.45632	.88982	.51283	.47178	.88172	.53507	.48710	.87335	.55774	9
10	.45658	.88968	.51319	.47204	.88158	.53545	.48735	.87321	.55812	10
11	0.45684	0.88955	0.51356	0.47229	0.88144	0.53582	0.48761	0.87306	0.55850	11
12	.45710	.88942	.51393	.47255	.88130	.53620	.48786	.87292	.55888	12
13	.45736	.88928	.51430	.47281	.88117	.53657	.48811	.87278	.55926	13
14	.45762	.88915	.51467	.47306	.88103	.53694	.48837	.87264	.55964	14
15	.45787	.88902	.51503	.47332	.88089	.53732	.48862	.87250	.56003	15
16	.45813	.88888	0.51540	.47358	.88075	0.53769	.48888	.87235	0.56041	16
17	.45839	.88875	.51577	.47383	.88062	.53807	.48913	.87221	.56079	17
18	.45865	.88862	.51614	.47409	.88048	.53844	.48938	.87207	.56117	18
19	.45891	.88848	.51651	.47434	.88034	.53882	.48964	.87193	.56156	19
20	.45917	.88835	.51688	.47460	.88020	.53920	.48989	.87178	.56194	20
21	0.45943	0.88822	0.51724	0.47486	0.88006	0.53957	0.49014	0.87164	0.56232	21
22	.45968	.88808	.51761	.47511	.87993	.53995	.49040	.87150	.56270	22
23	.45994	.88795	.51798	.47537	.87979	.54032	.49065	.87136	.56309	23
24	.46020	.88782	.51835	.47562	.87965	.54070	.49090	.87121	.56347	24
25	.46046	.88768	.51872	.47588	.87951	.54107	.49116	.87107	.56385	25
26	.46072	.88755	0.51909	.47614	.87937	0.54145	.49141	.87093	0.56424	26
27	.46097	.88741	.51946	.47639	.87923	.54183	.49166	.87079	.56462	27
28	.46123	.88728	.51983	.47665	.87910	.54220	.49192	.87064	.56501	28
29	.46149	.88715	.52020	.47690	.87896	.54258	.49217	.87050	.56539	29
30	.46175	.88701	.52057	.47716	.87882	.54296	.49242	.87036	.56577	30
31	0.46201	0.88688	0.52094	0.47741	0.87868	0.54333	0.49268	0.87021	0.56616	31
32	.46227	.88674	.52131	.47767	.87854	.54371	.49293	.87007	.56654	32
33	.46252	.88661	.52168	.47793	.87840	.54409	.49318	.86993	.56693	33
34	.46278	.88647	.52205	.47818	.87826	.54446	.49344	.86978	.56731	34
35	.46304	.88634	.52242	.47844	.87812	.54484	.49369	.86964	.56769	35
36	.46330	.88620	0.52279	.47869	.87798	0.54522	.49394	.86950	0.56808	36
37	.46355	.88607	.52316	.47895	.87784	.54560	.49420	.86935	.56846	37
38	.46381	.88593	.52353	.47920	.87770	.54597	.49445	.86921	.56885	38
39	.46407	.88580	.52390	.47946	.87757	.54635	.49470	.86906	.56923	39
40	.46433	.88566	.52427	.47971	.87743	.54673	.49495	.86892	.56962	40
41	0.46458	0.88553	0.52464	0.47997	0.87729	0.54711	0.49521	0.86878	0.57000	41
42	.46484	.88539	.52501	.48022	.87715	.54748	.49546	.86863	.57039	42
43	.46510	.88526	.52538	.48048	.87701	.54786	.49571	.86849	.57078	43
44	.46536	.88512	.52575	.48073	.87687	.54824	.49596	.86834	.57116	44
45	.46562	.88499	.52613	.48099	.87673	.54862	.49622	.86820	.57155	45
46	.46587	.88485	0.52650	.48124	.87659	0.54900	.49647	.86805	0.57193	46
47	.46613	.88472	.52687	.48150	.87645	.54938	.49672	.86791	.57232	47
48	.46639	.88458	.52724	.48175	.87631	.54975	.49697	.86777	.57271	48
49	.46664	.88445	.52761	.48201	.87617	.55013	.49723	.86762	.57309	49
50	.46690	.88431	.52798	.48226	.87603	.55051	.49748	.86748	.57348	50
51	0.46716	0.88417	0.52836	0.48252	0.87589	0.55089	0.49773	0.86733	0.57386	51
52	.46742	.88404	.52873	.48277	.87575	.55127	.49798	.86719	.57425	52
53	.46767	.88390	.52910	.48303	.87561	.55165	.49824	.86704	.57464	53
54	.46793	.88377	.52947	.48328	.87547	.55203	.49849	.86690	.57503	54
55	.46819	.88363	.52985	.48354	.87532	.55241	.49874	.86675	.57541	55
56	.46844	.88349	0.53022	.48379	.87518	0.55279	.49899	.86661	0.57580	56
57	.46870	.88336	.53059	.48405	.87504	.55317	.49924	.86646	.57619	57
58	.46896	.88322	.53096	.48430	.87490	.55355	.49950	.86632	.57657	58
59	.46922	.88308	.53134	.48456	.87476	.55393	.49975	.86617	.57696	59
60	0.46947	0.88295	.53171	0.48481	0.87462	.55431	0.50000	0.86603	.57735	60

TABLE OF NATURAL SINES, COSINES AND TANGENTS

,	30° Sin	Cos	Tan	31° Sin	Cos	Tan	32° Sin	Cos	Tan	,
0	0.50000	0.86603	0.57735	0.51504	0.85717	0.60086	0.52992	0.84805	0.62487	0
1	.50025	.86588	.57774	.51529	.85702	.60126	.53017	.84789	.62527	1
2	.50050	.86573	.57813	.51554	.85687	.60165	.53041	.84774	.62568	2
3	.50076	.86559	.57851	.51579	.85672	.60205	.53066	.84759	.62608	3
4	.50101	.86544	.57890	.51604	.85657	.60245	.53091	.84743	.62649	4
5	.50126	.86530	.57929	.51628	.85642	.60284	.53115	.84728	.62689	5
6	.50151	.86515	0.57968	.51653	.85627	0.60324	.53140	.84712	0.62730	6
7	.50176	.86501	.58007	.51678	.85612	.60364	.53165	.84697	.62770	7
8	.50201	.86486	.58046	.51703	.85597	.60403	.53189	.84681	.62811	8
9	.50227	.86471	.58085	.51728	.85582	.60443	.53214	.84666	.61852	9
10	.50252	.86457	.58124	.51753	.85567	.60483	.53238	.84650	.62892	10
11	0.50277	0.86442	0.58162	0.51778	0.85551	0.60522	0.53263	0.84635	0.62933	11
12	.50302	.86428	.58201	.51803	.85536	.60562	.53288	.84619	.62973	12
13	.50327	.86413	.58240	.51828	.85521	.60602	.53312	.84604	.63014	13
14	.50352	.86398	.58279	.51853	.85506	.60642	.53337	.84588	.63055	14
15	.50377	.86384	.58318	.51877	.85491	.60681	.53362	.84573	.63095	15
16	.50403	.86369	0.58357	.51902	.85476	0.60721	.53386	.84557	0.63136	16
17	.50428	.86354	.58396	.51927	.85461	.60761	.53411	.84542	.63177	17
18	.50453	.86340	.58435	.51952	.85446	.60801	.53435	.84526	.63217	18
19	.50478	.86325	.58474	.51977	.85431	.60841	.53460	.84511	.63258	19
20	.50503	.86310	.58513	.52002	.85416	.60881	.53484	.84495	.63299	20
21	0.50528	0.86296	0.58552	0.52027	0.85401	0.60921	0.53509	0.84480	0.63340	21
22	.50553	.86281	.58591	.52051	.85385	.60960	.53534	.84464	.63380	22
23	.50578	.86266	.58631	.52076	.85370	.61000	.53558	.84448	.63421	23
24	.50603	.86251	.58670	.52101	.85355	.61040	.53583	.84433	.63462	24
25	.50629	.86237	.58709	.52126	.85340	.61080	.53607	.84417	.63503	25
26	.50654	.86222	0.58748	.52151	.85325	0.61120	.53632	.84402	0.63544	26
27	.50679	.86207	.58787	.52175	.85310	.61160	.53656	.84386	.63584	27
28	.50704	.86192	.58826	.52200	.85294	.61200	.53681	.84370	.63625	28
29	.50729	.86178	.58865	.52225	.85279	.61240	.53705	.84355	.63666	29
30	.50754	.86163	.58905	.52250	.85264	.61280	.53730	.84339	.63707	30
31	0.50779	0.86148	0.58944	0.52275	0.85249	0.61320	0.53755	0.84324	0.63748	31
32	.50804	.86133	.58983	.52300	.85234	.61360	.53779	.84308	.63789	32
33	.50829	.86119	.59022	.52324	.85218	.61400	.53804	.84292	.63830	33
34	.50854	.86104	.59061	.52349	.85203	.61440	.53828	.84277	.63871	34
35	.50879	.86089	.59101	.52374	.85188	.61480	.53853	.84261	.63912	35
36	.50904	.86074	0.59140	.52399	.85173	0.61520	.53877	.84245	0.63953	36
37	.50929	.86059	.59179	.52423	.85158	.61561	.53902	.84230	.63994	37
38	.50954	.86045	.59218	.52448	.85142	.61601	.53926	.84214	.64035	38
39	.50979	.86030	.59258	.52473	.85127	.61641	.53951	.84198	.64076	39
40	.51004	.86015	.59297	.52498	.85112	.61681	.53975	.84183	.64117	40
41	0.51029	0.86000	0.59336	0.52522	0.85096	0.61721	0.54000	0.84167	0.64158	41
42	.51054	.85985	.59376	.52547	.85081	.61761	.54024	.84151	.64199	42
43	.51079	.85970	.59415	.52572	.85066	.61801	.54049	.84135	.64240	43
44	.51104	.85956	.59454	.52597	.85051	.61842	.54073	.84120	.64281	44
45	.51129	.85941	.59494	.52621	.85035	.61882	.54097	.84104	.64322	45
46	.51154	.85926	0.59533	.52646	.85020	0.61922	.54122	.84088	0.64363	46
47	.51179	.85911	.59573	.52671	.85005	.61962	.54146	.84072	.64404	47
48	.51204	.85896	.59612	.52696	.84989	.62003	.54171	.84057	.64446	48
49	.51229	.85881	.59651	.52720	.84974	.62043	.54195	.84041	.64487	49
50	.51254	.85866	.59691	.52745	.84959	.62083	.54220	.84025	.64528	50
51	0.51279	0.85851	0.59730	0.52770	0.84943	0.62124	0.54244	0.84009	0.64569	51
52	.51304	.85836	.59770	.52794	.84928	.62164	.54269	.83994	.64610	52
53	.51329	.85821	.59809	.52819	.84913	.62204	.54293	.83978	.64652	53
54	.51354	.85807	.59849	.52844	.84897	.62245	.54317	.83962	.64693	54
55	.51379	.85792	.59888	.52869	.84882	.62285	.54342	.83946	.64734	55
56	.51404	.85777	0.59928	.52893	.84866	0.62325	.54366	.83930	0.64775	56
57	.51429	.85762	.59967	.52918	.84851	.62366	.54391	.83915	.64817	57
58	.51454	.85747	.60007	.52943	.84836	.62406	.54415	.83899	.64858	58
59	.51479	.85732	.60046	.52967	.84820	.62447	.54440	.83883	.64899	59
60	0.51504	0.85717	.60086	0.52992	0.84805	.62487	0.54464	0.83867	.64941	60

TABLE OF NATURAL SINES, COSINES AND TANGENTS

′	33° Sin	33° Cos	33° Tan	34° Sin	34° Cos	34° Tan	35° Sin	35° Cos	35° Tan	′
0	0.54464	0.83867	0.64941	0.55919	0.82904	0.67451	0.57358	0.81915	0.70021	0
1	.54488	.83851	.64982	.55943	.82888	.67493	.57382	.81899	.70064	1
2	.54513	.83835	.65024	.55968	.82871	.67536	.57405	.81882	.70107	2
3	.54537	.83820	.65065	.55992	.82855	.67578	.57429	.81865	.70151	3
4	.54562	.83804	.65106	.56016	.82839	.67620	.57453	.81848	.70194	4
5	.54586	.83788	.65148	.56040	.82822	.67663	.57477	.81832	.70238	5
6	.54610	.83772	0.65189	.56064	.82806	0.67705	.57501	.81815	0.70281	6
7	.54635	.83756	.65231	.56088	.82790	.67748	.57524	.81798	.70325	7
8	.54659	.83740	.65272	.56112	.82773	.67790	.57548	.81782	.70368	8
9	.54683	.83724	.65314	.56136	.82757	.67832	.57572	.81765	.70412	9
10	.54708	.83708	.65355	.56160	.82741	.67875	.57596	.81748	.70455	10
11	0.54732	0.83692	0.65397	0.56184	0.82724	0.67917	0.57620	0.81731	0.70499	11
12	.54756	.83676	.65438	.56208	.82708	.67960	.57643	.81715	.70542	12
13	.54781	.83661	.65480	.56232	.82692	.68002	.57667	.81698	.70586	13
14	.54805	.83645	.65521	.56256	.82675	.68045	.57691	.81681	.70629	14
15	.54830	.83629	.65563	.56281	.82659	.68088	.57715	.81664	.70673	15
16	.54854	.83613	0.65604	.56305	.82643	0.68130	.57738	.81647	0.70717	16
17	.54878	.83597	.65646	.56329	.82626	.68173	.57762	.81631	.70760	17
18	.54902	.83581	.65688	.56353	.82610	.68215	.57786	.81614	.70804	18
19	.54927	.83565	.65729	.56377	.82593	.68258	.57810	.81597	.70848	19
20	.54951	.83549	.65771	.56401	.82577	.68301	.57833	.81580	.70891	20
21	0.54975	0.83533	0.65813	0.56425	0.82561	0.68343	0.57857	0.81563	0.70935	21
22	.55000	.83517	.65854	.56449	.82544	.68386	.57881	.81547	.70979	22
23	.55024	.83501	.65896	.56473	.82528	.68429	.57904	.81530	.71023	23
24	.55048	.83485	.65938	.56497	.82511	.68471	.57928	.81513	.71066	24
25	.55072	.83469	.65980	.56521	.82495	.68514	.57952	.81496	.71110	25
26	.55097	.83453	0.66021	.56545	.82479	0.68557	.57976	.81479	0.71154	26
27	.55121	.83437	.66063	.56569	.82462	.68600	.57999	.81462	.71198	27
28	.55145	.83421	.66105	.56593	.82446	.68642	.58023	.81445	71242	28
29	.55170	.83405	.66147	.56617	.82429	.68685	.58047	.81428	.71285	29
30	.55194	.83389	.66189	.56641	.82413	.68728	.58070	.81412	.71329	30
31	0.55218	0.83373	0.66230	0.56665	0.82396	0.68771	0.58094	0.81395	0.71373	31
32	.55242	.83356	.66272	.56689	.82380	.68814	.58118	.81378	.71417	32
33	.55266	.83340	.66314	.56713	.82363	.68857	.58141	.81361	.71461	33
34	.55291	.83324	.66356	.56737	.82347	.68900	.58165	.81344	.71505	34
35	.55315	.83308	.66398	.56760	.82330	.68942	.58189	.81327	.71549	35
36	.55339	.83292	0.66440	.56784	.82314	0.68985	.58212	.81310	0.71593	36
37	.55363	.83276	.66482	.56808	.82297	.69028	.58236	.81293	.71637	37
38	.55388	.83260	.66524	.56832	.82281	.69071	.58260	.81276	.71681	38
39	.55412	.83244	.66566	.56856	.82264	.69114	.58283	.81259	.71725	39
40	.55436	.83228	.66608	.56880	.82248	.69157	.58307	.81242	.71769	40
41	0.55460	0.83212	0.66650	0.56904	0.82231	0.69200	0.58331	0.81225	0.71813	41
42	.55484	.83195	.66692	.56928	.82214	.69243	.58354	.81208	.71857	42
43	.55509	.83179	.66734	.56952	.82198	.69286	.58378	.81191	.71901	43
44	.55533	.83163	.66776	.56976	.82181	.69329	.58401	.81174	.71946	44
45	.55557	.83147	.66818	.57000	.82165	.69372	.58425	.81157	.71990	45
46	.55581	.83131	0.66860	.57024	.82148	0.69416	.58449	.81140	0.72034	46
47	.55605	.83115	.66902	.57048	.82132	.69459	.58472	.81123	.72078	47
48	.55630	.83098	.66944	.57071	.82115	.69502	.58496	.81106	.72122	48
49	.55654	.83082	.66986	.57095	.82098	.69545	.58519	.81089	.72167	49
50	.55678	.83066	.67028	.57119	.82082	.69588	.58543	.81072	.72211	50
51	0.55702	0.83050	0.67071	0.57143	0.82065	0.69631	0.58567	0.81055	0.72255	51
52	.55726	.83034	.67113	.57167	.82049	.69675	.58590	.81038	.72299	52
53	.55750	.83017	.67155	.57191	.82032	.69718	.58614	.81021	.72344	53
54	.55775	.83001	.67197	.57215	.82015	.69761	.58637	.81004	.72388	54
55	.55799	.82985	.67239	.57238	.81999	.69804	.58661	.80987	.72432	55
56	.55823	.82969	0.67282	.57262	.81982	0.69847	.58684	.80970	0.72477	56
57	.55847	.82953	.67324	.57286	.81965	.69891	.58708	.80953	.72521	57
58	.55871	.82936	.67366	.57310	.81949	.69934	.58731	.80936	.72565	58
59	.55895	.82920	.67409	.57334	.81932	.69977	.58755	.80919	.72610	59
60	0.55919	0.82904	.67451	0.57358	0.81915	.70021	0.58779	0.80902	.72654	60

TABLE OF NATURAL SINES, COSINES AND TANGENTS

′	36° Sin	Cos	Tan	37° Sin	Cos	Tan	38° Sin	Cos	Tan	′
0	0.58779	0.80902	0.72654	0.60182	0.79864	0.75355	0.61566	0.78801	0.78129	0
1	.58802	.80885	.72699	.60205	.79846	.75401	.61589	.78783	.78175	1
2	.58826	.80868	.72743	.60228	.79829	.75447	.61612	.78765	.78222	2
3	.58849	.80850	.72788	.60251	.79811	.75492	.61635	.78747	.78269	3
4	.58873	.80833	.72832	.60274	.79794	.75538	.61658	.78729	.78316	4
5	.58896	.80816	.72877	.60298	.79776	.75584	.61681	.78711	.78363	5
6	.58920	.80799	0.72921	.60321	.79758	0.75629	.61704	.78694	0.78410	6
7	.58943	.80782	.72966	.60344	.79741	.75675	.61727	.78676	.78457	7
8	.58967	.80765	.73010	.60367	.79723	.75721	.61749	.78658	.78504	8
9	.58990	.80748	.73055	.60390	.79706	.75767	.61772	.78640	.78551	9
10	.59014	.80730	.73100	.60414	.79688	.75812	.61795	.78622	.78598	10
11	0.59037	0.80713	0.73144	0.60437	0.79671	0.75858	0.61818	0.78604	0.78645	11
12	.59061	.80696	.73189	.60460	.79653	.75904	.61841	.78586	.78692	12
13	.59084	.80679	.73234	.60483	.79635	.75950	.61864	.78568	.78739	13
14	.59108	.80662	.73278	.60506	.79618	.75996	.61887	.78550	.78786	14
15	.59131	.80645	.73323	.60529	.79600	.76042	.61910	.78532	.78834	15
16	.59154	.80627	0.73368	.60553	.79583	0.76088	.61932	.78514	0.78881	16
17	.59178	.80610	.73413	.60576	.79565	.76134	.61955	.78496	.78928	17
18	.59201	.80593	.73457	.60599	.79547	.76180	.61978	.78478	.78975	18
19	.59225	.80576	.73502	.60622	.79530	.76226	.62001	.78460	.79022	19
20	.59248	.80558	.73547	.60645	.79512	.76272	.62024	.78442	.79070	20
21	0.59272	0.80541	0.73592	0.60668	0.79494	0.76318	0.62046	0.78424	0.79117	21
22	.59295	.80524	.73637	.60691	.79477	.76364	.62069	.78406	.79164	22
23	.59319	.80507	.73681	.60715	.79459	.76410	.62092	.78387	.79212	23
24	.59342	.80489	.73726	.60738	.79442	.76456	.62115	.78369	.79259	24
25	.59365	.80472	.73771	.60761	.79424	.76502	.62138	.78351	.79306	25
26	.59389	.80455	0.73816	.60784	.79406	0.76548	.62160	.78333	0.79354	26
27	.59412	.80438	.73861	.60807	.79388	.76594	.62183	.78315	.79401	27
28	.59436	.80420	.73906	.60830	.79371	.76640	.62206	.78297	.79449	28
29	.59459	.80403	.73951	.60853	.79353	.76686	.62229	.78279	.79496	29
30	.59482	.80386	.73996	.60876	.79335	.76733	.62252	.78261	.79544	30
31	0.59506	0.80368	0.74041	0.60899	0.79318	0.76779	0.62274	0.78243	0.79591	31
32	.59529	.80351	.74086	.60922	.79300	.76825	.62297	.78225	.79639	32
33	.59552	.80334	.74131	.60945	.79282	.76871	.62320	.78207	.79686	33
34	.59576	.80316	.74176	.60968	.79264	.76918	.62343	.78188	.79734	34
35	.59599	.80299	.74221	.60992	.79247	.76964	.62365	.78170	.79781	35
36	.59623	.80282	0.74267	.61015	.79229	0.77010	.62388	.78152	0.79829	36
37	.59646	.80264	.74312	.61038	.79211	.77057	.62411	.78134	.79877	37
38	.59669	.80247	.74357	.61061	.79194	.77103	.62433	.78116	.79924	38
39	.59693	.80230	.74402	.61084	.79176	.77149	.62456	.78098	.79972	39
40	.59716	.80212	.74447	.61107	.79158	.77196	.62479	.78079	.80020	40
41	0.59739	0.80195	0.74492	0.61130	0.79140	0.77242	0.62502	0.78061	0.80067	41
42	.59763	.80178	.74538	.61153	.79122	.77289	.62524	.78043	.80115	42
43	.59786	.80160	.74583	.61176	.79105	.77335	.62547	.78025	.80163	43
44	.59809	.80143	.74628	.61199	.79087	.77382	.62570	.78007	.80211	44
45	.59833	.80125	.74674	.61222	.79069	.77428	.62592	.77988	.80258	45
46	.59856	.80108	0.74719	.61245	.79051	0.77475	.62615	.77970	0.80306	46
47	.59879	.80091	.74764	.61268	.79033	.77521	.62638	.77952	.80354	47
48	.59902	.80073	.74810	.61291	.79016	.77568	.62660	.77934	.80402	48
49	.59926	.80056	.74855	.61314	.78998	.77615	.62683	.77916	.80450	49
50	.59949	.80038	.74900	.61337	.78980	.77661	.62706	.77897	.80498	50
51	0.59972	0.80021	0.74946	0.61360	0.78962	0.77708	0.62728	0.77879	0.80546	51
52	.59996	.80003	.74991	.61383	.78944	.77754	.62751	.77861	.80594	52
53	.60019	.79986	.75037	.61406	.78926	.77801	.62774	.77843	.80642	53
54	.60042	.79969	.75082	.61429	.78908	.77848	.62796	.77824	.80690	54
55	.60065	.79951	.75128	.61452	.78891	.77895	.62819	.77806	.80738	55
56	.60089	.79934	0.75173	.61474	.78873	0.77941	.62842	.77788	0.80786	56
57	.60112	.79916	.75219	.61497	.78855	.77988	.62864	.77770	.80834	57
58	.60135	.79899	.75264	.61520	.78837	.78035	.62887	.77751	.80882	58
59	.60158	.79881	.75310	.61543	.78819	.78082	.62909	.77733	.80930	59
60	0.60182	0.79864	.75355	0.61566	0.78801	.78129	0.62932	0.77715	.80978	60

TABLE OF NATURAL SINES, COSINES AND TANGENTS

′	39° Sin	Cos	Tan	40° Sin	Cos	Tan	41° Sin	Cos	Tan	′
0	0.62932	0.77715	0.80978	0.64279	0.76604	0.83910	0.65606	0.75471	0.86929	0
1	.62955	.77696	.81027	.64301	.76586	.83960	.65628	.75452	.86980	1
2	.62977	.77678	.81075	.64323	.76567	84009	.65650	.75433	.87031	2
3	.63000	.77660	.81123	.64346	.76548	.84059	.65672	.75414	.87082	3
4	.63022	.77641	.81171	.64368	.76530	.84108	.65694	.75395	.87133	4
5	.63045	.77623	.81220	.64390	.76511	.84158	.65716	.75376	.87184	5
6	.63068	.77605	0.81268	.64412	.76492	0.84208	.65738	.75356	0.87236	6
7	.63090	.77586	.81316	.64435	.76473	.84258	.65759	.75337	.87287	7
8	.63113	.77568	.81364	.64457	.76455	.84307	.65781	.75318	.87338	8
9	.63135	.77550	.81413	.64479	.76436	.84357	.65803	.75299	.87389	9
10	.63158	.77531	.81461	.64501	.76417	.84407	.65825	.75280	.87441	10
11	0.63180	0.77513	0.81510	0.64524	0.76398	0.84457	0.65847	0.75261	0.87492	11
12	.63203	.77494	.81558	.64546	.76380	.84507	.65869	.75242	.87543	12
13	.63226	.77476	.81606	.64568	.76361	.84556	.65891	.75222	.87595	13
14	.63248	.77458	.81655	.64590	.76342	.84606	.65913	.75203	.87646	14
15	.63271	.77439	.81703	.64612	.76323	.84656	.65935	.75184	.87698	15
16	.63293	.77421	0.81752	.64635	.76304	.84706	.65957	.75165	0.87749	16
17	.63316	.77402	.81800	.64657	.76286	.84756	.65978	.75146	.87801	17
18	.63338	.77384	.81849	.64679	.76267	.84806	.66000	.75126	.87852	18
19	.63361	.77366	.81898	.64701	.76248	.84856	.66022	.75107	.87904	19
20	.63383	.77347	.81946	.64723	.76229	.84906	.66044	.75088	.87955	20
21	0.63406	0.77329	0.81995	0.64746	0.76210	0.84956	0.66066	0.75069	0.88007	21
22	.63428	.77310	.82044	.64768	.76192	.85006	.66088	.75050	.88059	22
23	.63451	.77292	.82092	.64790	.76173	.85057	.66109	.75030	.88110	23
24	.63473	.77273	.82141	.64812	.76154	.85107	.66131	.75011	.88162	24
25	.63496	.77255	.82190	.64834	.76135	.85157	.66153	.74992	.88214	25
26	.63518	.77236	0.82238	.64856	.76116	0.85207	.66175	.74973	0.88265	26
27	.63541	.77218	.82287	.64878	.76097	.85257	.66197	.74953	.88317	27
28	.63563	.77200	.82336	.64901	.76078	.85308	.66218	.74934	.88369	28
29	.63585	.77181	.82385	.64923	.76060	.85358	.66240	.74915	.88421	29
30	.63608	.77163	.82434	.64945	76041	.85408	.66262	.74896	.88473	30
31	0.63630	0.77144	0.82483	0.64967	0.76022	0.85458	0.66284	0.74876	0.88524	31
32	.63653	.77125	.82531	.64989	.76003	.85509	.66306	.74857	.88576	32
33	.63675	.77107	.82580	.65011	.75984	.85559	.66327	.74838	.88628	33
34	.63698	.77088	.82629	.65033	.75965	.85609	.66349	.74818	.88680	34
35	.63720	.77070	.82678	.65055	.75946	.85660	.66371	.74799	.88732	35
36	.63742	.77051	0.82727	.65077	.75927	0.85710	.66393	.74780	0.88784	36
37	.63765	.77033	.82776	.65100	.75908	.85761	.66414	.74761	.88836	37
38	.63787	.77014	.82825	.65122	.75889	.85811	.66436	.74741	.88888	38
39	.63810	.76996	.82874	.65144	.75870	.85862	.66458	.74722	.88940	39
40	.63832	.76977	.82923	.65166	.75851	.85912	.66480	.74703	.88992	40
41	0.63854	0.76959	0.82972	0.65188	0.75832	0.85963	0.66501	0.74683	0.89045	41
42	.63877	.76940	.83022	.65210	.75813	.86014	.66523	.74664	.89097	42
43	.63899	.76921	.83071	.65232	.75795	.86064	.66545	.74645	.89149	43
44	.63922	.76903	.83120	.65254	.75776	.86115	.66567	.74625	.89201	44
45	.63944	.76884	.83169	.65276	.75757	.86166	.66588	.74606	.89253	45
46	.63966	.76866	0.83218	.65298	.75738	0.86216	.66610	.74586	0.89306	46
47	.63989	.76847	.83268	.65320	.75719	.86267	.66632	.74567	.89358	47
48	.64011	.76828	.83317	.65342	.75700	.86318	.66653	.74548	.89410	48
49	.64033	.76810	.83366	.65364	.75681	.86368	.66675	.74528	.89463	49
50	.64056	.76791	.83415	.65386	.75662	.86419	.66697	.74509	.89515	50
51	0.64078	0.76773	0.83465	0.65408	0.75643	0.86470	0.66718	0.74489	0.89567	51
52	.64100	.76754	.83514	.65430	.75623	.86521	.66740	.74470	.89620	52
53	.64123	.76735	.83564	.65452	.75604	.86572	.66762	.74451	.89672	53
54	.64145	.76717	.83613	.65474	.75585	.86623	.66783	.74431	.89725	54
55	.64167	.76698	.83662	.65496	.75566	.86674	.66805	.74412	89777	55
56	.64190	.76679	0.83712	.65518	.75547	0.86725	.66827	.74392	0.89830	56
57	.64212	.76661	.83761	.65540	.75528	.86776	.66848	.74373	.89883	57
58	.64234	.76642	.83811	.65562	.75509	.86827	.66870	.74353	.89935	58
59	.64257	.76623	.83860	.65584	.75490	.86878	.66891	.74334	.89988	59
60	0.64279	0.76604	.83910	0.65606	0.75471	.86929	0.66913	0.74315	.90040	60

TABLE OF NATURAL SINES, COSINES AND TANGENTS

′	42° Sin	Cos	Tan	43° Sin	Cos	Tan	44° Sin	Cos	Tan	′
0	0.66913	0.74315	0.90040	0.68200	0.73135	0.93252	0.69466	0.71934	0.96569	0
1	.66935	.74295	.90093	.68221	.73116	.93306	.69487	.71914	.96625	1
2	.66956	.74276	.90146	.68242	.73096	.93360	.69508	.71894	.96681	2
3	.66978	.74256	.90199	.68264	.73076	.93415	.69529	.71873	.96738	3
4	.67000	.74237	.90251	.68285	.73056	.93469	.69550	.71853	.96794	4
5	.67021	.74217	.90304	.68306	.73036	.93524	.69570	.71833	.96850	5
6	.67043	.74198	0.90357	.68327	.73016	0.93578	.69591	.71813	0.96907	6
7	.67064	.74178	.90410	.68349	.72996	.93633	.69612	.71792	.96963	7
8	.67086	.74159	.90463	.68370	.72977	.93688	.69633	.71772	.97020	8
9	.67107	.74139	.90516	.68391	.72957	.93742	.69654	.71752	.97076	9
10	.67129	.74120	.90569	.68412	.72937	.93797	.69675	.71732	.97133	10
11	0.67151	0.74100	0.90621	0.68434	0.72917	0.93852	0.69696	0.71711	0.97189	11
12	.67172	.74081	.90674	.68455	.72897	.93906	.69717	.71691	.97246	12
13	.67194	.74061	.90727	.68476	.72877	.93961	.69737	.71671	.97302	13
14	.67215	.74041	.90781	.68497	.72857	.94016	.69758	.71651	.97359	14
15	.67237	.74022	.90834	.68518	.72837	.94071	.69779	.71630	.97416	15
16	.67258	.74002	0.90887	.68540	.72817	0.94125	.69800	.71610	0.97472	16
17	.67280	.73983	.90941	.68561	.72797	.94180	.69821	.71590	.97529	17
18	.67301	.73963	.90993	.68582	.72777	.94235	.69842	.71569	.97586	18
19	.67323	.73944	.91046	.68603	.72757	.94290	.69862	.71549	.97643	19
20	.67344	.73924	.91099	.68624	.72737	.94345	.69883	.71529	.97700	20
21	0.67366	0.73904	0.91153	0.68645	0.72717	0.94400	0.69904	0.71508	0.97756	21
22	.67387	.73885	.91206	.68667	.72697	.94455	.69925	.71488	.97813	22
23	.67409	.73865	.91259	.68688	.72678	.94510	.69946	.71468	.97870	23
24	.67430	.73846	.91313	.68709	.72658	.94565	.69966	.71447	.97927	24
25	.67452	.73826	.91366	.68730	.72638	.94620	.69987	.71427	.97984	25
26	.67473	.73806	0.91419	.68751	.72618	0.94676	.70008	.71407	0.98041	26
27	.67495	.73787	.91473	.68772	.72598	.94731	.70029	.71386	.98098	27
28	.67516	.73767	.91526	.68793	.72578	.94786	.70049	.71366	.98155	28
29	.67538	.73747	.91580	.68814	.72558	.94841	.70070	.71345	.98213	29
30	.67559	.73728	.91633	.68836	.72537	.94896	.70091	.71325	.98270	30
31	0.67581	0.73708	0.91687	0.68857	0.72517	0.94952	0.70112	0.71305	0.98327	31
32	.67602	.73688	.91740	.68878	.72497	.95007	.70132	.71284	.98384	32
33	.67623	.73669	.91794	.68899	.72477	.95062	.70153	.71264	.98441	33
34	.67645	.73649	.91847	.68920	.72457	.95118	.70174	.71243	.98499	34
35	.67666	.73629	.91901	.68941	.72437	.95173	.70195	.71223	.98556	35
36	.67688	.73610	0.91955	.68962	.72417	0.95229	.70215	.71203	0.98613	36
37	.67709	.73590	.92008	.68983	.72397	.95284	.70236	.71182	.98671	37
38	.67730	.73570	.92062	.69004	.72377	.95340	.70257	.71162	.98728	38
39	.67752	.73551	.92116	.69025	.72357	.95395	.70277	.71141	.98786	39
40	.67773	.73531	.92170	.69046	.72337	.95451	.70298	.71121	.98843	40
41	0.67795	0.73511	0.92224	0.69067	0.72317	0.95506	0.70319	0.71100	0.98901	41
42	.67816	.73492	.92277	.69088	.72297	.95562	.70340	.71080	.98958	42
43	.67837	.73472	.92331	.69109	.72277	.95618	.70360	.71060	.99016	43
44	.67859	.73452	.92385	.69130	.72257	.95673	.70381	.71039	.99073	44
45	.67880	.73432	.92439	.69151	.72236	.95729	.70402	.71019	.99131	45
46	.67901	.73413	0.92493	.69172	.72216	0.95785	.70422	.70998	0.99189	46
47	.67923	.73393	.92547	.69193	.72196	.95841	.70443	.70978	.99247	47
48	.67944	.73373	.92601	.69214	.72176	.95897	.70463	.70957	.99304	48
49	.67966	.73353	.92655	.69235	.72156	.95952	.70484	.70937	.99362	49
50	.67987	.73333	.92709	.69256	.72136	.96008	.70505	.70916	.99420	50
51	0.68008	0.73314	0.92763	0.69277	0.72116	0.96064	0.70525	0.70896	0.99478	51
52	.68030	.73294	.92817	.69298	.72095	.96120	.70546	.70875	.99536	52
53	.68051	.73274	.92872	.69319	.72075	.96176	.70567	.70855	.99594	53
54	.68072	.73254	.92926	.69340	.72055	.96232	.70587	.70834	.99652	54
55	.68093	.73235	.92980	.69361	.72035	.96288	.70608	.70813	.99710	55
56	.68115	.73215	0.93034	.69382	.72015	0.96344	.70628	.70793	0.99768	56
57	.68136	.73195	.93088	.69403	.71995	.96400	.70649	.70772	.99826	57
58	.68157	.73175	.93143	.69424	.71974	.96457	.70670	.70752	.99884	58
59	.68179	.73155	.93197	.69445	.71954	.96513	.70690	.70731	.99942	59
60	0.68200	0.73135	.93252	0.69466	0.71934	.96569	0.70711	0.70711	1.00000	60

TABLE OF NATURAL SINES, COSINES AND TANGENTS

′	45° Sin	Cos	Tan	46° Sin	Cos	Tan	47° Sin	Cos	Tan	′
0	0.70711	0.70711	1.00000	0.71934	0.69466	1.03553	0.73135	0.68200	1.07237	0
1	.70731	.70690	1.00058	.71954	.69445	1.03613	.73155	.68179	1.07299	1
2	.70752	.70670	1.00116	.71974	.69424	1.03674	.73175	.68157	1.07362	2
3	.70772	.70649	1.00175	.71995	.69403	1.03734	.73195	.68136	1.07425	3
4	.70793	.70628	1.00233	.72015	.69382	1.03794	.73215	.68115	1.07487	4
5	.70813	.70608	1.00291	.72035	.69361	1.03855	.73235	.68093	1.07550	5
6	.70834	.70587	1.00350	.72055	.69340	1.03915	.73254	.68072	1.07613	6
7	.70855	.70567	1.00408	.72075	.69319	1.03976	.73274	.68051	1.07676	7
8	.70875	.70546	1.00467	.72095	.69298	1.04036	.73294	.68030	1.07738	8
9	.70896	.70525	1.00525	.72116	.69277	1.04097	.73314	.68008	1.07801	9
10	.70916	.70505	1.00583	.72136	.69256	1.04158	.73333	.67987	1.07864	10
11	0.70937	0.70484	1.00642	0.72156	0.69235	1.04218	0.73353	0.67966	1.07927	11
12	.70957	.70463	1.00701	.72176	.69214	1.04279	.73373	.67944	1.07990	12
13	.70978	.70443	1.00759	.72196	.69193	1.04340	.73393	.67923	1.08053	13
14	.70998	.70422	1.00818	.72216	.69172	1.04401	.73413	.67901	1.08116	14
15	.71019	.70402	1.00876	.72236	.69151	1.04461	.73432	.67880	1.08179	15
16	.71039	.70381	1.00935	.72257	.69130	1.04522	.73452	.67859	1.08243	16
17	.71060	.70360	1.00994	.72277	.69109	1.04583	.73472	.67837	1.08306	17
18	.71080	.70340	1.01053	.72297	.69088	1.04644	.73492	.67816	1.08369	18
19	.71100	.70319	1.01112	.72317	.69067	1.04705	.73511	.67795	1.08432	19
20	.71121	.70298	1.01170	.72337	.69046	1.04766	.73531	.67773	1.08496	20
21	0.71141	0.70277	1.01229	0.72357	0.69025	1.04827	0.73551	0.67752	1.08559	21
22	.71162	.70257	1.01288	.72377	.69004	1.04888	.73570	.67730	1.08622	22
23	.71182	.70236	1.01347	.72397	.68983	1.04949	.73590	.67709	1.08686	23
24	.71203	.70215	1.01406	.72417	.68962	1.05010	.73610	.67688	1.08749	24
25	.71223	.70195	1.01465	.72437	.68941	1.05072	.73629	.67666	1.08813	25
26	.71243	.70174	1.01524	.72457	.68920	1.05133	.73649	.67645	1.08876	26
27	.71264	.70153	1.01583	.72477	.68899	1.05194	.73669	.67623	1.08940	27
28	.71284	.70132	1.01642	.72497	.68878	1.05255	.73688	.67602	1.09003	28
29	.71305	.70112	1.01702	.72517	.68857	1.05317	.73708	.67581	1.09067	29
30	.71325	.70091	1.01761	.72537	.68836	1.05378	.73728	.67559	1.09131	30
31	0.71345	0.70070	1.01820	0.72558	0.68814	1.05439	0.73747	0.67538	1.09195	31
32	.71366	.70049	1.01879	.72578	.68793	1.05501	.73767	.67516	1.09258	32
33	.71386	.70029	1.01939	.72598	.68772	1.05562	.73787	.67495	1.09322	33
34	.71407	.70008	1.01998	.72618	.68751	1.05624	.73806	.67473	1.09386	34
35	.71427	.69987	1.02057	.72638	.68730	1.05685	.73826	.67452	1.09450	35
36	.71447	.69966	1.02117	.72658	.68709	1.05747	.73846	.67430	1.09514	36
37	.71468	.69946	1.02176	.72678	.68688	1.05809	.73865	.67409	1.09578	37
38	.71488	.69925	1.02236	.72697	.68667	1.05870	.73885	.67387	1.09642	38
39	.71508	.69904	1.02295	.72717	.68645	1.05932	.73904	.67366	1.09706	39
40	.71529	.69883	1.02355	.72737	.68624	1.05994	.73924	.67344	1.09770	40
41	0.71549	0.69862	1.02414	0.72757	0.68603	1.06056	0.73944	0.67323	1.09834	41
42	.71569	.69842	1.02474	.72777	.68582	1.06117	.73963	.67301	1.09899	42
43	.71590	.68921	1.02533	.72797	.68561	1.06179	.73983	.67280	1.09963	43
44	.71610	.69800	1.02593	.72817	.68540	1.06241	.74002	.67258	1.10027	44
45	.71630	.69779	1.02653	.72837	.68518	1.06303	.74022	.67237	1.10091	45
46	.71651	.69758	1.02713	.72857	.68497	1.06365	.74041	.67215	1.10156	46
47	.71671	.69737	1.02772	.72877	.68476	1.06427	.74061	.67194	1.10220	47
48	.71691	.69717	1.02832	.72897	.68455	1.06489	.74081	.67172	1.10285	48
49	.71711	.69696	1.02892	.72917	.68434	1.06551	.74100	.67151	1.10349	49
50	.71732	.69675	1.02952	.72937	.68412	1.06613	.74120	.67129	1.10414	50
51	0.71752	0.69654	1.03012	0.72957	0.68391	1.06676	0.74139	0.67107	1.10478	51
52	.71772	.69633	1.03072	.72977	.68370	1.06738	.74159	.67086	1.10543	52
53	.71792	.69612	1.03132	.72996	.68349	1.06800	.74178	.67064	1.10608	53
54	.71813	.69591	1.03192	.73016	.68327	1.06862	.74198	.67043	1.10672	54
55	.71833	.69570	1.03252	.73036	.68306	1.06925	.74217	.67021	1.10737	55
56	.71853	.69550	1.03312	.73056	.68285	1.06987	.74237	.67000	1.10802	56
57	.71873	.69529	1.03372	.73076	.68264	1.07049	.74256	.66978	1.10867	57
58	.71894	.69508	1.03433	.73096	.68242	1.07112	.74276	.66956	1.10931	58
59	.71914	.69487	1.03493	.73116	.68221	1.07174	.74295	.66935	1.10996	59
60	0.71934	0.69466	1.03553	0.73135	0.68200	1.07237	0.74315	0.66913	1.11061	60

TABLE OF NATURAL SINES, COSINES AND TANGENTS

′	48° Sin	Cos	Tan		49° Sin	Cos	Tan		50° Sin	Cos	Tan	′
0	0.74315	0.66913	1.11061		0.75471	0.65606	1.15037		0.76604	0.64279	1.19175	0
1	.74334	.66891	1.11126		.75490	.65584	1.15104		.76623	.64257	1.19246	1
2	.74353	.66870	1.11191		.75509	.65562	1.15172		.76642	.64234	1.19316	2
3	.74373	.66848	1.11256		.75528	.65540	1.15240		.76661	.64212	1.19387	3
4	.74392	.66827	1.11321		.75547	.65518	1.15308		.76679	.64190	1.19457	4
5	.74412	.66805	1.11387		.75566	.65496	1.15375		.76698	.64167	1.19528	5
6	.74431	.66783	1.11452		.75585	.65474	1.15443		.76717	.64145	1.19599	6
7	.74451	.66762	1.11517		.75604	.65452	1.15511		.76735	.64123	1.19669	7
8	.74470	.66740	1.11582		.75623	.65430	1.15579		.76754	.64100	1.19740	8
9	.74489	.66718	1.11648		.75643	.65408	1.15647		.76773	.46078	1.19811	9
10	.74509	.66697	1.11713		.75662	.65386	1.15715		.76791	.64056	1.19882	10
11	0.74528	0.66675	1.11778		0.75681	0.65364	1.15783		0.76810	0.64033	1.19953	11
12	.74548	.66653	1.11844		.75700	.65342	1.15851		.76828	.64011	1.20024	12
13	.74567	.66632	1.11909		.75719	.65320	1.15919		.76847	.63989	1.20095	13
14	.74586	.66610	1.11975		.75738	.65298	1.15987		.76866	.63966	1.20166	14
15	.74606	.66588	1.12041		.75757	.65276	1.16056		.76884	.63944	1.20237	15
16	.74625	.66567	1.12106		.75776	.65254	1.16124		.76903	.63922	1.20308	16
17	.74645	.66545	1.12172		.75795	.65232	1.16192		.76921	.63899	1.20379	17
18	.74664	.66523	1.12238		.75813	.65210	1.16261		.76940	.63877	1.20451	18
19	.74683	.66501	1.12303		.75832	.65188	1.16329		.76959	.63854	1.20522	19
20	.74703	.66480	1.12369		.75851	.65166	1.16398		.76977	.63832	1.20593	20
21	0.74722	0.66458	1.12435		0.75870	0.65144	1.16466		0.76996	0.63810	1.20665	21
22	.74741	.66436	1.12501		.75889	.65122	1.16535		.77014	.63787	1.20736	22
23	.74761	.66414	1.12567		.75908	.65100	1.16603		.77033	.63765	1.20808	23
24	.74780	.66393	1.12633		.75927	.65077	1.16672		.77051	.63742	1.20879	24
25	.74799	.66371	1.12699		.75946	.65055	1.16741		.77070	.63720	1.20951	25
26	.74818	.66349	1.12765		.75965	.65033	1.16809		.77088	.63698	1.21023	26
27	.74838	.66327	1.12831		.75984	.65011	1.16878		.77107	.63675	1.21094	27
28	.74857	.66306	1.12897		.76003	.64989	1.16947		.77125	.63653	1.21166	28
29	.74876	.66284	1.12963		.76022	.64967	1.17016		.77144	.63630	1.21238	29
30	.74896	.66262	1.13029		.76041	.64945	1.17085		.77163	.63608	1.21310	30
31	0.74915	0.66240	1.13096		0.76060	0.64923	1.17154		0.77181	0.63585	1.21382	31
32	.74934	.66218	1.13162		.76078	.64901	1.17223		.77200	.63563	1.21454	32
33	.74953	.66197	1.13228		.76097	.64878	1.17292		.77218	.63541	1.21526	33
34	.74973	.66175	1.13295		.76116	.64856	1.17361		.77236	.63518	1.21598	34
35	.74992	.66153	1.13361		.76135	.64834	1.17430		.77255	.63496	1.21670	35
36	.75011	.66131	1.13428		.76154	.64812	1.17500		.77273	.63473	1.21742	36
37	.75030	.66109	1.13494		.76173	.64790	1.17569		.77292	.63451	1.21814	37
38	.75050	.66088	1.13561		.76192	.64768	1.17638		.77310	.63428	1.21887	38
39	.75069	.66066	1.13627		.76210	.64746	1.17708		.77329	.63406	1.21959	39
40	.75088	.66044	1.13694		.76229	.64723	1.17777		.77347	.63383	1.22031	40
41	0.75107	0.66022	1.13761		0.76248	0.64701	1.17846		0.77366	0.63361	1.22104	41
42	.75126	.66000	1.13828		.76267	.64679	1.17916		.77384	.63338	1.22176	42
43	.75146	.65978	1.13894		.76286	.64657	1.17986		.77402	.63316	1.22249	43
44	.75165	.65957	1.13961		.76304	.64635	1.18055		.77421	.63293	1.22321	44
45	.75184	.65935	1.14028		.76323	.64612	1.18125		.77439	.63271	1.22394	45
46	.75203	.65913	1.14095		.76342	.64590	1.18194		.77458	.63248	1.22467	46
47	.75222	.65891	1.14162		.76361	.64568	1.18264		.77476	.63226	1.22539	47
48	.75242	.65869	1.14229		.76380	.64546	1.18334		.77494	.63203	1.22612	48
49	.75261	.65847	1.14296		.76398	.64524	1.18404		.77513	.63180	1.22685	49
50	.75280	.65825	1.14363		.76417	.64501	1.18474		.77531	.63158	1.22758	50
51	0.75299	0.65803	1.14430		0.76436	0.64479	1.18544		0.77550	0.63135	1.22831	51
52	.75318	.65781	1.14498		.76455	.64457	1.18614		.77568	.63113	1.22904	52
53	.75337	.65759	1.14565		.76473	.64435	1.18684		.77586	.63090	1.22977	53
54	.75356	.65738	1.14632		.76492	.64412	1.18754		.77605	.63068	1.23050	54
55	.75376	.65716	1.14699		.76511	.64390	1.18824		.77623	.63045	1.23123	55
56	.75395	.65694	1.14767		.76530	.64368	1.18894		.77641	.63022	1.23196	56
57	.75414	.65672	1.14834		.76548	.64346	1.18964		.77660	.63000	1.23270	57
58	.75433	.65650	1.14902		.76567	.64323	1.19035		.77678	.62977	1.23343	58
59	.75452	.65628	1.14969		.76586	.64301	1.19105		.77696	.62955	1.23416	59
60	0.75471	0.65606	1.15037		0.76604	0.64279	1.19175		0.77715	0.62932	1.23490	60

TABLE OF NATURAL SINES, COSINES AND TANGENTS

′	51° Sin	Cos	Tan	52° Sin	Cos	Tan	53° Sin	Cos	Tan	′
0	0.77715	0.62932	1.23490	0.78801	0.61566	1.27994	0.79864	0.60182	1.32704	0
1	.77733	.62909	1.23563	.78819	.61543	1.28071	.79881	.60158	1.32785	1
2	.77751	.62887	1.23637	.78837	.61520	1.28148	.79899	.60135	1.32865	2
3	.77770	.62864	1.23710	.78855	.61497	1.28225	.79916	.60112	1.32946	3
4	.77788	.62842	1.23784	.78873	.61474	1.28302	.79934	.60089	1.33026	4
5	.77806	.62819	1.23858	.78891	.61452	1.28379	.79951	.60065	1.33107	5
6	.77824	.62796	1.23931	.78908	.61429	1.28456	.79969	.60042	1.33188	6
7	.77843	.62774	1.24005	.78926	.61406	1.28533	.79986	.60019	1.33268	7
8	.77861	.62751	1.24079	.78944	.61383	1.28610	.80003	.59996	1.33349	8
9	.77879	.62728	1.24153	.78962	.61360	1.28687	.80021	.59972	1.33430	9
10	.77897	.62706	1.24227	.78960	.61337	1.28764	.80038	.59949	1.33511	10
11	0.77916	0.62683	1.24301	0.78998	0.61314	1.28842	0.80056	0.59926	1.33592	11
12	.77934	.62660	1.24375	.79016	.61291	1.28919	.80073	.59902	1.33673	12
13	.77952	.62638	1.24449	.79033	.61268	1.28997	.80091	.59879	1.33764	13
14	.77970	.62615	1.24523	.79051	.61245	1.29074	.80108	.59856	1.33835	14
15	.77988	.62592	1.24597	.79069	.61222	1.29152	.80125	.59833	1.33916	15
16	.78007	.62570	1.24672	.79087	.61199	1.29229	.80143	.59809	1.33998	16
17	.78025	.62547	1.24746	.79105	.61176	1.29307	.80160	.59786	1.34079	17
18	.78043	.62524	1.24820	.79122	.61153	1.29385	.80178	.59763	1.34160	18
19	.78061	.62502	1.24895	.79140	.61130	1.29463	.80195	.59739	1.34242	19
20	.78079	.62479	1.24969	.79158	.61107	1.29541	.80212	.59716	1.34323	20
21	0.78098	0.62456	1.25044	0.79176	0.61084	1.29618	0.80230	0.59693	1.34405	21
22	.78116	.62433	1.25118	.79194	.61061	1.29696	.80247	.59669	1.34487	22
23	.78134	.62411	1.25193	.79211	.61038	1.29775	.80264	.59646	1.34568	23
24	.78152	.62388	1.25268	.79229	.61015	1.29853	.80282	.59623	1.34650	24
25	.78170	.62365	1.25343	.79247	.60992	1.29931	.80299	.59599	1.34732	25
26	.78188	.62343	1.25417	.79264	.60968	1.30009	.80316	.59576	1.34814	26
27	.78207	.62320	1.25492	.79282	.60945	1.30087	.80334	.59552	1.34896	27
28	.78225	.62297	1.25567	.79300	.60922	1.30166	.80351	.59529	1.34978	28
29	.78243	.62274	1.25642	.79318	.60899	1.30244	.80368	.59506	1.35060	29
30	.78261	.62252	1.25717	.79335	.60876	1.30323	.80386	.59482	1.35142	30
31	0.78279	0.62229	1.25792	0.79353	0.60853	1.30401	0.80403	0.59459	1.35224	31
32	.78297	.62206	1.25867	.79371	.60830	1.30480	.80420	.59436	1.35307	32
33	.78315	.62183	1.25943	.79388	.60807	1.30558	.80438	.59412	1.35389	33
34	.78333	.62160	1.26018	.79406	.60784	1.30637	.80455	.59389	1.35472	34
35	.78351	.62138	1.26093	.79424	.60761	1.30716	.80472	.59365	1.35554	35
36	.78369	.62115	1.26169	.79442	.60738	1.30795	.80489	.59342	1.35637	36
37	.78387	.62092	1.26244	.79459	.60715	1.30873	.80507	.59319	1.35719	37
38	.78406	.62069	1.26320	.79477	.60691	1.30952	.80524	.59295	1.35802	38
39	.78424	.62046	1.26395	.79494	.60668	1.31031	.80541	.59272	1.35885	39
40	.78442	.62024	1.26471	.79512	.60645	1.31110	.80558	.59248	1.35968	40
41	0.78460	0.62001	1.26546	0.79530	0.60622	1.31190	0.80576	0.59225	1.36051	41
42	.78478	.61978	1.26622	.79547	.60599	1.31269	.80593	.59201	1.36134	42
43	.78496	.61955	1.26698	.79565	.60576	1.31348	.80610	.59178	1.36217	43
44	.78514	.61932	1.26774	.79583	.60553	1.31427	.80627	.59154	1.36300	44
45	.78532	61910	1.26849	.79600	.60529	1.31507	.80645	.59131	1.36383	45
46	.78550	.61887	1.26925	.79618	.60506	1.31586	.80662	.59108	1.36466	46
47	.78568	.61864	1.27001	.79635	.60483	1.31666	.80679	.59084	1.36549	47
48	.78586	.61841	1.27077	.79653	.60460	1.31745	.80696	.59061	1.36633	48
49	.78604	.61818	1.27153	.79671	.60437	1.31825	.80713	.59037	1.36716	49
50	.78622	.61795	1.27230	.79688	.60414	1.31904	.80730	.59014	1.36800	50
51	0.78640	0.61772	1.27306	0.79706	0.60390	1.31984	0.80748	0.58990	1.36883	51
52	.78658	.61749	1.27382	.79723	.60367	1.32064	.80765	.58967	1.36967	52
53	.78676	.61727	1.27458	.79741	.60344	1.32144	.80782	.58943	1.37050	53
54	.78694	.61704	1.27535	.79758	.60321	1.32224	.80799	.58920	1.37134	54
55	.78711	.61681	1.27611	.79776	.60298	1.32304	.80816	.58896	1.37218	55
56	.78729	.61658	1.27688	.79794	.60274	1.32384	.80833	.58873	1.37302	56
57	.78747	.61635	1.27764	.79811	.60251	1.32464	.80850	.58849	1.37386	57
58	.78765	.61612	1.27841	.79829	.60228	1.32544	.80868	.58826	1.37470	58
59	.78783	.61589	1.27917	.79846	.60205	1.32624	.80885	.58802	1.37554	59
60	0.78801	0.61566	1.27994	0.79864	0.60182	1.32704	0.80902	0.58779	1.37638	60

F

TABLE OF NATURAL SINES, COSINES AND TANGENTS

′	54°			55°			56°			′
	Sin	*Cos*	*Tan*	*Sin*	*Cos*	*Tan*	*Sin*	*Cos*	*Tan*	
0	0.80902	0.58779	1.37638	0.81915	0.57358	1.42815	0.82904	0.55919	1.48256	0
1	.80919	.58755	1.37722	.81932	.57334	1.42903	.82920	.55895	1.48349	1
2	.80936	.58731	1.37807	.81949	.57310	1.42992	.82936	.55871	1.48442	2
3	.80953	.58708	1.37891	.81965	.57286	1.43080	.82953	.55847	1.48536	3
4	.80970	.58684	1.37976	.81982	.57262	1.43169	.82969	.55823	1.48629	4
5	.80987	.58661	1.38060	.81999	.57238	1.43258	.82985	.55799	1.48722	5
6	.81004	.58637	1.38145	.82015	.57215	1.43347	.83001	.55775	1.48816	6
7	.81021	.58614	1.38229	.82032	.57191	1.43436	.83017	.55750	1.48909	7
8	.81038	.58590	1.38314	.82049	.57167	1.43525	.83034	.55726	1.49003	8
9	.81055	.58567	1.38399	.82065	.57143	1.43614	.83050	.55702	1.49097	9
10	.81072	.58543	1.38484	.82082	.57119	1.43703	.83066	.55678	1.49190	10
11	0.81089	0.58519	1.38568	0.82098	0.57095	1.43792	0.83082	0.55654	1.49284	11
12	.81106	.58496	1.38653	.82115	.57071	1.43881	.83098	.55630	1.49378	12
13	.81123	.58472	1.38738	.82132	.57048	1.43970	.83115	.55605	1.49472	13
14	.81140	.58449	1.38824	.82148	.57024	1.44060	.83131	.55581	1.49566	14
15	.81157	.58425	1.38909	.82165	.57000	1.44149	.83147	.55557	1.49661	15
16	.81174	.58401	1.38994	.82181	.56976	1.44239	.83163	.55533	1.49755	16
17	.81191	.58378	1.39079	.82198	.56952	1.44329	.83179	.55509	1.49849	17
18	.81208	.58354	1.39165	.82214	.56928	1.44418	.83195	.55484	1.49944	18
19	.81225	.58331	1.39250	.82231	.56904	1.44508	.83212	.55460	1.50038	19
20	.81242	.58307	1.39336	.82248	.56880	1.44598	.83228	.55436	1.50133	20
21	0.81259	0.58283	1.39421	0.82264	0.56856	1.44688	0.83244	0.55412	1.50228	21
22	.81276	.58260	1.39507	.82281	.56832	1.44778	.83260	.55388	1.50322	22
23	.81293	.58236	1.39593	.82297	.56808	1.44868	.83276	.55363	1.50417	23
24	.81310	.58212	1.39679	.82314	.56784	1.44958	.83292	.55339	1.50512	24
25	.81327	.58189	1.39764	.82330	.56760	1.45049	.83308	.55315	1.50607	25
26	.81344	.58165	1.39850	.82347	.56737	1.45139	.83324	.55291	1.50702	26
27	.81361	.58141	1.39936	.82363	.56713	1.45229	.83340	.55266	1.50797	27
28	.81378	.58118	1.40022	.82380	.56689	1.45320	.83356	.55242	1.50893	28
29	.81395	.58094	1.40109	.82396	.56665	1.45410	.83373	.55218	1.50988	29
30	.81412	.58070	1.40195	.82413	.56641	1.45501	.83389	.55194	1.51084	30
31	0.81428	0.58047	1.40281	0.82429	0.56617	1.45592	0.83405	0.55170	1.51179	31
32	.81445	.58023	1.40367	.82446	.56593	1.45682	.83421	.55145	1.51275	32
33	.81462	.57999	1.40454	.82462	.56569	1.45773	.83437	.55121	1.51370	33
34	.81479	.57976	1.40540	.82479	.56545	1.45864	.83453	.55097	1.51466	34
35	.81496	.57952	1.40627	.82495	.56521	1.45955	.83469	.55072	1.51562	35
36	.81513	.57928	1.40714	.82511	.56497	1.46046	.83485	.55048	1.51658	36
37	.81530	.57904	1.40800	.82528	.56473	1.46137	.83501	.55024	1.51754	37
38	.81547	.57881	1.40887	.82544	.56449	1.46229	.83517	.55000	1.51850	38
39	.81563	.57857	1.40974	.82561	.56425	1.46320	.83533	.54975	1.51946	39
40	.81580	.57833	1.41061	.82577	.56401	1.46411	.83549	.54951	1.52043	40
41	0.81597	0.57810	1.41148	0.82593	0.56377	1.46503	0.83565	0.54927	1.52139	41
42	.81614	.57786	1.41235	.82610	.56353	1.46595	.83581	.54902	1.52235	42
43	.81631	.57762	1.41322	.82626	.56329	1.46686	.83597	.54878	1.52332	43
44	.81647	.57738	1.41409	.82643	.56305	1.46778	.83613	.54854	1.52429	44
45	.81664	.57715	1.41497	.82659	.56281	1.46870	.83629	.54830	1.52525	45
46	.81681	.57691	1.41584	.82675	.56256	1.46962	.83645	.54805	1.52622	46
47	.81698	.57667	1.41672	.82692	.56232	1.47054	.83661	.54781	1.52719	47
48	.81715	.57643	1.41759	.82708	.56208	1.47146	.83676	.54756	1.52816	48
49	.81731	.57620	1.41847	.82724	.56184	1.47238	.83692	.54732	1.52913	49
50	.81748	.57596	1.41934	.82741	.56160	1.47330	.83708	.54708	1.53010	50
51	0.81765	0.57572	1.42022	0.82757	0.56136	1.47422	0.83724	0.54683	1.53107	51
52	.81782	.57548	1.42110	.82773	.56112	1.47514	.83740	.54659	1.53205	52
53	.81798	.57524	1.42198	.82790	.56088	1.47607	.83756	.54635	1.53302	53
54	.81815	.57501	1.42286	.82806	.56064	1.47699	.83772	.54610	1.53400	54
55	.81832	.57477	1.42374	.82822	.56040	1.47792	.83788	.54586	1.53497	55
56	.81848	.57453	1.42462	.82839	.56016	1.47885	.83804	.54562	1.53595	56
57	.81865	.57429	1.42550	.82855	.55992	1.47977	.83820	.54537	1.53693	57
58	.81882	.57405	1.42638	.82871	.55968	1.48070	.83835	.54513	1.53791	58
59	.81899	.57382	1.42726	.82888	.55943	1.48163	.83851	.54488	1.53888	59
60	0.81915	0.57358	1.42815	0.82904	0.55919	1.48256	0.83867	0.54464	1.53987	60

TABLE OF NATURAL SINES, COSINES AND TANGENTS

′	57° Sin	57° Cos	57° Tan	58° Sin	58° Cos	58° Tan	59° Sin	59° Cos	59° Tan	′
0	0.83867	0.54464	1.53987	0.84805	0.52992	1.60033	0.85717	0.51504	1.66428	0
1	.83883	.54440	1.54085	.84820	.52967	1.60137	.85732	.51479	1.66538	1
2	.83899	.54415	1.54183	.84836	.52943	1.60241	.85747	.51454	1.66647	2
3	.83915	.54391	1.54281	.84851	.52918	1.60345	.85762	.51429	1.66757	3
4	.83930	.54366	1.54379	.84866	.52893	1.60449	.85777	.51404	1.66867	4
5	.83946	.54342	1.54478	.84882	.52869	1.60553	.85792	.51379	1.66978	5
6	.83962	.54317	1.54576	.84897	.52844	1.60657	.85807	.51354	1.67088	6
7	.83978	.54293	1.54675	.84913	.52819	1.60761	.85821	.51329	1.67198	7
8	.83994	.54269	1.54774	.84928	.52794	1.60865	.85836	.51304	1.67309	8
9	.84009	.54244	1.54873	.84943	.52770	1.60970	.85851	.51279	1.67419	9
10	.84025	.54220	1.54972	.84959	.52745	1.61074	.85866	.51254	1.67530	10
11	0.84041	0.54195	1.55071	0.84974	0.52720	1.61179	0.85881	0.51229	1.67641	11
12	.84057	.54171	1.55170	.84989	.52696	1.61283	.85896	.51204	1.67752	12
13	.84072	.54146	1.55269	.85005	.52671	1.61388	.85911	.51179	1.67863	13
14	.84088	.54122	1.55368	.85020	.52646	1.61493	.85926	.51154	1.67974	14
15	.84104	.54097	1.55467	.85035	.52621	1.61598	.85941	.51129	1.68085	15
16	.84120	.54073	1.55567	.85051	.52597	1.61703	.85956	0.51104	1.68196	16
17	.84135	.54049	1.55666	.85066	.52572	1.61809	.85970	.51079	1.68308	17
18	.84151	.54024	1.55766	.85081	.52547	1.61914	.85985	.51054	1.68419	18
19	.84167	.54000	1.55866	.85096	.52522	1.62019	.86000	.51029	1.68531	19
20	.84183	.53975	1.55966	.85112	.52498	1.62125	.86015	.51004	1.68643	20
21	0.84198	0.53951	1.56065	0.85127	0.52473	1.62230	0.86030	0.50979	1.68754	21
22	.84214	.53926	1.56165	.85142	.52448	1.62336	.86045	.50954	1.68866	22
23	.84230	.53902	1.56265	.85158	.52423	1.62442	.86059	.50929	1.68979	23
24	.84245	.53877	1.56366	.85173	.52399	1.62548	.86074	.50904	1.69091	24
25	.84261	.53853	1.56466	.85188	.52374	1.62654	.86089	.50879	1.69203	25
26	.84277	.53828	1.56566	.85203	.52349	1.62760	.86104	.50854	1.69316	26
27	.84292	.53804	1.56667	.85218	.52324	1.62866	.86119	.50829	1.69428	27
28	.84308	.53779	1.56767	.85234	.52300	1.62972	.86133	.50804	1.69541	28
29	.84324	.53755	1.56868	.85249	.52275	1.63079	.86148	.50779	1.69653	29
30	.84339	.53730	1.56969	.85264	.52250	1.63185	.86163	.50754	1.69766	30
31	0.84355	0.53705	1.57069	0.85279	0.52225	1.63292	0.86178	0.50729	1.69879	31
32	.84370	.53681	1.57170	.85294	.52200	1.63398	.86192	.50704	1.69992	32
33	.84386	.53656	1.57271	.85310	.52175	1.63505	.86207	.50679	1.70106	33
34	.84402	.53632	1.57372	.85325	.52151	1.63612	.86222	.50654	1.70219	34
35	.84417	.53607	1.57474	.85340	.52126	1.63719	.86237	.50629	1.70332	35
36	.84433	.53583	1.57575	.85355	.52101	1.63826	.86251	.50603	1.70446	36
37	.84448	.53558	1.57676	.85370	.52076	1.63934	.86266	.50578	1.70560	37
38	.84464	.53534	1.57778	.85385	.52051	1.64041	.86281	.50553	1.70673	38
39	.84480	.53509	1.57879	.85401	.52027	1.64148	.86296	.50528	1.70787	39
40	.84495	.53484	1.57981	.85416	.52002	1.64256	.86310	.50503	1.70901	40
41	0.84511	0.53460	1.58083	0.85431	0.51977	1.64363	0.86325	0.50478	1.71015	41
42	.84526	.53435	1.58184	.85446	.51952	1.64471	.86340	.50453	1.71129	42
43	.84542	.53411	1.58286	.85461	.51927	1.64579	.86354	.50428	1.71244	43
44	.84557	.53386	1.58388	.85476	.51902	1.64687	.86369	.50403	1.71358	44
45	.84573	.53362	1.58490	.85491	.51877	1.64795	.86384	.50377	1.71473	45
46	.84588	.53337	1.58593	.85506	.51853	1.64903	.86398	.50352	1.71588	46
47	.84604	.53312	1.58695	.85521	.51828	1.65011	.86413	.50327	1.71702	47
48	.84619	.53288	1.58797	.85536	.51803	1.65120	.86428	.50302	1.71817	48
49	.84635	.53263	1.58900	.85551	.51778	1.65228	.86442	.50277	1.71932	49
50	.84650	.53238	1.59002	.85567	.51753	1.65337	.86457	.50252	1.72047	50
51	0.84666	0.53214	1.59105	0.85582	0.51728	1.65445	0.86471	0.50227	1.72163	51
52	.84681	.53189	1.59208	.85597	.51703	1.65554	.86486	.50201	1.72278	52
53	.84697	.53165	1.59311	.85612	.51678	1.65663	.86501	.50176	1.72393	53
54	.84712	.53140	1.59414	.85627	.51653	1.65772	.86515	.50151	1.72509	54
55	.84728	.53115	1.59517	.85642	.51628	1.65881	.86530	.50126	1.72625	55
56	.84743	.53091	1.58620	.85657	.51604	1.65990	.86544	.50101	1.72741	56
57	.84759	.53066	1.59723	.95672	.51579	1.66099	.86559	.50076	1.72857	57
58	.84774	.53041	1.59826	.85687	.51554	1.66209	.86573	.50050	1.72973	58
59	.84789	.53017	1.59930	.85702	.51529	1.66318	.86588	.50025	1.73089	59
60	0.84805	0.52992	1.60033	0.85717	0.51504	1.66428	0.86603	0.50000	1.73205	60

TABLE OF NATURAL SINES, COSINES AND TANGENTS

′	60° Sin	Cos	Tan	61° Sin	Cos	Tan	62° Sin	Cos	Tan	′
0	0.86603	0.50000	1.73205	0.87462	0.48481	1.80405	0.88295	0.46947	1.88073	0
1	.86617	.49975	1.73321	.87476	.48456	1.80529	.88308	.46922	1.88205	1
2	.86632	.49950	1.73438	.87490	.48430	1.80653	.88322	.46896	1.88337	2
3	.86646	.49924	1.73555	.87504	.48405	1.80777	.88336	.46870	1.88469	3
4	.86661	.49899	1.73671	.87518	.48379	1.80901	.88349	.46844	1.88602	4
5	.86675	.49874	1.73788	.87532	.48354	1.81025	.88363	.46819	1.88734	5
6	.86690	.49849	1.73905	.87547	.48328	1.81150	.88377	.46793	1.88867	6
7	.86704	.49824	1.74022	.87561	.48303	1.81274	.88390	.46767	1.89000	7
8	.86719	.49798	1.74140	.87575	.48277	1.81399	.88404	.46742	1.89133	8
9	.86733	.49773	1.74257	.87589	.48252	1.81524	.88417	.46716	1.89266	9
10	.86748	.49748	1.74375	.87603	.48226	1.81649	.88431	.46690	1.89400	10
11	0.86762	0.49723	1.74492	0.87617	0.48201	1.81774	0.88445	0.46664	1.89533	11
12	.86777	.49697	1.74610	.87631	.48175	1.81899	.88458	.46639	1.89667	12
13	.86791	.49672	1.74728	.87645	.48150	1.82025	.88472	.46613	1.89801	13
14	.86805	.49647	1.74846	.87659	.48124	1.82150	.88485	.46587	1.89935	14
15	.86820	.49622	1.74964	.87673	.48099	1.82276	.88499	.46562	1.90069	15
16	.86834	.49596	1.75082	.87687	.48073	1.82402	.88512	.46536	1.90203	16
17	.86849	.49571	1.75200	.87701	.48048	1.82528	.88526	.46510	1.90337	17
18	.86863	.49546	1.75319	.87715	.48022	1.82654	.88539	.46484	1.90472	18
19	.86878	.49521	1.75437	.87729	.47997	1.82780	.88553	.46458	1.90607	19
20	.86892	.49495	1.75556	.87743	.47971	1.82906	.88566	.46433	1.90741	20
21	0.86906	0.49470	1.75675	0.87757	0.47946	1.83033	0.88580	0.46407	1.90876	21
22	.86921	.49445	1.75794	.87770	.47920	1.83159	.88593	.46381	1.91012	22
23	.86935	.49420	1.75913	.87784	.47895	1.83286	.88607	.46355	1.91147	23
24	.86950	.49394	1.76032	.87798	.47869	1.83413	.88620	.46330	1.91282	24
25	.86964	.49369	1.76151	.87812	.47844	1.83540	.88634	.46304	1.91418	25
26	.86978	.49344	1.76271	.87826	.47818	1.83667	.88647	.46278	1.91554	26
27	.86993	.49318	1.76390	.87840	.47793	1.83794	.88661	.46252	1.91690	27
28	.87007	.49293	1.76510	.87854	.47767	1.83922	.88674	.46227	1.91826	28
29	.87021	.49268	1.76630	.87868	.47741	1.84049	.88688	.46201	1.91962	29
30	.87036	.49242	1.76749	.87882	.47716	1.84177	.88701	.46175	1.92098	30
31	0.87050	0.49217	1.76869	0.87896	0.47690	1.84305	0.88715	0.46149	1.92235	31
32	.87064	.49192	1.76990	.87910	.47665	1.84433	.88728	.46123	1.92371	32
33	.87079	.49166	1.77110	.87923	.47639	1.84561	.88741	.46097	1.92508	33
34	.87093	.49141	1.77230	.87937	.47614	1.84689	.88755	.46072	1.92645	34
35	.87107	.49116	1.77351	.87951	.47588	1.84818	.88768	.46046	1.92782	35
36	.87121	.49090	1.77471	.87965	.47562	1.84946	.88782	.46020	1.92920	36
37	.87136	.49065	1.77592	.87979	.47537	1.85075	.88795	.45994	1.93057	37
38	.87150	.49040	1.77713	.87993	.47511	1.85204	.88808	.45968	1.93195	38
39	.87164	.49014	1.77834	.88006	.47486	1.85333	.88822	.45943	1.93332	39
40	.87178	.48989	1.77955	.88020	.47460	1.85462	.88835	.45917	1.93470	40
41	0.87193	0.48964	1.78077	0.88034	0.47434	1.85591	0.88848	0.45891	1.93608	41
42	.87207	.48938	1.78198	.88048	.47409	1.85720	.88862	.45865	1.93746	42
43	.87221	.48913	1.78319	.88062	.47383	1.85850	.88875	.45839	1.93885	43
44	.87235	.48888	1.78441	.88075	.47358	1.85979	.88888	.45813	1.94023	44
45	.87250	.48862	1.78563	.88089	.47332	1.86109	.88902	.45787	1.94162	45
46	.87264	.48837	1.78685	.88103	.47306	1.86239	.88915	.45762	1.94301	46
47	.87278	.48811	1.78807	.88117	.47281	1.86369	.88928	.45736	1.94440	47
48	.87292	.48786	1.78929	.88130	.47255	1.86499	.88942	.45710	1.94579	48
49	.87306	.48761	1.79051	.88144	.47229	1.86630	.88955	.45684	1.94718	49
50	.87321	.48735	1.79174	.88158	.47204	1.86760	.88968	.45658	1.94858	50
51	0.87335	0.48710	1.79296	0.88172	0.47178	1.86891	0.88982	0.45632	1.94997	51
52	.87349	.48684	1.79419	.88185	.47153	1.87021	.88995	.45606	1.95137	52
53	.87363	.48659	1.79542	.88199	.47127	1.87152	.89008	.45580	1.95277	53
54	.87377	.48634	1.79665	.88213	.47101	1.87283	.89021	.45555	1.95417	54
55	.87391	.48608	1.79788	.88226	.47076	1.87415	.89035	.45529	1.95557	55
56	.87406	.48583	1.79911	.88240	.47050	1.87546	.89048	.45503	1.95698	56
57	.87420	.48557	1.80034	.88254	.47024	1.87677	.89061	.45477	1.95838	57
58	.87434	.48532	1.80158	.88267	.46999	1.87809	.89074	.45451	1.95979	58
59	.87448	.48506	1.80281	.88281	.46973	1.87941	.89087	.45425	1.96120	59
60	0.87462	0.48481	1.80405	0.88295	0.46947	1.88073	0.89101	0.45399	1.96261	60

TABLE OF NATURAL SINES, COSINES AND TANGENTS

′	**63°** Sin	Cos	Tan	**64°** Sin	Cos	Tan	**65°** Sin	Cos	Tan	′
0	0.89101	0.45399	1.96261	0.89879	0.43837	2.05030	0.90631	0.42262	2.14451	0
1	.89114	.45373	1.96402	.89892	.43811	2.05182	.90643	.42236	2.14614	1
2	.89127	.45347	1.96544	.89905	.43785	2.05333	.90655	.42209	2.14777	2
3	.89140	.45321	1.96685	.89918	.43759	2.05485	.90668	.42183	2.14940	3
4	.89153	.45295	1.96827	.89930	.43733	2.05637	.90680	.42156	2.15104	4
5	.89167	.45269	1.96969	.89943	.43706	2.05790	.90692	.42130	2.15268	5
6	.89180	.45244	1.97111	.89956	.43680	2.05942	.90704	.42104	2.15432	6
7	.89193	.45218	1.97253	.89969	.43654	2.06094	.90717	.42077	2.15596	7
8	.89206	.45192	1.97395	.89981	.43628	2.06247	.90729	.42051	2.15760	8
9	.89219	.45166	1.97538	.89994	.43602	2.06400	.90741	.42024	2.15925	9
10	.89232	.45140	1.97681	.90007	.43576	2.06553	.90753	.41998	2.16090	10
11	0.89246	0.45114	1.97823	0.90019	0.43549	2.06706	0.90766	0.41972	2.16255	11
12	.89259	.45088	1.97966	.90032	.43523	2.06860	.90778	.41945	2.16420	12
13	.89272	.45062	1.98110	.90045	.43497	2.07014	.90790	.41919	2.16585	13
14	.89285	.45036	1.98253	.90057	.43471	2.07167	.90802	.41892	2.16751	14
15	.89298	.45010	1.98396	.90070	.43445	2.07321	.90814	.41866	2.16917	15
16	.89311	.44984	1.98540	.90083	.43418	2.07476	.90827	.41840	2.17083	16
17	.89324	.44958	1.98684	.90095	.43392	2.07630	.90839	.41813	2.17249	17
18	.89337	.44932	1.98828	.90108	.43366	2.07785	.90851	.41787	2.17416	18
19	.89350	.44906	1.98972	.90120	.43340	2.07939	.90863	.41760	2.17582	19
20	.89363	.44880	1.99116	.90133	.43314	2.08094	.90875	.41734	2.17749	20
21	0.89376	0.44854	1.99261	0.90146	0.43287	2.08250	0.90887	0.41707	2.17916	21
22	.89389	.44828	1.99406	.90158	.43261	2.08405	.90899	.41681	2.18084	22
23	.89402	.44802	1.99550	.90171	.43235	2.08560	.90912	.41655	2.18251	23
24	.89415	.44776	1.99695	.90183	.43209	2.08716	.90924	.41628	2.18419	24
25	.89428	.44750	1.99841	.90196	.43182	2.08872	.90936	.41602	2.18587	25
26	.89442	.44724	1.99986	.90208	.43156	2.09028	.90948	.41575	2.18755	26
27	.89455	.44698	2.00131	.90221	.43130	2.09184	.90960	.41549	2.18923	27
28	.89468	.44672	2.00277	.90234	.43104	2.09341	.90972	.41522	2.19092	28
29	.89481	.44646	2.00423	.90246	.43077	2.09498	.90984	.41496	2.19281	29
30	.89493	.44620	2.00569	.90259	.43051	2.09654	.90996	.41469	2.19430	30
31	0.89506	0.44594	2.00715	0.90271	0.43025	2.09811	0.91008	0.41443	2.19599	31
32	.89519	.44568	2.00862	.90284	.42999	2.09969	.91020	.41416	2.19769	32
33	.89532	.44542	2.01008	.90296	.42972	2.10126	.91032	.41390	2.19938	33
34	.89545	.44516	2.01155	.90309	.42946	2.10284	.91044	.41363	2.20108	34
35	.89558	.44490	2.01302	.90321	.42920	2.10442	.91056	.41337	2.20278	35
36	.89571	.44464	2.01449	.90334	.42894	2.10600	.91068	.41310	2.20449	36
37	.89584	.44438	2.01596	.90346	.42867	2.10758	.91080	.41284	2.20619	37
38	.89597	.44411	2.01743	.90359	.42841	2.10916	.91092	.41258	2.20790	38
39	.89610	.44385	2.01891	.90371	.42815	2.11075	.91104	.41231	2.20961	39
40	.89623	.44359	2.02039	.90383	.42788	2.11233	.91116	.41205	2.21132	40
41	0.89636	0.44333	2.02187	0.90396	0.42762	2.11392	0.91128	0.41178	2.21304	41
42	.89649	.44307	2.02335	.90408	.42736	2.11552	.91140	.41151	2.21475	42
43	.89662	.44281	2.02483	.90421	.42710	2.11711	.91152	.41125	2.21647	43
44	.89674	.44255	2.02631	.90433	.42683	2.11871	.91164	.41098	2.21819	44
45	.89687	.44229	2.02780	.90446	.42657	2.12030	.91176	.41072	2.21992	45
46	.89700	.44203	2.02929	.90458	.42631	2.12190	.91188	.41045	2.22164	46
47	.89713	.44177	2.03078	.90470	.42604	2.12350	.91200	.41019	2.22337	47
48	.89726	.44151	2.03227	.90483	.42578	2.12511	.91212	.40992	2.22510	48
49	.89739	.44125	2.03376	.90495	.42552	2.12671	.91224	.40966	2.22683	49
50	.89752	.44098	2.03526	.90508	.42525	2.12832	.91236	.40939	2.22857	50
51	0.89764	0.44072	2.03675	0.90520	0.42499	2.12993	0.91248	0.40913	2.23030	51
52	.89777	.44046	2.03825	.90532	.42473	2.13154	.91260	.40886	2.23204	52
53	.89790	.44020	2.03975	.90545	.42446	2.13316	.91272	.40860	2.23378	53
54	.89803	.43994	2.04125	.90557	.42420	2.13477	.91283	.40833	2.23553	54
55	.89816	.43968	2.04276	.90569	.42394	2.13639	.91295	.40807	2.23727	55
56	.89828	.43942	2.04426	.90582	.42367	2.13801	.91307	.40708	2.23902	56
57	.89841	.43916	2.04577	.90594	.42341	2.13963	.91319	.40753	2.24077	57
58	.89854	.43889	2.04728	.90606	.42315	2.14125	.91331	.40727	2.24252	58
59	.89867	.43863	2.04879	.90619	.42288	2.14288	.91343	.40700	2.24428	59
60	0.89880	0.43837	2.05030	0.90631	0.42262	2.14451	0.91355	0.40674	2.24604	60

TABLE OF NATURAL SINES, COSINES AND TANGENTS

′	66° Sin	Cos	Tan		67° Sin	Cos	Tan		68° Sin	Cos	Tan	′
0	0.91355	0.40674	2.24604		0.92051	0.39073	2.35585		0.92718	0.37461	2.47509	0
1	.91366	.40647	2.24780		.92062	.39046	2.35776		.92729	.37434	2.47716	1
2	.91378	.40621	2.24956		.92073	.39020	2.35967		.92740	.37407	2.47924	2
3	.91390	.40594	2.25132		.92085	.38993	2.36158		.92751	.37380	2.48132	3
4	.91402	.40567	2.25309		.92096	.38966	2.36349		.92762	.37353	2.48340	4
5	.91414	.40541	2.25486		.92107	.38939	2.36541		.92773	.37326	2.48549	5
6	.91425	.40514	2.25663		.92119	.38912	2.36733		.92784	.37299	2.48758	6
7	.91437	.40488	2.25840		.92130	.38886	2.36925		.92795	.37272	2.48967	7
8	.91449	.40461	2.26018		.92141	.38859	2.37118		.92805	.37245	2.49177	8
9	.91461	.40434	2.26196		.92153	.38832	2.37311		.92816	.37218	2.49386	9
10	.91473	.40408	2.26374		.92164	.38805	2.37504		.92827	.37191	2.49597	10
11	0.91484	0.40381	2.26552		0.92175	0.38778	2.37697		0.92838	0.37164	2.49807	11
12	.91496	.40355	2.26730		.92186	.38752	2.37891		.92849	.37137	2.50018	12
13	.91508	.40328	2.26909		.92198	.38725	2.38084		.92859	.37110	2.50229	13
14	.91519	.40301	2.27088		.92209	.38698	2.38279		.92870	.37083	2.50440	14
15	.91531	.40275	2.27267		.92220	.38671	2.38473		.92881	.37056	2.50652	15
16	.91543	.40248	2.27447		.92231	.38644	2.38668		.92892	.37029	2.50864	16
17	.91555	.40221	2.27626		.92243	.38617	2.38863		.92903	.37002	2.51076	17
18	.91566	.40195	2.27806		.92254	.38591	2.39058		.92913	.36975	2.51289	18
19	.91578	.40168	2.27987		.92265	.38564	2.39253		.92924	.36948	2.51502	19
20	.91590	.40142	2.28167		.92276	.38537	2.39449		.92935	.36921	2.51715	20
21	0.91601	0.40115	2.28347		0.92287	0.38510	2.39645		0.92946	0.36894	2.51929	21
22	.91613	.40088	2.28528		.92299	.38483	2.39841		.92956	.36867	2.52142	22
23	.91625	.40062	2.28710		.92310	.38456	2.40038		.92967	.36840	2.52357	23
24	.91636	.40035	2.28891		.92321	.38430	2.40235		.92978	.36813	2.52571	24
25	.91648	.40008	2.29073		.92332	.38403	2.40432		.92988	.36785	2.52786	25
26	.91660	.39982	2.29254		.92343	.38376	2.40629		.92999	.36758	2.53001	26
27	.91671	.39955	2.29437		.92355	.38349	2.40827		.93010	.36731	2.53217	27
28	.91683	.39928	2.29619		.92366	.38322	2.41025		.93020	.36704	2.53432	28
29	.91694	.39902	2.29801		.92377	.38295	2.41223		.93031	.36677	2.53648	29
30	.91706	.39875	2.29984		.92388	.38268	2.41421		.93042	.36650	2.53865	30
31	0.91718	0.39848	2.30167		0.92399	0.38242	2.41620		0.93052	0.36623	2.54082	31
32	.91729	.39822	2.30351		.92410	.38215	2.41819		.93063	.36596	2.54299	32
33	.91741	.39795	2.30534		.92421	.38188	2.42019		.93074	.36569	2.54516	33
34	.91752	.39768	2.30718		.92432	.38161	2.42218		.93084	.36542	2.54734	34
35	.91764	.39742	2.30902		.92444	.38134	2.42418		.93095	.36515	2.54952	35
36	.91776	.39715	2.31088		.92455	.38107	2.42618		.93106	.36488	2.55170	36
37	.91787	.39688	2.31271		.92466	.38080	2.42819		.93116	.36461	2.55389	37
38	.91799	.39661	2.31456		.92477	.38053	2.43019		.93127	.36434	2.55608	38
39	.91810	.39635	2.31641		.92487	.38026	2.43220		.93137	.36406	2.55827	39
40	.91822	.39608	2.31826		.92499	.37999	2.43422		.93148	.36379	2.56046	40
41	0.91833	0.39581	2.32012		0.92510	0.37973	2.43623		0.93169	0.36352	2.56266	41
42	.91845	.39555	2.32197		.92521	.37946	2.43825		.93169	.36325	2.56487	42
43	.91856	.39528	2.32383		.92532	.37919	2.44027		.93180	.35298	2.56707	43
44	.91868	.39501	2.32570		.92543	.37892	2.44230		.93190	.36271	2.56928	44
45	.91879	.39474	2.32756		.92554	.37865	2.44433		.93201	.36244	2.57150	45
46	.91891	.39448	2.32943		.92565	.37838	2.44636		.93211	.36217	2.57371	46
47	.91902	.39421	2.33130		.92576	.37811	2.44839		.93222	.36190	2.57593	47
48	.91914	.39394	2.33317		.92587	.37784	2.45043		.93232	.36163	2.57815	48
49	.91925	.39368	2.33505		.92598	.37757	2.45246		.93243	.36135	2.58038	49
50	.91936	.39341	2.33693		.92609	.37730	2.45451		.93253	.36108	2.58261	50
51	0.91948	0.39314	2.33881		0.92620	0.37703	2.45655		0.93264	0.36081	2.58484	51
52	.91959	.39287	2.34069		.92631	.37676	2.45860		.93274	.36054	2.58708	52
53	.91971	.39261	2.34258		.92642	.37649	2.46065		.93285	.36027	2.58932	53
54	.91982	.39234	2.34447		.92653	.37622	2.46270		.93295	.36000	2.59156	54
55	.91994	.39207	2.34636		.92664	.37596	2.46476		.93306	.35973	2.59381	55
56	.92005	.39180	2.34825		.92675	.37569	2.46682		.93316	.35945	2.59606	56
57	.92016	.39153	2.35015		.92686	.37542	2.46888		.93327	.35918	2.59831	57
58	.92028	.39127	2.35205		.92697	.37515	2.47095		.93337	.35891	2.60057	58
59	.92039	.39100	2.35395		.92708	.37488	2.47302		.93348	.35864	2.60283	59
60	0.92051	0.39073	2.35585		0.92718	0.37461	2.47509		0.93358	0.35837	2.60509	60

TABLE OF NATURAL SINES, COSINES AND TANGENTS

′	69° Sin	Cos	Tan		70° Sin	Cos	Tan		71° Sin	Cos	Tan	′
0	0.93358	0.35837	2.60509		0.93969	0.34202	2.74748		0.94552	0.32557	2.90421	0
1	.93369	.35810	2.60736		.93979	.34175	2.74997		.94561	.32529	2.90696	1
2	.93379	.35783	2.60963		.93989	.34147	2.75246		.94571	.32502	2.90971	2
3	.93389	.35755	2.61190		.93999	.34120	2.75496		.94580	.32474	2.91246	3
4	.93400	.35728	2.61418		.94009	.34093	2.75746		.94590	.32447	2.91523	4
5	.93410	.35701	2.61646		.94019	.34065	2.75996		.94599	.32419	2.91799	5
6	.93420	.35674	2.61874		.94029	.34038	2.76247		.94609	.32392	2.92076	6
7	.93431	.35647	2.62103		.94039	.34011	2.76498		.94618	.32364	2.93454	7
8	.93441	.35619	2.62332		.94049	.33983	2.76750		.94627	.32337	2.92632	8
9	.93452	.35592	2.62561		.94059	.33956	2.77002		.94637	.32309	2.93910	9
10	.93462	.35565	2.62791		.94068	.33929	2.77254		.94646	.32282	2.93189	10
11	0.93472	0.35538	2.63021		0.94078	0.33901	2.77507		0.94656	0.32254	2.93468	11
12	.93483	.35511	2.63252		.94088	.33874	2.77761		.94665	.32227	2.93748	12
13	.93493	.35484	2.63483		.94098	.33846	2.78014		.94674	.32199	2.94028	13
14	.93503	.35456	2.63714		.94108	.33819	2.78269		.94684	.32172	2.94309	14
15	.93514	.35429	2.63945		.94118	.33792	2.78523		.94693	.32144	2.94591	15
16	.93524	.35402	2.64177		.94127	.33764	2.78778		.94702	.32116	2.94872	16
17	.93534	.35375	2.64410		.94137	.33737	2.79033		.94712	.32089	2.95155	17
18	.93544	.35348	2.64642		.94147	.33710	2.79289		.94721	.32061	2.95437	18
19	.93555	.35320	2.64875		.94157	.33682	2.79545		.94730	.32034	2.95721	19
20	.93565	.35293	2.65109		.94167	.33655	2.79802		.94740	.32006	2.96004	20
21	0.93575	0.35266	2.65342		0.94176	0.33627	2.80059		0.94749	0.31979	2.96288	21
22	.93586	.35239	2.65576		.94186	.33600	2.80316		.94758	.31951	2.96573	22
23	.93596	.35211	2.65811		.94196	.33573	2.80574		.94768	.31924	2.96858	23
24	.93606	.35184	2.66046		.94206	.33545	2.80833		.94777	.31896	2.97144	24
25	.93616	.35157	2.66281		.94216	.33518	2.81091		.94786	.31868	2.97430	25
26	.93626	.35130	2.66516		.94225	.33490	2.81350		.94795	.31841	2.97717	26
27	.93637	.35103	2.66752		.94235	.33463	2.81610		.94805	.31813	2.98004	27
28	.93647	.35075	2.66989		.94245	.33436	2.81870		.94814	.31786	2.98292	28
29	.93657	.35048	2.67225		.94254	.33408	2.82130		.94823	.31758	2.98580	29
30	.93667	.35021	2.67462		.94264	.33381	2.82391		.94832	.31731	2.98869	30
31	0.93677	0.34994	2.67700		0.94274	0.33353	2.82653		0.94842	0.31703	2.99158	31
32	.93688	.34966	2.67937		.94284	.33326	2.82914		.94851	.31675	2.99447	32
33	.93698	.34939	2.68175		.94293	.33298	2.83176		.94860	.31648	2.99738	33
34	.93708	.34912	2.68414		.94303	.33271	2.83439		.94869	.31620	3.00028	34
35	.93718	.34885	2.68653		.94313	.33244	2.83702		.94878	.31593	3.00319	35
36	.93728	.34857	2.68892		.94322	.33216	2.83965		.94888	.31565	3.00611	36
37	.93738	.34830	2.69131		.94332	.33189	2.84229		.94897	.31537	3.00903	37
38	.93749	.34803	2.69371		.94342	.33161	2.84494		.94906	.31510	3.01196	38
39	.93759	.34775	2.69612		.94351	.33134	2.84758		.94915	.31482	3.01489	39
40	.93769	.34748	2.69853		.94361	.33106	2.85023		.94924	.31455	3.01783	40
41	0.93779	0.34721	2.70094		0.94371	0.33079	2.85289		0.94933	0.31427	3.02077	41
42	.93789	.34694	2.70335		.94380	.33051	2.85555		.94943	.31399	3.02372	42
43	.93799	.34666	2.70755		.94390	.33024	2.85822		.94952	.31372	3.02667	43
44	.93809	.34639	2.70819		.94399	.32997	2.86089		.94961	.31344	3.02963	44
45	.93819	.34612	2.71062		.94409	.32969	2.86356		.94970	.31316	3.03260	45
46	.93829	.34584	2.71305		.94419	.32942	2.86624		.94979	.31289	3.03556	46
47	.93839	.34557	2.71548		.94428	.32914	2.86892		.94988	.31261	3.03854	47
48	.93849	.34530	2.71792		.94438	.32887	2.87161		.94997	.31234	3.04152	48
49	.93859	.34503	2.72036		.94447	.32859	2.87430		.95006	.31206	3.04450	49
50	.93869	.34475	2.72281		.94457	.32832	2.87700		.95015	.31178	3.04749	50
51	0.93879	0.34448	2.72526		0.94467	0.32804	2.87970		0.95024	0.31151	3.05049	51
52	.93889	.34421	2.72771		.94476	.32777	2.88240		.95034	.31123	3.05349	52
53	.93899	.34393	2.73017		.94485	.32749	2.88511		.95043	.31095	3.05649	53
54	.93909	.34366	2.73263		.94495	.32722	2.88783		.95052	.31068	3.05950	54
55	.93919	.34339	2.73509		.94504	.32694	2.89055		.95061	.31040	3.06252	55
56	.93929	.34311	2.73756		.94514	.32667	2.89327		.95070	.31012	3.06554	56
57	.93939	.34284	2.74004		.94523	.32639	2.89600		.95079	.30985	3.06857	57
58	.93949	.34257	2.74251		.94533	.32612	2.89873		.95088	.30957	3.07160	58
59	.93959	.34229	2.74499		.94542	.32584	2.90147		.95097	.30929	3.07464	59
60	0.93969	0.34202	2.74748		0.94552	0.32557	2.90421		0.95106	0.30902	3.07768	60

TABLE OF NATURAL SINES, COSINES AND TANGENTS

′	72° Sin	Cos	Tan	73° Sin	Cos	Tan	74° Sin	Cos	Tan	′
0	0.95106	0.30902	3.07768	0.95631	0.29237	3.27085	0.96126	0.27564	3.48741	0
1	.95115	.30874	3.08073	.95639	.29209	3.27426	.96134	.27536	3.49125	1
2	.95124	.30846	3.08379	.95648	.29182	3.27767	.96142	.27508	3.49509	2
3	.95133	.30819	3.08685	.95656	.29154	3.28109	.96150	.27480	3.49894	3
4	.95142	.30791	3.08991	.95664	.29126	3.28452	.96158	.27452	3.50279	4
5	.95151	.30763	3.09298	.95673	.29098	3.28795	.96166	.27424	3.50666	5
6	.95159	.30736	3.09606	.95681	.29070	3.29139	.96174	.27396	3.51053	6
7	.95168	.30708	3.09914	.95690	.29042	3.29483	.96182	.27368	3.51441	7
8	.95177	.30680	3.10223	.95698	.29015	3.29829	.96190	.27340	3.51829	8
9	.95186	.30653	3.10532	.95707	.28987	3.30174	.96198	.27312	3.52219	9
10	.95195	.30625	3.10842	.95715	.28959	3.30521	.96206	.27284	3.52609	10
11	0.95204	0.30597	3.11153	0.95724	0.28931	3.30868	0.96214	0.27256	3.53001	11
12	.95213	.30570	3.11464	.95732	.28903	3.31216	.96222	.27228	3.53393	12
13	.95222	.30542	3.11775	.95740	.28875	3.31565	.96230	.27200	3.53785	13
14	.95231	.30514	3.12087	.95749	.28848	3.31914	.96238	.27172	3.54179	14
15	.95240	.30486	3.12400	.95757	.28820	3.32264	.96246	.27144	3.54573	15
16	.95248	.30459	3.12713	.95766	.28792	3.32614	.96253	.27116	3.54968	16
17	.95257	.30431	3.13027	.95774	.28764	3.32965	.96261	.27088	3.55364	17
18	.95266	.30403	3.13341	.95782	.28736	3.33317	.96269	.27060	3.55761	18
19	.95275	.30376	3.13656	.95791	.28708	3.33670	.96277	.27032	3.56159	19
20	.95284	.30348	3.13972	.95799	.28680	3.34023	.96285	.27004	3.56557	20
21	0.95293	0.30320	3.14288	0.95807	0.28652	3.34377	0.96293	0.26976	3.56957	21
22	.95302	.30292	3.14605	.95816	.28625	3.34732	.96301	.26948	3.57357	22
23	.95310	.30265	3.14922	.95824	.28597	3.35087	.96308	.26920	3.57758	23
24	.95319	.30237	3.15240	.95832	.28569	3.35443	.96316	.26892	3.58160	24
25	.95328	.30209	3.15558	.95841	.28541	3.35800	.96324	.26864	3.58562	25
26	.95337	.30182	3.15877	.95849	.28513	3.36158	.96332	.26836	3.58966	26
27	.95345	.30154	3.16197	.95857	.28485	3.36516	.96340	.26808	3.59370	27
28	.95354	.30126	3.16517	.95865	.28457	3.36875	.96348	.26780	3.59775	28
29	.95363	.30098	3.16838	.95874	.28429	3.37234	.96355	.26752	3.60181	29
30	.95372	.30071	3.17159	.95882	.28402	3.37594	.96363	.26724	3.60588	30
31	0.95380	0.30043	3.17481	0.95890	0.28374	3.37955	0.96371	0.26696	3.60996	31
32	.95389	.30015	3.17804	.95899	.28346	3.38317	.96379	.26668	3.61405	32
33	.95398	.29987	3.18127	.95907	.28318	3.38679	.96386	.26640	3.61814	33
34	.95407	.29960	3.18451	.95915	.28290	3.39042	.96394	.26612	3.62224	34
35	.95415	.29932	3.18775	.95923	.28262	3.39406	.96402	.26584	3.62636	35
36	.95425	.29904	3.19100	.95931	.28234	3.39771	.96410	.26556	3.63048	36
37	.95433	.29876	3.19426	.95940	.28206	3.40136	.96417	.26528	3.63461	37
38	.95441	.29849	3.19752	.95948	.28178	3.40502	.96425	.26500	3.63874	38
39	.95450	.29821	3.20079	.95956	.28150	3.40869	.96433	.26472	3.64289	39
40	.95459	.29793	3.20406	.95964	.28123	3.41236	.96440	.26443	3.64705	40
41	0.95467	0.29765	3.20734	0.95972	0.28095	3.41604	0.96448	0.26415	3.65121	41
42	.95476	.29738	3.21063	.95981	.28067	3.41973	.96456	.26387	3.65338	42
43	.95485	.29710	3.21392	.95989	.28039	3.42343	.96463	.26359	3.63957	43
44	.95493	.29682	3.21722	.95997	.28011	3.42713	.96471	.26331	3.66376	44
45	.95502	.29654	3.22053	.96005	.27983	3.43084	.96479	.26303	3.66796	45
46	.95511	.29626	3.22384	.96013	.27955	3.43456	.96486	.26275	3.67217	46
47	.95519	.29599	3.22715	.96021	.27927	3.43829	.96494	.26247	3.67638	47
48	.95528	.29571	3.23048	.96029	.27899	3.44202	.96502	.26219	3.68061	48
49	.95536	.29543	3.23381	.96038	.27871	3.44576	.96509	.26191	3.68484	49
50	.95545	.29515	3.23714	.96046	.27843	3.44951	.96517	.26163	3.68909	50
51	0.95554	0.29487	3.24049	0.96054	0.27815	3.45327	0.96525	0.26135	3.69335	51
52	.95562	.29460	3.24383	.96062	.27787	3.45703	.96532	.26107	3.69761	52
53	.95571	.29432	3.24719	.96070	.27759	3.46080	.96540	.26079	3.70188	53
54	.95579	.29404	3.25055	.96078	.27732	3.46458	.96547	.26051	3.70616	54
55	.95588	.29376	3.25392	.96086	.27704	3.46837	.96555	.26022	3.71046	55
56	.95596	.29348	3.25729	.96094	.27676	3.47216	.96562	.25994	3.71476	56
57	.95605	.29321	3.26067	.96102	.27648	3.47596	.96570	.25966	3.71907	57
58	.95613	.29293	3.26406	.96110	.27620	3.47977	.96578	.25938	3.72338	58
59	.95622	.29265	3.26745	.96118	.27592	3.48359	.96585	.25910	3.72771	59
60	0.95631	0.29237	3.27085	0.96126	0.27564	3.48741	0.96593	0.25882	3.73205	60

TABLE OF NATURAL SINES, COSINES AND TANGENTS

,	75° Sin	75° Cos	75° Tan	76° Sin	76° Cos	76° Tan	77° Sin	77° Cos	77° Tan	,
0	0.96593	0.25882	3.73205	0.97030	0.24192	4.01078	0.97437	0.22495	4.33148	0
1	.96600	.25854	3.73640	.97037	.24164	4.01576	.97444	.22467	4.33723	1
2	.96608	.25826	3.74075	.97044	.24136	4.02074	.97450	.22438	4.34300	2
3	.96615	.25798	3.74512	.97051	.24108	4.02574	.97457	.22410	4.34879	3
4	.96623	.25770	3.74950	.97058	.24079	4.03076	.97463	.22382	4.35459	4
5	.96630	.25741	3.75388	.97065	.24051	4.03578	.97470	.22353	4.36040	5
6	.96638	.25713	3.75828	.97072	.24023	4.04081	.97476	.22325	4.36623	6
7	.96645	.25685	3.76268	.97079	.23995	4.04586	.97483	.22297	4.37207	7
8	.96653	.25657	3.76709	.97086	.23966	4.05092	.97489	.22268	4.37793	8
9	.96660	.25629	3.77152	.97093	.23938	4.05599	.97496	.22240	4.38381	9
10	.96668	.25601	3.77595	.97100	.23910	4.06107	.97502	.22212	3.38969	10
11	0.96675	0.25573	3.78040	0.97107	0.23882	4.06616	0.97509	0.22183	4.39560	11
12	.96682	.25545	3.78485	.97113	.23853	4.07127	.97515	.22155	4.40152	12
13	.96690	.25517	3.78931	.97120	.23825	4.07639	.97521	.22127	4.40745	13
14	.96697	.25488	3.79378	.97127	.23797	4.08152	.97528	.22098	4.41340	14
15	.96705	.25460	3.79827	.97134	.23769	4.08666	.97534	.22070	4.41936	15
16	.96712	.25432	3.80276	.97141	.23740	4.09182	.97541	.22041	4.42534	16
17	.96720	.25404	3.80726	.97148	.23712	4.09699	.97547	.22013	4.43134	17
18	.96727	.25376	3.81177	.97155	.23684	4.10216	.97554	.21985	4.43735	18
19	.96734	.25348	3.81630	.97162	.23656	4.10736	.97560	.21956	4.44338	19
20	.96742	.25320	3.82083	.97169	.23627	4.11256	.97566	.21928	4.44942	20
21	0.96749	0.25291	3.82537	0.97176	0.23599	4.11778	0.97573	0.21900	4.45548	21
22	.96756	.25263	3.82992	.97182	.23571	4.12301	.97579	.21871	4.46155	22
23	.96764	.25235	3.83449	.97189	.23543	4.12825	.97585	.21843	4.46764	23
24	.96771	.25207	3.83906	.97196	.23514	4.13350	.97592	.21814	4.47374	24
25	.96778	.25179	3.84364	.97203	.23486	4.13877	.97598	.21786	4.47986	25
26	.96786	.25151	3.84824	.97210	.23458	4.14405	.97604	.21758	4.48600	26
27	.96793	.25123	3.85284	.97217	.23429	4.14934	.97611	.21729	4.49215	27
28	.96800	.25094	3.85745	.97223	.23401	4.15465	.97617	.21701	4.49832	28
29	.96808	.25066	3.86208	.97230	.23373	4.15997	.97623	.21672	4.50451	29
30	.96815	.25038	3.86671	.97237	.23345	4.16530	.97630	.21644	4.51071	30
31	0.96822	0.25010	3.87136	0.97244	0.23316	4.17064	0.97636	0.21616	4.51693	31
32	.96829	.24982	3.87601	.97251	.23288	4.17600	.97642	.21587	4.52316	32
33	.96837	.24954	3.88068	.97257	.23260	4.18137	.97649	.21559	4.52941	33
34	.96844	.24925	3.88536	.97264	.23231	4.18675	.97655	.21530	4.53568	34
35	.96851	.24897	3.89004	.97271	.23203	4.19215	.97661	.21502	4.54196	35
36	.96858	.24869	3.89474	.97278	.23175	4.19756	.97667	.21474	4.54826	36
37	.96866	.24841	3.89945	.97284	.23147	4.20298	.97674	.21445	4.55458	37
38	.96873	.24813	3.90417	.97291	.23118	4.20842	.97680	.21417	4.56091	38
39	.96880	.24785	3.90890	.97298	.23090	4.21387	.97686	.21388	4.56726	39
40	.96887	.24756	3.91364	.97305	.23062	4.21933	.97692	.21360	4.57363	40
41	0.96894	0.24728	3.91839	0.97311	0.23033	4.22481	0.97698	0.21332	4.58001	41
42	.96902	.24700	3.92316	.97318	.23005	4.23030	.97705	.21303	4.58641	42
43	.96909	.24672	3.92793	.97325	.22977	4.23580	.97711	.21275	4.59283	43
44	.96916	.24644	3.93271	.97331	.22948	4.24132	.97717	.21246	4.59927	44
45	.96923	.24615	3.93751	.97338	.22920	4.24685	.97723	.21218	4.60572	45
46	.96930	.24587	3.94232	.97345	.22892	4.25239	.97729	.21189	4.61219	46
47	.96937	.24559	3.94713	.97351	.22863	4.25795	.97735	.21161	4.61868	47
48	.96945	.24531	3.95196	.97358	.22835	4.26352	.97742	.21133	4.62518	48
49	.96952	.24503	3.95680	.97365	.22807	4.26911	.97748	.21104	4.63171	49
50	.96959	.24474	3.96165	.97371	.22778	4.27471	.97754	.21076	4.63825	50
51	0.96966	0.24446	3.96651	0.97378	0.22750	4.28032	0.97760	0.21047	4.64480	51
52	.96973	.24418	3.97139	.97384	.22722	4.28595	.07766	.21019	4.65138	52
53	.96980	.24390	3.97627	.97391	.22694	4.29159	.07772	.20990	4.65797	53
54	.96987	.24362	3.98117	.97398	.22665	4.29724	.97778	.20962	4.66458	54
55	.96994	.24333	3.98607	.97404	.22637	4.30291	.97784	.20933	4.67121	55
56	.97001	.24305	3.99099	.97411	.22609	4.30860	.97791	.20905	4.67786	56
57	.97008	.24277	3.99592	.97417	.22580	4.31430	.97797	.20877	4.68452	57
58	.97016	.24249	4.00086	.97424	.22552	4.32001	.97803	.20848	4.69121	58
59	.97023	.24220	4.00582	.97431	.22523	4.32573	.97809	.20820	4.69791	59
60	0.97030	0.24192	4.01078	0.97437	0.22495	4.33148	0.97815	0.20791	4.70463	60

TABLE OF NATURAL SINES, COSINES AND TANGENTS

′	78°				79°				80°			′
	Sin	Cos	Tan		Sin	Cos	Tan		Sin	Cos	Tan	
0	0.97815	0.20791	4.70463		0.98163	0.19081	5.14455		0.98481	0.17365	5.67128	0
1	.97821	.20763	4.71137		.98168	.19052	5.15256		.98486	.17336	5.68094	1
2	.97827	.20734	4.71813		.98174	.19024	5.16058		.98491	.17308	5.69064	2
3	.97833	.20706	4.72490		.98179	.18995	5.16863		.98496	.17279	5.70037	3
4	.97839	.20677	4.73170		.98185	.18967	5.17671		.98501	.17250	5.71013	4
5	.97845	.20649	4.73851		.98190	.18938	5.18480		.98506	.17222	5.71992	5
6	.97851	.20620	4.74534		.98196	.18910	5.19293		.98511	.17193	5.72974	6
7	.97857	.20592	4.75219		.98201	.18881	5.20107		.98516	.17164	5.73960	7
8	.97863	.20564	4.75906		.98207	.18852	5.20925		.98521	.17136	5.74949	8
9	.97869	.20535	4.76595		.98212	.18824	5.21744		.98526	.17107	5.75941	9
10	.97875	.20507	4.77286		.98218	.18795	5.22566		.98531	.17078	5.76937	10
11	0.97881	0.20478	4.77978		0.98223	0.18767	5.23391		0.98536	0.17050	5.77936	11
12	.97887	.20450	4.78673		.98229	.18738	5.24218		.98541	.17021	5.78938	12
13	.97893	.20421	4.79370		.98234	.18710	5.25048		.98546	.16992	5.79944	13
14	.97899	.20393	4.80068		.98240	.18681	5.25880		.98551	.16964	5.80953	14
15	.97905	.20364	4.80769		.98245	.18652	5.26715		.98556	.16935	5.81966	15
16	.97911	.20336	4.81471		.98251	.18624	5.27553		.98561	.16906	5.82982	16
17	.97916	.20307	4.82175		.98256	.18595	5.28393		.98565	.16878	5.84001	17
18	.97922	.20279	4.82882		.98261	.18567	5.29235		.98570	.16849	5.85024	18
19	.97928	.20250	4.83590		.98267	.18538	5.30080		.98575	.16820	5.86051	19
20	.97934	.20222	4.84300		.98272	.18510	5.30928		.98580	.16792	5.87080	20
21	0.97940	0.20193	4.85013		0.98277	0.18481	5.31778		0.98585	0.16763	5.88114	21
22	.97946	.20165	4.85727		.98283	.18452	5.32631		.98590	.16734	5.89151	22
23	.97952	.20136	4.86443		.98288	.18424	5.33487		.98595	.16706	5.90191	23
24	.97958	.20108	4.87162		.98294	.18395	5.34345		.98600	.16677	5.91236	24
25	.97963	.20079	4.87882		.98299	.18367	5.35206		.98605	.16648	5.92283	25
26	.97969	.20051	4.88605		.98304	.18338	5.36070		.98609	.16620	5.93335	26
27	.97975	.20022	4.89330		.98310	.18309	5.36936		.98614	.16591	5.94390	27
28	.97981	.19994	4.90056		.98315	.18281	5.37805		.98619	.16562	5.95448	28
29	.97987	.19965	4.90785		.98320	.18252	5.38677		.98624	.16533	5.96510	29
30	.97993	.19937	4.91516		.98326	.18224	5.39552		.98629	.16505	5.97576	30
31	0.97998	0.19908	4.92249		0.98331	0.18195	5.40429		0.98634	0.16476	5.98646	31
32	.98004	.19880	4.92984		.98336	.18166	5.41309		.98639	.16447	5.99720	32
33	.98010	.19851	4.93721		.98341	.18138	5.42192		.98643	.16419	6.00797	33
34	.98016	.19823	4.94460		.98347	.18109	5.43078		.98648	.16390	6.01878	34
35	.98021	.19794	4.95201		.98352	.18081	5.43966		.98653	.16361	6.02962	35
36	.98027	.19766	4.95945		.98357	.18052	5.44857		.98657	.16333	6.04051	36
37	.98033	.19737	4.96690		.98362	.18023	5.45751		.98662	.16304	6.05143	37
38	.98039	.19709	4.97438		.98368	.17995	5.46648		.98667	.16275	6.06240	38
39	.98044	.19680	4.98188		.98373	.17966	5.47548		.98671	.16247	6.07340	39
40	.98050	.19652	4.98940		.98378	.17938	5.48451		.98676	.16218	6.08444	40
41	0.98056	0.19623	4.99695		0.98383	0.17909	5.49356		0.98681	0.16189	6.09552	41
42	.98062	.19595	5.00451		.98389	.17880	5.50264		.98686	.16160	6.10664	42
43	.98067	.19566	5.01210		.98394	.17852	5.51176		.98690	.16132	6.11779	43
44	.98073	.19538	5.01971		.98400	.17823	5.52090		.98695	.16103	6.12899	44
45	.98079	.19509	5.02734		.98404	.17794	5.53007		.98700	.16074	6.14023	45
46	.98084	.19481	5.03499		.98409	.17766	5.53927		.98704	.16046	6.15151	46
47	.98090	.19452	5.04267		.98414	.17737	5.54851		.98709	.16017	6.16283	47
48	.98096	.19423	5.05037		.98420	.17709	5.55777		.98714	.15988	6.17419	48
49	.98101	.19395	5.05809		.98425	.17680	5.56706		.98718	.15959	6.18559	49
50	.98107	.19366	5.06584		.98430	.17651	5.57638		.98723	.15931	6.19703	50
51	0.98112	0.19338	5.07360		0.98435	0.17623	5.58573		0.98728	0.15902	6.20851	51
52	.98118	.19309	5.08139		.98440	.17594	5.59511		.98732	.15873	6.22003	52
53	.98124	.19281	5.08921		.98445	.17565	5.60452		.98737	.15845	6.23160	53
54	.98129	.19252	5.09704		.98450	.17537	5.61397		.98741	.15816	6.24321	54
55	.98135	.19224	5.10490		.98455	.17508	5.62344		.98746	.15787	6.25486	55
56	.98141	.19195	5.11279		.98461	.17479	5.63295		.98751	.15758	6.26655	56
57	.98146	.19167	5.12069		.98466	.17451	5.64248		.98755	.15730	6.27829	57
58	.98152	.19138	5.12862		.98471	.17422	5.65205		.98760	.15701	6.29007	58
59	.98157	.19110	5.13658		.98476	.17394	5.66165		.98764	.15672	6.30189	59
60	0.98163	0.19081	5.14455		0.98481	0.17365	5.67128		0.98769	0.15643	6.31375	60

TABLE OF NATURAL SINES, COSINES AND TANGENTS

′	Sin	Cos	Tan	Sin	Cos	Tan	Sin	Cos	Tan	′
	81°			**82°**			**83°**			
0	0.98769	0.15643	6.31375	0.99027	0.13917	7.11537	0.99255	0.12187	8.14435	0
1	.98773	.15615	6.32566	.99031	.13889	7.13042	.99258	.12158	8.16398	1
2	.98778	.15586	6.33761	.99035	.13860	7.14553	.99262	.12129	8.18370	2
3	.98782	.15557	6.34961	.99039	.13831	7.16071	.99265	.12100	8.20352	3
4	.98787	.15529	6.36165	.99043	.13802	7.17594	.99269	.12071	8.22344	4
5	.98792	.15500	6.37374	.99047	.13773	7.19125	.99272	.12043	8.24345	5
6	.98796	.15471	6.38587	.99051	.13745	7.20661	.99276	.12014	8.26355	6
7	.98801	.15442	6.39804	.99055	.13716	7.22204	.99279	.11985	8.28376	7
8	.98805	.15414	6.41026	.99059	.13687	7.23754	.99283	.11956	8.30406	8
9	.98809	.15385	6.42253	.99063	.13658	7.25310	.99286	.11927	8.32446	9
10	.98814	.15356	6.43484	.99067	.13629	7.26873	.99290	.11898	8.34496	10
11	0.98818	0.15327	6.44720	0.99071	0.13600	7.28442	0.99293	0.11869	8.36555	11
12	.98823	.15299	6.45961	.99075	.13572	7.30018	.99297	.11840	8.38625	12
13	.98827	.15270	6.47206	.99079	.13543	7.31600	.99300	.11812	8.40705	13
14	.98832	.15241	6.48456	.99083	.13514	7.33190	.99303	.11783	8.42795	14
15	.98836	.15212	6.49710	.99087	.13485	7.34786	.99307	.11754	8.44896	15
16	.98841	.15184	6.50970	.99091	.13456	7.36389	.99310	.11725	8.47007	16
17	.98845	.15155	6.52234	.99094	.13427	7.37999	.99314	.11696	8.49128	17
18	.98849	.15126	6.53503	.99098	.13399	7.39616	.99317	.11667	8.51259	18
19	.98854	.15097	6.54777	.99102	.13370	7.41240	.99321	.11638	8.53402	19
20	.98858	.15069	6.56055	.99106	.13341	7.42871	.99324	.11609	8.55555	20
21	0.98863	0.15040	6.57339	0.99110	0.13312	7.44509	0.99327	0.11580	8.57718	21
22	.98867	.15011	6.58627	.99114	.13283	7.46154	.99331	.11552	8.59893	22
23	.98871	.14982	6.59921	.99118	.13255	7.47806	.99334	.11523	8.62078	23
24	.98876	.14954	6.61219	.99122	.13226	7.49465	.99337	.11494	8.64275	24
25	.98880	.14925	6.62523	.99125	.13197	7.51132	.99341	.11465	8.66482	25
26	.98884	.14896	6.63831	.99129	.13168	7.52806	.99344	.11436	8.68701	26
27	.98889	.14867	6.65144	.99133	.13139	7.54487	.99347	.11407	8.70931	27
28	.98893	.14839	6.66463	.99137	.13110	7.56176	.99351	.11378	8.73172	28
29	.98897	.14810	6.67787	.99141	.13082	7.57872	.99354	.11349	8.75425	29
30	.98902	.14781	6.69116	.99145	.13053	7.59575	.99357	.11320	8.77689	30
31	0.98906	0.14752	6.70450	0.99148	0.13024	7.61287	0.99361	0.11291	8.79964	31
32	.98910	.14723	6.71789	.99152	.12995	7.63005	.99364	.11263	8.82252	32
33	.98915	.14695	6.73133	.99156	.12966	7.64732	.99367	.11234	8.84551	33
34	.98919	.14666	6.74483	.99160	.12937	7.66466	.99370	.11205	8.86862	34
35	.98923	.14637	6.75838	.99163	.12908	7.68208	.99374	.11176	8.89615	35
36	.98927	.14608	6.77199	.99167	.12880	7.69957	.99377	.11147	8.91520	36
37	.98932	.14580	6.78564	.99171	.12851	7.71715	.99380	.11118	8.93867	37
38	.98936	.14551	6.79936	.99175	.12822	7.73480	.99383	.11089	8.96227	38
39	.98940	.14522	6.81312	.99178	.12793	7.75254	.99387	.11060	8.98598	39
40	.98944	.14493	6.82694	.99182	.12764	7.77035	.99390	.11031	9.00983	40
41	0.98948	0.14464	6.84082	0.99186	0.12735	7.78825	0.99393	0.11002	9.03379	41
42	.98953	.14436	6.85475	.99189	.12707	7.80622	.99396	.10973	9.05789	42
43	.98957	.14407	6.86874	.99193	.12678	7.82428	.99399	.10945	9.08211	43
44	.98961	.14378	6.88278	.99197	.12649	7.84242	.99403	.10916	9.10646	44
45	.98965	.14349	6.89688	.99201	.12620	7.86064	.99406	.10887	9.13093	45
46	.98969	.14321	6.91104	.99204	.12591	7.87895	.99409	.10858	9.15554	46
47	.98974	.14292	6.92525	.99208	.12562	7.89734	.99412	.10829	9.18028	47
48	.98978	.14263	6.93952	.99212	.12533	7.91582	.99415	.10800	9.20516	48
49	.98982	.14234	6.95385	.99215	.12505	7.93438	.99418	.10771	9.23016	49
50	.98986	.14205	6.96823	.99219	.12476	7.95302	.99421	.10742	9.25530	50
51	0.98990	0.14177	6.98268	0.99222	0.12447	7.97176	0.99425	0.10713	9.28058	51
52	.98994	.14148	6.99718	.99226	.12418	7.99058	.99428	.10684	9.30599	52
53	.98998	.14119	7.01174	.99230	.12389	8.00948	.99431	.10655	9.33155	53
54	.99002	.14090	7.02637	.99233	.12360	8.02848	.99434	.10626	9.35724	54
55	.99007	.14061	7.04105	.99237	.12331	8.04756	.99437	.10598	9.38307	55
56	.99011	.14033	7.05579	.99240	.12302	8.06674	.99440	.10569	9.40904	56
57	.99015	.14004	7.07059	.99244	.12274	8.08600	.99443	.10540	9.43515	57
58	.99019	.13975	7.08546	.99248	.12245	8.10536	.99446	.10511	9.46141	58
59	.99023	.13946	7.10038	.99251	.12216	8.12481	.99449	.10482	9.48781	59
60	0.99027	0.13917	7.11537	0.99255	0.12187	8.14435	0.99452	0.10453	9.51436	60

TABLE OF NATURAL SINES, COSINES AND TANGENTS

′	84° Sin	84° Cos	84° Tan	85° Sin	85° Cos	85° Tan	86° Sin	86° Cos	86° Tan	′
0	0.99452	0.10453	9.51436	0.99620	0.08716	11.4301	0.99756	0.06976	14.3007	0
1	.99455	.10424	9.54106	.99622	.08687	11.4685	.99758	.06947	14.3607	1
2	.99458	.10395	9.56791	.99625	.08658	11.5072	.99760	.06918	14.4212	2
3	.99461	.10366	9.59490	.99627	.08629	11.5461	.99763	.06889	14.4823	3
4	.99464	.10337	9.62205	.99630	.08600	11.5853	.99765	.06860	14.5438	4
5	.99467	.10308	9.64935	.99632	.08571	11.6248	.99766	.06831	14.6059	5
6	.99470	.10279	9.67680	.99635	.08542	11.6645	.99768	.06802	14.6685	6
7	.99473	.10250	9.70441	.99637	.08513	11.7045	.99770	.06773	14.7317	7
8	.99476	.10221	9.73217	.99640	.08484	11.7448	.99772	.06744	14.7954	8
9	.99479	.10192	9.76009	.99642	.08455	11.7853	.99774	.06715	14.8596	9
10	.99482	.10164	9.78817	.99644	.08426	11.8262	.99776	.06685	14.9244	10
11	0.99485	0.10135	9.81641	0.99647	0.08397	11.8673	0.99778	0.06656	14.9898	11
12	.99488	.10106	9.84482	.99649	.08368	11.9087	.99780	.06627	15.0557	12
13	.99491	.10077	9.87338	.99652	.08339	11.9504	.99782	.06598	15.1222	13
14	.99494	.10048	9.90211	.99654	.08310	11.9923	.99784	.06569	15.1893	14
15	.99497	.10019	9.93101	.99657	.08281	12.0346	.99786	.06540	15.2571	15
16	.99500	.09990	9.96007	.99659	.08252	12.0772	.99788	.06511	15.3254	16
17	.99503	.09961	9.98931	.99661	.08223	12.1201	.99790	.06482	15.3943	17
18	.99506	.09932	10.0187	.99664	.08194	12.1632	.99792	.06453	15.4638	18
19	.99508	.09903	10.0483	.99666	.08165	12.2067	.99793	.06424	15.5340	19
20	.99511	.09874	10.0780	.99669	.08136	12.2505	.99795	.06395	15.6048	20
21	0.99514	0.09845	10.1080	0.99671	0.08107	12.2946	0.99797	0.06366	15.6762	21
22	.99517	.09816	10.1381	.99673	.08078	12.3390	.99799	.06337	15.7483	22
23	.99520	.09787	10.1683	.99676	.08049	12.3838	.99801	.06308	15.8211	23
24	.99523	.09758	10.1988	.99678	.08020	12.4288	.99803	.06279	15.8945	24
25	.99526	.09729	10.2294	.99680	.07991	12.4742	.99805	.06250	15.9687	25
26	.99528	.09700	10.2602	.99683	.07962	12.5199	.99806	.06221	16.0435	26
27	.99531	.09671	10.2913	.99685	.07933	12.5660	.99808	.06192	16.1190	27
28	.99534	.09643	10.3224	.99687	.07904	12.6124	.99810	.06163	16.1952	28
29	.99537	.09614	10.3538	.99689	.07875	12.6591	.99812	.06134	16.2722	29
30	.99540	.09585	10.3854	.99692	.07846	12.7062	.99814	.06105	16.3499	30
31	0.99542	0.09556	10.4172	0.99694	0.07817	12.7536	0.99816	0.06076	16.4283	31
32	.99545	.09527	10.4491	.99696	.07788	12.8014	.99817	.06047	16.5075	32
33	.99548	.09498	10.4813	.99699	.07759	12.8496	.99819	.06018	16.5874	33
34	.99551	.09469	10.5136	.99701	.07730	12.8981	.99821	.05989	16.6681	34
35	.99554	.09440	10.5462	.99703	.07701	12.9469	.99822	.05960	16.7496	35
36	.99556	.09411	10.5789	.99705	.07672	12.9962	.99824	.05931	16.8319	36
37	.99559	.09382	10.6118	.99708	.07643	13.0458	.99826	.05902	16.9150	37
38	.99562	.09353	10.6450	.99710	.07614	13.0958	.99827	.05873	16.9990	38
39	.99564	.09324	10.6783	.99712	.07585	13.1461	.99829	.05844	17.0837	39
40	.99567	.09295	10.7119	.99714	.07556	13.1969	.99831	.05815	17.1693	40
41	0.99570	0.09266	10.7457	0.99716	0.07527	13.2480	0.99833	0.05785	17.2558	41
42	.99573	.09237	10.7797	.99719	.07498	13.2996	.99834	.05756	17.3432	42
43	.99575	.09208	10.8139	.99721	.07469	13.3515	.99836	.05727	17.4314	43
44	.99578	.09179	10.8483	.99723	.07440	13.4039	.99838	.05698	17.5205	44
45	.99581	.09150	10.8829	.99725	.07411	13.4566	.99839	.05669	17.6106	45
46	.99583	.09121	10.9178	.99727	.07382	13.5098	.99841	.05640	17.7015	46
47	.99586	.09092	10.9529	.99729	.07353	13.5634	.99843	.05611	17.7934	47
48	.99588	.09063	10.9882	.99731	.07324	13.6174	.99844	.05582	17.8863	48
49	.99591	.09034	11.0237	.99734	.07295	13.6719	.99846	.05553	17.9802	49
50	.99594	.09005	11.0594	.99736	.07266	13.7267	.99847	.05524	18.0750	50
51	0.99596	0.08976	11.0954	0.99738	0.07237	13.7821	0.99849	0.05495	18.1708	51
52	.99599	.08947	11.1316	.99740	.07208	13.8378	.99851	.05466	18.2677	52
53	.99602	.08918	11.1681	.99742	.07179	13.8940	.99852	.05437	18.3655	53
54	.99604	.08889	11.2048	.99744	.07150	13.9507	.99854	.05408	18.4645	54
55	.99607	.08861	11.2417	.99746	.07121	14.0079	.99855	.05379	18.5645	55
56	.99609	.08832	11.2789	.99748	.07092	14.0655	.99857	.05350	18.6656	56
57	.99612	.08803	11.3163	.99750	.07063	14.1235	.99858	.05321	18.7678	57
58	.99614	.08774	11.3540	.99752	.07034	14.1821	.99860	.05292	18.8711	58
59	.99617	.08745	11.3919	.99754	.07005	14.2411	.99861	.05263	18.9755	59
60	0.99620	0.08716	11.4301	0.99756	0.06976	14.3007	0.99863	0.05234	19.0811	60

TABLE OF NATURAL SINES, COSINES AND TANGENTS

'	87° Sin	Cos	Tan	88° Sin	Cos	Tan	89° Sin	Cos	Tan	'
0	0.99863	0.05234	19.0811	0.99939	0.03490	28.6363	0.99985	0.01745	57.2900	0
1	.99865	.05205	19.1879	.99940	.03461	28.8771	.99985	.01716	58.2612	1
2	.99866	.05176	19.2959	.99941	.03432	29.1220	.99986	.01687	59.2659	2
3	.99868	.05146	19.4051	.99942	.03403	29.3711	.99986	.01658	60.3058	3
4	.99869	.05117	19.5156	.99943	.03374	29.6245	.99987	.01629	61.3829	4
5	.99871	.05088	19.6273	.99944	.03345	29.8823	.99987	.01600	62.4992	5
6	.99872	.05059	19.7403	.99945	.03316	30.1446	.99988	.01571	63.6567	6
7	.99873	.05030	19.8546	.99946	.03286	30.4116	.99988	.01542	64.8580	7
8	.99875	.05001	19.9702	.99947	.03257	30.6833	.99989	.01513	66.1055	8
9	.99876	.04972	20.0872	.99948	.03228	30.9599	.99989	.01484	67.4019	9
10	.99878	.04943	20.2056	.99949	.03199	31.2416	.99989	.01454	68.7501	10
11	0.99879	0.04914	20.3253	0.99950	0.03170	31.5284	0.99990	0.01425	70.1533	11
12	.99881	.04885	20.4465	.99951	.03141	31.8205	.99990	.01396	71.6151	12
13	.99882	.04856	20.5691	.99952	.03112	32.1181	.99991	.01367	73.1390	13
14	.99883	.04827	20.6932	.99953	.03083	32.4213	.99991	.01338	74.7292	14
15	.99885	.04798	20.8188	.99953	.03054	32.7303	.99991	.01309	76.3900	15
16	.99886	.04769	20.9460	.99954	.03025	33.0452	.99992	.01280	78.1263	16
17	.99888	.04740	21.0747	.99955	.02996	33.3662	.99992	.01251	79.9434	17
18	.99889	.04711	21.2049	.99956	.02967	33.6935	.99993	.01222	81.8470	18
19	.99890	.04682	21.3369	.99957	.02938	34.0273	.99993	.01193	83.8435	19
20	.99892	.04653	21.4704	.99958	.02909	34.3678	.99993	.01164	85.9398	20
21	0.99893	0.04624	21.6056	0.99959	0.02879	34.7151	0.99994	0.01134	88.1436	21
22	.99894	.04594	21.7426	.99959	.02850	35.0695	.99994	.01105	90.4633	22
23	.99896	.04565	21.8813	.99960	.02821	35.4313	.99994	.01076	92.9085	23
24	.99897	.04536	22.0217	.99961	.02792	35.8006	.99995	.01047	95.4895	24
25	.99898	.04507	22.1640	.99962	.02763	36.1776	.99995	.01018	98.2179	25
26	.99900	.04478	22.3081	.99963	.02734	36.5627	.99995	.00989	101.107	26
27	.99901	.04449	22.4541	.99963	.02705	36.9560	.99995	.00960	104.171	27
28	.99903	.04420	22.6020	.99964	.02676	37.3579	.99996	.00931	107.426	28
29	.99904	.04391	22.7519	.99965	.02647	37.7686	.99996	.00902	110.892	29
30	.99905	.04362	22.9038	.99966	.02618	38.1885	.99996	.00873	114.589	30
31	0.99906	0.04333	23.0577	0.99967	0.02589	38.6177	0.99996	0.00844	118.540	31
32	.99907	.04304	23.2137	.99967	.02560	39.0568	.99997	.00815	122.774	32
33	.99909	.04275	23.3718	.99968	.02531	39.5059	.99997	.00785	127.321	33
34	.99910	.04246	23.5321	.99969	.02501	39.9655	.99997	.00756	132.219	34
35	.99911	.04217	23.6945	.99969	.02472	40.4358	.99997	.00727	137.507	35
36	.99912	.04188	23.8593	.99970	.02443	40.9174	.99998	.00698	143.237	36
37	.99914	.04159	24.0263	.99971	.02414	41.4106	.99998	.00669	149.465	37
38	.99915	.04129	24.1957	.99972	.02385	41.9158	.99998	.00640	156.259	38
39	.99916	.04100	24.3675	.99972	.02356	42.4335	.99998	.00611	163.700	39
40	.99917	.04071	24.5418	.99973	.02327	42.9641	.99998	.00582	171.885	40
41	0.99918	0.04042	24.7185	0.99974	0.02298	43.5081	0.99999	0.00553	180.932	41
42	.99919	.04013	24.8978	.99974	.02269	44.0661	.99999	.00524	190.984	42
43	.99921	.03984	25.0798	.99975	.02240	44.6386	.99999	.00495	202.219	43
44	.99922	.03955	25.2644	.99976	.02211	45.2261	.99999	.00465	214.858	44
45	.99923	.03926	25.4517	.99976	.02182	45.8294	.99999	.00436	229.182	45
46	.99924	.03897	25.6418	.99977	.02152	46.4489	.99999	.00407	245.552	46
47	.99925	.03868	25.8348	.99978	.02123	47.0853	.99999	.00378	264.441	47
48	.99926	.03839	26.0307	.99978	.02094	47.7395	.99999	.00349	286.478	48
49	.99927	.03810	26.2296	.99979	.02065	48.4121	1.00000	.00320	312.521	49
50	.99929	.03781	26.4316	.99979	.02036	49.1039	1.00000	.00291	343.773	50
51	0.99930	0.03752	26.6367	0.99980	0.02007	49.8157	1.00000	0.00262	381.971	51
52	.99931	.03723	26.8450	.99980	.01978	50.5485	1.00000	.00233	429.718	52
53	.99932	.03693	27.0566	.99981	.01949	51.3032	1.00000	.00204	491.106	53
54	.99933	.03664	27.2715	.99982	.01920	52.0807	1.00000	.00175	572.957	54
55	.99934	.03635	27.4899	.99982	.01891	52.8821	1.00000	.00145	687.540	55
56	.99935	.03606	27.7117	.99983	.01862	53.7086	1.00000	.00116	859.436	56
57	.99936	.03577	27.9372	.99983	.01833	54.5613	1.00000	.00087	1145.92	57
58	.99937	.03548	28.1664	.99984	.01803	55.4415	1.00000	.00058	1718.87	58
59	.99938	.03519	28.3994	.99984	.01774	56.3506	1.00000	.00029	3437.75	59
60	0.99939	0.03490	28.6363	0.99985	0.01745	57.2900	1.00000	0.00000	Infinite.	60

Section D

Great Circle Sailing

NOTES ON GNOMONIC CHARTS

1. Principle of the gnomonic projection

A sphere, representing the Earth reduced to a required scale, is marked with meridians of longitude and parallels of latitude. The graticule thus formed is transferred by direct projection from a point of light at the centre onto a plane surface placed tangential to the sphere. The point of tangency is normally in the middle of the area to be charted. Because the point of light is at the sphere's centre, it lies in the plane of **all** great circles. Thus the shadow cast by any great circle is a continuation of its own plane, and must, therefore, cut the plane surface along a straight line; hence any straight line on a gnomonic chart represents a great circle.

Gnomonic projections are classified according to the position of the point of tangency, i.e. *Oblique* when the point of tangency does not lie on the equator or at the pole; otherwise *Polar or Equatorial*.

It is not possible to show a whole hemisphere on a gnomonic projection, the **practical limitation** being about 75° in all directions from the point of tangency; beyond this the scale and its rate of expansion are excessively large.

2. Important Navigational Properties

The following properties are common to all classes of gnomonic charts:

(a) Great circles are represented by straight lines;

(b) The projection is not orthomorphic;

(c) At any point on the chart, other than the point of tangency, the scale along the meridian is different to that along the parallel; hence DISTANCES CANNOT BE MEASURED DIRECTLY FROM THE CHART.

(d) Angles are correctly represented *only* at the point of tangency, elsewhere they are distorted; hence COURSES CANNOT BE MEASURED DIRECTLY FROM THE CHART.

(e) A rhumb line between any two points, which are not in the same longitude and not on the equator, would appear on the chart as a curved line on the equatorial side of the great circle joining them.

3. Uses of gnomonic projection

(a) Charts for great circle sailing and route planning;

(b) Charts of polar regions. The distortion on Mercator projection is too great for practical use in such latitudes;

(c) Charts having a natural scale greater than 1:50,000 (numerical scale 3.7 cm to the mile), harbour plans, etc.

4. Method of transferring a great circle track from a gnomonic chart on to a Mercator chart

(1) Plot the two terminal points on the gnomonic chart, and join them by a straight line; this then is the required great circle track.

(2) Write down the latitudes at which the great circle track cuts successive meridians which have been selected at convenient intervals—e.g. 5° or 10°. (The intervals are a matter of choice depending on several factors, one being the expected rate at which the ship will change her longitude.)

(3) Plot each of these positions, including the terminal points, on the corresponding Mercator Chart, and join each of these points to the next one in succession by a straight line. This series of short rhumb lines will approximate very closely to the great circle.

5.   To plot a composite track on a gnomonic chart

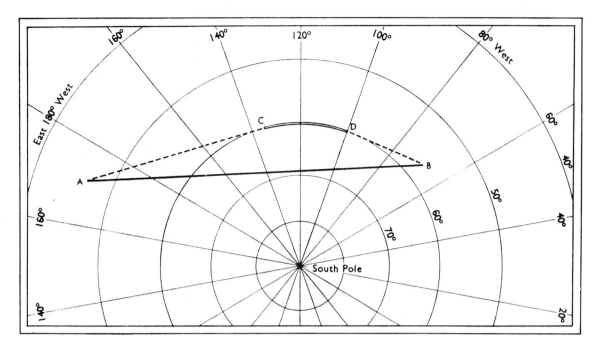

Fig. D1
POLAR GNOMONIC CHART

KEY
Great Circle Track
Composite Track
Rhumb Line

Example: Figure D.1 represents a polar gnomonic chart of part of the Southern Oceans. The straight line AB is the great circle track from Port Chalmers (N.Z.) to Cape Horn, and this goes down to nearly 69°S. latitude. Assuming that 60°S. is decided on as being the limiting safe latitude for this particular voyage, it is required to plot a composite track to give the shortest possible route, from A to B, without sailing south of the 60th parallel.

(1) From A and B, draw straight lines tangential to the parallel of 60°S. These lines touch the parallel at points C and D respectively.

(2) The composite track is then:
   From A to C by great circle,
   from C to D by parallel sailing, and
   from D to B by great circle.

Note that the great circle arcs AC and DB are not parts of one great circle.

WARNING: ANGLES ARE DISTORTED ON GNOMONIC CHARTS, AND IT IS NOT POSSIBLE TO DETERMINE COURSES BY DIRECT MEASUREMENT.

G

GREAT CIRCLE SAILING BY FORMULAE, LONGHAND METHODS

1. Order of Work

Find (1) Distance
    (2) Initial Course   } By haversine formula*
    (3) Final Course
    (4) Lat. and Long. of Vertex   } By Napier's Rules
    (5) Lat. of succession of Points

If preferred, the initial and final courses may be found simultaneously by means of the tangent formula; but the haversine formula is in more common use.

The sine formula may also be used but is best avoided since it gives ambiguous results which are difficult to resolve when a course is near 90° or 270°.

2. Rough location of the vertex

The initial and final courses will, together, indicate whether the vertex lies between or outside the terminal points of the track. **The vertex lies between the terminal points only when the initial and final courses are in different compass quadrants.**

It is not always necessary to calculate the final course when other considerations give clear indication of the location of the vertex; but if the d.long. between departure point and vertex seems likely to be near or in excess of 90°, then the final course angle should be used when calculating the longitude of the vertex.

Example 1: Find the initial and final courses and the distance on the great circle from Position A (51° 46'N., 55° 22'W.) to Position B (55° 32'N., 07° 14'W.). Required also the latitude and longitude of the vertex and the positions of successive points at 10° intervals of longitude along the track, commencing with longitude 45°W.

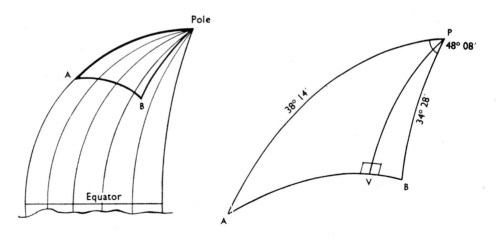

Fig. D.2   *Fig.* D.3

(1) To find the distance (AB):

In △ PAB, Hav AB = hav P. sin PA. sin PB + hav (PA ∼ PB)

P = d.long = 48° 08′			9.22089	⌐ 0.05824
PA = co-lat A	=	38° 14′	0.79160	0.00108
PB = co-lat B	=	34° 28′	9.75276	————
				0.05932
(PA ∼ PB)	=	3° 46′	8.76525 ⌐	AB = 28°12′
				60

∴ Distance =   1,692 mls.

(2) To find the initial course (P$\widehat{A}$B)

In △ PAB, Hav A = [hav PB — hav (PA ∼ AB)] cosec PA. cosec AB.

PB	=	34° 28′	0.08777	⌐ 8.90375
PA	=	38° 14′	0.00765	0.20840
AB	=	28° 12′	————	0,32555
			0.08012	————
				9.43770
(PA ∼ PB)	=	10° 02′	A = 63° 07′	————

∴ Initial Course = 063°

(3) To find the final course (180° — P$\widehat{B}$A)

In △ PAB, Hav B = [hav PA — hav (PB ∼ AB)] cosec PB. cosec AB.

PA	=	38° 14′	0.10725	⌐ 9.01813
PB	=	34° 28′	0.00299	0.24724
AB	=	28° 12′	————	0.32555
			0.10426	————
				9.59092
(PB ∼ AB)	=	6° 16′	B = 77° 17′	————

∴ Final Course = 103°

(4) To find the latitude and longitude of the vertex

In this example the initial and final courses are in different compass quadrants, so the vertex (V) must lie between the terminal points, A and B.

In △ PAV, V = 90°, PA = 38° 14′ and A = 63° 07′.

By Napier's Rules:

Sin PV = sin PA. sin A
Cos Lat. V = sin PA. sin A.

9.79160
9.95033
9.74193
Lat V = 56° 30′ N.

Cos PA = cot A. cot P
Cot P = cos PA. tan A

		9.89515	
		0.29502	
		·0.19017	
	P =	32° 50′	
Long	A =	55° 22′ W.	
Long	**V =**	**22° 32′ W.**	

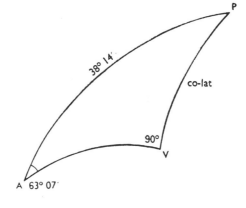

Fig. D.4

(5) To find the latitudes of successive points

Pts.	Long. of Points	Long. of Vertex	Polar Angles (P)
C	45°W.		CPV = 22° 28′
D	35°W.	22° 32′W.	DPV = 12° 28′
E	25°W.		EPV = 2° 28′
F	15°W.		FPV = 7° 32′

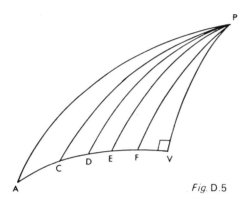

Fig. D.5

In △CPV, V = 90°, C is one of the selected points. Then, by Napier's Rules:

$$\text{Cos P} = \tan PV . \cot CP$$
$$\therefore \text{Cot CP} = \cos P . \cot PV$$

i.e. Tan lat. Point = cos Polar Angle. tan lat. Vertex

Point	C	D	E	F
Cos P.	9.96572	9.98964	9.99960	9.99624
Tan lat. V	0.17922	0.17922	0.17922	0.17922
Tan lat.	0.14494	0.16886	0.17882	0.17546
Position { Lat.	54° 23′N	55° 52′N	56° 29′N	56° 16′N
Long.	45° 00′W	35° 00′W	25° 00′W	15° 00′W

Example 2: Find the initial course and distance on the great circle from Position A (58° 42′N. 05° 00′W.) to Position B (32° 34′N. 64° 30′W.). Find also the latitude and longitude of the vertex and the latitude of the points where the great circle cuts the meridians of 15°W. and 25°W.

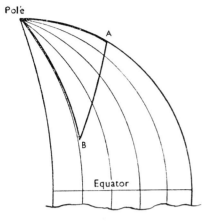

Fig. D.6

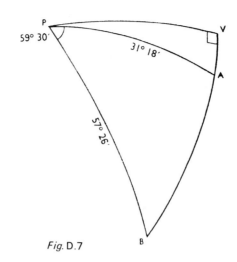

Fig. D.7

(1)   To find the distance (AB)
In △ **PAB**, Hav AB = hav P. sin PA. sin PB + hav(PA ~ PB).

P =d.long	=59° 30′	9:39134	⌐0.10781
PA =co-lat A	=31° 18′	9.71560	0.05111
PB =co-lat B	=57° 26′	9.92571	0.15892
(PA ~ PB)	=26° 08′	9.03265 ┘	AB= 46° 59′
			60

∴ Distance = **2,819 miles**

(2)   To find initial course (360° — PÂB)
In △ **PAB**, Hav A =[hav PB — hav (PA ~ AB)] cosec PA. cosec AB.

PB	=57° 26′	0.23086	⌐9.32685
PA	=31° 18′	0.01861	0.28440
AB	=46° 49′		0.13599
		0.21225 ┘	
(PA ~ AB)	=15° 31′		9.74724
		A = 96° 45′	

∴ Initial Course = **263°**

(3)   The final course is not required in this case.
(4)   To find the latitude and longitude of the vertex:
The initial course is in the SW quadrant, so the vertex lies to the east of point A.
In △ **PAV**, V = 90°, PA = 31° 18′ and A = (180° — 96° 45′) = 83° 15′.
By Napier's Rules:

Sin PV = sin PA. sin A	Cos PA = cot A. cot P
Cos lat. V = sin PA. sin A	Cot P = cos PA. tan A
9.71560	9.93169
9.99698	0.92680
————	————
9.71258	0.85849
	P = 7° 53′
	Long. A = 5° 00′W

Lat. V = 58° 56′N.   **Long. V   = 2° 53′E.**

(5)   To find the latitude in which the great circle cuts the meridians of 15°W., and 25°W.

Pts.	Long. of Points	Long. of Vertex	Polar Angles (P)
C	15°W	2° 53'E.	17° 53'
D	25°W		27° 53'

In Δ CPV, V = 90° and C is one of the selected points.

Then, by Napier's Rules:

Cos P = tan PV . cot CP

and   Cot CP = cos P . cot PV   i.e.

Tan lat. Point = cos Polar Angle . tan lat. Vertex

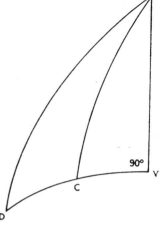

Fig. D.8

Point	C	D
Cos P	9.97849	9.94640
Tan lat. V	0.22008	0.22008
Tan lat.	0.19857	0.16648
Position { Lat.	57° 43'N.	55° 40'N
Position { Long.	15° 00'W	25° 00'W

COMPOSITE SAILING BY FORMULAE

In figure D. 9

P. South Pole

A. Departure Point

B. Destination Point

C. Point at which the track meets the limiting latitude

D. Point at which the track leaves the limiting latitude

X. A selected point on the track

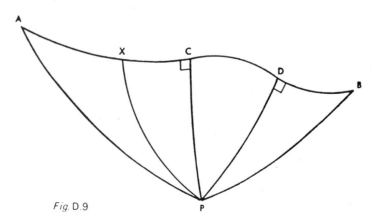

Fig. D.9

Order of Work

To find:

1. **Initial Course** $\quad\quad$ Sin PAC $\quad$ = $\quad$ sec lat. A. cos lat. C

2. **Distance A to C** $\quad\quad$ Cos AC $\quad$ = $\quad$ sin lat. A. cosec lat. C

3. **Longitude of Vertex C** $\quad\quad$ Cos APC $\quad$ = $\quad$ tan lat. A. cot lat. C

1, 2 and 3 are worked simultaneously (see Example)

4. **Final Course*** $\quad\quad$ Sin PBD $\quad$ = $\quad$ sec lat. B. cos lat. D

5. **Distance, D to B** $\quad\quad$ Cos DB $\quad$ = $\quad$ sin lat. B. cosec lat. D

6. **Longitude of Vertex D** $\quad\quad$ Cos BPD $\quad$ = $\quad$ tan lat. B. cot lat. D

4, 5 and 6 are worked simultaneously (see Example)

7. **Distance, C to D** (parallel sailing) $\quad\quad$ dep $\quad$ = $\quad$ d.long. × cos. lat.

8. **Total Distance**—add together the distances found

9. **Latitudes of Successive Points** Tan lat. X $\quad$ = $\quad$ cos XPC. tan lat. C
$\quad\quad\quad$ i.e. $\quad$ Tan lat. Point = cos Polar Angle. tan lat. Vertex.

* If required.

Example: *Port Chalmers (N.Z.) to C. Horn—see Fig. D1.* Required the composite route from Position A (45° 46'S. 170° 50'E.) to Position B (56° 05'S. 67° 17'W.) the maximum latitude to be 60°S. find the initial course, the longitudes of the points at which the track meets and leaves the 60th parallel, and the total distance along the composite track. Find also the latitudes at which the track cuts the meridians of 90°W., 80°W., and 70°W.

To find: (1) Initial Course: (2) Distance, AC; (3) Longitude of C.

In Δ PAC, C = 90°. Then, by Napier's Rules:

(1)

Sin PC	= sin PA. sin A
Sin A	= sin PC. cosec PA
Sin A	= sec lat. A. cos lat. C

Lat. A = 45° 46'	0.15641
Lat. D = 60° 00'	9.69897
	9.85538

A = 45° 47'

∴ **Initial Course = 134°**

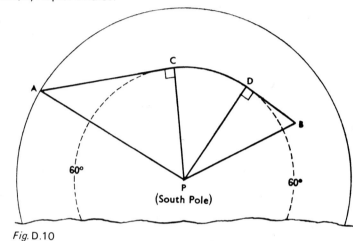

Fig. D.10

(2)
Cos PA	= cos PC. cos. AC
Cos AC	= cos PA. sec. PC
Cos AC	= sin lat. A. cosec lat. C
	9.85522
	0.06247
	9.91769

AC = 34° 10'
60

Distance = 2,050 miles

(3)
Cos P = cot PA tan. PC
Cos P = tan lat. A. cot lat. C

0.01162
9.76144
9.77306

P	= 53° 38'
Long. A	= 189° 10'W.

Long. C = 135° 10'W.

To find: (4) Distance, DB and (5) Longitude of D.

In Δ PBD, D = 90°. Then, by Napier's Rules:

(4)
Cos PB = cos PD. cos DB
Cos DB = cos PB. sec PD
Cos DB = sin lat. B. cosec lat. D

Lat. B = 56° 05'	9.91900
Lat. D = 60° 00'	0.06247
	9.98147

DB = 16° 37'
60

Distance, DB = 997 miles

(5)
Cos P = cos PB. tan PD.
Cos P = tan lat. B. cot lat. D.

0.17238
0.76144
0.93382

P =	30° 50'
Long. B =	67° 17'W.

Long. D = 98° 07'W.

6.   To find distance, C to D

Long. C = 135° 32'W.

Long. D = 98° 07'W.

————————

37° 25'

60

————————

d. long = 2,256'

dep. = d. long. cos lat.

= 2245 cos 60°

3.35122

9.69897

————————

3.05019

Distance CD = 1,123 miles

7.   To find total distance.

Great circle distance, A to C   =   2,050 miles.

Rhumb line distance C to D   =   1,123 miles

Great circle distance D to B   =   997 miles

————————

Total Distance   =   4,170 miles

8.   To find latitudes of selected points

Longitude of Vertex	Longitude of Points	Polar Angles (P)
(D) 98° 07'W.	E. 90°W. F. 80°W. G. 70°W.	8° 07' 18° 07' 28° 07'

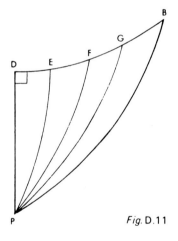

Fig. D.11

In Δ PDE, D = 90°. By Napier's Rules:

$$\cos P = \tan PD . \cot PE.$$

$$\therefore \cot PE = \cos P . \cot PD.$$

i.e. Tan lat. Point = cos Polar Angle. tan lat. Vertex.

	E	F	G
log cos polar angles log tan lat. vertex	9.99563 0.23856	9.97792 0.23856	9.94546 0.23856
log tan	0.23419	0.21648	0.18402
Position } Lat. Long.	59° 45' S. 90° 00'W.	58° 43' S. 80° 00'W.	56° 47' S. 70° 00'W.

SHORT METHODS OF FINDING GREAT CIRCLE COURSES AND DISTANCES:

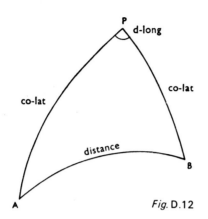

Fig. D.12

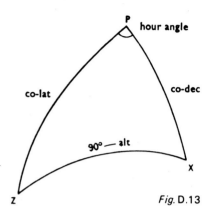

Fig. D.13

In Fig. D12, P represents the pole, A the departure point, and B the destination. The triangle PAB is similar to the astronomical triangle PZX (fig. D13), and any tables designed for the solution of the latter may be used for the former. Thus, by renaming the parts of the left-hand triangle as shown on the right, it follows that:

Latitude of A remains as *latitude*.
Latitude of B becomes *declination*.
Difference of longitude, APB, becomes *hour angle*.

Initial Course, PÂB, becomes *azimuth*.
Distance, AB, becomes (*90° — altitude*).

Great Circle Course by ABC Azimuth Tables:

Example. Find the initial and final courses on the great circle track from A (51° 46'N. 55° 22'W.) to B (55° 32'N. 07° 14'W.).

Arguments for entering ABC Tables:
(1) For initial course: — Hour Angle 48°, lat. 51.8°N., dec. 55.5°N.
(2) For final course: — Hour Angle 48°, lat. 55.5°N., dec. 51.8°N.

	(1)		(2)
A =	1.14S.	A =	1.31S.
B =	1.96N.	B =	1.71N.
C =	0.82N.	C =	0.40N. Az. N. 77¼°W.

Initial Course = N.63°E.   ∴ Final Course = 103°

NOTE: (a) Compare with answers to example on p. 99
       (b) If Altitude-Azimuth tables are used, the approximate distance can be found by taking out the altitude and subtracting it from 90°.

THE USE OF ELECTRONIC CALCULATORS FOR THE SOLUTION OF GREAT CIRCLE PROBLEMS

General;

An enormous range of hand-held calculators is currently available, comprising instruments at many different levels of sophistication. Most of these can be used for the solution of great circle problems, but the optimal method will depend upon the capabilities of the calculator. In general, it is recommended that methods should be used which are similar to the ones suggested in previous sections for longhand solutions so that it is easy to revert to these should a calculator become unserviceable. Adaptations can, however, usefully be made to take the best advantage of the facilities offered by a particular calculator, using the maker's handbook as a guide. The following notes are intended to give some general guidance in using calculators at three levels of sophistication, i.e. simple four function calculators, simple "scientific" calculators and programmable or pre-programmed navigation calculators.

Simple Four Function Calculators designed for Algebraic Logic. A calculator with facilities for addition. subtraction, multiplication and division may be used as an alternative to tables of logarithms in the calculations previously discussed under longhand methods. For the basic four function calculator with no memory it is recommended that the haversine formula should be used. The values of the natural sines, cosines and tangents may conveniently be found from the tables in section B which are arranged so that all three functions may be found, if required, from a single entry of an angle. The natural haversines can be taken from Reed's Nautical Almanac or other nautical tables.

A typical keyboard might be as shown in the figure, and a suitable order of work is illustrated in the example below. It may, of course, be necessary to amend the sequence to suit the operation of a particular model of calculator.

**FOUR FUNCTION
CALCULATOR**

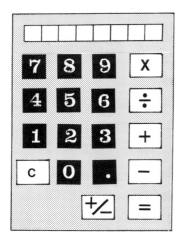

EXAMPLE: Find the distance, the initial course and the position of the vertex for the great circle from position A in 51° 46′ N., 55° 22′ W. to position B on 55° 32′ N., 07° 14′ W.

(1) To find the distance AB: (refer to diagram on p. 98)

In $\triangle$ PAB, hav AB = hav P sin PA sin PB + hav (PA $\sim$ PB)

P	= d. long	= 48° 08'	Nat. hav.	0.16630	
PA	= colat A	= 38° 14'	Nat. sin	0.61887	From
PB	= colat B	= 34° 28'	Nat. sin	0.56593	Tables
(PA $\sim$ PB)		= 3° 46'	Nat hav.	0.06569	

Quantity	Entry	Reading (to five decimal places)	
hav P	0.16630	0.16630	
	x	0.16630	
sin PA	0.61887	0.61887	
	x	0.10291	Using
sin PB	0.56593	0.56593	Calculator
	+	0.05824	
hav (PA $\sim$ PB)	0.00108	0.00108	
	=	0.05932	

hav AB	= 0.05932	
AB	= 28° 12'	From
	60	Tables
	1692 mls.	

(2) To find the initial course, Angle A:

In $\triangle$ PAB, hav A = $\dfrac{\text{hav PB} - \text{hav (PA} \sim \text{AB)}}{\text{sin PA sin PB}}$

PB	= 34° 28'	Nat. hav	0.08777		
PA	= 38° 14'	Nat. sin	0.61887		From
AB	= 28° 12'	Nat. sin	0.47255		Tables
(PA $\sim$ AB)	= 10° 02'	Nat. hav	0.00765		

Quantity	Entry	Reading	
hav. PB	0.08777	0.08777	
	—	0.08777	
hav (PA $\sim$ AB)	0.00765	0.00765	
	÷	0.08012	Using
sin PA	0.61887	0.61887	Calculator
	÷	0.12946	
sin AB	0.47255	0.47255	
	=	0.27396	

hav A	= 0.27396	From
A	= 63° 07'	Tables

(3) To find the latitude of the vertex:
In $\triangle$ PAV, sin PV = sin PA sin A
             cos (lat. V) = sin PA sin A

PA	= 38° 14′	Nat. sin	0.61887	}	From
A	= 63° 07′	Nat. sin	0.89193		Tables

Quantity	Entry	Reading		
sin PA	0.61887	0.61887	]	
	x	0.61887		Using
sin A	0.89193	0.89193		Calculator
	=	0.55199	]	

cos lat. V	= 0.55199	}	From
lat. V.	= 56° 30′ N.		Tables

(4) To find the longitude of the vertex:
In $\triangle$ PAV, cos PA =   cot A cot P

$$\tan P = \frac{1}{\cos PA \tan A}$$

PA	= 38° 14′	Nat. cos	0.78550	}	From
A	= 63° 07′	Nat. tan	0.45218		Tables

Quantity	Entry	Reading		
1	1	1	]	
	÷	1		
cos PA	0.78550	0.78550		Using
	÷	1.27307		Calculator
tan A	1.97253	1.97253		
	=	0.64540	]	

tan P = 0.64540
   P = 32° 50′
long. A = 55° 22′ W
long. V = 22° 32′ W.

These results may be compared with those arrived at by longhand solution of the same
problem on p. 99. Clearly, if the position of en-route points is required, similar methods
could be used.

A Standard Scientific Calculator with two Memories.

A scientific calculator has keys for sine, cosine and tangent amongst other functions, but will not generally have a key for haversines. It is therefore convenient to use the basic cosine formula instead of the haversine formula for the solution of great circle problems. The keyboard illustrated is for an instrument designed for simple trigonometric calculations. Typical scientific calculators will have the facilities shown plus many additional ones. These latter are not essential for the solution of great circle problems although some, such as parenthesis keys, may simplify the operations required.

Note that for this example:
Key STO transfers a quantity to store.

Key RCL recalls a quantity from store.

Key 1/x converts a number into its reciprocal thus, for instance, converting sine into cosecant, tangent into cotangent, etc.

The sine of an angle is entered by first entering the angle in degrees and decimals of a degree, and then pressing the SIN key.

To find an angle whose sine is the number displayed, the ARC key is pressed, and then the SIN key. Similar procedures are followed for cosine and tangent.

SCIENTIFIC CALCULATOR

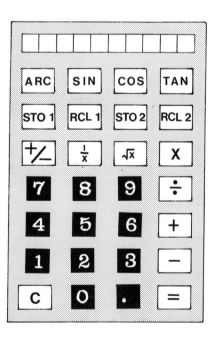

A suitable order of work is illustrated in the example opposite. It should be noted that angles in degrees and minutes will normally have to be converted to degrees and decimal parts of a degree before entering on the calculator for the input of sine, cosine or tangent functions.

EXAMPLE: Find the distance, initial course and the position of the vertex for the great circle from position A in 51° 46′ N., 55° 22′ W. to position B in 55° 32′ N. 07° 14′ W.

(1) Conversion of angles into degrees and decimal parts by dividing the minutes by 60.

P	= d. long.	= 48° 08′	= 48.133°
PA	= co-lat. A	= 38° 14′	= 38.233°
PB	= co-lat. B	= 34° 28′	= 34.467°

(2) To find the distance (AB): (Refer to diagram on p. 98)

In △ PAB;   cos AB = cos PA cos PB + sin PA sin PB cos P

Quantity		Entry	Reading (to five decimal places)
PA	→	38.233	28.233
		cos	0.78550
		STO1	0.78550
PB	→	34.467	34.467
		cos	0.82446
		x	0.82446
		RCL1	0.78550
		=	0.64761
		STO1	0.64761
PA	→	38.233	38.233
		sin	0.61887
		STO2	0.61887
PB	→	34.467	34.467
		sin	0.56593
		x	0.56593
		RCL2	0.61887
		=	0.35024
		STO2	0.35024
P	→	48.133	48.133
		cos	0.66740
		x	0.66740
		RCL2	0.35024
		+	0.23375
		RCL1	0.64761
		=	0.88136
		ARC	0.88136
AB	←	cos	28.192

AB = 28° 12′
   60
‾‾‾‾‾‾
1692 mls.

(3) To find the initial course, angle A:

$$\cos A = \frac{\cos PB - \cos PA \cos AB}{\sin PA \sin AB}$$

Quantity		Entry	Reading
PA	→	38.233	38.233
		sin	0.61887
		STO1	0.61887
AB	→	28.192	28.192
		sin	0.47242
		x	0.47242
		RCL1	0.61887
		=	0.29237
		STO1	0.29237
PA	→	38.233	38.233
		cos	0.78550
		STO 2	0.78550
AB	→	28.192	28.192
		cos	0.88136
		x	0.88136
		RCL2	0.78550
		=	0.69231
		STO2	0.69231
PB	→	34.467	34.467
		cos	0.82446
		—	0.82446
		RCL2	0.69231
		÷	0.13215
		RCL1	0.29237
		=	0.45200
		ARC	0.45200
A	←	cos	63.128

Initial Course = 63° 08'

(4) To find the latitude of the vertex:
In Δ PAV; — sin PV = sin PA sin A
cos (lat. V) = sin PA sin A

Quantity		Entry	Reading
PA	→	38.233	38.233
		sin	0.61887
		STO1	0.61887
A	→	63.128	63.128
		sin	0.89202
		x	0.89202
		RCL1	0.61887
		=	0.55204
		ARC	0.55204
lat. V	←	cos	56.493

Latitude of Vertex = 56° 30' N.

(5) To find the longitude of the vertex:

In $\triangle$ PAV; $-$ cos PA $=$ cot A cot P

$$\tan P = \frac{1}{\cos PA \tan A}$$

Quantity		Entry	Reading
PA	$\rightarrow$	38.233	38.233
		cos	0.78550
		STO1	0.78550
A	$\rightarrow$	63.128	63.128
		tan	1.97353
		x	1.97353
		RCL1	0.78550
		=	1.55021
		$\frac{1}{x}$	0.64507
		ARC	0.64507
P	$\leftarrow$	cos	32.825

D. Long. = 32° 50′
Long. A = 55° 22′ W.
Long. V = $\overline{22° 32′ W.}$

Specialised Navigation Computers or Programmable Calculators

These instruments permit more direct methods of solving great circle problems. A programmable calculator such as the Hewlett-Packard HP — 66 may be used either with suitable programs (navpacs) provided by the manufacturers or with programs developed by the owner. The procedure for the solution of great circle problems will naturally depend upon the form of the programs used.

Specialised navigation computers are pre-programmed and will usually include facilities for the solution of great circle problems. The latitude and longitude of positions may typically be entered in degrees and minutes, the correct sequence being prompted by request cues from the instrument display. The calculation of course and distance follows automatically after the positions have been entered and the program initiated. Instruments of this class include the Interceptor Celestial Navigation Computer from Digital Systems Marine, the Galaxy I Celestial Navigation Computer from Micro Instruments and the NC — 2 Astro Navigation Calculator from Tamaya.

H

THE USE OF AN EQUATORIAL STEREOGRAPHIC PROJECTION FOR THE SOLUTION OF GREAT CIRCLE PROBLEMS.

Method

The equatorial stereographic projection diagram printed on page 28 may be used for an approximate solution of great circle problems. To find the initial course and distance between positions A and B, the following procedure is adopted:

(1) Place a piece of tracing paper over the diagram and locate by means of a pin or the point of a pair of compasses through the centre.

(2) Mark point A on the tracing paper at the correct latitude. It should be located on the eastern (right hand) circumference of the diagram if A is to the east of B, or on the western (left hand) circumference if A is to the west of B.

(3) Mark point B on the tracing paper at the correct latitude and the correct difference of longitude from point A, using the easterly or westerly d.long. scale as appropriate.

(4) Rotate the tracing paper so that the point marked A is superimposed over point P on the diagram. Read off the initial course and the great circle distance (in degrees) according to the new position of point B over the great circle bearing and great circle distance scales on the diagram.

It is recommended that the example given on page 99 should be attempted by the above method in order to fix ideas. Results can generally be interpolated to the nearest degree which is adequate for setting courses to follow a great circle track.

METHODS OF "MAKING " THE GREAT CIRCLE TRACK

Working to a succession of selected points is a common practice, and probably the best method, generally. Much depends on likely weather conditions, currents, availability, of fixes, etc. The shorter the distance between selected points, the more closely does the series of rhumb lines approximate to the great circle; but many points also means frequent alterations of course.

If observations should show that the vessel has been set, say, 30 miles to one side of the track, it is then usually better to work out a new great circle to destination point, rather than alter course to regain the original track. This latter action can only serve to increase the total distance.

Recalculation of Initial Course for each leg: An easy method adopted by many ships is, each day, to work out and steer a new initial course to the same destination point. In practising this method, it is well to remember that each new course, **if made good,** will take the vessel further away (on the poleward side) from the original great circle, and the total distance could be considerably increased thereby. Some compensation for this possibility should be made when setting each new course — at least by steering "nothing to the nor'ard" in North latitudes.

The figure obtained by adding the distance to go, each day, to the total distance made good (from point of departure on the great circle) will indicate any distance being lost.

Section E

Astronomical Navigation
(Some Notes and Worked Examples)

LATITUDE BY MERIDIAN ALTITUDE OF A HEAVENLY BODY

AT UPPER TRANSIT

Order of Work

1. Correct Sextant Altitude
2. Extract Declination (from *Nautical Almanac*)
3. Obtain True Zenith distance (T.Z.D.) by subtracting the True Altitude from 90°.
4. Latitude is determined by combining T.Z.D. and Declination according to the following rules:
   (1) Name T.Z.D. **opposite** to the body's bearing.
   (2) If Declination and T.Z.D. are named alike—ADD, if unlike SUBTRACT the smaller from the greater.
5. Latitude is always named according to the result obtained from this combination.

Example 1. True meridian altitude of SIRIUS 46° 08', bearing South; Declination 16° 40' S. Required the observer's Latitude.

	90° 00'.0
True Altitude	46 08 .0S
True Zenith Distance	43 52 .0N
Declination	16 40 .0S
Latitude	**27°12'.0N**

Example 2. D.R. Lat 0° 02'N., True Altitude of the Sun's centre at upper meridian passage 66° 50'.5, bearing North; Declination 23° 07'N. Find the observer's Latitude.

	90° 00'.0
True Altitude	66 50 .5N
True Zenith Distance	23 09 .5S
Declination	23 07 .0N
Latitude	**0°02'.5S**

Example ·3. True meridian altitude of RIGEL (Dec. 8° 13'.9S) was 46° 20', bearing North. Required the Latitude.

	90° 00'.0
True Altitude	46 20 .0N
True Zenith Distance	43 40 .0S
Declination	8 13 .9S
Latitude	**51°53'.9S**

AT LOWER TRANSIT (BELOW POLE)

The rules in this case are very simple and never alter.

Order of Work

1. Correct Sextant Altitude
2. Extract Declination from Nautical Almanac
3. Subtract Declination from 90° to obtain Polar Distance.
4. **Latitude = Polar Distance + True Altitude.**
5. Latitude is always named the same as the Declination.

Example. In D.R. Position 40° 15′N. 39°20′W.; the Sextant meridian altitude of DUBHE, below pole, was 12° 19′, bearing North. I.E. 1′.5 on the arc; H. of E. 15 m. Required the Latitude. Declination of Dubhe 61° 55′.5.

SA.	12° 19′.0		90° 00′.0	
I.E.	−1 .5	Declination	61 55 .5	
O.A.	12 17 .5	Polar Distance	28 04 .5	
Dip	−6 .7	True Altitude	12 06 .4	
	12 10 .8	**Latitude**	**40°10′.9N**	
Cor.	−4 .4			
T.A.	12° 06′.4			

LATITUDE BY POLE STAR OBSERVATION

Example. On the evening of August 18th, in a typical year, in D.R. Position 44° 55′N. 30° 04′.5W., at G.M.T. 2137 hrs., Sextant Altitude POLARIS 44° 27′.5; I.E. 1′.0 on the arc; H. of E. 16 m. Required Latitude and Position Line.

Order of Work

1. Correct Sextant Altitude, as described in Section B.
2. From G.M.T. (to the nearest minute) extract G.H.A. Aries from the Almanac and apply D.R. longitude to obtain L.H.A. Aries.
3. With L.H.A. Aries, enter the Pole Star Tables in Nautical Almanac and extract value for a_0. Interpolate.
4. Move down the same column and extract a_1 from abreast the Latitude (to the nearest tabulated value). *Interpolation is not necessary.*
5. Enter the same column abreast the month, and extract a_2. *Interpolation is not necessary.*
6. **Latitude = True Altitude − 1° + a_0 + a_1 + a_2.**
7. Still in the original column, take out the Azimuth from abreast the Latitude.
8. The Position Line is drawn at 90° to the true bearing of the star, through position observed latitude and D.R. longitude.

Working

G.M.T. 2137 hrs.			
G.H.A. Aries	282° 16′.9	From the Almanac for	
Inc.	9 16 .5	a typical year	
	291 33 .4		
Long.	30 04 .5		
L.H.A. Aries	261° 28′.9		

POLARIS

S.A.	44° 27′.5	
I.E.	−	1 .0
O.A.	44 26 .5	
Dip.	−	7 .1
A.A.	44 19 .4	
Cor.	−	1 .0
True Altitude	44 18 .4	
	−	1 00 .0
	43 18 .4	
a_0 +	1 32 .1	
a_1 +	0 .5	
a_2 +	0 .9	
Latitude	**44°51′.9**	

Tabulated Azimuth = 0.9°
∴ True bearing = 001°
Position Line 091°—271°
is drawn through Position
44° 51.9N. 30° 04′.5W.

THE INTERCEPT METHOD
OF OBTAINING A POSITION LINE

Standard Method (by Haversine Formula)

Example 1. On August 18th of a typical year (at Ship), in D.R. Position 23° 54'N., 163° 32'E., at G.M.T., 17d. 20h. 41m. 01s., Sextant Altitude Sun's LL 25° 51', I.E. 1'.0 off the arc, H. of E. 15 m. Required Intercept and Position Line.

Procedure

1. Determine Sun's L.H.A. and corrected Declination,

2. Correct the Sextant Altitude (S.A.),

3. Subtract True Altitude (T.A.) from 90° to obtain True Zenith Distance (T.Z.D.).

4. Calculate the Zenith Distance (C.Z.D.) for the D.R. position by haversine formula.

$$\text{Hav C.Z.D.} = \text{hav P.} \cos l \cos d + \text{hav}(l \pm d).$$

Where P = L.H.A., or angle P of the astronomical PZX triangle,
l = Latitude, and d = Declination.

$(l \pm d)$ is obtained by adding l and d when they are of unlike names, and subtracting the smaller from the greater when they are named alike.

5. Determine the Sun's true bearing by means of A.B.C. Tables or other Azimuth Tables. (When L.H.A. lies between 0° and 180° the body is always west of the meridian, it is east when L.H.A. is between 180° and 360°.)

6. the *Intercept* (in nautical miles) is found by taking the difference between the T.Z.D. and C.Z.D. It is named TOWARDS if the T.Z.D. is the smaller of the two, and AWAY when the T.Z.D. is greater.*

To plot the Position Line (see diagram on page 119)

7. Plot the D.R. Position.

8. Through the D.R. Position draw the bearing line of the body.

9. Along the bearing line, *from* the D.R. Position, lay off the Intercept, *Towards* or *—Away* from the body, as appropriate.

10. Through the point so obtained, draw the Position Line 90° to the bearing line. The point through which the Position Line (PL) is drawn is called the "Intercept Terminal Point" (I.T.P.).

* *Many navigators prefer to find the Intercept by first subtracting the C.Z.D. from 90° to obtain Computed Altitude which is then compared with the True Altitude. The Intercept thus found is named TOWARDS when the True Altitude is the greater of the two.*

Computation:

G.M.T. 17d. 20h. 41m. 01s.

			S.A.	☉ 25° 51′.0	
			I.E.	+1 .0	
G.H.A.	119° 01′.8	Dec.	O.A.	25 52 .0	
Inc.	10 15 .3	13° 12′.7N	Dip	−6 .9	
Long.	163 32 .0 E	− 0.6	A.A.	25 45 .1	
L.H.A.	292° 49′.1	13° 12′.1N	Cor.	+14 .0	
			T.A.	25 59 .1	
				90 00 .0	
			T.Z.D.	64° 00′.9	

$$\text{hav C.Z.D.} = \text{hav P. cos}\,l.\,\text{cos}\,d. + \text{hav}\,(l \pm d)$$

P	= 67° 10′.9		9.48587	
l	= 23 54 .0 N		9.96107	0.27246
d	= 13 12 .1 N		9.98837	0.00869
(l − d)	= 10° 41′.9		9.43531	0.28115

A	.186 S	C.Z.D.	64° 02½′
B	.248 N	T.Z.D.	64° 01 ′
C	.062 N ∴ **Azimuth N 87° E**	**Intercept**	1½′ TOWARDS

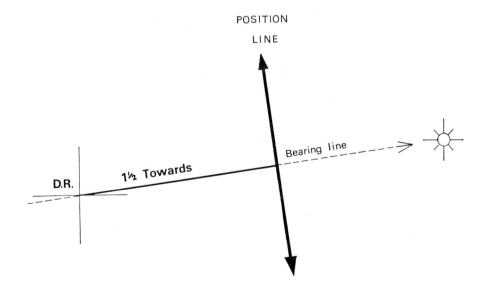

POSITION LINE

Bearing line

D.R.   1½ Towards

Example 2. On 16th August, of a typical year at morning twilight, in D.R. Position 34° 06'S. 150° 20'W., the Observed Altitude of PROCYON was 24° 42' at G.M.T. 16d. 16h. 18m. 12s., H. of E. 19 m. Required Intercept and Position Line.

			PROCYON	O.A.	24° 52'.0
G.M.T. 16d. 16h. 18m. 12s.				Dip	−7 .6
G.H.A. Aries	205° 06'.3			A.A.	24 44 .4
Inc.	4 33 .7			Cor.	−2 .1
S.H.A. Star	245 35 .4		Dec. 5° 18'.6 N		
				T.A.	24 42 .3
G.H.A. Star	455 15 .4				90 00 0
Long.	150 20 .0 W				
				T.Z.D.	65° 17'.7
L.H.A. Star	304° 55'.4				

$$\text{hav C.Z.D.} = \text{hav P. cos}\,l.\ \text{cos}\,d. + \text{hav}\,(l \pm d)$$

P	=	55° 04'.6	9.32990		0.17623
l	=	34 06 .0S	9.91806		0.11368
d	=	5 18 .6N	9.99813		
(l + d) =		39° 24'.6	9.24609		0.28991

A .472 N

B .116 N

C .588 N   ∴ Azimuth N 64° E

C.Z.D. 65° 09'.3
T.Z.D. 65° 17 .7

Intercept 8'.4 AWAY

Note: The plotting of the position line is similar to Example 1.

THE USE OF SHORT METHOD TABLES

There is a wide variety of short method tables available for the reduction of astronomical observations by the intercept (Marcq Saint-Hilaire) method. The most direct are the altitude — azimuth tables which are entered with Latitude, Declination and Local Hour Angle.

To avoid three way interpolation, the latitude is chosen to be the whole number of degrees nearest to the D.R. latitude and the longitude is chosen to be that nearest to the D.R. longitude which, when applied to the Greenwich Hour Angle of the body, gives a Local Hour Angle which is a whole number of degrees. Since the chosen latitude and longitude may be up to 30' distant from the D.R. position, longish intercepts may have to be plotted. These volumes of tables are somewhat bulky but they give rapid results since both calculated altitude and azimuth may be obtained from a single entry.

Other tables are available in which compactness is achieved at the expense of additional entries and some measure of additional complexity.

THE USE OF ELECTRONIC CALCULATORS FOR REDUCING ASTRONOMICAL OBSERVATIONS

General:

These instruments may be used for finding both the calculated zenith distance and the azimuth in astronomical problems by similar methods to those suggested for the solution of great circle problems, see p. 107. The following notes are again intended to give some general guidance in using calculators at three levels of sophistication, but adaptations may be necessary or desirable for particular models.

Simple Four Function Calculator designed with algebraic logic:

A calculator with facilities for addition, subtraction, multiplication and division may be used as an alternative to logarithms in the reduction of astro observations by the intercept method. For this simple four function calculator, with no memory, it is recommended that the basic haversine formula should be used. The values of natural sines and cosines may conveniently be found from the tables in section B which are arranged so that both functions may be obtained from a single entry of an angle. The natural haversines can be taken from *Reeds Nautical Almanac* or other nautical tables. A typical keyboard might be as shown on p. 107 and a suitable order of work is illustrated in the example below. It may, of course, be necessary to amend the sequence to suit the operation of a particular model of calculator.

Example: On August 18th of a typical year (at ship) in D.R. position 23° 54′ N., 163° 32′ E., at GMT 17d. 20h. 41m. 01s. Sextant Altitude Suns LL 25° 51′, I.E. 1.0′ off the arc, H of E 15 metres. Required the intercept and azimuth.

GMT   17d. 20h. 41m. 01s.

						S.A.	☉ 25° 51.0′
						I.E.	+ 1.0′
GHA	119° 01.8′	← From Almanac →	Dec.	13° 12.7′ N.		O.A.	25° 52.0′
Inc.	10° 15.3′		Inc.	— 0.6′		Dip.	— 6.9′
Long.	163° 32.0′ E.		Dec.	13° 12.1′ N.		A.A.	25° 45.1′
LHA	292° 49.1′					Corr.	+ 14.0′
						T.A.	25° 59.1′
							90° 00.0′
						TZD	64° 00.9′

hav CZD = hav LHA cos l cos d + hav (l $\pm$ d)

LHA	292° 49.1′	n. hav.	0.30610	⎫
l	23° 54.0′	n. cos.	0.91425	⎬ From
d	13° 12.1′	n. cos	0.97357	⎬ Tables
l-d	10° 41.9′	n. hav.	0.00869	⎭

Quantity		Entry	Reading	
hav LHA	→	0.30610	0.30610	
		x	0.30610	
cos l	→	0.91425	0.91425	
		x	0.27985	Using
cos d	→	0.97357	0.97357	Calculator
		+	0.27246	
		0.00869	0.00869	
		=	0.28115	

hav CZD = 0.28115
    CZD = 64° 02.6′   From
    TZD = 64° 00.9′   Tables
    Int =   1.7 Towards

$$\text{hav Az.} = \frac{\text{hav PX} - \text{hav (PZ} \sim \text{ZX)}}{\sin \text{PZ} \sin \text{ZX}}$$

PX	= 90° – d	= 76° 47.9′	n. hav	0.38581	
PZ	= 90° – l	= 66° 06.0′	sin	0.91425	From
ZX		= 64° 00.9′	sin	0.89891	Tables
PZ ∼ ZX		= 2° 05.1′	n. hav	0.00033	

Quantity		Entry	Reading (to five decimal places)	
hav PX	→	0.38581	0.38581	
		—	0.38581	
hav (PZ ∼ ZX)	→	0.00033	0.00033	
		÷	0.38548	Using
sin PZ	→	0.91425	0.91425	Calculator
		÷	0.42164	
sin ZX	→	0.89891	0.89891	
		=	0.46905	

hav Az. = 0.46905   From
    Az. = 086° 27′   Tables

A Standard Scientific Calculator with two Memories

A scientific calculator has keys for sine, cosine and tangent amongst other functions, but will not generally have a key for haversines. It is therefore convenient to use the basic cosine formula for the reduction of astronomical observations. An example of a suitable keyboard is illustrated on p. 110, but typical scientific calculators will have additional functions which are not essential for the solution of astronomical navigation problems.

Note that for this example:
Key STO transfers a quantity to store.
Key RCL recalls a quantity from store.
The sine of an angle is entered by first entering the angle in degrees and decimal parts of a degree, and then pressing the SIN key.
To find an angle whose sine is the number displayed, the ARC key is pressed, and then the SIN key. Similar procedures are followed for cosine and tangent.

A suitable order of work is illustrated in the example below. It should be noted that angles in degrees and minutes will normally have to be converted to degrees and decimal parts of a degree before entering on the calculator for the input of sine and cosine functions. The detailed sequence of operations may, of course, have to be amended to suit a particular model of calculator.

Example: On August 18th of a typical year (at ship) in D.R. position 23° 54′ N., 163° 32′ E., at GMT 17d. 20h. 41m. 01s. Sextant Altitude Suns LL 25° 51′, I.E. 1.0′ off the arc, H. of E. 15 metres. Required the intercept and azimuth.

GMT	17d. 20h. 41m. 01s.		Lat. 23° 54′ N.	SA	☉25° 51.0′
			= 23.900° N.	IE	+ 1.0′
				OA	25° 52.0′
GHA	119° 01.8′	← From Almanac → Dec.	13° 12.7′ N.	Dip	— 6.9′
Inc.	10° 15.3′	Inc.	— 0.6′	AA	25° 45.1′
Long.	163° 32.0′ E.	Dec.	13° 12.1 N.	Corr.	+ 14.0′
LHA	292° 49.1		= 13.202°	TA	25° 59.1′
	= 292.818°				90° 00.0′
				TZD	64° 00.9′

From the basic cosine formula:
$\cos ZX = \cos PZ \cos PX + \sin PZ \sin PX \cos P$
$\cos CZD = \sin l \sin d + \cos l \cos d \cos LHA$

Quantity		Entry	Reading (to five decimal places)
l	→	23.900	23.900
		sin	0.40514
		STO1	0.40514
d	→	13.202	13.202
		sin	0.22836
		x	0.22836
		RCL1	0.40514
		=	0.09252
		STO1	0.09252

Cont. overleaf

Examples Cont.

I	→	23.900	23.900
		cos	0.91425
		STO2	0.91425
d	→	13.202	13.202
		cos	0.97357
		x	0.97357
		RCL2	0.91425
		=	0.89009
		STO2	0.89009
LHA	→	292.818	292.818
		cos	0.38781
		x	0.38781
		RCL2	0.89009
		+	0.34519
		RCL1	0.09252
		=	0.43771
		ARC	0.43771
CZD	←	COS	64.042

CZD	=	64° 02.5′
TZD	=	64° 00.9′
Int.		1.6′ Towards

Also from the basic cosine formula:

$$\cos Z = \frac{\cos PX - \cos PZ \cos ZX}{\sin PZ \sin ZX}$$

$$\cos Az = \frac{\sin d - \sin I \cos ZD}{\cos I \sin ZD}$$

Quantity		Entry	Reading
I	→	23.9	23.9
		cos	0.91425
		STO1	0.91425
CZD	→	64.042	64.042
		sin	0.89912
		x	0.89912
		RCL1	0.91425
		=	0.82202
		STO1	0.82202
I	→	23.9	23.9
		sin	0.40514
		STO2	0.40514
CZD	→	64.042	64.042
		cos	0.43771
		x	0.43771
		RCL2	0.40514
		=	0.17733
		STO2	0.17733

Quantity	Entry	Reading
d	$\rightarrow$ 13.202	13.202
	sin	0.22836
	—	0.22836
	RCL2	0.17733
	÷	0.05103
	STO1	0.82202
	=	0.06208
	ARC	0.06208
Az	$\leftarrow$ cos	86.441

Azimuth = 086° 26'

Specialised Navigation Computers and Programmable Calculators:
The use of these instruments for great circle calculations is discussed on page 113. They may be used in a similar way for reducing astronomical observations.

GRAPHICAL METHODS OF REDUCING ASTRONOMICAL OBSERVATIONS

General:
A number of graphical methods of reducing astronomical observations are available. These generally provide sufficient accuracy for finding azimuth which is only required to the nearest degree for plotting the direction of intercepts and position lines, but not generally sufficient accuracy for finding the calculated altitude or zenith distance which is required to the nearest minute of arc.

Weir's Azimuth Diagram:
This is a diagram produced by the British Hydrographic Office and available from Admiralty Chart Agents. It consists of a lattice of ellipses and hyperbolae superimposed on rectangular coordinate axes. The diagram is used by plotting a first point on the Y axis at a distance from the origin dependent upon the body's declination. A second point is plotted at the intersection of an ellipse corresponding to the observer's latitude and a hyperbola corresponding to the body's local hour angle (LHA). The line joining the two points makes an angle with the Y axis which is equal to the azimuth of the body.

Equatorial Stereographic Projection:
A diagram similar to that on page 28 may be used to find the azimuth and approximate altitude or zenith distance of a body. The procedure is as follows:

(1) Place a piece of tracing paper over the diagram and locate it by means of a pin or the point of a pair of compasses through the centre.
(2) Mark point Z on the tracing paper at the D.R. latitude of the observer and on the eastern (right hand) circumference of the diagram if the body is to the west of the observer, or on the western (left hand) circumference if the body is to the east of the observer.
(3) Mark point X on the tracing paper in its correct position relative to the declination and local hour angle (LHA) scales of the diagram.
(4) Rotate the tracing paper until point Z is superimposed over point P on the diagram.
(5) Read off the altitude and azimuth corresponding to the new position of point X over the altitude and azimuth scales of the diagram. Zenith distance may also be read from the appropriate scale if required.

NOTES ON TAKING STELLAR OBSERVATIONS

1. Set up the star finder (or star globe if one is available) beforehand for the time of Civil Twilight.

2. Select three or more stars suitably spaced in Azimuth and, preferably, with altitudes between 30° and 60°. If four stars are to be used, ideally they should be in two pairs 90° apart in Azimuth, the stars in each pair being on opposite bearings. The advantage of this combination is that the effects of any abnormal refraction will be cancelled out by the use of opposite horizons. Some alternative stars should be selected in case of cloudy conditions.

3. Make a list of the stars selected, with their approximate altitudes and bearings (relative to the ship's head), to assist in rapid identification.

4. Evening stars should be observed as early as possible to obtain the best horizon. Observe the brightest star first—set the altitude on the sextant and sweep the horizon on the appropriate bearing; by this means it is often possible to get the observation before the star becomes visible to the naked eye.

5. Morning stars should be observed as late as possible to obtain the clearest horizon. In this case it is best to observe the faintest star first because the brighter ones will be visible for longer.

6. When the horizon is not good, take several observations of each star at evenly spaced time intervals; if the changes in altitude between successive observations are not approximately equal the sights should not be relied upon.

7. When the horizon is hazy take observations from a position as low down as possible.

8. Abnormal refraction should be suspected whenever there is an unusually large difference between air and sea surface temperatures. When the sea is warmer than the air the horizon tends to be lower than its normal position, and tends to become elevated when the sea is colder than the air.

PRECOMPUTATION OF STAR SIGHTS

Many navigators prefer not to precompute their star sights. It often happens that, for one reason or another, it is not possible to take the observations at exactly the preselected times. This, however, presents no disadvantage if there is available a table giving the rate of change in altitude (see table *Change of Altitude in One Minute of Time,* in Section C).

Probably the most discouraging factor in using this method is that the work done in precomputation is completely wasted if there are no stars visible at twilight. In conditions when there is a reasonable probability of obtaining stellar observations the practice is a rewarding one; especially on those occasions when twilight falls at a busy time, or when an extra number of star sights are deemed prudent prior to making a difficult landfall.

Procedure

1. Calculate in advance the D.R. position for the time of Civil Twilight.
2. Select suitable stars for observation at that time, and the G.M.T. at which it is intended each observation is to be made.*
3. Compute the Altitude and Azimuth of each star for its appropriate G.M.T.*
4. Apply the sextant corrections *in reverse* to the computed true altitudes to obtain computed sextant altitudes.
5. From the table in Section B (Change of Altitude in One Minute of Time) extract and write down the rate of change in Altitude for each star.
6. At the appropriate time, and just before observing each star, set its precomputed altitude on the sextant. *It is advantageous to have an assistant at the chronometer to give a "count down" to the required G.M.T.; but if an assistant is not available, first sight the star on the horizon, then watch the chronometer until (say) 10-15 seconds before "time", and then make your own "count down" whilst making the observation.*
7. Compare the sextant readings with the computed sextant altitudes to determine the intercepts.
8. Should the actual G.M.T. of an observation differ from that used in computation, adjust either one of the altitudes for the time difference, according to its rate of change. (Stars to the east of the meridian have increasing altitudes.)

Example: D.R. Position 43° 02'N. 20° 30'W; the precomputed sextant Altitude of Star "X" was 32° 19'.5 — Azimuth 342°W — G.M.T. 20h. 16m. 00s. Change of Altitude in 60 seconds (from table in Section B) = 7'.3 (decreasing). The actual observation, taken at G.M.T. 20h. 16m. 40s., gave sextant reading 32° 20'.

Computed Sextant Alt.	=	32° 19'.5
Change of alt. in 40s. = $7.3 \times \dfrac{40}{60}$ =		— 4'.9
		32° 14'.6
Sextant Reading	=	32° 20'.0
Intercept TOWARDS		5'.4

All experienced navigators have their own procedures and techniques. Many prefer to work all stars for the same G.M.T. and adjust the observations for change of altitude in time. This, they contend, is less bothersome than having to keep an eye on the chronometer and "counting down" — especially if there are any clouds in the sky.

Section F

MARINE METEOROLOGY

J

ABSOLUTE HUMIDITY: See "Vapour Concentration."

ABSOLUTE TEMPERATURE: See "Kelvin Scale."

ADIABATIC: Without gain or loss of heat—thermally insulated. When a body of air is subjected to increased pressure it undergoes compressional heating; similarly, if the same body of air is subjected to a decrease in pressure it undergoes expansional cooling. In both cases, no interchange of heat takes place between the body of air and the surrounding air (environment); the temperature changes thus brought about are said to be *adiabatic* changes. If a parcel of air rises through its environment it undergoes a reduction in pressure and is cooled adiabatically. Conversely, if it sinks, it undergoes an increase in pressure and is warmed adiabatically.

ADVECTION: The term generally refers to the horizontal movement of air, or the transference of heat by horizontal motion.

AIR MASS: An extensive body of air within which the temperature and humidity are more or less constant in a horizontal plane.

ANABATIC WIND: A local wind which blows *up* sloping ground which has been heated by the sun's rays. Favourable conditions are: a slack pressure gradient, strong surface heating, barren slope directly facing the sun.

ANALOGUE: A past synoptic chart which closely depicts the current situation for which the changes are to be forecast. Synoptic charts over a period of many years have been preserved and classified according to their particular patterns. Analogues are sometimes helpful as an aid to forecasting when there is a lack of other information. Meteorological history often repeats itself, and the developments which followed an analogue may sometimes be a guide to the possible developments in the future.

ANALYSIS: The process of positioning the fronts and drawing the isopleths on a surface or upper air chart.

ANTICYCLONE (also called a HIGH): An area of relative high pressure surrounded by an area of relatively low pressure. Characterised on a synoptic chart by a system of closed isobars, roughly circular or oval in shape. The wind blows clockwise round an anticyclone in the northern hemisphere, and counter-clockwise in the southern hemisphere.

ANTICYCLONIC GLOOM: A condition of poor light resulting from a dense layer of stratiform cloud below the subsidence inversion of an anticyclone. It occurs most often in large industrial areas, during quiet winter weather when smoke pollution is trapped and accumulates under the inversion.

ANTITRADES: The prevailing upper winds which blow above and in the opposite direction (polewards) to that of the trade winds.

ANVIL CLOUD: The anvil-shaped layer surmounting the top of a very well developed cumulonimbus cloud. Usually composed of ice crystals.

ATMOSPHERIC PRESSURE: See PRESSURE.

BACKING: The changing of the wind in a counterclockwise direction. A clockwise change is termed a *veer.*

BAGUIO: The local term for a tropical cyclone in the Philippine Islands.

BAROMETRIC PRESSURE: In the International (SI) System of units, the unit of force is the Newton (N), the force which, if applied to a mass of 1 kilogram will produce an acceleration of one metre per second per second. The unit of pressure is the Pascal (Pa) which is a force of 1 Newton per square metre. However the use of the millibar for measuring barometric pressure in meteorology is unlikely to be superseded in the near future. A millibar is equal to 100 pascals.

BLACK FROST: A relatively dry air condition in which the ground temperature falls below freezing point but remains above the dew-point of the air. Thus no deposit of hoar frost occurs.

BLACK ICE: The term ususally refers to glazed frost which has formed on road surfaces. When drizzle or light rain falls onto a surface, the temperature of which is below 0°C., a thin sheet of relatively dark ice forms. (See: GLAZED FROST).

BLIZZARD: Falling or drifting snow driven by an intensely cold high wind.

BLOCKING: The term refers to a synoptic situation whereby the normal movement of weather systems is "blocked" for a few days by the presence of another slow moving or stationary system, e.g., a *blocking anticyclone.*

BORA: A cold, often dry, north easterly to easterly wind which blows down the slopes of the Dalmatian Mountains and off the eastern shores of the Adriatic. It is partly katabatic, strongest and most frequent in winter, and sometimes attains gale force when the pressure distribution is favourable and the pressure gradient strong. Often dangerous when it arrives suddenly, with little warning, in the form of violent gusts.

BUYS BALLOT'S LAW: If an observer stands with his back to the wind, the lower pressure is on his left in the northern hemisphere, and on his right in the southern hemisphere. Mariners usually say "*face* the wind, and lower pressure is on your right in the northern hemisphere, and on your left in the southern hemisphere."

CHINOOK: A warm and dry southwest wind blowing down the eastern slopes of the Rocky Mountains in the U.S.A. and Canada. Its onset is usually sudden and the FÖHN effect very pronounced, especially in winter when it causes rapid melting of the snow. (See FÖHN).

CLEAR ICE: See GLAZED FROST.

CLIMATE: The prevailing and characteristic meteorological conditions of a locality, as opposed to *weather* which is the state of the atmosphere at a given time. The climate of a locality is governed mainly by: (a) latitude; (b) position in relation to large land masses and oceans; (c) prevailing large scale wind circulations; (e) local topography; and (f) altitude.

CLOUD BASE: The level at which rising unsaturated air reaches its dew-point temperature. Further ascent above this level results in the condensation of excess water vapour, forming cloud. Height of cloud base is reported as height above ground level.

COL: An atmospheric pressure distribution located between two highs and two lows arranged alternately. Associated with light variable winds; inclined to be thundery in summer and dull or foggy in winter.

COLD ANTICYCLONE: One in which the air temperature at the surface and in the lower troposphere is, level for level, colder than in the air surrounding the whole system. In this type, the high pressure is caused mainly by the low temperature and consequent high density of the air. Probably the best example of a cold anticyclone is the winter high of Siberia. A transitory cold high may sometimes build up in the polar air in the rear of a family of depressions; usually they soon collapse, but sometimes persist and, due to a long period of continued subsidence, slowly change into a warm anticyclone.

COLD FRONT: The line of discontinuity (at the surface or at upper level) along which an advancing cold air mass is overtaking and undercutting a warmer air mass.

COLD POOL: An air column of relatively low mean temperature, indicated on a thickness chart by closed isopleths encircling an area of low thickness. The thermal wind flows parallel to the thickness lines, counterclockwise round the cold pool in the northern hemisphere and clockwise in the southern hemisphere.

COLD SECTOR: That area of a depression occupied by cold air at the surface. It comprises the whole depression after the occluding process has been completed.

COLD TROUGH: A pressure trough (or trough on an isobaric contour chart) in which temperature is generally lower than in adjacent areas.

COLD WAVE: An American term for a period of low temperatures (below the average for the season and locality) which lasts for 24 hours or longer, particularly during the cold season.

CONDUCTION: The transmission or flow of heat through an unequally heated body from places or levels of higher temperature to places or levels of lower temperature.

CONFLUENCE: The convergent flow and merging of adjacent airstreams.

CONVECTION: The transference of heat within a gas (or liquid) by *movement* of the gas containing it. In meteorology it is broadly understood as the vertical movement of air within the environment, providing vertical exchange of heat and water vapour.

CONVERGENCE: An area of convergence is one in which the horizontal inflow of air exceeds the horizontal outflow at the same level. In this condition the excess air escapes vertically. Except in arid regions, convergence at surface level is usually associated with much cloud and precipitation; typical examples are fronts and centres of depressions.

CRACHIN: A weather condition which occurs between January and April in the China Sea and coastal areas from Shanghai to Cape Cambodia. The polar maritime air flowing down from the north interacts with trade wind and tropical maritime air, giving low stratus and drizzle with mist or fog.

CYCLOGENESIS: The process whereby a new cyclone or depression is formed, or an existing one is strengthened.

CYCLOLYSIS: The disappearance or weakening of an existing cyclone or depression.

CYCLONE: A relatively very low pressure centre surrounded by an area of higher pressure. The wind circulates counterclockwise round the centre in northern latitudes and clockwise in southern latitudes. The term usually refers only to "tropical cyclones" which are limited to definite regions, in many of which they are given local names. Cyclones of the temperate latitudes are called "depressions".

DEPRESSION (or LOW): A central region of relatively low pressure surrounded by an area of higher pressure. The wind circulates anti-clockwise round the low centre in the northern hemisphere, and clockwise in the southern hemisphere. The weather associated with a depression is, typically, unsettled with strong or gale force winds, much cloud and precipitation. The area covered by the system varies from about 100 to 2,000 miles in diameter. The term "depression" usually refers only to depressions of middle or high latitudes, and "cyclone" to tropical revolving storms (see CYCLONE).

DEW: A deposit of water formed by condensation of water vapour on surfaces which have been cooled by radiation to a temperature below that of the dewpoint of the air. Favourable conditions are—a calm night with a clear sky and high relative humidity.

DEW-POINT: The temperature to which unsaturated air must be cooled, at constant pressure and constant water vapour content in order to become saturated. Any further cooling usually results in condensation of the excess water vapour. (See FROST-POINT).

DIVERGENCE: An area of divergence is one from which the horizontal outflow of air exceeds the horizontal inflow at the same level; the deficiency of air is restored by vertical movement *(subsidence, when divergence is at surface level)*. Usually associated with quiet settled conditions. The central area of an intense anticyclone is a good example.

DRIZZLE: Liquid precipitation in the form of very small water drops (between 0.2 and 0.5 mm. diameters) falling slowly and gently from low based stratus cloud in conditions of high relative humidity at the surface.

DUST DEVIL: (Dust whirl or sand-pillar)—Occurs in hot, dry, sandy or dusty regions. During the heat of the day, when convection currents are strongest, small whirlwinds develop and carry large quantities of dust and sand upwards in dense columns of varying heights (usually less than 30 metres, but far greater heights have been reported). Their speed of movement varies considerably from 2 or 3 knots to nearly 30 knots, and their diameters are generally only a few yards.

DUST STORMS: Occur mainly in sandy deserts and semi-desert regions in the dry season, when there is an adequate supply of fine dust. The sudden arrival of a strong wind in very unstable air will carry dust to great heights and reduce visibility to less than 1,000 metres over a considerable area. Dust may be carried by the wind for great distances over the sea, causing "dust haze" to extend many miles from the coast.

EVAPORATION: In meteorology, the process of changing liquid water or ice into water vapour.

EVAPORATION FOG: Fog formed by evaporation of warm water or warm rain drops into relatively cold air. (See SEA SMOKE and FRONTAL FOG).

FETCH: The distance which the wind has travelled over a water surface in nearly the same direction.

FOG: A condition of atmospheric obscurity (caused by either water droplets, smoke particles, dust particles, or any combination thereof in suspension) in which the visibility is less than 1,000 metres.

FÖHN: A warm dry wind blowing down the leeward slopes of a mountain range. When moist air ascends the weather slopes to heights well above the condensation level, much of its original moisture may become trapped on the high ground, or deposited there by precipitation. Thus the air descending the lee slopes has a much lower moisture content; evaporation commences at a higher level than that at which condensation began. Below the "evaporation level", warming takes place at the dry adiabatic lapse rate (1°C per 100 metres) and the air finishes its descent relatively warm and dry. The *Föhn* is a local name which originated in the Swiss Alps, but the effect is experienced anywhere where the conditions are suitable. A notable example is the "Chinook".

FREE ATMOSPHERE: The atmosphere above the *friction layer*, i.e. above 2,000 ft. (600 metres) above ground level, where the air motion is considered to be free from the effects of surface friction.

FREEZING FOG: Supercooled water droplets of fog which freeze on impact with solid objects, forming *rime*.

FREEZING DRIZZLE OR FREEZING RAIN: Supercooled water drops of drizzle or rain which freeze on impact with solid objects to form *glazed frost*.

FREEZING LEVEL: The height above sea level of the 0°C. isotherm.

FRICTION LAYER: The layer of the atmosphere extending from ground level up to about 600 metres (2,000 feet) within which the effects of surface friction on air motion is appreciable.

FRONT: The line separating warm and cold air masses. A *surface front* is the line along which the sloping frontal surface cuts the Earth's surface. Although represented by a line on a synoptic chart it is, in fact, a narrow zone of transition.

FRONTAL FOG: Occurs at or near a front or occlusion. Caused by the evaporation of relatively warm rain drops falling through the cooler air below the frontal surface, thus increasing its moisture content and causing it to become saturated. See also MIXING FOG.

FRONTOGENESIS: The development of a front or the marked intensification of an existing one. Convergence or confluence or both are the most effective factors.

FRONTOLYSIS: The disappearance or marked weakening of a front. Horizontal divergence is the most effective factor, usually accompanied by subsidence.

FROST: *Air frost* occurs when the temperature of the air at screen level (about 1.25 m above the ground) falls below 0°C. When only the air which is in contact with the ground falls below this temperature, the term *ground frost* is used.

GALE: A wind having a speed of between 34 and 40 knots—force 8 on the Beaufort Scale.

GALE WARNING: Gale warnings are issued only when winds of force 8 or above are expected. The terms *severe gale* or *gale becoming severe,* indicate that winds of force 9 or above are expected. The terms *imminent, soon* and *later* indicate within 6 hours, between 6 and 12 hours, and more than 12 hours respectively, of the time of issue.

GEOSTROPHIC WIND: A hypothetical wind in the "free atmosphere" which moves under the influence of two balanced forces—the horizontal pressure force and the geostrophic force. It flows parallel to *straight* equidistant isobars which are stationary.

GRADIENT WIND: A hypothetical wind in the "free atmosphere" which flows under three balanced forces—horizontal pressure force, geostrophic force and cyclostrophic force. It flows parallel to *curved* equidistant isobars which are stationary.

GROUND FROST: See FROST.

GUST: A sudden increase in the strength of the wind. Its duration is very brief, being much shorter than that of a squall. At sea, gusts have no appreciable effect in raising waves, but squalls may last long enough to raise a group of waves which move along with the squall.

HAAR: A sea fog which invades eastern Scotland and parts of eastern England, especially during spring and early summer.

HARMATTAN: A dry and comparatively cool easterly wind which blows over north-west Africa during the dry season (November to March). It carries with it much dust from the Sahara, and reduces visibility for many miles to seaward. The period of the Harmattan decreases southwards.

HAZE: Atmospheric obscurity caused by the presence of dust or smoke particles.

HOAR FROST: A deposit of thin ice crystals or frozen dew upon surfaces whose temperatures have fallen below both dew-point and 0°C.

HORSE LATITUDES: The regions of light variable winds, calms, and fine weather of the subtropical anticyclones between latitudes about 30° to 40°. These belts fluctuate slightly north and south with the sun. The term is believed to originate in the days of sailing ships carrying horses as cargo. When, due to a prolonged period in these latitudes, fresh water ran short, the horses were thrown overboard.

HUMIDITY: Absolute humidity or vapour concentration is the water vapour content of the air expressed as mass per unit volume, usually in grammes per cubic metre. Relative humidity is the amount of water vapour actually present in the air, expressed as a percentage of the amount the air would contain at that temperature if it were saturated.

HURRICANE: the term applied to tropical revolving storms which occur in the regions of the West Indies, Gulf of Mexico, and off the north-east coast of Australia. On the Beaufort Scale any wind of force 12 (64 to 71 knots) is termed a *hurricane.*

HURRICANE WAVE: The raising of the level of the sea surface, by something in the nature of 3-6 metres, in a confined region near the centre of a tropical revolving storm.

ICELANDIC LOW: A large area of mean low pressure centred between Greenland and Iceland. In January the mean surface pressure is about 994 mb. Depressions frequently develop in this region, but they are less intense during the summer months.

INSOLATION: Energy received at the Earth's surface by short-wave solar radiation.

INSTABILITY: See STABILITY.

INTERTROPICAL CONVERGENCE ZONE (I.T.C.Z.): A narrow belt in low latitudes separating two convergent air masses which originate in different hemispheres. (Formerly known as the *intertropical front,* but as it bears little resemblance to fronts of the temperate latitudes, the term is now seldom used.) The zone fluctuates seasonally north and south with the Sun, its range of movement being small over the oceans and large over the Continents. Its mean position lies north of the equator for most of its length. Areas of horizontal convergence along this belt vary from day to day in both position and activity, but are generally associated with much cloud and convectional rain; for example, the *doldrums* of the Atlantic and Pacific Oceans.

INTERTROPICAL FRONT: See INTERTROPICAL CONVERGENCE ZONE.

INVERSION (of temperature): An inversion, or *negative lapse rate,* is said to occur at a place when atmospheric temperature increases with increasing height through a layer. A surface inversion may be caused through radiation cooling of a land surface at night, or by horizontal movement of warm air over a relatively cool surface. An inversion at height may be caused by the subsidence and compressional warming of dry air from upper levels. In all cases, it indicates very stable conditions, upward movement of air being arrested at the level of the inversion.

ISALLOBAR: A line on a synoptic chart joining all points of equal *barometric tendency,* Isallobaric charts are used mainly to assist in forecasting the movements of pressure systems; for example, all depressions tend to move from areas of rising tendencies towards areas of falling tendencies (from isallobaric high towards isallobaric low).

ISOTHERM: A line of constant temperature.

ISOTHERMAL LAYER: A layer of the atmosphere in which the temperature lapse rate is zero.

JET STREAM: A very fast moving current of air located near the troposphere; usually in the nature of 1,000 miles in length, 100 to 300 miles in width, and having a depth of 3 or more miles. Speed at the centre of the 'tube' is often around 100 knots, and may sometimes reach 200 knots. Speed falls off very rapidly with departure from the central core of the stream. Jet streams are associated with a strong horizontal temperature gradient, and flow with both high temperature and high pressure (at upper level) on the right in the northern hemisphere, and on the left in the southern hemisphere.

In temperate latitudes, *polar front* jet streams flow in the warm air near to the frontal surface. They occur over a wide range of latitude, but an individual jet stream usually persists for several days, sometimes more than a week, with little change of position. *Subtropical* jet streams occur at a height of around 15,000 m. in latitudes 25°-40° in winter, and 40°-45° in summer. During a season they are fairly constant in position; they are very persistent in winter, and speeds exceeding 200 knots are not uncommon.

KATABATIC WIND: On a 'quiet' night with a slack pressure gradient and clear skies, a surface inversion resulting from radiation cooling may be formed. On sloping ground the air in contact with the surface becomes colder and denser than the air at the same horizontal level away from the ground. The denser air then gravitates down the slope forming a 'down-slope' wind. In this case, the cooling by contact overcomes adiabatic warming. The effect may be intensified considerably in winter months on mountain slopes where the descent over a snow-clad surface is long; the resulting katabatic wind may then persist throughout the hours of daylight. Many local winds, such as the *Bora* and *Mistral,* are greatly strengthened by katabatic drainage.

KATA FRONT: A warm or cold front along which the warm air tends to descend relatively to the cold air at all levels; thus frontal activity is considerably damped down, and is often completely absent.

KELVIN TEMPERATURE SCALE: The international (SI) unit of temperature is the Kelvin (K), widely used for scientific work. It is defined as the fraction 1/273.16 of the thermodynamic temperature of the triple point of water; the triple point of substance being the pressure/temperature condition, unique for a given substance, at which the substance may exist in the solid, liquid or gaseous state. On this scale water freezes at 273.15 K and boils (at standard pressure) at 373.15 K. For meteorological purposes. K = 273 + °C, where C is Celsius (or Centigrade) temperature.

LAND AND SEA BREEZES: The diurnal variation in sea surface temperature is usually very small when compared to that of the adjacent land. During the day, under the influence of solar radiation, the land becomes warmer than the sea. This inequality produces a pressure gradient near the coastline, and causes an on-shore breeze (sea breeze) which is strongest during the mid or late afternoon. At night the process is reversed; terrestrial radiation cools the land to a temperature below that of the sea surface, the result is an offshore breeze (land breeze) which is usually weaker than the sea breeze, as the effect of surface friction is greater over the land.

Sea breezes may extend 15 miles on either side of the coastline; they rarely exceed force 3 in temperate latitudes but may reach force 5 in the tropics. Favourable conditions are clear skies and a slight pressure gradient. These winds, being local and transitory, do not conform to the general flow of surface isobars. If the general pressure gradient is strong the land and sea breezes may be completely masked.

LAPSE RATE (Temperature lapse rate); The fall in atmospheric temperature per unit increase in height, it is taken as positive when temperatures decrease with height. The *average* lapse rate within the troposphere is about 0.6°C per 100 metres but the actual lapse rate varies considerably from day to day and from place to place; over a limited height interval, lapse rate is sometimes negative (the condition is termed an "inversion"), notably just over fog. *The term "lapse rate" generally refers to the lapse rate of the environment (environmental atmosphere) and should on no account be confused with an "adiabatic lapse rate" (see ADIABATIC).*

Unsaturated air, when displaced vertically upwards through its environment, will cool at the "dry adiabatic rate" (D.A.L.R.), which is 1°C. per 100 metres, *Saturated air,* however, will cool at the "saturated adiabatic lapse rate" (S.A.L.R.), which varies according to temperature and pressure, but averages about half the D.A.L.R.

LATENT HEAT: The quantity of heat absorbed or emitted without change of temperature during a change of state of unit mass of a material.

Water may be changed to the vapour state by evaporation at any temperature, but a supply of heat is required to effect the process. Since the temperature does not change whilst evaporation is taking place, the heat used is said to become *latent* and is stored in the vapour. The same quantity of latent heat is required irrespective of the temperature at which the change takes place. When evaporation takes place into the atmosphere heat is drawn from the surroundings or from the evaporating surface and can be transported from one level to another, or from one region to another. Much of the heat supplied to sea and land surface by solar radiation is used in the process of evaporation and contained in the atmosphere as latent heat; later, cooling by ascent or by transportation into cooler latitudes may cause *condensation and release of latent heat,* thus raising the temperature of the upper air, or effecting transfer of heat from tropical to temperate latitudes.

LEVANTER: An easterly wind in the Straits of Gibraltar, bringing excessive moisture, local cloud, heavy dews, poor or bad visibility, and sometimes rain. It can occur at any time of the year, but is most frequent in March and July to October. The levanter is generally associated with high pressure over western Europe and low pressure to the south-west of Gibraltar or to the south over Morocco. It is usually light or moderate in force, and a banner cloud extends for a mile or so to leeward of the Rock. On occasions, when it blows fresh or strong, dangerous eddies are formed in the lee of the Rock.

LEVECHE: A hot, dry, sand-and-dust-laden southerly wind which blows on the south-east coast of Spain. It occurs in front of an advancing depression, and its approach is often heralded by a belt of brownish cloud moving up from the south. (See also SIROCCO.)

LINE SQUALL: A very well marked, particularly active cold front in the form of a *V-shaped trough.* Its approach and passage are characterised by an arch or line of low black cloud (often "roll" cloud) preceding the front. A sudden freshening and slight backing of the wind, followed by a veer of perhaps 90° or more as it passes, together with a hard squall or squalls, often heavy rain or hail with thunder and lightning; it is also marked by a sudden fall in temperature. The barometer commences to rise rapidly immediately the trough has passed, the wind moderates quickly and tends to back a little before settling to a steady direction. A line squall generally lasts for about 15 minutes and occasionally for half an hour. (See "Pampero" and "Southerly Buster".)

LONG WAVE (Rossby Waves); A smooth wavelike pattern on an upper air contour chart, which shows the flow of westerly winds right round the Arctic low. These long waves vary considerably in amplitude and length, and may extend for 2,000 miles or more from crest to crest. There are generally four or five of such waves to be seen on a contour chart of a complete hemisphere.

The position and shape of long waves are of special importance in forecasting.

LONG WAVE RADIATION (Terrestrial radiation): The ground is cooled at night by outward (long wave) radiation in excess of incoming radiation. Conditions favourable for nocturnal cooling are:- a cloudless sky, low absolute humidity, and absence of wind. Dew and hoarfrost are indications of effective long wave radiation.

LOOMING: (1) An apparent elevation of distant terrestrial objects by abnormal refraction; objects below the horizon may become visible. Associated with a strong inversion. (See MIRAGE).
(2) Term used when land or objects are seen indistinctly through poor visibility, darkness or distance.

MIRAGE: An optical phenomenon in which objects appear to be raised, lowered, magnified, distorted, inverted or multiplied due to unusual and sharp variations in density of atmospheric layers close to the Earth's surface.
Inferior mirage: Occurs when the surface air is strongly heated by contact with hot, fairly level ground, and so becomes less dense than the air immediately above. Rays of light from the clear sky are refracted upwards towards the observer; the illusion produced is that of an expanse of shimmering bright water.
Superior mirage. When the surface is much colder than the air above, and the wind is very light, a strong temperature inversion is formed. In this case, the light rays from an object are bent downwards towards the observer, and objects below the horizon may become visible. Sometimes an inverted image is seen above the real object, and occasionally, an upright image over the inverted one. Superior image occurs more often in high latitudes.

MIST: A condition of atmospheric obscurity caused by the presence of suspended minute water droplets. The term is limited to conditions in which objects are visible at distances greater than 1 kilometre. A relative humidity of 95% is used by the British Meteorological Office as a guide to the dividing line between mist and haze.

MISTRAL: A cold dry, strong N. or N.W. wind blowing over the northwest coasts of the Mediterranean. It occurs usually when there is high pressure to the northwest, over France, and low to the southeast. It often attains gale force, especially in winter, when the flow of air over the Gulf of Lions is reinforced by katabatic drainage from the French Maritime Alps and also from the funnelling of the Rhone Valley.

MIXING FOG: Forms along the boundary (mixing zone) between two air masses of widely differing temperatures, both of which are nearly saturated.

Sometimes called "frontal fog" because it is often experienced during the passage of a front.

MIZZLE: See SCOTCH MIST.

MONSOON: A seasonal wind blowing from a large land mass towards the ocean in winter, and in the reverse direction in summer. Caused by the unequal surface heating of large land and sea areas. In the summer, low surface pressure develops over the relatively hot land; in winter, high pressure builds up over the relatively cold land. Monsoons occur in many parts of the world, but the Asiatic monsoons are the most notable.

OCCLUSION: Within a frontal depression the cold front moves faster than the warm front, and eventually overtakes it. Thus, advancing polar air overtakes retreating polar air, and the tropical air of the warm sector is lifted off the ground. When these two polar air masses come together, their differing characteristics (due to recent history) will cause the overtaking air to override or undercut the retreating air; in both cases, the process is called an *occlusion,* warm or cold, respectively.

OKTA: Unit used in reporting cloud amount; it is equal to an area of one eighth of the area of the sky.

OROGRAPHIC CLOUD: is formed when an airstream, on meeting a barrier of high ground, is deflected upwards and the consequent adiabatic cooling brings the temperature below the dew-point of the rising air.

PAMPERO: The name given to a severe line squall in the Argentine and Uruguay. (See LINE SQUALL).

POLAR FRONT: The line of separation between the principal polar and tropical air masses in the middle latitudes. Most of the travelling depressions of these latitudes are formed on bends or waves on the polar front. It often extends as an unbroken line for thousands of miles.

PRECIPITATION: The term includes rain, drizzle, sleet, snow, hail, dew, hoar frost, rime and glazed frost. Cloud, fog and mist are not classed as precipitation. "Wet fog" however, which deposits water on the surfaces with which it comes in contact, is classified as precipitation.

PRESSURE: Force per unit area exerted on a surface by the liquid or gas in contact with it. *Atmospheric pressure* at any level is produced by the weight of the air which lies above that level; hence atmospheric pressure decreases as height increases.

PRESSURE GRADIENT (Horizontal): The change in pressure per unit distance measured at right angles to the isobars. It is generally termed *steep* when the isobars are close together, and *slight, slack* or *flat*

when they are widely spaced. The steeper the gradient, the greater the wind speed. In the middle latitudes, a gradient of 1mb. in 30 miles gives a geostrophic wind speed of approximately 30 knots (surface wind speed at sea about 24 knots).

PRESSURE TENDENCY: The rate of change of pressure with time. In practice it usually refers to the change in pressure during the period of three hours prior to the time of observation. Of great practical value in forecasting. (See ISALLOBAR).

PROGNOSTIC CHART: Forecast chart.

QUASI-STATIONARY FRONT: A front whose position shows little or no movement on successive synoptic charts. Subject to wave-like disturbances which bring increased frontal activity, and the likelihood of the formation of a new depression.

RADIATION INVERSION: (Surface inversion): A temperature inversion extending upwards from the ground, and resulting from a period of nocturnal radiation cooling. Favourable conditions are: a clear sky at night, and little or no wind. The inversion will be greatly strengthened if the period of darkness is long, as in winter months.

RADIOSONDE: A small, compact radio transmitter, attached to a free balloon for the purpose of obtaining upper air observations—usually pressure, temperature and humidity. Wind velocities can be obtained also, either by tracking the balloon with a radio-theodolite, or by radar echoes from a radar target (reflector) carried by the balloon.

RIDGE: A ridge (or wedge) of high pressure is a tongue-like extension of an anticyclone or high pressure area. It is generally associated with fair weather, similar to that of an anticyclone. Ridges travelling eastwards between two temperate latitude depressions are usually fast-moving, and the fair periods which they often bring are brief. Ridges extending from continental highs in winter, or from sub-tropical highs, are slower in movement, and sometimes remain in one area for several days.

RIME: When supercooled water droplets of fog strike solid objects (such as trees, telephone wires, ship's masts, rigging and superstructure) which are at temperatures below 0°C. they freeze on impact, forming a deposit of white ice crystals. The deposit is rough in appearance, and grows out to windward of the object.

ROARING FORTIES: The prevailing westerly winds of the southern hemisphere which blow over the oceans in the temperate latitudes, on the poleward side of the 40th parallel.

ROSSBY WAVE: See LONG WAVE.

SATURATION: Air is said to be saturated when its relative humidity is 100%. It should be noted that, at subfreezing temperatures, the saturation value of absolute humidity is higher over water than over ice—thus air which is only just saturated with respect to water is supersaturated with respect to ice.

SCIROCCO: The local name for a southerly wind in the Mediterranean. Originating in the desert regions of North Africa, it crosses the African coast as a hot, dry wind and often carries much dust. Blowing over the relatively cool water surface, it picks up moisture and tends to become stable; thus it reaches the northern coasts as a warm, unpleasantly humid wind, often with fog or low stratus.

SCOTCH MIST: A combination of drizzle and thick mist; most common in the uplands of Scotland, from whence it derives its name. Frequent in Devon and Cornwall, where it is known as "MIZZLE".

SCUD (Stratus fractus): Ragged-looking low clouds of bad weather, which appear to move rapidly below rain cloud (nimbostratus) in strong winds.

SEA BREEZE: See LAND AND SEA BREEZES.

SEA SMOKE (Arctic sea smoke, frost smoke, steam fog, warm water fog, or water smoke): When cold air flows over a relatively very warm sea surface, intense evaporation takes place into the air *at* the surface, so that its vapour pressure becomes greater than the saturation vapour pressure of the air immediately above. As convection carries the warmed surface air upward into the colder air, the excess water vapour is condensed and gives the appearance of steam or smoke rising from the sea surface. Occurs mainly in high altitudes (e.g., with cold air blowing over gaps in the ice pack), off eastern coasts of cold continents in winter, over inland seas, lakes, and waterways in Autumn.

SECONDARY COLD FRONT: A trough of low pressure in the polar air following the first cold front of a depression. It marks the advance of fresh polar air which, due to recent history, is colder than the polar air immediately behind the primary front.

SECONDARY DEPRESSION: A small low which forms within the area covered by the closed circulation of a larger (primary) depression. It generally moves round its parent low in a cyclonic direction, following the main flow of isobars, and often develops sufficiently to completely absorb the primary depression. Secondaries often form on a frontal wave, and sometimes at the tip of the warm sector of a partly occluded depression. Non-frontal secondaries may form within an unstable polar air mass.

SHAMAL: A prevailing N.W. wind which blows over Iraq, the Persian Gulf, and Gulf of Oman. Most frequent in summer, when the monsoon low is established over N.W. India. Generally hot, very dry, and associated with cloudless skies. It carries quantities of dust and fine sand from the desert, causing bad visibility. In the early summer it may persist for several weeks at a time. Seldom exceeds force 7, except in winter when it sometimes reaches force 9, and may be accompanied by rain squalls, thunder, and lightning. The onset of a Shamal is not usually preceded by any marked barometric tendency.

SLEET: Snow and rain falling together or snow which melts as it falls. (In United States Weather Bureau terminology: "Frozen precipitation consisting of transparent, rounded, hard, raindropsized grains of ice that rebound as they strike a hard surface. Also called ice pellets". In United States popular terminology: "A smooth coating of ice deposited by freezing rain; glaze".)

SMOG: Fog which is thickened and darkened by smoke pollution. In large industrial areas, a normal white or grey water fog is often changed into brown smog by smoke from furnace and domestic fires.

SOUTHERLY BUSTER: The local name for the sudden squally onset of cold air which marks the passage of a well-defined, active cold front on the south and south-east coast of Australia. The N.W. wind in advance of the trough is light, warm and oppressive. The arrival of the S.W. wind is usually marked by a line of roll cloud, and sometimes by thunder and lightning; it commences as a sudden violent squall, and often blows with gale force for several hours before moderating. There is a large and rapid fall in temperature as the front passes. Similar to the Pamperos of South America.

SPECIFIC HEAT: The specific heat of a substance is the heat required to raise the temperature of unit mass of it by one degree. In the International (SI) units it is expressed in joules per kilogramme per degree Kelvin. The specific heat of water is higher than that of any other common substance; hence the gain or loss of a given quantity of heat brings about a smaller change in the temperature of the sea than of the land.

SQUALL: A sudden, very marked increase in wind speed, which lasts for some minutes and then suddenly dies down. It is of longer duration than a gust. (See GUST).
When using the Beaufort scale for the estimation of wind speed, the following criteria should be used for the reporting of squalls: "A sudden increase of wind speed by at least 3 stages of the Beaufort Scale, the speed rising to Force 6 or more, and lasting for at least one minute."

STABILITY (Atmospheric): Stable air offers resistance to vertical displacement. In unstable air vertical movement is stimulated. If, in stable atmosphere, a parcel of air is displaced upwards or downwards it will tend to return to its original level immediately the displacing force is removed. In unstable atmosphere the parcel will continue to move in the same direction after the initial displacing force has ceased to act. Lapse rate is the governing factor which determines whether the atmosphere is stable or unstable.

Unsaturated air is stable when its lapse rate is less than the dry adiabatic lapse rate (D.A.L.R.), and unstable when its lapse rate exceeds the D.A.L.R.

Saturated air is stable when its lapse rate is less than the saturated adiabatic lapse rate (S.A.L.R.), and unstable when its lapse rate exceeds the S.A.L.R.

In general, atmospheric stability is favoured by small lapse rates, and atmospheric instability by large lapse rates. Layer type cloud is associated with stable atmosphere; cumuliform cloud of great vertical extent is associated with unstable atmosphere.

STANDING WAVE: An air wave which is stationary or nearly stationary in relation to the Earth's surface. Usually associated with the flow of air over high ground or other obstructions.

STEAM FOG: See SEA SMOKE.

STRATOSPHERE: The region of the atmosphere contained between the tropopause (average height about 7 miles) and the stratopause (average height about 31 miles). Within this region temperature does not decrease with height, but remains practically constant in the lower levels, and increases with height in the upper levels. Temperature in the stratosphere is not governed by convection or transference of latent heat, but it is increased in the higher levels by absorption of solar radiation by ozone.

SUBLIMATION: The direct deposition of ice from water vapour, or direct evaporation to water vapour from an ice surface.

SUBSIDENCE: The slow downward motion of air which is warmed adiabatically during descent. In an anticyclone, the deficiency of surface air due to divergence is restored by subsidence which brings about great stability and an *anticyclonic inversion*.

SUMATRAS: Violent thundery squalls which occur in the Malacca Strait, usually at night, during the south-west monsoon period. They are initiated by Katabatic winds; the sudden shift of wind from a southerly direction and an increase in force is accompanied by heavy cumulonimbus cloud, heavy rain and a marked fall in temperature.

SUPERCOOLED WATER DROPLETS: Water droplets in the liquid state at temperatures below 0°C.

SUPERSATURATION: A sample of air is said to be "supersaturated" if it contains more than enough water to saturate it at its existing temperature. Owing to the presence of condensation nuclei, an appreciable degree of supersaturation with respect to water is rarely observed in the atmosphere.

THERMAL DEPRESSION (Thermal low): A surface depression, the formation of which is caused by unequal heating of adjacent areas, i.e. strong surface heating over islands and peninsulas in summer, or relatively warm inland seas and lakes in winter. Monsoon lows are large scale thermal depressions.

THERMAL WIND: The wind at upper level can be resolved into two components— the lower (geostrophic) wind and the thermal wind. The latter is the effect of horizontal temperature distribution.
The thermal wind increases with increasing height, and flows along the isotherms of mean temperature with higher temperature on the right in the northern hemisphere, and on the left in the southern hemisphere. Its speed is proportional to the temperature gradient.

THICKNESS: The vertical separation between pairs of standard pressure levels; e.g., 500 and 1,000 mb. At any given point, the value of thickness is governed entirely by the mean temperature of the air column separating the two levels; thus, the thickness in a region where the layer is warm will be greater than in a region where the layer is cold and dense.
Thickness charts show isopleths of equal thickness (called "thickness lines"). Areas of "high" or "low" thickness may be enclosed by thickness lines indicating areas of high or low mean temperature for the layer concerned.

TORNADO: An exceptionally violent whirl of air which moves over land, causing great devastation along a very narrow path. The diameters average only a few hundred metres, and the paths anything from 300 metres to 300 miles, but usually less than 15 miles. They form in hot, moist, thundery conditions and are associated with very violent convection in cumulonimbus cloud. Often accompanied by deluges of rain, hail, thunder and lightning. Although experienced in many parts of the world, they occur most frequently in the U.S.A., in the plains to the east of the Rockies. Very severe damage is caused by:
(a) The very powerful updraft which can lift heavy objects into the air;
(b) Exceptionally low pressure in the centre of the funnel which causes buildings to explode when "struck" by its arrival;
(c) Wind speed of such ferocity that small objects become missiles with high penetration, and heavier objects become huge battering rams. Wind speeds are believed to sometimes exceed 200 knots, and estimates of pressure vary from 100 to 500 mb.
The term "tornado" has also been used for thunder storm squalls in West Africa.

TROPOPAUSE: The boundary between the troposphere and the stratosphere. Its height varies from about 5 miles at the poles to about 10 or 11 miles over the equator.

TROPOSPHERE: The lower layers of the atmosphere bounded by the tropopause. Characterised by a positive lapse rate, convection currents, cloud and precipitation.

TYPHOON: The local name for a tropical revolving storm in the China Sea.

UPSLOPE FOG: Cloud which is formed on the windward slopes of high ground by the orographic uplift of moist, stable air. Cooling below the dew point is effected adiabatically.

VAPOUR CONCENTRATION: Vapour concentration or relative humidity is the water vapour content of the air expressed as mass per unit volume, usually in grammes per cubic metre.

VAPOUR PRESSURE: The atmosphere is made up of a mixture of gases. Each gas exerts a pressure proportional to its density. Atmospheric pressure is the sum total of the individual pressures of these gases. That part of atmospheric pressure which is due to water vapour *only* is called *vapour pressure.*

VEERING: A clockwise changing of the wind direction. The term "backing" is used to describe changing in an anticlockwise direction.

VENDAVALES: Strong S.W. winds off the east coast of Spain, and in the Straits of Gibraltar. Associated with advancing depressions from late Autumn to early Spring. Often accompanied by violent squalls, heavy rain and thunderstorms.

VIRGA: Precipitation falling below cloud which does not reach the Earth's surface.

WARM ANTICYCLONE: One in which the air temperature, level for level, is warmer than in the air surrounding the whole system. It is the most stable, persistent, and slow-moving of all pressure systems. The sub-tropical highs are warm anti-cyclones.
A temporary cold anticyclone may sometimes change into a temporary warm one due to continued subsidence. This occurs when a temporary cold high remains stationary for a long period.
A warm high gives quiet settled conditions, often dry, fine, sunny and warm.

WARM POOL: An air column of relatively high mean temperature, indicated on a thickness chart by closed isopleths encircling an area of high thickness. The thermal wind flows parallel to the thickness lines, clockwise round the warm pool in the northern hemisphere and counterclockwise in the southern hemisphere.

WARM RIDGE: A feature on an upper air chart, characterised by a flow of thickness lines which are concave towards high thickness, indicating a profusion of warm air into the main body of colder air. The thermal wind flows parallel to the isopleths with high temperature on the right in the northern hemisphere, and on the left in the southern hemisphere.

WATERSPOUT: The localised result of exceptionally strong convective instability over the sea. It forms under a very heavy cumulonimbus cloud, from the base of which a funnel-shaped cloud depends and reaches down towards the sea which is whirled into violent commotion, causing a cloud of spray to rise immediately below the funnel. Some waterspouts may develop no further than this, but with others the end of the spout reaches down into the spray cloud and forms a writhing column between the sea and cloud. The upper part of the spout usually travels along at a different speed to the part near the surface, thus after a few minutes the column assumes a slant, becomes less active, and breaks at about one third of its height from the surface; it then disappears quickly. The life cycle of a waterspout usually lasts from 10 to 30 minutes. Diameters vary from 5 metres to 100 metres, but are usually less than 30 metres. Speed of movement is very slow.
Waterspouts are the ocean counterpart of tornados and, although generally much less violent, they are a hazard to shipping and a serious danger to any small craft. Their occurrence is more frequent in the tropics than in temperate latitudes.

WAVE DEPRESSION: A depression which forms at the crest of a wave on a front.

WEATHER: The term generally refers to meteorological conditions (such as cloud, precipitation, mist, fog, sunshine, etc.) at a given time, as opposed to *climate* which is the prevailing meteorological condition of a place or region.

WEDGE: A wedge (or ridge) of high pressure is an outward extension from an anticyclone, usually between two lows. The associated weather is similar to that of an anticyclone, but is short-lived when the wedge moves along between two travelling depressions. A broad wedge extending from a large intense anticyclone may sometimes persist for many days.

WILLY-WILLY: The local name for a tropical revolving storm in Western Australia.

These photographs illustrate the appearance of the sea corresponding to the Beaufort wind scale. Their purpose is to assist observers in estimating the wind speed when making weather reports. The description of the sea is according to the SEA CRITERION laid down by the World Meteorological Organisation.

The appearance of the sea may be affected also by fetch, depth of water, swell, heavy rain, tide and the lag effect between the wind getting up and the sea increasing.

Probable wave heights and *probable* maximum wave heights have been added only as a rough guide to show what may be expected in sea areas remote from land. In enclosed waters, or when near land with an off-shore wind, wave heights will be smaller and the waves steeper.

It is difficult at night to estimate wind force by the sea criterion.

FORCE 0 (CALM)

Wind speed less than 1 knot

(Sea like a mirror)

Photo by R. R. Baxter (Crown Copyright)

Photo by R. R. Baxter (Crown Copyright)

FORCE 1 (LIGHT AIR)
Wind Speed 1-3 knots; mean, 2 knots

(Ripples with the appearance of scales are formed, but without foam crests)

FORCE 2 (LIGHT BREEZE)
Wind speed 4-6 knots; mean, 5 knots

(Small wavelets, still short but more pronounced—crests have a glassy appearance and do not break)
Probable wave height 0.15 metres (½ foot)
Probable Maximum 0.3 metres (1 foot)

Photo by R. R. Baxter (Crown Copyright)

Photo by R. Palmer

FORCE 3 (GENTLE BREEZE)

Wind speed 7-10 knots; mean, 9 knots

(Largest wavelets. Crests begin to break. Foam of glassy appearance.
Perhaps scattered white horses)
Probable wave height 0.6 metres (2 feet)
Probable Maximum 1.0 metres (3 feet)

FORCE 4 (MODERATE BREEZE)

Wind speed 11-16 knots; mean, 13 knots

(Small waves, becoming longer; fairly frequent white horses)
Probable wave height 1.0 metres (3½ feet)
Probable Maximum 1.5 metres (5 feet)

Photo by P. J. Weaver

Photo by R. R. Baxter (Crown Copyright)

FORCE 5 (FRESH BREEZE)

Wind speed 17-21 knots; mean, 19 knots

(Moderate waves, taking a more pronounced long form; many white horses are formed. Chance of some spray)

Probable wave height 1.8 metres (6 feet)
Probable Maximum 2.5 metres (8½ feet)

FORCE 6 (STRONG BREEZE)

Wind speed 22-27 knots; mean, 24 knots

(Large waves begin to form; the white foam crests are more extensive everywhere. Probably some spray)

Probable wave height 3.0 metres (9½ feet)
Probable Maximum 4.0 metres (13 feet)

Photo by R. R. Baxter (Crown Copyright)

FORCE 7 (NEAR GALE)

Wind speed 28-33 knots; mean, 30 knots

(Sea heaps up and white foam from breaking waves begins to be blown in streaks along the direction of the wind)
Probable wave height 4.0 metres (13½ feet)
Probable Maximum 6.0 metres (19 feet)

FORCE 8 (GALE)

Wind speed 34-40 knots; mean, 37 knots

(Moderately high waves of greater length; edges of crests begin to break into spindrift. The foam is blown in well marked streaks along the direction of the wind)
Probable wave height 5.5 metres (18 feet)
Probable Maximum 7.5 metres (25 feet)

Photo by P. J. Weaver

FORCE 9 (STRONG GALE)
Wind speed 41-47 knots; mean, 44 knots
(High waves. Dense streaks of foam along the direction of the wind.
Crests of waves begin to topple, tumble and roll over. Spray may affect
visibility)
Probable wave height 7.0 metres (23 feet)
Probable Maximum 9.75 metres (32 feet)

FORCE 10 (STORM)
Viewed at right angles to the trough
Wind speed 48-55 knots; mean, 52 knots
(Very high waves with long overhanging crests. The resulting foam, in
great patches, is blown in dense white streaks along the direction of the
wind. On the whole, the surface of the sea takes a white appearance.
The tumbling of the sea becomes heavy and shock-like. Visibility
affected)
Probable wave height 9.0 metres (29 feet)
Probable Maximum 12.5 metres (41 feet)

Photo by J. Hodkinson (Crown Copyright)

K

Photo by O. R. Bates

FORCE 10 (STORM)

Viewed along the trough

FORCE 11 (VIOLENT STORM)
Viewed at right angles to the trough
Wind speed 56-63 knots; mean, 60 knots
(Exceptionally high waves. (Small and medium-sized ships might be for a time lost to view behind the waves.) The sea is completely covered with long white patches of foam lying along the direction of the wind. Everywhere the edges of the wave crests are blown into froth. Visibility affected)
Probable wave height 11.3 metres (37 feet)
Probable Maximum 16.0 metres (52 feet)

Photo by G.P.O. (Crown Copyright)

Photo by Kevin O'Keefe (Crown Copyright)

FORCE 11 (VIOLENT STORM)

Viewed along the trough

FORCE 12 (HURRICANE)
Wind speed 64-71 knots; mean, 68 knots
(The air is filled with foam and spray. Sea completely white with driving spray; visibility very seriously affected)
Probable wave height 13.7 metres (45 feet)

The Beaufort scale actually extends to Force 17 (up to 118 knots), but Force 12 is the highest which can be identified from the appearance of the sea

Photo by G.P.O. (Crown Copyright)

CLOUD FORMATION

Summary of physical processes, resulting in cloud formation:
(1) The ascent of *unsaturated* air;
(2) As height increases pressure decreases, consequently the rising air expands and undergoes adiabatic cooling;
(3) Cooling continues so long as the ascent continues;
(4) The rising unsaturated air becomes saturated when it reaches its dew-point temperature at the *condensation level*;
(5) Further ascent results in the condensation of the *excess* water vapour, forming cloud;
(6) In general, the cloud thus formed will be stratiform or cumuliform, according to whether the air is stable or unstable, respectively.

Causes of initial uplift of air:
There are five main causes of initial uplift:
(1) **Orographic** uplift occurs when an air stream is forced to rise over an obstructing coastline or barrier of hills;
(2) **Thermal** uplift is the result of surface heating by solar radiation. The air is warmed by contact with the Earth's surface, expands, becomes buoyant, and floats upwards through the environment. It usually takes the form of columns of rising air within which the temperature is generally higher than in the environment, and is characterised by cumuliform cloud;
(3) **Turbulence:** Uplift occurs mainly in the surface layers as a result of surface friction and wind blowing over rough or uneven ground. In stable atmosphere the cloud formed will be stratus type; very moist air gives low stratus, whereas fairly dry air gives stratocumulus.
Turbulence can occur from a variety of causes anywhere within the troposphere. It gives cirrocumulus cloud at high levels and altocumulus at medium heights.
(4) **Frontal** uplift operates mainly within depressions but can occur elsewhere. More often than not, the cloud structures of the warm front are of the layer type, whereas cumuliform cloud is a common feature of the cold front.
(5) **Uplift resulting from convergent winds:** When the horizontal inflow of air into a surface area exceeds the horizontal outflow, the surplus air is forced upwards mechanically. Except in arid regions, convergence is usually associated with much cloud and precipitation; typical examples are at fronts and centres of depressions.

WIND

Relationship between wind direction and isobars:
In the "free atmosphere" (about 600 metres or 2,000 feet above the ground) where air movement is considered to be completely free from the effects of surface friction the wind flows parallel to the isobars. At the surface however, the effect of friction is to deflect the flow of air across the isobars towards lower pressure, at an angle which is governed by the roughness of the surface—normally about 10° to 15° at sea, and about 20° to 30° inland.

Buys Ballot's Law: Face the wind, and low pressure will be on your right in the northern hemisphere, and on your left in the southern hemisphere. It should be noted that **in equatorial latitudes** the Earth's rotation is not effective, Buys Ballot's Law does not apply, and the wind does, in fact, flow directly from high towards low pressure, crossing the isobars at an angle of about 90°. The limiting latitudes within which the Earth's rotation is not fully effective is considered to be about 5° N. and S.

Diurnal variation of surface wind speed:
At sea, well away from the proximity of land, the surface wind speed averages about 0.8 of
the geostrophic wind speed whether by day or by night. **Inland,** however, this figure is
reduced to about 0.6 by day, and about 0.2 by night.

SEA AND SWELL

Ocean waves are caused by the action of wind, but they can be produced also by tidal
effects and earth tremors. Local waves caused by the wind blowing at the time of
observation are termed "sea".

Waves persist for some time after the initial generating force has ceased to exist. Small
waves will soon die out; the larger the waves the longer they persist and the greater the
distance they will travel.

"Swell" is the term used for waves energised by past wind or wind at a distance. For
example, the long swell resulting from the high sea in a tropical cyclone may sometimes
be observed over 1,000 miles from the storm centre.
The following terms are used with reference to waves:

Height: The vertical distance from trough to crest—usually expressed in feet or
metres;

Period: The time *in seconds* between the passage of two successive crests (or
troughs) past a fixed point;

Velocity: The speed at which the crest travels—

$$Velocity \ = \ \frac{length}{period}$$

The result is in feet per second, or metres per second, according to which
units are used for the length.

Waves in shallow water: The term "shallow" is considered to apply when the depth of
water is less than half the length of the wave.
Deep water waves undergo very considerable changes on entering shallow water. Their
speed is reduced, and their height is increased until, on reaching or approaching the
shore, they will break at a limiting depth. Their direction of motion may change also, and
the crests tend to become parallel to the shore line.

Wave observation includes the measurement or estimate of *Direction, Period* and
Height. Clear and concise instructions on the best way to make such observations from a
moving ship are contained in the "Marine Observer's Handbook" (M.O.887). **Sea and
swell should be recorded as separate observations.**

The importance of Wave Observations:
Sea and swell observations from ships are of great value to meteorologists, oceanographers, naval architects, the British Ship Research Association, the National Physical
Laboratory, the National Institute of Oceanography, civil engineers, and harbour
authorities. Finally and collectively, from these and many other sources, they result in
items of direct practical benefit to the mariner. Today there is more research into strength
and behaviour of ships in a seaway than ever before. The data obtained is used to improve
ship design.

Actual observations are used in drawing up wave analysis and prognostic sea condition charts for facsimile broadcasts to ships. Such data has also resulted in the production of information which enables the mariner to recognise synoptic patterns of wave systems associated with certain characteristic pressure patterns. On such information, direct navigational decisions can often be made.

Other uses of wave observations are many, and include design and construction of harbours and breakwaters, planning of cargo operations for ships in open anchorages, problems relating to the silting up and erosion of coastlines. Ships' observations are often of value in public enquiries into shipping losses, etc.

The following statement, regarding wave observations from ships, is from the Marine Division of the Meteorological Office (Met. O.1.):

"Actual figures of height and period, even though they are only estimates and are sometimes not very accurate, do provide really useful practical information. Those who deal with such observations know that they are only estimates, accordingly they are treated with a certain amount of caution."

FOG

The following notes refer to the two most common types of fog—radiation fog and advection fog. One condition essential for the formation of both types is that the surface temperature must be lower than the dew-point of the air.

RADIATION FOG

Radiation fog (often called ground fog) is the result of the nocturnal cooling of a land surface. The air in contact with the ground is cooled below its dew-point and the excess water vapour is condensed, forming fog. Once formed, the fog may drift out over the sea and create a nuisance to coastal shipping, but it usually disperses soon on contact with a relatively warm water surface. On rare occasions it may extend for more than ten miles off the coast.

Conditions necessary for formation are:
(a) Little or no cloud at night, so as to allow free unimpeded terrestrial radiation.
(b) A high relative humidity, so that only a little cooling is required to bring the temperature below the dew-point;
(c) A light wind of less than 8 knots (3 to 6 knots is ideal) to diffuse the surface cooling to a sufficient depth.

Associated pressure systems: More often than not, radiation fog is associated with anticyclones and ridges which provide the clear skies and light winds needed for its formation.

Season: Ground fog is most frequent in Autumn and Winter when the air is damp and the nights are long. In winter, when the Sun's rays are weak, it is slow to clear, and may persist throughout the day with further intensification and deepening after sunset. In this way it can sometimes last for several days at a time, especially in large industrial areas.

Diurnal Variation: The lowest night temperatures usually occur about dawn, at which time too the surface wind speed is at a minimum, and often calm. The slight increase in turbulence caused by the Sun's rays often causes existing fog to thicken or fog to form when, owing to lack of turbulence, it has not done so previously. The maximum intensity of ground fog generally occurs at about one hour after sunrise. It is most likely to be at a minimum in the early afternoon.

Local effects: Under generally favourable conditions, radiation fog tends to form first in:

(a) *Large cities and industrial areas* where the high degree of smoke pollution provides a super-abundance of condensation nuclei, so that fog sometimes starts to form before the relative humidity has reached 100%. Smoke pollution often changes a white water fog into a brown "smog" which can persist for days.

(b) *Sheltered areas,* because nocturnal cooling is more pronounced than in localities exposed to wind.

(c) *Valleys and low-lying ground* which are fed by the katabatic drainage of cold air at night.

(d) *Marshy areas* because of their effect on humidity.

Dispersal of radiation fog may be brought about by:

(a) *Solar heating* of the land which, in turn, warms the air by contact, increases its capacity to hold water vapour, and clears the fog by evaporation.

(b) *A freshening of the wind* which increases turbulent mixing in the lower layers of the atmosphere. Thus the air in contact with the cold surface is mixed with warmer air from above, and its temperature raised above the dew-point.

(c) *A shift in wind direction,* changing the characteristics of the air mass.

ADVECTION FOG

Advection fog is caused by air being carried horizontally on to a surface whose temperature is below the dew-point of the air. All advection fog which occurs over the sea is alternatively called "sea fog".

Sea fog can sometimes persist with moderate (and occasionally strong) wind, because sea-water does not warm readily, and the stirring effect of the wind brings up cooler water from below. If, however, conditions for fog are otherwise favourable a wind which is too strong for fog will be accompanied by low stratus.

Air moving from warm land on to cold sea is a common cause of fog in spring and early summer, before the sea temperature has had time to warm up. If the air is fairly dry, evaporation will take place over the sea, thus raising the dew-point whilst the temperature falls, so fog will soon form.

Air moving from warm sea on to a cold sea current is another cause of sea fog; its occurrence is very frequent on the Grand Banks of Newfoundland when warm moist air from over the waters of the Gulf Stream move northward over the cold Labrador Current.

Air moving over a surface which becomes gradually colder: This situation can cause very widespread fog, covering immense areas, and may persist for several days, it is not confined to a particular season. A warm, humid tropical-maritime air mass, on a long sea passage into higher latitudes soon becomes saturated as it moves over a surface which becomes continually colder. Very low stratus with fog patches is formed at first, and later, as latitude increases, sea fog becomes widespread.

Air moving from warm sea on to cold land will form fog if the land has been well cooled by a cold spell. The temperature of the land is raised rapidly by the warm air, so the fog is usually confined to the time of the onset of the warm wind and seldom persists. If the wind is more than moderate it will bring low stratus instead of fog.

NOTES ON FRONTAL DEPRESSIONS

Growth and dissolution:
(a) A depression with a wide warm sector will usually deepen and grow in size.
(b) An unoccluded depression usually continues to deepen until (and often during) the early stages of occlusion.
(c) A fully occluded depression tends to fill up and usually becomes slow moving. At this stage it can persist, filling up very slowly; but the process of weakening is likely to be more rapid over a surface which is relatively cold. Sometimes the circulation is quickly destroyed by the arrival of a new, more vigorous system. Very occasionally a completely occluded depression will deepen, as the result of a fresh supply of polar air being drawn into the system from outside.

Movement:
(a) Small, active depressions move faster than large dying ones.
(b) Small depressions tend to follow the flow of isobars in the general pattern—i.e. follow the main stream.
(c) All depressions move from isallobaric high towards isallobaric low. If barometric tendencies are the same all round the centre of a depression, it will remain stationary.
(d) Depressions tend to follow the flow of air round the perimeter of large, well established warm anticyclones.
(e) An unoccluded depression moves in a direction parallel to the isobars in the warm sector, and at approximately four-fifths of the geostrophic wind speed derived from these isobars. At sea, this is approximately the same speed as the surface wind.
(f) A depression within a "family" follows the approximate path of its parent, but is usually displaced towards lower latitudes.
(g) A partly occluded depression tends to slow down as the occluding process continues.
(h) A fully occluded depression becomes slow and sometimes erratic in movement, but generally moving in the direction of the average flow of air up to the tropopause—i.e. dominated by the thermal component; it also tends to move off to the left of its original track in the northern hemisphere, and to the right in the southern hemisphere. Large depressions which are completely occluded are liable to become stationary or nearly stationary, especially if there is little horizontal temperature change within the area covered.
(i) Secondary depressions tend to move with the main circulation of air round the primary.
(j) A non-frontal depression tends to move in the same direction as the strongest winds circulating round it.
(k) The future movement of a depression can be estimated by *"extrapolation"*. That is, movement can be assumed to continue as shown by a succession of synoptic charts; but allowance for other factors must be made also.

Movements of fronts and occlusions:
The wind vector at a front can be split into two components—one measured along the line of the front, and the other at right angles to the front. The latter is the main factor governing the speed at which the front moves.

(a) The speed of a front generally decreases with distance from the low centre;
(b) The speed of a warm front may be taken generally as about 0.6 of the geostrophic wind component at, and normal to, the front;

(c) The speed of a cold front may be taken generally as about the same as, or a little faster than, that of the geostrophic wind speed component at and normal to the front;

(d) A front which lies parallel to the isobars is stationary or nearly stationary and tends to move towards the side of falling barometric tendencies;

(e) An occluded front may be expected to move roughly as a warm or cold front, depending on whether the occlusion is warm or cold, respectively. An occlusion will slow down on approaching a blocking anticyclone.

UPPER AIR CHARTS

General:

Surface charts are often very complex, due to a variety of relatively small pressure systems, topographical features, temperature differences in adjacent areas, etc. Upper air charts are by comparison much simpler. They give clearer and more reliable indication of air movement on a large scale and of the airflow patterns which greatly influence the development and movement of surface pressure systems. Thus they are of special value as an aid in forecasting.

Upper air charts originating from meteorological centres in many parts of the world are now available, daily at regular intervals, to any ship equipped with a facsimile receiver.

Constant-Pressure or Contour Charts:

An isobaric surface is a surface of constant barometric pressure; e.g. 500 mb. Its height above M.S.L. at any point depends on the mean temperature of the air column below the pressure-surface, the higher the mean temperature the greater the height.

A contour is a horizontal line passing through all points of equal heights on an isobaric surface.

A contour chart shows, by means of contour lines, the variations in height of a selected pressure surface (e.g. 500 mb.) in the same way as the height of land is shown on an ordinary survey map. The contours are usually drawn at height intervals of 60 metres (200 feet). The standard pressure surfaces for which these charts are drawn are 700, 500, 300, 200 and 100 mb.

A contour chart is similar in appearance to one showing surface isobars. The height contours are also isobars but, unlike those on a surface chart, they are all of the same pressure. "Highs" and "lows" refer to heights, not pressure.

Winds flow parallel to contours, with greater height (and higher mean temperature below) on the right in the northern hemisphere, and on the left in the southern hemisphere.

The wind speed at the pressure surface concerned is directly proportional to the contour gradient, and is completely independent of atmospheric density.

Wind speed generally increases with height until near the tropopause; above the tropopause it decreases with height.

Thickness Charts:

The weight of any vertical column of air separating two isobaric surfaces (e.g. 500 mb. and 300 mb.) is exactly the same, but its length (which is called "thickness") is governed by its vertical mean temperature. Thus the *thickness* of a layer contained between two pressure surfaces is less in areas where the air is cold and dense than in the warmer areas. Lines drawn on a chart joining all points of equal thickness are called "thickness lines".

A thickness chart is not unlike an isobaric chart in appearance, but the "highs" and "lows" enclosed by thickness lines show areas of high or low vertical mean temperature in the layer concerned, and are called warm or cold "pools" respectively.

Where horizontal temperature changes are sharp, thickness lines will appear close together, thus frontal zones are clearly shown.

Thermal winds (theoretical winds obtained by taking the vector difference between winds at the top and bottom of the layer concerned) flow parallel to the thickness lines with high temperature to the right in the northern hemisphere, and to the left in the southern hemisphere.

The 1,000—500 mb. thickness charts are especially useful as an aid in forecasting changes in surface pressure distribution; for example, depressions tend to move nearly parallel to or a little to the right of the thermal wind flow (shown on this chart) over the region in which the depression is centred. Certain patterns of thermal troughs and ridges on thickness charts are favourable for the formation and intensification (or the weakening and disappearance) of surface pressure systems.

Long Waves (Rossby Waves):

The prevailing "Upper Westerlies" which completely encircle the Arctic low will show some four or five "long waves" in the general flow pattern of a 500 mb. contour chart. The flow of upper air round these long waves tends to steer small surface depressions and anticyclones.

Although long waves vary greatly in length and amplitude, they sometimes remain in nearly the same position for many days at a time with very little change in shape. At such times, in general, settled weather is associated with areas on the equatorial side of the crests; the weather within and a little to the east of the troughs is often very unsettled.

Well-defined, deep upper air troughs and ridges with sharply curved contours are usually slow moving; whilst those which are rather flat in shape, with slightly curved contours, move much faster.

Very pronounced and extensive upper air highs and lows are slow-moving; small, weak ones move faster.

Use of 500 mb. contour charts as an aid in estimating the movement of surface pressure systems:

(a) The use of contour charts for forecasting the movement of temperate latitude depressions is confined to small, shallow, warm sector depressions, whose closed circulations are not shown by the 500 mb. contours.

(b) Contours give a general indication of the direction of movement of small surface pressure systems such as transitory cold anticyclones, frontal depressions and the *cold* ridges of high pressure between them.

(c) If the contours over a surface depression or anticyclone are fairly straight and evenly spaced, the surface system will be steered by the flow of upper air along these contours.

(d) Those surface pressure systems mentioned in (a), (b) and (c) above generally move at about half the speed of the wind on the 500 mb. pressure surface.

(e) Upper air patterns are continually changing, so the current 500 mb. contour chart will give more reliable indication of movement of a surface system for the next 6 to 12 hours than for 12 to 24 hours.

NOTE TO MASTERS AND SHIPOWNERS

One of the most useful and practical publications, in the field of meteorology, to be printed in recent years is the W.M.O.'s *Technical Note No. 72—"The Preparation and Use of Weather Maps by Mariners"—(W.M.O. No. 179.TP.89)—* obtainable from The Secretariat of the World Meteorological Organisation, Geneva, Switzerland.

This Technical Note is in reality a practical handbook of meteorology tailored to the needs of mariners, and has been prepared to enable them to derive increased benefit from weather bulletins and facsimile broadcasts from meteorological services. The text is brief and sets out a set of simple instructions adequately illustrated with maps. It also discusses the various ways in which weather maps can be used in differing conditions, examining a number of weather situations which are particularly dangerous to shipping, together with some relevant forecasting rules.

THE WORLD METEOROLOGICAL ORGANISATION (W.M.O.)

W.M.O. is a Specialised Agency of the United Nations of which 125 States and Territories are Members. It was created:

(a) to facilitate international co-operation in the establishment of networks of stations and centres to provide meteorological services and observations;

(b) to promote the establishment and maintenance of systems for the rapid exchange of meteorological information;

(c) to promote standardisation of meteorological observations, and ensure the uniform publication, of observations and statistics;

(d) to further the application of meteorology to aviation, shipping, agriculture, and other human activities;

(e) to encourage research and training in meteorology.

The selected Ship Scheme (whereby selected ships of most nations voluntarily make meteorological observations at routine hours, and transmit the results by radio to appropriate centres) is to provide a network of observations over the oceans; it operates under the arrangements made by W.M.O. Full details of this scheme, together with practical instructions as to how the observations should be made, are given in *The Marine Observer's Handbook (M.O.887).*

Instructions for coding and decoding observations, and transmission by radio are contained in *Ship's Code and Decode Book (Met. 0.509) (Eighth Edition).* Both of these publications are obtainable from H.M.S.O.

SPECIAL METEOROLOGICAL SERVICES FOR SHIPPING (GREAT BRITAIN)

The following is a brief summary of special services, full details of which are given in *The Admiralty List of Radio Signals, Vol. III.*

Special Shipping Forecasts from Coast Radio Stations:

Ships at Sea: Request forecast from nearest coast radio station listed for the purpose in A.L.R.S. Vol. III. No charge is made by the Met. Office; G.P.O. charges for transmission services.

Vessels fitted with R/T may now obtain weather forecasts direct by link call from the Central Forecast Office. Forecasts relating to specific areas within the limits 35° N.—65° N., and between 40° W. and the European coast, may be obtained by making a radio-telephone link call to the Deputy Forecaster, Bracknell 20242, extn. 2508. The coast station charge for this service will be the cost of the R/T link call.

Ships about to sail: Telephone Met. Office at Bracknell or send reply-paid telegram to Metbrack London requesting information (allowing 20 words for reply, excluding address). No other charges if the information is required immediately.

Salvage Officers and Others requiring warnings of gales or winds from specified directions, or particular kinds of weather on specified dates or short periods— write to Director General of the Meteorological Office (Met. 02a), London Road, Bracknell, Berks. RG12 2SZ.

Local forecasts for ports and coastal areas can be obtained, free of charge, by telephoning or writing to the forecast centres listed in A.L.R.S. Vol. III—ask for "The Forecast Office."

Local weather reports on F.M. (V.H.F.) from Port Radio Stations— See A.L.R.S. Vol. III.

Local reports of present weather from Coastal Stations may be obtained by telephone from any of the stations listed (with their telephone numbers) in A.L.R.S. Vol. III—there are more than 60 stations listed round the British Isles.

Ice information can be obtained by writing to the Director General of the Meteorological Office, or by telephoning (see Vol. III). Charts of sea ice are obtainable from Great Britain and some other countries from facsimile broadcasts at specified hours.

Section G

Weather Routeing

METEOROLOGICAL INFORMATION AVAILABLE TO MARINERS

For well over a hundred years the Meteorological Office have processed data supplied by voluntary observing ships of all nationalities. As a direct result of this work information on winds, sea condition, weather, currents, ice and visibility is now available to all ships.

Seasonal information is supplied in: Admiralty "Ocean Passages for the World"—Admiralty Sailing Directions (Pilots)—Admiralty Routeing Charts.

Synoptic information is supplied by radio: storm warnings (force 10 or over)—General statement of weather situation—24-hour forecasts—Coded Analysis—Coded ships' and station reports—Facsimile broadcasts, further details of which are given below.

Special Routeing Advice from the Shore is provided by the Meteorological Office at Bracknell and the Royal Netherlands Meteorological Service. The Federal Republic of Germany, Norway and the U.S.S.R. are also weather routeing on a trial basis. The U.S.A. Authorities and some commercial companies provide weather routeing services covering the North Atlantic and North Pacific.

The World Meteorological Organisation co-ordinates the national services responsible for the collation and distribution of the detailed information reported from individual weather stations.

To-day there are over 2,000 land Weather Stations in the northern hemisphere alone, and these are supplemented by observing ships of many nations and five fixed Ocean Weather Ships. Use is also made of aircraft, balloons, weather radar, rockets and satellites. From all these sources a steady stream of "actual" weather reports flow into the central forecasting offices where, often with the help of computers, analysis and forecast charts are prepared.

These charts are transmitted by radio and can be received on board ship by means of an automatic facsimile weather chart receiver/recorder apparatus, which prints out a facsimile chart on electrosensitive paper.

A telephone conversation with a forecast office before sailing is often of good practical value. Thereafter synoptic advice to shipmasters from professional meteoro-logists is available by radio in all parts of the world, at the cost of the message only.

FACSIMILE WEATHER CHART RECORDERS

This equipment can normally be installed in the chartroom and operated by the Navigating Officer. Ships which are so fitted can receive the most up-to-date weather information at frequent intervals. They are, in fact, provided with a more-or-less constant picture of:

    (a)   present and future weather;

    (b)   present and future sea condition; and

    (c)   ice situation in relevant areas.

The information is received automatically, quite independently of single operator watches and with no additional work for deck officers. The maps are prepared by highly trained experts who have all the necessary data available. Such charts provide a far more accurate and up-to-date picture than one drawn by a Ship's Officer with the very limited data receivable by morse.

Tests have shown that radio interference which would render morse or radio-teletype transmissions worthless for plotting purposes does not prevent an intelligible chart being received by facsimile. Cases have occurred in near "black-out" conditions when facsimile charts have been received from across the Atlantic although no information at all could be received by any other type of radio circuit. *To ensure the best results a very stable receiver is essential.*

There are, at present, over 70 transmitting stations in service worldwide, most of these being in the northern hemisphere. The following facsimile broadcasts are only a few of those sent out from the countries mentioned but they will indicate what sort of useful information is available by this means:

United Kingdom (Bracknell)
Surface Analysis—every six hours.
Surface Forecast for 24 hours—every six hours.
Surface Forecast for 48 hours and 72 hours—daily.
Ice information—daily.
Upper air charts—daily at regular intervals.

Canadian transmitters
In addition to surface analysis.
Surface and 500 m. prognosis for 30 hours and 36 hours—every six hours.
Wave height analysis—every 12 hours.
Ice information—daily.
Additional broadcasts of observed and forecast ice as and when required.

Spain
Surface Analysis for North Atlantic—every six hours.
Sea Wave and Swell Analysis—every 12 hours.
Sea surface temperature analysis and prognosis—daily.

U.S.A.
Five-Day Forecast every Monday, Wednesday and Friday.
Surface and 1,000-500 mb. Thickness prognosis—every 12 hours.
Surface prognosis for 24, 48, 72, 96, 120 and 144 hours—every Monday, Wednesday and Friday.
Surface prognosis for 48 and 72 hours every Saturday, Sunday, Tuesday and Thursday.

Marianas Is.
Sea surface temperature analysis.
Sea Condition prognosis for 24 hours.
Surface prognosis for 24 hours—daily.

Details of some facsimile transmissions made from various stations throughout the world and which are of use to mariners are contained in *Admiralty List of Radio Signals, Vol. III.* e.g. surface analysis and prognosis, observed or forecast ice information, wave height and well analysis and prognosis. As yet, the number of stations and schedules listed are not complete. Upper air charts have received little or no mention thus far but, as some merchant ships are already using these charts, it is likely that the information given will be greatly expanded in the future.

Sea condition charts show isopleths of wave heights in metres. The dirction of the wave-trains are indicated by arrows. The prognostic wave charts broadcast from American stations, when compared with actual wave observations, have been found to be fairly accurate, i.e. 86% were within + 4 feet. (1.2 metres).

Facsimile charts, when studied in conjunction with the synopsis and forecast received in morse, can be of real practical value in: keeping up-to-date with the weather situation and anticipated developments; giving material assistance in the avoidance of a particular weather situation; keeping the ship out of the high wave area, etc.

The most important single factor in reducing a vessel's speed through the water is wave height, thus the wave analysis and forecast charts can be of good practical value. Quite often the wave height contours enclosing a high wave area are very close together so that, in these circumstances, only a small alteration to the planned route may put the ship in much quieter sea conditions.

A series of weather maps, taken at regular intervals, shows the movements and changes in surface pressure systems and provides a useful aid in forecasting. Furthermore, with the aid of such maps and sea condition charts, one is better able to understand the reasoning behind a forecast or any routeing advice that has been received. A comparison between the forecast and the actual conditions currently experienced at the ship enables a shipmaster to make a more accurate estimation of how the weather situation is likely to develop along his route. Should there be a wide discrepancy between the actual weather and that forecasted, routed vessels should alert the routeing office by radio as soon as possible.

WEATHER ROUTEING FROM THE SHORE

The primary aim of weather routeing from the shore is to advise the Master of the ship as to which route will, as far as possible, avoid the areas of highest waves, consistent with providing the quickest and most economic passage.

History and Achievements

Up until about 1954 weather routeing, as distinct from the usual climatic or seasonal routeing, was employed only as an occasional measure (e.g. avoidance of a tropical revolving storm) and not as a regular day-to-day practice. Many forward thinking meteorologists and shipping organisations felt that the continuous economic toll on speed, fuel consumption and weather damage resulting from high waves demanded some form of weather routeing which could be employed continuously rather than occasionally.

Modern methods of weather routeing with advice from the shore were carried out originally in U.S.A. by some private firms of consulting meteorologists: Weather Corporation of America, the Louis Allen Weather Corporation, and the Pacific Weather Analysis Corporation. These services were first carried out on a trial basis at the request of various shipping companies, and the resulting data was regarded as private. Although this research was somewhat limited in scope it appears to have been highly successful, and the original firms are still very much "in business". It was decided later that the U.S. Navy should carry out an extensive research programme to find out if, in fact, it was scientifically possible to effect really worthwhile economies by a system of weather routeing and, if so, to devise some operational method which could be used by all interested ships.

For such a programme as this, the U.S. Military Sea Transportation Service (M.S.T.S.) seemed very suitable. They had many vessels, of between 7,000 and 18,000 tons deadweight and with speeds from 15½ to 19 knots, which plied both the Pacific and Atlantic routes. Ideally, each "test" should be carried out by two vessels of similar characteristics, one vessel being used as a control ship (not routed) so that accurate comparisons could be made. This was done whenever possible. The actual routeings were done by the

Oceanographic Forecasting Central of the U.S. Hydrographic Office, and the routeing advice which they gave to ships was based on information received from the U.S. Navy Fleet Weather Central, the Extended Forecasting Section of the U.S. Weather Bureau, and other forecasting activities in Washington.

Extract from Technical Report of the U.S. Hydrographic Office (TR-53):

> "*Between October, 1956, and May, 1957, the U.S. Hydrographic Office provided the Military Sea Transportation Service with optimum routes for 22 vessels in the Atlantic Ocean and ten in the Pacific Ocean. Routes were based on long range (principally five-day) predictions of wave and oceanographic conditions...*"
>
> "*It is estimated on the basis of all the evaluated factors that without an increase in fuel consumption an average of 14.5 hours travel time was saved on each of the 32 crossings, with increased passenger comfort and cargo safety.*"
>
> *Routeing procedures were continued after completion of these tests, and later on the U.S. Hydrographic Office reported that* "*Over a period of two years over 1,000 optimum ship routes were provided to one authority with an average reduction in travel time of 14 hours per crossing ... Increased safety of ship, cargo and passengers... more stringent and consistent schedules were maintained.*"

By the end of 1965, a total of 4,288 routed crossings had been made by ships of the M.S.T.S. and the results carefully analysed. The following figures for two successive years are of interest:

Year	*1964*	*1965*
Valid routeings	744	800
Arrived on time or ahead of schedule	86.3%	84.2%
Arrived four or more hours late	13.7%	15.8%
No slowing down for weather	66.5%	63.6%
No weather damage to ship or cargo	98.6%	98.9%

After making a careful study of the results attained in the U.S.A., the Holland America Line decided to give weather routeing a trial. Experimental routeing commenced at the beginning of 1960, and, after two years, the results of comparisons between routed and non-routed vessels indicated an average net gain of six hours per westbound crossing of the North Atlantic during *winter* months, there being little or no gain during the six months of fairly favourable weather. On eastbound crossings, the average gain for the two-year period was 1½ hours per crossing. There was also evidence to show that heavy weather damage to cargo and ships was reduced. These figures have been maintained to date, and the shipmasters concerned have expressed great satisfaction with the service which is being steadily improved as the result of further experience, better forecasting and the continued study and research into new methods.

During this period, from time to time, some excellent papers on the subject of weather routeing have been read at meetings of the Institute of Navigation; in addition a number of useful and informative articles on the same subject and its potential advantages have appeared in copies of *The Marine Observer*.

In the meantime, British meteorologists have given much time and study to the various aspects of weather routeing, and have been greatly assisted in this by the U.S.A. and the Netherlands, who have provided information about their techniques. In order to find out the view of shipowners and shipmasters on this subject, the Meteorological Office made arrangements for a special informal meeting which took place aboard the "Wellington", Headquarters ship of the Honourable Company of Master Mariners, in March of 1966. At this meeting, six papers on various aspects of weather routeing were read, and discussed. (See *"The Marine Observer"*, October 1966 and January 1967.) The direct result was

L

further consultation between the Meteorological Office and North Atlantic shipowners, and four *experimental* routeings with westbound North Atlantic cargo ships took place in September 1967. The routeing advice was given by the Meteorological Office at Bracknell.

September is usually a stormy month and this one was no exception during the time of the experiment. The following results were achieved:

M/V *PARTHIA* (Cunard)—Liverpool to New York:
(1)   *Normal Route:* North of Ireland—Great Circle Inishtrahull to Cape Race—total distance 2,994 miles.
(2)   *Calculated Best Time/Weather Route:* South of Ireland to avoid severe gales and storms, and steering SW'ly course to a position nearly 600 miles south of the normal route—Distance 3,293 miles (299 above normal).
(3)   *Actual Route:* South of Ireland and zig-zagged somewhat about mid-way between (1) and (2)—Distance 3,163 miles (169 above normal).

> *Time saved:*   *14 hours*
> *Wind reduction:*   *10 knots*

Analysis showed later that, had she followed the Best Time/Weather route, on the last day of the voyage she would have been 120 miles ahead of her actual position and 340 miles ahead of the calculated position on the normal route.

M/V *SAMARIA* (Cunard—Southampton to New York—3rd to 12th September:
> *Shortest Route:* Via Great Circle from Bishop Rock—Distance 3,077 miles.
> *Note:* At midnight on 3rd September, gales already in English Channel and no diversion possible.
> *Actual Route:* At noon on 6th September, ship diverted to south'ard of shortest route and was about 130 miles south of the Great Circle on the 8th. Distance 3,092 miles.

> *Time saved:*   *1 hour*
> *Wind reduction:*   *small*

It is interesting to note that had *Samaria* remained in port for another 24 hours, she would have reached about the same position at 0000 hours on 6th September *without* having to contend with gales which were severe at times.

M/V *NEWFOUNDLAND* (Furness Withy)—Liverpool to St. Johns—12th to 18th September:
> *Normal Route:* Via Great Circle from Fastnet to St. Johns—total distance 1,963 miles.
> *Actual Route:* took vessel about 240 miles south of the Great Circle to avoid gales and severe gales—Distance 2.049 miles (86 above normal).

> *Time saved:*   *9 to 10 hours*
> *Wind reduction:*   *15 knots*

M/V *SUGAR CARRIER* (Tate and Lyle)—Antwerp to Sydney, N.S.—11th to 19th September.
> *Normal Route:* Via Great Circle from Bishop Rock to Cape Race—Total distance 2,589 miles.
> *Actual Route:* took vessel about 200 miles south of the Great Circle, making a total distance of 2,673 miles (84 above normal).

> *Time saved:*   *4 hours*
> *Wind reduction:*   *10 knots*

The above results conform to those achieved by other routeings carried out over a number of years by other countries, in that they show that the shortest route is not always the quickest. In the case of the *Parthia,* adding 169 miles to the route saved nearly 14 hours by keeping the ship in better sea conditions.

The Meteorological Office officially opened a North Atlantic routeing service on 11th March, 1968. Further information concerning this service appears later in this Section.

Classification of Routeing

Overlooking the technical difference between weather and climate, weather routeing has been aptly classified by some experts into three types: (1) climatic; (2) strategic: and (3) tactical.

Climatic routeing is following the standard route recommended for a particular season. Such routes are described in Section H and also in *Ocean Passages for the World,* Admiralty Pilots, and monthly charts of winds, currents, storm frequency, etc. From this type of routeing the best value is obtained in some trade wind areas, and in the Indian Ocean and China Sea where the occurrence and behaviour of the monsoons are very regular. For most other regions, the weather over short periods does not always conform to the seasonal pattern which, after all, is only an average.

For example, in the North Atlantic, when the general pressure distribution for January is normal, westbound ships from U.K. may escape the strongest westerly winds and high seas by taking the southerly route recommended for small vessels. But if, as happens sometimes, the Icelandic low is located far to the south of its normal position for the month, the shorter northerly route with following wind and sea is the most advantageous. It is in such cases as this that strategic routeing commends itself.

A route which is planned for one particular voyage has been termed a **strategic route.** It is based on: the latest weather analysis, the three to five day forecast chart, some idea of further outlook, and seasonal probabilities are also taken into consideration. Some voyages may have special requirements, e.g. avoidance of damage to an exceptionally valuable deck cargo would take priority over fuel economy.

An important consideration in route selection is the location of the track along which the storms travel, rather than the displacement of storms along that track. In general, westbound ships should be routed to the north of the storm track and eastbound ships to the south of it.

Tactical routeing has been described as making a temporary departure from the route planned, and is made according to developments in the synoptic situation. It is based on: weather maps, wave height analysis and prognosis, 12 to 24 hour forecasts, gale warnings, etc.

General Remarks

A completely separate and independent routeing must be provided for each individual ship according to her particular characteristics (speed, draught, state of loading, cargo, etc.), and her behaviour in various sea conditions.

Routeings are provided at the request of the shipowner and always with the voluntary agreement of the Master. It is emphasised that the meteorologist is able to give only guidance and advice and can never usurp any of the Master's responsibility. The Master of any routed vessel is free to accept (wholly or partially) or reject the advice given.

Weather routeing is essentially a *practical problem;* this is recognised by all countries who provide a routeing service and for this reason, officers with nautical experience are employed in addition to the meteorologists in the routeing offices. The degree of success in weather routeing is dependent on the accuracy with which the forecasts can be made. Although the three to five day forecasts are generally fairly good they are not, as yet, completely reliable, particularly towards the end of the period when unexpected developments might alter the anticipated situation very considerably. At present the meteorologist cannot give an accurate forecast of the wind for more than 48 to 72 hours ahead, and, occasionally, for not more than 24. He can, however, usually give some idea of the accuracy to be expected. The routes are recommended by highly trained experts and it is seldom that a ship is routed into conditions less favourable than those experienced along the standard route.

In *tactical routeing* avoiding action should be taken as early as possible to increase its effectiveness and to avoid having to make a large deviation. In this the faster vessels have a big advantage over those whose speeds are less than 15 knots. The faster the ships the later the stage at which effective deviation is still possible. Because a slow ship spends longer in the areas where bad weather is likely to be encountered, and because she must take avoiding action at an earlier stage she is much more dependent on the three to five day forecast.

Routeing Advice from the U.K.

A ship routeing service is available from the Meteorological Office at Bracknell for vessels crossing the North Atlantic and the North Pacific on request. The service has been adapted for advice on the movement of tows, both in and out of harbour and on passage. The service is manned by a team of master mariners who are Nautical Officers within the Meteorological Office and who have had long seagoing experience. These Nautical Officers devote their whole time to selecting the most advantageous routes for ships which use the service. They are provided with a continuous flow of analysis and forecast charts, ice information, warnings, bulletins and satellite pictures and are briefed on the meteorological situation by senior forecasters.

The duties of the Nautical Officer are to:
(1) Establish contact with the Master of the ship as far as possible;
(2) Obtain details of the ship, her performance, stability, fuel consumption, sailing draught, deck cargo, and any peculiarities that she may have;
(3) Find out from past records and all other means available, the speed reduction the ship is likely to undergo in waves of different heights from different directions relative to the ship. Then, from this data to construct curves of speed *v.* wave height;
(4) Find out the Master's personal views about weather routeing, and if he has any special ideas about avoidance of ice areas, extensive fog areas, etc.;
(5) Find out the owner's policy regarding such details as desirable time of arrival in harbour, berthing, etc.;
(6) Do all the navigational work connected with weather routeing, calculating distances to go on various alternative routes, effect of ocean currents, etc.;
(7) Keep up-to-date with ice conditions;
(8) Make sure that all weather routeing signals to the ship are unambiguous to the Navigators.

The method of routeing is very similar to that practised so successfully in the United States. Wave height forecasts are made for 12, 24, 36 and 48 hours ahead, and studied by the meteorologist in conjunction with surface analysis and forecast charts; upper air charts and the 72-hour forecast charts are also studied.

Wave height contours are converted into isopleths of ship speed by means of the speed/wave height graphs; other factors are also considered. *Least time track* curves are drawn for each 12 hours of ship's run up to 48 hours. The point on the 48-hour curve nearest to destination is the one which the ship is advised to make for; but consideration is given to currents, ice, fog and estimated synoptic development during a further 24 to 48 hours. This process is continued throughout the routeing period.

Masters of ships which are to be routed from the U.K. need to telephone the Central Forecasting Office of the Meteorological Office a few hours before sailing, and give final details regarding sailing time, draught, cargo, etc. General routeing advice for the next 24 hours will then be given. For example, a vessel whose normal route is from the North of Ireland may be advised to pass to the south. Further advice regarding the recommended route is radioed to the ship a few hours after sailing; thereafter routeing signals are normally sent every two days. Intermediate messages recommending a change or adjustment are sent if and when necessary, but all routeing signals are transmitted according to a prearranged schedule. The Master of an east-bound vessel should send a signal to Bracknell giving relevant details, and stating the position and time at which he wishes routeing to commence.

After the voyage has been completed, a very thorough hindcast analysis of the route is made at the Meteorological Office if requested. The calculated daily positions of the ship had she followed the normal route, are plotted on a chart together with the winds (deduced from ship's observations) which she would have encountered. The actual route followed and winds experienced are also plotted. Distance steamed, time saved, etc., are shown on the chart. A copy is then sent to the Master and owners of the vessel.

Should the ship follow a route other than the calculated best time/weather route, as in the case of the *Parthia,* the same information for the calculated best time/weather route will be shown also.

Requests for routeing service should normally be made in writing to the Director-General, Meteorological Office, Met. O la, Eastern Road, Bracknell, Berks., RG12 2UR, but application may be made by signal in some cases.

A charge is made to the shipowner for this service, which does not include the charge for advisory radio messages. Every effort is made by the routeing team to keep the cost of messages to a minimum. Scales of charges may be obtained, on request to the above address.

An interesting example of a very successful routeing is that of the M/V *Gladys Bowater*—Rouen to Charleston—sailed on 30th March, 1968. The actual route took the vessel to between 500 and 600 miles south of the *North Atlantic Lane Route.* The actual distance steamed was 4,072 miles—an increase of 407 miles over the Lane Route. In spite of this longer distance, she reached her destination 22 hours earlier than she would have done had she followed the Lane Route.

NOTE:

The articles on weather routeing which have appeared in the following periodicals are recommended for reading. They are informative and of very special interest to any shipmasters or marine superintendents who are considering the potential advantages of this practice.

"The Marine Observer" — January 1969, January, April and July 1971 and January 1977, available from H.M.S.O.

For those who require further and more technical details of weather routeing methods *"Application of Wave Forecasts to Marine Navigation" (S.P.1) by Richard W. James* is well worth reading. It is obtainable from U.S. Navy Hydrographic Office, Washington, D.C.

WEATHER ROUTEING BY THE MASTER

It is generally considered that, as things stand at the moment, the *best* results are likely to be obtained by being weather routed from the shore by an experienced team of trained specialists. Nevertheless, the Shipmaster can, from time to time, do some very effective weather routeing on his own if he is provided with facsimile apparatus. A number of Masters have been doing this for some time and worthwhile economies have been made thereby—heavy weather damage has been minimised, time saved has reduced costs of "waiting time" for stevedores, etc.

It should be remembered that the duty forecaster at almost any meteorological service can be contacted by H.F. radio telephone, at any time of the day or night, and advice obtained at only the cost of the telephone message.

The number of facsimile broadcasting stations is increasing world-wide. With this and the great forward strides now being made in meteorology, and hence the accuracy of forecasting, facilities for weather routeing by the Master look very promising for the future.

It has been suggested that short courses of training in weather routeing should be made available to shipmasters. This seems very desirable, and the advantages are obvious, especially since weather routeing services are confined to the North Atlantic and North Pacific. There are ways in which such a scheme could be organised, enabling courses to be run in various parts of the country at no great cost; but it would be up to the shipowners to show the requirement before any positive steps could be taken in this direction. In the meantime, experience is a very fine teacher. Masters who do their own weather routeing are strongly recommended to have the following publication at hand:

W.M.O. Technical Note No. 72: "The Preparation and Use of Weather Maps by Mariners" (W.M.O. No. 179.TP.89)—obtainable from The Secretariat of the World Meteorological Organisation, Geneva, Switzerland.

Section H

Ocean Routes and Distances

SOME GENERAL CONSIDERATIONS

The first point to consider when planning a long ocean passage is the bunker requirements of the vessel concerned. In ships with a small bunker capacity it may be necessary to call *en route* to refuel, while in other ships the high cost of bunkers at the departure port may make an intermediate stop for cheaper fuel an economic proposition. The allied problems of fresh water and stores also need consideration.

The next point concerns the relative merits of following a Great Circle track or steering on a rhumb line course. The advantage of the Great Circle track is that the distance to steam is less, the maximum saving being when the destination lies East or West of the departure port. The disadvantage of a Great Circle route is that higher latitudes are attained on passage with probable poorer weather conditions and the danger, in certain cases, of encountering ice. When navigating westbound by Great Circle, the higher incidence of head winds and adverse weather may negate the gain due to the shorter distance to steam. This is especially the case in ships with full lines and limited ballast capacity, such as bulk carriers. Experience has shown that these ships when westbound in ballast make faster passages by following the rhumb line course. Information regarding the synoptic situation and its relation to the seasonal pattern may be obtained from the Meteorological Office. This information may assist in deciding whether or not to follow a Great Circle track (See Section G).

Important navigational requirements for the voyage include the appropriate corrected charts, the latest navigational warnings and notices, Sailing Directions, Light Lists and Tide Tables.

In coastal areas, direct routes may need to be modified to comply with established traffic separation schemes (see Section T).

More detailed information on ocean routes may be found in "Ocean Passages for the World" published by the Hydrographer of the Navy.

NORTH ATLANTIC ROUTES

WEATHER ROUTEING

Weather conditions in the North Atlantic north of 35°N. Latitude are such that the optimum ocean route between two selected ports in this area is heavily dependent on the wind and wave conditions existing during the period over which the passage is to be made. It is strongly recommended that weather routeing techniques should be employed in making passages through the area (see Section G) and the following notes on Transatlantic routes should therefore be taken as giving general guidance only.

RECOMMENDED ROUTES

The direct Great Circle routes between N.W. European ports and Canadian and N.E. United States ports take a ship into relatively high latitudes and this is particularly important on the western side of the Atlantic where there may be danger from fog and ice conditions on the Grand Banks. To meet this problem, three pairs of "alter course positions" are established at different latitudes in this area so that the appropriate pair may be used according to season. In each pair, the northernmost position is used for westbound traffic and the southernmost position is used for eastbound traffic. The alter course positions are defined as follows:

	Position		
Name	*Eastbound*	*Westbound*	*Season*
Cape Race (CR)	46° 12'N. 53° 05'W.	46° 27'N. 53° 05'W.	16th May-30th Nov. (or when Cape Race Route is clear of ice)
Banks North (BN)	45° 25'N. 50° 00'W.	45° 55'N. 50° 00'W.	11th April-15th May and 1st Dec.-14th Feb.
Banks South (BS)	42° 00'N. 50° 00'W.	43° 00'N. 50° 00'W.	15th Feb.-10th April

East of the alter course positions, passages to and from European landfalls may generally be made by following direct Great Circle tracks but of course subject to a safe offing from any intervening island groups. West of the alter course positions, ships may generally proceed as directly as navigation permits to the Cabot Strait and the St. Lawrence or to eastern Canadian or north-eastern United States ports. Ships should not, however, pass closer to the south of Sable Island than 60 miles when eastbound or 40 miles when westbound.

ACCESS TO THE ST. LAWRENCE

The Cabot Strait and the Quebec-Montreal channel are usually open to navigation from April to November. Access to the St. Lawrence is also available *via* the Belle Island Strait which is usually open to navigation from June to November.

TRANSATLANTIC DISTANCES

The preceding paragraphs apply, for example, to passages between the points listed below. The distances (apart from those to Belle Island Strait) apply to tracks *via* the Cape Race (CR) alter course position and are given to the nearest ten nautical miles.

Cape Wrath and:	Belle Island Strait	— 1,740 miles
	Cabot Strait	— 2,130 miles
	Halifax	— 2,310 miles
	Boston	— 2,660 miles
	New York	— 2,870 miles
	Delaware Bay	— 2,920 miles
	Chesapeake Bay	— 3,050 miles
Inishtrahull and:	Belle Island Strait	— 1,700 miles
	Cabot Strait	— 2,060 miles
	Halifax	— 2,240 miles
	Boston	— 2,580 miles
	New York	— 2,790 miles
	Delaware Bay	— 2,850 miles
	Chesapeake Bay	— 2,980 miles
Fastnet and:	Belle Island Strait	— 1,790 miles
	Cabot Strait	— 1,990 miles
	Halifax	— 2,180 miles
	Boston	— 2,520 miles
	New York	— 2,730 miles
	Delaware Bay	— 2,790 miles
	Chesapeake Bay	— 2,910 miles
Bishop Rock and:	Belle Island Strait	— 1,830 miles
	Cabot Strait	— 2,130 miles
	Halifax	— 2,310 miles
	Boston	— 2,650 miles
	New York	— 2,860 miles
	Delaware Bay	— 2,920 miles
	Chesapeake Bay	— 3,050 miles

ADDITIONAL ATLANTIC OCEAN ROUTES

1. FROM BISHOP ROCK TO CURACAO OR PANAMA
(A) Via Mona Passage
From a position 5 miles south of Bishop Rock steer on the Great Circle to latitude 18° 30'N., longitude 67° 50'W., and thence through Mona Passage to destination as direct as navigation permits.

Distance on Great Circle—3,456 miles
Total distance to Colon, Panama—4,345 miles
Total distance to Willemstad, Curacao—3,860 miles.

(B) Via Sombrero Island Passage
From a position 5 miles south of Bishop Rock steer on the Great Circle to latitude 18° 39'N., longitude 63° 25'W., and thence as direct as navigation permits to destination.

Distance on Great Circle—3,283 miles
Total distance to Colon, Panama—4,393 miles
Total distance to Willemstad, Curacao—3,800 miles.

2. FROM BISHOP ROCK TO RECIFE, BRAZIL
(A) Via Las Palmas
From a position 5 miles south of Bishop Rock, steer on a course to pass about 30 miles off Cape Villano, and thence by rhumb line courses to Las Palmas. From Las Palmas steer as direct as navigation permits on rhumb line courses to destination.

Distance to Las Palmas—1,368 miles
Total distance to Recife—3,826 miles.

(B) Via St. Vincent, Cape Verde Islands
From a position 5 miles south of Bishop Rock, steer on the Great Circle to St. Vincent. From St. Vincent steer Great Circle to destination.

Distance to St. Vincent—2,170 miles
Total distance to Recife—3,783 miles.

3. FROM CAPETOWN TO BUENOS AIRES
From Capetown follow the rhumb line course to the entrance to the River Plate, and thence as direct as navigation permits to destination.

Distance to Buenos Aires—3,180 miles.

When eastbound follow route 10.

4. FROM CAPETOWN TO RIO DE JANEIRO
Follow the direct rhumb line track.

Distance to Rio de Janeiro—3,313 miles.

When eastbound follow route 9.

5. FROM CAPETOWN TO NEW YORK

Follow the Great Circle between Capetown and New York.

Distance to New York—6,790 miles.

6. FROM CAPETOWN TO RECIFE, BRAZIL

Follow the Great Circle between Capetown and Recife.

Distance to Recife—3,319 miles.

7. FROM CAPETOWN TO CURACAO OR PANAMA

Follow the Great Circle track from Capetown to latitude 4° 40'S., longitude 34° 35'W., and thence by rhumb line courses as directly as safe navigation permits.

Distance to Willemstad, Curacao—5,733 miles
Distance to Colon, Panama—6,423 miles.

8. FROM CAPETOWN TO LAS PALMAS

From departure point off Capetown, steer on the Great Circle track to latitude 10° 40'N., longitude 17° 40'W., and thence as directly as navigation permits to destination.

Distance to Las Palmas—4,426 miles.

9. FROM RIO DE JANEIRO TO CAPETOWN

Follow the Great Circle from Rio de Janeiro to Capetown.

Distance to Capetown—3,273 miles.

10. FROM BUENOS AIRES TO CAPETOWN

Proceed to the mouth of the River Plate as directly as safe navigation permits, and then follow the Great Circle track to Capetown (maximum southerly latitude 41°S.).

Distance to Capetown—3,696 miles.

11. FROM GIBRALTAR STRAITS TO PANAMA

(A) Via Mona Passage

From a position 3 miles south of Tarifa Point, steer on the Great Circle to latitude 18° 30'N., longitude 67° 50'W., and thence through the Mona Passage as direct as navigation permits to destination.

Distance on Great Circle—3,424 miles
Total distance to Colon, Panama—4,313 miles.

(B) Via Sombrero Island Passage

From a position 3 miles south of Tarifa Point, steer on the Great Circle to latitude 18° 40'N., longitude 63° 28'W., and thence as direct as navigation permits to destination.

Distance on Great Circle—3,207 miles
Total distance to Colon, Panama—4,315 miles.

12. FROM GIBRALTAR STRAITS TO BARBADOS, CURACAO AND TRINIDAD

From a position 3 miles south of Tarifa Point, steer on the Great Circle to latitude 13° 40'N., longitude 59° 00'W., and thence as directly as navigation permits to destination.

Distance on Great Circle—3,156 miles
Total distance to Carlisle Bay, Barbados—3,218 miles
Total distance to Willemstad, Curacao—3,796 miles
Total distance to Port of Spain, Trinidad—3,414 miles.

13. FROM GIBRALTAR STRAITS TO BOSTON OR NEW YORK

(A) From 11th April to 30th June, dates inclusive

From a position 3 miles south of Tarifa Point, steer on a course to pass 10 miles south of Cape St. Vincent, thence by Great Circle to latitude 41° 30'N., longitude 47° 00'W., and thence by rhumb line courses to Boston, or to a position to the south of Nantucket, and thence to New York.

Distance on Great Circle—1,776 miles
Total distance to Boston—3,018 miles
Total distance to New York—3,173 miles.

(B) From 1st July to 10th April

From a position 3 miles south of Tarifa Point, steer on a course to pass 10 miles south of Cape St. Vincent, thence by Great Circle to latitude 43° 00'N., longitude 50° 00'W., thence to Boston or New York as in Route (A) above.

Distance on Great Circle—1,905 miles
Total distance to Boston—2,998 miles
Total distance to New York—3,165 miles.

When eastbound, from Boston or New York to Gibraltar, follow routes 14(A) or (B).

14. FROM NEW YORK OR BOSTON TO STRAITS OF GIBRALTAR

(A) From 11th April to 30th June, dates inclusive

Steer on rhumb line courses to latitude 40° 30'N., longitude 47° 00'W. (Ships from New York should pass about 25 miles south of Nantucket.) From this position, follow the Great Circle to pass 10 miles south of Cape St. Vincent, and thence as direct as navigation permits to position 3 miles south of Tarifa Point.

Distance on Great Circle—1,781 miles
Total distance from New York—3,187 miles
Total distance from Boston—3,035 miles.

(B) From 1st July to 10th April, dates inclusive

Steer on rhumb line courses to latitude 42° 00'N., longitude 50° 00'W. From this position, follow the Great Circle to pass 10 miles south of Cape St. Vincent, and thence as directly as navigation permits to position 3 miles south of Tarifa Point.

Distance on Great Circle—1,908 miles
Total distance from New York—3,172 miles
Total distance from Boston—3,010 miles.

15. FROM NEW YORK TO PANAMA

From Ambrose Light steer on the rhumb line course to latitude 24° 05'N., longitude 74° 15'W., and thence through Crooked Island Passage to a position 5 miles east of Cabo Maysi, Cuba. From this latter position, proceed as directly as navigation permits to destination.

Distance to Colon, Panama—1,963 miles.

PACIFIC OCEAN ROUTES

1. FROM LOS ANGELES TO HONOLULU
Steer on the Great Circle track from Los Angeles to Honolulu.

Distance to Honolulu—2,227 miles.

2. FROM LOS ANGELES TO SAN BERNARDINO STRAIT
(A) Northern Route
Proceed as directly as navigation permits to latitude 33° 45'N., longitude 120° 10'W., and thence by Great Circle to latitude 12° 45'N., longitude 124° 20°E., in the entrance to the Straits.

Distance to Straits—6,187 miles.

(B) Southern Route
Take Route 1 to Honolulu, thence as direct as navigation permits to latitude 21° 32'N., longitude 160° 30'W., and then follow the Great Circle track to latitude 12° 45'N., longitude 124° 20'E. This route enables vessels to call at Honolulu for fuel if required.

Distance to San Bernardino Strait—6,683 miles.

3. FROM LOS ANGELES TO SURIAGO STRAIT
(A) Northern Route
Proceed as directly as navigation permits to latitude 33° 45'N., longitude 120° 10'W., and thence by Great Circle to latitude 10° 40'N., longitude 126° 00'E., in the entrance to the Straits.

Distance to Straits—6,190 miles.

(B) Southern Route
Take Route 2(B) to latitude 21° 32'N., longitude 160° 30'W., thence by Great Circle to Guam and thence by rhumb line to latitude 10° 40'N., longitude 126° 00'E.

Distance to Suriago Strait—6,677 miles.

4. FROM BALBOA, PANAMA, TO HONOLULU
Proceed as directly as navigation permits from Panama Bay to latitude 06° 45'N., longitude 81° 00'W., and thence by Great Circle to Honolulu.

Distance to Honolulu—4,685 miles.

5. FROM BALBOA, PANAMA, TO TAHITI
Proceed as directly as navigation permits from Panama Bay to latitude 06° 20'N., longitude 80° 40'W., thence by Great Circle to latitude 13° 35'S., longitude 145° 15'W., and thence to destination passing northwest of the Tuamotu Islands.

Distance to Tahiti—4,573 miles.

6. FROM BALBOA, PANAMA, TO YOKOHAMA

Take Route 4 to Honolulu and thence by rhumb line course direct to Yokohama Bay. The direct rhumb line track from Honolulu passes about 20 miles south of the island chain which lies to the westward of the Hawaiian group.

Distance to Yokohama—8,115 miles.

7. FROM BALBOA, PANAMA, TO NEW ZEALAND PORTS

(A) Direct Route

Steer on a rhumb line course from the entrance to Panama Bay to latitude 02° 15'S., longitude 90° 00'W., and thence follow the Great Circle track to latitude 25° 40'S., longitude 130° 00'W. From this position, about 30 miles south of Pitcairn Island, steer on a second Great Circle to latitude 36° 30'S., longitude 160° 00'W., and thence to destination by a final Great Circle.

Distance to Auckland—6,553 miles.
Distance to Wellington—6,509 miles.
Distance to Port Chalmers—6,730 miles.

(B) Via Tahiti, for vessels with limited bunker capacity

Take Route 5 to Tahiti and thence by Great Circle track to destination.

Distance to Auckland—6,787 miles.
Distance to Wellington—6,920 miles.
Distance to Port Chalmers—7,173 miles.

8. FROM BALBOA, PANAMA, TO SYDNEY

(A) Direct

Take Route 7 to the position south of Pitcairn Island, thence by rhumb line to latitude 30° 00'S., longitude 150° 00'W., and thence to a position about 5 miles north of Three Kings Islands, which lie off the northwest tip of North Island, New Zealand. From the position off Three Kings Islands steer direct to Sydney.

Distance to Sydney—7,700 miles.

(B) Via Tahiti

Take Route 5 to Tahiti and thence by Great Circle track to destination.

Distance to Sydney—7,876 miles.

9. FROM BALBOA, PANAMA, TO SUVA

Take Route 5 from Panama Bay to latitude 06° 30'S., longitude 120° 00'W., and thence by Great Circle track to Nanuku Passage in the Fiji Islands. From Nanuku Passage proceed to destination as directly as navigation permits.

Distance to Suva—6,326 miles.

10. FROM BRISBANE TO TAHITI

From Moreton Bay follow the direct Great Circle track which passes about 10 miles north of Baratonga in the Cook Islands and about 10 miles south of Mauke Island.

Distance to Tahiti—3,258 miles.

11. FROM BRISBANE TO WELLINGTON

From Moreton Bay steer on the direct rhumb line course to the entrance to Cook Strait and thence to destination as directly as navigation permits.

Distance to Wellington—1,447 miles.

12. FROM CALLAO TO TAHITI

Follow the Great Circle track from Callao to latitude 14° 00'S., longitude 141° 25'W., thence along the northern edge of the Tuamotu group of islands to destination as directly as safe navigation permits.

Distance to Tahiti—4,355 miles.

13. FROM CALLAO TO HONOLULU

Steer on the direct Great Circle track.

Distance to Honolulu—5,160 miles.

14. FROM CALLAO TO NEW ZEALAND

Steer on the Great Circle from Callao to latitude 30° 00'S., longitude 120° 00'W., and thence due west to longitude 140° 00'W. From this latter position take the Great Circle to latitude 36° 30'S., longitude 160° 00'W., and thence to destination by a further Great Circle.

Distance to Auckland—5,966 miles.
Distance to Wellington—5,924 miles.

15. FROM VALPARAISO TO NEW ZEALAND

Steer on the Great Circle from Valparaiso to latitude 30° 00'S., longitude 120° 00'W., and thence by Route 14 to destination.

Distance to Auckland—5,820 miles.
Distance to Wellington—5,778 miles.

M

16. FROM VALPARAISO TO TAHITI

Steer on the Great Circle from Valparaiso to pass a safe distance south of the Duke of Gloucester Islands and thence south of Hereheretue to destination as directly as navigation permits.

Distance to Tahiti—4,528 miles.

17. FROM VALPARAISO TO HONOLULU

Follow the direct Great Circle track.

Distance to Honolulu—5,918 miles.

18. FROM VANCOUVER TO HONOLULU

Proceed to the entrance to the Juan de Fuca Strait and thence follow the Great Circle track to destination.

Distance to Honolulu—2,420 miles.

19. FROM VANCOUVER TO GUAM

Proceed to the entrance to the Juan de Fuca Strait and thence to destination by the direct Great Circle track.

Distance to Guam—4,965 miles.

20. FROM YOKOHAMA TO SAN FRANCISCO

After clearing Yokohama Bay follow the direct Great Circle track. Maximum latitude attained 47° 30'N.

Distance to San Francisco—4,538 miles.

21. FROM YOKOHAMA TO VANCOUVER

After clearing Yokohama Bay and Nojima Saki take the Great Circle to latitude 50° 00'N., longitude 170° 00'W., thence due east to longitude 140° 00'W., and finally by rhumb line courses to destination *via* the Juan de Fuca Strait.

Distance to Vancouver—4,295 miles.

INDIAN OCEAN ROUTES

1. FROM ADEN TO BOMBAY

(A) From October to April (N.E. Monsoon)

Take the direct rhumb line course from a position 5 miles south of Ras Marshaq to a position 3 miles southwest of Prongs Reef Light.

Distance to Bombay—1,659 miles.

(B) From May to September (S.W. Monsoon)

Steer by rhumb line courses to a position in latitude 13° 00'N., longitude 55° 00'E., and thence to Bombay, making a landfall off Khanderi Island.

Distance to Bombay—1,685 miles.

2. FROM ADEN TO KARACHI

Proceed as directly as prudent navigation permits along the Arabian coast to a position south of the Kuria Muria islands and thence by rhumb line course direct to Karachi.

Distance to Karachi—1,473 miles.

3. FROM ADEN TO COLOMBO

(A) From October to April, passing west of Socotra

Steer to a position about 20 miles north of Cape Guardafui and thence by rhumb line as direct as prudent navigation permits to Colombo, passing through the Eight Degree Channel.

Distance to Colombo—2,098 miles.

(B) From May to September, passing north of Socotra

Steer by rhumb line courses to position latitude 13° 00'N., longitude 55° 00'E., and thence direct to Colombo.

Distance to Colombo—2,118 miles.

4. FROM ADEN TO FREMANTLE

Proceed as directly as safe navigation permits to a position about 10 miles east of Cape Guardafui, thence by rhumb line to latitude 04° 00'S., longitude 73° 00'E., and from this position follow the Great Circle to Fremantle.

Distance to Fremantle—4,925 miles.

5. FROM ADEN TO CAPE LEEUWIN

Follow Route 4 to latitude 04° 00'S., longitude 73° 20'E., and thence by Great Circle to a position about 12 miles south of Cape Leeuwin.

Distance to Cape Leeuwin—4,970 miles.

6.   FROM BOMBAY TO ADEN

(A) From October to April (N.E. Monsoon)

Take Route 1 reversed.

Distance to Aden—1,659 miles.

(B) From May to September (S.W. Monsoon)

Steer due west from Bombay to longitude 60° 00'E., and thence along the Arabian coast at about 30 miles distant from the headlands.

Distance to Aden—1,682 miles.

7.   FROM BOMBAY TO MOMBASA

Steer on the direct rhumb line course.

Distance to Mombasa—2,403 miles.

8.   FROM COLOMBO TO ADEN

(A) From October to April (N.E. Monsoon)

Take Route 3 reversed.

Distance to Aden—2,098 miles.

(B) From May to September (S.W. Monsoon)

From Colombo steer rhumb line courses, first to pass through Eight Degree Channel to latitude 10° 00'N., longitude 60° 00'E., thence to a position about 45 miles northeast of Socotra and finally direct to Aden.

Distance to Aden—2,130 miles.

Note: During the period of the S.W. Monsoon the current south of Socotra sets very strongly northeastwards. For this reason the suggested westbound route to Aden from Colombo passes north of Socotra.

9.   FROM COLOMBO TO FREMANTLE

From a departure point off Pont de Galle, Ceylon, take the direct Great Circle to Fremantle. The Great Circle route ensures passing the Cocos Islands at a distance of about 60 miles to the westward.

Distance to Fremantle—3,120 miles.

10.   FROM COLOMBO TO CAPE LEEUWIN

From a departure point off Point de Galle, Ceylon, take the direct Great Circle to a position about 12 miles south of Cape Leeuwin.

Distance to Cape Leeuwin—3,202 miles.

11.   FROM CAPETOWN TO ADELAIDE

Proceed as direct as prudent navigation permits to latitude 35° 30'S., longitude 20° 00'E., thence due east to Investigator Strait and destination.

Distance to Adelaide—5,945 miles.

12. FROM CAPETOWN TO MELBOURNE

Proceed as direct as prudent navigation permits to latitude 35° 30'S., longitude 20° 00'E., thence due east to longitude 115° 00'E., thence by Great Circle to a position south of Cape Otway and finally to Melbourne.

Distance to Melbourne— 6,259 miles.

13. FROM CAPETOWN TO FREMANTLE

Proceed as direct as prudent navigation permits to latitude 35° 30'S., longitude 20° 00'E., thence due east to longitude 90° 00'E., and thence by Great Circle track to Fremantle.

Distance to Fremantle—4,854 miles.

14. FROM CAPETOWN TO HOBART

Proceed as in Route 12 to longitude 115° 00'E., thence by Great Circle to a position about 10 miles to the southwestwards of South West Cape, Tasmania, and thence to Hobart as directly as navigation permits.

Distance to Hobart—6,381 miles.

15. FROM DURBAN TO SUNDA STRAIT

Proceed by rhumb line course from Durban to latitude 30° 00'S., longitude 56° 40'E., and thence by Great Circle to latitude 06° 25'S., longitude 105° 00'E., in the Sunda Strait.

Distance to Sunda Strait—4,340 miles.

16. FROM DURBAN TO THURSDAY ISLAND OR DARWIN

Steer on the Great Circle track from Durban to latitude 15° 30'S., longitude 120° 00'E., and thence as directly as navigation permits to destination.

Distance to Thursday Island—6,268 miles.
Distance to Darwin—5,576 miles.

17. FROM DURBAN TO FREMANTLE

Steer on the Great Circle track from Durban to latitude 35° 30'S., longitude 67° 30'E., thence due east to longitude 90° 00'E. and then proceed along the Great Circle to Fremantle.

Distance to Fremantle—4,261 miles.

18. FROM DURBAN TO ADELAIDE

Steer on the Great Circle from Durban to latitude 35° 30'S., longitude 67° 30'E., from thence proceed due east to Investigation Strait and destination.

Distance to Adelaide—5,340 miles.

19. FROM DURBAN TO MELBOURNE

Steer on the Great Circle from Durban to latitude 35° 00'S., longitude 67° 30'E., thence due east to longitude 115° 00'E., then by Great Circle to a position south of Cape Otway, and finally as direct as mavigation permits to destination.

Distance to Melbourne—5,653 miles.

20. FROM DURBAN TO HOBART

Steer on the Great Circle from Durban to latitude 35° 00'S., longitude 67° 30'E. to join Route 14.

Distance to Hobart—5,776 miles.

21. FROM FREMANTLE TO DURBAN

(A) From October to April

Steer a rhumb line course from Fremantle to latitude 30° 00'S., longitude 100° 00'E., and thence on the Great Circle to Durban.

Distance to Durban—4,343 miles.

(B) From May to September

Steer a rhumb line course to latitude 30° 00'S., longitude 100° 00'E., and thence due west to Durban.

Distance to Durban—4,420 miles.

22. FROM FREMANTLE TO CALCUTTA

Steer on rhumb line courses, first to cross the Equator in longitude 94° 30'E. from thence to the entrance to River Hooghly.

Distance to Calcutta—3,682 miles.

Section I

Ocean Surface Currents

For some years the Meteorological Office has made a close study of ships' drifts and, by means of the large electronic computer now available at Bracknell, hopes to make considerable progress in the understanding and perhaps prediction of ocean currents and their variations. Although oceanographers can now make very precise physical measurements of the characteristics of the sea (particularly of ocean currents), the great volume and wide distribution of ships' operations makes every single current observation of permanent value for study of the ocean circulations and their influence on the weather and life within the sea.

GENERAL NOTES

Today, as in the past, ocean surface current charts are compiled from information obtained from ships' observations. The many thousands of observations recorded are subjected to statistical analysis, and from the results of this analysis, the modern charts are produced. The collection of information for these charts goes on continuously, and more observations from ships—especially those sailing in less frequented waters—are essential for their continued improvement. The Meteorological Office states that: **"Observations of ocean currents will be very welcome from any ship whether reporting meteorological observations or not"**.

The notes and charts contained in this section concern the principal predominant currents of the oceans, and the daily drifts which are given represent approximate **average drift per day under normal conditions**. One of the main causes of ocean surface currents is the effect of the wind dragging the surface water along; hence, a strong wind from a direction other than that of the prevailing wind can cause fluctuation in the speed and direction of the normal current in the area concerned.

Admiralty Routeing Charts contain comprehensive information on the Ocean Currents which are of navigational importance. These charts are available from all Admiralty Chart Agents.

Admiralty Sailing Direction (Pilots) contain more detailed information concerning currents in local coastal and offshore regions. The latest editions should always be used.

CURRENTS OF THE SOUTH ATLANTIC: (Chart on page 193)

South Equatorial Current. The broad belt of water flowing westwards from Longitude 0° to the Brazilian coast with its axis in about Latitude 6°S. is known as the South Equatorial Current. The northern edge of this current extends across the Equator to about Latitude 4°N. In the region of Cape Sao Roque the current divides, the smaller branch sets southward as the Brazil Current, and the major branch sets north-west towards the Caribbean, where it joins the North Equatorial Current.

Average daily drift: In Longitude 25°W.—20 miles. Between Cape Sao Roque and Trinidad the drift may exceed 40 miles per day. Maximum drift occurs during June and July.

Brazil Current. This current is the extension of the southern branch of the South Equatorial Current, and flows south along the Brazilian coast. In about Latitude 35°S. it meets the Falkland Current and both currents then set easterly.

Average daily drift: 15 miles.

Falkland Current. The northerly flowing current which passes west of the Falkland Islands and extends from Staten Island to about Latitude 40°S. is called the Falkland Current. A minor branch of this current continues north to the River Plate estuary, and during May to September extends further north to as far as Rio de Janeiro. This northern extension of the Falkland Current is known as the **Brazil Inshore Countercurrent**.

Average daily drift: Falkland Current   12 miles.
Brazil Inshore Countercurrent   15 miles.

The easterly drift which comprises the southern part of the South Atlantic circulation has no specific name. It is composed of water from the Brazil and Falkland Currents, and is bounded on the south by the **Southern Ocean Current.**

  Average daily drift: 15 miles.

Benguela Current. The Benguela Current sets north along the south-west coast of Africa, and is most pronounced between the Cape of Good Hope and Latitude 18°S. North of Latitude 20°S. the current gradually flows away from the coast and later becomes the South Equatorial Current.

  Average daily drift: 13 miles.

CURRENTS OF THE NORTH ATLANTIC: (Chart on page 194)

The Gulf Stream. This current may be described as the mainspring of the North Atlantic circulation. Between the Florida Strait and Cape Hatteras, the axis of the current tends to follow the 100 fathom line. Immediately to the north of Hatteras there is a gradual swing eastwards away from the coast, and the current changes character from a relatively narrow fast flowing stream to a slower and much wider one. It generally ceases to be a well defined band of water in about Longitude 45°W., and continues northwards and eastwards as the *North Atlantic Current.* South of Cape Hatteras, the current reaches its maximum rate during July, and falls to a minimum in November. North-east of Hatteras, the maximum rate occurs in May, and the minimum in October.

Average daily drift:	*South of Hatteras—*	*July*	*70 miles.*
		November	*60 miles.*
	North-east of Hatteras—	*May*	*33 miles.*
		October	*30 miles.*

North Atlantic Current. Eastwards of about Longitude 45°W. the remnants of the Gulf Stream spread out to form several broad bands, the most northerly of these being known as the North Atlantic current, which flows in a north-easterly direction towards the British Isles. Part of the current reaches the Norwegian coast, and then turns northward where it is named the Norwegian Atlantic Current. The remainder enters the North Sea after branching south to the north-east of the Shetland Islands.

Average daily drift:	*In 40°W.*	*14 miles.*
	In 20°W.	*9 miles.*

  There is no marked seasonal change.

Irminger Current. This current is a northern branch of the North Atlantic Current. South-west of Iceland it splits into two, one part making a clockwise circulation around Iceland, while the major part sets to the westward and joins the East Greenland Current.

  Average daily drift: 9 miles.

East Greenland Current. The main outflow of the water from the Arctic Basin follows the East Greenland coast, hence its name. It sets south-westward to Cape Farewell, and then turns north.

Average daily drift: 6-12 miles.
(Relatively few observations from this area).

East Iceland Current. A branch of the East Greenland Current which sets south-easterly past the east coast of Iceland before recurving and setting parallel to the Norwegian section of the Atlantic Current.

Average daily drift: 8 miles.

West Greenland Current. This is the continuation of the East Greenland Current northwards along the west coast of Greenland and into Baffin Bay. In Baffin Bay the current recurves and sets southwards along the east coast of Baffin Island.

Average daily drift: 6-12 miles.
(Few observations from this area).

Labrador Current. The southerly current in the Davis Strait, reinforced by water from the Hudson Strait, is known as the Labrador Current, and flows south-easterly along the Labrador coast. South of Newfoundland the current sets south-westwards, bounded on the west by Nova Scotia, and on the east by the Gulf Stream. The greatest southern extension, to about Latitude 36°N., occurs in November to January. The least extension, to about Latitude 40°N., occurs in August to October. There is invariably a well-defined demarcation between the Gulf Stream and the Labrador Current, which may be observed by a sharp drop in sea surface temperature when steaming westwards. The Labrador Current covers the whole of the Newfoundland Bank, except for the southern edge during the summer.

Average daily drift: 10 miles.

Azores Current. A southerly branch of the North Atlantic Current, which sets south-east and then south through the Azore Islands before recurving westwards.

Average daily drift: 11 miles.

Portugal Current. In about Longitude 20°W. another branch of the North Atlantic Current sets south-easterly towards Cape Finisterre, and then turns south to pass along the Portuguese coast as the Portugal Current. A portion of this current enters the Mediterranean.

Average daily drift: 10 miles.

Canary Current. This current is the extension of the Portugal Current southwards through the Canary Islands towards the Cape Verde Islands.

Average daily drift: 10 miles.

North Equatorial Current. The North Atlantic circulation is completed by the current which stems from the region of the Cape Verde Islands and flows westwards in a broad belt to the Caribbean.

Average daily drift: 12 miles.

Equatorial Counter Current. Bounded by the North and South Equatorial Currents, the Equatorial Counter Current sets easterly in approximately Latitude 6°N. During August to November the current begins in about Longitude 50°W., but this longitude varies to about 23°W. in February to April.

> *Average daily drift: 15 miles.*

Guinea Current. This is the extension of the Equatorial Counter Current along the coast of Guinea to the Bight of Biafra.

> *Average daily drift: 23 miles.*

ADJACENT SEAS:

The Caribbean Sea. The current in this sea is composed of the extension of the North Equatorial Current and a branch of the South Equatorial Current. The combined flow is westwards and through the Yucatan Channel to the Gulf of Mexico. In the Southern Caribbean, the current is strongest in November to January, while in the north the period of greatest drift is in August to October.

> | *Average daily drift:* | *In the south* | *20 miles.* |
> | --- | --- | --- |
> | *In the region to the west of Trinidad* | | *35 miles.* |
> | | *In the north* | *13 miles.* |

The Mediterranean Sea. The inflowing water from the Portugal Current sets eastwards along the North African coast. In the region of Port Said, the current sets northwards towards Cyprus and then westwards. The westward drift tends to follow the coastline of the northern shores, and is not well defined. There is no outflow of water at the surface in the Straits of Gibraltar.

Average daily drift: From the Strait of Gibraltar eastwards to Cape Bon— 15 miles. East of Cape Bon — 12 miles. The return current along the northern coasts is much more variable, but along the French coast may average 12 miles per day during the winter months.

CURRENTS OF THE NORTH PACIFIC (China Sea on p.196)

Kuro Shio: This current corresponds to the Gulf Stream of the North Atlantic. It flows in a narrow band north-eastwards from Taiwan and along the southern coasts of Japan to about Latitude 35°N. before turning eastwards.

> | *Average daily drift:* | *In Summer* | *35 miles.* |
> | --- | --- | --- |
> | | *In Winter* | *22 miles.* |

North Pacific Current: The easterly flowing extension of the Kuro Shio is known as the North Pacific Current. Between Longitudes 145°E. and 160°E. the current is still fairly narrow and well defined. East of Longitude 160°E. it fans out into a broad stream, most of which turns south before reaching Longitude 150°W.

> | *Average daily drift:* | *West of Longitude 160°E.* | *25 miles.* |
> | --- | --- | --- |
> | | *East of Longitude 160°E.* | *5-10 miles.* |

Kamchatka Current: The main outflow of cold water from the Bering Sea flows south along the Kamchatka Peninsula to be known as the Kamchatka Current. Offshore in about Latitude 50°N. a branch of this current sets south-easterly.

> *Average daily drift: 5-10 miles.*
> *(Few observations from this area).*

Oya Shio: This current is the southerly extension of the Kamchatka Current which continues south-westwards to flow along the east coast of Honshu until it meets the northern edge of the Kuro Shio. Off-shore branches of the Oya Shio set south-easterly along its entire length.

> *Average daily drift: 5-10 miles.*

Aleutian Current: The offshore branches of the Kamchatka and Oya Shio currents combine with a northern branch of the Kuro Shio to form the Aleutian Current. This current flows eastwards, parallel and to the north of the North Pacific Current, to about Longitude 140°W., where it divides into a northerly and southerly branch.

> *Average daily drift: 3-7 miles.*

Alaska Current: The northern branch of the Aleutian Current flows north into the Gulf of Alaska to become the Alaska Current. It sets north, then north-west following the coastline of Alaska before flowing westwards along the south coast of the Aleutian Islands. West of Longitude 160°W. branches turn south and then east to rejoin the Aleutian Current. Other branches turn north to enter the Bering Sea.

> *Average daily drift: 6 miles.*

Californian Current: The major part of the Aleutian Current turns south before reaching the coast, and sets southerly on a broad front. In the region of California, it is known as the Californian Current.

> *Average daily drift: 5 miles.*

Davidson Current: From November to February this current flows northwards, inshore of the Californian Current, to about the latitude of Vancouver Island. For the remainder of the year, this area is filled with irregular current eddies.

> *Average daily drift: 12 miles.*

North Equatorial Current: The circulation of the North Pacific is completed by the North Equatorial Current, which flows westwards, with its axis in about Latitude 12°N. Its source is the extension of the Californian Current and the northern branch of the Equatorial Counter Current. Further west, in the region of Hawaii, it is reinforced by water originating from the North Pacific Current. The northern extent of the current varies with the season, and may reach Latitude 30°N. in early Autumn. In about Longitude 145°E. the current divides, one part swings to the south and feeds the Counter Current, while the remainder flows northwards towards Tiawan.

> *Average daily drift: 10 miles.*

Equatorial Counter Current: This easterly flowing current lies between the North and South Equatorial Currents with its axis in about Latitude 6°N. It flows throughout the year, and is composed of water from the southern branch of the North Equatorial Current, which is reinforced by the South Equatorial Current during March to November. In the eastern part of the ocean, the counter current recurves northwards near the coast to about Latitude 18°N. in June to July. It then sets westwards to become part of the North Equatorial Current.

Average daily drift:	*West of Longitude 140°E.*	*35 miles.*
	In mid-ocean	*24 miles.*
	East of Longitude 120°W.	*15 miles.*
	Off Mexican Coast	*5 miles.*

CURRENTS OF THE SOUTH PACIFIC (Chart on page 198)

South Equatorial Current: From about Longitude 95°W. to 145°E. the South Equatorial Current flows westwards astride the Equator. Its northerly extent is governed by the Equatorial Counter Current, and varies from about Latitude 2°N. to 5°N. The westward drift extends to about Latitude 20°S., but south of Latitude 6°S. the current is much weaker and less constant. There are marked seasonal changes in the set of the current on the west side of the ocean. In the period from June to August, the whole of the current sets northwards in about Longitude 130°E. and then recurves eastwards to become part of the Equatorial Counter Current. During December to February, the current sets south in about Longitude 140°E. and then flows south-easterly along the north coast of New Guinea. For the remainder of the year, the current divides, branches flowing north and south.

Average daily drift: 24 miles.

East Australia Coast Current: Flows predominantly southward along the coast from about Latitude 22°S. to Cape Howe. Liable to interruptions by northerly sets. The strongest south-going currents are usually found near the 100 fathom line. It is most constant from December to February.

Daily drift very variable, average about 28 miles.

Southern Ocean Current: Like the South Atlantic and Indian Oceans, the southern part of the South Pacific circulation is formed by the Southern Ocean Current, reinforced by water from the East Australia Coast Current, and sets easterly on a broad front. On approaching the South American Coast, the northern part of the current divides. One branch turns northwards, while the other sets southwards to rejoin the main flow south of Cape Horn.

Average daily drift: 10 miles

(There is little information concerning this region, but the drift appears to be less and the direction less constant than in the South Atlantic and Indian Oceans.)

Peru Current: The northern branch of the Southern Ocean Current sets northwards along the coast of Peru, and is known as the Peru Current. North of Latitude 10°S. the current diverges, and the bulk of it sets north-westerly to enter the South Equatorial Current. For most of the year, an inshore branch of the current continues northwards along the coast and enters the Gulf of Panama.

Average daily drift: 13 miles

El Nino or Holy Child Current: During the months of January to March, a branch of the Equatorial Counter Current sets south-easterly across the Equator, and then south along the coast of Ecuador. Occasionally this current extends to about Latitude 12°S.

Average daily drift: 12 miles

CURRENTS OF THE NORTH INDIAN OCEAN (Chart on page 200)

Equatorial Countercurrent: This is the only current of the North Indian Ocean that is not reversed in direction by the action of the monsoons. It sets eastwards throughout the year, and lies to the north of the west flowing Equatorial Current. In November to January the current originates close to the African Coast, and extends to the Sumatran coast before setting south-easterly. During this period the northern limit varies between Latitude 2°N. and 4°N. The reversal of direction of the East African Coast Currents results in the western limit of the Countercurrent migrating eastwards during February to April to a position north-west of the Seychelles, where it remains until September. On the east side of the ocean few observations are available, but it would appear that during the south-west monsoon part of the Countercurrent sets southwards and enters the Equatorial Current. The current is displaced to the south during the north-east monsoon but in some areas it may run close to the Indian North-east Monsoon Current so that a small north-south change in position can take a ship from a west flowing to an east flowing current. During the south-west monsoon, the Indian South-west Monsoon Current to the north of the Equatorial Countercurrent also flows towards the eastwards and there is no definite demarcation between the two. The Equatorial Countercurrent is strongest during the monsoon transition periods in April/May and October/November.

Average daily drift: 24 miles

Somali Current and East Africa Coast Current: During December and January, the Somali Current flows south-westwards along the African Coast from Ras Hafun to the Equator where it meets the north flowing East Africa Coast Current before turning eastwards to become the Equatorial Countercurrent. North of Ras Hafun, the set is northerly to Cape Guardafui, and then westerly in the Gulf of Aden. In February the north-easterly flow extends from about 10°N. and thereafter the limit moves progressively further south until, by April, the East Africa Coast Current and the Somali Current form a continuous flow to the northwards from Latitude 10°S. to Cape Guardafui. From May to September the flow remains northerly, and is greatly strengthened by the south-west monsoon. During this period the current divides in about Latitude 7°N.; while the major part turns eastwards, the remainder continues along the coast to Cape Guardafui. The month of October sees the transition to the southerly set of November.

Average daily drift:	*November to January*	*16 miles.*
	February to March	*48 miles.*
	May to September	*48 miles.*

During July to September the current south of Socotra may reach 170 miles per day.

Indian South-west Monsoon Current: This occurs during the period May to September and is a continuation of the Somali current. It thus sets initially to the north-east, but becomes easterly across the Arabian Sea and then south-easterly towards the coasts of India and Pakistan.

Average daily drift: 10 miles.

Indian North-east Monsoon Current: This occurs during the north-east monsoon season, reaching its greatest development in February. It flows to the west or west-south-westwards between the Equator and about 6°N.

>*Average daily drift: 20 miles.*

The remaining currents of the North Indian Ocean, Arabian Sea, and Bay of Bengal have no specific names, but all reverse direction with the seasons. Hence the general current circulation is described below by season.

November to January: There is a counter-clockwise circulation around the coastlines of the Arabian Sea and Bay of Bengal. Clear of the coasts the set is westerly.

>*Daily drift: Rarely exceeds 20 miles, and is usually much less. An exception is to the South of Ceylon, where the drift may reach 40 miles per day.*

February to April: The coastal circulation slowly reverses direction to become clockwise, and is usually complete by late March. In open waters, the flow remains westerly, but the currents are more variable.

>*Average daily drift: 18 miles*

May to September: Under the influence of the south-west monsoon, the coastal circulation is strengthened and remains clockwise. Off-shore in both the Arabian Sea and the Bay of Bengal, the current sets easterly.

>*Average daily drift: 18 miles*

October: This is the month of transition. All currents tend to be variable in set and drift.

CHINA SEA: The currents in this region also follow seasonal patterns associated with the monsoons. From May to August, the set is north-easterly over the whole area. September is the transition month, but the north-easterly set tends to persist longer in the southern part than elsewhere. During October to March, the current flow is south-west under the influence of the north-east monsoon. April is the transition month to complete the cycle.

>*Average daily drift: October to March 20 miles*
>*   May to August   15 miles*

CURRENTS OF THE SOUTH INDIAN OCEAN: (Chart on page 204)

Equatorial Current: Due to the monsoons of the North Indian Ocean, there is only one Equatorial Current, and this is situated south of the Equator. This west flowing current has its northern boundary in about Latitude 6° or 10°S., depending on the season, it being nearer the Equator during the south-west monsoon. On the west side of the ocean, part of the current passes north of Madagascar, and continues to the African coast before dividing into northerly and southerly branches. South of Madagascar, the southern portion of the Equatorial Current flows southwesterly and joins the Agulhas Current.

>*Average daily drift: 36 miles*

Mozambique Current: This current flows southwards through the Mozambique Channel. It is formed by the southern branch of that part of the Equatorial Current which passes north of Madagascar.

>*Average daily drift: 48 miles.*

Agulhas Current: The Mozambique Current and the southern portion of the Equatorial Current meet off the South African coast in about Latitude 28°S. and are then known as the Agulhas Current. This current flows south-westerly along the coast, and part of it enters the South Atlantic Ocean. The remainder branches south-easterly between Longitudes 20°E. to 30°E. and later sets eastwards.

Average daily drift: 40 miles

Southern Ocean Current: This current, reinforced on its northern edge by water from the Agulhas Current, sets easterly as a broad front, and comprises the southern portion of the oceanic circulation. In about Longitude 100°E. the northern portion recurves north-east while the major southern portion continues easterly south of Cape Leeuwin and across the Australian Bight.

Average daily drift: 24 miles

West Australia Current: This northerly set off the west coast of Australia is generally weak. Close inshore during September to February, there is a southerly counter current.

Average daily drift: 14 miles

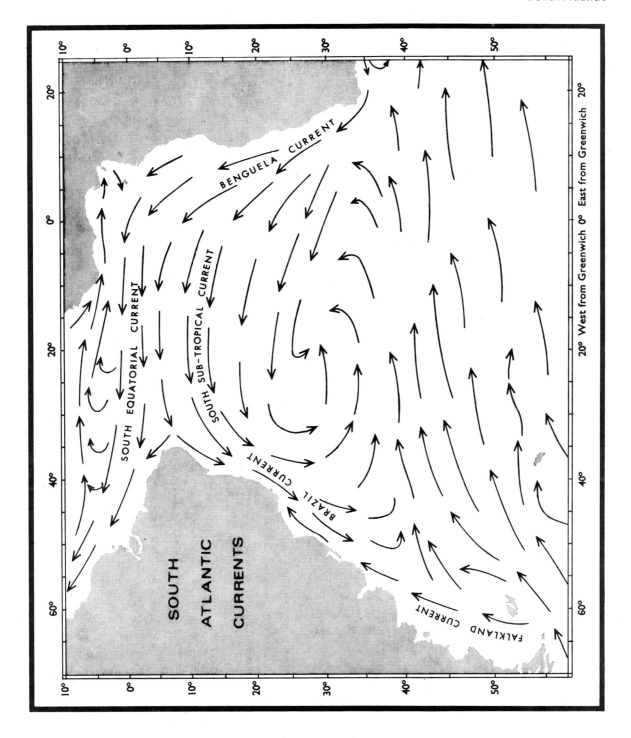

SOUTH
ATLANTIC
CURRENTS

North Atlantic and Adjacent Seas

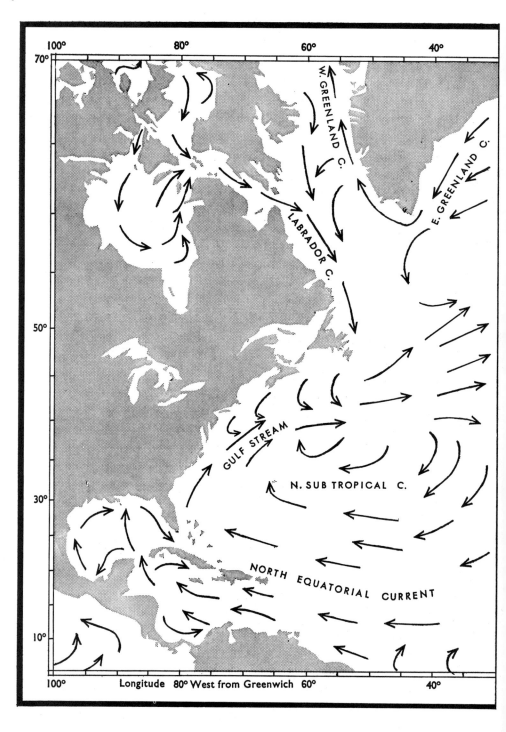

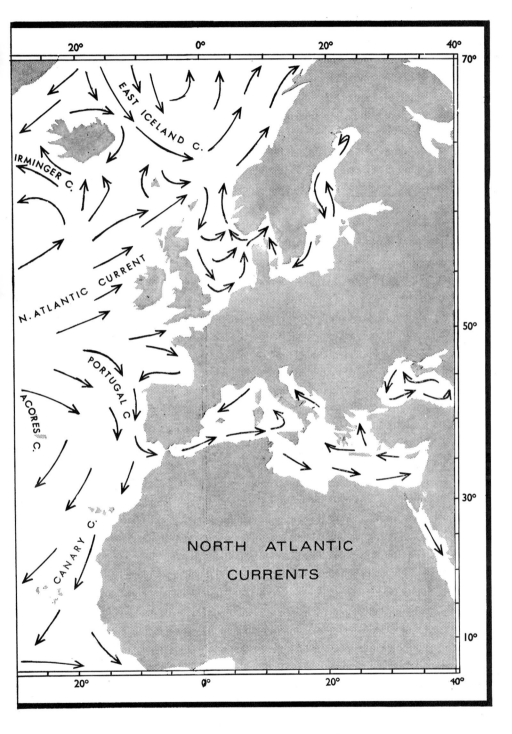

NORTH ATLANTIC
CURRENTS

North Pacific

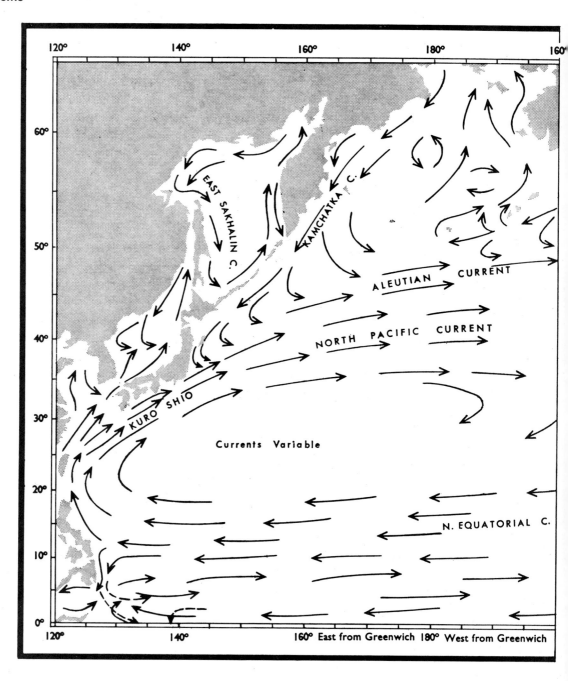

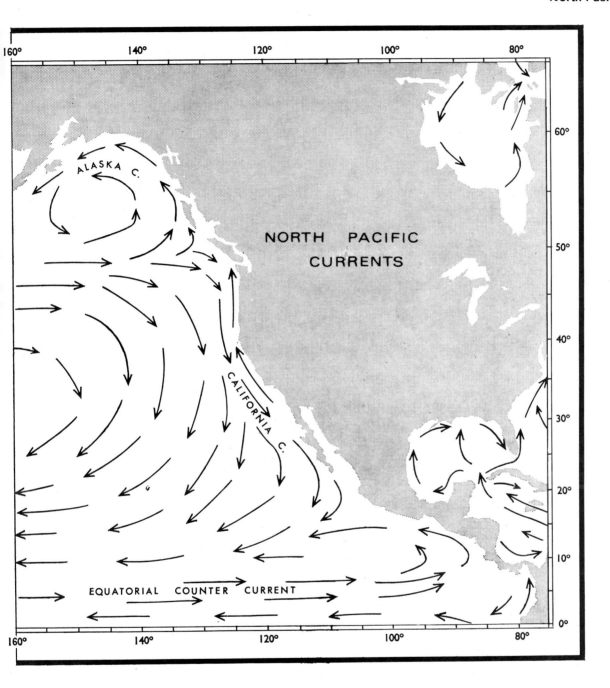

South Pacific

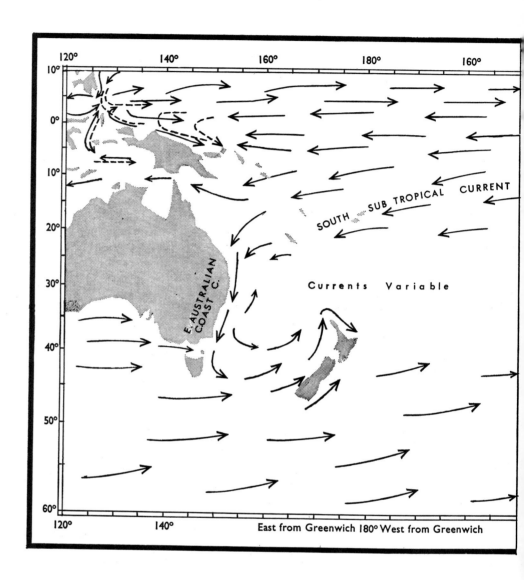

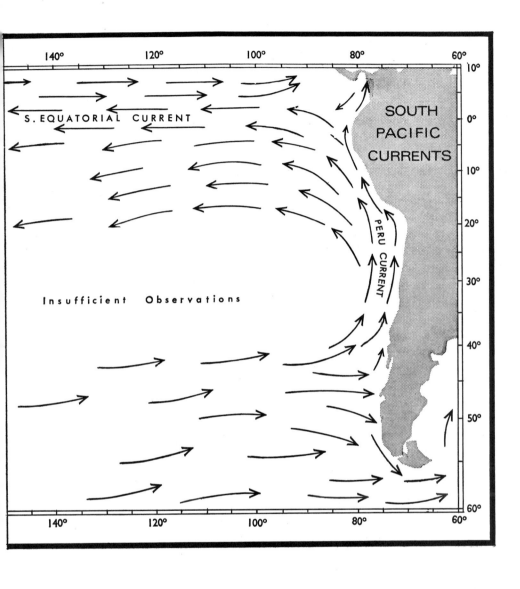

North Indian Ocean and China Seas (N.E. monsoon)

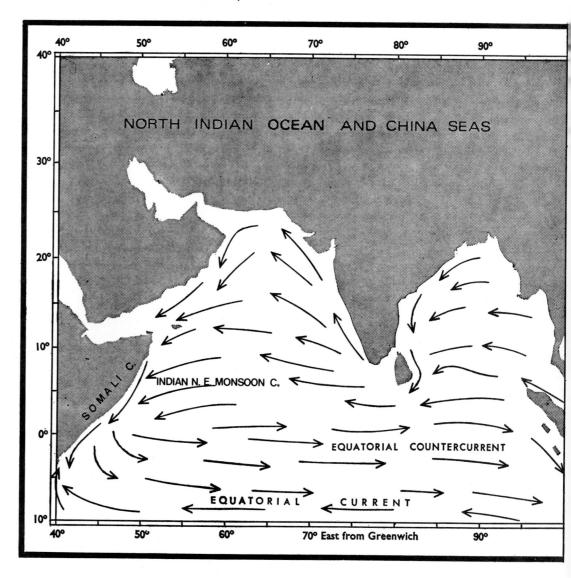

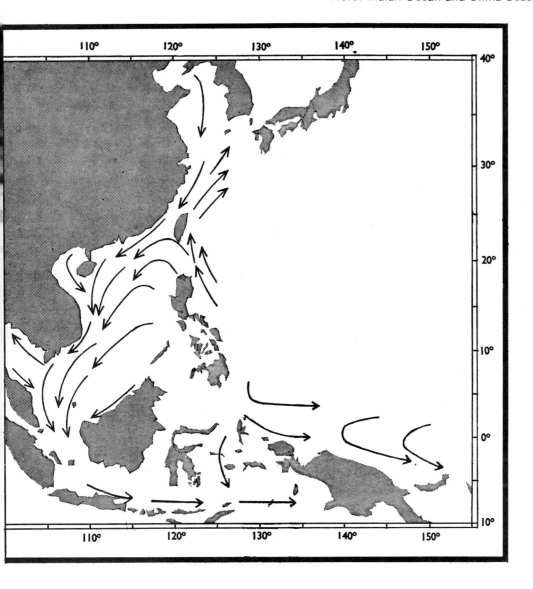

North Indian Ocean and China Seas (S.W. monsoon)

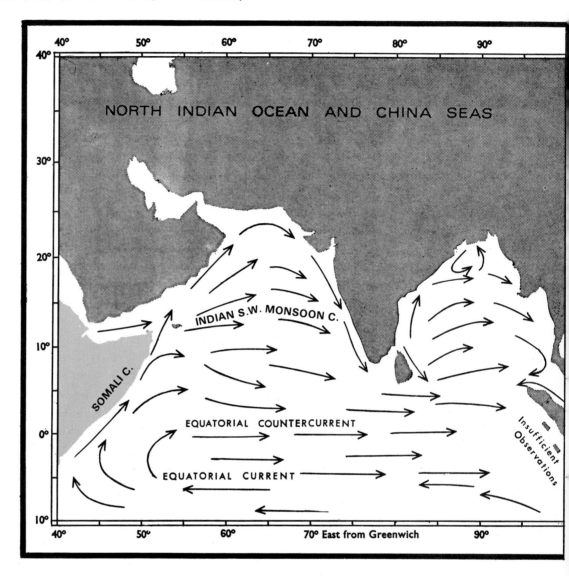

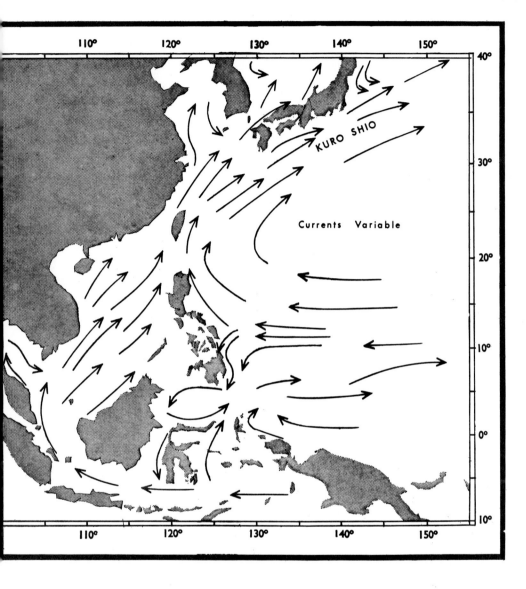

South Indian Ocean

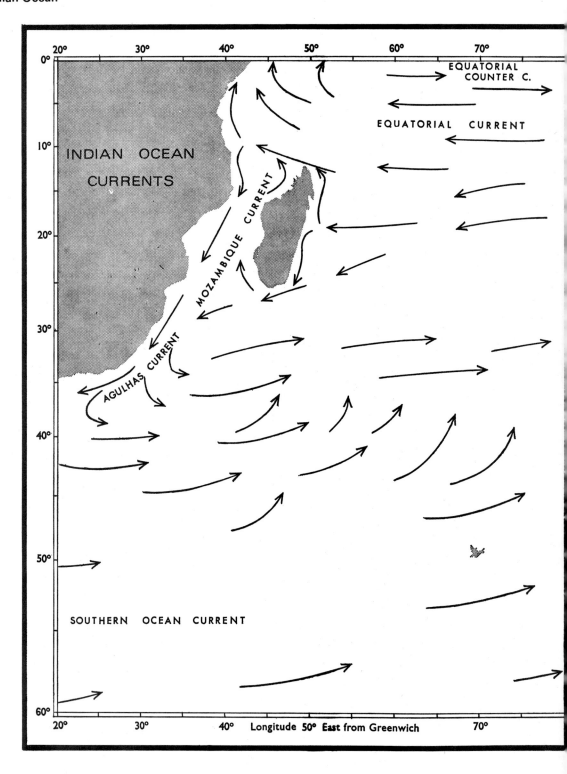

INDIAN OCEAN CURRENTS

EQUATORIAL COUNTER C.

EQUATORIAL CURRENT

MOZAMBIQUE CURRENT

AGULHAS CURRENT

SOUTHERN OCEAN CURRENT

Longitude 50° East from Greenwich

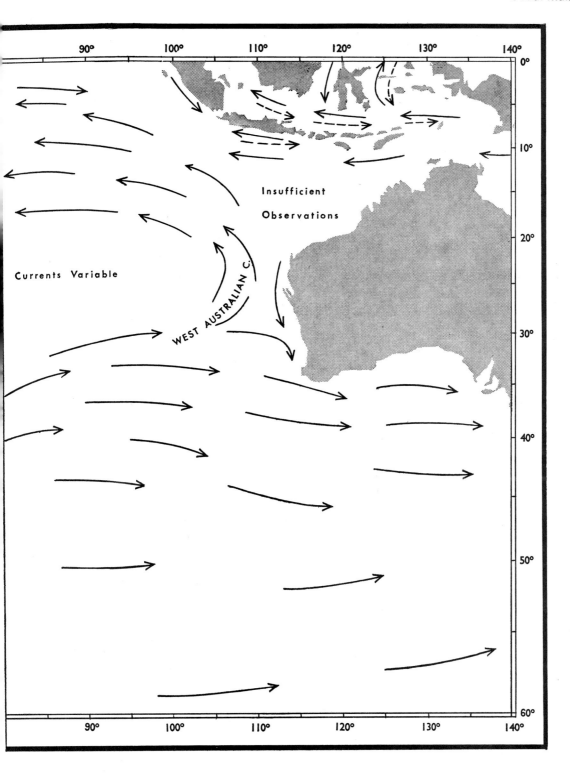

Section J

Sea Ice

ICE TERMINOLOGY

Anchor Ice: Ice anchored or attached to the sea-bed and submerged at high water.

Belt: A band of pack ice which may extend for a few miles or to well over fifty miles.

Bergy-Bit: A small iceberg with a height above sea level usually less than 5 metres.

Bergy Water: An area of freely navigable water with no sea ice present but in which ice of land origin is present.

Beset: The position of a vessel trapped by ice and unable to move.

Bight: A large crescent-shaped indentation in the ice edge caused by the wind or current.

Brash-ice: The floating remnants of larger ice formations that are not more than 2 metres across.

Calving: The process whereby a mass of ice breaks away from a glacier, ice front or iceberg.

Close pack ice: Pack ice in which the separate floes are close together, resulting in an ice cover of 7/10ths-8/10ths.

Concentration: The ratio, expressed in tenths, describing the mean areal density of ice in a given area.

Consolidated pack-ice: Pack ice in which the floes have joined and frozen together, giving an ice cover of 10/10ths.

Crack: Any fracture which has not parted.

Difficult Area: A general qualitative expression to indicate in a relative manner, that the severity of ice conditions prevailing in an area is such that navigation in it is difficult.

Easy Area: A general qualitative expression to indicate in a relative manner, that the ice conditions prevailing in an area are such that navigation is not difficult.

Fast ice: Sea ice which is connected either to the coast or to an ice wall, and extends seawards for distances up to 200 miles.

Firn: Old snow which has been compacted into a dense material which is neither snow or ice.

First Year Ice: Sea Ice of not more than one winter's growth, developing from Young Ice; thickness 30 centimetres to 2 metres.

Floe: Any relatively flat piece of sea ice 20 metres or more across. Floes are sub-divided according to horizontal extent as follows:

Giant:	Over 5.4 n. miles across.
Vast:	1-5.4 n. miles across.
Big:	500-2,000 metres across.
Medium:	100-500 metres across.
Small:	20-100 metres across.

Frost smoke: The phenomena of fog-like clouds produced by cold air passing over relatively warm sea water. Generally observed in open water to leeward of a large ice field.

Glacier tongue: That part of a glacier which extends seawards, and is usually floating. In the Antarctic the extension may be measured in tens of miles.

Grease ice: The name given to the ice particles first formed as sea water freezes. These ice particles give the sea an oily appearance.

Growler: A nearly submerged piece of ice frequently greenish in colour, and much smaller than a bergy-bit.

Hummocked ice: Sheet ice which has been broken by pressure and forced into haphazard heaps and ridges.

Iceberg: A large mass of floating ice which has broken away from an ice shelf or from a glacier tongue, and which extends to a height of more than 5 metres above the water surface. (See page 214.)

Ice-blink: The illumination of low clouds by reflected light from a distant ice field.

Ice bound: An area in which navigation is prevented by ice, except possibly with the assistance of an ice-breaker.

Ice-cake: A small floe, less than 20 metres across.

Ice cover: The amount of sea ice present, measured in tenths of the visible surface of the sea covered with ice.

Ice-edge: The boundary between any kind of sea ice and the open sea.

Ice-foot: A narrow band of ice attached to the coast, which persists after fast ice has dispersed.

Ice-front: The perpendicular seaward edge of a floating ice-shelf, varying in height from 2-50 metres or more above sea level.

Ice island: An unusual type of tabular berg found in the Arctic. The height above sea level is about 5 metres and the area may exceed 145 square miles.

Ice limit: The mean location of the ice edge for any particular season, derived from observations over a number of years.

Ice port: An indentation in an ice front where ships can moor alongside to discharge directly on to the ice shelf.

Ice rind: A thin skin of ice formed by the freezing of grease ice on a calm sea surface.

Ice shelf: An ice formation of great thickness, the majority of which is afloat. The horizontal extent is usually considerable, and the surface generally flat or gently undulating.

Ice wall: The seaward edge of a glacier terminating in a steep ice cliff resting on a rock base.

Icing: The accretion of ice on exposed objects.

Lead: A channel of open water in pack ice, through which vessels may navigate.

Level ice: Sheet ice that has not been subjected to pressure or otherwise disturbed, so that the surface is flat.

New ice: A term to describe grease ice, slush, shuga and ice-rind.

Nilas: A thin elastic crust of ice. Has a matt appearance and is up to 10 centimetres in thickness.

Nip: When ice closes up to prevent the passage of a vessel it is said to nip.

Open pack ice: An area of water in which the ice floes are rarely in contact. Ice cover 4/10ths-6/10ths.

Open Water: A large area of freely navigable water in which ice is present in concentrations of less than 1/10th.

Pack ice: A general term to describe any type of sea ice other than fast ice.

Pancake ice: Distinctive, nearly circular, pieces of ice with raised rims, caused by the individual pieces striking each other. Pancake ice varies in size from about 30 centimetres-3 metres across.

Polynya: Any non-linear shaped opening enclosed in ice. Polynyas may contain brash ice or new ice. If it recurs in the same position every year, it is called a Recurring Polynya.

Puddle: A hollow on the surface of sea ice containing water which is usually partially fresh.

Rafted Ice: A type of pressure ice that is caused by one floe riding up on another.

Ram: The underwater extension of a mass of ice beyond its visible boundaries.

Rotten ice: Sea ice that is in an advanced state of decay and is very porous through melting.

Shore lead: A lead between the shore or ice attached to the shore and the floating off-shore pack ice.

Shuga: Small lumps of ice formed from grease ice and spongy white in appearance.

Slush: A mixture of snow and water.

Strip: A long narrow belt of pack ice drifted clear of the main ice area by the wind or current.

Tabular berg: An iceberg with a flat top, usually calved from an ice-shelf formation.

Thaw holes: A generally circular hole through the ice, formed when puddles melt through to the underlying water.

Tide crack: The junction between a fixed ice foot and fast ice which is subject to tidal movement.

Tongue: A temporary tongue-like extension of the ice edge caused by the wind or current.

Very close pack ice: Very little water present, ice cover practically 10/10ths.

Very open pack ice: Considerably more water than ice. Ice cover 1/10th-3/10ths.

Water sky: Dark bands or patches on low clouds, indicating leads and pools in the pack ice.

Weathering: The gradual removal of surface irregularities on pressure-ice by snow falls and alternate melting and freezing.

Young ice: Recently formed level ice, about 10-30 centimetres thick. Usually refers to ice in the stage of development where it is changing from nilas to first year ice.

ICE DISTRIBUTION MAPS

The British Meteorological Office broadcasts each day by radio facsimile a map showing the distribution of sea ice (as observed or estimated) in the North Atlantic and adjacent waters. These maps are intended for immediate operational guidance. Another series of maps is published with an issue depicting the distribution of ice at the end of each month. This map is designed for use as a permanent record in research rather than operational use; the map is not compiled until late data have been received and is published several months after the event.

ICE ILLUSTRATIONS

These photographs are to illustrate some of the ice terms mentioned in this section, and to assist in identification of some of the many types of ice formation.

BERGY BIT

Smoothed and rounded by water erosion

BESET

The ship is trapped in *consolidated pack ice* which is heavily
hummocked

BRASH ICE

FAST ICE

FROST SMOKE

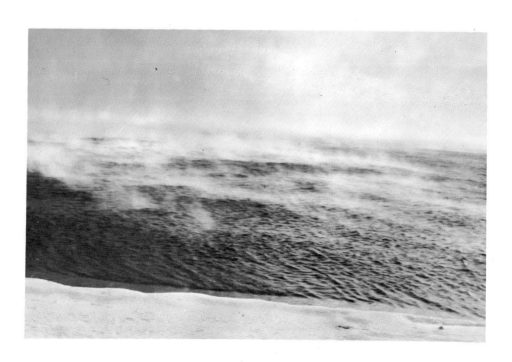

GROWLER

GREASE ICE (Formerly called *frazil ice*)

The oily appearance of the surface indicates the presence of grease ice
which is forming round pieces of *brash ice*

HUMMOCKED ICE

ICEBERG

ICE BLINK

ICE EDGE

ICE FOOT

Ice rind is forming on the sea

ICE FRONT

ICEPORT

ICE WALL

The ice surface behind an ice wall slopes down towards the sea. Rock is often exposed at sea level

ICING

Sea spray frozen on to a ship's superstructure

LEAD

CLOSE PACK ICE

VERY CLOSE PACK ICE

CONSOLIDATED PACK ICE

In the middle distance, amidst *pressure ice,* may be seen an area of *level ice;* this is a frozen *lead* which has not been subjected to pressure

---

OPEN PACK ICE

VERY OPEN PACK ICE

Ice cakes are seen in the foreground

PANCAKE ICE

PUDDLES

RAFTED ICE

Rafting is most commonly found in *new ice.*

RAM

ROTTEN ICE

The *puddles* on the surface of the ice have mostly joined together and, in places, have melted right through the ice

STRIP

The area of ice in the foreground is a small *patch;* in the background a *strip*

SHORE LEAD

TABULAR BERG

YOUNG ICE

The mottled appearance of the ice and the straight edges of the ship's
track cut through it are typical

P

DUTIES OF THE MASTER ON SIGHTING ICE

The International Conference on Safety of Life at Sea, 1960, requires the Master of any British ship to promulgate by all means possible information relating to sightings of dangerous ice and conditions of severe ice accretion. The message is to be in English or International Code, preceded by TTT and sent to all ships in the vicinity, and to the first point on the coast to which communication can be made.

In the case of dangerous ice, the message shall contain the following:
  (i) Type of ice
 (ii) The position of the ice
(iii) G.M.T. and date of observation.

When experiencing conditions of severe icing, the message shall contain:
  (i) G.M.T. and date
 (ii) Air and sea temperatures
(iii) Wind force and direction.

The Merchant Shipping Act of 1932 contains the following reference to navigation near ice. The Master of a British ship when ice is reported on or near his course shall at night either (a) proceed at a moderate speed; or (b) alter course to keep well clear of reported ice and danger area. The penalty for each contravention is a fine not exceeding £100.

THE INTERNATIONAL ICE PATROL

The International Ice Patrol is operated by the United States Coast Guard, the cost being met by contributions from the Signatory Nations to the International Safety Convention. The service operates during the ice season, beginning in late February or early March, and continues until about the end of June. Its primary purpose is to provide mariners of all nationalities with advance information of the extent and limits of icebergs and sea ice in the North Atlantic in the vicinity of the Grand Banks.

To accomplish this object, the U.S. Coast Guard operates surface patrol craft and reconnaissance aircraft with supporting personnel to conduct ice observations. The International Ice Patrol also maintains a central office in New York where all ice data collected is evaluated and analysed. Ice condition forecasts are prepared from the latest information received, and bulletins are broadcast together with details of the actual observed ice conditions. The scheduled broadcasts from the participating Radio Stations are twice daily. Special ice broadcasts preceded by the International Safety Signal TTT are made when considered advisable. There are also daily transmissions of ice conditions by facsimile. For full details of these broadcasts, refer to *Admiralty List of Radio Signals, Volume V.*

Requests for information from ships:—
This is a standing request for shipping to report any ice sighted, and when within Latitudes 40° N. and 50° N. and Longitudes 42° W. and 60° W. to make regular six hourly reports. The six-hourly reports should contain the ship's position, course, speed, air and sea temperature, visibility and wind. The importance of these reports cannot be over-emphasised. They should be addressed to COMINTICEPAT NEW YORK NY, preferably through a Coast Guard Radio Station.

How the information is utilised

Visibility report:
(a) Enables ice observation flights to be planned to avoid areas of low visibility;
(b) Determines when special warnings on ice conditions should be broadcast.

Sea temperature report: Used to construct sea isotherm charts, which are then employed to detect changes in the branches of the Labrador Current, and also to estimate ice deterioration rates.

Wind data: Required for the estimation of the set and drift of ice for forecasting weather for the purpose of planning ice observation flights.

A plot is maintained on all reporting ships, and these ships can then be warned directly when approaching dangerous ice.

A LATE REPORT IS BETTER THAN NO REPORT

Single radio operator ships may find it impracticable to report every six hours. It is therefore suggested that reports are prepared at six-hourly intervals, and held for transmission until the radio operator comes on watch.

Ice Sighting Reports:
To be of maximum use, reports of ice sighted should contain the following information:—
(a) Type of ice sighted (berg, growler, sea ice) and whether a visual or radar sighting;
(b) The position of the *ice*;
(c) Description of the ice (size and shape);
(d) Sea temperature at the point of nearest approach to ice;
(e) Weather and visibility conditions.

Warning:
The International Ice Patrol have conducted tests which have proved that radar cannot provide positive assurance of iceberg detection. Sea water is a better reflector of radar signals than ice, and therefore an iceberg or growler inside the area of "clutter" on the radar screen may not be detected. It was also determined in these tests that the average maximum detection range of a dangerous growler is four miles.

ICE WARNINGS

In sea areas other than those covered by the International Ice Patrol, the following arrangements have been made for the dissemination of information relating to ice conditions.

Eastern Canada: From about mid-December until the end of the ice season, the Canadian Department of Transport provides an ice information service. Advice is provided on recommended routes, ice breaker availability, etc. and the service is operated through three Zone centres.

Zone A comprises Labrador and the South and East Coasts of Newfoundland, and is centred on an Ice Operations Office at St. Johns, Newfoundland.

Zone B comprises the Gulf of St. Lawrence including the Strait of Belle Isle, and is centred on the Ice Operations Office at Dartmouth, N.S.

Zone C comprises the Lower St. Lawrence River and is operated through the Marine Traffic Regulating System which is responsible for all marine traffic in the area. The service is centred on the Marine Information Centre, Montreal, P.Q.
Ice Central is located at Halifax and provides ice advisories and forecasts throughout the ice season. For specialised advice in matters such as routeing, ice-breaker assistance, local ice conditions, etc., the Ice Operations Officer of the appropriate Zone should be contacted.

Canadian Arctic, Hudson Bay and Strait: The Canadian Department of Transport provides a service for these areas, based on an Ice Operations Office at Frobisher Bay, N.W.T. and an Ice Information Office at Churchill, Manitoba. Information available during the Summer navigation season includes ice conditions, advice on routes, icebreaker support and the organisation of convoys when these are necessary.

The Baltic: During the ice season the following countries, Denmark, Finland, East and West Germany, Poland, Norway, Netherlands, Sweden and the U.S.S.R. broadcast via their respective radio stations ice warnings and reports. By agreement, messages are broadcast in a common code known as the **Baltic Ice Code.** Plain language warnings are also broadcast.

Greenland Waters: Ice reporting stations in Greenland used a special code, and ice warnings in this code are broadcast from Radio Angmagssalik (OZL). Ice reports are also broadcast in plain language.
For full details of the Special Code, and the Baltic Ice Code, refer to the Admiralty List of Radio Signals, Volume V.

North West Pacific (Northern Sea of Japan, Bering Sea and adjacent waters):—
Several Russian Radio Stations, including Vladivostock, broadcast ice warnings in plain language Russian and English.

Southern Hemisphere: There are no special ice warnings broadcast from any commercial radio station in the Southern Hemisphere. Any information relating to ice would be included in a **navigational** warnings message.

THE FORMATION OF ICE

Icebergs:

In certain polar regions the heavy snowfalls on high land undergo a process which changes the snow to ice. The ice gravitates into the valleys to become slow-moving rivers of ice known as glaciers. Some of these glaciers may reach the sea and extend seawards as a glacier tongue or ice-shelf. If the water is sufficiently deep the ice floats, and any pieces of ice breaking off the floating section will drift away as icebergs. The colours of icebergs are varied; although basically white many have tinges of blue or green, and others may show streaks of soil or debris indicating their glacial origin.

Iceshelves from which icebergs may be calved do not always originate from glaciers. This is especially so in the Antarctic where an iceshelf may begin as persistent fast ice which increases in thickness due to an accumulation of snow until, after a period of many years, its height may extend to hundreds of feet.

Sea-Ice: *(This ice is formed by the freezing of sea water)*.

The temperature at which sea-water freezes depends on the salt content or salinity. Sea water with an average salinity of about 35 parts per 1,000 freezes in the open sea at a temperature of $-1.9°C$. or $28.6°$ F. The higher the salinity the lower the freezing point. The nearly fresh water of the Baltic freezes at a temperature of $-0.3°$ C. or $31.5°$ F. A second factor involved in the freezing process is the temperature at which the water reaches its maximum density. In the case of sea water, this temperature also depends on the salinity, but for fresh water it is fixed at $4°$ C. or $39.2°$ F.

The Freezing Process:

Surface cooling of water which is at a temperature above that of its maximum density results in an increase of density in the surface layer. This layer now sinks, to be replaced by the less dense water below, and further surface cooling repeats the process, which continues until the whole body of water has reached its maximum density. When fresh water reaches its maximum density, at $4°$ C. or $39.2°$ F., convectional descent ceases and the surface will rapidly cool to the freezing point. However, sea water continues to increase its density as the temperature falls, until the freezing point is reached. Hence, the convectional descent of the surface layer continues much longer, and ice formation is delayed. Sea-ice first forms in shallow water where the delay due to the convectional descent process is least. In very deep water, the cold weather may not last long enough for the process to be completed, and sea-ice will not then form.

ICE LIMITS:

The climatic chart of the oceans in Section F shows the extreme limits reached by sea-ice and icebergs. These extreme limits are the limits beyond which ice has only very occasionally been reported. *The following information relates to the seasonal limits of ice, and is based on average conditions.*

Warning: Ice conditions vary considerably from year to year, and on occasions the extent and severity of the ice in a particular region may differ widely from the average.

Baffin Bay and Davis Strait: There is always a certain amount of ice present in these areas during the summer. From mid-May to late November the eastern side of the Strait is ice-free, with conditions best elsewhere during September.

Hudson Strait: From late July until mid-October the Strait is open to navigation. Hudson, Bay is usually ice-free in August and September.

Gulf of St. Lawrence: The Gulf is normally free of pack ice from the beginning of June until the end of November. In occasional years, icebergs may enter the Gulf through the Belle Isle Strait during this ice-free period. Ice begins to form in December and by the end of January the Gulf is entirely covered. In April the ice begins to clear from the westward.

Belle Isle Strait: The navigation season for the Strait is from mid-June until November. Icebergs may be present during this period.

Cabot Strait: The Strait is normally ice free from the end of May until the end of December. During the period February to April, the extent of the ice is at a maximum. Icebergs or growlers rarely appear in this area.

The Grand Banks: Icebergs are in evidence from early April until the end of June or even later, with the greatest number arriving during May. Pack-ice may be met in the area from January until June. The greatest southerly extent of pack-ice normally occurs during March and April.

Newfoundland: The majority of harbours are closed by ice during the winter. However, the principal port, St. John's, is rarely closed for longer than one week, if at all.

Nova Scotia: Halifax is the only harbour in which navigation is normally unaffected by ice.

United States, East Coast: Although ice may be found in a number of ports and estuaries, navigation is seldom seriously disrupted, even in very severe winters.

Greenland, South Coast: Most of the icebergs are calved from the East Greenland glaciers round Cape Farewell during the months April to August inclusive. It is not unusual to see bergs in this area at any time of the year. The greatest southerly extent occurs during April and May, when icebergs may be sighted 120 miles south of Cape Farewell.

White Sea: The normal navigation season is from July to September.

The Northern Sea Route: This route around the North Coast of the USSR is usually navigable with ice-breaker assistance during August and September. Ice is invariably present throughout this short season.

Baltic Sea: The extreme north of the Gulf of Bothnia is normally icefree only from early July until late October. In most other coastal areas of the Baltic a belt of ice which closes many ports exists during the winter and spring. Off-shore the greater part of the Baltic is ice-free.

Bering Sea: Apart from a few coastal areas, it is usually ice-free from early August until the end of September. During January and February conditions are at their worst and navigation north of 60° N. is impossible.

Sea of Okhotsk: The coast is only ice-free during September. Maximum ice cover occurs during February and March when only a small area in the middle of the sea is ice-free. Towards the end of May the ice begins to break up and by the end of June the greater part of the sea is clear.

Gulf of Tartary: In the northern part, navigation is not normally possible from December until the end of May due to heavy drift ice. In the south, the break up is generally earlier and normal navigation may be resumed by mid-April.

Sea of Japan: Ice forms along the shores of the southern part of the Russian Maritime Province during winter, but navigation is not usually impeded. In the north conditions are more difficult during the period from early January to mid-April.

Japan: During the winter months, the northern and eastern coasts of the island of Hokkaido are mainly ice-bound. Drifting pack ice is generally present to the south of the island.

Yellow Sea: The northern coasts experience a certain amount of ice which attains maximum coverage during January and February.

Ice in the Southern Hemisphere:

The normal trade routes in the southern hemisphere do not extend far enough south for the Antarctic pack ice to become a danger to navigation. The **extreme** northerly limit of pack ice is about Latitude 51° S. in Longitude 45° W. (to the east of the Falkland Islands) and occurs during August and September. In other longitudes the **extreme limit** of pack ice lies near the 56th parallel. Except in the region to the east of the Falkland Islands the **mean limit** is normally much further south.

Icebergs, however, may constitute a danger to navigation in certain longitudes as the **extreme limit** lies much further north than that of pack ice. The seasonal variation of the limit is not marked. Possibly the greatest danger from icebergs exists around Cape Horn and northwards towards the River Plate. In the South Pacific between longitudes 180° and 120° W. icebergs may be encountered throughout the year if proceeding South of the 50th parallel. During the period February to March the **mean limit** of icebergs in the western part of the South Indian Ocean is in the region of the 43rd parallel.

SIGNS INDICATING THE PROXIMITY OF ICE:

Pack Ice: The phenomena of *ice-blink* is a reliable indication of the presence of pack-ice, and is observed before the ice appears over the horizon. The reflected light from the ice appears in the sky above the pack as a characteristic luminous area, which is mainly white if clouds are present, or yellow if the sky is mainly clear. It may on occasions be seen at night. Dark bands or patches in the ice blink indicate leads or pools in the ice.

Another reliable sign of pack-ice is the sudden smoothing of the sea and lessening of the swell, indicating that ice is not far to windward. The edge of pack-ice is frequently shrouded in a fog bank and, if far from land, the appearance of walruses, seals and birds may also indicate the proximity of ice.

Ice-bergs: It is generally agreed that there are no infallible signs to indicate the presence of bergs. A visual sighting is the only absolutely sure way of location and reliance on any other method could prove dangerous. Radar is a useful means of aiding detection, but surprisingly large icebergs under the most favourable conditions may give very poor echoes. Bergy-bits and growlers may pass undetected in heavy "sea clutter". On quiet nights when proceeding at slow speed, vessels have heard the noise of the sea breaking on the base of the iceberg; this however, cannot be relied upon.

ICE BREAKER SERVICES:

Ice-breaker fleets are maintained by the Governments of those maritime nations in which ice is a normal additional winter hazard to navigation. The purpose of these ice-breakers is two-fold; firstly to keep important ports from becoming ice-bound by maintaining navigable channels through the ice; secondly, to escort vessels through the ice to and from those ports as required.

How to obtain the services of an ice-breaker:
When in port and wishing to proceed to sea, the request for ice-breaker assistance should be made to the Harbour Master or local ice-breaker representative, if ice-breaker assistance is required at sea, the request should be made to the Master of the ice-breaker working at the port of destination, or to the nearest coast radio station. The operating areas of each ice-breaker are normally included in the daily **Ice Reports.** As much advance notice as possible should be given of the requirement for the services of an ice-breaker.

Signals between Ice-Breaker and Assisted Vessels:
All vessels being assisted must immediately obey any signals from the ice-breaker. A continuous watch should be kept for these signals, which may be made visually, by whistle or siren, or by radiotelephony. **There is an international code system of signals for use between ice-breaker and assisted vessels; there may be local signals however and the appropriate Admiralty Pilot book should be consulted regarding them.**

Section K

Admiralty Charts

NOTES ON ADMIRALTY CHARTS

GENERAL INFORMATION

Publication

Admiralty charts are published by the Hydrographic Department, Taunton, under the superintendence of the Hydrographer of the Navy. They are available from Admiralty appointed chart agents whose addresses are listed in Volume 1 of the weekly notices to mariners. The charts may be purchased individually, but they are also offered in standard chart folios, each of which covers a particular geographical region of the world. The catalogue of Admiralty charts, published annually, gives the limits of every individual chart as well as the limits of the standard folios. Also included in the catalogue is an index of Admiralty Light Lists and Admiralty Sailing Directions (Pilots). Generally Admiralty charts provide sufficient coverage for safe navigation anywhere in U.K. waters and certain other selected areas. They provide worldwide coverage of charts for oceanic and for coastal navigation and for port approach navigation to the outer limits of pilotage. Charts of other national hydrographic offices may, however, need to be consulted for detailed large scale charts of foreign ports and other inshore areas.

Choice of Chart

The largest scale chart of an area should always be used for navigation, for a number of reasons:-
(1) Greater detail is shown and, in particular, some of the navigation marks and some of the dangers to navigation may not appear on smaller scale charts.
(2) Plotting accuracy for fixing position and for laying off courses and distances will be greater.
(3) When charts are brought up to date from the results of new surveys, it is usually the largest scale charts which are corrected first.
(4) The effects of chart distortion will be minimised.

Metrication

Admiralty charts are in the process of conversion from the representation of depths by fathoms and heights in feet to a representation of both depths and heights in metres. The conversion affects over 3,000 Admiralty charts and is being progressively carried out over a period of some years. During this time the charts which are unconverted will continue to be available in fathoms and feet. Accompanying the change of units, the style of metric charts is changed, notably by the greater use which is made of colour. In addition to the use of blue to indicate shallow water, the colour green is used to indicate areas which dry out at low tide, and yellow is used for land.

Symbols

Symbols printed on Admiralty charts are almost all in accordance with the International Hydrographic Organisation Standard List. A booklet (Styled chart No. 5011) provides a key to the symbols and the abbreviations used on Admiralty charts.

Depths

A sounding on a chart refers to the depth of water below the chart datum at that point, the chart datum being an arbitrary level which, on Admiralty charts, can be taken as a level below which the tide seldom falls. A mariner may therefore assume that the depth of water at a point is generally at least equal to the charted depth, depending upon the state of the tide. The actual level adopted for chart datum is given under the chart title on metric charts.

Soundings are printed in metres or in metres and decimetres for depths of 20 metres or less.

Heights

Banks which dry at low water but are covered at high water are coloured green, and the drying heights are printed in metres and decimetres above the chart datum level. The figures representing drying heights are underlined.

All other heights are given in metres above a level which is mean high water springs when the tide is semi-diurnal, mean higher high water when the tide is diurnal, and mean sea level when the tidal range is insignificant. A mariner may therefore assume that the height of a point above the actual sea level at a given time is generally at least equal to the charted height of the point, but dependent upon the state of the tide.

For spot heights, a dot accompanying the figure, marks the point to which the height applies. The heights of objects represented by a symbol are indicated in brackets against the symbol.

Distances

The principal unit of distance used on Admiralty charts is the sea mile. This is the length of one minute of latitude and is a unit which varies in length from about 1,843 metres at the equator to about 1,862 metres at the poles. The international nautical mile of 1,852 metres is simply the value of the sea mile in 45° latitude but rounded off to the nearest metre. On Mercator charts, the graduation of the latitude scale provides a scale of distance but, because the scale expands as the secant of the latitude, it is important that a section of the scale is used which straddles the mean latitude of the distance being measured.

On very large scale charts or plans, the scale of distance can be taken as sensibly constant. A scale of distance in sea miles and cables is given, a cable being a tenth part of a mile. Also a scale of distance in metres is included.

Directions

The directions of leading lines, sectors of lights, etc. are given with reference to true north and are always given from seawards.

Chart Dimensions

The dimensions of the inner border of a chart are printed in brackets outside the lower border on the right hand side. On metric charts, these dimensions are given in millimetres. On gnomonic and transverse mercator charts, the upper and lower borders may have different dimensions and these are both printed. The latitude and longitude of the inner borders of metric charts are indicated inside the lower left-hand and upper right-hand corners. Distortion of the paper on which charts are printed may arise from a number of causes but is rarely sufficient to be noticeable for navigational purposes. The presence of distortion may be detected by comparing the measured dimensions of a chart with the printed dimensions.

Lattice Charts

Where coverage of a sea area is provided by hyperbolic navigational aids, Admiralty charts of a suitable scale are often available overprinted with a lattice of position lines corresponding to selected readings of the appropriate receiver. Position lines corresponding to intermediate readings may then be interpolated as required. Lattice charts are available for the Consol, Decca Navigator, Loran and Omega systems (see also section P).

CORRECTION OF CHARTS

Methods of Correction

The original publication date of a chart is printed centrally underneath the lower margin. New editions are necessary from time to time when information contained on a chart needs substantial updating. The date of the new edition is printed to the right of the publication date and all old copies of the chart should then be cancelled and taken out of service. Small corrections usually originate from Admiralty Notices to Mariners which are supplied in weekly editions for the use of ships. These corrections should be made in waterproof violet ink and the year and number of the correction should be entered under the heading "small corrections" underneath the lower margin on the left-hand side of the chart. e.g.-

Small Corrections, 1979 — 812 — 906, 1980 — 417, etc.

Certain small corrections which are considered to be of some use to the mariner but not essential for the safety of navigation may be incorporated on a chart when it is reprinted but not promulgated as a notice to mariners. Since 1972, such corrections have been made on those Admiralty charts which are considered to be the primary published charts for a particular area. Each such correction is noted against the appropriate year by numbers representing the day and the month in brackets, e.g.:-
Small Corrections, 1979 — [20.4]

Inserting Small Corrections

Ordinary small corrections should, as has already been mentioned, be made in waterproof violet ink. Clarity and neatness are important, and the standard symbols and abbreviations should always be used. Any marks to be expunged should be neatly crossed through and no attempt should be made to erase them. When a number of charts are affected by a notice to mariners the full information should first be entered on the chart with the largest scale. On the other affected charts, the amount of detail included should be similar to that already shown on the charts.

In general it will be found that large scale charts show all the detail that is necessary for safe navigation in an area. Charts of intermediate scale, designed for coastal navigation, give details of the lights and buoys required for landfall and for offshore passages. Lights and buoys within harbours and channels are omitted. The information provided against marked lights decreases as the chart scale decreases, the height of the light being omitted first, then the period, then the group characteristic and lastly the range of the light. On small scale oceanic charts, lights are simply indicated by a star and a magenta flare, and only lights which have a range of 15 miles or more are included.

When extensive amendment to detail is required to a section of a chart, the correction may be issued in the form of a block for pasting onto the chart. Owing to distortion, it may not be possible to locate a block so that it fits the charted features along all edges. In such cases, the block should be located so that the best fit is achieved with respect to the most important navigational features.

Noting Temporary or Preliminary Notices

Corrections resulting from temporary or preliminary notices to mariners should be entered on charts in pencil. The year and number of the notice should be noted, also in pencil, against the correction and again beneath the listed small corrections. Corrections from temporary notices should be erased when they are cancelled and corrections from preliminary notices should be erased when they are replaced by the corresponding permanent correction. It should be remembered that charts supplied by the Hydrographic Department or through Admiralty Chart Depots or Agents are not corrected from temporary or preliminary notices to mariners, although they are, of course, corrected from the standard notices to mariners.

CAUTION IN THE USE OF CHARTS

Reliability of Charts

It must be borne in mind that charts can never be perfect, not only because of possible deficiencies in the original surveys, but also because of changes in charted features and particularly in the form of the sea bed which tend to make a chart out of date as soon as it is printed. Some indication of the reliability of a chart may be gained from a consideration of its scale. The largest scale chart of an area may well be to the same scale as the original survey, and the survey scale in turn governs the thoroughness with which the survey was conducted. In particular, the spacing of lines of soundings in a survey is dependent on the survey scale and is usually chosen so that the lines are about 5 millimetres apart when plotted. On coastal charts, based on surveys to a scale of perhaps 1:50,000 the distance between lines of soundings is thus of the order of: 0.005 x 50,000 = 250 metres so that a steeply rising shoal, a wreck, or a pinnacle of rock may easily be missed.

To allow a reasonable safety margin, it is recommended that ships of average ocean going size should not approach a rocky coastline within the 20 metre depth contour unless special precautions are taken. Deep draught ships should exercise even greater caution and, where the sea bed is charted as uneven and where the quality of the original survey is suspect, it is recommended that such ships should take great care whenever they are required to navigate within the 200 metre depth contour.

The date of the surveys on which a chart is based also gives an indication of its reliability. Generally, surveys dated before the middle of the nineteenth century were conducted with limited equipment and techniques, and charts based on these should not be depended upon as being either accurate or complete. Prior to 1935, soundings were generally based on leadline methods so that dangers could be missed between casts as well as between lines of soundings. Incomplete surveying of an area may be indicated by scattered and irregularly spaced soundings and by incomplete depth contours. Mariners should, of course, navigate in such areas with extreme caution.

Deep Draught Routes

Early nineteenth century surveys were conducted at a time when ships typically had draughts of up to 5 or 6 metres and there was therefore little need for a close examination of sea bed contours in areas where depths were greater than this. As the size of ships increased, closer attention was paid to deeper sea areas but it has only been since about the early nineteen sixties that the needs of ships with draughts of greater than 15 metres have become important.

Current hydrographic resources are not sufficient to allow a rapid and detailed re-survey of every sea area to the greater depths now required. Nevertheless, a great deal of effort has been deployed internationally to make more detailed surveys of some of the more important routes used by deep draught vessels. When navigating such vessels through critical areas, a safe margin must be allowed for under keel clearance, and designated deep draught routes should always be followed where available. The decision as to what constitutes a safe under keel clearance must be made in relation to a number of factors which will include not only an assessment of the reliability and completeness of the charted soundings, but also consideration of such factors as increase of draught due to rolling and pitching, squat effects, adverse effects on ship manoeuvrability due to shallow water and the possibility of negative surges or inaccuracies in predicted tidal heights. The presence of sandwaves or other possible causes of alteration of soundings since the survey date should also be taken into account.

Cautionary Note

The mariner makes navigational decisions on the basis of information from a large number of sources. Direct information is provided by his senses, principally of sight and hearing. Secondary information is provided from instruments such as log, compass and position fixing aids when the primary information cannot be directly sensed because of its form or remoteness. Stored information is available from the mariner's memory of his accumulated experience and from publications of which the chart is one of the most versatile and useful sources.

Like any other navigation aid, charts are subject to errors although these are very seldom of navigational significance. Like any other source of stored information, charts may also contain out of date items although the correction facilities are such that these items are not likely to persist for long periods. In the day to day management of his ship, the mariner should use the maximum possible information from all sources in order to arrive at optimal navigational decisions. In this context, the soundings printed on charts are a much under used source of information and, in coastal waters, the echo sounder should always be used to check positions found from the intersection of only two position lines. The prudent navigator makes the maximum use of all the information presented to him on his charts whilst at the same time bearing in mind its possible limitations.

Section L

Harmonic Tidal Prediction

HARMONIC TIDAL PREDICTION
Vol. II (Atlantic & Indian Ocean) and Vol. III (Pacific Ocean & Adjacent Seas)

General
These tables are designed for use with the Admiralty Tide Tables (A.T.T.) Vol. II (Atlantic and Indian Ocean) and Vol. III (Pacific Ocean and Adjacent Seas) and are especially useful for finding heights of the tide at times other than those of H.W. and L.W. They are based on the Admiralty method of prediction by use of harmonic constants, but they eliminate the need for any special plotting diagrams or scales.

Four tidal constituents are used—M_2, S_2, K_1, and O_1, each of which makes its own contribution towards the existing height of the tide at any given time. For the purpose of explaining how to use the tables, they may be regarded, very briefly and simply, as follows:

M_2 and S_2—the tidal effects resulting from the *semi-diurnal* tractive forces of the Moon and Sun respectively.

K_1—the tidal effect of the combined average *diurnal* forces of the Sun and Moon.

O_1—the effect of the principal variation in the Moon's *diurnal* force.

INSTRUCTIONS FOR USING THE TABLES

The extracts from the A.T.T.s required for the working of these examples are given on page 265.

Example 1: To construct a tidal curve showing the heights of the tide from 0 to 24 hours at Port Alpha on 17th February.

Procedure
(Working is shown on page 242)

COMPLETE BLOCK A

(1) The General Index, at the back of the A.T.T.s gives the rotation number of Port Alpha as 3071.

(2) Enter A.T.T. Part II with No. 3071, Port Alpha, and extract height of mean level (M.L.) under Z_0 and the values given for $g°$ and H under M_2, S_2, K_1, and O_1. Write these figures down in Block A as shown on page 242.

(3) Obtain the correction for seasonal change from the bottom of the A.T.T. page and apply it to the height of M.L. to determine the corrected M.L.

(4) Enter A.T.T. Part I, Table VII for 17th February and copy down (as shown in the appropriate columns) the angles and factors given therein.

(5) Complete the third line of Block A by adding the angles (subtract 360° if the result exceeds 360°), and multiplying H by the factor. Label the resultant angles as m, s, k and o, as appropriate. H, when multiplied by the factor, gives the maximum (High Water) amplitude for the constituent. *The Amplitude for any given time is the rise or fall of the tide from M.L. at that time.*

(6) Turn to O/Nav. Table I and look for the **nearest tabulated value** to m (146°) in the M_2 column. Write down the corresponding H.W. time which is given in the left-hand column of the table, abreast of the nearest angle found. This time (5 hours) is the approximate Zone Time at which the H.W. of the M_2 constituent occurs.

(7) Still in Table I, look for the **nearest tabulated value** to s (128°) in the S_2 column. The nearest is 135° and the corresponding time of H.W. is 4.5 hours. Repeat this procedure with the K_1 and O_1 constituents.

COMPLETE BLOCK B

(8) Turn to O/Nav. Table II.

Some explanation of this table is necessary before proceeding further:

(a) The amplitudes (rise or fall of tide from M.L.) are tabulated without a decimal point, which must be inserted as appropriate when using the table.

(b) Each amplitude column is headed by a maximum (H.W.) value, and this is repeated below on the line which is marked H.W. at the sides.

(c) The figures in the columns at the sides of the page, given at half-hourly intervals, are hours before or after H.W.; but when first entering the table it is necessary in Example 1 and 2 to begin by extracting information for the period BEFORE H.W. In Example 1, the Zone Time of the M_2 H.W. is 5 hours. By entering Table II with 5 hours at the side and amplitude 6.5 m. (65) at the top, we obtain — 5.3 m. (This is the M_2 amplitude for 5 hours BEFORE H.W., i.e. for 0 hours Zone Time.) By working UP the column, the following information can be extracted:

At 4 hours before H.W. (Zone Time 1 hour) Amplitude	=	*−2.9 m.*
At 3 hours before H.W. (Zone Time 2 hours) Amplitude	=	*+0.3 m.*
and so on, until, at the top of the table—		
At time of H.W. (Zone Time 5 hours) Amplitude	=	*6.5 m.*

To obtain amplitudes AFTER H.W., continue DOWN the column:

At 1 hour AFTER H.W. (Zone Time 6 hours) Amplitude	=	*5.7 m.*
At 2 hours AFTER H.W. (Zone Time 7 hours) Amplitude	=	*3.4 m.*
and so on, until—		
At 19 hours AFTER H.W. (Zone Time 24 hours) Amplitude	=	*−6.4 m.*

Complete column (1) of Block B by copying the Amplitudes (obtained as described above) from Table II, and writing each against its appropriate hour.

(9) Complete columns (2), (4) and (5) of Block B from Tables III, IV, and V, respectively. The procedure for each one is the same as that described for column (1).

(10) Complete column (3) by adding the Amplitudes under M_2 and S_2 for each hour.

(11) Complete column (6) by adding K_1 and O_1 Amplitudes for each hour.

(12) Complete column (7) by adding together the values in columns (3) and (6) for each hour.

(13) Complete column (9) by adding the corrected height of M.L. (8.7) to each of the hourly values in column (7).

There being no Shallow Water corrections for Port Alpha, column 9 gives the height of the tide for each hour of the day. The application of Shallow Water corrections is shown in Example 2.

(14) Plot, on a piece of graph paper, the heights of the tide against Zone Time, and draw a smooth curve through the points so obtained.

Working for Example 1

17th February
PORT ALPHA
A.T.T. Part II 3071

Harmonic Constants

Part I. Table VII

O/Nav. Table I
(nearest tabulated time)

BLOCK A

M.L. Zo m.	TIDAL CONSTITUENTS							
	M_2		S_2		K_1		O_1	
	g°	H. m.	g°	H. m.	g°	H. m.	g°	H. m.
9.1	072	6.0	110	2.0	209	0.9	192	0.7
	074	1.08	018	1.20	324	1.12	126	1.31
−.4	146	6.5	128	2.4	533	1.0	318	0.9
8.7					360			
					123			
Cor.M.L	**m**	Amp.	**s**	Amp.	**k**	Amp.	**o**	Amp.
H.W.	5 hrs.		4.5 hrs.		11.5 hrs.		23 hrs.	

BLOCK B

Zone Time hrs.	(1) Table II M_2 m.	(2) Table III S_2 m.	(3) Sum M_2+S_2 m.	(4) Table IV K_1 m.	(5) Table V O_1 m.	(6) Sum K_1+O_1 m.	(7) Sum (3)+(6) m.	(8) Cor. M.L. m.	(9) Ht. of Tide (7)+(8) m.	(10) Shallow Water Cor. m.	(11) Cor. Ht. m.
0	−5.3	−1.7	−7.0	−1.0	0.7	−0.3	−7.3		1.4		
1	−2.9	−0.6	−3.5	−0.9	0.5	−0.4	−3.9		4.8		
2	+0.3	+0.6	+0.9	−0.8	0.3	−0.5	+0.4		9.1		
3	3.4	1.7	5.1	−0.6	0.1	−0.5	4.6		13.3		
4	5.7	2.3	8.0	−0.4	−0.1	−0.5	7.5		16.2		
5	6.5	2.3	8.8	−0.1	−0.3	−0.4	8.4		17.1		
6	5.7	1.7	7.4	+0.1	−0.5	−0.4	7.0		15.7		
7	3.4	0.6	4.0	0.4	−0.7	−0.3	3.7		12.4		
8	0.3	−0.6	−0.3	0.6	−0.8	−0.2	−0.5		8.2		
9	−2.9	−1.7	−4.6	0.8	−0.9	−0.1	−4.7		4.0		
10	−5.3	−2.3	−7.6	0.9	−0.9	0	−7.6		1.1		
11	−6.5	−2.3	−8.8	1.0	−0.9	+0.1	−8.7		0	Nil	
12	−6.0	−1.7	−7.7	1.0	−0.8	0.2	−7.5	8.7	1.2		
13	−4.1	−0.6	−4.7	0.9	−0.7	0.2	−4.5		4.2		
14	−1.0	+0.6	−0.4	0.8	−0.6	0.2	−0.2		8.5		
15	+2.2	1.7	+3.9	0.6	−0.4	0.2	+4.1		12.8		
16	4.9	2.3	7.2	0.4	−0.1	0.3	7.5		16.2		
17	6.4	2.3	8.7	0.1	+0.1	0.2	8.9		17.6		
18	6.2	1.7	7.9	−0.1	0.3	0.2	8.1		16.8		
19	4.5	0.6	5.1	−0.4	0.5	0.1	5.2		13.9		
20	1.7	−0.6	1.1	−0.6	0.6	0	1.1		9.8		
21	−1.6	−1.7	−3.3	−0.8	0.8	0	−3.3		5.4		
22	−4.4	−2.3	−6.7	−0.9	0.9	0	−6.7		2.0		
23	−6.2	−2.3	−8.5	−1.0	0.9	−0.1	−8.6		0.1		
24	−6.4	−1.7	−8.1	−1.0	0.9	−0.1	−8.2		0.5		

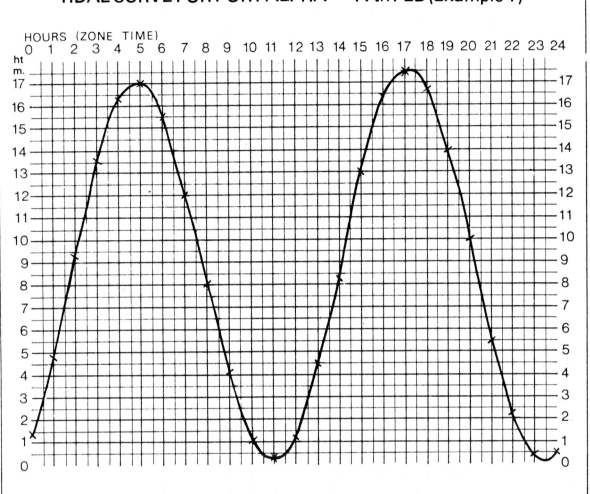

TIDAL CURVE FOR PORT ALPHA — 17th FEB (Example 1)

HOURS (ZONE TIME)

Example 2: Construct a tidal curve showing heights of the tide from 0 to 24 hours on 11th April, at Port Beta.

The A.T.T. give a table of shallow water corrections for Port Beta (No. 2280) on the same page as that on which the harmonic constants are found. (See relevant "Extracts" on p. 265.)

Procedure
(Working is shown on page 245.)

(1) The order of work is identically the same as that for Example 1 until column (9) of Block B is completed.

(2) Complete column (10) of Block B, as follows:

(i) Look in column (3) of Block B to determine the approximate time of the first semi-diurnal H.W. (SL. H.W.(1)). In this example, the *first semi-diurnal* H.W. (height 3.4 m.) is at Zone Time 4 hours.

(ii) Enter the shallow water correction table on the line AT (the time of first semi-diurnal H.W.) and, by interpolating between 0316 hours and 0623 hours, the correction (+0.1) is determined for 0400 hours. Write this in column (10) abreast of 4 hours.

(iii) Similarly, the corrections for 5, 6, 7, 8, and 9 hours are taken from abreast of AT + 1, +2, +3, +4, and +5 respectively. 10 hours is 6 hours before the second H.W. (SL. H.W.(2)), and is the same as AT –6 hours; 11 hours is AT –5 hours . . . and so on.

(3) Complete column (11) by applying the shallow water corrections, according to their signs, to the heights in column 9.

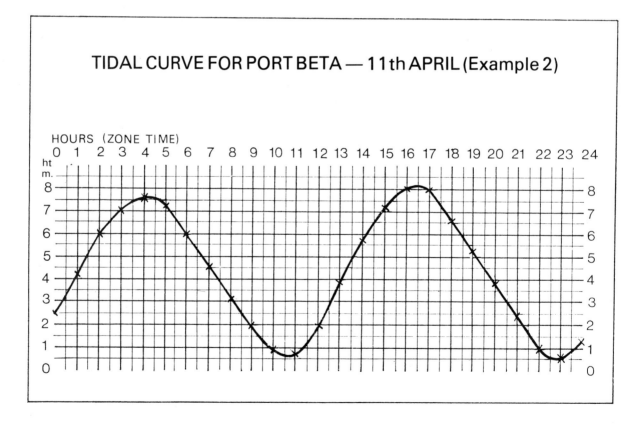

TIDAL CURVE FOR PORT BETA — 11th APRIL (Example 2)

BLOCK A

11th April — rendered as:

11th April
PORT BETA
A.T.T. Part II 2280

Harmonic Constants

Part I. Table VII

O/Nav. Table I
(nearest tabulated time)

M.L. Zo m.	TIDAL CONSTITUENTS							
	M_2		S_2		K_1		O_1	
	g°	H.m.	g°	H.m.	g°	H.m.	g°	H.m.
4·3	161	2·8	185	0·8	217	0·3	208	0·3
0	305	1·08	354	1·30	240	0·92	051	1·31
	466	3·0	539	1·04	457	·28	259	·39
	360		360		360			
4·3 Cor.M.L	106 m	Amp.	179 s	Amp.	097 K	Amp.	o	Amp.
H.W.	3·5 hrs.		6 hrs.		6·5 hrs.		18·5 hrs.	

BLOCK B

Zone Time hrs.	(1) Table II M_2 m.	(2) Table III S_2 m.	(3) Sum M_2+S_2 m.	(4) Table IV K_1 m.	(5) Table V O_1 m.	(6) Sum K_1+O_1 m.	(7) Sum (3)+(6) m.	(8) Cor. M.L. m.	(9) Ht. of Tide (7)+(8) m.	(10) Shallow Water Cor. m.	(11) Cor. Ht. m.
0	−0·6	−1·0	−1·6	0	−0·1	−0·1	−1·7	+	2·6	−0·3	2·3
1	+0·9	−0·9	0	0	−0·2	−0·2	−0·2	4·3	4·1	0	4·1
2	2·2	−0·5	+1·7	0·1	−0·3	−0·2	+1·5		5·8	+0·2	6·0
3	2·9	0	2·9	0·2	−0·3	−0·1	2·8		7·1	+0·1	7·2
4	2·9	+0·5	3·4	0·2	−0·4	−0·2	3·2		7·5	+0·1	7·6
5	2·2	0·9	3·1	0·3	−0·4	−0·1	3·0		7·3	+0·1	7·4
6	0·9	1·0	1·9	0·3	−0·4	−0·1	1·8		6·1	−0·1	6·0
7	−0·6	0·9	0·3	0·3	−0·4	−0·1	0·2		4·5	0	4·5
8	−1·9	0·5	−1·4	0·3	−0·3	0	−1·4		2·9	+0·3	3·2
9	−2·8	0	−2·8	0·2	−0·3	−0·1	−2·9		1·4	+0·5	1·9
10	−3·0	−0·5	−3·5	0·2	−0·2	0	−3·5		0·8	+0·1	0·9
11	−2·4	−0·4	−3·3	0·1	−0·1	0	−3·3		1·0	−0·3	0·7
12	−1·2	−1·0	−2·2	0	0	0	−2·2		2·1	−0·3	1·8
13	+0·3	−0·9	−0·6	0	+0·1	+0·1	−0·5		3·8	0	3·8
14	1·7	−0·5	+1·2	−0·1	+0·2	+0·1	+1·3		5·6	+0·2	5·8
15	2·7	0	2·7	−0·2	0·3	0·1	2·8		7·1	+0·1	7·2
16	3·0	+0·5	3·5	−0·2	0·3	0·1	3·6		7·9	+0·1	8·0
17	2·6	0·9	3·5	−0·3	0·4	0·1	3·6		7·9	+0·1	8·0
18	1·5	1·0	2·5	−0·3	0·4	0·1	2·6		6·9	−0·1	6·8
19	0	0·9	0·9	−0·3	0·4	0·1	1·0		5·3	0	5·3
20	−1·4	0·5	−0·9	−0·3	0·4	0·1	−0·8		3·5	+0·3	3·8
21	−2·5	0	−2·5	−0·2	0·3	0·1	−2·4		1·9	+0·5	2·4
22	−3·0	−0·5	−3·5	−0·2	0·3	0·1	−3·4		0·9	+0·1	1·0
23	−2·7	−0·9	−3·6	−0·1	0·2	0·1	−3·5		0·8	−0·3	0·5
24	−1·8	−1·0	−2·8	0	0·1	0·1	−2·7		1·6	−0·3	1·3

Example 3: Construct a tidal curve showing the heights of the tide at Port Gamma, from 1100 to 1700 hours, Zone Time, on 11th May. From your curve determine the following;

    (a) The time and height of the p.m. H.W.
    (b) Between which times (within the limits of the curve) there will be more than 12 metres of water above Chart Datum.
    (c) The height of the tide at 11.30 hours.

Relevant Extracts from A.T.T.s are seen on page 265.

NOTE: In this example, the M_2 H.W. is at 2.5 hours—so 1100 hours is 8.5 hours AFTER H.W. Table II, therefore, is entered first with 8.5 hours to obtain the amplitude; amplitudes for the succeeding hours are found by moving DOWN the column. Similarly, Table III is entered with 7 hours AFTER H.W.; but Table IV must be entered at 6 hours BEFORE H.W. and amplitude read by moving UP the column.

Working for Example 3. (A page from the Navigator's work book)

PORT GAMMA (3850) 11ᵗʰ May,

ML	M_2		S_2		K_1		O_1		
m	°	m	°	m	°	m	°	m	
7.5	108	3.7	134	2.0	048	0.3	041	0.3	
0	320	115	342	·99	207	1.35	096	1·41	
7.5	428	42	476	2.0	255	·40	137	·42	
	360		360						
	068		116						
HW.	2·5 hrs		4 hrs		17 hrs		10 hrs		

ZT	M_2	S_2	Sum	K_1	O_1	Sum	SUM	ML	Height
11	−1·7	−1·7	−3·4	0	0·4	0·4	−3·0	+7·5	4·5
12	+0·4	−1·0	−0·6	0·1	0·4	0·5	−0·1		7·4
13	2·4	0	+2·4	0·2	0·3	0·5	+2·9		10·4
14	3·8	+1·0	4·8	0·3	0·2	0·5	5·3		12·8
15	4·2	1·7	5·9	0·3	0·1	0·4	6·3		13·8
16	3·6	2·0	5·6	0·4	0	0·4	6·0		13·5
17	2·1	1·7	3·8	0·4	−0·1	0·3	4·1		11·6

Ht. ZONE TIME hours →

HW at 1510 hrs — Ht. 13·9m

Ht. of Tide 12m above CD is from 1340 until 1650 hrs

Ht. of Tide at 1130 hrs = 6·0m

TABLES FOR HARMONIC TIDAL PREDICTION

TABLE I

Time of H.W.	M₂	S₂	K₁	O₁
Hours	°	°	°	°
0	0	0	0	0
0·5	14	15	8	7
1	29	30	15	14
1·5	43	45	23	21
2	58	60	30	28
2·5	72	75	38	35
3	87	90	45	42
3·5	101	105	53	49
4	116	120	60	56
4·5	130	135	68	63
5	145	150	75	70
5·5	159	165	83	77
6	174	180	90	84
6·5	188	195	98	91
7	203	210	105	98
7·5	217	225	113	105
8	232	240	120	112
8·5	246	255	128	119
9	261	270	135	125
9·5	275	285	143	132
10	290	300	150	139
10·5	304	315	158	146
11	319	330	165	153
11·5	333	345	173	160
12	348	360	180	167
12·5	362	—	188	174
13	—	—	196	181
13·5	—	—	203	188
14	—	—	211	195
14·5	—	—	218	202
15	—	—	226	209
15·5	—	—	233	216
16	—	—	241	223
16·5	—	—	248	230
17	—	—	256	237
17·5	—	—	263	244
18	—	—	271	251
18·5	—	—	278	258
19	—	—	286	265
19·5	—	—	293	272
20	—	—	301	279
20·5	—	—	308	286
21	—	—	316	293
21·5	—	—	323	300
22	—	—	331	307
22·5	—	—	338	314
23	—	—	346	321
23·5	—	—	353	328
24	—	—	361	335
24·5	—	—	—	342
25	—	—	—	349
25·5	—	—	—	356
26	—	—	—	363

HARMONIC TIDAL PREDICTION

TABLE II

Hours before or after H.W.	Semidiurnal Constituent M₂ AMPLITUDE (insert decimal point as appropriate)																	Hours before or after H.W.
	2	4	6	8	10	12	14	16	18	20	22	24	26	28	30	32	34	
HW.	2	4	6	8	10	12	14	16	18	20	22	24	26	28	30	32	34	HW.
0·5	2	4	6	8	10	12	14	15	17	19	21	23	25	27	29	31	33	0·5
1	2	3	5	7	9	10	12	14	16	17	19	21	23	24	26	28	30	1
1·5	1	3	4	6	7	9	10	12	13	15	16	17	19	20	22	23	25	1·5
2	1	2	3	4	5	6	7	8	10	11	12	13	14	15	16	17	18	2
2·5	1	1	2	2	3	4	4	5	5	6	7	7	8	8	9	10	10	2·5
3	0	0	0	0	1	1	1	1	1	1	1	1	1	1	2	2	2	3
3·5	0	-1	-1	-2	-2	-2	-3	-3	-4	-4	-4	-5	-5	-6	-6	-6	-7	3·5
4	-1	-2	-3	-3	-4	-5	-6	-7	-8	-9	-10	-10	-11	-12	-13	-14	-15	4
4·5	-1	-3	-4	-5	-6	-8	-9	-10	-12	-13	-14	-16	-17	-18	-19	-21	-22	4·5
5	-2	-3	-5	-7	-8	-10	-11	-13	-15	-16	-18	-20	-21	-23	-25	-26	-28	5
5·5	-2	-4	-6	-7	-9	-11	-13	-15	-17	-19	-21	-22	-24	-26	-28	-30	-32	5·5
6	-2	-4	-6	-8	-10	-12	-14	-16	-18	-20	-22	-24	-26	-28	-30	-32	-34	6
6·5	-2	-4	-6	-8	-10	-12	-14	-16	-18	-20	-22	-24	-26	-28	-30	-32	-34	6·5
7	-2	-4	-6	-7	-9	-11	-13	-15	-17	-18	-20	-22	-24	-26	-28	-29	-31	7
7·5	-2	-3	-5	-6	-8	-10	-11	-13	-14	-16	-17	-19	-21	-22	-24	-25	-27	7·5
8	-1	-2	-4	-5	-6	-7	-9	-10	-11	-12	-14	-15	-16	-17	-19	-20	-21	8
8·5	-1	-2	-2	-3	-4	-5	-6	-6	-7	-8	-9	-10	-10	-11	-12	-13	-14	8·5
9	0	-1	-1	-1	-2	-2	-2	-3	-3	-3	-3	-4	-4	-4	-5	-5	-5	9
9·5	0	0	1	1	1	1	1	1	2	2	2	2	2	3	3	3	3	9·5
10	1	1	2	3	3	4	5	5	6	7	7	8	9	10	10	11	12	10
10·5	1	2	3	5	6	7	8	9	10	11	12	14	15	16	17	18	19	10·5
11	2	3	5	6	8	9	11	12	14	15	17	18	20	21	23	24	26	11
11·5	2	4	5	7	9	11	13	14	16	18	20	21	23	25	27	29	30	11·5
12	2	4	6	8	10	12	14	16	18	20	22	23	25	27	29	31	33	12
12·5	2	4	6	8	10	12	14	16	18	20	22	24	26	28	30	32	34	12·5
13	2	4	6	8	10	11	13	15	17	19	21	23	25	27	29	31	33	13
13·5	2	3	5	7	9	10	12	14	15	17	19	21	22	24	26	27	29	13·5
14	1	3	4	6	7	8	10	11	13	14	15	17	18	20	21	22	24	14
14·5	1	2	3	4	5	6	7	8	9	10	11	12	13	14	15	16	17	14·5
15	1	1	2	2	3	3	4	4	5	5	6	6	7	7	8	8	9	15
15·5	0	0	0	0	0	0	0	0	0	0	0	0	0	0	0	0	0	15·5
16	0	-1	-1	-2	-2	-3	-3	-4	-4	-5	-5	-6	-6	-7	-7	-8	-8	16
16·5	-1	-2	-3	-4	-5	-6	-7	-8	-9	-10	-11	-12	-13	-14	-15	-16	-17	16·5
17	-1	-3	-4	-5	-7	-8	-9	-11	-12	-14	-15	-16	-18	-19	-20	-22	-23	17
17·5	-2	-3	-5	-7	-8	-10	-12	-13	-15	-17	-18	-20	-22	-24	-25	-27	-29	17·5
18	-2	-4	-6	-8	-9	-11	-13	-15	-17	-19	-21	-23	-25	-27	-28	-30	-32	18
18·5	-2	-4	-6	-8	-10	-12	-14	-16	-18	-20	-22	-24	-26	-28	-30	-32	-34	18·5
19	-2	-4	-6	-8	-10	-12	-14	-16	-18	-20	-22	-24	-26	-28	-29	-31	-33	19
19·5	-2	-4	-5	-7	-9	-11	-13	-14	-16	-18	-20	-22	-24	-25	-27	-29	-31	19·5
20	-2	-3	-5	-6	-8	-9	-11	-12	-14	-15	-17	-18	-20	-22	-23	-25	-26	20
20·5	-1	-2	-4	-5	-6	-7	-8	-9	-11	-12	-13	-14	-15	-16	-18	-19	-20	20·5
21	-1	-1	-2	-3	-4	-4	-5	-6	-7	-7	-8	-9	-9	-10	-11	-12	-12	21
21·5	0	0	-1	-1	-1	-1	-2	-2	-2	-2	-3	-3	-3	-3	-4	-4	-4	21·5
22	0	1	1	1	1	2	2	2	2	3	3	3	3	4	4	4	5	22
22·5	1	2	2	3	4	5	5	6	7	8	8	9	10	11	11	12	13	22·5
23	1	2	4	5	6	7	8	10	11	12	13	14	16	17	18	19	20	23
23·5	2	3	5	6	8	9	11	12	14	16	17	19	20	22	23	25	26	23·5
24	2	4	5	7	9	11	13	15	16	18	20	22	24	26	27	29	31	24
24·5	2	4	6	8	10	12	14	16	18	20	22	24	26	28	30	32	33	24·5
25	2	4	6	8	10	12	14	16	18	20	22	24	26	28	30	32	34	25
	2	4	6	8	10	12	14	16	18	20	22	24	26	28	30	32	34	

TABLE II　　　　　　　　　　　　　　　　　HARMONIC TIDAL PREDICTION

Hours before or after H.W.	Semidiurnal Constituent M₂																	Hours before or after H.W.
	AMPLITUDE (insert decimal point as appropriate)																	
	36	38	40	42	44	46	48	50	52	54	56	58	60	62	64	66	68	
HW.	36	38	40	42	44	46	48	50	52	54	56	58	60	62	64	66	68	HW.
0·5	35	37	39	41	43	45	46	48	50	52	54	56	58	60	62	64	66	0·5
1	31	33	35	37	38	40	42	44	45	47	49	51	52	54	56	58	59	1
1·5	26	28	29	30	32	33	35	36	38	39	41	42	44	45	46	48	49	1·5
2	19	20	21	22	23	24	25	27	28	29	30	31	32	33	34	35	36	2
2·5	11	11	12	13	13	14	14	15	16	16	17	17	18	19	19	20	20	2·5
3	2	2	2	2	2	2	3	3	3	3	3	3	3	3	3	4	4	3
3·5	−7	−8	−8	−8	−9	−9	−10	−10	−10	−11	−11	−12	−12	−12	−13	−13	−13	3·5
4	−16	−17	−17	−18	−19	−20	−21	−22	−23	−24	−24	−25	−26	−27	−28	−29	−30	4
4·5	−23	−25	−26	−27	−29	−30	−31	−32	−34	−35	−36	−38	−39	−40	−42	−43	−44	4·5
5	−29	−31	−33	−34	−36	−38	−39	−41	−43	−44	−46	−47	−49	−51	−52	−54	−56	5
5·5	−34	−36	−37	−39	−41	−43	−45	−47	−49	−51	−52	−54	−56	−58	−60	−62	−64	5·5
6	−36	−38	−40	−42	−44	−46	−48	−50	−52	−54	−56	−58	−60	−62	−64	−66	−68	6
6·5	−36	−38	−40	−42	−44	−46	−47	−49	−51	−53	−55	−57	−59	−61	−63	−65	−67	6·5
7	−33	−35	−37	−39	−41	−42	−44	−46	−48	−50	−52	−53	−55	−57	−59	−61	−63	7
7·5	−29	−30	−32	−33	−35	−37	−38	−40	−41	−43	−44	−46	−48	−49	−51	−52	−54	7·5
8	−22	−23	−25	−26	−27	−28	−30	−31	−32	−33	−35	−36	−37	−38	−40	−41	−42	8
8·5	−14	−15	−16	−17	−18	−18	−19	−20	−21	−22	−22	−23	−24	−25	−26	−26	−27	8·5
9	−6	−6	−6	−7	−7	−7	−8	−8	−8	−9	−9	−9	−10	−10	−10	−10	−11	9
9·5	3	4	4	4	4	4	4	5	5	5	5	5	6	6	6	6	6	9·5
10	12	13	14	14	15	16	16	17	18	18	19	20	20	21	22	22	23	10
10·5	20	21	23	24	25	26	27	28	29	30	32	33	34	35	36	37	38	10·5
11	27	29	30	32	33	35	36	38	39	41	42	44	45	47	48	50	51	11
11·5	32	34	36	38	39	41	43	45	46	48	50	52	54	55	57	59	61	11·5
12	35	37	39	41	43	45	47	49	51	53	55	57	59	61	63	65	66	12
12·5	36	38	40	42	44	46	48	50	52	54	56	58	60	62	64	66	68	12·5
13	34	36	38	40	42	44	46	48	50	52	54	56	57	59	61	63	65	13
13·5	31	32	34	36	38	39	41	43	44	46	48	50	51	53	55	56	58	13·5
14	25	27	28	29	31	32	33	35	36	38	39	40	42	43	45	46	47	14
14·5	18	19	20	21	22	23	24	25	26	27	28	29	30	31	32	33	34	14·5
15	9	10	11	11	12	12	13	13	14	14	15	15	16	16	17	17	18	15
15·5	0	0	1	1	1	1	1	1	1	1	1	1	1	1	1	1	1	15·5
16	−9	−9	−10	−10	−10	−11	−11	−12	−12	−13	−13	−14	−14	−15	−15	−16	−16	16
16·5	−17	−18	−19	−20	−21	−22	−23	−24	−25	−26	−26	−27	−28	−29	−30	−31	−32	16·5
17	−24	−26	−27	−28	−30	−31	−33	−34	−35	−37	−38	−39	−41	−42	−43	−45	−46	17
17·5	−30	−32	−34	−35	−37	−39	−40	−42	−44	−45	−47	−49	−50	−52	−54	−55	−57	17·5
18	−34	−36	−38	−40	−42	−44	−46	−47	−49	−51	−53	−55	−57	−59	−61	−63	−65	18
18·5	−36	−38	−40	−42	−44	−46	−48	−50	−52	−54	−56	−58	−60	−62	−64	−66	−68	18·5
19	−35	−37	−39	−41	−43	−45	−47	−49	−51	−53	−55	−57	−59	−61	−63	−65	−67	19
19·5	−33	−34	−36	−38	−40	−42	−43	−45	−47	−49	−51	−52	−54	−56	−58	−60	−62	19·5
20	−28	−29	−31	−32	−34	−35	−37	−38	−40	−42	−43	−45	−46	−48	−49	−51	−52	20
20·5	−21	−22	−23	−25	−26	−27	−28	−29	−30	−32	−33	−34	−35	−36	−37	−39	−40	20·5
21	−13	−14	−15	−15	−16	−17	−17	−18	−19	−20	−20	−21	−22	−23	−23	−24	−25	21
21·5	−4	−5	−5	−5	−5	−5	−6	−6	−6	−6	−7	−7	−7	−7	−8	−8	−8	21·5
22	5	5	5	6	6	6	6	7	7	7	7	8	8	8	9	9	9	22
22·5	14	14	15	16	17	17	18	19	20	21	22	23	23	24	25	26	26	22·5
23	21	23	24	25	26	27	29	30	31	32	33	35	36	37	38	39	41	23
23·5	28	30	31	33	34	36	37	39	40	42	44	45	47	48	50	51	53	23·5
24	33	35	36	38	40	42	44	46	47	49	51	53	55	56	58	60	62	24
24·5	35	37	39	41	43	45	47	49	51	53	55	57	59	61	63	65	67	24·5
25	36	38	40	42	44	46	48	50	52	54	56	58	60	62	64	66	68	25
	36	38	40	42	44	46	48	50	52	54	56	58	60	62	64	66	68	

HARMONIC TIDAL PREDICTION   **TABLE II**

Hours before or after H.W.	Semidiurnal Constituent M$_2$ AMPLITUDE (insert decimal point as appropriate)																	Hours before or after H.W.
	70	72	74	76	78	80	82	84	86	88	90	92	94	96	98	100	102	
HW.	70	72	74	76	78	80	82	84	86	88	90	92	94	96	98	100	102	HW.
0·5	68	70	72	74	76	77	79	81	83	85	87	89	91	93	95	97	99	0·5
1	61	63	65	66	68	70	72	73	75	77	79	80	82	84	86	87	89	1
1·5	51	52	54	55	57	58	60	61	62	64	65	67	68	70	71	73	74	1·5
2	37	38	39	40	41	42	43	45	46	47	48	49	50	51	52	53	54	2
2·5	21	22	22	23	24	24	25	25	26	27	27	28	28	29	30	30	31	2·5
3	4	4	4	4	4	4	4	4	5	5	5	5	5	5	5	5	5	3
3·5	−14	−14	−15	−15	−15	−16	−16	−17	−17	−17	−18	−18	−19	−19	−19	−20	−20	3·5
4	−31	−31	−32	−33	−34	−35	−36	−37	−38	−38	−39	−40	−41	−42	−43	−44	−45	4
4·5	−45	−47	−48	−49	−51	−52	−53	−54	−56	−57	−58	−60	−61	−62	−64	−65	−66	4·5
5	−57	−59	−61	−62	−64	−65	−67	−69	−70	−72	−74	−75	−77	−79	−80	−82	−83	5
5·5	−66	−67	−69	−71	−73	−75	−77	−79	−81	−82	−84	−86	−88	−90	−92	−94	−95	5·5
6	−70	−72	−74	−76	−78	−80	−82	−84	−86	−88	−89	−91	−93	−95	−97	−99	−101	6
6·5	−69	−71	−73	−75	−77	−79	−81	−83	−85	−87	−89	−91	−93	−95	−97	−99	−101	6·5
7	−64	−66	−68	−70	−72	−74	−76	−77	−79	−81	−83	−85	−87	−88	−90	−92	−94	7
7·5	−56	−57	−59	−60	−62	−64	−65	−67	−68	−70	−72	−73	−75	−76	−78	−79	−81	7·5
8	−43	−44	−46	−47	−48	−49	−51	−52	−53	−54	−56	−57	−58	−59	−61	−62	−63	8
8·5	−28	−29	−30	−30	−31	−32	−33	−34	−34	−35	−36	−37	−38	−38	−39	−40	−41	8·5
9	−11	−11	−12	−12	−12	−13	−13	−13	−14	−14	−14	−15	−15	−15	−16	−16	−16	9
9·5	7	7	7	7	7	7	8	8	8	8	8	9	9	9	9	9	10	9·5
10	24	24	25	26	26	27	28	29	29	30	31	31	32	33	33	34	35	10
10·5	39	41	42	43	44	45	46	47	49	50	51	52	53	54	55	56	58	10·5
11	53	54	56	57	59	60	62	63	65	66	68	69	71	72	74	75	77	11
11·5	63	64	66	68	70	71	73	75	77	79	80	82	84	86	88	89	91	11·5
12	68	70	72	74	76	78	80	82	84	86	88	90	92	94	96	98	100	12
12·5	70	72	74	76	78	80	82	84	86	88	90	92	94	96	98	100	102	12·5
13	67	69	71	73	75	77	79	80	82	84	86	88	90	92	94	96	98	13
13·5	60	62	63	65	67	68	70	72	73	75	77	79	80	82	84	85	87	13·5
14	49	50	52	53	54	56	57	59	60	61	63	64	66	67	68	70	71	14
14·5	35	36	37	38	39	40	41	42	43	44	45	46	47	48	49	50	51	14·5
15	18	19	19	20	21	21	22	22	23	23	24	24	25	25	26	26	27	15
15·5	1	1	1	1	1	1	1	1	1	1	1	1	1	1	1	1	1	15·5
16	−17	−17	−18	−18	−19	−19	−19	−20	−20	−21	−21	−22	−22	−23	−23	−24	−24	16
16·5	−33	−34	−35	−36	−37	−38	−39	−40	−41	−42	−43	−44	−44	−45	−46	−47	−48	16·5
17	−47	−49	−50	−52	−53	−54	−56	−57	−58	−60	−61	−62	−64	−65	−66	−68	−69	17
17·5	−59	−61	−62	−64	−66	−67	−69	−71	−72	−74	−76	−77	−79	−81	−82	−84	−86	17·5
18	−66	−68	−70	−72	−74	−76	−78	−80	−82	−84	−85	−87	−89	−91	−93	−95	−97	18
18·5	−70	−72	−74	−76	−78	−80	−82	−84	−86	−88	−90	−92	−94	−96	−98	−100	−102	18·5
19	−69	−71	−73	−75	−77	−79	−81	−83	−85	−86	−88	−90	−92	−94	−96	−98	−100	19
19·5	−63	−65	−67	−69	−71	−72	−74	−76	−78	−80	−81	−83	−85	−87	−89	−90	−92	19·5
20	−54	−55	−57	−58	−60	−62	−63	−65	−66	−68	−69	−71	−72	−74	−75	−77	−78	20
20·5	−41	−42	−43	−44	−46	−47	−48	−49	−50	−52	−53	−54	−55	−56	−57	−59	−60	20·5
21	−25	−26	−27	−28	−28	−29	−30	−31	−31	−32	−33	−33	−34	−35	−36	−36	−37	21
21·5	−8	−9	−9	−9	−9	−10	−10	−10	−10	−10	−11	−11	−11	−11	−12	−12	−12	21·5
22	9	10	10	10	10	11	11	11	11	12	12	12	13	13	13	13	14	22
22·5	26	27	28	29	29	30	31	32	32	33	34	35	35	36	37	38	38	22·5
23	42	43	44	45	47	48	49	50	51	53	54	55	56	57	58	60	61	23
23·5	54	56	58	59	61	62	64	65	67	69	70	72	73	75	76	78	79	23·5
24	64	66	67	69	71	73	75	77	78	80	82	84	86	87	89	91	93	24
24·5	69	71	73	75	77	79	81	83	85	87	89	91	93	95	97	99	100	24·5
25	70	72	74	76	78	80	82	84	86	88	90	92	94	96	98	100	102	25
	70	72	74	76	78	80	82	84	86	88	90	92	94	96	98	100	102	

TABLE II

HARMONIC TIDAL PREDICTION

Hours before or after H.W.	Semidiurnal Constituent M$_2$ AMPLITUDE (insert decimal point as appropriate)																	Hours before or after H.W.
	104	106	108	110	112	114	116	118	120	122	124	126	128	130	132	134	136	
HW.	104	106	108	110	112	114	116	118	120	122	124	126	128	130	132	134	136	HW.
0·5	101	103	105	107	108	110	112	114	116	118	120	122	124	126	128	130	132	0·5
1	91	93	94	96	98	100	101	103	105	107	108	110	112	114	115	117	119	1
1·5	75	77	78	80	81	83	84	86	87	89	90	91	93	94	96	97	99	1·5
2	55	56	57	58	59	60	62	63	64	65	66	67	68	69	70	71	72	2
2·5	31	32	33	33	34	34	35	36	36	37	37	38	39	39	40	40	41	2·5
3	6	6	6	6	6	6	6	6	6	6	7	7	7	7	7	7	7	3
3·5	−21	−21	−21	−22	−22	−23	−23	−23	−24	−24	−25	−25	−25	−26	−26	−27	−27	3·5
4	−45	−46	−47	−48	−49	−50	−51	−52	−52	−53	−54	−55	−56	−57	−58	−59	−59	4
4·5	−67	−69	−70	−71	−73	−74	−75	−77	−78	−79	−80	−82	−83	−84	−86	−87	−88	4·5
5	−85	−87	−88	−90	−92	−93	−95	−97	−98	−100	−101	−103	−105	−106	−108	−110	−111	5
5·5	−97	−99	−101	−103	−105	−107	−109	−110	−112	−114	−116	−118	−120	−122	−124	−125	−127	5·5
6	−103	−105	−107	−109	−111	−113	−115	−117	−119	−121	−123	−125	−127	−129	−131	−133	−135	6
6·5	−103	−105	−107	−109	−111	−113	−115	−117	−119	−121	−123	−125	−127	−129	−131	−133	−135	6·5
7	−96	−98	−99	−101	−103	−105	−107	−109	−111	−112	−114	−116	−118	−120	−122	−123	−125	7
7·5	−83	−84	−86	−87	−89	−91	−92	−94	−95	−97	−99	−100	−102	−103	−105	−106	−108	7·5
8	−64	−65	−67	−68	−69	−70	−72	−73	−74	−75	−77	−78	−79	−80	−81	−83	−84	8
8·5	−42	−42	−43	−44	−45	−46	−47	−47	−48	−49	−50	−51	−51	−52	−53	−54	−55	8·5
9	−17	−17	−17	−17	−18	−18	−18	−19	−19	−19	−20	−20	−20	−21	−21	−21	−22	9
9·5	10	10	10	10	10	11	11	11	11	11	12	12	12	12	12	12	13	9·5
10	35	36	37	37	38	39	39	40	41	41	42	43	43	44	45	45	46	10
10·5	59	60	61	62	63	64	65	67	68	69	70	71	72	73	74	76	77	10·5
11	78	80	81	83	84	86	87	89	90	92	93	95	96	98	99	101	102	11
11·5	93	95	96	98	100	102	104	105	107	109	111	113	114	116	118	120	122	11·5
12	102	104	106	108	109	111	113	115	117	119	121	123	125	127	129	131	133	12
12·5	104	106	108	110	112	114	116	118	120	122	124	126	128	130	132	134	136	12·5
13	100	101	103	105	107	109	111	113	115	117	119	121	123	124	126	128	130	13
13·5	89	91	92	94	96	97	99	101	103	104	106	108	109	111	113	115	116	13·5
14	73	74	75	77	78	80	81	82	84	85	86	88	89	91	92	93	95	14
14·5	52	53	54	55	56	57	58	59	60	61	61	62	63	64	65	66	67	14·5
15	27	28	28	29	29	30	30	31	32	32	33	33	34	34	35	35	36	15
15·5	1	1	1	1	1	1	2	2	2	2	2	2	2	2	2	2	2	15·5
16	−25	−25	−26	−26	−27	−27	−28	−28	−29	−29	−29	−30	−30	−31	−31	−32	−32	16
16·5	−49	−50	−51	−52	−53	−54	−55	−56	−57	−58	−59	−60	−61	−62	−62	−63	−64	16·5
17	−71	−72	−73	−75	−76	−77	−79	−80	−81	−83	−84	−85	−87	−88	−90	−91	−92	17
17·5	−87	−89	−91	−92	−94	−96	−98	−99	−101	−103	−104	−106	−108	−109	−111	−113	−114	17·5
18	−99	−101	−103	−104	−106	−108	−110	−112	−114	−116	−118	−120	−122	−123	−125	−127	−129	18
18·5	−104	−106	−108	−110	−112	−114	−116	−118	−120	−122	−124	−126	−128	−130	−132	−134	−136	18·5
19	−102	−104	−106	−108	−110	−112	−114	−116	−118	−120	−122	−124	−126	−128	−130	−132	−134	19
19·5	−94	−96	−98	−100	−101	−103	−105	−107	−109	−110	−112	−114	−116	−118	−119	−121	−123	19·5
20	−80	−82	−83	−85	−86	−88	−89	−91	−92	−94	−95	−97	−99	−100	−102	−103	−105	20
20·5	−61	−62	−63	−64	−66	−67	−68	−69	−70	−71	−73	−74	−75	−76	−77	−78	−80	20·5
21	−38	−39	−39	−40	−41	−41	−42	−43	−44	−44	−45	−46	−47	−47	−48	−49	−49	21
21·5	−12	−13	−13	−13	−13	−14	−14	−14	−14	−15	−15	−15	−15	−15	−16	−16	−16	21·5
22	14	14	14	15	15	15	15	16	16	16	17	17	17	17	18	18	18	22
22·5	39	40	41	41	42	43	44	44	45	46	47	47	48	49	50	51	51	22·5
23	62	63	64	66	67	68	69	70	72	73	74	75	76	78	79	80	81	23
23·5	81	83	84	86	87	89	90	92	93	95	97	98	100	101	103	104	106	23·5
24	95	97	98	100	102	104	106	107	109	111	113	115	117	118	120	122	124	24
24·5	102	104	106	108	110	112	114	116	118	120	122	124	126	128	130	132	134	24·5
25	104	106	108	110	112	114	116	118	120	122	124	126	128	130	132	134	136	25
	104	106	108	110	112	114	116	118	120	122	124	126	128	130	132	134	136	

Hours before or after H.W.	Semidiurnal Constituent M$_2$ — AMPLITUDE (insert decimal point as appropriate)																	Hours before or after H.W.
	138	140	142	144	146	148	150	152	154	156	158	160	162	164	166	168	170	
HW.	138	140	142	144	146	148	150	152	154	156	158	160	162	164	166	168	170	HW.
0·5	134	136	137	139	141	143	145	147	149	151	153	155	157	159	161	163	165	0·5
1	121	122	124	126	128	129	131	133	135	136	138	140	142	143	145	147	149	1
1·5	100	102	103	104	106	107	109	110	112	113	115	116	118	119	120	122	123	1·5
2	73	74	75	76	77	78	80	81	82	83	84	85	86	87	88	89	90	2
2·5	42	42	43	43	44	45	45	46	46	47	48	48	49	49	50	51	51	2·5
3	7	7	8	8	8	8	8	8	8	8	8	9	9	9	9	9	9	3
3·5	−27	−28	−28	−29	−29	−29	−30	−30	−31	−31	−31	−32	−32	−33	−33	−33	−34	3·5
4	−60	−61	−62	−63	−64	−65	−66	−66	−67	−68	−69	−70	−71	−72	−73	−73	−74	4
4·5	−89	−91	−92	−93	−95	−96	−97	−99	−100	−101	−102	−104	−105	−106	−108	−109	−110	4·5
5	−113	−115	−116	−118	−119	−121	−123	−124	−126	−128	−129	−131	−133	−134	−136	−137	−139	5
5·5	−129	−131	−133	−135	−137	−139	−140	−142	−144	−146	−148	−150	−152	−154	−155	−157	−159	5·5
6	−137	−139	−141	−143	−145	−147	−149	−151	−153	−155	−157	−159	−161	−163	−165	−167	−169	6
6·5	−137	−138	−140	−142	−144	−146	−148	−150	−152	−154	−156	−158	−160	−162	−164	−166	−168	6·5
7	−127	−129	−131	−133	−135	−136	−138	−140	−142	−144	−146	−147	−149	−151	−153	−155	−157	7
7·5	−110	−111	−113	−114	−116	−118	−119	−121	−122	−124	−126	−127	−129	−130	−132	−133	−135	7·5
8	−85	−86	−88	−89	−90	−91	−93	−94	−95	−96	−98	−99	−100	−101	−102	−104	−105	8
8·5	−55	−56	−57	−58	−59	−59	−60	−61	−62	−63	−63	−64	−65	−66	−67	−67	−68	8·5
9	−22	−22	−23	−23	−23	−24	−24	−24	−24	−25	−25	−25	−26	−26	−26	−27	−27	9
9·5	13	13	13	13	14	14	14	14	14	15	15	15	15	15	15	16	16	9·5
10	47	48	48	49	50	50	51	52	52	53	54	54	55	56	56	57	58	10
10·5	78	79	80	81	82	83	85	86	87	88	89	90	91	92	94	95	96	10·5
11	104	105	107	108	110	111	113	114	116	117	119	120	122	123	125	126	128	11
11·5	123	125	127	129	130	132	134	136	138	139	141	143	145	147	148	150	152	11·5
12	135	137	139	141	143	145	147	149	151	152	154	156	158	160	162	164	166	12
12·5	138	140	142	144	146	148	150	152	154	156	158	160	162	164	166	168	170	12·5
13	132	134	136	138	140	142	144	146	147	149	151	153	155	157	159	161	163	13
13·5	118	120	121	123	125	126	128	130	132	133	135	137	138	140	142	144	145	13·5
14	96	98	99	100	102	103	105	106	107	109	110	112	113	114	116	117	119	14
14·5	68	69	70	71	72	73	74	75	76	77	78	79	80	81	82	83	84	14·5
15	36	37	37	38	38	39	39	40	40	41	42	42	43	43	44	44	45	15
15·5	2	2	2	2	2	2	2	2	2	2	2	2	2	2	2	2	2	15·5
16	−33	−33	−34	−34	−35	−35	−36	−36	−37	−37	−38	−38	−38	−39	−39	−40	−40	16
16·5	−65	−66	−67	−68	−69	−70	−71	−72	−73	−74	−75	−76	−77	−78	−79	−79	−80	16·5
17	−94	−95	−96	−98	−99	−100	−102	−103	−104	−106	−107	−109	−110	−111	−113	−114	−115	17
17·5	−116	−118	−119	−121	−123	−124	−126	−128	−129	−131	−133	−135	−136	−138	−140	−141	−143	17·5
18	−131	−133	−135	−137	−139	−141	−142	−144	−146	−148	−150	−152	−154	−156	−158	−160	−161	18
18·5	−138	−140	−142	−144	−146	−148	−150	−152	−154	−156	−158	−160	−162	−164	−166	−168	−170	18·5
19	−136	−138	−140	−141	−143	−145	−147	−149	−151	−153	−155	−157	−159	−161	−163	−165	−167	19
19·5	−125	−127	−128	−130	−132	−134	−136	−138	−139	−141	−143	−145	−147	−148	−150	−152	−154	19·5
20	−106	−108	−109	−111	−112	−114	−115	−117	−119	−120	−122	−123	−125	−126	−128	−129	−131	20
20·5	−81	−82	−83	−84	−85	−87	−88	−89	−90	−91	−92	−94	−95	−96	−97	−98	−100	20·5
21	−50	−51	−52	−52	−53	−54	−55	−55	−56	−57	−57	−58	−59	−60	−60	−61	−62	21
21·5	−16	−17	−17	−17	−17	−18	−18	−18	−18	−19	−19	−19	−19	−20	−20	−20	−20	21·5
22	18	19	19	19	19	20	20	20	21	21	21	21	22	22	22	22	23	22
22·5	52	53	54	54	55	56	57	57	58	59	60	60	61	62	63	63	64	22·5
23	82	84	85	86	87	88	90	91	92	93	94	95	97	98	99	100	101	23
23·5	107	109	111	112	114	115	117	118	120	121	123	125	126	128	129	131	132	23·5
24	126	128	129	131	133	135	137	138	140	142	144	146	148	149	151	153	155	42
24·5	136	138	140	142	144	146	148	150	152	154	156	158	160	162	164	166	167	24·5
25	138	140	142	144	146	148	150	152	154	155	157	159	161	163	165	167	169	25
	138	140	142	144	146	148	150	152	154	156	158	160	162	164	166	168	170	

TABLE II   HARMONIC TIDAL PREDICTION

Hours before or after H.W.	Semidiurnal Constituent M₂															Hours before or after H.W.
	AMPLITUDE (insert decimal point as appropriate)															
	172	174	176	178	180	182	184	186	188	190	192	194	196	198	200	
HW.	172	174	176	178	180	182	184	186	188	190	192	194	196	198	200	HW.
0·5	167	168	170	172	174	176	178	180	182	184	186	188	190	192	194	0·5
1	150	152	154	156	157	159	161	163	164	166	168	170	171	173	175	1
1·5	125	126	128	129	131	132	134	135	136	138	139	141	142	144	145	1·5
2	91	92	93	94	95	97	98	99	100	101	102	103	104	105	106	2
2·5	52	52	53	54	54	55	55	56	57	57	58	58	59	60	60	2·5
3	9	9	9	9	10	10	10	10	10	10	10	10	10	11	11	3
3·5	−34	−35	−35	−35	−36	−36	−37	−37	−37	−38	−38	−38	−39	−39	−40	3·5
4	−75	−76	−77	−78	−79	−80	−80	−81	−82	−83	−84	−85	−86	−87	−87	4
4·5	−112	−113	−114	−115	−117	−118	−119	−121	−122	−123	−125	−126	−127	−128	−130	4·5
5	−141	−142	−144	−146	−147	−149	−151	−152	−154	−155	−157	−159	−160	−162	−164	5
5·5	−161	−163	−165	−167	−169	−170	−172	−174	−176	−178	−180	−182	−183	−185	−187	5·5
6	−171	−173	−175	−177	−179	−181	−183	−185	−187	−189	−191	−193	−195	−197	−199	6
6·5	−170	−172	−174	−176	−178	−180	−182	−184	−186	−188	−190	−192	−194	−196	−198	6·5
7	−158	−160	−162	−164	−166	−168	−170	−171	−173	−175	−177	−179	−181	−182	−184	7
7·5	−137	−138	−140	−141	−143	−145	−146	−148	−149	−151	−153	−154	−156	−157	−159	7·5
8	−106	−107	−109	−110	−111	−112	−114	−115	−116	−117	−119	−120	−121	−122	−123	8
8·5	−69	−70	−71	−71	−72	−73	−74	−75	−75	−76	−77	−78	−79	−79	−80	8·5
9	−27	−28	−28	−28	−29	−29	−29	−30	−30	−30	−31	−31	−31	−31	−32	9
9·5	16	16	16	17	17	17	17	17	18	18	18	18	18	18	19	9·5
10	58	59	60	60	61	62	62	63	64	64	65	66	67	67	68	10
10·5	97	98	99	100	102	103	104	105	106	107	108	109	111	112	113	10·5
11	129	131	132	134	135	137	138	140	142	143	145	146	148	149	151	11
11·5	154	155	157	159	161	163	164	166	168	170	172	173	175	177	179	11·5
12	168	170	172	174	176	178	180	182	184	186	188	190	192	194	195	12
12·5	172	174	176	178	180	182	184	186	188	190	192	194	196	198	200	12·5
13	165	167	168	170	172	174	176	178	180	182	184	186	188	190	191	13
13·5	147	149	150	152	154	156	157	159	161	162	164	166	167	169	171	13·5
14	120	121	123	124	126	127	128	130	131	133	134	135	137	138	139	14
14·5	85	86	87	88	89	90	91	92	93	94	95	96	97	98	99	14·5
15	45	46	46	47	47	48	48	49	49	50	50	51	52	52	53	15
15·5	2	2	2	2	2	2	2	2	2	2	3	3	3	3	3	15·5
16	−41	−41	−42	−42	−43	−43	−44	−44	−45	−45	−46	−46	−47	−47	−48	16
16·5	−81	−82	−83	−84	−85	−86	−87	−88	−89	−90	−91	−92	−93	−94	−95	16·5
17	−117	−118	−119	−121	−122	−123	−125	−126	−128	−129	−130	−132	−133	−134	−136	17
17·5	−145	−146	−148	−150	−151	−153	−155	−156	−158	−160	−161	−163	−165	−166	−168	17·5
18	−163	−165	−167	−169	−171	−173	−175	−177	−179	−180	−182	−184	−186	−188	−190	18
18·5	−172	−174	−176	−178	−180	−182	−184	−186	−188	−190	−192	−194	−196	−198	−200	18·5
19	−169	−171	−173	−175	−177	−179	−181	−183	−185	−187	−189	−191	−193	−195	−197	19
19·5	−156	−157	−159	−161	−163	−165	−167	−168	−170	−172	−174	−176	−177	−179	−181	19·5
20	−132	−134	−135	−137	−139	−140	−142	−143	−145	−146	−148	−149	−151	−152	−154	20
20·5	−101	−102	−103	−104	−105	−107	−108	−109	−110	−111	−112	−114	−115	−116	−117	20·5
21	−63	−63	−64	−65	−65	−66	−67	−68	−68	−69	−70	−71	−71	−72	−73	21
21·5	−20	−21	−21	−21	−21	−22	−22	−22	−22	−23	−23	−23	−23	−24	−24	21·5
22	23	23	23	24	24	24	24	25	25	25	26	26	26	26	27	22
22·5	65	66	66	67	68	69	69	70	71	72	72	73	74	75	75	22·5
23	103	104	105	106	107	109	110	111	112	113	115	116	117	118	119	23
23·5	134	135	137	139	140	142	143	145	146	148	149	151	153	154	156	23·5
24	157	158	160	162	164	166	168	169	171	173	175	177	179	180	182	24
24·5	169	171	173	175	177	179	181	183	185	187	189	191	193	195	197	24·5
25	171	173	175	177	179	181	183	185	187	189	191	193	195	197	199	25
	172	174	176	178	180	182	184	186	188	190	192	194	196	198	200	

TABLE III

Hours before or after H.W.	Semidiurnal Constituent S$_2$ AMPLITUDE (insert decimal point as appropriate)																	Hours before or after H.W.
	2	4	6	8	10	12	14	16	18	20	22	24	26	28	30	32	34	
HW.	2	4	6	8	10	12	14	16	18	20	22	24	26	28	30	32	34	HW.
0·5	2	4	6	8	10	12	14	15	17	19	21	23	25	27	29	31	33	0·5
1	2	3	5	7	9	10	12	14	16	17	19	21	23	24	26	28	29	1
1·5	1	3	4	6	7	8	10	11	13	14	16	17	18	20	21	23	24	1·5
2	1	2	3	4	5	6	7	8	9	10	11	12	13	14	15	16	17	2
2·5	1	1	2	2	3	3	4	4	5	5	6	6	7	7	8	8	9	2·5
3	0	0	0	0	0	0	0	0	0	0	0	0	0	0	0	0	0	3
3·5	−1	−1	−2	−2	−3	−3	−4	−4	−5	−5	−6	−6	−7	−7	−8	−8	−9	3·5
4	−1	−2	−3	−4	−5	−6	−7	−8	−9	10	−11	−12	−13	−14	−15	−16	−17	4
4·5	−1	−3	−4	−6	−7	−8	−10	−11	−13	−14	−16	−17	−18	−20	−21	−23	−24	4·5
5	−2	−3	−5	−7	−9	−10	−12	−14	−16	−17	−19	−21	−23	−24	−26	−28	−29	5
5·5	−2	−4	−6	−8	−10	−12	−14	−15	−17	−19	−21	−23	−25	−27	−29	−31	−33	5·5
6	−2	−4	−6	−8	−10	−12	−14	−16	−18	−20	−22	−24	−26	−28	−30	−32	−34	6
6·5	−2	−4	−6	−8	−10	−12	−14	−15	−17	−19	−21	−23	−25	−27	−29	−31	−33	6·5
7	−2	−3	−5	−7	−9	−10	−12	−14	−16	−17	−19	−21	−23	−24	−26	−28	−29	7
7·5	−1	−3	−4	−6	−7	−8	−10	−11	−13	−14	−16	−17	−18	−20	−21	−23	−24	7·5
8	−1	−2	−3	−4	−5	−6	−7	−8	−9	−10	−11	−12	−13	−14	−15	−16	−17	8
8·5	−1	−1	−2	−2	−3	−3	−4	−4	−5	−5	−6	−6	−7	−7	−8	−8	−9	8·5
9	0	0	0	0	0	0	0	0	0	0	0	0	0	0	0	0	0	9
9·5	1	1	2	2	3	3	4	4	5	5	6	6	7	7	8	8	9	9·5
10	1	2	3	4	5	6	7	8	9	10	11	12	13	14	15	16	17	10
10·5	1	3	4	6	7	8	10	11	13	14	16	17	18	20	21	23	24	10·5
11	2	3	5	7	9	10	12	14	16	17	19	21	23	24	26	28	29	11
11·5	2	4	6	8	10	12	14	15	17	19	21	23	25	27	29	31	33	11·5
12	2	4	6	8	10	12	14	16	18	20	22	24	26	28	30	32	34	12
12·5	2	4	6	8	10	12	14	15	17	19	21	23	25	27	29	31	33	12·5
13	2	3	5	7	9	10	12	14	16	17	19	21	23	24	26	28	29	13
13·5	1	3	4	6	7	8	10	11	13	14	16	17	18	20	21	23	24	13·5
14	1	2	3	4	5	6	7	8	9	10	11	12	13	14	15	16	17	14
14·5	1	1	2	2	3	3	4	4	5	5	6	6	7	7	8	8	9	14·5
15	0	0	0	0	0	0	0	0	0	0	0	0	0	0	0	0	0	15
15·5	−1	−1	−2	−2	−3	−3	−4	−4	−5	−5	−6	−6	−7	−7	−8	−8	−9	15·5
16	−1	−2	−3	−4	−5	−6	−7	−8	−9	−10	−11	−12	−13	−14	−15	−16	−17	16
16·5	−1	−3	−4	−6	−7	−8	−10	−11	−13	−14	−16	−17	−18	−20	−21	−23	−24	16·5
17	−2	−3	−5	−7	−9	−10	−12	−14	−16	−17	−19	−21	−23	−24	−26	−28	−29	17
17·5	−2	−4	−6	−8	−10	−12	−14	−15	−17	−19	−21	−23	−25	−27	−29	−31	−33	17·5
18	−2	−4	−6	−8	−10	−12	−14	−16	−18	−20	−22	−24	−26	−28	−30	−32	−34	18
18·5	−2	−4	−6	−8	−10	−12	−14	−15	−17	−19	−21	−23	−25	−27	−29	−31	−33	18·5
19	−2	−3	−5	−7	−9	−10	−12	−14	−16	−17	−19	−21	−23	−24	−26	−28	−29	19
19·5	−1	−3	−4	−6	−7	−8	−10	−11	−13	−14	−16	−17	−18	−20	−21	−23	−24	19·5
20	−1	−2	−3	−4	−5	−6	−7	−8	−9	−10	−11	−12	−13	−14	−15	−16	−17	20
20·5	−1	−1	−2	−2	−3	−3	−4	−4	−5	−5	−6	−6	−7	−7	−8	−8	−9	20·5
21	0	0	0	0	0	0	0	0	0	0	0	0	0	0	0	0	0	21
21·5	1	1	2	2	3	3	4	4	5	5	6	6	7	7	8	8	9	21·5
22	1	2	3	4	5	6	7	8	9	10	11	12	13	14	15	16	17	22
22·5	1	3	4	6	7	8	10	11	13	14	16	17	18	20	21	23	24	22·5
23	2	3	5	7	9	10	12	14	16	17	19	21	23	24	26	28	29	23
23·5	2	4	6	8	10	12	14	15	17	19	21	23	25	27	29	31	33	23·5
24	2	4	6	8	10	12	14	16	18	20	22	24	26	28	30	32	34	24
	2	4	6	8	10	12	14	16	18	20	22	24	26	28	30	32	34	

TABLE III

HARMONIC TIDAL PREDICTION

Hours before or after H.W.	Semidiurnal Constituent S_2 AMPLITUDE (insert decimal point as appropriate)																	Hours before or after H.W.
	36	38	40	42	44	46	48	50	52	54	56	58	60	62	64	66	68	
HW.	36	38	40	42	44	46	48	50	52	54	56	58	60	62	64	66	68	HW.
0·5	35	37	39	41	43	44	46	48	50	52	54	56	58	60	62	64	66	0·5
1	31	33	35	36	38	40	42	43	45	47	48	50	52	54	55	57	59	1
1·5	25	27	28	30	31	33	34	35	37	38	40	41	42	44	45	47	48	1·5
2	18	19	20	21	22	23	24	25	26	27	28	29	30	31	32	33	34	2
2·5	9	10	10	11	11	12	12	13	13	14	14	15	16	16	17	17	18	2·5
3	0	0	0	0	0	0	0	0	0	0	0	0	0	0	0	0	0	3
3·5	−9	−10	−10	−11	−11	−12	−12	−13	−13	−14	−14	−15	−16	−16	−17	−17	−18	3·5
4	−18	−19	−20	−21	−22	−23	−24	−25	−26	−27	−28	−29	−30	−31	−32	−33	−34	4
4·5	−25	−27	−28	−30	−31	−33	−34	−35	−37	−38	−40	−41	−42	−44	−45	−47	−48	4·5
5	−31	−33	−35	−36	−38	−40	−42	−43	−45	−47	−48	−50	−52	−54	−55	−57	−59	5
5·5	−35	−37	−39	−41	−43	−44	−46	−48	−50	−52	−54	−56	−58	−60	−62	−64	−66	5·5
6	−36	−38	−40	−42	−44	−46	−48	−50	−52	−54	−56	−58	−60	−62	−64	−66	−68	6
6·5	−35	−37	−39	−41	−43	−44	−46	−48	−50	−52	−54	−56	−58	−60	−62	−64	−66	6·5
7	−31	−33	−35	−36	−38	−40	−42	−43	−45	−47	−48	−50	−52	−54	−55	−57	−59	7
7·5	−25	−27	−28	−30	−31	−33	−34	−35	−37	−38	−40	−41	−42	−44	−45	−47	−48	7·5
8	−18	−19	−20	−21	−22	−23	−24	−25	−26	−27	−28	−29	−30	−31	−32	−33	−34	8
8·5	−9	−10	−10	−11	−11	−12	−12	−13	−13	−14	−14	−15	−16	−16	−17	−17	−18	8·5
9	0	0	0	0	0	0	0	0	0	0	0	0	0	0	0	0	0	9
9·5	9	10	10	11	11	12	12	13	13	14	14	15	16	16	17	17	18	9·5
10	18	19	20	21	22	23	24	25	26	27	28	29	30	31	32	33	34	10
10·5	25	27	28	30	31	33	34	35	37	38	40	41	42	44	45	47	48	10·5
11	31	33	35	36	38	40	42	43	45	47	48	50	52	54	55	57	59	11
11·5	35	37	39	41	43	44	46	48	50	52	54	56	58	60	62	64	66	11·5
12	36	38	40	42	44	46	48	50	52	54	56	58	60	62	64	66	68	12
12·5	35	37	39	41	43	44	46	48	50	52	54	56	58	60	62	64	66	12·5
13	31	33	35	36	38	40	42	43	45	47	48	50	52	54	55	57	59	13
13·5	25	27	28	30	31	33	34	35	37	38	40	41	42	44	45	47	48	13·5
14	18	19	20	21	22	23	24	25	26	27	28	29	30	31	32	33	34	14
14·5	9	10	10	11	11	12	12	13	13	14	14	15	16	16	17	17	18	14·5
15	0	0	0	0	0	0	0	0	0	0	0	0	0	0	0	0	0	15
15·5	−9	−10	−10	−11	−11	−12	−12	−13	−13	−14	−14	−15	−16	−16	−17	−17	−18	15·5
16	−18	−19	−20	−21	−22	−23	−24	−25	−26	−27	−28	−29	−30	−31	−32	−33	−34	16
16·5	−25	−27	−28	−30	−31	−33	−34	−35	−37	−38	−40	−41	−42	−44	−45	−47	−48	16·5
17	−31	−33	−35	−36	−38	−40	−42	−43	−45	−47	−48	−50	−52	−54	−55	−57	−59	17
17·5	−35	−37	−39	−41	−43	−44	−46	−48	−50	−52	−54	−56	−58	−60	−62	−64	−66	17·5
18	−36	−38	−40	−42	−44	−46	−48	−50	−52	−54	−56	−58	−60	−62	−64	−66	−68	18
18·5	−35	−37	−39	−41	−43	−44	−46	−48	−50	−52	−54	−56	−58	−60	−62	−64	−66	18·5
19	−31	−33	−35	−36	−38	−40	−42	−43	−45	−47	−48	−50	−52	−54	−55	−57	−59	19
19·5	−25	−27	−28	−30	−31	−33	−34	−35	−37	−38	−40	−41	−42	−44	−45	−47	−48	19·5
20	−18	−19	−20	−21	−22	−23	−24	−25	−26	−27	−28	−29	−30	−31	−32	−33	−34	20
20·5	−9	−10	−10	−11	−11	−12	−12	−13	−13	−14	−14	−15	−16	−16	−17	−17	−18	20·5
21	0	0	0	0	0	0	0	0	0	0	0	0	0	0	0	0	0	21
21·5	9	10	10	11	11	12	12	13	13	14	14	15	16	16	17	17	18	21·5
22	18	19	20	21	22	23	24	25	26	27	28	29	30	31	32	33	34	22
22·5	25	27	28	30	31	33	34	35	37	38	40	41	42	44	45	47	48	22·5
23	31	33	35	36	38	40	42	43	45	47	48	50	52	54	55	57	59	23
23·5	35	37	39	41	43	44	46	48	50	52	54	56	58	60	62	64	66	23·5
24	36	38	40	42	44	46	48	50	52	54	56	58	60	62	64	66	68	24
	36	38	40	42	44	46	48	50	52	54	56	58	60	62	64	66	68	

R

Hours before or after H.W.	Semidiurnal Constituent S$_2$ AMPLITUDE (insert decimal point as appropriate)																Hours before or after H.W.
	70	72	74	76	78	80	82	84	86	88	90	92	94	96	98	100	
HW.	70	72	74	76	78	80	82	84	86	88	90	92	94	96	98	100	HW.
0·5	68	70	71	73	75	77	79	81	83	85	87	89	91	93	95	97	0·5
1	61	62	64	66	68	69	71	73	74	76	78	80	81	83	85	87	1
1·5	49	51	52	54	55	57	58	59	61	62	64	65	66	68	69	71	1·5
2	35	36	37	38	39	40	41	42	43	44	45	46	47	48	49	50	2
2·5	18	19	19	20	20	21	21	22	22	23	23	24	24	25	25	26	2·5
3	0	0	0	0	0	0	0	0	0	0	0	0	0	0	0	0	3
3·5	−18	−19	−19	−20	−20	−21	−21	−22	−22	−23	−23	−24	−24	−25	−25	−26	3·5
4	−35	−36	−37	−38	−39	−40	−41	−42	−43	−44	−45	−46	−47	−48	−49	−50	4
4·5	−49	−51	−52	−54	−55	−57	−58	−59	−61	−62	−64	−65	−66	−68	−69	−71	4·5
5	−61	−62	−64	−66	−68	−69	−71	−73	−74	−76	−78	−80	−81	−83	−85	−87	5
5·5	−68	−70	−71	−73	−75	−77	−79	−81	−83	−85	−87	−89	−91	−93	−95	−97	5·5
6	−70	−72	−74	−76	−78	−80	−82	−84	−86	−88	−90	−92	−94	−96	−98	−100	6
6·5	−68	−70	−71	−73	−75	−77	−79	−81	−83	−85	−87	−89	−91	−93	−95	−97	6·5
7	−61	−62	−64	−66	−68	−69	−71	−73	−74	−76	−78	−80	−81	−83	−85	−87	7
7·5	−49	−51	−52	−54	−55	−57	−58	−59	−61	−62	−64	−65	−66	−68	−69	−71	7·5
8	−35	−36	−37	−38	−39	−40	−41	−42	−43	−44	−45	−46	−47	−48	−49	−50	8
8·5	−18	−19	−19	−20	−20	−21	−21	−22	−22	−23	−23	−24	−24	−25	−25	−26	8·5
9	0	0	0	0	0	0	0	0	0	0	0	0	0	0	0	0	9
9·5	18	19	19	20	20	21	21	22	22	23	23	24	24	25	25	26	9·5
10	35	36	37	38	39	40	41	42	43	44	45	46	47	48	49	50	10
10·5	49	51	52	54	55	57	58	59	61	62	64	65	66	68	69	71	10·5
11	61	62	64	66	68	69	71	73	74	76	78	80	81	83	85	87	11
11·5	68	70	71	73	75	77	79	81	83	85	87	89	91	93	95	97	11·5
12	70	72	74	76	78	80	82	84	86	88	90	92	94	96	98	100	12
12·5	68	70	71	73	75	77	79	81	83	85	87	89	91	93	95	97	12·5
13	61	62	64	66	68	69	71	73	74	76	78	80	81	83	85	87	13
13·5	49	51	52	54	55	57	58	59	61	62	64	65	66	68	69	71	13·5
14	35	36	37	38	39	40	41	42	43	44	45	46	47	48	49	50	14
14·5	18	19	19	20	20	21	21	22	22	23	23	24	24	25	25	26	14·5
15	0	0	0	0	0	0	0	0	0	0	0	0	0	0	0	0	15
15·5	−18	−19	−19	−20	−20	−21	−21	−22	−22	−23	−23	−24	−24	−25	−25	−26	15·5
16	−35	−36	−37	−38	−39	−40	−41	−42	−43	−44	−45	−46	−47	−48	−49	−50	16
16·5	−49	−51	−52	−54	−55	−57	−58	−59	−61	−62	−64	−65	−66	−68	−69	−71	16·5
17	−61	−62	−64	−66	−68	−69	−71	−73	−74	−76	−78	−80	−81	−83	−85	−87	17
17·5	−68	−70	−71	−73	−75	−77	−79	−81	−83	−85	−87	−89	−91	−93	−95	·97	17·5
18	−70	−72	−74	−76	−78	−80	−82	−84	−86	−88	−90	−92	−94	−96	−98	−100	18
18·5	−68	−70	−71	−73	−75	−77	−79	−81	−83	−85	−87	−89	−91	−93	−95	−97	18·5
19	−61	−62	−64	−66	−68	−69	−71	−73	−74	−76	−78	−80	−81	−83	−85	−87	19
19·5	−49	−51	−52	−54	−55	−57	−58	−59	−61	−62	−64	−65	−66	−68	−69	−71	19·5
20	−35	−36	−37	−38	−39	−40	−41	−42	−43	−44	−45	−46	−47	−48	−49	−50	20
20·5	−18	−19	−19	−20	−20	−21	−21	−22	−22	−23	−23	−24	−24	−25	−25	−26	20·5
21	0	0	0	0	0	0	0	0	0	0	0	0	0	0	0	0	21
21·5	18	19	19	20	20	21	21	22	22	23	23	24	24	25	25	26	21·5
22	35	36	37	38	39	40	41	42	43	44	45	46	47	48	49	50	22
22·5	49	51	52	54	55	57	58	59	61	62	64	65	66	68	69	71	22·5
23	61	62	64	66	68	69	71	73	74	76	78	80	81	83	85	87	23
23·5	68	70	71	73	75	77	79	81	83	85	87	89	91	93	95	97	23·5
24	70	72	74	76	78	80	82	84	86	88	90	92	94	96	98	100	24
	70	72	74	76	78	80	82	84	86	88	90	92	94	96	98	100	

TABLE IV — HARMONIC TIDAL PREDICTION

Hours before or after H.W.	2	4	6	8	10	12	14	16	18	20	22	24	26	28	30	32	34	Hours before or after H.W.
HW.	2	4	6	8	10	12	14	16	18	20	22	24	26	28	30	32	34	HW.
0·5	2	4	6	8	10	12	14	16	18	20	22	24	26	28	30	32	34	0·5
1	2	4	6	8	10	12	14	15	17	19	21	23	25	27	29	31	33	1
1·5	2	4	6	7	9	11	13	15	17	18	20	22	24	26	28	30	31	1·5
2	2	3	5	7	9	10	12	14	16	17	19	21	23	24	26	28	29	2
2·5	2	3	5	6	8	10	11	13	14	16	17	19	21	22	24	25	27	2·5
3	1	3	4	6	7	8	10	11	13	14	16	17	18	20	21	23	24	3
3·5	1	2	4	5	6	7	9	10	11	12	13	15	16	17	18	19	21	3·5
4	1	2	3	4	5	6	7	8	9	10	11	12	13	14	15	16	17	4
4·5	1	2	2	3	4	5	5	6	7	8	8	9	10	11	11	12	13	4·5
5	1	1	2	2	3	3	4	4	5	5	6	6	7	7	8	8	9	5
5·5	0	1	1	1	1	2	2	2	2	3	3	3	3	4	4	4	4	5·5
6	0	0	0	0	0	0	0	0	0	0	0	0	0	0	0	0	0	6
6·5	0	−1	−1	−1	−1	−2	−2	−2	−2	−3	−3	−3	−3	−4	−4	−4	−4	6·5
7	−1	−1	−2	−2	−3	−3	−4	−4	−5	−5	−6	−6	−7	−7	−8	−8	−9	7
7·5	−1	−2	−2	−3	−4	−5	−5	−6	−7	−8	−8	−9	−10	−11	−11	−12	−13	7·5
8	−1	−2	−3	−4	−5	−6	−7	−8	−9	−10	−11	−12	−13	−14	−15	−16	−17	8
8·5	−1	−2	−4	−5	−6	−7	−9	−10	−11	−12	−13	−15	−16	−17	−18	−19	−21	8·5
9	−1	−3	−4	−6	−7	−8	−10	−11	−13	−14	−16	−17	−18	−20	−21	−23	−24	9
9·5	−2	−3	−5	−6	−8	−10	−11	−13	−14	−16	−17	−19	−21	−22	−24	−25	−27	9·5
10	−2	−3	−5	−7	−9	−10	−12	−14	−16	−17	−19	−21	−23	−24	−26	−28	−29	10
10·5	−2	−4	−6	−7	−9	−11	−13	−15	−17	−18	−20	−22	−24	−26	−28	−30	−31	10·5
11	−2	−4	−6	−8	−10	−12	−14	−15	−17	−19	−21	−23	−25	−27	−29	−31	−33	11
11·5	−2	−4	−6	−8	−10	−12	−14	−16	−18	−20	−22	−24	−26	−28	−30	−32	−34	11·5
12	−2	−4	−6	−8	−10	−12	−14	−16	−18	−20	−22	−24	−26	−28	−30	−32	−34	12
12·5	−2	−4	−6	−8	−10	−12	−14	−16	−18	−20	−22	−24	−26	−28	−30	−32	−34	12·5
13	−2	−4	−6	−8	−10	−12	−14	−15	−17	−19	−21	−23	−25	−27	−29	−31	−33	13
13·5	−2	−4	−6	−7	−9	−11	−13	−15	−17	−18	−20	−22	−24	−26	−28	−30	−31	13·5
14	−2	−3	−5	−7	−9	−10	−12	−14	−16	−17	−19	−21	−23	−24	−26	−28	−29	14
14·5	−2	−3	−5	−6	−8	−10	−11	−13	−14	−16	−17	−19	−21	−22	−24	−25	−27	14·5
15	−1	−3	−4	−6	−7	−8	−10	−11	−13	−14	−16	−17	−18	−20	−21	−23	−24	15
15·5	−1	−2	−4	−5	−6	−7	−9	−10	−11	−12	−13	−15	−16	−17	−18	−19	−21	15·5
16	−1	−2	−3	−4	−5	−6	−7	−8	−9	−10	−11	−12	−13	−14	−15	−16	−17	16
16·5	−1	−2	−2	−3	−4	−5	−5	−6	−7	−8	−8	−9	−10	−11	−11	−12	−13	16·5
17	−1	−1	−2	−2	−3	−3	−4	−4	−5	−5	−6	−6	−7	−7	−8	−8	−9	17
17·5	0	−1	−1	−1	−1	−2	−2	−2	−2	−3	−3	−3	−3	−4	−4	−4	−4	17·5
18	0	0	0	0	0	0	0	0	0	0	0	0	0	0	0	0	0	18
18·5	0	1	1	1	1	2	2	2	2	3	3	3	3	4	4	4	4	18·5
19	1	1	2	2	3	3	4	4	5	5	6	6	7	7	8	8	9	19
19·5	1	2	2	3	4	5	5	6	7	8	8	9	10	11	11	12	13	19·5
20	1	2	3	4	5	6	7	8	9	10	11	12	13	14	15	16	17	20
20·5	1	2	4	5	6	7	9	10	11	12	13	15	16	17	18	19	21	20·5
21	1	3	4	6	7	8	10	11	13	14	16	17	18	20	21	23	24	21
21·5	2	3	5	6	8	10	11	13	14	16	17	19	21	22	24	25	27	12·5
22	2	3	5	7	9	10	12	14	16	17	19	21	23	24	26	28	29	22
22·5	2	4	6	7	9	11	13	15	17	18	20	22	24	26	28	30	31	22·5
23	2	4	6	8	10	12	14	15	17	19	21	23	25	27	29	31	33	23
23·5	2	4	6	8	10	12	14	16	18	20	22	24	26	28	30	32	34	23·5
24	2	4	6	8	10	12	14	16	18	20	22	24	26	28	30	32	34	24
	2	4	6	8	10	12	14	16	18	20	22	24	26	28	30	32	34	

Diurnal Constituent K_I — AMPLITUDE (insert decimal point as appropriate)

Hours before or after H.W.	Diurnal Constituent K$_1$ AMPLITUDE (insert decimal point as appropriate)																	Hours before or after H.W.
	36	38	40	42	44	46	48	50	52	54	56	58	60	62	64	66	68	
HW.	36	38	40	42	44	46	48	50	52	54	56	58	60	62	64	66	68	HW.
0·5	36	38	40	42	44	46	48	50	52	54	56	58	59	61	63	65	67	0·5
1	35	37	39	41	43	44	46	48	50	52	54	56	58	60	62	64	66	1
1·5	33	35	37	39	41	42	44	46	48	50	52	54	55	57	59	61	63	1·5
2	31	33	35	36	38	40	42	43	45	47	48	50	52	54	55	57	59	2
2·5	29	30	32	33	35	36	38	40	41	43	44	46	48	49	51	52	54	2·5
3	25	27	28	30	31	33	34	35	37	38	40	41	42	44	45	47	48	3
3·5	22	23	24	26	27	28	29	30	32	33	34	35	37	38	39	40	41	3·5
4	18	19	20	21	22	23	24	25	26	27	28	29	30	31	32	33	34	4
4·5	14	15	15	16	17	18	18	19	20	21	21	22	23	24	24	25	26	4·5
5	9	10	10	11	11	12	12	13	13	14	14	15	16	16	17	17	18	5
5·5	5	5	5	5	6	6	6	7	7	7	7	8	8	8	8	9	9	5·5
6	0	0	0	0	0	0	0	0	0	0	0	0	0	0	0	0	0	6
6·5	−5	−5	−5	−5	−6	−6	−6	−7	−7	−7	−7	−8	−8	−8	−8	−9	−9	6·5
7	−9	−10	−10	−11	−11	−12	−12	−13	−13	−14	−14	−15	−16	−16	−17	−17	−18	7
7·5	−14	−15	−15	−16	−17	−18	−18	−19	−20	−21	−21	−22	−23	−24	−24	−25	−26	7·5
8	−18	−19	−20	−21	−22	−23	−24	−25	−26	−27	−28	−29	−30	−31	−32	−33	−34	8
8·5	−22	−23	−24	−26	−27	−28	−29	−30	−32	−33	−34	−35	−37	−38	−39	−40	−41	8·5
9	−25	−27	−28	−30	−31	−33	−34	−35	−37	−38	−40	−41	−42	−44	−45	−47	−48	9
9·5	−29	−30	−32	−33	−35	−36	−38	−40	−41	−43	−44	−46	−48	−49	−51	−52	−54	9·5
10	−31	−33	−35	−36	−38	−40	−42	−43	−45	−47	−48	−50	−52	−54	−55	−57	−59	10
10·5	−33	−35	−37	−39	−41	−42	−44	−46	−48	−50	−52	−54	−55	−57	−59	−61	−63	10·5
11	−35	−37	−39	−41	−43	−44	−46	−48	−50	−52	−54	−56	−58	−60	−62	−64	−66	11
11·5	−36	−38	−40	−42	−44	−46	−48	−50	−52	−54	−56	−58	−59	−61	−63	−65	−67	11·5
12	−36	−38	−40	−42	−44	−46	−48	−50	−52	−54	−56	−58	−60	−62	−64	−66	−68	12
12·5	−36	−38	−40	−42	−44	−46	−48	−50	−52	−54	−56	−58	−59	−61	−63	−65	−67	12·5
13	−35	−37	−39	−41	−43	−44	−46	−48	−50	−52	−54	−56	−58	−60	−62	−64	−66	13
13·5	−33	−35	−37	−39	−41	−42	−44	−46	−48	−50	−52	−54	−55	−57	−59	−61	−63	13·5
14	−31	−33	−35	−36	−38	−40	−42	−43	−45	−47	−48	−50	−52	−54	−55	−57	−59	14
14·5	−29	−30	−32	−33	−35	−36	−38	−40	−41	−43	−44	−46	−48	−49	−51	−52	−54	14·5
15	−25	−27	−28	−30	−31	−33	−34	−35	−37	−38	−40	−41	−42	−44	−45	−47	−48	15
15·5	−22	−23	−24	−26	−27	−28	−29	−30	−32	−33	−34	−35	−37	−38	−39	−40	−41	15·5
16	−18	−19	−20	−21	−22	−23	−24	−25	−26	−27	−28	−29	−30	−31	−32	−33	−34	16
16·5	−14	−15	−15	−16	−17	−18	−18	−19	−20	−21	−21	−22	−23	−24	−24	−25	−26	16·5
17	−9	−10	−10	−11	−11	−12	−12	−13	−13	−14	−14	−15	−16	−16	−17	−17	−18	17
17·5	−5	−5	−5	−5	−6	−6	−6	−7	−7	−7	−7	−8	−8	−8	−8	−9	−9	17·5
18	0	0	0	0	0	0	0	0	0	0	0	0	0	0	0	0	0	18
18·5	5	5	5	5	6	6	6	7	7	7	7	8	8	8	8	9	9	18·5
19	9	10	10	11	11	12	12	13	13	14	14	15	16	16	17	17	18	19
19·5	14	15	15	16	17	18	18	19	20	21	21	22	23	24	24	25	26	19·5
20	18	19	20	21	22	23	24	25	26	27	28	29	30	31	32	33	34	20
20·5	22	23	24	26	27	28	29	30	32	33	34	35	37	38	39	40	41	20·5
21	25	27	28	30	31	33	34	35	37	38	40	41	42	44	45	47	48	21
21·5	29	30	32	33	35	36	38	40	41	43	44	46	48	49	51	52	54	21·5
22	31	33	35	36	38	40	42	43	45	47	48	50	52	54	55	57	59	22
22·5	33	35	37	39	41	42	44	46	48	50	52	54	55	57	59	61	63	22·5
23	35	37	39	41	43	44	46	48	50	52	54	56	58	60	62	64	66	23
23·5	36	38	40	42	44	46	48	50	52	54	56	58	59	61	63	65	67	23·5
24	36	38	40	42	44	46	48	50	52	54	56	58	60	62	64	66	68	24
	36	38	40	42	44	46	48	50	52	54	56	58	60	62	64	66	68	

TABLE IV

Hours before or after H.W.	Diurnal Constituent K₁																Hours before or after H.W.
	AMPLITUDE (insert decimal point as appropriate																
	70	72	74	76	78	80	82	84	86	88	90	92	94	96	98	100	
HW.	70	72	74	76	78	80	82	84	86	88	90	92	94	96	98	100	HW.
0·5	69	71	73	75	77	79	81	83	85	87	89	91	93	95	97	99	0·5
1	68	70	71	73	75	77	79	81	83	85	87	89	91	93	95	97	1
1·5	65	67	68	70	72	74	76	78	79	81	83	85	87	89	91	92	1·5
2	61	62	64	66	68	69	71	73	74	76	78	80	81	83	85	87	2
2·5	56	57	59	60	62	63	65	67	68	70	71	73	75	76	78	79	2·5
3	49	51	52	54	55	57	58	59	61	62	64	65	66	68	69	71	3
3·5	43	44	45	46	47	49	50	51	52	54	55	56	57	58	60	61	3·5
4	35	36	37	38	39	40	41	42	43	44	45	46	47	48	49	50	4
4·5	27	28	28	29	30	31	31	32	33	34	34	35	36	37	38	38	4·5
5	18	19	19	20	20	21	21	22	22	23	23	24	24	25	25	26	5
5·5	9	9	10	10	10	10	11	11	11	11	12	12	12	13	13	13	5·5
6	0	0	0	0	0	0	0	0	0	0	0	0	0	0	0	0	6
6·5	−9	−9	−10	−10	−10	−10	−11	−11	−11	−11	−12	−12	−12	−13	−13	−13	6·5
7	−18	−19	−19	−20	−20	−21	−21	−22	−22	−23	−23	−24	−24	−25	−25	−26	7
7·5	−27	−28	−28	−29	−30	−31	−31	−32	−33	−34	−34	−35	−36	−37	−38	−38	7·5
8	−35	−36	−37	−38	−39	−40	−41	−42	−43	−44	−45	−46	−47	−48	−49	−50	8
8·5	−43	−44	−45	−46	−47	−49	−50	−51	−52	−54	−55	−56	−57	−58	−60	−61	8·5
9	−49	−51	−52	−54	−55	−57	−58	−59	−61	−62	−64	−65	−66	−68	−69	−71	9
9·5	−56	−57	−59	−60	−62	−63	−65	−67	−68	−70	−71	−73	−75	−76	−78	−79	9·5
10	−61	−62	−64	−66	−68	−69	−71	−73	−74	−76	−78	−80	−81	−83	−85	−87	10
10·5	−65	−67	−68	−70	−72	−74	−76	−78	−79	−81	−83	−85	−87	−89	−91	−92	10·5
11	−68	−70	−71	−73	−75	−77	−79	−81	−83	−85	−87	−89	−91	−93	−95	−97	11
11·5	−69	−71	−73	−75	−77	−79	−81	−83	−85	−87	−89	−91	−93	−95	−97	−99	11·5
12	−70	−72	−74	−76	−78	−80	−82	−84	−86	−88	−90	−92	−94	−96	−98	−100	12
12·5	−69	−71	−73	−75	−77	−79	−81	−83	−85	−87	−89	−91	−93	−95	−97	−99	12·5
13	−68	−70	−71	−73	−75	−77	−79	−81	−83	−85	87	−89	−91	−93	−95	−97	13
13·5	−65	−67	−68	−70	−72	−74	−76	−78	−79	−81	−83	−85	−87	−89	−91	−92	13·5
14	−61	−62	−64	−66	−68	−69	−71	−73	−74	−76	−78	−80	−81	−83	−85	−87	14
14·5	−56	−57	−59	−60	−62	−63	−65	−67	−68	−70	−71	−73	−75	−76	−78	−79	14·5
15	−49	−51	−52	−54	−55	−57	−58	−59	−61	−62	−64	−65	−66	−68	−69	−71	15
15·5	−43	−44	−45	−46	−47	−49	−50	−51	−52	−54	−55	−56	−57	−58	−60	−61	15·5
16	−35	−36	−37	−38	−39	−40	−41	−42	−43	−44	−45	−46	−47	−48	−49	−50	16
16·5	−27	−28	−28	−29	−30	−31	−31	−32	−33	−34	−34	−35	−36	−37	−38	−38	16·5
17	−18	−19	−19	−20	−20	−21	−21	−22	−22	−23	−23	−24	−24	−25	−25	−26	17
17·5	−9	−9	−10	−10	−10	−10	−11	−11	−11	−11	−12	−12	−12	−13	−13	−13	17·5
18	0	0	0	0	0	0	0	0	0	0	0	0	0	0	0	0	18
18·5	9	9	10	10	10	10	11	11	11	11	12	12	12	13	13	13	18·5
19	18	19	19	20	20	21	21	22	22	23	23	24	24	25	25	26	19
19·5	27	28	28	29	30	31	31	32	33	34	34	35	36	37	38	38	19·5
20	35	36	37	38	39	40	41	42	43	44	45	46	47	48	49	50	20
20·5	43	44	45	46	47	49	50	51	52	54	55	56	57	58	60	61	20·5
21	49	51	52	54	55	57	58	59	61	62	64	65	66	68	69	71	21
21·5	56	57	59	60	62	63	65	67	68	70	71	73	75	76	78	79	21·5
22	61	62	64	66	68	69	71	73	74	76	78	80	81	83	85	87	22
22·5	65	67	68	70	72	74	76	78	79	81	83	85	87	89	91	92	22·5
23	68	70	71	73	75	77	79	81	83	85	87	89	91	93	95	97	23
23·5	69	71	73	75	77	79	81	83	85	87	89	91	93	95	97	99	23·5
24	70	72	74	76	78	80	82	84	86	88	90	92	94	96	98	100	24
	70	72	74	76	78	80	82	84	86	88	90	92	94	96	98	100	

HARMONIC TIDAL PREDICTION

TABLE V

Hours before or after H.W.	Diurnal Constituent O$_1$ AMPLITUDE (insert decimal point as appropriate)																	Hours before or after H.W.
	2	4	6	8	10	12	14	16	18	20	22	24	26	28	30	32	34	
HW.	2	4	6	8	10	12	14	16	18	20	22	24	26	28	30	32	34	HW.
0·5	2	4	6	8	10	12	14	16	18	20	22	24	26	28	30	32	34	0·5
1	2	4	6	8	10	12	14	16	17	19	21	23	25	27	29	31	33	1
1·5	2	4	6	7	9	11	13	15	17	19	21	22	24	26	28	30	32	1·5
2	2	4	5	7	9	11	12	14	16	18	19	21	23	25	27	28	30	2
2·5	2	3	5	7	8	10	11	13	15	16	18	20	21	23	25	26	28	2·5
3	1	3	4	6	7	9	10	12	13	15	16	18	19	21	22	24	25	3
3·5	1	3	4	5	7	8	9	11	12	13	14	16	17	18	20	21	22	3·5
4	1	2	3	4	6	7	8	9	10	11	12	13	15	16	17	18	19	4
4·5	1	2	3	4	5	5	6	7	8	9	10	11	12	13	14	15	16	4·5
5	1	1	2	3	3	4	5	6	6	7	8	8	9	10	10	11	12	5
5·5	0	1	1	2	2	3	3	4	4	5	5	6	6	6	7	7	8	5·5
6	0	0	1	1	1	1	2	2	2	2	2	3	3	3	3	4	4	6
6·5	0	0	0	0	0	0	0	0	0	0	0	0	0	0	0	0	0	6·5
7	0	−1	−1	−1	−1	−2	−2	−2	−2	−3	−3	−3	−3	−4	−4	−4	−4	7
7·5	−1	−1	−2	−2	−3	−3	−4	−4	−5	−5	−6	−6	−7	−7	−8	−8	−9	7·5
8	−1	−1	−2	−3	−4	−4	−5	−6	−7	−7	−8	−9	−10	−10	−11	−12	−12	8
8·5	−1	−2	−3	−4	−5	−6	−7	−8	−9	−10	−11	−11	−12	−13	−14	−15	−16	8·5
9	−1	−2	−3	−5	−6	−7	−8	−9	−10	−12	−13	−14	−15	−16	−17	−19	−20	9
9·5	−1	−3	−4	−5	−7	−8	−9	−11	−12	−14	−15	−16	−18	−19	−20	−22	−23	9·5
10	−2	−3	−5	−6	−8	−9	−11	−12	−14	−15	−17	−18	−20	−21	−23	−24	−26	10
10·5	−2	−3	−5	−7	−8	−10	−12	−13	−15	−17	−18	−20	−22	−23	−25	−27	−28	10·5
11	−2	−4	−5	−7	−9	−11	−13	−14	−16	−18	−20	−21	−23	−25	−27	−29	−30	11
11·5	−2	−4	−6	−8	−9	−11	−13	−15	−17	−19	−21	−23	−24	−26	−28	−30	−32	11·5
12	−2	−4	−6	−8	−10	−12	−14	−16	−18	−20	−21	−23	−25	−27	−29	−31	−33	12
12·5	−2	−4	−6	−8	−10	−12	−14	−16	−18	−20	−22	−24	−26	−28	−30	−32	−34	12·5
13	−2	−4	−6	−8	−10	−12	−14	−16	−18	−20	−22	−24	−26	−28	−30	−32	−34	13
13·5	−2	−4	−6	−8	−10	−12	−14	−16	−18	−20	−22	−24	−26	−28	−30	−32	−34	13·5
14	−2	−4	−6	−8	−10	−12	−14	−15	−17	−19	−21	−23	−25	−27	−29	−31	−33	14
14·5	−2	−4	−6	−7	−9	−11	−13	−15	−17	−19	−20	−22	−24	−26	−28	−30	−31	14·5
15	−2	−3	−5	−7	−9	−10	−12	−14	−16	−17	−19	−21	−23	−24	−26	−28	−30	15
15·5	−2	−3	−5	−6	−8	−10	−11	−13	−15	−16	−18	−19	−21	−23	−24	−26	−27	15·5
16	−1	−3	−4	−6	−7	−9	−10	−12	−13	−15	−16	−18	−19	−20	−22	−23	−25	16
16·5	−1	−3	−4	−5	−6	−8	−9	−10	−12	−13	−14	−15	−17	−18	−19	−21	−22	16·5
17	−1	−2	−3	−4	−5	−7	−8	−9	−10	−11	−12	−13	−14	−15	−16	−17	−19	17
17·5	−1	−2	−3	−4	−4	−5	−6	−7	−8	−9	−10	−11	−11	−12	−13	−14	−15	17·5
18	−1	−1	−2	−3	−3	−4	−5	−5	−6	−7	−7	−8	−8	−9	−10	−10	−11	18
18·5	0	−1	−1	−2	−2	−3	−3	−3	−4	−4	−5	−5	−5	−6	−6	−7	−7	18·5
19	0	0	−1	−1	−1	−1	−1	−1	−2	−2	−2	−2	−2	−2	−3	−3	−3	19
19·5	0	0	0	0	0	0	0	1	1	1	1	1	1	1	1	1	1	19·5
20	0	1	1	1	2	2	2	2	3	3	3	4	4	4	5	5	5	20
20·5	1	1	2	2	3	3	4	4	5	5	6	7	7	8	8	9	9	20·5
21	1	2	2	3	4	5	5	6	7	8	9	9	10	11	12	12	13	21
21·5	1	2	3	4	5	6	7	8	9	10	11	12	13	14	15	16	17	21·5
22	1	2	4	5	6	7	8	10	11	12	13	14	16	17	18	19	20	22
22·5	1	3	4	6	7	8	10	11	12	14	15	17	18	19	21	22	23	22·5
23	2	3	5	6	8	9	11	12	14	15	17	19	20	22	23	25	26	23
23·5	2	3	5	7	8	10	12	14	15	17	19	20	22	24	25	27	29	23·5
24	2	4	5	7	9	11	13	14	16	18	20	22	23	25	27	29	31	24
24·5	2	4	6	8	9	11	13	15	17	19	21	23	25	27	28	30	32	24·5
25	2	4	6	8	10	12	14	16	18	20	22	24	25	27	29	31	33	25
25·5	2	4	6	8	10	12	14	16	18	20	22	24	26	28	30	32	34	25·5
26	2	4	6	8	10	12	14	16	18	20	22	24	26	28	30	32	34	26
	2	4	6	8	10	12	14	16	18	20	22	24	26	28	30	32	34	

TABLE V

Hours before or after H.W.	Diurnal Constituent O₁ — AMPLITUDE (insert decimal point as appropriate)																	Hours before or after H.W.
	36	38	40	42	44	46	48	50	52	54	56	58	60	62	64	66	68	
HW.	36	38	40	42	44	46	48	50	52	54	56	58	60	62	64	66	68	HW.
0·5	36	38	40	42	44	46	48	50	52	54	56	58	60	62	64	66	67	0·5
1	35	37	39	41	43	45	47	49	50	52	54	56	58	60	62	64	66	1
1·5	34	35	37	39	41	43	45	47	49	50	52	54	56	58	60	62	64	1·5
2	32	34	35	37	39	41	42	44	46	48	49	51	53	55	57	58	60	2
2·5	30	31	33	34	36	38	39	41	43	44	46	48	49	51	53	54	56	2·5
3	27	28	30	31	33	34	36	37	39	40	42	43	45	46	48	49	51	3
3·5	24	25	26	28	29	30	32	33	34	36	37	38	40	41	42	43	45	3·5
4	20	21	22	24	25	26	27	28	29	30	31	33	34	35	36	37	38	4
4·5	16	17	18	19	20	21	22	23	24	25	26	27	27	28	29	30	31	4·5
5	12	13	14	15	15	16	17	17	18	19	19	20	21	21	22	23	24	5
5·5	8	9	9	10	10	11	11	12	12	12	13	13	14	14	15	15	16	5·5
6	4	4	4	5	5	5	5	6	6	6	6	6	7	7	7	7	8	6
6·5	0	0	0	0	0	−1	−1	−1	−1	−1	−1	−1	−1	−1	−1	−1	−1	6·5
7	−5	−5	−5	−6	−6	−6	−6	−7	−7	−7	−7	−8	−8	−8	−8	−9	−9	7
7·5	−9	−10	−10	−11	−11	−12	−12	−13	−13	−14	−14	−15	−15	−16	−16	−17	−17	7·5
8	−13	−14	−15	−15	−16	−17	−18	−18	−19	−20	−21	−21	−22	−23	−24	−24	−25	8
8·5	−17	−18	−19	−20	−21	−22	−23	−24	−25	−26	−27	−28	−29	−30	−31	−32	−32	8·5
9	−21	−22	−23	−24	−26	−27	−28	−29	−30	−31	−33	−34	−35	−36	−37	−38	−39	9
9·5	−24	−26	−27	−28	−30	−31	−32	−34	−35	−36	−38	−39	−41	−42	−43	−45	−46	9·5
10	−27	−29	−30	−32	−33	−35	−36	−38	−40	−41	−43	−44	−46	−47	−49	−50	−52	10
10·5	−30	−32	−33	−35	−37	−38	−40	−42	−43	−45	−47	−48	−50	−52	−53	−55	−57	10·5
11	−32	−34	−36	−38	−39	−41	−43	−45	−46	−48	−50	−52	−54	−55	−57	−59	−61	11
11·5	−34	−36	−38	−40	−41	−43	−45	−47	−49	−51	−53	−55	−57	−58	−60	−62	−64	11·5
12	−35	−37	−39	−41	−43	−45	−47	−49	−51	−53	−55	−57	−59	−60	−62	−64	−66	12
12·5	−36	−38	−40	−42	−44	−46	−48	−50	−52	−54	−56	−58	−60	−62	−64	−66	−68	12·5
13	−36	−38	−40	−42	−44	−46	−48	−50	−52	−54	−56	−58	−60	−62	−64	−66	−68	13
13·5	−36	−38	−40−	42	−44	−46	−48	−49	−51	−53	−55	−57	−59	−61	−63	−65	−67	13·5
14	−35	−37	−39	−41	−42	−44	−46	−48	−50	−52	−54	−56	−58	−60	−62	−64	−66	14
14·5	−33	−35	−37	−39	−41	−43	−44	−46	−48	−50	−52	−54	−56	−57	−59	−61	−63	14·5
15	−31	−33	−35	−37	−38	−40	−42	−44	−45	−47	−49	−51	−52	−54	−56	−58	−59	15
15·5	−29	−31	−32	−34	−36	−37	−39	−40	−42	−44	−45	−47	−48	−50	−52	−53	−55	15·5
16	−26	−28	−29	−31	−32	−34	−35	−37	−38	−39	−41	−42	−44	−45	−47	−48	−50	16
16·5	−23	−24	−26	−27	−28	−30	−31	−32	−33	−35	−36	−37	−39	−40	−41	−42	−44	16·5
17	−20	−21	−22	−23	−24	−25	−26	−27	−28	−29	−30	−32	−33	−34	−35	−36	−37	17
17·5	−16	−17	−18	−18	−19	−20	−21	−22	−23	−24	−25	−25	−26	−27	−28	−29	−30	17·5
18	−12	−12	−13	−14	−14	−15	−16	−16	−17	−18	−18	−19	−20	−20	−21	−22	−22	18
18·5	−8	−8	−8	−9	−9	−10	−10	−10	−11	−11	−12	−12	−13	−13	−13	−14	−14	18·5
19	−3	−3	−4	−4	−4	−4	−4	−4	−5	−5	−5	−5	−5	−5	−6	−6	−6	19
19·5	1	1	1	1	1	2	2	2	2	2	2	2	2	2	2	2	2	19·5
20	6	6	6	6	7	7	7	8	8	8	9	9	9	10	10	10	10	20
20·5	10	10	11	11	12	13	13	14	14	15	15	16	16	17	17	18	19	20·5
21	14	15	16	16	17	18	19	19	20	21	22	22	23	24	25	26	26	21
21·5	18	19	20	21	22	23	24	25	26	27	28	29	30	31	32	33	34	21·5
22	22	23	24	25	26	28	29	30	31	32	34	35	36	37	38	39	41	22
22·5	25	26	28	29	30	32	33	35	36	37	39	40	41	43	44	46	47	22·5
23	28	29	31	32	34	36	37	39	40	42	43	45	46	48	50	51	53	23
23·5	30	32	34	35	37	39	41	42	44	46	47	49	51	52	54	56	57	23·5
24	33	34	36	38	40	42	43	45	47	49	51	52	54	56	58	60	61	24
24·5	34	36	38	40	42	44	46	47	49	51	53	55	57	59	61	63	65	24·5
25	35	37	39	41	43	45	47	49	51	53	55	57	59	61	63	65	67	25
25·5	36	38	40	42	44	46	48	50	52	54	56	58	60	62	64	66	68	25·5
26	36	38	40	42	44	46	48	50	52	54	56	58	60	62	64	66	68	26
	36	38	40	42	44	46	48	50	52	54	56	58	60	62	64	66	68	

Hours before or after H.W.	Diurnal Constituent O₁ AMPLITUDE (insert decimal point as appropriate)							Hours before or after H.W.
	70	72	74	76	78	80	100	
HW.	70	72	74	76	78	80	100	HW.
0·5	69	71	73	75	77	79	99	0·5
1	68	70	72	74	76	78	97	1
1·5	65	67	69	71	73	75	93	1·5
2	62	64	65	67	69	71	88	2
2·5	57	59	61	62	64	66	82	2·5
3	52	54	55	57	58	60	75	3
3·5	46	47	49	50	51	53	66	3·5
4	39	40	42	43	44	45	56	4
4·5	32	33	34	35	36	37	46	4·5
5	24	25	26	26	27	28	35	5
5·5	16	17	17	18	18	18	23	5·5
6	8	8	8	8	9	9	11	6
6·5	−1	−1	−1	−1	−1	−1	−1	6·5
7	−9	−10	−10	−10	−10	−11	−13	7
7·5	−18	−18	−19	−19	−20	−20	−25	7·5
8	−26	−26	−27	−28	−29	−29	−37	8
8·5	−33	−34	−35	−36	−37	−38	−48	8·5
9	−41	−42	−43	−44	−45	−46	−58	9
9·5	−47	−49	−50	−51	−53	−54	−68	9·5
10	−53	−55	−56	−58	−59	−61	−76	10
10·5	−58	−60	−62	−63	−65	−67	−83	10·5
11	−63	−64	−66	−68	−70	−72	−89	11
11·5	−66	−68	−70	−72	−73	−75	−94	11·5
12	−68	−70	−72	−74	−76	−78	−98	12
12·5	−70	−72	−74	−76	−78	−80	−100	12·5
13	−70	−72	−74	−76	−78	−80	−100	13
13·5	−69	−71	−73	−75	−77	−79	−99	13·5
14	−68	−69	−71	−73	−75	−77	−97	14
14·5	−65	−67	−69	−70	−72	−74	−93	14·5
15	−61	−63	−65	−66	−68	−70	−87	15
15·5	−57	−58	−60	−61	−63	−65	−81	15·5
16	−51	−53	−54	−56	−57	−58	−73	16
16·5	−45	−46	−48	−49	−50	−51	−64	16·5
17	−38	−39	−40	−41	−42	−44	−54	17
17·5	−31	−32	−32	−33	−34	−35	−44	17·5
18	−23	−23	−24	−25	−25	−26	−33	18
18·5	−15	−15	−15	−16	−16	−17	−21	18·5
19	−6	−6	−7	−7	−7	−7	−9	19
19·5	2	2	2	3	3	3	3	19·5
20	11	11	11	12	12	12	15	20
20·5	19	20	20	21	21	22	27	20·5
21	27	28	29	29	30	31	39	21
21·5	35	36	37	38	39	40	50	21·5
22	42	43	44	45	47	48	60	22
22·5	48	50	51	53	54	55	69	22·5
23	54	56	57	59	60	62	77	23
23·5	59	61	63	64	66	68	84	23·5
24	63	65	67	69	70	72	90	24
24·5	66	68	70	72	74	76	95	24·5
25	69	71	73	74	76	78	98	25
25·5	70	72	74	76	78	80	100	25·5
26	70	72	74	76	78	80	100	26
	70	72	74	76	78	80	100	

EXTRACTS FROM ADMIRALTY TIDE TABLES—VOL. II, for a typical year.

Part II

No.	M.L. Z_0 m.	HARMONIC CONSTANTS							
		M_2 g°	H. m.	S_2 g°	H. m.	K_1 g°	H. m.	O_1 g°	H. m.
2280	4·3	161	2·8	185	0·8	217	0·3	208	0·3
3071	9·1	072	6·0	110	2·0	209	0·9	192	0·7
3850	7·5	108	3·7	134	2·0	048	0·3	041	0·3
4764	6·9	321	3·3	025	1·8	166	0·6	096	1·4

SEASONAL CHANGES IN MEAN LEVEL

No.	Jan. 1	Feb. 1	Mar. 1	Apr. 1	May 1	Jun. 1
2261-2292			Negligible			
3071, 3072	−0·4	−0·6	−0·4	+0·2	+0·7	+0·7
3850-3862			Negligible			
4763-4766	+0·5	+0·4	+0·2	0·0	−0·2	−0·3

SHALLOW WATER CORRECTIONS TO HARMONIC PREDICTIONS

Corrections in metres at luni-hourly intervals from semi-diurnal high water (SL).

In interpolating for other times of SL(1) ± 1224 may be applied to tabulated times.

Luni-hourly intervals	No. 2280 Port Beta SL. H.W. (1)*			
	0623	0929	0010	0316
−6	+0·5	0	−0·2	−0·1
−5	−0·2	−0·3	−0·3	−0·4
−4	−0·2	−0·1	−0·2	−0·3
−3	+0·1	+0·3	0	−0·1
−2	+0·3	+0·4	+0·1	+0·1
−1	+0·1	+0·2	0	+0·1
AT	0	0	0	+0·2
+1	−0·1	−0·2	−0·1	+0·2
+2	−0·3	−0·4	−0·2	0
+3	−0·1	−0·3	−0·2	0
+4	−0·6	0	−0·1	+0·2
+5	+1·0	+0·2	−0·1	+0·3

PART I: TABLE VII—TIDAL ANGLES AND FACTORS

Month Day	M_2 Angle	Factor	S_2 Angle	Factor	K_1 Angle	Factor	O_1 Angle	Factor
Feb. 17	074°	1·08	018°	1·20	324°	1·12	126°	1·31
Apr. 11	305	1·08	354	1·30	240	0·92	051	1·31
Apr. 13	000	1·15	353	1·28	238	1·00	108	1·41
May 11	320	1·15	342	0·99	207	1·35	096	1·41

* First semi-diurnal H.W.

BLOCK A

A.T.T. Part II

Harmonic Constants

Part I. Table VII

O/Nav. Table I
(nearest tabulated time)

	M.L. Zo m.	TIDAL CONSTITUENTS							
		M_2		S_2		K_1		O_1	
		g°	H. m.	g°	H. m.	g°	H. m.	g°	H. m.
		———	———	———	———	———	———	———	———
Cor.M.L		m	Amp.	s	Amp.	k	Amp.	o	Amp.
H.W.			hrs.		hrs.		hrs.		hrs.

BLOCK B

Zone Time hrs.	(1) Table II M_2 m.	(2) Table III S_2 m.	(3) Sum M_2+S_2 m.	(4) Table IV K_1 m.	(5) Table V O_1 m.	(6) Sum K_1+O_1 m.	(7) Sum (3)+(6) m.	(8) Cor. M.L. m.	(9) Ht. of Tide (7)+(8) m.	(10) Shallow Water Cor. m.	(11) Cor. Ht. m.
0											
1											
2											
3											
4											
5											
6											
7											
8											
9.											
10											
11											
12											
13											
14											
15											
16											
17											
18											
19											
20											
21											
22											
23											
24											

	M.L. Zo m.	TIDAL CONSTITUENTS							
		M₂		S₂		K₁		O₁	
		g°	H. m.	g°	H. m.	g°	H. m.	g°	H. m.
A.T.T. Part II									
Harmonic Constants									
Part I. Table VII		—	—	—	—	—	—	—	—
	Cor.M.L	m	Amp.	s	Amp.	k	Amp.	o	Amp.
O/Nav. Table I (nearest tabulated time)	H.W.		hrs.		hrs.		hrs.		hrs.

BLOCK B

Zone Time hrs.	(1) Table II M₂ m.	(2) Table III S₂ m.	(3) Sum M₂+S₂ m.	(4) Table IV K₁ m.	(5) Table V O₁ m.	(6) Sum K₁+O₁ m.	(7) Sum (3)+(6) m.	(8) Cor. M.L. m.	(9) Ht. of Tide (7)+(8) m.	(10) Shallow Water Cor. m.	(11) Cor. Ht. m.
0											
1											
2											
3											
4											
5											
6											
7											
8											
9											
10											
11											
12											
13											
14											
15											
16											
17											
18											
19											
20											
21											
22											
23											
24											

BLOCK A

A.T.T. Part II

Harmonic Constants

Part I. Table VII

O/Nav. Table I
(nearest tabulated time)

M.L. Zo m.	TIDAL CONSTITUENTS							
	M₂		S₂		K₁		O₁	
	g°	H. m.	g°	H. m.	g°	H. m.	g°	H. m.
	—	—	—	—	—	—	—	—
Cor.M.L	m	Amp.	s	Amp.	k	Amp.	o	Amp.
H.W.		hrs.		hrs.		hrs.		hrs.

BLOCK B

Zone Time hrs.	(1) Table II M₂ m.	(2) Table III S₂ m.	(3) Sum M₂+S₂ m.	(4) Table IV K₁ m.	(5) Table V O₁ m.	(6) Sum K₁+O₁ m.	(7) Sum (3)+(6) m.	(8) Cor. M.L. m.	(9) Ht. of Tide (7)+(8) m.	(10) Shallow Water Cor. m.	(11) Cor. Ht. m.
0											
1											
2											
3											
4											
5											
6											
7											
8											
9.											
10											
11											
12											
13											
14											
15											
16											
17											
18											
19											
20											
21											
22											
23											
24											

Section M

Legal Notes, Shipping Terms and Abbreviations

SHIPPING ABBREVIATIONS

The following list is confined to abbreviations which are in general use.

a.a.	Always afloat
A/c	Account
Acc.	Accepted
A.d.	After date
Ad. val.	Ad valorem, according to value
A.F.	Advanced freight
Amt.	Amount
A/p	Additional premium
A.P.	Average payable
A.R.	All risks
A/S	After sight
A/T	American terms
Av.	Average
B/-	Bag, bale
b.b.	Below bridges
B.C.	Bristol Channel
B.D.	Bar draft
B/E	Bill of Exchange
Bona Fide	In good faith
b/f	Brought forward
B/G	Bonded goods
B/H	Bill of Health
B.H.P.	Brake Horse Power
B/L	Bill of Lading
b.m.	Board measure
B.O.	Buyer's option
B.O.T.	Board of Trade
B/P	Bills payable
B/R	Bills received
Brl.	Barrel
B.S.	Bill of Sale
b.t.	Berth terms
B.V.	Bureau Veritas
cancl.	Cancelled
Carte Blanche	Full discretionary powers
C.Cl.	Continuation clause
C. & D.	Collected and delivered
C/E	Customs entry
c. & f.	Cost and freight
c.f.o.	Channel for orders
c. & i.	Cost and insurance
c.i.f.	Cost, insurance and freight
c.i.f. & c.	Cost, insurance, freight and commission
c/l	Craft loss
cld.	Cleared
C.N.	Credit note, Consignment note
C/O	Certificate of origin
Cont. (B-H)	Continent Bordeaux-Hamburg
Cont. (A-H)	Continent Antwerp-Hamburg
Cont. (H-H)	Continent Havre-Hamburg
C/P	Charter Party
c.p.d.	Charterers pay dues
C.R.	Current rate, Company's risk

C.T.C.	Corn trade clauses
C.T.L.	Constructive total loss
C.T.L.O.	Constructive total loss only
c.v.	Chief value
c.w.o.	Cash with order
D/A	Discharge afloat
d.a.a.	Discharge always afloat
d.b.	Deals and battens
d.b.b.	Deals, battens and boards
Dbk.	Drawback
D/C	Deviation clause
d.d.	Date due
D/D	Delivered at Docks
dd.	Delivered
d.d.	Days after date
d/d	Dated
d.d.s.	Delivered sound
d.d.o.	Despatch discharging only
d.f.	Dead freight
d.l.o.	Despatch loading only
d.p.	Direct port
D.P.	Documents against payment
Dr.	Debtor, debit
D/s	Days after sight
d.w.	Dead weight
d.w.c.	Dead weight capacity
E.E.	Errors excepted
E. & O.E.	Errors and omissions excepted
est.	Estimated
et. al.	And others
et. seq.	And the following
Ex.	Excluding, without
Exd.	Examined
f.a.	Free alongside
F.A.A.	Free of all average
f.a.c.	Fast as can
f.a.q.	Free alongside quay
F. & D.	Freight and demurrage
f.a.s.	Free alongside ship
F.C. & S.	Free of capture and seizure
F.D.	Free discharge
f.f.a.	Free from alongside
f.g.a.	Free of general average
f.i.a.	Full interest admitted
f.i.b.	Free into bunker/barge
f.i.o.	Free in and out
f.i.w.	Free into wagon
f.o.	Firm order
f.o.b.	Free on board
f.o.c.	Free of charge
f.o.d.	Free of damage
f.o.q.	Free on quay
f.o.r.	Free on rail
f.o.r.t.	Full out rye terms
f.o.s.	Free on ship
f.o.t.	Free on trucks
f.o.w.	First open water
F.P.	Floating Policy
F.P.A.	Free of Particular Average

f.r. & c.c.	Free of riots and civil commotions	mt.	Empty
		M.T.L.	Mean Tide Level
f.r.o.f.	Fire risk on freight		
Frt.	Freight	n/a	No account (banking)
f.t.	Full terms	n.a.a.	Not always afloat
f.w.d.	Fresh water damage	N.C.	New charter, new crop
		N.C.V.	No commercial value
G/A	General Average	N.D.	No discount
g.m.b.	Good merchantable brand	n.d.w.	Net deadweight
g.m.q.	Good merchantable quality	n.e.p.	Not elsewhere provided
g.o.b.	Good ordinary brand	n.e.s.	Not elsewhere specified
g.r.t.	Gross register tonnage	n.h.p.	Nominal horse power
g.s.m.	Good sound merchantable	n/n	No number
		N/m	No mark
H.A. or D.	Havre, Antwerp or Dunkirk	n.o.p.	Not otherwise provided
h.c.	Held covered	n.o.r.	Not otherwise rated
H/H	Havre to Hamburg	N/R	Not reported
h.p.	Horse power	n.r.	No risk, net register
h.p.n.	Horse power nominal	n.r.t.	Net register tons
H.W.	High Water	n.s.p.f.	Not specially provided for
		N/t	New terms
I.A.T.A.	International Air Transport Association	Nt. wt.	Net weight
I.B.	In Bond	o.a.	Over all
I.C.C.	Institute cargo clauses	O.C.	Open charter, Old crop, Open cover
i.h.p.	Indicated horse power		
I.M.C.O.	Inter-governmental Maritime Consultative Organisation	o/d	On demand
		O/o	Order of
int.	Interest	O.P.	Open Policy
ince.	Insurance	O.R.	Owners Risk
i.o.p.	Irrespective of percentage	O.S.	Open Ship
i.v.	Invoice value	O/t	Old terms
K.D.	Knocked down	P/A	Particular Average
		P.chgs.	Particular Charges
L/A	Lloyd's Agent	P.D.	Port dues
L.A.T.	Linseed Association Terms	P. & I.	Protection and Indemnity
L.B.P.	Length between-perpendiculars	P/L	Partial Loss
L.C.	London clause	P. & L.	Profit and Loss
L/C	Letter of Credit	P.L.A.	Port of London Authority
L.H.A.R.	London, Hull, Antwerp, Rotterdam	P.N.	Promissory note
		p.o.r.	Port of refuge
L.L.T.	London landed terms	p.p.	Picked ports
Ll. & Co's	Lloyds and Companies	ppd.	Prepaid
l.m.c.	Low middling clause (cotton)	p.p.i.	Policy proof of interest
L.R.	Lloyd's Register	P.R.	Port risks
L.R.M.C.	Lloyd's Refrigerating Machinery Certificate	P/R	Provisional release
		P.T.	Parcel ticket
l.s.	Lump sum	p.t.	Private terms
ltr.	Lighter	Ptg.Std.	Petrograde Standard (timber)
l.w.l.	Load water line		
L.W.	Low Water	Qn.	Quotation
		qty.	Quantity
M.C.	Machinery Certificate	q.v.	Quod vide (which see)
M/D	Memorandum of Deposit		
mfrs.	Manufacturers	R/A	Refer to acceptor
M.I.P.	Marine Insurance Policy	R.A.T.	Rape-Seed Association terms
M.M.A.	Merchandise Marks Act	R. & C.C.	Riots and Civil Commotions
M.O.H.	Medical Officer of Health	R.C.C.& S.	Riots, Civil Commotions and Strikes
M.R.	Mate's receipt		
M/s	Month's sight	R/D	Refer to drawer
M.S.A.	Merchant Shipping Act	r.d.	Running days

R.D.C.	Running down clause
R.I.	Re-Insurance
r.o.b.	Remain on board
R.P.	Return premium
R.T.	Rye terms
r.t.b.a.	Rate to be arranged
s/a	Safe arrival
S.B.	Short bill
s.b.s.	Surveyed before shipment
S.C.	Salvage charges
s/d	Sea damaged
S.d.	Short delivery
S. & F.A.	Shipping and forwarding agent
S. & H.E.	Sundays and holidays excepted
S.I.	Short interest
S.L.	Salvage loss
S/L.C.	Sue and Labour clause
S/N	Shipping Note
S.O.	Seller's option
S.O.L.	Ship owners' liability
s.p.d.	Steamer pays dues
S.R. & C.C.	Strikes, riots and civil commotions
S.R.L.	Ship repairers' liability
S.R. ports	Southern range U.S.A. Atlantic Ports, south of Norfolk, Virginia
s.s. or b.	Stranded, sunk or burnt
Stg.	Sterling
S.W.	Shippers weight
T.	Tare
T/c	Till countermanded
T.E.	Trade expenses
T.L.	Total loss
T.L.O.	Total loss only
T/O	Transfer order
T.Q.	Tale quale (as found)
T.R.	Tons registered
U/a	Underwriting account
u.c.b.	Unless caused by
U.K./Cont.	United Kingdom or Continent
U.K./Cont.(B.H.)	United Kingdom or Continent (Bordeaux Hamburg range)
U.K./Cont.(G.H.)	United Kingdom or Continent (Gibraltar, Hamburg range)
U.K./Cont.(H.H.)	United Kingdom or Continent (Havre, Hamburg range)
U.K.f.o.	United Kingdom for orders
U.K.H.A.D.	United Kingdom, Havre, Antwerp or Dunkirk
U.P.S.	Underwriters pay stamp duty
u/w	Underwriter
V.c.	Valuation clause
v.o.p.	Value as in original policy
v.v.	Vice Versa
W.A.	With average
W.B./E.I.	West Britain/East Ireland
w.b.s.	Without benefit of salvage

W.C.A.	West Coast of Africa
W.C.N.A.	West Coast North America
W/d	Warranted
W.H.O.	World Health Organisation
whse.	Warehouse
w.o.b.	Washed overboard
W.O.L.	Wharf owners' liability
w.p.	Without prejudice
W.P.A.	With Particular Average
w.p.p.	Waterproof paper packing
W.R.	Warehouse receipt
w.r.o.	War risk only
Wtd.	Warranted
W/W	Warehouse warrant
W.W.D.	Weather working days
Y/A.R.	York Antwerp Rules

GENERAL SHIPPING AND LEGAL TERMS IN COMMON USE

Abandonment: Leaving a ship as unseaworthy; the giving up of a vessel and cargo to establish a claim on the Underwriters.

Adjustment: A settlement of a loss incurred by an insured person.

Advance Note: A draft on a shipowner for wages, given to a seaman on signing Articles of Agreement and redeemable after ship has sailed with the seaman aboard.

Affidavit: A written declaration on oath.

Affreightment: A contract to carry goods by ship. Charter Parties and Bills of Lading are Contracts of Affreightment.

Arbitration: The submitting of matters of controversy to judgement by persons selected by all parties to the dispute.

Arrest: The detention of a vessel until the purpose of the arrest has been fulfilled.

Assessor: A person who officially estimates the value of goods for the purpose of apportioning the sum payable in the settlement of claims.

Average: A partial loss of the subject matter insured.

Average (General): Partial loss as a result of voluntary sacrifice for the common safety. The owner of the property sacrificed has the right to receive contributions from other interests directly benefited.

Average (Particular): Partial loss due to accident, Act of God, or stress of weather. It is borne by the owner of property damaged.

Average Adjuster: A person who officially calculates the contribution due from each beneficiary as a consequence of a GENERAL AVERAGE ACT.

Average Bond: An agreement signed by all interested parties acknowledging their liability to pay a share of the loss under General Average.

Back freight: Payment due to the shipowner for the carriage of goods beyond the contract port owing to circumstances beyond the control of the shipowner.

Bare Boat Charter: Charterer hires a vessel for a long period, appoints the Master and Crew, and pays all running expenses.

Barratry: An illegal or fraudulent act committed by the Master or crew to the prejudice of the Owner or Charterer.

Bill of Exchange: An order in writing from one person or firm to another requiring them to pay a certain sum to a person named.

Bill of Health: A document stating the condition of health in the country the vessel has sailed from. It is required by vessels calling at ports in countries that are *not* signatories to the International Sanitary Regulations.

Bill of Lading: A document which is a receipt for cargo received on board, and is evidence of the contract between Shipper and Shipowner. It is also evidence of title to the goods described on it.

Bill of Sight: This is a Customs import form completed by the importer. It authorises the Customs to open packages so that they can ascertain whether goods are dutiable.

Bill of Store: A Customs import form which is used for British dutiable goods returned to the United Kingdom within a stated period.

Bonded Goods: Imported goods deposited in a Government warehouse until duty is paid.

Breaking Bulk: The initial opening of hatches on entering port and the commencement of discharge of cargo.

Charter Party: An agreement wherein the Shipowner hires his vessel to the Charterer subject to certain conditions.

Clean Bill of Lading: One in which there is nothing to qualify the admission that the goods are shipped in good order and condition.

Cocket Card (Clearance Label): Denotes that a vessel has complied with all the regulations. It is attached to the Victualling Bill by the Customs Officer who clears the vessel, and is then known as Outward Clearance.

Consignee: The firm or persons authorised to receive the cargo, and to whom it is consigned.

Constructive Total Loss: This term applies to cases in which the cost of salvaging and repairing a wrecked vessel would exceed her value when repaired.

Dead Freight: Freight which is paid on empty space in the vessel when the Charterer is responsible for the freight of a full cargo. It should be paid before sailing.

Demurrage: The sum agreed by charter to be paid as damage for delay beyond the stipulated time for loading or discharging. It should be collected daily by the Master or Agent.

Derelict: A vessel that has been abandoned by the crew but has not sunk.

Despatch money: When so agreed in the Charter, it is paid by the Shipowner to the Charterer as a result of the vessel completing loading or discharging before the stipulated time.

S

Detention: Where demurrage is paid for an agreed number of days, any further delay is termed "detention", in respect of which the Ship-owner can claim unlimited damages.

Deviation: A divergence from an insured voyage which may release the Underwriter from his risk, unless it is especially covered.

Drawback: A repayment of duty on the exportation of goods previously imported.

Entering inwards: The reporting of the vessel's arrival in port by the Master at the Custom House. Permission to commence discharging is obtained.

Entry outwards: The reporting of the intention to commence a new voyage by the Master at the Custom House, Permission to commence loading is obtained.

Flotsam: Cargo cast or lost overboard and recoverable by reason of its remaining afloat.

Free in and out: Cargo to be loaded and discharged free to the vessel.

Free on board: Goods delivered on board the vessel free of extra charge to the purchaser.

Freight: The charge for transporting goods by water.

Grain Certificate: A certificate to show that the regulations have been complied with when carrying a grain cargo.

Groundage: A fee payable for permission to anchor in certain ports.

Indemnity: Security from damage or loss.

Invoice: A document setting out in detail the goods consigned, marks and numbers, cost, any charges, and name of consignee.

Inward charges: Pilotage and other expenses incurred on entering port.

Jerque Note: A document given to the Master by the Customs after the inward cargo is discharged and the vessel has been rummaged.

Jetsam: Cargo or goods which sink when jettisoned. The term applies also to such goods when washed ashore.

Jettison: The act of throwing cargo and stores overboard in order to save the vessel.

Lagan: Cargo thrown overboard, but buoyed so that it may be recovered.

Lay Days: Days allowed by Charter for loading or discharging cargo.

Leadage: The cost of transporting coal from colliery to place of shipment.

Lien: A legal right over goods, to hold them until the claim against the owner has been settled.

Light Bill: A Customs receipt for the payment of light dues.

Light Dues: Monies collected by the Customs on behalf of Trinity House for the maintenance of lighthouses and buoys. Dues are levied on vessels according to their net registered tonnage.

Lighterage: The price paid for loading or unloading ships by lighters or barges.

Lloyd's Agents: Persons appointed by Lloyd's, and stationed in all major world ports; their function is to safeguard Lloyd's interest and report all movement and losses of ships.

Lloyd's Register: An independent non-profit making Society, controlled by the various sectors of the shipping industry. It undertakes surveys, classification of all vessels, and produces various annual publications, including Construction Rules for Steel Ships.

Lump Sum Freight: A fixed amount of freight payable, regardless of how much cargo is loaded.

Manifest: A document containing the passenger list, and details of all stores and cargo aboard the vessel.

Maritime Lien: The claim a Master and crew has on the vessel for the payment of wages due.

Mate's Receipt: A receipt signed by the Mate to say the cargo has been received on board in good order and condition.

Notary Public: An official certified to take affidavits and depositions from members of the public.

Official Number: A registered number given to all merchant vessels, and cut in on the vessel's "main beam" together with the Net Register Tonnage.

Open Charter: Where the Charter Party specifies neither the kind of cargo nor the ports of destination.

Open Policy (or **Floating Policy**): An agreement between Underwriter and Shipper to insure goods to a certain maximum value. The goods to be shipped in one or more vessels to be named later.

Portage Bill: A bill giving the statement of wages of each member of the crew at the end of a voyage.

Power of Attorney: A document which empowers one person to act for another.

Pratique: Permission to land crew and cargo after the vessel has satisfied the Port Doctor as to the state of health aboard.

Prime entry: Goods entering the United Kingdom which are dutiable.

Promissory Note: A note promising to pay a certain person a stated sum on a specified date.

Protest (see also page 278): A written declaration by the Master, and witnessed before a Notary Public.

Quayage: The charge for using a berth alongside a wharf.

Receiver of Wreck: An official who is responsible to the Board of Trade for all wreckage that is salved on the coastline, or found at sea and brought to a British port.

Registry, Certificate of: A document giving all particulars of the vessel, including the names of the Owner and the Master.

Running Down Clause: Provides insurance cover for a Shipowner whose vessel is in collision with another, against third-party claims.

Salvage (see note below): Money awarded to those who have assisted in saving a vessel from being lost.

Ship's Articles: The agreement between the Master and his crew, giving details of conditions and terms.

Ship's Husband: The Shipowner's Agent who superintends the vessel when in port.

Short Delivery: The quantity of cargo delivered in less than the Bill of Lading quantity.

Time Charter: The Charterer has the use of the vessel for a specified period. The Shipowner supplies the crew and provisions.

Tonnage Deck: The uppermost continuous deck in ships having less than three decks, or the second continuous deck from below.

Transire: A Customs document used when a vessel is coasting, giving full cargo details. It serves as Clearance from the port of issue.

Under Deck Tonnage: The cubic capacity of the vessel below the tonnage deck in measurement tons of 100 cubic feet per ton (or 2.83 cubic metres per ton.)

Unseaworthy: The condition of a vessel where from any cause it is unsafe to send her to sea.

Valued Policy: The agreed value of the subject matter insured is stated on the policy. Hull and Goods Policies are invariably of this type.

Victualling Bill: A document showing bonded stores for the vessel's use.

Voyage Charter: The Shipowner hires his vessel, subject to various conditions, for the carriage of cargo for a single voyage.

Way Bill: A statement in triplicate indicating numbers and descriptions of goods it accompanies. Usually refers to Post Office Mails.

Weather Working Day: A day of 24 hours on which work is not prevented by bad weather.

Wharfage: The charges made for the use of a wharf.

Working Day: A day in which work is normally done at a particular port, and excludes Sunday or official holidays.

NOTES ON SALVAGE AND TOWAGE

The term salvage has two meanings in the shipping world. It applies (a) to the services rendered by persons who, by their efforts, rescue a ship and/or cargo from loss or damage by a marine peril, and (b) to the reward paid to the salvors of such property.

The Principles of Salvage:

The Law of Salvage requires that the rescue of maritime property must fulfil the following conditions before a claim can be considered as valid.

1 The property salvaged must have been in real danger;
2 The salvor voluntarily offered his services;
3 The services rendered must be wholly or partially successful.

How Salvage affects the Ship's Master:

The master of a ship is required by law to go to the assistance of vessels in distress *for the purpose of saving life*. The saving of life *alone* does not entitle him to claim salvage. If property and lives are saved together, then life salvage may be paid as an addition to the property salvage award.

A possible present day salvage situation that the Ship Master may encounter is that of a disabled vessel requiring a tow to a port of safety. **Before commencing the tow, the Master of the vessel undertaking the tow should:**

1 Satisfy himself that there is a clause in the Charter Party or Bills of Lading allowing his vessel to engage in such operations;
2 Reach agreement with the Master of the disabled vessel as to the destination;
3 Inform his owners, so that they may confirm his decision and pay any aditional premium required by the Underwriters;
4 If the vessel is on charter, notify the charterers.
5 Insist that Lloyd's Form of Salvage Agreement should be adopted (this avoids later costly litigation).

Other points to consider:

1 Whether sufficient fuel and stores are available.
2 The nature of the cargo carried, and whether the delay incurred by the salvage operation would be harmful to the goods.
3 If on a charter, will the delay cause the towing vessel to arrive at her destination after the cancelling date?

Points which are considered when a salvage award is assessed:

1 The value of the property saved.
2 The nature of the danger from which the property was salvaged.
3 The risks to which the salvor's property was exposed during the salvage operation.
4 The time taken, and skill shown, by the salvors in effecting the salvage.
5 Any pecuniary loss suffered by the salvors.
6 The value of the salvor's property at risk.

Towage

The towage of a vessel which is in no way damaged or disabled, when all that is required is the expediting of her voyage, is a towage service. The distinction between towage and salvage services is important, because the owner of the vessel towing is entitled to greater remuneration for salvage than for towing.

NOTES ON MERCHANT SHIPPING TONNAGE REGULATIONS

The tonnage regulations were revised during 1967 to give effect to a recommendation of the Intergovernmental Maritime Consultative Organisation (I.M.C.O.) regarding the treatment for tonnage purposes of the shelter-deck and certain other spaces on board ship. **The outward sign of these changes** in the Regulations has been the appearance of the **tonnage mark** on the sides of certain ships. See fig. M.1 on page 276.

In the past, shelter-deck ships have been allocated reduced tonnage by virtue of the tonnage openings in the shelter-deck. These ships generally carried light bulky cargoes which filled the spaces without deeply submerging the vessel. On occasions, when heavy cargoes were available and space was not so important, it was desirable to be able to load to a deeper draft. This entailed closing all the tonnage openings and raising the position of the load lines, disc and deck line. The vessel then adopted a larger tonnage, and was entitled to load to a deeper draft. The owners were at liberty to change from one tonnage to the other as trade demanded, but the changeover took time, money, and necessitated the services of a surveyor.

The 1967 Rules enable a vessel to be allocated alternative tonnages, and the submersion or non-submersion of the tonnage mark indicates which tonnage is applicable; i.e., if the tonnage mark is submerged, then the higher tonnage applies, but if not submerged the lower tonnage applies. This allocation of alternative tonnages does not now depend on tonnage openings, and these are permanently closed, thus increasing the safety of the vessel.

An owner may apply to have a permanently reduced tonnage, in which case the tonnage mark is placed on the ship's side at a draft equal to the deepest loadline draft, and the higher of the horizontal lines is then omitted.

LOADLINES AND FREEBOARD

The following notes are based on the Load Line Convention (1966) which came into force on 21st July, 1968.

Apart from certain exceptions, all vessels are required to be surveyed in accordance with the Load Line Rules, and marked with a deck line, load lines, and the load line mark (disc).

Summer freeboard: The distance between the top edges of the deck line and the horizontal line through the disc is called the "Summer freeboard". It is a measure of the minimum reserve buoyancy considered necessary for the safety of the vessel when navigating in a designated Summer Zone sea area (see Zone Chart).

"The load line grid" indicates the minimum admissible freeboards for any particular Zone, and is always placed *forward* of the disc. It also indicates the draft to which the vessel may load when floating in water of unit density. See fig. M.2.1 on page 277.

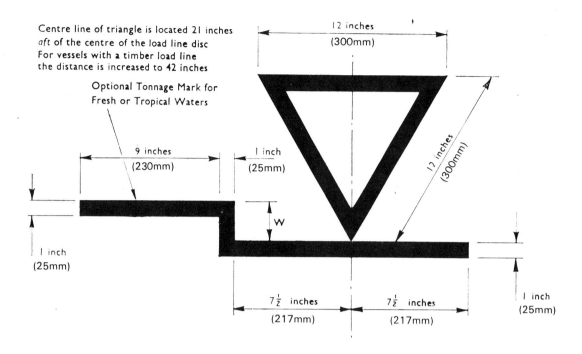

Centre line of triangle is located 21 inches *aft* of the centre of the load line disc. For vessels with a timber load line the distance is increased to 42 inches

Optional Tonnage Mark for Fresh or Tropical Waters

12 inches (300mm)

12 inches (300mm)

9 inches (230mm)

1 inch (25mm)

W

1 inch (25mm)

$7\frac{1}{2}$ inches (217mm)

$7\frac{1}{2}$ inches (217mm)

1 inch (25mm)

Fig. M.1.

When **timber freeboards** are assigned to a vessel, an additional grid of lumber load lines is placed *aft* of the load line disc. See fig. M.2. on page 277.

Overloading:

The law requires that a vessel shall not be so loaded as to submerge the appropriate load line when that vessel is floating in salt water. A vessel in fresh water may submerge the appropriate load line by the amount of the *Fresh Water Allowance* or, if in partly fresh water, by a proportion of this allowance.

Contravention of the law makes the Master of the overloaded vessel liable to a heavy fine, and in certain cases, imprisonment; also the vessel may be detained until she ceases to be overloaded. **Inadvertent overloading must be rectified before sailing.** This is best achieved by discharging ballast, feed water, domestic water or fuel, bearing in mind voyage requirements. Cargo should only be discharged as a last resort.

FREEBOARD

Conditions of Assignment:

Before a vessel may be assigned a freeboard, certain conditions must be fulfilled:

(a) Information must be supplied to the Master of every new ship to enable him to arrange the loading and discharging so as to avoid excessive stresses in the vessel's structure;

(b) The means of securing openings in the hull and the quality of the fittings employed must meet certain minimum standards. **Class 2 closing appliances are no longer accepted;**

(c) Arrangements for the protection of the crew, the location of side scuttles, and the type and size of freeing ports also come under close scrutiny;

(d) The Assigning Authority will also consider whether the general structure of the hull is of sufficient strength for the draft corresponding to the freeboard assigned.

Freeboard Computation:

All vessels are now divided into two categories for the purpose of computing freeboard.

Type A—Consists of all vessels designed to carry only liquid cargoes in bulk.

Type B—Includes all other vessels.

The minimum freeboard for vessels of each type is obtained from separate tables. To this minimum freeboard must be added certain corrections depending on how the hull of the individual vessel differs from that of the standard vessel on which the tables are based.

Large tankers benefit considerably under these new Rules providing that if, when in the loaded condition, any one empty compartment becomes flooded, the vessel will remain afloat in a satisfactory condition of equilibrium.

Bulk carriers also benefit but, to take full advantage of the freeboard reduction, they must fulfil certain requirements of sub-division, and be fitted with steel weathertight hatches.

Dry cargo ships fitted with steel weathertight hatches are entitled to smaller freeboards regardless of their sub-division.

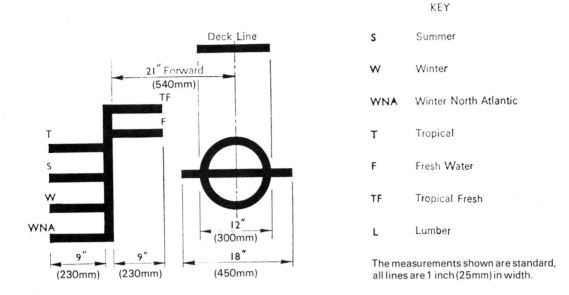

KEY

S	Summer
W	Winter
WNA	Winter North Atlantic
T	Tropical
F	Fresh Water
TF	Tropical Fresh
L	Lumber

The measurements shown are standard, all lines are 1 inch (25mm) in width.

Fig. M.2.1.   LOAD LINE GRID

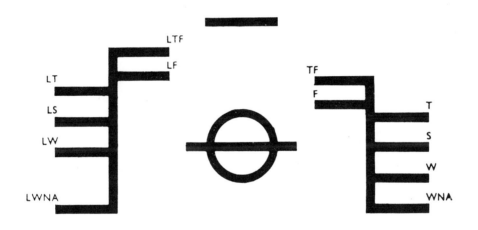

Fig. M.2.2   **LOAD LINES ON VESSELS WHICH HAVE BEEN ASSIGNED A TIMBER FREEBOARD**

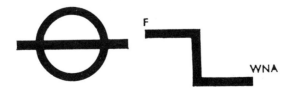

Fig. M.2.3.   **LOAD LINES ON SAILING SHIPS**

Small vessels with wooden hatches are penalised with larger freeboards and, if these vessels have short superstructures or none at all, then the tabular freeboard is doubled.

These Rules apply to all new vessels, but existing vessels may take advantage of the freeboard reductions providing they comply with the requirements. *No existing vessel will be allocated a larger freeboard than she has at present.*

PROTEST

"Noting Protest" is the legal term for the procedure whereby the Master of a vessel declares before a Notary Public, British Consular Officer or other authority, of circumstances beyond his control which may have caused (or may give rise in the future to) loss or damage to either the vessel or her cargo.

The original note of protest is entered into the Register at the office of the Notary Public or Consulate. Certified copies are supplied to the Master for a fee.

Protests must be noted within 24 hours of arrival at a port, and preferably before breaking bulk if cargo damage is suspected.

The importance of a Protest is that in many cases, particularly on the Continent, it is **essential** for the establishment of a claim. In the United Kingdom the situation is different, and legal rights are not affected by the failure to "note protest". The main use of a protest in the United Kingdom is to support the claim of a cargo owner against his underwriters, and is therefore of value.

Extension of Protest: A protest may be extended at a later date, usually within 6 months of the original, when the full extent of the loss or damage has been ascertained.

The following are occasions for usefully noting protest:
1 When the vessel has encountered weather liable to have caused damage to the cargo.
2 When, regardless of cause, it is suspected that damage to the ship has been sustained.
3 When, due to bad weather, it has been impracticable to provide proper ventilation for the cargo.
4 In all cases of general average.
5 Any serious breach of a Charter Party by the charterer, such as:
   (i) Undue loading delays;
   (ii) Refusal to load;
   (iii) Loading improper cargo;
   (iv) Refusal to accept Bills of Lading as signed by the Master;
   (v) Refusal to pay demurrage.

A protest will *not* exonerate the Master if he fails to endorse the Bills of Lading in respect of goods shipped in a damaged condition or of goods short shipped.

Section N

Search and Rescue at Sea

SEARCH AND RESCUE

General
The following is for information and guidance of Mariners who become involved in a Distress Incident at Sea. It should be read in conjunction with and as supplementary to Admiralty Notices to Mariners No. 4 of Annual Summary, and the IMCO Merchant Ship Search and Rescue Manual (MERSAR).

Whatever the type of air or surface craft in distress survivors may have to be taken off a craft or recovered from the sea. Success in rescuing survivors will depend firstly on speedy and well organised action by the search and rescue units involved.

Distress incidents fall into two main categories:
(a) Coastal: in which some or all of the following may be able to assist. Surface craft, long range Search and Rescue (S.A.R.) aircraft, helicopters, shore lifeboats and shore life saving services.
(b) Ocean: in which ships and long range S.A.R. aircraft will be concerned. In the more remote ocean areas only ships may be available.

Co-ordination of Search and Rescue
For the effective conduct of S.A.R. operations co-ordination will be of prime importance and there are several aspects of this.

(a) Shore Co-ordination
A number of Administrations vest authority to exercise overall co-ordination in Rescue Co-ordination Centres (R.C.C.) whose task is to plan and supervise the conduct of S.A.R. operations. They maintain the closest contact with Coast Radio Stations whose function is of special importance in this context.

(b) Airborne Co-ordination
When more than one long range aircraft and/or helicopter are participating in S.A.R. operations under the control of an R.C.C. the R.C.C. may designate an Airborne On Scene Commander (O.S.C.).

(c) Surface Co-ordination
If the specialised S.A.R. ships (including warships) are in the vicinity, one of these may be expected to assume the duties of O.S.C. If only merchant ships are in the search area or at the location of the distress a Co-ordinator Surface Search (C.S.S.) should be established by mutual arrangements to organise and conduct co-ordinated S.A.R. operations as required. Detailed guidance concerning the selection of the C.S.S. is given on page 281.

Surface co-ordination can be effective only if full use is made of the communications channels available to the rescue units and strict discipline is maintained by all searching vessels. Communications by radio should be brief and to the point.

THE MARINE ASPECT OF RESCUE AT SEA
The following instructions are intended to provide a general guide on the action to be taken by Masters of vessels who receive a distress message. The provisions of sub-paragraphs (a) to (d) of Regulation 10 of Chapter V of the International Convention for the Safety of Life at Sea, 1960, are specially relevant and for ease of reference are produced on page 288.

1. Action on receipt of Distress Call and Message

As authorised by the Master the following immediate action should be taken by all vessels in the area concerned:

(a) **Acknowledge receipt of the distress message** in accordance with the provision of articles 1425-1428 of the Radio Regulations.

(b) **Communicate**
(i) Name of vessel.
(ii) Position.
(iii) E.T.A. on scene of distress.
(iv) The true bearing of the ship in distress if this is known.

(c) **Maintain continuous listening watch on the distress frequency(ies) namely:**
(i) 500 kHz (radiotelegraphy) and/or
(ii) 2,182 kHz (radiotelephony) and additionally if fitted
(iii) V.H.F. Safety and Calling Channel 16 (156.8 MHz)

(d) **Set D/F watch** on 500 kHz and/or 2,182 kHz

(e) **Operate radar continuously.**

2. Proceeding to the Distress

Vessels proceeding to the area of the distress should endeavour to ascertain and plot the position, courses and speeds of other vessels in the area who may be proceeding similarly to render assistance. This information will be obtainable by listening to the distress frequency(ies) and/or the V.H.F. Safety and Calling frequency.

3. Vessels should similarly attempt to construct an accurate 'picture' of the circumstances attending the casualty. The important information needed which should be included in the distress message or in subsequent messages by the vessel in distress is as follows:

(a) The nature of the incident—collision, storm damage, fire, etc.
(b) The number of persons on board (crew, passengers including women and children and any injured).
(c) Existing weather conditions.
(d) Whether lifeboats or liferafts have been launched, and if so
(i) the number and types;
(ii) the number of persons in each;
(iii) whether these include any injured persons.
(e) E.T.A.'s on scene and communication capabilities of other assisting vessels and if practicable the radio navigational aids with which they are equipped. e.g. Loran, Decca Navigator, Radar, etc.
Advantage should be taken of the information available in the "International List of Ship Stations".

4. Establishment of the "Co-ordinator Surface Search" (C.S.S.)

The duties of the C.S.S. are to organise and conduct co-ordinated S.A.R. operations as required. This is liable to be a complex task and this consideration has a bearing on the selection of the C.S.S.

5. When more than one ship is concerned, the C.S.S. can be established only by mutual agreement.

6. It is most desirable that the C.S.S. should be established as early as practicable and preferably before arrival "on scene".

7. In view of the nature of his tasks it is important that the C.S.S. should have good radio communication facilities including, preferably, M.F. (2,182 kHz) and/or V.H.F. (156.8 MHz) radiotelephony in addition to 500 kHz radiotelegraphy.

8. The following order of choice gives general guidance for the establishment of the C.S.S.
(a) The surface craft in distress if practicable and not in imminent danger of sinking;
(b) The first vessel expected to arrive on the scene;
(c) Should two or more vessels be expected to arrive on scene at approximately the same time, the ship with the more extensive communication facilities;
(d) For an incident in coastal waters in which helicopters are co-operating, a shore lifeboat which normally has facilities for communicating on both Maritime and Aeronautical frequencies would be most suitable.

9. Subsequent changes in the C.S.S. are in general undesirable and therefore should normally be made only in the event of failure of equipment which would effect the execution of his task.

10. On assuming the duty, the C.S.S. should immediately inform the nearest Coast Station.

11. In ocean areas, should long range S.A.R. aircraft arrive and commence searching prior to the arrival of any surface vessels on the scene, it will still be necessary to establish a C.S.S.

12. Visual Identification of C.S.S.
The C.S.S. should display continuously the following visual signals as a means of identity:

(a) BY DAY— International Code Group "FR"
(b) BY NIGHT—A distinctive signal which the C.S.S. will promulgate to assisting ships, e.g. a searchlight pointed skywards.
(c) When the C.S.S. is changed the identification signal should be transferred.

13. Air and Surface Co-ordination
Should an Airborne On Scene Commander (O.S.C.) be on scene currently with the C.S.S., the latter should appreciate that the O.S.C. is under the control of the R.C.C. While it will be desirable for the C.S.S. to indicate his intentions to the O.S.C. he has no automatic authority to direct the latter.

14. It would be highly advantageous to have the facility of direct intercommunication by radiotelephony between the C.S.S. and O.S.C. in order to effect co-ordination. This is expected to become practicable as and when an increasing number of long range S.A.R. aircraft are fitted with M.F. Radiotelephony (2,182 kHz). Failing this facility, co-ordination may then need to be effected via a Coast Radio Station or R.C.C.

15. Control of Radio Communications
(a) In order to ensure the required degree of co-ordination it will be necessary for the C.S.S. to control the available communication channels effectively on which *the*

strictest radio discipline and procedure should be exercised by all participating vessels.

(b) Assisting vessels should always address messages concerning the operation to the C.S.S.

16. Approaching the Casualty Area

(a) When approaching the casualty area, vessels should make full use of any radio direction finding facilities to "home" on to the casualty and similarly to locate any transmissions from Emergency Position Indicating Radio Beacons (E.P.I.R.B.'s).

(b) The importance of operating radar and of maintaining an effective visual lookout cannot be over-emphasised. (See Typical Radar Detection Ranges on page 287).

(c) At night searchlights should be used if available otherwise some form of surface illumination should be contrived if practicable.

(d) The C.S.S., if established, should be kept informed of any contacts made with the vessel in distress or survival craft by D/F, radar or visual sighting. If the C.S.S. has not been established this information should be passed to ships in the vicinity.

17. Arrival on Scene—Search Procedure

(a) If no C.S.S. has been established by this stage, immediate action should be taken in accordance with the provisions of paragraph 8.

(b) If the casualty has not been located, a search will be necessary, and the C.S.S. should without delay initiate the appropriate search pattern.

(c) The C.S.S. should make optimum use of all available units taking into account aircraft if these have been deployed to the area. (See paragraph 13).

(d) To conduct the search effectively it will be necessary for the C.S.S. to maintain a general plot of the area under search and assisting ships would be well advised to do the same. If the search is taking place within the coverage area of Decca Navigator or Loran, either of these would provide a convenient reference datum.

18. Search Successful—Rescue

(a) Once the casualty has been sighted the C.S.S. should, where necessary, direct appropriate vessels to effect rescue and similarly should arrange that vessels not required should stand off.

(b) In bad weather, vegetable oils and animal oils (including fish oils) are most suitable for reducing the state of the sea. If these are not available, lubricating oils may be used, but *fuel oil should only be used as a last resort*. Further details are given on page 286.

(c) In conditions of bad weather, the C.S.S. may decide that a vessel with a low freeboard would be better suited to effect the rescue and make arrangements accordingly.

(d) If practicable, arrangements should be made for injured personnel requiring the attention of a Medical Officer to be transferred to a vessel carrying one.

(e) In an ocean incident, if there is no vessel with a Medical Officer "on scene", the C.S.S. should transmit an urgency message requesting any vessel with a Medical Officer on board in the vicinity to rendezvous with the rescue vessel.

(f) In a coastal incident, the local Coast Radio Station may be able to arrange for a Medical Officer to be sent off from the shore.

(g) Survivors who are medically fit should be questioned to obtain supplementary information on the vessel or aircraft in distress, its complement, casualties and whether any other persons in lifeboats and/or liferafts have been seen. This information should be promptly relayed to the C.S.S.

19. Search Unsuccessful

The C.S.S. should continue the search until all hope of rescuing survivors has passed. (See "Survival Time for Persons in water of varying temperatures" on page 286.)

At his discretion the C.S.S., after consultation with other search vessels, would then take the following action:

(a) *Ocean Incident.* To cancel the distress, advise assisting vessels to proceed on passage and inform the nearest Coast Radio Station or R.C.C.

(b) *Coastal Incident.* After consultation with other search vessels notify the local Coast Radio Station.

20. Cancellation of the Distress

(a) The C.S.S. should inform all concerned when the search has been terminated This would apply whether the search has been successful or not.

(b) The C.S.S. should also inform the nearest Coast Radio Station of the following points:

    (i) Number of survivors rescued.

    (ii) Their physical condition.

    (iii) Whether hospitalization is needed.

    (iv) The state of the distressed craft and whether it is a menace to navigation, or

    (v) In the case of an unsuccessful search, this should also be reported together with details of the area covered.

(c) The C.S.S. should release assisting vessels and instruct them to proceed on passage.

(d) Finally, the C.S.S. should inform the nearest Coast Radio Station that the distress message can be cancelled. Action to this end may need to be referred to a R.C.C. before it is executed and normal radio traffic resumed on the frequencies concerned.

MARINE COMMUNICATIONS FACILITIES FOR DISTRESS PURPOSES

(a) **Transmission and reception (Radio)**

    (i) M.F. Radiotelegraphy 500 kHz.

    (ii) M.F. Radiotelephony 2,182 kHz.

    (iii) V.H.F. (International) Maritime Radiotelephony 156.8 MHz (Channel 16).

(b) **Reception only (Radio)**

    (i) General coverage 15 kHz to 28 MHz.

    (ii) 1,605 kHz to 3,800 kHz.

(c) **Signalling Lamps**

(d) **International Flags**

(e) **Additionally,** deep sea vessels may be fitted with H.F. radiotelegraphy and/or radiotelephony facilities. This may be most useful in an ocean incident, particularly in remote areas, for passing messages for the information of Shore Co-ordinating Authorities and other authorities.

(f) **Marine Emergency Position Indicating Radio Beacons** operating on 2,182 kHz and/or 121.5 MHz and 243 MHz.

MARINE RADIO ADAPTATIONS

(a) A search vessel over 1,600 g.t. may not be fitted with a permanent radio telephone installation on 2,182 kHz but it may well have a lifeboat-portable with this frequency included. It would therefore be practicable to use this set to provide radiotelephone communications on scene, and to listen for the signals from Marine E.P.I.R.B.'s.

(b) A search vessel over 1,600 g.t. with a general purpose receiver and a vessel with an M.F. radiotelephone installation with a tunable receiver covering 1,605 to 3,800 kHz would be able to tune to the aeronautical on scene radio-telephone frequency of 3,023 kHz.

(c) A vessel 1,600 g.t. and above would also be able to tune to the aeronautical on scene radiotelephone frequency of 5,680 kHz and the radiotelegraphy frequencies 3,095 kHz and 5,695 kHz.

(d) Portable "walkie-talkie" sets on either the Citizens Band (27 MHz) or V.H.F./U.H.F. frequencies may also be used as emergency communications between parent ships and rescue boats or liferafts.

AERONAUTICAL COMMUNICATIONS

(a) Only relatively few military S.A.R. aircraft have a radiotelegraphy receiving capability on 500 kHz.

(b) In certain areas S.A.R. aircraft will have a radiotelephony receiving capability on 2,182 kHz and some may also be able to transmit as well. (Military S.A.R. aircraft may have full facilities on 2,182 kHz in the future.)

(c) Visual signals by lamp and manoeuvring of aircraft (see (e) under) may be the only method of establishing a liaison with surface vessels. Alternatively a Coast radio station may be used as a link.

(d) In some coastal waters lifeboats have a communication capability with aircraft and/or helicopters.

(e) **Manoeuvring Signals used by S.A.R. Aircraft**

 (i) **To direct ships towards a distress craft or survivor(s)**
 Aircraft circles the ship at least once.
 Aircraft crosses the ship's course close ahead at low altitude, opening and closing the throttle or changing the propeller pitch.
 Aircraft heads in the direction in which the ship is to be directed.

 (ii) **To indicate to the ship to which the signal is directed that it is no longer required to assist.**
 Aircraft crosses the ship's wake close astern at low altitude opening and closing the throttle or changing the propeller pitch.

DROPPABLE EQUIPMENT CARRIED IN LONG RANGE S.A.R. AIRCRAFT

(a) This comprises equipment containers connected in series by a buoyant rope. The longest container carries a liferaft which can hold nine persons. The others carry supplies. Alternatively the following may be dropped free:

(b) Individual liferafts.

(c) Buoyant radio beacons.

(d) Dye and smoke markers and flame floats.

(e) Parachute flares. Illumination.

(f) Salvage pumps may also be dropped.

SEA RESCUE BY HELICOPTER (Inshore areas)

(a) An orange smoke signal, Aldis lamp or heliograph may be used to attract the attention of the helicopter.

(b) A clear stretch of deck should be made available as a pirk-up area if possible, and be marked out with a large letter "H" in white.

(c) The helicopter will approach from astern and come to a hover over the cleared area.

(d) The ship should either maintain a constant speed through the water and generally head 30° to starboard* of the prevailing wind direction, or remain stationary, head to wind. If these conditions are met the helicopter can lower on to or lift from the clear area. [*Some helicopters may require this to be 30° to port.]

(e) The length of the winch cable is about 15 metres or 50 feet (minimum).

(f) On no account should the lifting device on the end of the winch cable be secured to any part of the ship or become entangled in the rigging or fixtures. Ship's personnel should not attempt to grasp the lifting device unless requested to do so by the helicopter. Even in this case a metal part of the lifting device should first be allowed to touch the deck in order to avoid possible shock due to static electricity.

(g) If the above conditions cannot be met the helicopter may be able to lift a person from a boat or liferaft secured to a long painter. Since it is possible for liferafts to be overturned by the downdraught from a helicopter, it is advisable for all persons to remain in the centre of a raft until they are about to be lifted.

(h) In all cases an indication of wind direction is useful, and pennants, flags or smoke from the galley funnel (provided there is not too much) may be used for this purpose.

(i) The current operational range of helicopters is about 90 miles, some can operate out to about 200 miles.

SURVIVAL TIME FOR PERSONS IN WATER OF VARYING TEMPERATURES

Water Temp. Centigrade/Fahrenheit		Duration of Survival Hours
0°	32°	Less than 1 hour
4.4°	40°	½ to 3 hours
10.0°	50°	1 to 6 hours
15.6°	60°	2 to 24 hours
21.1°	70°	3 to 40 hours
26.7°	80°	Indefinite

Records show that the critically injured survivors of an accident usually die during the first 24 hours if not given aid. In this respect the table of survival times is an estimate based partly on laboratory experiments and refers to **uninjured** persons in the water without watertight clothing.

OIL USED FOR QUELLING WAVES

Experience has shown that vegetable oils and animal oils, including fish oils, are most suitable for quelling waves. If these are not available, lubricating oils should be used. **Fuel oil should not be used except as a last resource, as it is harmful to persons in the water.**

Lubricating oil is less harmful, and tests have shown that 250 litres or 45 gallons discharged slowly through a rubber hose with an outlet just above the sea while the ship proceeds at slow speed can effectively quell a sea area of some 6,000 square metres or 50,000 sq. ft. [Notice M.412 of August 1957 refers].

RADAR DETECTION RANGES FOR END-ON CONTACTS
The following relates to normal atmospheric conditions.

	Radar Scanner Height	
	15 metres	30 metres
Vessel	or 50 ft.	or 100 ft.
10,000 g.t.	13 n.m.	18 n.m.
1,000 g.t.	6 n.m.	8.4 n.m.
200 g.t.	5.5 n.m.	7.7 n.m.
10 metre or 30ft boat	1.9 n.m.	2.7 n.m.

Note: As the radar echo strength will fluctuate considerably with aspect, the figures are only to be used as a guide.

WORKS OF REFERENCE
Merchant Ship Search and Rescue Manual (Mersar), IMCO, London
United Kingdom Marine Search and Rescue Organisation, Department of Trade, H.M.S.O.
Admiralty List of Radio Signals Vol. 1 (Search and Rescue Section).
Admiralty Notices to Mariners—No. 4 of Annual Summary.
International Code of Signals.
Intergovernmental Maritime Consultative Organisation (Merchant Ship Position-Reporting Systems) Lndn. 1965.
List of Co-ordination Centres participating in Rescue Co-operation (Swedish P.T.T.—Gothenburg 1955).
Maritime Conventions Act 1966. Section 6 (1).
Merchant Shipping (Safety Convention) Act 1949—Section 22.
Merchant Shipping Act 1894—Sections 422 and 423.
Intergovernmental Maritime Consultative Organisation (International Conference on Safety of Life at Sea, 1960—Chapter V. Regulations 9, 10, 15 and 16), etc.
U.S. Coast Guard, National Search and Rescue Manual CG.308.
U.S. Coast Guard "S.A.R. Seminar" May 1965. Papers.
British and Commonwealth Marine Dept. Development and Projects Section.
Report No. 42 (S.A.R. Procedure for Merchant Vessels).

AIRCRAFT CASUALTIES AT SEA

Distress Communications	See
Action taken to render assistance	Admiralty Notices
Action to be taken when survivors are picked up	to Mariners—No. 4
Action to be taken when an aircraft is forced to	of Annual Summary and
"ditch" (alight on the sea)	IMCO Merchant Ship Search
	and Rescue Manual.

INTERNATIONAL CONVENTION FOR THE SAFETY OF LIFE AT SEA (1960)

CHAPTER V—SAFETY OF NAVIGATION

REGULATION 10

Distress Messages—Obligations and Procedures

(a) The Master of a ship at sea, on receiving a signal from any source that a ship or aircraft or survival craft thereof is in distress, is bound to proceed with all speed to the assistance of the persons in distress informing them if possible that he is doing so. If he is unable or, in the special circumstances of the case, considers it unreasonable or unnecessary to proceed to their assistance, he must enter in the logbook the reason for failing to proceed to the assistance of the persons in distress.

(b) The Master of a ship in distress, after consultation, so far as may be possible, with the Masters of the ships which answer his call for assistance, has the right to requisition such one or more of those ships as he considers best able to render assistance, and it shall be the duty of the Master or Masters of the ship or ships requisitioned to comply with the requisition by continuing to proceed with all speed to the assistance of persons in distress.

(c) The Master of a ship shall be released from the obligation imposed by paragraph (a) of this Regulation when he learns that one or more ships other than his own have been requisitioned and are complying with the requisition.

(d) The Master of a ship shall be released from the obligation imposed by paragraph (a) of this Regulation, and, if his ship has been requisitioned, from the obligation imposed by paragraph (b) of this Regulation, if he is informed by the persons in distress or by the Master of another ship which has reached such persons that assistance is no longer necessary.

Section O

Miscellaneous—Weights, Measures, Formulae

T

THE PHENOMENON OF SQUAT

Squat is the name given to the reduction in clearance between the sea bed and the keel of a vessel which is making way through the water.

As a ship moves through the water, she leaves behind her a "hole" in the sea which is filled immediately by a compensating inrush of water from all directions, including a powerful flow along the sides of the vessel. This causes an uneven depression in the level of the water closely surrounding the vessel, the effects of which are to lower the vessel bodily* in relation to the sea bed and to change her trim. Thus the vessel undergoes an apparent sinkage and a greater depth of water is required to avoid the danger of grounding when she is making way.

The flow of water past the sides of the vessel creates a considerable drag which reduces the forward speed of the vessel. This effect is most marked when proceeding through canals.

Many readers will have observed the behaviour of their own ship in shallow water in canals and be aware that, for a given engine power, the speed is less than is normally expected in open water.

The amount by which a vessel "squats" depends on a number of factors, but the main considerations (for a particular vessel at a particular draught) governing this are:

(a) the vessel's speed through the water and,

(b) the physical size of the channel through which the vessel is moving.

In this age of mammoth tankers and the economics of operating such vessels at their designed draughts to ports which are reached via expensively dredged channels, it has been necessary to reconsider the criteria determining the amount of underwater clearance desirable, especially with reference to squat. Many practical experiments aboard ships have made it possible to calculate with reasonable accuracy the value of squat to be expected in any particular channel.

The vessel's draught must remain constant because the weight of water displaced must always be equal to the weight of the ship.

CHANGE IN MEAN DRAFT DUE TO CHANGE IN DENSITY OF WATER

The table on pp. 292 and 293 is for rapid determination of a vessel's change in mean draft as she moves through waters of changing density, e.g. from river to dock, river to sea, etc.
The range of densities covered by the table will enable it to be used in those ports where the phenomena of "fresher than fresh" or "salter than salt" water occurs.
Fresh water has a *maximum* relative density of 1.000 at a temperature of 4°C. At all other temperatures, the relative density will be a little less than this value. For example, an ice cube will float in a glass of fresh water because its density is less than that of fresh water. Watch for low densities in fresh water rivers where temperatures are extreme.
The value for the relative density of salt sea water is normally taken as 1.025 but in areas where there is a high evaporation rate, the salt content is increased accordingly, with a corresponding increase in density. Hence water that is "salter than salt".

Remember that draft increases when density decreases, and vice versa.

Example 1: A ship with a fresh water allowance (F.W.A.) of 7 centimetres is loading a full cargo in dock water of relative density 1.016. Entering the table with 1.016 on the left, and 7 centimetres along the top, the change of mean draft on entering salt water is found to be 2½ centimetres. Hence the ship may submerge the appropriate load marks by 2½ centimetres.

Example 2: A ship (F.W.A. 8 centimetres) is loading in a port where the relative density of the water is 1.032. The table shows that the ship will INCREASE her mean draft by 2¼ centimetres on reaching sea water of normal density.

Example 3: A ship (F.W.A. 9 centimetres) is loading in a port where the relative density of the water is .997. The table shows that the mean draft will DECREASE by 1 centimetre in normal fresh water.

WARNING

A measurement of density from a single bucket sample (even though taken clear of overside discharges, etc.) may be unreliable due to eddies of fresh water, from streams or storm drains in dock wall outfalls, floating on the more dense salt water. In some ports, density varies considerably with the state of the tide.
In addition to taking readings from a number of samples taken at points along the ship's length, enquiries regarding the normal water density in the ship's vicinity should be made to the local port authority.

CHANGE IN MEAN DRAFT

DUE TO CHANGE IN DENSITY OF WATER

Relative Density	Fresh Water Allowance in centimetres (or inches)															
	3.0	4.0	5.0	6.0	7.0	8.0	9.0	10.0	11.0	12.0	13.0	14.0	15.0	16.0	17.0	18.0
.996	3.5	4.6	5.8	7.0	8.1	9.3	10.4	11.6	12.8	13.9	15.1	16.2	17.4	18.5	19.7	20.9
.997	3.4	4.5	5.6	6.7	7.8	8.9	10.1	11.2	12.3	13.4	14.6	15.7	16.8	17.9	19.0	20.0
.998	3.2	4.3	5.4	6.5	7.5	8.6	9.7	10.8	11.9	12.9	14.0	15.1	16.2	17.3	18.3	19.4
.999	3.1	4.2	5.2	6.2	7.3	8.3	9.3	10.4	11.4	12.5	13.5	14.6	15.6	16.6	17.7	18.7
1.000	3.0	4.0	5.0	6.0	7.0	8.0	9.0	10.0	11.0	12.0	13.0	14.0	15.0	16.0	17.0	18.0
1.001	2.9	3.8	4.8	5.8	6.7	7.7	8.6	9.6	10.6	11.5	12.5	13.4	14.4	15.4	16.3	17.3
1.002	2.8	3.7	4.6	5.5	6.4	7.4	8.3	9.2	10.1	11.0	11.9	12.9	13.8	14.7	15.6	16.5
1.003	2.6	3.5	4.4	5.3	6.2	7.0	7.9	8.8	9.7	10.6	11.4	12.3	13.2	14.1	15.0	15.8
1.004	2.5	3.4	4.2	5.0	5.9	6.7	7.6	8.4	9.2	10.1	10.9	11.7	12.6	13.4	14.3	15.1
1.005	2.4	3.2	4.0	4.8	5.6	6.4	7.2	8.0	8.8	9.6	10.4	11.2	12.0	12.8	13.6	14.4
1.006	2.3	3.0	3.8	4.5	5.4	6.0	6.8	7.6	8.3	9.1	9.9	10.6	11.4	12.2	12.9	13.7
1.007	2.2	2.9	3.6	4.3	5.0	5.8	6.5	7.2	7.9	8.6	9.3	10.1	10.8	11.5	12.2	13.0
1.008	2.0	2.7	3.4	4.0	4.8	5.4	6.2	6.8	7.5	8.1	8.8	9.5	10.2	10.9	11.6	12.2
1.009	1.9	2.6	3.2	3.8	4.5	5.2	5.8	6.4	7.0	7.7	8.3	8.9	9.6	10.2	10.9	11.5
1.010	1.8	2.4	3.0	3.6	4.2	4.8	5.4	6.0	6.6	7.2	7.8	8.4	9.0	9.6	10.2	10.8
1.011	1.7	2.2	2.8	3.4	3.9	4.5	5.0	5.6	6.2	6.7	7.3	7.8	8.4	9.0	9.5	10.1
1.012	1.6	2.0	2.6	3.1	3.6	4.2	4.7	5.2	5.7	6.2	6.8	7.3	7.8	8.3	8.8	9.4
1.013	1.4	1.9	2.4	2.9	3.4	3.8	4.3	4.8	5.3	5.8	6.2	6.7	7.2	7.7	8.1	8.6
1.014	1.3	1.8	2.2	2.6	3.0	3.5	4.0	4.4	4.8	5.3	5.7	6.2	6.6	7.0	7.5	7.9
1.015	1.2	1.6	2.0	2.4	2.8	3.2	3.6	4.0	4.4	4.8	5.2	5.6	6.0	6.4	6.8	7.2
1.016	1.0	1.5	1.8	2.2	2.5	2.9	3.2	3.6	4.0	4.3	4.7	5.0	5.4	5.8	6.1	6.5
1.017	1.0	1.3	1.6	1.9	2.2	2.6	2.9	3.2	3.5	3.8	4.2	4.5	4.8	5.1	5.4	5.8
1.018	0.8	1.1	1.4	1.7	2.0	2.2	2.5	2.8	3.1	3.4	3.6	3.9	4.2	4.5	4.8	5.0
1.019	0.7	1.0	1.2	1.4	1.7	1.9	2.2	2.4	2.6	2.8	3.1	3.4	3.6	3.8	4.1	4.3
1.020	0.6	0.8	1.0	1.2	1.4	1.6	1.8	2.0	2.2	2.4	2.6	2.8	3.0	3.2	3.4	3.6
1.021	0.5	0.6	0.8	1.0	1.1	1.3	1.4	1.6	1.8	1.9	2.1	2.2	2.4	2.6	2.7	2.9
1.022	0.4	0.5	0.6	0.7	0.8	1.0	1.0	1.2	1.3	1.4	1.6	1.7	1.8	1.9	2.0	2.2
1.023	0.2	0.3	0.4	0.5	0.6	0.6	0.7	0.8	0.9	1.0	1.0	1.1	1.2	1.2	1.4	1.4
1.024	0.1	0.2	0.2	0.2	0.2	0.3	0.4	0.4	0.4	0.5	0.5	0.6	0.6	0.6	0.7	0.7
1.025	0.0	0.0	0.0	0.0	0.0	0.0	0.0	0.0	0.0	0.0	0.0	0.0	0.0	0.0	0.0	0.0
1.026	0.1	0.2	0.2	0.2	0.3	0.3	0.4	0.4	0.4	0.5	0.5	0.6	0.6	0.6	0.7	0.7
1.027	0.2	0.3	0.4	0.5	0.6	0.6	0.7	0.8	0.9	1.0	1.0	1.1	1.2	1.3	1.4	1.4
1.028	0.4	0.5	0.6	0.7	0.8	1.0	1.1	1.2	1.3	1.4	1.6	1.7	1.8	1.9	2.0	2.2
1.029	0.5	0.6	0.8	1.0	1.1	1.3	1.4	1.6	1.8	1.9	2.1	2.2	2.4	2.6	2.7	2.9
1.030	0.6	0.8	1.0	1.2	1.4	1.6	1.8	2.0	2.2	2.4	2.6	2.8	3.0	3.2	3.4	3.6
1.031	0.7	1.0	1.2	1.4	1.7	1.9	2.2	2.4	2.6	2.8	3.1	3.4	3.6	3.8	4.1	4.3
1.032	0.8	1.1	1.4	1.7	2.0	2.2	2.5	2.8	3.1	3.4	3.6	3.9	4.2	4.5	4.8	5.0
1.033	1.0	1.3	1.6	1.9	2.2	2.6	2.9	3.2	3.5	3.8	4.2	4.5	4.8	5.1	5.4	5.8
1.034	1.0	1.5	1.8	2.2	2.5	2.9	3.2	3.6	4.0	4.3	4.7	5.0	5.4	5.8	6.1	6.5
1.035	1.2	1.6	2.0	2.4	2.8	3.2	3.6	4.0	4.4	4.8	5.2	5.6	6.0	6.4	6.8	7.2
1.036	1.3	1.8	2.2	2.6	3.0	3.5	4.0	4.4	4.8	5.3	5.7	6.2	6.6	7.0	7.5	7.9
1.037	1.4	1.9	2.4	2.9	3.4	3.8	4.3	4.8	5.3	5.8	6.2	6.7	7.2	7.7	8.1	8.6
1.038	1.6	2.0	2.6	3.1	3.6	4.2	4.7	5.2	5.7	6.2	6.8	7.3	7.8	8.3	8.8	9.4
1.039	1.7	2.2	2.8	3.4	3.9	4.5	5.0	5.6	6.2	6.7	7.3	7.8	8.4	9.0	9.5	10.1
1.040	1.8	2.4	3.0	3.6	4.2	4.8	5.4	6.0	6.6	7.2	7.8	8.4	9.0	9.6	10.2	10.8

CHANGE IN MEAN DRAFT

DUE TO CHANGE IN DENSITY OF WATER

Relative Density	Fresh Water Allowance in centimetres (or inches)																
	19	20	21	22	23	24	25	26	27	28	29	30	31	32	33	34	35
.996	22.0	23.2	24.4	25.5	26.7	27.8	29.0	30.2	31.3	32.5	33.6	34.8	36.0	37.1	38.3	39.4	40.6
.997	21.3	22.4	23.5	24.6	25.8	26.9	28.0	29.1	30.2	31.4	32.5	33.6	34.7	35.8	37.0	38.1	39.2
.998	20.5	21.6	22.7	23.8	24.8	25.9	27.0	28.1	29.2	30.2	31.3	32.4	33.5	34.6	35.6	36.7	37.8
.999	19.8	20.8	21.8	22.9	23.9	25.0	26.0	27.0	28.1	29.1	30.2	31.2	32.2	33.3	34.3	35.4	36.4
1.000	19.0	20.0	21.0	22.0	23.0	24.0	25.0	26.0	27.0	28.0	29.0	30.0	31.0	32.0	33.0	34.0	35.0
1.001	18.2	19.2	20.2	21.1	22.1	23.0	24.0	25.0	25.9	26.9	27.8	28.8	29.8	30.7	31.7	32.6	33.6
1.002	17.5	18.4	19.3	20.2	21.2	22.1	23.0	23.9	24.9	25.8	26.7	27.6	28.5	29.4	30.4	31.3	32.2
1.003	16.7	17.6	18.5	19.4	20.2	21.1	22.0	22.9	23.8	24.6	25.5	26.4	27.3	28.2	29.0	29.9	30.8
1.004	16.0	16.8	17.6	18.5	19.3	20.1	21.0	21.8	22.7	23.5	24.4	25.2	26.0	26.9	27.7	28.6	29.4
1.005	15.2	16.0	16.8	17.6	18.4	19.2	20.0	20.1	21.6	22.4	23.2	24.0	24.8	25.6	26.4	27.2	28.0
1.006	14.4	15.2	16.0	16.7	17.5	18.2	19.0	19.8	20.5	21.3	22.0	22.8	23.6	24.3	25.1	25.8	26.6
1.007	13.7	14.4	15.1	15.8	16.6	17.3	18.0	18.7	19.4	20.2	20.9	21.6	22.3	23.0	23.8	24.5	25.2
1.008	12.9	13.6	14.3	15.0	15.6	16.3	17.0	17.7	18.4	19.0	19..7	20.4	21.1	21.8	22.4	23.1	23.8
1.009	12.2	12.8	13.4	14.1	14.7	15.4	16.0	16.6	17.3	17.9	18.6	19.2	19.8	20.5	21.1	21.8	22.4
1.010	11.4	12.0	12.6	13.2	13.8	14.4	15.0	15.6	16.2	16.8	17.4	18.0	18.6	25.6	19.8	20.4	21.0
1.011	10.6	11.2	11.8	12.3	12.9	13.4	14.0	14.6	15.1	15.7	16.2	16.9	17.4	17.9	18.5	19.0	19.6
1.012	9.9	10.4	10.9	11.4	12.0	12.5	13.0	13.5	14.0	14.6	15.1	15.6	16.1	16.6	17.1	17.7	18.2
1.013	9.1	9.6	10.1	10.6	11.0	11.5	12.0	12.5	13.0	13.4	13.9	14.4	14.9	15.4	15.8	16.3	16.8
1.014	8.4	8.8	9.2	9.7	10.1	10.6	11.0	11.4	11.9	12.3	12.8	13.2	13.6	14.1	14.5	15.0	15.4
1.015	7.6	8.0	8.4	8.8	9.2	9.6	10.0	10.4	10.8	11.2	11.6	12.0	12.4	12.8	13.2	13.6	14.0
1.016	6.8	7.2	7.6	7.9	8.3	8.6	9.0	9.4	9.7	10.1	10.4	10.8	11.2	11.5	11.9	12.2	12.6
1.017	6.1	6.4	6.7	7.0	7.4	7.7	8.0	8.3	8.6	9.0	9.3	9.6	9.9	10.2	10.6	10.9	11.2
1.018	5.3	5.6	5.9	6.2	6.4	6.7	7.0	7.3	7.6	7.8	8.1	8.4	8.7	9.0	9.2	9.5	9.8
1.019	4.6	4.8	5.0	5.3	5.5	5.8	6.0	6.2	6.5	6.7	7.0	7.2	7.4	7.7	7.9	8.2	8.4
1.020	3.8	4.0	4.2	4.4	4.6	4.8	5.0	5.2	5.4	5.6	5.8	6.0	6.2	6.4	6.6	6.8	7.0
1.021	3.0	3.2	3.4	3.5	3.7	3.8	4.0	4.2	4.3	4.5	4.6	4.8	5.0	5.1	5.3	5.4	5.6
1.022	2.3	2.4	2.5	2.6	2.8	2.9	3.0	3.1	3.2	3.4	3.5	3.6	3.7	3.8	4.0	4.1	4.2
1.023	1.5	1.6	1.7	1.8	1.8	1.9	2.0	2.1	2.2	2.2	2.3	2.4	2.5	2.6	2.6	2.7	2.8
1.024	0.8	0.8	0.8	0.9	0.9	1.0	1.0	1.0	1.1	1.1	1.2	1.2	1.2	1.3	1.3	1.4	1.4
1.025	0.0	0.0	0.0	0.0	0.0	0.0	0.0	0.0	0.0	0.0	0.0	0.0	0.0	0.0	0.0	0.0	0.0
1.026	0.8	0.8	0.8	0.9	0.9	1.0	1.0	1.0	1.1	1.1	1.2	1.2	1.2	1.3	1.3	1.4	1.4
1.027	1.5	1.6	1.7	1.8	1.8	1.9	2.0	2.1	2.2	2.2	2.3	2.4	2.5	2.6	2.6	2.7	2.8
1.028	2.3	2.4	2.5	2.6	2.8	2.9	3.0	3.1	3.2	3.4	3.5	3.6	3.7	3.8	4.0	4.1	4.2
1.029	3.0	3.2	3.4	3.5	3.7	3.8	4.0	4.2	4.3	4.5	4.6	4.8	5.0	5.1	5.3	5.4	5.6
1.030	3.8	4.0	4.2	4.4	4.6	4.8	5.0	5.2	5.4	5.6	5.8	6.0	6.2	6.4	6.6	6.8	7.0
1.031	4.6	4.8	5.0	5.3	5.5	5.8	6.0	6.2	6.5	6.7	7.0	7.2	7.4	7.7	7.9	8.2	8.4
1.032	5.3	5.6	5.9	6.2	6.4	6.7	7.0	7.3	7.6	7.8	8.1	8.4	8.7	9.0	9.2	9.5	9.8
1.033	6.1	6.4	6.7	7.0	7.4	7.7	8.0	8.3	8.6	9.0	9.3	9.6	9.9	10.2	10.6	10.9	11.2
1.034	6.8	7.2	7.6	7.9	8.3	8.6	9.0	9.4	9.7	10.1	10.4	10.8	11.2	11.5	11.9	12.2	12.6
1.035	7.6	8.0	8.4	8.8	9.2	9.6	10.0	10.4	10.8	11.2	11.6	12.0	12.4	12.8	13.2	13.6	14.0
1.036	8.4	8.8	9.2	9.7	10.1	10.6	11.0	11.4	11.9	12.3	12.8	13.2	13.6	14.1	14.5	15.0	15.4
1.037	9.1	9.6	10.1	10.6	11.0	11.5	12.0	12.5	13.0	13.4	13.9	14.4	14.9	15.4	15.8	16.3	16.8
1.038	9.9	10.4	10.9	11.4	12.0	12.5	13.0	13.5	14.0	14.6	15.1	15.6	16.1	16.6	17.1	17.7	18.2
1.039	1.06	11.2	11.8	12.3	12.9	13.4	14.0	14.6	15.1	15.7	16.2	16.9	17.4	17.9	18.5	19.0	19.6
1.040	11.4	12.0	12.6	13.2	13.8	14.4	15.0	15.6	16.2	16.8	17.4	18.0	18.6	19.2	19.8	20.4	21.0

CONVERSION—FATHOMS TO METRES AND VICE VERSA

Fathoms	Metres	Metres	Fathoms
1	1.829	1	0.547
2	3.658	2	1.094
3	5.486	3	1.640
4	7.315	4	2.187
5	9.144	5	2.734
6	10.973	6	3.281
7	12.802	7	3.828
8	14.630	8	4.374
9	16.459	9	4.921
10	18.288	10	5.468
20	36.576	20	10.936
30	54.864	30	16.404
40	73.152	40	21.872
50	91.440	50	27.340
60	109.728	60	32.808
70	128.016	70	38.277
80	146.304	80	43.745
90	164.592	90	49.213
100	182.880	100	54.681

CONVERSION—FEET TO METRES AND VICE VERSA

Feet	Metres	Metres	Feet
1	0.305	1	3.281
2	0.610	2	6.562
3	0.914	3	9.843
4	1.220	4	13.123
5	1.524	5	16.404
6	1.829	6	19.685
7	2.134	7	22.966
8	2.439	8	26.247
9	2.743	9	29.528
10	3.048	10	32.808
20	6.096	20	65.617
30	9.144	30	98.425
40	12.192	40	131.234
50	15.240	50	164.042
60	18.288	60	196.851
70	21.336	70	229.660
80	24.384	80	262.467
90	27.432	90	295.276
100	30.479	100	328.084

For conversions of values exceeding 100 units, shift the decimal point as required.

Example: Convert 1,237 feet to metres:

Feet		Metres
1,000	=	304.79
200	=	60.96
30	=	9.144
7	=	2.134
∴ 1,237 feet	=	377.03 metres

DISTANCE CONVERSION TABLE

1 Nautical Mile	= 6,076 feet	= 1,852 metres
1 Statute Mile	= 5,280 feet	= 1,609 metres
1 Kilometre	= 3,280.8 feet	= 1,000 metres

Nautical Miles	Statute Miles	Kilometres	Statute Miles	Kilometres	Nautical Miles	Kilometres	Nautical Miles	Statute Miles
1	1.15	1.85	1	1.61	0.87	1	0.54	0.62
2	2.30	3.70	2	3.22	1.74	2	1.08	1.24
3	3.45	5.56	3	4.83	2.61	3	1.62	1.86
4	4.60	7.41	4	6.44	3.48	4	2.16	2.49
5	5.75	9.26	5	8.05	4.34	5	2.70	3.11
6	6.90	11.11	6	9.66	5.21	6	3.24	3.73
7	8.06	12.96	7	11.27	6.08	7	3.78	4.35
8	9.21	14.82	8	12.87	6.95	8	4.32	4.97
9	10.36	16.67	9	14.48	7.82	9	4.86	5.59
10	11.51	18.52	10	16.09	8.69	10	5.40	6.21
20	23.02	37.04	20	32.19	17.38	20	10.80	12.43
30	34.52	55.56	30	48.28	26.07	30	16.20	18.64
40	46.03	74.08	40	64.37	34.76	40	21.60	24.85
50	57.54	92.60	50	80.47	43.45	50	27.00	31.07
60	69.05	111.12	60	96.56	52.14	60	32.40	37.28
70	80.56	129.64	70	112.65	60.83	70	37.80	43.50
80	92.06	148.16	80	128.75	69.52	80	43.20	49.71
90	103.57	166.68	90	144.84	78.21	90	48.60	55.92
100	115.08	185.20	100	160.93	86.90	100	54.00	62.14

To obtain equivalent distances in excess of 100 units, move decimal point required number of places to the right, e.g.

80 Nautical Miles = 148.16 kilometres
hence 800 Nautical Miles = 1,481.6 kilometres

Equivalent distances which fall between tabular equivalents may be found as in the following example:

Required: equivalent nautical miles for 187 statute miles.

100 Statute miles = 86,90 Nautical miles
80 Statute miles = 69.52 Nautical miles
7 Statute miles = 6.08 Nautical miles
———
Hence: 187 Statute miles = 162.50 Nautical miles
———

The accuracy obtained will be sufficient for all practical purposes.

TONNAGE CONVERSION TABLE

1 long ton	=	2,240 lb.	=	1,016 kilograms
1 short ton	=	2,000 lb.	=	907 kilograms
1 metric ton (tonne)	=	2,204.6 lb.	=	1,000 kilograms

Long	Short	Metric	Short	Metric	Long	Metric	Long	Short
1	1.1	1.02	1	0.91	0.9	1	0.98	1.1
2	2.2	2.03	2	1.81	1.8	2	1.97	2.2
3	3.7	3.05	3	2.72	2.7	3	2.95	3.3
4	4.5	4.06	4	3.63	3.6	4	3.94	4.4
5	5.6	5.08	5	4.54	4.5	5	4.92	5.5
6	6.7	6.10	6	5.44	5.4	6	5.91	6.6
7	7.8	7.11	7	6.35	6.3	7	6.89	7.7
8	9.0	8.13	8	7.26	7.1	8	7.87	8.8
9	10.1	9.14	9	8.16	8.0	9	8.86	9.9
10	11.2	10.16	10	9.07	8.9	10	9.84	11.0
20	22.4	20.3	20	18.1	17.9	20	19.7	22.0
30	33.6	30.5	30	27.2	26.8	30	29.5	33.1
40	44.8	40.6	40	36.3	35.7	40	39.4	44.1
50	56.0	50.8	50	45.4	44.7	50	49.2	55.1
60	67.2	61.0	60	54.4	53.6	60	59.1	66.1
70	78.4	71.1	70	63.5	62.5	70	68.9	77.2
80	89.6	81.3	80	72.6	71.5	80	78.7	88.2
90	100.8	91.4	90	81.7	80.4	90	88.6	99.2
100	112.0	101.6	100	90.7	89.3	100	98.4	110.2
200	224.0	203.2	200	181.4	178.6	200	196.8	220.5
300	336.0	304.8	300	272.2	267.9	300	295.3	330.7
400	448.0	406.4	400	362.9	357.2	400	393.7	441.0
500	560.0	508.0	500	453.6	446.6	500	492.1	551.2
600	672.0	609.6	600	544.3	535.9	600	590.5	661.4
700	784.0	711.2	700	635.0	625.2	700	688.9	771.6
800	896.0	812.8	800	725.8	714.5	800	787.4	881.8
900	1,008.0	914.4	900	816.5	803.8	900	885.8	992.1
1,000	1,120.0	1,016.1	1,000	907.2	893.1	1,000	984.2	1,102.3
2,000	2,240.0	2,032.1	2,000	1,814.4	1,786.2	2,000	1,968.4	2,204.6
3,000	3,360.0	3,048.1	3,000	2,721.6	2,679.3	3,000	2,952.6	3,306.9
4,000	4,480.0	4,065.2	4,000	3,628.8	3,572.4	4,000	3,936.8	4,409.2
5,000	5,600.0	5,080.2	5,000	4,536.0	4,465.5	5,000	4,921.0	5,511.5
6,000	6,720.0	6,096.3	6,000	5,443.2	5,358.6	6,000	5,905.2	6,613.8
7,000	7,840.0	7,112.3	7,000	6,350.4	6,251.7	7,000	6,889.4	7,716.1
8,000	8,960.0	8,128.4	8,000	7,257.6	7,144.8	8,000	7,873.6	8,818.4
9,000	10,080.0	9,144.4	9,000	8,164.8	8,037.9	9,000	8,857.8	9,920.7
10,000	11,200.0	10,160.5	10,000	9,071.9	8,931.0	10,000	9,842.0	11,023.0

TEMPERATURE CONVERSION—CELSIUS (C) TO FAHRENHEIT (F)

C.	F.	C.	F.	C.	F.	C.	F.
−20	−4.1		+	+	+	+	+
−19.5	−3.1	−2	28.4	15.5	59.9	33	91.4
−19	−2.2	−1.5	29.3	16	60.8	33.5	92.3
−18.5	−1.3	−1	30.2	16.5	61.7	34	93.2
−18	−0.4	−0.5	31.1	17	62.6	34.5	94.1
−17.5	+0.5	0	32.0	17.5	63.5	35	95.0
−17	+1.4	+0.5	32.9	18	64.4	35.5	95.9
−16.5	+2.3	+1	33.8	18.5	65.3	36	96.8
−16	+3.2	+1.5	34.7	19	66.2	36.5	97.7
−15.5	+4.1	+2	35.6	19.5	67.1	37	98.6
−15	+5.0	+2.5	36.5	20	68.0	37.5	99.5
−14.5	5.9	+3	37.4	20.5	68.9	38	100.4
−14	6.8	3.5	38.3	21	69.8	38.5	101.3
−13.5	7.7	4	39.2	21.5	70.7	39	102.2
−13	8.6	4.5	40.1	22	71.6	39.5	103.1
−12.5	9.5	+5	41.0	22.5	72.5	40	104.0
−12	10.4	5.5	41.9	23	73.4	40.5	104.9
−11.5	11.3	6	42.8	23.5	74.3	41	105.8
−11	12.2	6.5	43.7	24	75.2	41.5	106.7
−10.5	13.1	7	44.6	24.5	76.1	42	107.6
−10	14.0	7.5	45.5	25	77.0	42.5	108.5
−9.5	14.9	8	46.4	25.5	77.9	43	109.4
−9	15.8	8.5	47.3	26	78.8	43.5	110.3
−8.5	16.7	9	48.2	26.5	79.7	44	111.2
−8	17.6	9.5	49.1	27	80.6	44.5	112.1
−7.5	18.5	+10	50.0	27.5	81.5	45	113.0
−7	19.4	10.5	50.9	28	82.4	45.5	113.9
−6.5	20.3	11	51.8	28.5	83.3	46	114.8
−6	21.2	11.5	52.7	29	84.2	46.5	115.7
−5.5	22.1	12	53.6	29.5	85.1	47	116.6
−5	23.0	12.5	54.5	30	86.0	47.5	117.5
−4.5	23.9	13	55.4	30.5	86.9	48	118.4
−4	24.8	13.5	56.3	31	87.8	48.5	119.3
−3.5	25.7	14	57.2	31.5	88.7	48	120.2
−3	26.6	14.5	58.1	32	89.6	49.5	121.1
−2.5	27.5	+15	59.0	32.5	90.5	50	122.0

General Formula: $F = \dfrac{9}{5}C + 32$

TEMPERATURE CONVERSION
FAHRENHEIT (F) to CELSIUS (C)

F.	C.	F.	C.	F.	C.	F.	C.	F.	C.	F.	C.
00	-17.8	20	-6.7	40	4.4	60	15.6	80	26.7	100	37.8
00.5	-17.5	20.5	-6.4	40.5	4.7	60.5	15.8	80.5	26.9	100.5	38.1
01	-17.2	21	-6.1	41	5.0	61	16.1	81	27.2	101	38.3
01.5	-16.9	21.5	-5.8	41.5	5.3	61.5	16.4	81.5	27.5	101.5	38.6
02	-16.7	22	-5.6	42	5.6	62	16.7	82	27.8	102	38.9
02.5	-16.4	22.5	-5.3	42.5	5.8	62.5	16.9	82.5	28.1	102.5	39.2
03	-16.1	23	-5.0	43	6.1	63	17.2	83	28.3	103	39.4
03.5	-15.8	23.5	-4.7	43.5	6.4	63.5	17.5	83.5	28.6	103.5	39.7
04	-15.6	24	-4.4	44	6.7	64	17.8	84	28.9	104	40.0
04.5	-15.3	24.5	-4.2	44.5	6.9	64.5	18.1	84.5	29.2	104.5	40.3
05	-15.0	25	-3.9	45	7.2	65	18.3	85	29.4	105	40.6
05.5	-14.7	25.5	-3.6	45.5	7.5	65.5	18.6	85.5	29.7	105.5	40.8
06	-14.4	26	-3.3	46	7.8	66	18.9	86	30.0	106	41.1
06.5	-14.2	26.5	-3.1	46.5	8.1	66.5	19.2	86.5	30.3	106.5	41.4
07	-13.9	27	-2.8	47	8.3	67	19.4	87	30.6	107	41.7
07.5	-13.6	27.5	-2.5	47.5	8.6	67.5	19.7	87.5	30.8	107.5	41.9
08	-13.3	28	-2.2	48	8.9	68	20.0	88	31.1	108	42.2
08.5	-13.1	28.5	-1.9	48.5	9.2	68.5	20.3	88.5	31.4	108.5	42.5
09	-12.8	29	-1.7	49	9.4	69	20.6	89	31.7	109	42.8
09.5	-12.5	29.5	-1.4	49.5	9.7	69.5	20.8	89.5	31.9	109.5	43.1
10	-12.2	30	-1.1	50	10.0	70	21.1	90	32.2	110	43.3
10.5	-11.9	30.5	-0.8	50.5	10.3	70.5	21.4	90.5	32.5	110.5	43.6
11	-11.7	31	-0.6	51	10.6	71	21.7	91	32.8	111	43.9
11.5	-11.4	31.5	-0.3	51.5	10.8	71.5	21.9	91.5	33.1	111.5	44.2
12	-11.1	32	0.0	52	11.1	72	22.2	92	33.3	112	44.4
12.5	-10.8	32.5	+0.3	52.5	11.4	72.5	22.5	92.5	33.6	112.5	44.7
13	-10.6	33	+0.6	53	11.7	73	22.8	93	33.9	113	45.0
13.5	-10.3	33.5	+0.8	53.5	11.9	73.5	23.1	93.5	34.2	113.5	45.3
14	-10.0	34	1.1	54	12.2	74	23.3	94	34.4	114	45.6
14.5	-9.7	34.5	1.4	54.5	12.5	74.5	23.6	94.5	34.7	114.5	45.8
15	-9.4	35	1.7	55	12.8	75	23.9	95	35.0	115	46.1
15.5	-9.2	35.5	1.9	55.5	13.1	75.5	24.2	95.5	35.3	115.5	46.4
16	-8.9	36	2.2	56	13.3	76	24.4	96	35.6	116	46.7
16.5	-8.6	36.5	2.5	56.5	13.6	76.5	24.7	96.5	35.8	116.5	46.9
17	-8.3	37	2.8	57	13.9	77	25.0	97	36.1	117	47.2
17.5	-8.1	37.5	3.1	57.5	14.2	77.5	25.3	97.5	36.4	117.5	47.5
18	-7.8	38	3.3	58	14.4	78	25.6	98	36.7	118	47.8
18.5	-7.5	38.5	3.6	58.5	14.7	78.5	25.8	98.5	36.9	118.5	48.1
19	-7.2	39	3.9	59	15.0	79	26.1	99	37.2	119	48.3
19.5	-6.9	39.5	4.2	59.5	15.3	79.5	26.4	99.5	37.5	119.5	48.6
F.	C.	F.	C.	F.	C.	F.	C.	F.	C.	F.	C.

General Formula: $C = \dfrac{5}{9}(F - 32)$

WEIGHTS AND MEASURES

Cubic Measure

1 cubic foot	=	1,728 cubic inches	=	0.028 cu. metres
1 cubic yard	=	27 cubic feet	=	0.765 cu. metres
35 cubic feet	=	1 long ton of salt water		
40 cubic feet	=	1 shipping ton (Merchandise)	=	1.132 cu. metres
42 cubic feet	=	1 shipping ton (Timber)	=	1.189 cu. metres
100 cubic feet	=	1 registered ton	=	2.832 cu. metres
108 cubic feet	=	1 stack of wood	=	3.058 cu. metres
128 cubic feet	=	1 cord of wood	=	3.625 cu. metres
216 cubic feet	=	1 fathom of wood	=	6.117 cu. metres

277¼ cubic inches of Fresh water	=	1 Imperial gallon	=	5.546 litres
1 cubic foot of Fresh water weighs		62.5 lb.		
36 cubic feet of Fresh water weighs		1 long ton		
1 gallon of Fresh water weighs		10 lb.		

10 English gallons = 12 American gallons = 55.546 litres

Avoirdupois Weight

27⅓ grains		=	1 drachm	(dr.)	=	1.8 grams
16	drachms	=	1 ounce	(oz.)	=	28.3 grams
16	ounces	=	1 pound	(lb.)	=	453.6 grams
14	pounds	=	1 stone	(st.)	=	6.4 kg.
28	pounds (2 stone)	=	1 quarter	(qr.)	=	12.7 kg.
112	pounds (4 quarters)	=	1 hundredweight	(cwt.)	=	50.8 kg.
20	hundredweight (2240 pounds)	=	1 ton	(long ton)	=	1016 kg.

Ale and Beer Measures

2 pints	=	1 quart	(qt.)	=	1.14 litres
4 quarts	=	1 gallon	(gal.)	=	4.55 litres
9 gallons	=	1 firkin	(fir.)	=	40.9 litres
18 gallons	=	1 kilderkin	(kil.)	=	81.8 litres
36 gallons	=	1 barrel	(bar.)	=	164 litres
54 gallons	=	1 hogshead	(hhd.)	=	245 litres
72 gallons	=	1 puncheon	(pun.)	=	327 litres
108 gallons	=	1 butt		=	491 litres

Wine Measure

4 gills	=	1 pint	(pt.)	=	0.57 litres
2 pints	=	1 quart	(qt.)	=	1.14 litres
4 quarts	=	1 gallon	(gal.)	=	4.55 litres
10 gallons	=	1 anker	(ank.)	=	45.5 litres
18 gallons	=	1 runlet	(run.)	=	81.8 litres
42 gallons	=	1 tierce		=	191 litres
63 gallons	=	1 hogshead	(hhd.)	=	286 litres
84 gallons	=	1 puncheon	(pun.)	=	382 litres
126 gallons	=	1 pipe or butt		=	573 litres
252 gallons	=	1 tun		=	1,146 litres

The gallonage of a pipe may vary:

A pipe of Madeira	=	92 gallons	=	418 litres
A pipe of Sherry Wine	=	108 gallons	=	491 litres
A pipe of Brandy	=	114 gallons	=	518 litres
A pipe of Port Wine	=	115 gallons	=	523 litres

Hogsheads may also vary.

Capacity (Liquid and Dry)

4 gills	=	20 ounces Avoir of fresh water =	1 pint =	0.57 litres
2 pints	=	1 quart	=	1.14 litres
4 quarts	=	1 gallon = 10 pounds Avoir. of fresh water	=	4.55 litres
2 gallons	=	1 peck (pk.)	=	9.09 litres
4 pecks	=	1 bushel (bush.)	=	36.4 litres
8 bushels	=	1 quarter (qr.)	=	291 litres
36 bushels	=	1 chaldron (chal.)	=	1,309 litres = 1.3 cu. metres

Stationery

24 sheets	=	1 quire	
20 quires	=	1 ream =	480 sheets
21 quires	=	1 printer's ream =	504 sheets

MENSURATION AND OTHER FORMULAE

Rectangle Area = LB

L = length
B = breadth

Triangle Area = ½ b.h.

b = base
h = height

Trapezium Area = ½ (a + b)h

a, b, the parallel sides
h = height

Circle Area = πr^2
Circumference = $2 \pi r$

r = radius

Cone Area of curved surface = πrl
Volume = $\frac{1}{3}\pi r^2 h$

r = base radius
h = height
l = slant height

Cylinder Area of curved surface = $2 \pi rh$
Volume = $\pi r^2 h$

r = base radius
h = height

Sphere Surface area = $4 \pi r^2$
Volume = $\frac{4}{3}\pi r^3$

r = radius

Pyramid Volume = $\frac{1}{3}Bh$

h = height
B = base area

$\pi = 3.14159$

The unit of circular measure is the **Radian** which is defined as the angle subtended at the centre of a circle by an arc equal in length to the radius. 1 Radian = 57°.3.

To convert degrees to Radians: $\text{Radians} = \dfrac{\theta^{\circ}}{180} \times \pi$

To convert Radians to degrees: $\text{Degrees} = \dfrac{\text{Radians}}{\pi} \times 180^{\circ}$

Formula to solve quadratic equations i.e. $ax^2 + bx + c = 0$

$$x = \frac{-b \pm \sqrt{b^2 - 4ac}}{2a}$$

STABILITY FORMULAE

Tonnes per centimetre immersion, TPC $= \dfrac{1.025A}{100}$ Where A = area of waterplane

Fresh water allowance, FWA $= \dfrac{W}{4 \times \text{TPC}}$ Where W = loaded displacement and FWA is in centimetres

Effect of Density on Draft and Displacement

For box-shaped vessels: $\dfrac{\text{New d}}{\text{Old d}} = \dfrac{\text{Old } \delta}{\text{New } \delta}$

For ship-shaped vessels: $\dfrac{\text{New V}}{\text{Old V}} = \dfrac{\text{Old } \delta}{\text{New } \delta}$

When draft remains constant: $\dfrac{\text{New W}}{\text{Old W}} = \dfrac{\text{New } \delta}{\text{Old } \delta}$

Where d = draft, δ = density, V = volume of displacement, W = displacement

Simpson's Rules

First Rule: *(For an even number of "intervals")*

$$\text{Area} = \frac{h}{3}\left[a + 4b + 2c + 4d + 2e + 4f + g\right]$$

Second Rule: *(Can be used when the number of "intervals" is a multiple of three)*

$$\text{Area} = \frac{3h}{8}\left[a + 3b + 3c + 2d + 3e + 3f + 2g + 3h + 3i + j\right]$$

Third or 5-8 Rule: (*To find the area between any two consecutive ordinates when three consecutive ordinates are known*)

$$\text{Area} = \frac{h}{12}\left[5a + 8b - c\right]$$

Note that 5 applies to the end ordinate of the required area and 8 to the middle ordinate

Where h is the common interval and a, b, c, d, etc. are ordinates.

When number of intervals is such that no single Rule can be used: combine Rules 1 and 3 or 1 and 2.

KG of ship

$$KG = \frac{\text{Total moments of all the weights in a ship}}{\text{Final displacement}}$$

Shift of G due to shifting, loading or discharging weight.

Shifting:
$$GG_1 = \frac{w \times d}{W}$$

Loading:
$$GG_1 = \frac{w \times d}{W + w}$$

Discharging:
$$GG_1 = \frac{w \times d}{W - w}$$

Where w = weight moved, d = distance between CG of weight and CG of ship, W = vessel's displacement before moving weight

Morrish's Formula

Depth of B below waterline =
$$\frac{1}{3}\left(\frac{d}{2} + \frac{V}{A}\right)$$

Where B = centre of buoyancy, d = mean draft, V = volume of displacement and A = area of waterplane.

Moment of Statical Stability = W × GZ

At **small** angles of heel: $GZ = GM \times Sin\,\theta$

At **large** angles of heel: $GZ = (GM + \frac{1}{2}BM.\,Tan^2\,\theta)Sin\,\theta$

Where θ = angle of heel

BM   For any vessel:
$$BM = \frac{I}{V} = \frac{LB^3}{12V}$$

For box-shapes
$$BM = \frac{B^2}{12d}$$

Where I = Moment of inertia of waterplane area about the centre line, V = volume of displacement, L = length of waterplane, and B = breadth of waterplane.

To find angle of heel resulting from a transverse shift of weight:

$$\text{Tan heel} = \frac{GG_1}{GM} = \frac{w \times d}{W \times GM}$$

Where w = weight moved, d = transverse distance weight is moved, W = vessel's displacement.

To find angle of heel due to loading and/or discharging weight off the centre line:

$$\text{Tan heel} = \frac{GG_1}{GM} = \frac{\text{Final moment}}{\text{Final displacement} \times \text{Final GM}}$$

Bringing a listed vessel to the upright position

In all cases: Required moment = Moment causing list

i.e. $w \times d = W \times GG_1 = GM \tan \theta$

When shifting weight transversely: use the *initial* GM

When loading and/or discharging weight off the centre line: use the *final* displacement and the *final* GM.

Where W = displacement, θ = angle of heel, $(w \times d)$ = final moment.

Finding GM_L from change of trim: $GM_L = \dfrac{L \times GG_1}{t}$

Where L = length of vessel at waterline when upright on an even keel, t = change of trim. (All measurements in the same units, i.e. feet or metres).

Moment to Change Trim 1 centimetre, MCT 1 cm. $= \dfrac{W \times GM_L}{100 L}$

Approximate formulae when GM_L is not known

For a ship: MCT 1 cm. $= \dfrac{7 T^2}{B}$

For a box-shape: MCT 1 cm. $= \dfrac{8 T^2}{B}$

Where T = MCT 1 cm, L = the vessel's length in metres, B = maximum beam in metres.

Change of Trim C of T $= \dfrac{\text{Moment}}{\text{MCT 1 cm}}$

Effect of trim on arithmetic mean draft
When the tipping centre is not amidships a correction (s) must be applied to the arithmetic mean draft to obtain the true mean draft.

$$s(\text{in centimetres}) = \frac{d \times t}{L}$$

Where d = distance (in metres) of tipping centre from amidships, t = trim (in centimetres), L = vessel's length (in metres). s is plus when the tipping centre is nearest the deep end, and minus when nearer to the shallow end.

Change in Draft forward and aft due to change of trim

When the tipping centre is not amidships:

$$\text{Change Aft} = \text{C of T} \times \frac{l}{L}$$

$$\text{Change Fwd.} = \text{C of T} - \text{Change Aft.}$$

Where l = distance of tipping centre from aft, L = length of vessel.

When weight has been loaded or discharged, the bodily sinkage or rise $\left(\dfrac{w}{\text{TPC}}\right)$ must be applied, as appropriate, to each end.

Loading weight to keep the after draft constant

$$d = \frac{L \times \text{MCTI cm}}{l \times \text{TPC}}$$

Where d = distance from tipping centre at which weight should be loaded, l = distance of tipping centre from aft, L = vessel's length.

Inclining Experiment

$$GM = \frac{\text{Moment} \times \text{length of plumb line}}{\text{Displacement} \times \text{deflection}}$$

Increase in Draft due to Heel

$$\text{New Draft} = \tfrac{1}{2} B \sin \theta + \text{Old draft} \cos \theta$$

Where B = vessel's beam and θ = angle of heel

Angle of Loll

$$\text{Tan } \theta = \sqrt{\frac{-2(-GM)}{BM}}$$

Where θ = angle of loll, and BM = BM when vessel is upright.

Virtual loss of GM due to Free Surface of liquids

$$\text{Virtual rise of G} = \frac{i}{V} \times \frac{\delta_1}{\delta_2} \times \frac{1}{n^2} \text{ feet}$$

Where i = moment of inertia of the free surface, V = vessel's volume of displacement δ_1 = density of liquid in tank, δ_2 = density of water in which vessel is floating, n = number of longitudinal compartments into which the tank is divided.

$$\text{For a rectangular free surface} \quad i = \frac{l b^3}{12}$$

Where l = length of free surface, b = total breadth of free surface (disregarding longitudinal divisions).

U

Dry Docking

$$P = \frac{MCT\ 1\ cm \times t}{l}$$

$$\text{Virtual loss of GM} = \frac{P \times KM}{W} \text{ or } \frac{P \times KG}{W - P}$$

Where P = upthrust in tonnes at stern i.e. (old displacement — new displacement), t = change in trim (in centimetres) since entering dock, l = distance (in metres) of tipping centre from aft, W = vessel's displacement on entering dock.

Increase in draft due to bilging a compartment.

$$\text{Permeability: } p = \frac{\text{Broken stowage}}{\text{Stowage factor}} \times 100 \text{ per cent}$$

$$\text{When compartment is empty: } \quad \text{Sinkage} = \frac{v}{A - a}$$

$$\text{When compartment contains cargo: Sinkage} = \frac{v \times p}{A - a \times p}$$

Where v = volume of lost buoyancy, A = area of waterplane, a = area of damaged waterplane, p = permeability expressed as a fraction.

Required head of liquid in sounding pipe to indicate a full tank when vessel is trimmed by the stern.

Assuming sounding pipe to be at the after end of the tank:

$$\text{Head in centimetres} = \frac{l \times t}{L}$$

Where l = length of tank in metres, t = trim in centimetres, L = vessel's length in metres

Dynamical Stability

$$\text{Dynamical Stability} = W \times \text{area under stability curve}$$

$$\text{or} \quad \text{Dynamical Stability} = 2W.\ \text{hav}\ \theta(GM + BM\ \text{hav}\ \theta\ \text{sec}\ \theta)$$

Where W = vessel's displacement, and θ = angle of heel at which the dynamical stability is required.

COMPASS FORMULAE

The Coefficients A, B, C, D and E.

Coefficient A is constant on all headings. Its value can be obtained by taking the mean of the deviations on four or more *compass* headings which are evenly spaced round the 360°.

Coefficient B.

$$\text{Permanent } B \propto \frac{1}{H} \qquad\qquad\qquad \text{Induced } B \propto \frac{Z}{H}$$

The value of Coefficient B (Total) is found by taking the mean of the deviations on *compass* headings E and W **after** reversing the sign of the deviation on W.

Coefficient C.

$$\text{Permanent } C \propto \frac{1}{H} \qquad\qquad\qquad \text{Induced } C \propto \frac{Z}{H}$$

The value of Coefficient C (Total) is found by taking the mean of the deviation on *compass* headings N and S **after** reversing the sign of the deviation on S.

Coefficient D*. Its value is obtained by taking the mean of the deviations on *compass* headings NE, SE, SW, and NW **after** reversing the signs of the deviations on SE and NW.

Coefficient E*. Its value is obtained by taking the mean of the deviations on *compass* headings N, E, S and W **after** reversing the signs of the deviations on E and W.

* The values of Coefficients D and E do not vary with changes in magnetic latitude.

To find the Deviation due to Coefficients A, B, C, D and E on any compass heading:

DEVIATION = A + B. sin Course + C. cos Course + D. sin 2 Course + E cos 2 Course

Note that, at a well placed compass, the values of coefficients A, E and induced C should be negligible so that the practical formula becomes:

DEVIATION = B. sin Course + C cos Course + D sin 2 Course.

Section P

Radio Navigational Aids

MARINE USE OF V.H.F.

Maritime VHF services on the frequency range 156 to 165 Mc/s using frequency modulation have been introduced to provide reliable clear short-range radio telephone communication free of interference so often found on the overcrowded medium wave bands. The effective working range of VHF communications is normally limited to slightly more than the "line-of-sight" distance between transmitter and receiver aerials and in practice is between 30 and 40 miles for fixed ship installations: these distances are often exceeded.

VHF communication is being used more and more by harbour authorities to provide more efficient and safer control of the movements of shipping at the approaches of and in port. It is used for Port Control, Docking and Port Radar Guidance.

Post and Telegraph Administrations throughout the world are establishing coastal VHF radio stations through which a VHF link can be established into national telephone networks. In addition, VHF can be used for communications between ships similarly equipped.

Within the VHF maritime band 156-174 MHz, international channels are allocated in accordance with the following table:

NOTES REFERRING TO THE TABLE

(a) The figures in the column headed "Intership" indicate the normal sequence in which channels should be taken into use by mobile stations.

(b) The figures in the columns headed "Port operations", "Ship movement" and "Public correspondence" indicate the normal sequence in which channels should be taken into use by each coast station. However, in some cases, it may be necessary to omit channels in order to avoid harmful interference between the services of neighbouring coast stations.

(c) Administrations may designate frequencies in the intership, port operations and ship movement services for use by light aircraft and helicopters to communicate with ships or participating coast stations in predominantly maritime support operations under the conditions specified in the Radio Regulations. However, the use of the channels which are shared with public correspondence shall be subject to prior agreement between interested and affected administrations.

(d) The listed channels with the exception of 06, 15, 16, 17, 75 and 76, may also be used for high-speed data and facsimile transmissions, subject to special arrangement between interested and affected administrations.

(e) Except in the United States of America, the listed channels, preferably two adjacent channels from the series 87, 28, 88, with the exception of 06, 15, 16, 17, 75 and 76, may be used for narrow-band direct-printing telegraphy and data transmission, subject to special arrangement between interested and affected administrations.

(f) The two-frequency channels for port operations (18, 19, 20, 21, 22, 79 and 80) may be used for public correspondence, subject to special arrangement between interested and affected administrations.

(g) Until 1 January 1983, the effective radiated power of ship stations on channels 15 and 17 shall not exceed 1 W.

(h) The frequency 156.300 MHz (channel 06) may also be used for communication between ship stations and aircraft stations engaged in coordinated search and rescue operations. Ship stations shall avoid harmful interference to such communications on channel 06 as well as to communications between aircraft stations, ice-breakers and assisted ships during ice seasons.

(i) In France and in Belgium, the frequencies 156.050, 156.150 and 156.175 MHz are used as ship station frequencies in channels 01, 03 and 63 respectively and as coast station frequencies in channels 21, 23 and 83 respectively when the latter are used in the special semi-duplex public correspondence systems employed with 1 MHz separation between transmit and receive frequencies. These special provisions will cease to be used not later than 1 January 1983.

(j) Channels 60 and 88 can be used subject to special arrangements between interested and affected administrations.

(k) The frequencies in this table may also be used for radiocommunications on inland waterways in accordance with the conditions specified in the Radio Regulations.

(l) Channels 15 and 17 may also be used for on-board communications provided the effective radiated power does not exceed 1 W, and subject to the national regulations of the administration concerned when these channels are used in its territorial waters.

(m) This guard-band will apply after 1 January 1983.

(n) Within the European Maritime area and in Canada these frequencies (channels 10, 67, 73) may also be used, if so required, by the individual administrations concerned, for communication between ship stations, aircraft stations and participating land stations engaged in coordinated search and rescue and anti-pollution operations in local areas, under the conditions specified in the Radio Regulations.

(o) The preferred first three frequencies for the purpose indicated in Note *c)* are 156.450 MHz (channel 09), 156.525 MHz (channel 70) and 156.625 MHz (channel 72).

(p) These channels (68, 69, 11, 71, 12, 13, 14, 74, 79, 80) are the preferred channels for the ship movement service. They may, however, be assigned to the port operations service until required for the ship movement service if this should prove to be necessary in any specific area.

(q) This channel (86) may be used as a calling channel if such a channel is required in an automatic radiotelephone system when such a system is recommended by the C.C.I.R.

TRANSMITTING FREQUENCIES 156-174 MHz BAND
IN THE MARITIME MOBILE SERVICE

Channel desig-nators	Notes	Transmitting freq (MHz). Ship stations	Transmitting freq (MHz). Coast stations	Inter-ship	Port operations Single freq.	Port operations Two freq.	Ship movement Single freq.	Ship movement Two freq.	Public corres-pon-dence
60	j)	156.025	160.625			17		9	25
01	i)	156.050	160.650			10		15	8
61		156.075	160.675			23		3	19
02		156.100	160.700			8		17	10
62		156.125	160.725			20		6	22
03	i)	156.150	160.750			9		16	9
63	i)	156.175	160.775			18		8	24
04		156.200	160.800			11		14	7
64		156.225	160.825			22		4	20
05		156.250	160.850			6		19	12
65		156.275	160.875			21		5	21
06	h)	156.300		1					
66		156.325	160.925			19		7	23
07		156.350	160.950			7		18	11
67	n)	156.375	156.375	10	10		9		
08		156.400		2					
68	p)	156.425	156.425		6		2		
09	o)	156.450	156.450	5	5		12		
69	p)	156.475	156.475	9	11		4		
10	n)	156.500	156.500	3	9		10		
70	o)	156.525		6					
11	p)	156.550	156.550		3		1		
71	p)	156.575	156.575		7		6		
12	p)	156.600	156.600		1		3		
72	o)	156.625		7					
13	p)	156.650	156.650	4	4		5		
73	n)	156.675	156.675	8	12		11		
14	p)	156.700	156.700		2		7		
74	p)	156.725	156.725		8		8		
15	g)l)	156.750	156.750	12	14				
75	m)	Guard-band 156.7625 —156.7875 MHz							
16		156.800	156.800	Distress Safety and Calling					
76	m)	Guard band 156.8125 —156.8375 MHz							
17	g)l)	156.850	156.850	13	13				
77		156.875		11					
18	f)	156.900	161.500			3		22	
78		156.925	161.525			12		13	27
19	f)	156.950	161.550			4		21	
79	f)p)	156.975	161.575			14		1	
20	f)	157.000	161.600			1		23	
80	f)p)	157.025	161.625			16		2	
21	f)i)	157.050	156.050 or 161.650			5		20	
81		157.075	161.675			15		10	28
22	f)	157.100	161.700			2		24	
82		157.125	161.725			13		11	26
23	i)	157.150	156.150 or 161.750						5
83	i)	157.175	156.175 or 161.775						16
24		157.200	161.800						4
84		157.225	161.825			24		12	13
25		157.250	161.850						3
85		157.275	161.875						17
26		157.300	161.900						1
86	q)	157.325	161.925						15
27		157.350	161.950						2
87		157.375	161.975						14
28		157.400	162.000						6
88	j)	157.425	162.025						18

SHIPS' D/F BEARINGS

Calibration for Quadrantal Error of the D/F Apparatus should be carried out:
(1) As soon as possible after installation;
(2) Whenever any change is made in the position of the D/F aerial;
(3) If verification checks show the calibration table to be inaccurate.
The Calibration Table should be verified by means of check bearings at intervals not exceeding 12 months, and whenever any change is made in ship's structure or deck fittings which are likely to affect the accuracy of D/F bearings (e.g. stays, wire halliards, stowage position of derricks, etc.). Further details concerning calibration and arrangements for calibration in certain countries are contained in *Admiralty List of Radio Signals Vol. II.* Attention is drawn also to Statutory Instruments, 1965, No. 1112—The Merchant Shipping (D/F) Rules.

Errors and Practical Limitations

Night Effect (also termed Sunrise or Sunset Effects): Serious errors may occur in bearings taken *between one hour before sunset and one hour after sunrise* if the transmitter is more than 25 miles from the ship. The effects are greatest at times within one hour before or after sunrise and sunset. During the day from one hour after sunrise until one hour before sunset the errors are normally insignificant.
The presence of night effect is often indicated by a blurred zero or a surging and fading of the signal. Bearings taken under these conditions should be regarded as unreliable, and be checked by further bearings and all other means available. **If the transmitter is less than 25 miles from the ship, bearings will normally be free from night effect throughout the 24 hours.**

Coast Refraction (or Land Effect): When the signal path *from* the transmitter cuts the coast at a small angle, it is refracted away from the normal to the coastline (towards the coast). The resulting position line shows the ship as being nearer to the coast than her true position. Bearings which run nearly parallel to the coast may be 4° or 5° in error. When **high land** intervenes between the ship and the transmitter, serious errors, the direction of which cannot be predicted, are likely.

Ambiguity of D/F Bearings: When taking D/F bearings of a light vessel or other off-shore beacon, it is important that the sense-finding circuit be used to indicate on which side of the beacon the ship lies. A further check can be obtained by noting the change (due to the ship's movement) in several successive bearings taken at short intervals.

The Accuracy of a Bearing depends on:
(1) the accuracy with which the ship's true heading was determined at the instant the D/F reading was taken;
(2) the accuracy of the observed reading and
(3) the accuracy of the calibration table.

The Accuracy of the Position Line depends, not only on the accuracy of the bearing, but on the distance between the ship and the transmitter. An error of 1° in a true bearing causes an error of approximately one mile in the position line at a range of 60 miles.

The Accuracy of a Fix by D/F Bearings depends firstly on the accuracy of each position line, and secondly on the angle at which they cut one another. Considerable reliance can be placed on a fix obtained by three or more widely divergent simultaneous D/F bearings if the resultant "cocked hat" is small.

Practical Rules

1. Accurate calibration is essential.

2. **Keep the ship's head as steady as possible** when taking bearings, and note the exact heading at the instant of finding the null.

3. **Ship's D/F bearings are not reliable unless:**
   (1) the "zero" is perfect (i.e. a bearing of complete silence can be found however high the amplification of a signal);
   (2) the "zero" is *sharp*;
   (3) the transmitter lies within a distance of 50 miles from the ship by day, and 25 miles by night (i.e. from one hour before sunset to one hour after sunrise);
   (4) the compass error is known accurately;
   (5) the bearing does not make a very small angle with the coast;
   (6) high land does not intervene between the ship and the transmitter.

4. **When selecting beacons** for D/F bearings, avoid choosing those which lie beyond the listed range.

5. **Aerial circuits other than D/F**, if near the D/F aerial, should be disconnected from their sets whilst D/F bearings are being taken.

WARNINGS:

1. **Radiobeacons are liable to suspend operation** without advance notice for adjustment, repair or maintenance work, etc. Especially is this the case with radiobeacons located on light-vessels which may be taken out of service for overhaul, whilst the reserve light-vessel may not be equipped with the radiobeacon.

2. **Serious dangers** may arise from the misuse of radiobeacon fog signals and the risk of collision with light-vessels or Weather Ships when "homing" on them. The mariner who, in bad visibility, approaches a radio fog signal directly ahead on a radio bearing and relies on hearing the sound fog signal in sufficient time to alter course to avoid danger, is taking an *unjustifiable risk.* Sound fog signals of themselves give no indication of distance off and can be very misleading at times. If such signals are carried in light-vessels, risk of collision can be avoided by ensuring that the bearing does not remain constant.

USE OF AERO RADIOBEACONS
(See Admiralty List of Radio Signals, Vol. II)

General: Although aero radiobeacons are sited specially for the use of aircraft, many are well placed and otherwise very suitable for marine navigation. A selection of such beacons having certain favourable factors are listed in *Admiralty List of Radio Signals.* Aero radiobeacons which, for one reason or another, do not provide useful marine coverage are omitted.

Some countries have established radiobeacons in coastal regions specifically for both marine and air navigation; such beacons are classified as "aero-marine".

Advantages of aero radiobeacons:
1. They provide good coverage in some of the regions where marine radiobeacons are scarce or non-existent.
2. Most of them operate *continuously* in all weathers during their hours of service, thus providing a useful "homing" device when the beacon is located at or near the ship's landfall.
3. They may be very useful when interference in the marine beacon band is heavy.
4. In some coastal regions they radiate very powerful signals, giving ranges far beyond those in marine radiobeacons in the same area. Thus they often provide useful landfall aids in day-time.

Limitations of aero radiobeacons:
1. Bearing errors resulting from *land effect* are unpredictable. It is thought that they are likely to be at their maximum close inshore, and that bearings taken at greater distances from the coast may be comparatively free from this cause of error. *The possibility of such errors must always be considered when bearings are plotted.*
2. Aero radiobeacons are subject to withdrawal, alteration or shifting without advance notice, and the service details listed are sometimes unreliable.
3. Aero radiobeacons listed in *Admiralty List of Radio Signals* operate continuously throughout the 24 hours unless otherwise stated. Beacons stated to operate "by day" are not always in operation on week-ends, and their times of operation are liable to variation according to the requirements of flying schedules or individual aircraft on a particular flight.
4. The positions of aero radiobeacons are being inserted on all new Admiralty charts (abbreviation Aero Ro. Bn.). The position of such a beacon not shown on the chart in use should be inserted by the navigator, as it may be located some miles away from the place after which it is named.

CONSOL
General: Consol is a long range navigational aid intended mainly for aircraft, but it can be useful to ships as an aid to ocean navigation.
The Consol beacon transmits a radiation pattern of alternate dot and dash sectors separated by an equisignal (continuous note) formed by the merging of the dots and dashes. Any vessel hearing the signal can, by merely counting the number of dots and dashes, translate the count into a great circle bearing. A total of 60 dot-dash characters are transmitted in each operating cycle.

Requirements to enable a ship to use consol:
(1) A standard MF receiver, but in order to obtain satisfactory results during normal prevailing conditions of interference and static noise, the receiver should have narrow band characteristics.
(2) A Consol chart of the area or
(3) Consol tables which are used to convert the Consol count into a great circle bearing of the ship *from* the beacon. These tables are contained in *Admiralty List of Radio Signals, Vol. V.*

The complete cycle of operation consists of:
(1) A long continuous note interrupted by the station call sign.
(2) A short silence.
(3) The "Keying" cycle consisting of dot and dash characters separated by the equisignal.
(4) A short silence before the operating cycle is repeated.

Method of counting: Theoretically, the total number of dots and dashes heard should add up to 60. In practice, however, some of the characters are usually lost in the equisignal. The observed count is corrected thus: **subtract the observed total count from 60, then add half of the difference to each of the dot and dash counts.**

Example (1).　　Observed count: 36 dashes—equisignal—20 dots.
Total characters heard　= 36 + 20 = 56
Lost characters　　　　= 60 – 56 = 4

$$\text{True count} = \begin{cases} 36 + \dfrac{4}{2} = \textbf{38 dashes*} \\[2mm] 20 + \dfrac{4}{2} = \textbf{22 dots.} \end{cases}$$

This would be referred to the Consol chart or tables as a count of **38 dashes.**

Example (2).　　Observed count: Equisignal—56 dots.
Total characters heard　=　0 + 56 = 56
Lost characters　　　　= 60 – 56 =　4

$$\text{True count} = \begin{cases} 0 + \dfrac{4}{2} = \textbf{2 dashes*} \\[2mm] 56 + \dfrac{4}{2} = \textbf{58 dots.} \end{cases}$$

This would be referred to the Consol chart or tables as a count of **2 dashes.**

Example (3).　　Observed count: 54 dots—equisignal.
Total characters heard　= 54 +　0 = 54
Lost characters　　　　= 60 – 54 =　6

$$\text{True count} = \begin{cases} 54 + \dfrac{6}{2} = \textbf{57 dots*} \\[2mm] 0 + \dfrac{6}{2} = \textbf{3 dashes.} \end{cases}$$

This would be referred to the Consol chart or tables as a count of **57 dots.**

* The count and type of characters transmitted before the equisignal is the one which should be referred to the Consol chart or tables and the time at which the equisignal is heard is the time of observation.

Note: It is recommended that an average of several counts be taken before referring to the Consol chart or tables. Large differences in the count indicate that the bearing is unreliable.

Procedure for obtaining a Consol position line:

(1) To avoid ambiguity, it should be known in which particular dot or dash sector the ship is located. Normally the D.R. position will give adequate indication. If, however, the D.R. position is unreliable and the bearing from the beacon is not known within ±10°, a D/F bearing of the long continuous note should be taken.

(2) Tune the receiver to the required beacon and identify the station by the call sign.

(3) Count the characters as explained above.

(4) Refer the true count to the Consol chart or tables. On the chart, the coloured lattice lines are marked with the number of the count and character which precedes the equisignal.

The Consol tables give the great circle bearing of the ship from the beacon. Half-Convergency must be applied to all great circle bearings before they are plotted on a mercator chart. A table of Half-Convergency values for use with *each beacon* is included in the Consol tables.

WARNING: Although useful for ocean navigation, Consol bearings are not accurate enough for landfall or coastal navigation and should never be relied on when closing danger.

Coverage: Observations taken within 25 miles of a Consol Station are unreliable and should never be used.

Full particulars of each station with diagrams showing coverage and accuracy are provided in *Admiralty List of Radio Signals, Vol. V.*

Range and accuracy: The maximum range is about 1,200 miles by day to 1,500 miles by night; but it must be borne in mind that for several reasons it is not essentially accurate and position lines may frequently be 12 miles in error. The accuracy varies with the vessel's position in the radiation pattern. Errors rise as the range is increased and/or the ambiguous sector is approached. At night, errors may be considerable, rising steeply at 350-450 miles from a beacon.

The table of "95% Position Line Errors" given in *Admiralty List of Radio Signals* should be consulted. They are errors which it is prudent to assume present, although individual bearings may be more accurate than the figures quoted.

Use of equipment:

Automatic gain control must be switched off when receiving Consol signals.

If the D/F equipment is used to receive Consol signals, the loop or goniometer should be at the maximum reception position during the period of counting. In conditions of interference or heavy static, reception may be improved by rotating the loop or goniometer to one side or the other of this position; but it should never be moved more than 45° from the "maximum" otherwise an error in the count may be introduced, especially at night when the range is less than 300 miles.

CONSOLAN

Consolan is a long range navigational aid similar to Consol. There is one station in operation in the U.S.A., at *San Francisco*. Details of transmission, characteristics, service, position, etc., together with Consolan Tables for this station is given in *Admiralty List of Radio Signals, Vol. V.*

Coverage is over two sectors, each of about 140°. Consolan is not usable within 50 miles of the stations.

Range: From 1,000 to 1,400 miles over the sea.

Accuracy of Bearings: Normally within ±½° during the day and ±1° during night-time.

DECCA NAVIGATOR

An illustrated manual "Operating Instructions and Marine Data Sheets" for the Decca Navigator Systems (supplied by the Decca Navigator Company Limited, 9 Albert Embankment, London S.E.1.) is an essential requirement for all vessels equipped with this system, and the instructions contained therein should be followed rigidly.

Principle: Decca is a position fixing system which transmits continuous wave signals in the low frequency band 70-130 KHz. Master and Slave stations transmit on different frequencies which are multiplied by different factors in the receiver so that they may be phase compared at a common "comparison" frequency. The phase difference between the master and slave signals defines a range difference of the ship from the master and slave stations and thus a hyperbolic position line on which the ship must lie. Ambiguity arises due to the fact that the same phase difference will be observed at intervals of half a wavelength of the comparison frequency as the ship moves along a master-slave baseline. These intervals are known as lanes. Lane identification is provided by synthesising pulses which have a repetition frequency of 14.2 kHz and thus a much reduced ambiguity.

Coverage: The approved coverage is 240 miles from the Master Station of each chain, but use can be obtained from the system at greater distances under favourable conditions.

Accuracy: The accuracy of a position line is dependent on the distance from the transmitter, and its location with reference to the base line joining the relevant pair of stations; the best degree of accuracy generally being obtained near the mid-point of the base line. Fixing accuracy depends on the accuracy of the lattice lines and their angle of cut. Within 50 miles of the Master station fixes can normally be expected to be accurate to within half a cable; but the system is capable of an even higher degree of accuracy under favourable conditions and provided the equipment is correctly used.

There is a very high probability of correct *Lane Identification* within 240 miles of the Master Station during day-time; **but during night conditions the effects of sky-wave can cause sudden lane slipping and incorrect Lane Identification readings at distances greater than 150 miles, particularly at dawn and dusk. Mariners are warned that Decca should not be relied on as the sole aid to Navigation in these circumstances.**

Diagrams illustrating the accuracy to be expected of a Decca fix in particular localities at the various times of the day and year are given in Volume V of the *Admiralty List of Radio Signals.*

Inaccuracies which arise are set forth in the following two paragraphs. *All these limitations are very important, and should be understood by all who use the system.*

Fixed Errors: Lattice lines are slightly distorted in some areas due to "terrain effect". Since the distortion does not alter, it is possible to correct the error. Sometimes the errors are incorporated in the Decca charts, but otherwise are tabulated for all relevant areas in the data sheets.

Variable Errors: are caused by sky-wave interference and tend to increase with distance from the transmitters. In general, their effect is small under daylight conditions but may be considerable at long ranges by night. It is not possible to correct for such variable errors, but it is possible to estimate the likely value of the error at a given distance from the stations, and to judge the direction in which a Decca fix is likely to be displaced from the true position. Data Sheets give the estimated variable errors for day and night at various points and show:

(1) In which direction the fix will have the error, and how large this error is likely to be;
(2) In which direction the fixing accuracy is worst, and what the error in this direction is likely to be.
This information enables the navigator to plot the "diamond of error".

Lane Slip may result from any of the following:
(1) fouling of the Decca aerial;
(2) interruption of power supply;
(3) interruption or disturbance in transmission;
(4) interference from electric storms, external radio transmissions, or excessive night effect;
(5) incorrect referencing of the decometers.

Effects of Weather: The performance of the Lane Identification Meter and the Decometers can be affected by snow or precipitation static. Under such conditions caution must be exercised, and frequent lane checks carried out.

Decca Warnings: In the event of an occurrence of an irregularity in transmission which may cause *lane slip* in the coverage of a Chain, a warning signal (Decca Warning) is sent from the coast radio stations in the vicinity. These stations are listed in Data Sheets and the *Admiralty List of Radio Signals, Vol. V.* The usual form of warning signal appears in the latter publication. Attention is drawn also to the Annual Notice to Mariners No. 9.

Decca Lattice Charts: Information relating to Decca lattice charts is given in the Data Sheets and includes a full list of all charts published (Chart No., title, scale in inches to the mile, and date of latest issue).

Decca Chains in Operation are listed in the Data Sheets and in Vol. V. of the *Admiralty List of Radio Signals.* They are established in Europe, Eastern Canada, India, Persian Gulf, Australia, Japan and South Africa.

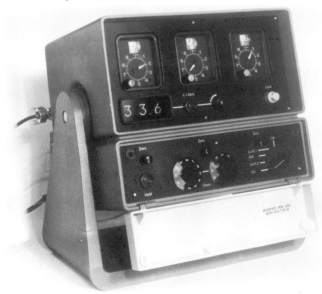

The Decca Navigator Marine Receiver Mark 21
The numerical lane identification display confirms the Green decometer reading of 33.6. Mark 21 has the capability to receive 63 multipulse chain frequencies plus frequency facility marked X for special requirements.

The Mk. 21, provides for the full 63 Decca main chain frequencies, plus an additional setting marked X for special requirements. The following are some of the main features of this receiver.

The *Multipulse* **Lane Identification** readings are displayed in very bold figures on an electronic in-line digital readout which gives the Lane value to the nearest tenth. This readout has the precision to give a fix which may be more accurate than the Decometers under skyware reception conditions at the longer ranges.

Zone letters and Lane numbers are both displayed in a window on the Decometer face, just above the rotating fraction pointer which reads to one hundredth of a Lane. This eliminates the possibility of reading errors which can occur when observing indicators have more than one pointer.

The main functions of "**setting-up**" are incorporated into a single sequential stepped switch which ensures that only the correct procedures can be followed.

A signal acquisition lamp indicates that the receiver has locked on to the Master station. It also indicates by degree of flicker the signal to noise quality of this transmission, thus cautioning the user on the state of reception. Similarly, the individual Decometers will indicate by fluctuation of their fractional pointers a reduction in the quality of incoming Slave signals.

Very high signal selectivity is achieved by the inclusion, in all receiver channels, of a device which generates noise-free replicas of incoming signals, thus permitting satisfactory operation under conditions of high atmospheric and electrical interference.

"**Inter-Chain**" **Fixing.** In principle, once the receiver has been initially set up on any chain it is in a condition to very quickly acquire any other chain within range. The multipulse digital readout automatically identifies the Red, Green and Purple position line readings and the calibration necessary on switching chains is now instantaneous on the push of a button.

Maintenance. The Mk. 21 is especially designed for quick servicing. Should a fault occur, all that is required is the exchange of a plug-in printed circuit board.

Installation is very simple. The receiver, power unit, Decometer and Lane identification display is housed in a single unit.

Power requirement. An A.C. input approximately 15 VA and on D.C. about 25 watts. A range of built-in power units permits the equipment to operate on 12, 24, 32, 110 and 220 V.D.C., and 80-260 V.A.C., from 40 to 400 Hz.

LORAN A

Loran A is a medium range navigational aid. It has become obsolescent with the development of Loran C and other position fixing aids.

Principle: A "pair" of shore stations consisting of Master and Slave and located from 200 to 600 miles apart transmit synchronised radio pulses. The ship's equipment measures the **time interval** between reception of the Master and Slave pulses by means of a cathode ray tube. The reading so obtained is then referred to a navigational chart which is overprinted with a family of hyperbolae, each lattice line being numbered with its appropriate **time difference.** Thus the hyperbola whose number corresponds to the reading taken constitutes a position line. Two or more "pairs" of stations are required for a fix.

Loran Tables are used to convert the time-difference reading into a position line when a Loran chart is not available.

Radio frequency. From 1,750 to 1,950 kHz. Thus both ground and sky waves can be used within their effective ranges.

Range: *Ground waves:* By day—600 to 700 n.m. over the sea. By night—rather less due to atmospheric noise. *Sky waves:* Effective at distances between 300 and 1,200 n.m. at night over land or sea.

Accuracy of position lines depends on range, length of base line, location within coverage, ionization effects and the operator's skill. Position lines obtained from *ground wave* readings may generally be taken as within ½% of range from the mid point of the station base line, and sky wave readings as within 1%.

Coverage. Good coverage has been generally provided for most of the N. Atlantic and N. Pacific. A list of the chains remaining in operation is contained in Volume V of the *Admiralty List of Radio Signals.*

Transmission failures. If the transmissions get out of synchronisation or become unreliable for any reason either the Master or Slave signal, or both, will "blink" at intervals of about 2 seconds. "Blinking" is either appearing and disappearing of the signal or else shifting right and left by about 1,000 micro-seconds.

Disadvantages. The performance can be greatly reduced by station interference. It is often difficult to distinguish between ground and sky waves, and much experience is needed for recognising and matching first sky waves at long ranges. (It is recommended that the signals be observed for *at least* 30 seconds under these conditions.)

LORAN C

Loran C is a development of, and a successor to, Loran A. It provides more accurate fixing and considerably increased range compared with Loran A.

The Radio Frequency is 100 kHz which is low enough to give a ground wave range of 800-1,200 n.m. Also sky waves may be used at longer ranges.

Principle: A Loran C chain consists of a master transmitting station and two to four slaves designated W, X, Y and Z. The time interval between reception of signals from master and slave pairs is measured coarsely by comparing pulse envelopes and then finely by comparing the phase of the radio frequency cycles within the envelopes. The measured time difference defines the observer's position as on a hyperbola which can be identified on the appropriate Loran C lattice chart. Two master-slave pairs are needed to obtain a fix.

Each chain is identified by a unique group repetition interval (GRI) at which the complete pattern of signals is repeated. There is a delay between the master and slave pulses such that, at any point in the coverage area, an observer receives the pulses in the order: master, W slave, X slave, Y slave, Z slave. Multiple pulses are used to give an increased signal/noise ratio, the master signals comprising nine sub-pulses and the slave signals comprising eight sub-pulses.

Range: The ground wave coverage of 800-1,200 n.m. is increased to over 2,000 n.m. by the use of sky waves but with reduced accuracy.

Accuracy: Within ground wave coverage the fixing accuracy is usually better than ± 500 metres (95% probability) where there is a reasonable angle of cut between position lines. Using skywaves, the comparable accuracy is ± 2 n.m.

Coverage: Coverage is provided for areas in the N. Atlantic and the N. Pacific and also for the Mediterranean Sea. Details are included in Volume V of the *Admiralty List of Radio Signals.*

Transmission Failures: If the transmissions from a chain get out of synchronisation or become unreliable for any reason, the ninth sub-pulse from the master station multiple pulse will "blink" and also the first two sub-pulses in each multiple pulse from an affected slave.

OMEGA

Omega is a long range hyperbolic fixing system operating in the very low frequency (VLF) band. It has been under development for a number of years. Eight transmitting stations are sufficient to provide world-wide coverage.

Radio Frequency: The basic frequency is 10.2 kHz but signals of 11.33 kHz and 13.6 kHz are also transmitted. Each station transmits the same frequencies in turn, according to a schedule which repeats at 10 second epochs. The signals from individual stations are identified by the duration and sequence of the transmissions.

Principle: The phase of signals from pairs of stations are compared (as in the Decca system) and a number of possible hyperbolic position lines are defined by an observed phase difference. Along the baseline the lanes within which possible position lines recur are approximately 8 n.m. wide (half a wavelength) when phase comparison is made at the 10.2 kHz frequency. The ambiguity is reduced when phase comparison is made at a difference frequency of 3.4 kHz so that lane widths become 24 n.m., and it is further reduced when phase comparison is made at a difference frequency of 1.13 kHz so that the lane widths become 72 n.m.

Accuracy: Observations of phase difference must be corrected for the phase variations which may be predicted according to the time of day, season of the year and geographical location. These predictions are published by the Defense Mapping Agency Hydrographic Center, Washington D.C. When these corrections are applied, fixing accuracy may be expected to be of the order of ± 1 n.m. by day and ± 2 n.m. by night (95% probability).

Differential Omega: In addition to the predictable phase variations, irregular variations also occur which cannot be taken account of in tables. Sudden ionospheric disturbances (SID) and polar cap absorption (PCA) effects and other shorter term effects are examples of unpredictable error sources. In the differential mode a fixed station monitors the unpredicted Omega propagation errors in a local area and broadcasts corrections which can be applied by ships in the general vicinity. This procedure has the potential for greatly increased accuracy.

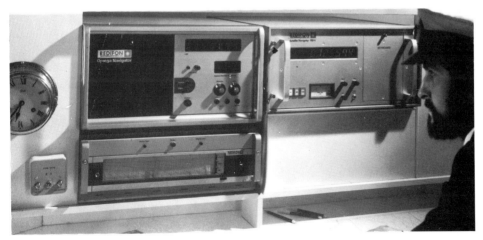

Left: Redifon Omega Navigator NV1 which fixes positions to within 1-2 nautical miles. Direct readout is given of three hyperbolic lines of position by continuously tracking signals from eight ground stations strategically positioned at key points on the earth's surface.

Right: Redifon Satellite Navigator RSN1 which gives direct readout of latitude and longitude to an accuracy of within ¼ of a nautical mile down to 400 ft. and is entirely automatic. An inbuilt computer makes all the necessary calculations using information received from six orbiting satellites.

Section Q

Artificial Satellites and Navigation

GENERAL ARTIFICIAL SATELLITES AND NAVIGATION

Navigators with a knowledge of the theory of astronomical navigation and nautical astronomy know well the solar system and the laws governing the motion of the Earth and the other planets in their orbits around the Sun. For many years people have dreamed of creating bodies to do just this: artificial satellites to orbit the Earth or the Sun under human control. With the vast increase in our knowledge of rocketry and electronic control systems, it has become possible to launch space craft into almost any desired orbit, and the question then arises as to what use can a satellite be put for the purposes of navigation on the Earth's surface.

Before considering specific systems, it might be as well to review the characteristics of satellite orbits, and to consider the advantages and disadvantages that satellites have as compared with more commonplace navigational landmarks. The path of a *space craft* may be any one of a number of what are sometimes referred to as conic sections.

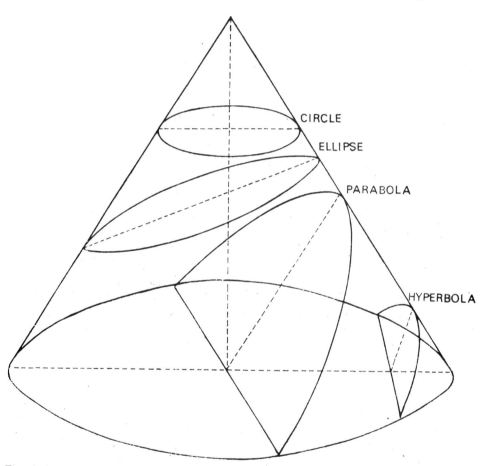

The circle and the ellipse are closed curves called *orbits,* and when a space craft traverses an orbit it is referred to as a *satellite.* The parabola and the hyperbola are not closed curves, and are referred to as *trajectories,* and when a space craft follows a trajectory it is usually referred to as a *probe.*

Obviously it is satellites in orbit that are of interest to Earth-bound navigators. The orbit of a particular satellite depends upon its *injection velocity,* that is its velocity when it enters its orbit, and also its position relative to the Earth at the time of injection. If its injection velocity is equal to what is called the *escape velocity* the path will be a parabola. This precise value is difficult to achieve and so in general the injection velocity will be either greater or less than the escape velocity. If greater the trajectory will be a hyperbola and the space craft will escape from the Earth; if less the trajectory will be an ellipse. Again, the circular orbit is difficult to achieve precisely and so all satellites follow elliptical orbits.

From a consideration of Kepler's Laws we are able to deduce most of the information we require about satellite orbits. We know that as the altitude of the satellite increases, its speed decreases. A satellite skimming the Earth's surface would be moving at about 8 km per second, while one at an altitude of 35,000 kilometres would have a speed of about 4 km per second. Again, a satellite with a very low altitude has an orbital period of about 84 minutes, while one at an altitude of about 35,000 kilometres has a period of 24 hours, that is the period of rotation of the Earth on its axis. The choice of an orbit for a particular navigation system depends on many factors but some of the more obvious are these—There must be a line of sight between the satellite and anyone who wishes to communicate with it. The higher the satellite the greater is the area of the Earth's surface that it can "see". In fact a satellite at an altitude of 35,000 kilometres can see about one third of the surface of the Earth. This satellite will have, as stated, a period of 24 hours, and is called a *synchronous satellite*. If its orbital plane lies in the plane of the equator, and it traverses its orbit in the same direction as the Earth rotates, its geographical position will be stationary: it is then called a *geostationary satellite* and only three such satellites would be required to cover the Earth's surface—apart from polar regions. On the other hand, if a satellite is in a very low orbit it can see only a comparatively small area of the Earth's surface but it is moving at high speed, and adequate coverage may still be obtained by using a reasonably small number of satellites.

All that has been said so far about elliptical orbits has been based on two assumptions that have greatly simplified the situation. Firstly, it was assumed that only the Earth and the satellite were present in the universe; in fact, of course, we must take account of the effects of the gravitational attractions of the Sun and Moon. Secondly, we have assumed that the Earth was a spherical mass of uniform density, whereas it is not. These two factors cause *perturbations,* that is departures from an elliptical orbit fixed in space. The orbit is not truly elliptical and in general it rotates relative to both space and the Earth. Thus the geostationary satellite, at first so attractive, is in fact complicated by the requirement that if it is to be precisely geostationary it must incorporate thrust motors to correct for perturbations. Moreover we cannot ignore the effect of the Earth's atmosphere producing aerodynamic drag. The effect of this is to cause what is known as *orbital decay.* As time goes by the dimensions of the ellipse decrease, the satellite comes closer and closer to the surface of the Earth in air of ever increasing density and eventually frictional heating is sufficient to destroy it. All this means that whatever system of navigation is used, the orbit of the satellite is continuously changing and hence there must be facilities for continuously and accurately tracking it. Since any proposed system uses radio signals the effect of the atmosphere, or more particularly the ionosphere, must also be taken into consideration and in general the higher the satellite, that is the less oblique the path of the signals through the ionosphere, the smaller will errors be.

Whatever type of system is used a balance must be struck between economy, reliability, accuracy and expense. As we have seen an expensive tracking system is required in any case. The satellite itself must be able to receive and transmit signals and it needs a power source to do this, yet it must be as small in size and mass as possible. The greater the altitude of the satellite the greater is the amount of total energy required to get it up into orbit at the required speed. On the other hand, the lower the satellite orbit the greater is its speed, and hence accurate tracking is more difficult.

U.S. NAVY NAVIGATION SATELLITE SYSTEM (NNSS)

This position fixing system, formerly called the Transit System, has been available for commercial use since 1967. Receivers are associated with digital computing facilities for processing the signals received from the satellites, and position is displayed in latitude and longitude.

Radio Frequency: The satellite transmissions are made on two highly stable channels at about 400 MHz and 150 MHz. These carriers are modulated for transmission of the satellite orbital parameters.

Principle: The frequencies received by an observer decrease during a satellite pass due to the Doppler effect. Cycle counts are made by the receiver over incremental periods of two minutes or less and the counts for a series of such periods are compared with the computed counts which would have been obtained for the same periods from an estimated position. The estimated position is then successively adjusted until the computed counts coincide with the observed counts.

Availability: The satellites each have a nearly circular polar orbit with an altitude of about 1,000 Km. Positions may be obtained whenever a satellite is sufficiently above the user's horizon, and the time interval between useful satellite passes varies from an average of 90 minutes in low latitudes to 30 minutes in high latitudes, although occasionally intervals of more than 4 hours may occur. Many equipments provide an automatic D.R. facility using inputs from the ship's log and compass so that a continuous readout of position is displayed.

Accuracy: The system accuracy is approximately ± 100 metres (95% probability) using a dual frequency system (400 MHz and 150 MHz) with which it is possible to estimate and correct for ionospheric distortion of the signal. Using a cheaper single frequency system (400 MHz), the accuracy is approximately ± 200 metres (95% probability). These errors may be greatly increased if the user's velocity is not accurately known since this contributes to the observed Doppler effect. The order of this error is about 400 metres for every knot of velocity error. Errors in N-S velocity are particularly significant, and fix errors in longitude are likely to be greater than those in latitude. It is also necessary to bear in mind that in some parts of the world the errors in charted positions may exceed those of fixing by the NNSS system and the discrepancy due to this cause may exceed 1 n.m. in areas charted from old and poorly controlled surveys.

THE NAVSTAR GPS SYSTEM

This is a position fixing system currently under development. It is based on 24 satellites disposed in three 16,000 kilometre orbits inclined at 63½° to the equator. Radio signals from the satellites at a frequency of about 1,500 MHz are controlled by atomic frequency standards of very great stability.

The Principle is to find the ranges (or pseudo ranges which include clock bias) from the instantaneous positions of a number of satellites to the observer by measuring the time of reception of the satellite signals using high precision clocks.

System Availability is virtually continuous and fixing is estimated as an order of accuracy better than the NNSS.

Section R

Signalling

NOTES ON SIGNALLING METHODS

The International Code Book should be consulted for detailed instructions on the use of flag and other signalling methods. Code books are published in English, French, Italian, German, Japanese, Spanish, Russian and Greek.

The Flags of the International Code of Signals

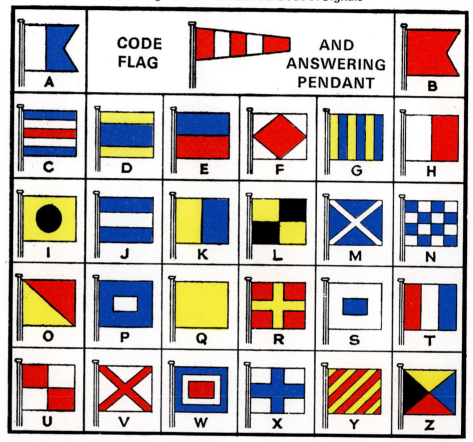

NUMERAL PENDANTS

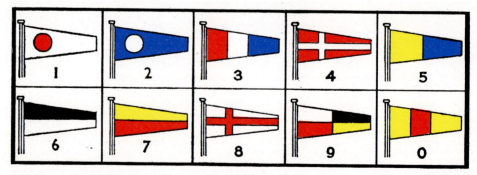

SUBSTITUTES

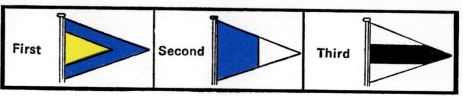

INTERNATIONAL CODE OF SIGNALS
SINGLE-LETTER SIGNALS

The **most important Code signals** of all—the **single letter signals**—consist of **Very Urgent** signals or those in common use. Seamen should know these by heart, so that there may be no hesitation in acting on them.

They may be made by any method of signalling (see footnotes below).

These also, with the several others that would be used for the purpose indicated, *i.e.* **G** = **I require a Pilot** and the "alter course" signals **E, I and S** and others, would be given by **Sound Signals** (Morse Code) as required.

A   I have a diver down; keep well clear at slow speed.

*B   I am taking in or discharging or carrying dangerous goods.

C   **Yes** (affirmative or "The significance of the previous group should be read in the affirmative").

*D   **Keep clear** of me—I am manoeuvring with difficulty.

*E   I am altering my course to **starboard**.

F   I am **disabled**. Communicate with me.

G   I **require a Pilot**.

*H   I **have a pilot** on board.

*I   I am altering my course to **port**.

J   I am on fire and have dangerous cargo on board, keep well clear of me.

K   I wish to communicate with you.

L   You should **stop** your vessel instantly.

M   My vessel is stopped and making no way through the water.

†N   **No** (negative or "The significance of the previous group should be read in the negative").

O   **Man overboard**.

P   **In Harbour** (Blue Peter): All persons should report on board as the vessel is **about to proceed to sea.**

Q   My vessel is **healthy** and I request free pratique.

‡R   No signal.

*S   My engines are going **astern**.

*T   Keep clear of me; I am engaged in pair trawling.

U   You are running **into danger**.

V   I **require assistance**.

W   I **require medical assistance**.

X   **Stop** carrying out your intentions and watch for my signals.

Y   I am **dragging my anchor**.

Z   I **require a tug**. When made by fishing vessels operating in close proximity on the fishing grounds it means: "I am shooting my nets."

†N—this signal may be given only visually or by sound. For voice or radio transmission the signal should be *NO*.

‡*Important Note:* No single letter signal has been allocated to letter R.

Note 1. Letters marked by * when made by sound may only be made in compliance with the requirements of the International Regulations for Preventing Collisions at Sea. Rules 34 and 35.

Note 2. Signals K and S have special meanings as landing signals for small boats with crews or persons in distress.

THE MORSE CODE

Letter	Code	Letter	Code	Number	Code
A	·—	N	—·	1	·————
B	—···	O	———	2	··———
C	—·—·	P	·——·	3	···——
D	—··	Q	——·—	4	····—
E	·	R	·—·	5	·····
F	··—·	S	···	6	—····
G	——·	T	—	7	——···
H	····	U	··—	8	———··
I	··	V	···—	9	————·
J	·———	W	·——	0	—————
K	—·—	X	—··—		
L	·—··	Y	—·——		
M	——	Z	——··		

MORSE SIGNALLING BY FLASHING LIGHT

Procedure Signals: (A bar over a sequence of letters means that they are to be made as one group.)

Calling up	= $\overline{AA}$ $\overline{AA}$ $\overline{AA}$
Answering	= $\overline{TTTT}$ etc
Word or group received	= T
Full stop or decimal point	= $\overline{AAA}$
Erase signal	= $\overline{EEEEEE}$
Affirmative	= C
Negative	= NO
Correct	= OK
Received	= R
End of signal	= AR
Waiting signal	= AS
Repeat signal	= RPT

The following may be used in conjunction with the repeat signal:

All after	= AA
All before	= AB
All between	= BN
Word or group after	= WA
Word or group before	= WB

Sequence for Transmitting a Message:

(1) The Call: This may consist of the calling up sign given above or the identity signal for the station which is being addressed.

(2) The Answer: This consists of the general answering sign given above.

(3) The Identity of the caller: After contact has been established, the calling station sends the group "DE" followed by its name or identity signal.

(4) The Text of the Message: This may be transmitted in plain language or in international code groups. The latter should be indicated by prefixing the code groups with the signal "YU" or "INTERCO".

(5) Acknowledgement: Each word or group should be acknowledged by the signal "T".

(6) Termination: The end of the message is indicated by the group "AR" which is answered by "R".

MORSE SIGNALLING BY SOUND

Sound signals, other than those specified in the International Regulations for Preventing Collisions at Sea, should be used very sparingly and always with great caution because of the possibility of misunderstandings. Confusion is possible between message signals and rule of the road or distress signals, particularly in poor visibility.

VOICE COMMUNICATION (using radio telephone, telephone, loud hailer, etc).

Standard Marine Vocabulary:
A standard marine navigational vocabulary has been compiled by the IMCO Safety of Navigation Sub-Committee. This is now published and recommended for international use for ship to ship and ship to shore communication. The object is to provide a vocabulary of standardised words and phrases which can be used and understood by mariners with a limited knowledge of the English language.

Phonetic Letters:
These may be used for transmitting individual letters by voice, according to the following table:

Letter	Code Word	Pronunciation	Letter	Code Word	Pronunciation
A	Alfa	ALF AH	N	November	NO VEM BER
B	Bravo	BRAH VOH	O	Oscar	OSS CAH
C	Charlie	CHAR LEE	P	Papa	PAH PAH
		(or SHAR LEE)	Q	Quebec	KEY BECK
D	Delta	DELL TAH	R	Romeo	ROW ME OH
E	Echo	ECK OH	S	Sierra	SEE AIR RAH
F	Foxtrot	FOKS TROT	T	Tango	TANG GO
G	Golf	GOLF	U	Uniform	YOU NEE FORM
H	Hotel	HOH TELL			(or OO NEE FORM)
I	India	IN DEE AH	V	Victor	VIK TAH
J	Juliett	JEW LEE ETT	W	Whiskey	WISS KEY
K	Kilo	KEY LOH	X	X-Ray	ECKS RAY
L	Lima	LEE MAH	Y	Yankee	YANG KEY
M	Mike	MIKE	Z	Zulu	ZOO LOO

Note: Emphasis is given to the syllables which are underlined.

Section S

Sea flags

SEA FLAGS

1. ENSIGNS OF MARITIME COUNTRIES

The most important flag that is worn at sea by any vessel is the **Ensign.** Almost every country has its special Merchant or Maritime flag that is worn in that country's vessels.

These are variously published in colours, but the Flag Chart entitled **National Flags and Ensigns** compiled and published by the United States Naval Oceanographic Office, is published for the primary purpose of aiding the Mariner to determine nationalities of vessels encountered at sea.

This Flag Chart shows over 175 different Ensigns in their correct colours in a large size, 1¾ by 1¼ inches per flag, and is obtainable from the world-wide agents of the U.S. Oceanographic Office.

NOTE

Details of U.S.A. practice with respect to sea flags is contained in 'Piloting, Seamanship and Small Boat Handling' by Charles F. Chapman, published by 'Motor Boating and Sailing', 224W. 57th St. New York, N.Y. 10019.

2. THE BRITISH NATIONAL FLAG

(a) **The Union Flag.** This, **the National Flag,** incorrectly, but frequently referred to as the Union Jack—is never worn at sea except by Royalty and the Royal Navy.

It is incorrect for a foreign yachtsman, desiring to wear a Courtesy Ensign in British waters, to wear this flag. The correct Courtesy Ensign for a vessel of any foreign nationality to wear under these circumstances is the **Red Ensign**—worn where decribed for all Courtesy Ensigns. (See page 338).

The Jack. This is the small flag worn on a "Jack" staff in the fore part of a vessel either on the stem or on the bowsprit by **NAVAL vessels only.** The ships of the Royal Navy wear the Union Flag. Ships of the other Commonwealth countries wear their National Colours as a Jack.

If merchant vessels wear a Jack it would be a small "House Flag". It is not a recognised flag for a yacht to wear. **A Jack is worn only when a vessel is at anchor or in harbour.**

(b) **The Pilot Jack.** This is the Union Flag described under (a) above; having around it a wide white border of one-fifth the size of the flag; and is known as the **Pilot Jack,** which is an **International** day signal for a Pilot for any port in the world when hoisted at the **fore** (the foremast) of any vessel.

This **Pilot Jack** for all countries is the **National** flag of that country surrounded by the above described white border. Thus a French vessel would have as her Pilot Jack a **French** National Flag surrounded by a white border.

3. BRITISH ENSIGNS

The Ensign is the most important flag to be worn by any vessel as it indicates her Nationality. British Ensigns may be of several colours as described (a) to (e).

(a) **White Ensign**—Red Cross of St. George on a white field. Union Flag in upper canton. Worn by the Royal Yacht, Royal Navy and Royal Yacht Squadron, and sometimes with Royal Cypher used as a Standard.

(b) **Blue Ensign**—Dark blue field with Union Flag in upper canton. The fly is frequently defaced by badge of the office or organisation wearing it, e.g.: Royal Fleet Auxiliary, Naval Ordnance, Ocean Weather Ships, Consular Service, Ordnance and Royal Artillery, Royal Engineers, Royal Army Service Corps, Dept. of Agriculture and Fisheries, Scottish Home Department Fisheries Division, Dept. of Trade, Customs, Post Office, Port of London Authority, Lloyd's Pacific Cable Board, Mersey Docks and Harbour Board, Commissioners of Northern

Lighthouses, Commissioners of Irish Lights, etc. All vessels with Admiralty warrant to fly the Blue Ensign. Many Yacht Club members have this privilege, some with defaced and some with undefaced Ensigns.

(c) **Red Ensign**—Red field with Union Flag in upper canton. Worn by Merchant Navy and private craft of British subjects. Sometimes defaced in fly. Worn with defacement in fly by some Yacht Clubs (e.g., Lloyd's Y.C.) with Admiralty Warrant.

(d) **Royal Air Force** vessels wear a *Light* Blue Ensign with the Union Flag in the canton and with a defacement of red, white and dark blue circles (small red in the centre).

(e) **Civil Air**—Dark Blue St. George's Cross with white border on a light blue field with the Union Flag in the canton.

The **Red** Ensign is also the correct flag for any British yacht to wear. Under the Merchant Shipping Act a **registered** yacht—that is a vessel used entirely for pleasure and not profit—(of over 15 tons register) is allowed and **required** to wear the Red Ensign on all correct occasions. **The Red Ensign must, by law, be carried on board.**

The **Blue Ensign** is worn by a relatively small number of British Merchant Navy vessels, having been granted the privilege in cases where the Commanding Officer and a percentage of the crew are members of the Royal Naval Reserve.

The **Blue** Ensign may also be worn by yachts whose owner is a member of a Yacht Club and has been granted—*through the Yacht Club*—a special Ensign Warrant by the Admiralty as described in paragraph 4 below. Yacht Clubs with this privilege are listed in the *Navy List.*

Irish Yacht Club members belonging to Clubs in the Irish Republic now wear the Ensign of their Club with the **Eire** Flag in the upper canton in place of the **Union** Flag.

4. BRITISH ENSIGN WARRANTS

The Admiralty—by Act of Parliament—grant to certain Yacht Clubs, the privilege of wearing special Ensigns: The **White** Ensign to the Royal Yacht Squadron only; and the **Blue**—undefaced or defaced—or the **Red** if defaced, to other Yacht Clubs. The Ensign when "defaced" has the special distinguishing badge of the Yacht Club in the fly—like a British Colonial Ensign.

A member of such a Yacht Club desiring his vessel to wear such a "special" Ensign must be the owner of a registered seagoing yacht of over 2 tons (houseboats are ineligible); which is never used for profit. Under these conditions he applies to his Yacht Club for such a privilege. If the Admiralty Warrant is granted to the Yacht—**not** to the owner (it is not a personal warrant)—then this must at all times be kept on board with the Ship's Certificate of Registry.

The **Blue Ensign undefaced** is worn by members of several Yacht Clubs which have in the past been granted an Ensign Warrant. Such Clubs as the Royal Cruising Club, Royal Thames Yacht Club and Royal Motor Yacht Club are examples.

The **Red Ensign defaced** has been granted to several Yacht Clubs under their Ensign Warrant, and these Clubs include the Royal Victoria Y.C. (I.O.W.), the Royal Lymington Y.C. and Lloyd's Yacht Club.

5. ROYAL NAVY FLAGS

(1) **All Ships and Establishments**—White Ensign.

(2) **Lord High Admiral and Lords Commissioners.**—Red field charged with gold anchor and cable. Also worn on foremast of Royal Yacht when the Sovereign is aboard.

(3) **Admiral of the Fleet**—Union Flag.

(4) **Admiral**—White field charged with Red Cross of St. George.

w

(5) **Vice Admiral**—As Admiral plus red ball in the first canton.

(6) **Rear Admiral**—As Vice Admiral plus red ball in the third canton.

(7) **Commodore**—As Vice Admiral but slight taper ending with swallow tail.

(8) **Commanding Officer Small Craft**—White pendant up to 21 yards long with Red Cross of St. George in the hoist.

6. TRINITY HOUSE FLAGS

(1) **Jack**—Red Cross of St. George, old sailing ships in quarters.

(2) **Ensign**—Red Ensign, defaced by Jack in fly.

(3) **Burgee**—As Jack on a red field.

7. H.M. CUSTOMS FLAGS

(1) **Ensign**—Blue defaced by crown over portcullis.

(2) **Burgee**—White with red border on upper and lower edges, defaced crown over portcullis.

8. MISCELLANEOUS FLAGS

(1) **Queen's Harbour Master**—Union Flag with white border, charged with white circle with Q.H.M. in black; Imperial Crown over.

(2) **Thames Conservancy**—St. George's Cross charged with arms of T.C.

(3) **Port of London Authority**—St. George's Cross charged with arms of P.L.A. or Blue Ensign defaced.

(4) **Examination Vessels**—Blue or White Ensign and special flag white and red horizontal surrounded by a blue border.

(5) **Royal Mail**—White pendant charged with "ROYAL MAIL" cypher and horn.

(6) **North Sea Fisheries**—Pendant quartered, blue above yellow in hoist, reverse in fly.

(7) **Pilots**—**Pilot Flag**, upper half white, lower half red. The **Pilot Jack (National Flag with white border) hoisted at the fore is the signal for a Pilot**

9. WHAT MARITIME FLAGS ARE FLOWN

Flags worn at sea by ships, large and small, comprise: (a) **Ensign**; (b) **House flag**; (c) **International Code Flags**; (d) **Special Flags**; Pilot Jack, Courtesy Ensign, Royal Naval Flags, Merchant Navy Commodore Flag, and others mentioned.

Foreign merchant vessels of course wear the **Ensign** of their own country and the **House Flag** of their owner's fleet, with their distinctive **funnel** markings. **British Commonwealth** countries ships wear the Ensign of their particular country and other normal flags as mentioned.

10. COURTESY ENSIGNS

A pleasant maritime practice is for a vessel visiting another country on business or pleasure to show her respect for that country by flying the flag of that country in a conspicuous position, when anchored off, approaching a harbour, or in a port of that foreign country.

The "Queens" flew the Ensign of the United States of America when in U.S. waters, and similarly the vessels of the United States Lines—and other famous vessels—fly the British Red Ensign when in U.K. waters.

The **Maritime Ensign** of the particular country visited is the correct Courtesy Ensign to be worn by a British vessel, and the Red Ensign the correct Courtesy Ensign for a ship or yacht of a foreign country visiting the United Kingdom to wear. This would normally be flown on a yardarm, or halliard where it could best be seen. This Courtesy Ensign would normally be several sizes smaller than the actual Ensign worn in that particular vessel.

11. HOUSE FLAGS

A **House Flag** is a private flag worn by vessels of the Merchant Navy by all ships of the same owners as a distinguishing flag. Owners of private yachts—especially power vessels—may, provided the flag design does not conflict with any other in existence, wear their own **personal** flag which is generally the same as the owner's Racing Flag, if used. These are rectangular in shape and may be of any suitable size. They are never worn in vessels wearing the White Ensign.

House Flags are never used in sailing craft, but are nearly always worn in larger power craft and form part of the "suit of Colours" to be worn with the Ensign and Burgee.

12. INTERNATIONAL CODE FLAGS

The **International Code** comprises 40 special flags as shown in the coloured plate on page 330. These enable Naval, Merchant, Fishing Vessels, Yachts and Shore Signal Stations to send and receive messages by flags between any nationalities. A brief description of the Code is given on pages 330 to 333.

In addition to the use for which they were intended and have been so used for decades—the flags flown individually or in a "hoist" are used for different purposes. Any British registered vessel or yacht may be allotted a 4-flag hoist—known as the **"Ship's Numbers"**—which consists of four flags flown in a hoist with the country distinguishing code flag or flags flown at the top of the hoist. British ships use "G", "M" or "2"— Code Flag uppermost. Such as M.N.R.S. would indicate a British vessel's name.

These letters are always endorsed in the Ship's Certificate of Registry and are the same as her Radio Call Sign. Vessels hoist their "numbers" on request by one of H.M. Ships or when reporting at any signal station or speaking to any vessel at sea.

When **hoisted singly** these flags have **Urgent** and **Important** meanings; flag **G**, for example is one of the International Signals for a Pilot anywhere in the world. Flag **Q** is the **Quarantine** Flag in British Waters. All these single flag meanings are shown on page 331. They have special uses as **Distress Signals;** and are used considerably by vessels for **Dressing Ships** overall—on special occasions—e.g. a Naval Review, the Queen's birthday and other ceremonial occasions.

13. H.M. FLAG—ROYAL STANDARD

The Royal Standard is the personal Flag of the Sovereign and is only flown in a ship when the Sovereign is actually on board when, in addition to the Royal Standard which shall be flown at the main, the Lord High Admiral's Flag shall be flown at the fore and the Union Flag at the mizzen, or in a two-masted vessel as may best be seen. Other members of the Royal Family also have personal Standards.

14. H.M. SHIP FLAGS

The Royal Navy have Special Flags of their own, both for distinguishing their Commanding Officers when afloat—these are described on page 337—and also for special signalling and manoeuvring flags which are not used outside R.N. ships, so are not described here, but may be found in the "Admiralty Manual of Seamanship", Vol. I.

In the past the Royal Navy had their own Signalling Code, so all Royal Naval Reserve Officers had to learn two Codes, the R.N. and the International. Since the last war, however, the Royal Navy have adopted the International Code of Signals, so **all** countries now use the International Code of Signals for merchant or warship signalling, which has greatly simplified this method of signalling.

15. MERCHANT NAVY FLAGS

The Merchant Navy use special flags sparingly, but most large shipping companies honour their senior Master nowadays by appointing him Commodore of their Fleet of ships, and on appointment and thereafter until retirement, he is entitled to wear this Commodore's Flag when in command afloat. A happy recognition of a lifetime spent at sea in their service.

16. THE PILOT FLAG

Any vessel in British waters having a Pilot **on board** hoists the letter **H** of the International Code (i.e. white and red **vertical**); whilst the Pilot vessel that puts Pilots aboard (and takes them off outward bound vessels), flies the same colours but **horizontal,** i.e. a white over red flag.

17. FISHERY CRUISERS

An International Code of Special Signals is prescribed for use in the North Sea and U.K. waters generally, for rapid communication between fishery cruisers and fishing vessels. Eight signals can be made by the cruiser and eight by a fishing vessel to provide instant signalling in emergency.

The flags used are the White and Red Ensigns, a yellow flag and a blue flag as between British vessels. Foreign fishery cruisers use **their** Ensign, and foreign fishing vessels use their National Flag. In emergency any three-cornered flag may replace the yellow flag, and in place of a blue flag a spherical shape, i.e. fender, etc. The Night Signal by British fishing vessels requiring **urgent assistance** from H.M. Fishery Cruiser is one **green** Very light.

As all the meanings of these eight signals will be known to fishing vessels, they are not reproduced here.

In practice, fishery protection vessels rarely use the special flag code. They prefer to use the International Code of Signals;

e.g. SQ = Stop vessel — heave to.
SQ3 = Stop vessel — heave to — I am going
to board you.
or L = You should stop your vessel instantly.

18. ROYAL MAIL PENNANT

Any large merchant vessel actually carrying mails for the Post Office under contract flies when entering or leaving harbour a white pennant with a Royal Crown over a Horn, all red defacement in the centre, with the words ROYAL MAIL (one word on either side of the defacement).

19. PETROL FLAG

Vessels carrying petrol or similar inflammable cargoes, normally when in confined waters or coasting, fly a square red flag with a white ball in the centre, but under the new **Code** could fly Code Flag B.

20. WHEN FLAGS ARE WORN

Flags worn at sea comprise the Ensign, House Flag or Club Burgee.

When on a passage out of sight of land flags are not usually worn; but the Ensign at least should be hoisted by day when passing another vessel.

In harbour "Colours" are made, that is the **Ensign** is hoisted together with others included, at 0800 in the summer (25th March—20th September) and 0900 in the winter from 21st September to 24th March (inclusive).

When entering or leaving a foreign harbour a British vessel (or yacht) of any size **must** wear her "Colours", and those of 50 tons gross or upwards, **must** do likewise when entering or leaving a British port under severe penalty.
Ensigns are always lowered at sunset.

21. WHERE FLAGS ARE WORN

The **Ensign**, whatever its colour, is **always** worn in the after part of the vessel. When in port, moored in a river or at anchor, it should always be worn at the Ensign staff at the stern.

Power vessels under way however should, if a gaff is fitted, wear the Ensign at its peak; otherwise it must be worn at the Ensign staff. *Sailing* vessels should wear the Ensign in port or where conditions are suitable from an Ensign staff aft, otherwise at the after peak. In the case of Bermudian rigged vessels at sea, it is customary to wear the Ensign two-thirds of the way up the after leech. Ensigns should never be worn at the masthead except when dressing ship; although with the advent of smaller vessels it has become customary for yawls and ketches to wear the Ensign from the mizzen masthead.

The **House Flag** in a merchant vessel or power yacht would be worn at the mainmast head; but in single masted vessels at the starboard yard-arm, or if no yard is fitted, from a position about two-thirds up the starboard shrouds. Otherwise in the case of yachts it could be worn at any masthead not occupied by the more important flag—the **Burgee**.

The **Burgee** should always be worn from the **principal** masthead—that is the main masthead—and it is customary to wear it above the truck on a swivelling cane so that it flies out well. In launches or vessels without a mast the Burgee would be worn from a small staff in the bows. When racing, the Yacht's Racing Flag would be worn in its place.

Wearing Sea Flags Ashore. No Sea Flag should ever be flown ashore except, of course, the Union Flag.

22. SPECIAL FLAG OCCASIONS

The **Salute** is made by lowering the Ensign slowly until its lower edge is just clear of the rail or about two-thirds down from the peak or from the flagstaff truck. It is kept there until the vessel being saluted has dipped her Ensign and commences to hoist it again, then the vessel making the salute slowly hoists her Ensign allowing the vessel being saluted always to finish the operation first.

Mourning. Private mourning is carried out when the owner dies or when a crew member dies. National mourning would be observed when notified or when a member of the Royal Family dies immediately the news is received.
In cases or **National** mourning only the Ensign is half-masted during the day and at the time of the funeral, or if the news is received at night, then half-mast the Ensign all the next day.

Distress. Although not a recognised signal of Distress—except in the United States—it is a convenient method (especially for use in bad weather under difficult conditions) for the **Ensign when flown upside down** to be considered as a Signal of Distress and has been so regarded from time immemorial. (See also under International Code Flags.)

23. FLAGS IN USE

Measurements. The Admiralty measure flags by the height of the vertical hoist as so many breadths of 9 inches each, so a British Ensign of six breadths would be 54 inches **hoist,** and thus 108 inches in **length.** Vessels nowadays normally measure their flags by the **length** horizontally (from left to right) from the flag rope or stick to the fly end, i.e. a 3 yard flag for a small Merchant ship.

Ensigns. All British Ensigns (and the Union Flag and Pilot Jack) have identical proportions with the **Fly** (length) always double the **Hoist** (height), i.e. 18 by 9 inches, 24 by 12 inches, and larger sizes in these proportions.

Foreign Ensigns. Ensigns of foreign countries are normally always made with the **Hoist** (height) two-thirds of the **Fly** (length), i.e. 30 inches length by 20 inches hoist.

Yacht Club Burgees. British Yacht Club Burgees are normally triangular in shape and are made with the **Hoist** (height) two-thirds of the **Fly** (length), i.e. 12 inches (long) by 8 inches (hoist) or 30 inches (length) by 20 inches (hoist). There are several notable exceptions to this where the Burgees are somewhat narrower; but by and large the above proportion applies.

Distinguishing Flags. Both House Flags and Racing Flags are rectangular. The same proportions as Yacht Club Burgees above but **rectangular** instead of pointed (or Burgee) shape.

All **National Flags** have their proportions well understood and published. Other flags may be made to any dimensions desired.

Section T

Traffic Separation Schemes

TRAFFIC SEPARATION

GENERAL

In order to increase the safety of navigation, routes incorporating traffic separation have, with the approval of the Intergovernmental Maritime Consultative Organisation, been established in certain areas of the world. In the interests of safe navigation it is recommended that through traffic should, as far as circumstances permit, use these routes.

The following sections are reprinted by permission of the Intergovernmental Maritime Consultative Organisation.

INTRODUCTION

The practice of following predetermined routes originated in 1989 and was adopted, for reasons of safety, by shipping companies operating passenger ships across the North Atlantic. It was subsequently incorporated into the International Conventions for the Safety of Life at Sea.

The 1960 Safety Convention referred to the same practice in converging areas on both sides of the North Atlantic. The Contracting Governments undertook the responsibility of using their influence to induce the owners of all passenger ships crossing the Atlantic to follow the recognised routes, and to do everything in their power to ensure adherence to such routes in converging areas by all ships, so far as circumstances permit.

In 1961 the Institutes of Navigation of the Federal Republic of Germany, France and the United Kingdom undertook a study of measures for separating traffic in the Strait of Dover and, subsequently, in certain other areas where statistics indicated an increased risk of collision. Their studies resulted in concrete proposals concerning the separation of traffic in those areas as well as certain basic principles. These proposals were submitted to IMCO and were generally adopted. This initial step was further developed by IMCO and the basic concept of separating opposing traffic was applied to many areas throughout the world.

The increase in traffic density, combined with the use of ships of greater tonnage and higher speed, indicated that the wider application of the principle of traffic separation, whenever it was warranted, could contribute substantially to safety at sea by reducing the number of ships meeting on opposite or nearly opposite courses and by providing an orderly flow of traffic. In fulfilment of their obligations, arising from the Safety Convention, Contracting Governments have determined routes to be followed to separate opposing streams of traffic as far as possible and recommend adherence to such routes by all vessels. The following sections describe the general principles of routeing, the methods used and the areas where traffic separation schemes have been agreed.

Methods of Routeing

1. When establishing routeing systems the following are among the methods which may be used:

(a) separation of traffic by separation zones or lines;

(b) separation of traffic by natural obstacles and geographically defined objects;

(c) separation of traffic by inshore traffic zones intended for keeping coastal traffic away from traffic separation schemes;

(d) separation of traffic by sectors at approaches to focal points;

(e) separation of traffic by roundabouts intended to facilitate navigation at focal points, where traffic separation schemes meet;

(f) routeing of traffic by deep water routes, two-way routes or tracks for ships proceeding in specific directions.

2. A description of methods (a) to (e) with drawings intended only to explain their function is given in the following:

(a) *By separation zones or lines* (Fig.1)

In such cases, the separation of traffic is achieved by a separation zone or line between streams of traffic proceeding in opposite or nearly opposite directions. The outside limits in such a scheme are the outer boundaries of lanes intended for one-way traffic. Beyond such limits ships can navigate in any direction. A separation zone may also be used to separate a traffic lane from an inshore traffic zone.

The width and length of separation zones and traffic lanes are determined after careful examination of local conditions, traffic density, prevailing hydrographic and meteorological conditions, space available for manoeuvring, etc., and generally their length is kept to the minimum necessary. In narrow passages and restricted waters a separation line may be adopted instead of a zone, for the separation of traffic, to allow for more navigable space.

(b) *By natural obstacles and geographically defined objects* (Fig.2)

This method is used where there is a defined area with obstacles such as islands, shoals or rocks restricting free movement and providing a natural division for opposing traffic streams.

(c) *By inshore traffic zones* (Fig.3)

By using inshore traffic zones coastal shipping can keep clear of through traffic in the adjacent traffic separation scheme. Ships navigating in any direction may be encountered in an inshore traffic zone.

(d) *By sectors at approaches to focal points* (Fig.4)

Such a method is used where ships converge at a point or a small area from various directions. Port approaches, sea pilot stations, positions where landfall buoys or light vessels are fixed, entrances to channels, canals, estuaries, etc., may be considered as such focal points. The number of shipping lanes, their dimensions and directions depend mainly on the type of the local traffic.

(e) *By roundabouts* (Fig.5)

To facilitate navigation at focal points where several traffic separation schemes meet, ships should move in a counter-clockwise direction around a specified point or zone until they are able to join the appropriate lane.

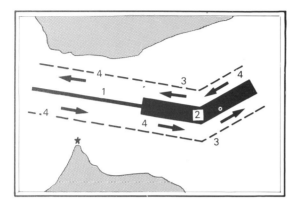

Fig.1 *Traffic separation by separation line and zone*
1—Separation line
2—Separation zone
3—Outside limits of lanes
4—Arrows indicating main traffic direction

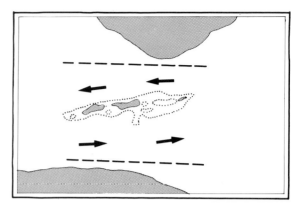

Fig.2 *Separation of traffic by natural obstacles*

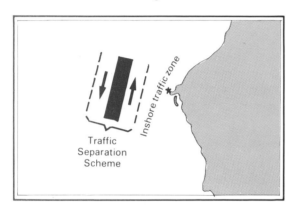

Fig.3 *Inshore traffic zone for coastal traffic*

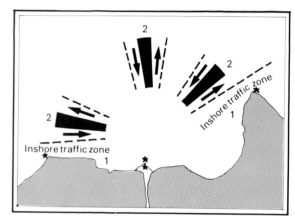

Fig.4 *Sectorial traffic separation scheme at approaches to focal point*
1—Inshore traffic zone
2—Separation schemes for main traffic

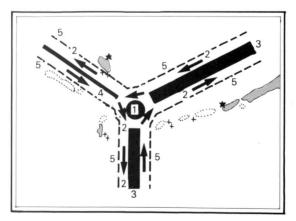

Fig.5 *A roundabout where several traffic separation schemes meet*

1—Circular separation zone
2—Arrows indicating traffic direction
3—Separation zone
4—Separation line
5—Outside limits of lanes

General Principles of Ships' Routeing

The use of routeing systems

1. The International Regulations for Preventing Collisions at Sea apply to navigation in routeing systems.

2. Routeing systems are included for use by day and by night in all weathers, in ice-free waters or under light ice conditions where no extraordinary manoeuvres or assistance by icebreaker(s) are required.

3. Routeing systems are recommended for use by all ships unless stated otherwise.

4. A deep water route is primarily intended for use by ships which because of their draught in relation to the available depth of water in the area concerned require the use of such a route. Through traffic to which the above consideration does not apply should, if practicable, avoid following deep water routes. When using a deep water route mariners should be aware of possible changes in the indicated depth of water due to meteorological or other effects.

5. A vessel using a traffic separation scheme shall:
   (i) proceed in the appropriate traffic lane in the general direction of traffic flow for that lane;
   (ii) so far as practicable keep clear of a traffic separation line or separation zone;
   (iii) normally join or leave a traffic lane at the termination of the lane, but when joining or leaving from the side shall do so at as small an angle to the general direction of traffic flow as practicable.

6. A vessel shall so far as practicable avoid crossing traffic lanes, but if obliged to do so shall cross as nearly as practicable at right angles to the general direction of traffic flow.

7. Inshore traffic zones shall not normally be used by through traffic which can safely use the appropriate traffic lane within the adjacent traffic separation scheme.

8. A vessel, other than a crossing vessel, shall not normally enter a separation zone or cross a separation line except:
   (i) in cases of emergency to avoid immediate danger;
   (ii) to engage in fishing within a separation zone.

9. A vessel navigating in areas near the terminations of traffic separation schemes shall do so with particular caution.

10. A vessel shall so far as practicable avoid anchoring in a traffic separation scheme or in areas near its terminations.

11. A vessel not using a traffic separation scheme shall avoid it by as wide a margin as is practicable.

12. The arrows printed on charts merely indicate the general direction of traffic; ships need not set their courses strictly along the arrows.

13. The signal "YG" meaning "You appear not to be complying with the traffic separation scheme" is provided in the International Code of Signals for appropriate use.

THE CONDUCT OF VESSELS IN TRAFFIC SEPARATION SCHEMES

Vessels using traffic separation schemes should do so in compliance with rule 10 of the 1972 International Regulations for Preventing Collisions at Sea. The text of this rule is as follows:

Rule 10
Traffic Separation Schemes

(a) This Rule applies to traffic separation schemes adopted by the Organisation.

(b) A vessel using a traffic separation scheme shall:

  (i) proceed in the appropriate traffic lane in the general direction of traffic flow for that lane;

  (ii) so far as practicable keep clear of a traffic separation line or separation zone;

  (iii) normally join or leave a traffic lane at the termination of the lane, but when joining or leaving from the side shall do so at as small an angle to the general direction of traffic flow as practicable.

(c) A vessel shall so far as practicable avoid crossing traffic lanes, but if obliged to do so shall cross as nearly as practicable at right angles to the general direction of traffic flow.

(d) Inshore traffic zones shall not normally be used by through traffic which can safely use the appropriate traffic lane within the adjacent traffic separation scheme.

(e) A vessel, other than a crossing vessel, shall not normally enter a separation zone or cross a separation line except:

  (i) in cases of emergency to avoid immediate danger;

  (ii) to engage in fishing within a separation zone.

(f) A vessel navigating in areas near the terminations of traffic separation schemes shall do so with particular caution.

(g) A vessel shall so far as practicable avoid anchoring in a traffic separation scheme or in areas near its terminations.

(h) A vessel not using a traffic separation scheme shall avoid it by as wide a margin as is practicable.

(i) A vessel engaged in fishing shall not impede the passage of any vessel following a traffic lane.

(j) A vessel of less than 20 metres in length or a sailing vessel shall not impede the safe passage of a power-driven vessel following a traffic lane.

LOCALITIES OF TRAFFIC SEPARATION SCHEMES

The routeing diagrams which follow are intended only for rapid reference and illustrative purposes. Further information and larger scale diagrams are available in the IMCO publication "Ships' Routeing."

CAUTION:

The chartlets are for illustrative purposes only and must not be used for navigation. Mariners should consult the appropriate nautical publications and charts for up-to-date details on aids to navigational and other relevant information.

AUSTRALASIA

In Australasia, there is a traffic separation scheme in the Bass Strait, south of the Wilson Promontory. Since this is the only scheme in this area it has not been shown in the following diagrams.

BALTIC SEA

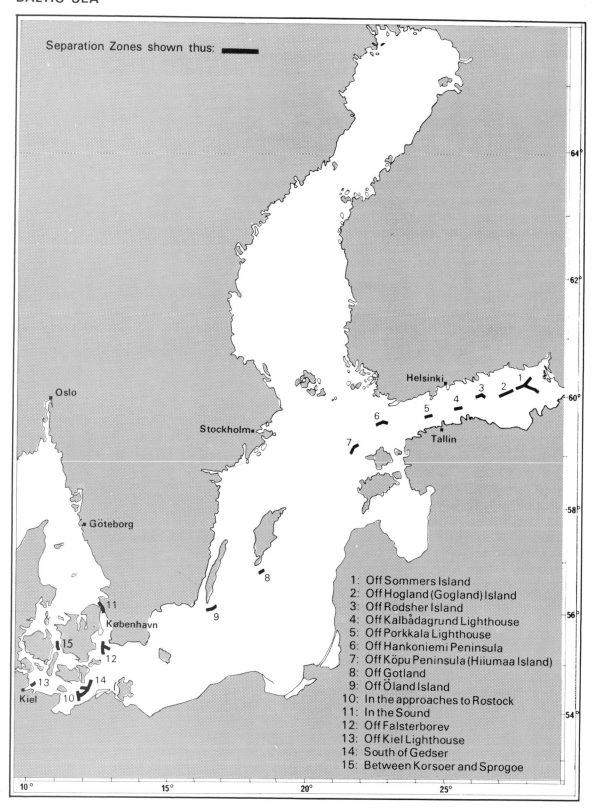

Separation Zones shown thus: ━━━━

Oslo

Helsinki

Stockholm

Tallin

Göteborg

København

Kiel

1: Off Sommers Island
2: Off Hogland (Gogland) Island
3: Off Rodsher Island
4: Off Kalbådagrund Lighthouse
5: Off Porkkala Lighthouse
6: Off Hankoniemi Peninsula
7: Off Köpu Peninsula (Hiiumaa Island)
8: Off Gotland
9: Off Öland Island
10: In the approaches to Rostock
11: In the Sound
12: Off Falsterborev
13: Off Kiel Lighthouse
14: South of Gedser
15: Between Korsoer and Sprogoe

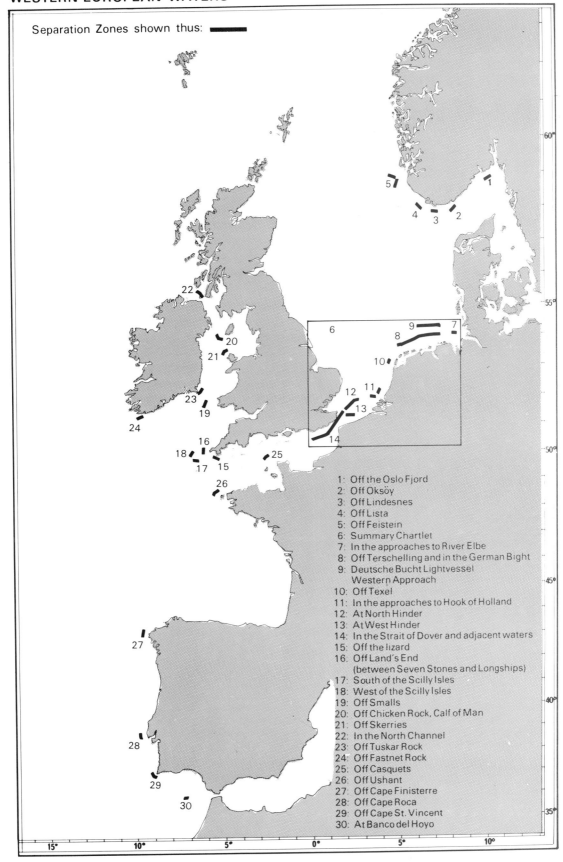

Separation Zones shown thus: ▬▬▬▬▬

1: Off the Oslo Fjord
2: Off Oksöy
3: Off Lindesnes
4: Off Lista
5: Off Feistein
6: Summary Chartlet
7: In the approaches to River Elbe
8: Off Terschelling and in the German Bight
9: Deutsche Bucht Lightvessel
   Western Approach
10: Off Texel
11: In the approaches to Hook of Holland
12: At North Hinder
13: At West Hinder
14: In the Strait of Dover and adjacent waters
15: Off the lizard
16: Off Land's End
    (between Seven Stones and Longships)
17: South of the Scilly Isles
18: West of the Scilly Isles
19: Off Smalls
20: Off Chicken Rock, Calf of Man
21: Off Skerries
22: In the North Channel
23: Off Tuskar Rock
24: Off Fastnet Rock
25: Off Casquets
26: Off Ushant
27: Off Cape Finisterre
28: Off Cape Roca
29: Off Cape St. Vincent
30: At Banco del Hoyo

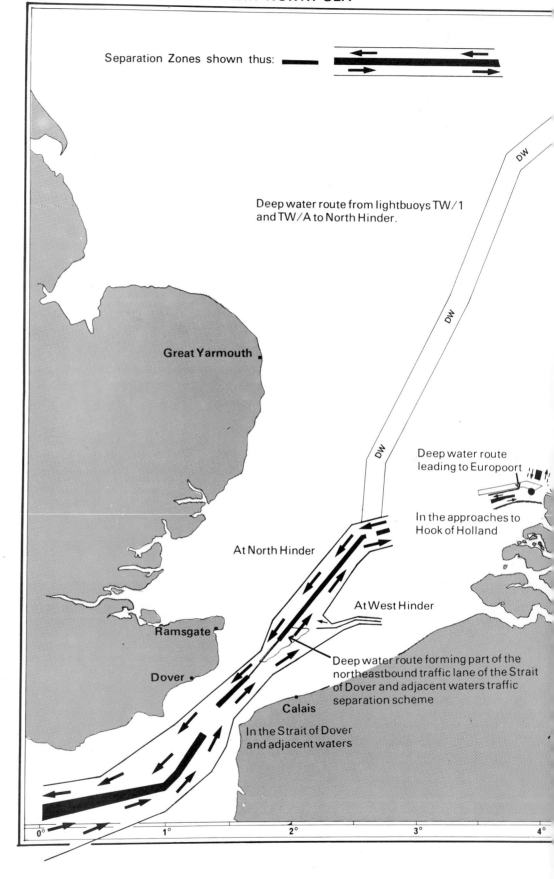

Separation Zones shown thus:

Deep water route from lightbuoys TW/1 and TW/A to North Hinder.

Great Yarmouth

Deep water route leading to Europoort

In the approaches to Hook of Holland

At North Hinder

At West Hinder

Ramsgate

Dover

Deep water route forming part of the northeastbound traffic lane of the Strait of Dover and adjacent waters traffic separation scheme

Calais

In the Strait of Dover and adjacent waters

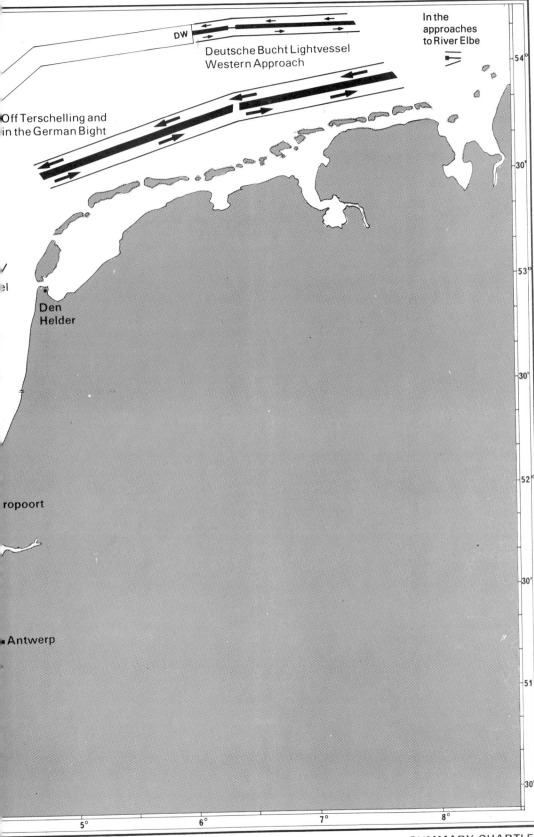

DW

Deutsche Bucht Lightvessel
Western Approach

In the
approaches
to River Elbe

Off Terschelling and
in the German Bight

Den
Helder

ropoort

Antwerp

54°

30'

53°

30'

52°

30'

51°

30'

5°   6°   7°   8°

SUMMARY CHARTLET

X

354

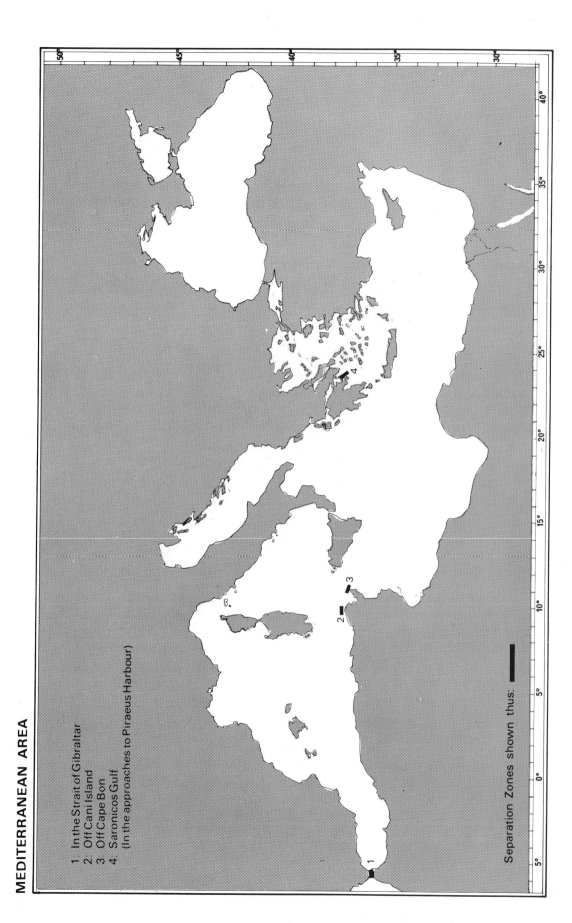

MEDITERRANEAN AREA

1. In the Strait of Gibraltar
2. Off Cani Island
3. Off Cape Bon
4. Saronicos Gulf
   (In the approaches to Piraeus Harbour)

Separation Zones shown thus: ▬

INDIAN OCEAN AND ADJACENT WATERS

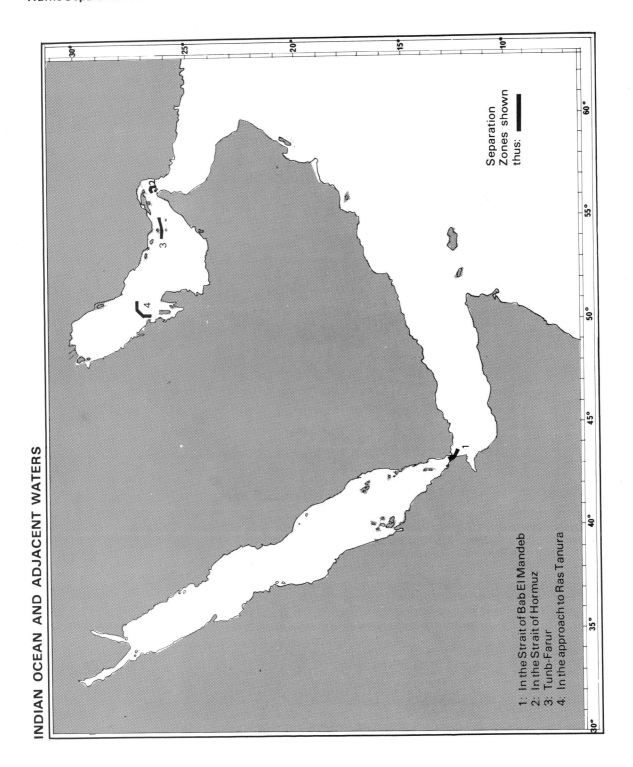

Separation
Zones shown
thus: ▬▬▬

1. In the Strait of Bab El Mandeb
2. In the Strait of Hormuz
3. Tunb-Farur
4. In the approach to Ras Tanura

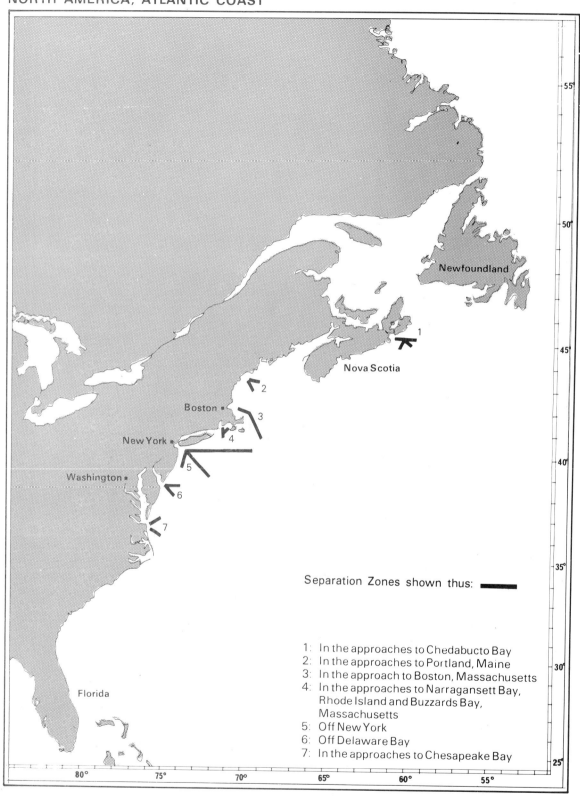

Newfoundland

Nova Scotia

Boston

New York

Washington

Florida

Separation Zones shown thus: ▬▬▬

1: In the approaches to Chedabucto Bay
2: In the approaches to Portland, Maine
3: In the approach to Boston, Massachusetts
4: In the approaches to Narragansett Bay,
   Rhode Island and Buzzards Bay,
   Massachusetts
5: Off New York
6: Off Delaware Bay
7: In the approaches to Chesapeake Bay

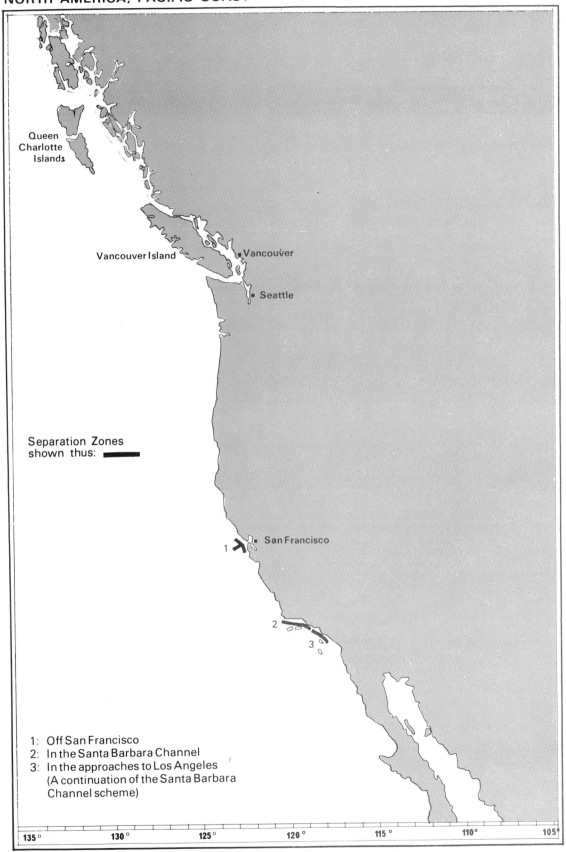

Queen
Charlotte
Islands

Vancouver Island   • Vancouver

• Seattle

Separation Zones
shown thus: ▬▬▬

1   ➤ • San Francisco

2   ⟋

3   ⟋

1: Off San Francisco
2: In the Santa Barbara Channel
3: In the approaches to Los Angeles
   (A continuation of the Santa Barbara
   Channel scheme)

135°   130°   125°   120°   115°   110°   105°

Section U

Worldwide Distance Tables

EXPLANATION

The tables on the following pages give the distances between some of the principal ports in each of six areas of the world.

Area I comprises North-Western European waters including the North and Baltic Seas.

Area II comprises the North Atlantic Ocean including the Caribbean Sea and the Gulf of Mexico.

Area III comprises the Mediterranean and Black Seas.

Area IV comprises the South Atlantic Ocean.

Area V comprises the Indian Ocean and adjacent waters.

Area VI comprises the Pacific Ocean and adjacent waters.

The limits of these areas are indicated on the chart of the world on which are also marked the transition ports, each of which is common to two areas. The transition ports, distinguished by an asterisk in the tables, enable distances between ports in different areas to be found. For example if it is required to find the distance between Liverpool in area I and Montevideo in area IV, the chart indicates that Recife is the appropriate transition port. Thus:

From table II	Liverpool to Recife	4085
From table IV	Recife to Montevideo	2080
By addition	Liverpool to Montevideo	6165 miles.

In some cases routes will take a ship through several areas. For example it may be required to find the distance from Boston in area II to Karachi in area V, via the Suez Canal. The chart indicates Gibraltar and Suez as the appropriate transition ports, thus:

From table II	Boston to Gibraltar	2945
From table III	Gibraltar to Suez	2000
From table V	Suez to Karachi	2772
By addition	Boston to Karachi	7717 miles

In all cases the distances are in nautical miles and are the least distances which can be achieved by following reasonable routes.

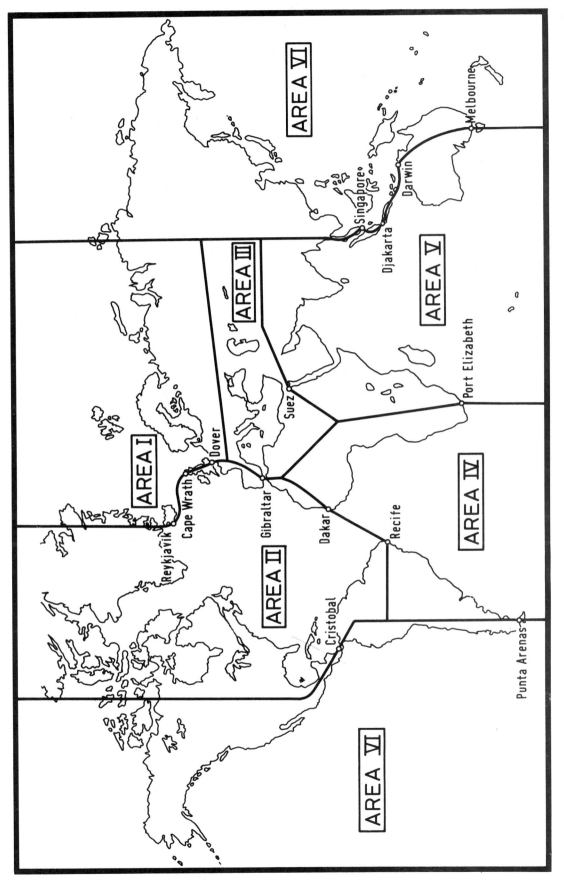

AREA VI

AREA III

AREA I

AREA II

AREA V

AREA IV

AREA VI

Melbourne

Darwin

Singapore

Djakarta

Port Elizabeth

Suez

Dover

Cape Wrath

Reykjavik

Gibraltar

Dakar

Recife

Cristobal

Punta Arenas

AREA I
NORTH-WEST EUROPEAN WATERS

Note that distances in this table are calculated via Kiel Canal when its use gives a saving of more than 200 miles.

	ABERDEEN	AMSTERDAM	ANTWERP	ARCHANGEL	BREMEN	COPENHAGEN	DOVER	DUNKIRK	ESBJERG	GYDNIA	GOTHENBURG	HAMBURG	HELSINKI	HULL	KIEL	LEITH	LENINGRAD	LONDON	MIDDLESBROUGH	MURMANSK	NARVIK	NEWCASTLE	OSLO	REYKJAVIK	ROSTOCK	ROTTERDAM	STOCKHOLM	SZCSECIN	TRONDHEIM
AMSTERDAM	380																												
ANTWERP	450	148																											
ARCHANGEL	1745	1980	2040																										
BREMEN	460	260	333	1881																									
COPENHAGEN	566	490	600	1892	372																								
DOVER	405	150	135	2031	371	605																							
DUNKIRK	418	135	102	2016	351	588	38																						
ESBJERG	378	253	361	1801	174	377	369	350																					
GYDNIA	841	621	737	2148	503	259	735	719	522																				
GOTHENBURG	458	464	616	1829	382	134	568	553	270	383																			
HAMBURG	473	251	382	1917	148	364	381	364	167	523	402																		
HELSINKI	1106	923	1026	2477	803	553	1066	1020	925	424	657	724																	
HULL	270	207	265	1926	372	610	204	223	332	866	504	380	1158																
KIEL	498	291	398	2037	164	162	403	386	190	339	218	91	628	396															
LEITH	85	372	453	1783	475	622	389	399	399	838	514	486	1127	237	691														
LENINGRAD	1243	1050	1177	2569	930	682	1163	1147	1054	551	847	1127	155	1163	779	1313													
LONDON	436	208	193	2061	409	641	70	112	380	970	596	425	1067	239	439	417	1218												
MIDDLESBRO'	161	248	333	1852	396	593	273	287	346	849	486	357	1141	120	430	133	1270	273											
MURMANSK	1358	1517	1629	473	1492	1563	1664	1646	1434	1941	1455	1581	2103	1566	1595	1435	2254	1715	1485										
NARVIK	866	1090	1211	986	1092	1068	1176	1165	948	1446	960	1081	1608	1066	1119	946	1759	1215	994	551									
NEWCASTLE	145	285	351	1804	415	601	295	312	350	857	487	424	1149	143	439	116	1278	325	41	1500	994								
OSLO	488	522	630	1711	460	272	657	617	312	528	159	461	948	559	355	538	963	668	525	1450	551	525							
*REYKJAVIK	805	1462	1250	1883	1236	1259	1196	1215	1120	1521	1234	1234	1809	1050	1252	888	1950	1231	957	1517	1450	935	1179						
ROSTOCK	673	373	482	1999	253	107	486	470	273	272	238	174	578	486	83	720	705	509	513	1629	1153	698	380	1360					
ROTTERDAM	391	67	121	1950	290	525	132	104	287	662	489	307	951	211	323	381	1102	184	272	1628	1139	285	555	1182	409				
STOCKHOLM	983	794	901	2314	667	425	911	889	799	325	512	594	239	899	503	1039	386	942	1015	1980	1485	942	694	1681	453	826			
SZCSECIN	728	513	620	2054	393	167	626	610	539	228	390	314	559	626	222	721	686	661	700	1823	1328	753	541	1638	168	545	408		
TRONDHEIM	572	790	892	1237	765	741	882	867	630	997	763	870	1289	744	814	646	1418	879	676	870	405	667	663	958	848	545	408	823	
*WRATH (C.)	168	518	615	1727	596	653	566	583	493	909	600	600	1201	419	726	254	1330	567	326	1360	840	300	575	1360	760	547	642	1075	555

AREA II
NORTH ATLANTIC

	AVONMOUTH	BALTIMORE	BORDEAUX	BOSTON	CRISTOBAL	CURACAO	DAKAR	DOVER	DUBLIN	GALVESTON	GIBRALTAR	GLASGOW	HALIFAX	HAVANA	KINGSTON (JA.)	LA GUIRA	LAS PALMAS	LE HAVRE	LISBON	LIVERPOOL	MONTREAL	NEW ORLEANS	NEW YORK	PHILADELPHIA	PORT OF SPAIN	RECIFE	REYKJAVIK	VERA CRUZ
BALTIMORE	3455																											
BORDEAUX	556	3450																										
BOSTON	3025	682	2950																									
CRISTOBAL	4510	1904	4695	2136																								
CURACAO	3970	1878	4120	1984	691																							
DAKAR	2375	3526	2245	2956	3694	3050																						
DOVER	442	3483	586	2998	4685	4132	2443																					
DUBLIN	220	3415	599	2950	4480	3930	2420	488																				
GALVESTON	4820	1820	5045	2099	1485	1791	4452	4890	4780																			
GIBRALTAR	1158	3445	1011	2945	4340	3765	1570	1230	1204	4810																		
GLASGOW	373	3275	775	2775	4285	3920	2620	650	170	4890	1381																	
HALIFAX	2475	899	2585	386	2298	1984	2626	2956	2440	2303	2625	2410																
HAVANA	4115	1110	4355	1408	990	1138	3716	4195	4075	768	4120	4310	1608															
KINGSTON (JA.)	4010	1404	4300	1708	555	585	3436	3980	3975	1256	4285	4207	1795	743														
LA GUIRA	3950	1845	4030	1968	834	148	2911	3910	3910	1939	4225	4110	2058	1281	731													
LAS PALMAS	1540	3265	1367	2765	3750	3098	839	1614	1588	4365	715	1769	2445	3738	3450	3086												
LE HAVRE	438	3445	513	2880	4130	4130	2410	115	428	4880	1147	590	2515	4190	4130	4070	1560											
LISBON	893	3300	732	2705	3625	3920	1575	954	917	4610	280	1081	2385	3920	3805	3535	720	881										
LIVERPOOL	282	3358	672	2875	4165	4165	2500	558	121	4925	1270	206	2480	4195	4105	4105	1650	498	1005									
MONTREAL	2995	1852	3120	1309	2854	2690	3224	2997	2955	3160	2885	2560	958	2528	2690	3012	3080	3015	2920	2980								
NEW ORLEANS	4635	1630	4855	1944	1668	1816	3560	4595	4480	390	4620	4156	2148	621	1155	1816	4275	4690	4420	4735	3069							
NEW YORK	3185	410	3150	379	1972	1848	3145	3182	2975	1862	2975	3145	593	1167	1472	1848	2965	3080	2905	3075	1516	1707						
PHILADELPHIA	3330	376	3300	520	1760	1838	3441	3290	3290	1833	3125	3295	743	1140	1446	1838	3115	3230	3055	3225	1665	1678	235					
PORT OF SPAIN	3780	1919	3815	2016	447	329	2628	3750	3919	2211	3460	3995	2055	1478	998	329	3840	3875	3320	3895	2895	1952	1941	1952				
RECIFE	3960	3835	3669	3217	2483	2469	1717	4042	4000	4248	3150	4205	3558	3513	3000	2270	1995	3995	3155	4085	4301	3698	3745	3634	2106			
REYKJAVIK	1103	2755	1444	2248	4099	3707	3013	1360	889	4156	1920	839	1893	3461	3601	3729	2202	1300	2235	923	2138	3979	2600	3634	3745	4397		
VERA CRUZ	4905	1915	5145	2196	1410	1737	4536	4985	4865	622	4910	5105	2399	811	1200	1882	4505	4980	4710	4985	3318	810	1958	1926	2158	4204	4251	
WRATH (C.)	570	3172	951	2665	4457	3991	2760	566	360	4547	1546	308	2317	3852	3959	3994	1899	780	1270	394	2589	4370	2871	3020	3851	4267	642	4642

AREA III
MEDITERRANEAN
AND BLACK SEA

	ALEXANDRIA	ALGIERS	BARCELONA	BEIRUT	CONSTANZA	GENOA	GIBRALTAR	HAIFA	ISTANBUL	IZMIR	MARSEILLES	NAPLES	NOVOROSSIYSK	ODESSA	PALERMO	PIRAEUS	PORT SAID	SUEZ	TRIESTE	TRIPOLI (LIBYA)	TUNIS	VALENCIA	VENICE
ALGIERS	1388																						
BARCELONA	1473	279																					
BEIRUT	340	1594	1673																				
CONSTANZA	918	1580	1665	1006																			
GENOA	1312	528	352	1500	1481																		
GIBRALTAR	1798	412	515	2004	1996	847																	
HAIFA	292	1589	1674	72	1012	1496	2000																
ISTANBUL	722	1384	1469	810	196	1285	1800	816															
IZMIR	534	1231	1316	623	469	1132	1641	629	273														
MARSEILLES	1405	410	185	1595	1574	201	690	1589	1378	1225													
NAPLES	1001	579	555	1189	1170	334	979	1185	974	821	457												
NOVOROSSIYSK	1178	1840	1925	1266	402	1741	2256	1272	456	729	1834	1430											
ODESSA	1064	1726	1811	1152	173	1627	2142	1158	342	615	1720	1316	362										
PALERMO	943	503	566	1131	1112	427	914	1127	916	763	494	167	1372	1258									
PIRAEUS	512	1070	1156	645	548	972	1481	640	352	204	1180	660	806	692	603								
PORT SAID	156	1503	1588	228	982	1419	1913	169	786	598	1512	1242	1242	1122	1050	593							
SUEZ	243	1675	1675	315	1069	1506	2000	256	873	685	1599	1329	1329	1209	1137	680	87						
TRIESTE	1191	1240	1300	1367	1348	1111	1648	1363	1152	1000	1204	800	1494	1608	742	839	1294	1381					
TRIPOLI (LIBYA)	860	663	759	1118	1144	717	1074	1100	948	795	742	502	1290	1404	371	635	987	1074	916				
TUNIS	1040	384	484	1252	1233	462	789	1247	1037	884	472	309	1384	1498	179	724	1155	1242	916	316			
VALENCIA	1554	226	164	1760	1746	510	387	1755	1550	1397	345	710	1892	2006	651	1235	1669	1756	1388	830	830		
VENICE	1196	1256	1305	1383	1354	1116	1653	1369	1158	1004	1220	816	1511	1625	747	844	1300	1387	62	921	830	921	
ZHDANOV	1282	1947	2029	1373	490	1845	2360	1379	560	833	1941	1537	450	205	1476	912	1346	1433	1712	1508	1597	2114	1718

AREA IV
SOUTH ATLANTIC

	ACCRA	BAHIA BLANCA	BUENOS AIRES	CAPETOWN	CONAKRY	DAKAR	DUALA	LAGOS	LOBITO	LUANDA	MONROVIA	MONTEVIDEO	PORT ELIZABETH	PORTO ALEGRE	PUNTA ARENAS	RECIFE	RIO DE JANEIRO	SANTOS
BAHIA BLANCA	4362																	
BUENOS AIRES	4108	557																
CAPETOWN	2592	3804	3718															
CONAKRY	991	4030	3742	3201														
DAKAR	1390	4138	3859	3604	450													
DUALA	613	4737	4501	2374	1535	1987												
LAGOS	220	4552	4304	2566	1205	1610	439											
LOBITO	1353	4301	4117	1406	2140	2547	1059	1285										
LUANDA	1179	4402	4215	1600	2007	2410	858	1087	234									
MONROVIA	694	3967	3697	2933	297	701	1285	914	1847	1714								
MONTEVIDEO	3994	459	125	3621	3645	3745	4404	4190	4020	4101	3583							
PORT ELIZABETH	3002	4160	4070	422	3607	4005	2787	2977	1817	2011	3340	3970						
PORTO ALEGRE	3888	860	579	3636	3340	3620	4400	4087	3946	4037	3462	482	3340					
PUNTA ARENAS	4905	1020	1435	4346	4721	4943	5325	5025	5155	5303	4543	1322	4005	4670				
RECIFE	2235	2455	2177	3318	1680	1717	2840	2453	3551	2861	1680	2080	3710	2020	3340			
RIO DE JANEIRO	3063	1423	1142	3272	2649	2761	3509	3268	3297	3357	2614	1045	3651	900	2272	1080		
SANTOS	3247	1280	998	3400	2834	2950	3694	3454	3478	3538	2799	901	3782	758	2159	1265	210	
WALVIS BAY	1911	3955	3828	700	2982	2580	1770	1880	720	915	2300	3731	1119	3656	4616	2972	3167	3330

**AREA V
INDIAN OCEAN**

	ADEN	AQABA	BAHREIN	BASRAH	BEIRA	BOMBAY	BUSHIRE	CALCUTTA	CHITTAGONG	COLOMBO	DAR ES SALAAM	DARWIN	DJAKARTA	DURBAN	JEDDAH	KARACHI	KUWAIT	LOURENCO MARQUES	MADRAS	MELBOURNE	MOMBASA	PENANG	PERTH	PORT ELIZABETH	PORT SUDAN	RANGOON	SINGAPORE
AQABA	1246																										
BAHREIN	1732	2974																									
BASRAH	1967	3207	322																								
BEIRA	2600	3839	3624	3942																							
BOMBAY	1657	2899	1352	1587	3250																						
BUSHIRE	1792	3034	170	190	3684	1412																					
CALCUTTA	3304	4544	3337	3572	4200	2112	3397																				
CHITTAGONG	3352	4589	3385	3617	4548	2160	3445	367																			
COLOMBO	2094	3334	2114	2349	3175	889	2174	1244	1292																		
DAR ES SALAAM	1740	2982	2783	3018	1012	2330	2843	3490	3538	2380																	
DARWIN	5355	6595	5405	5640	5544	4180	5465	3532	3399	3312	5427																
DJAKARTA	3900	5127	3933	4168	4409	2740	4260	2055	1860	1530	4043	1530															
DURBAN	3200	4409	4195	4429	702	3800	4254	4735	4783	3615	1580	5558	4159														
JEDDAH	701	646	2428	2663	3300	2353	2488	3998	4046	2788	2440	6049	4580	3900													
KARACHI	1470	2712	922	1147	3225	501	982	2615	2564	1341	2405	4632	2968	3554	2166												
KUWAIT	1917	3569	263	146	3809	1537	154	3522	3570	2299	2968	5590	4118	4379	2040	1099											
LOURENCO M'Q'S	2960	4191	4361	4579	485	3520	4548	4500	4548	3555	1484	5537	4358	304	3675	4161	4379										
MADRAS	2650	3890	2683	2916	3635	1458	2743	775	823	590	2840	3468	2008	4008	3344	1910	2868	3675									
MELBOURNE	6480	7690	7057	6775	5780	5556	6835	5295	5282	4698	5973	3177	3390	5640	7160	6009	6964	5680	5000								
MOMBASA	1620	2842	2643	2879	1150	2400	2703	3699	3747	2519	179	5434	4000	1719	2320	2365	2828	1501	3040	5998							
PENANG	3336	4576	3604	4235	4000	2144	4003	1301	1167	1276	3780	2258	900	4030	4580	2596	3554	4485	1277	4211	3699						
PERTH	4900	6154	5206	5440	4355	4000	5226	3582	3130	2975	4500	1841	1770	4250	5580	4446	5391	4300	3390	1681	4369	2596					
PORT ELIZABETH	3560	4790	4575	4883	1083	4200	4635	5105	5153	3975	1960	5431	4789	391	3824	4260	4760	155	4255	5759	2100	4370	4370				
PORT SUDAN	658	639	2385	2620	3247	2310	2445	3955	4003	2745	2395	6006	4550	3845	190	2569	3527	4003	3301	7123	2219	3987	5574	4199			
RANGOON	3309	4549	3342	3577	4280	2117	3402	779	600	1249	3750	3000	1630	4695	3999	2569	3527	4545	998	4825	3720	766	3245	5065	3960		
SINGAPORE	3627	4867	3660	3895	4515	2435	3720	1567	1517	1650	3999	1900	520	4880	4321	2887	3845	4321	1586	3850	3990	376	2239	5209	4278	1117	
SUEZ	1307	300	3034	3269	3904	2959	3094	4652	4604	3394	3040	6655	5207	4481	636	3219	2772	4264	3950	7780	2922	4636	6231	4873	694	4609	4927

**AREA VI
PACIFIC OCEAN**

	AUCKLAND	BALBOA	BANGKOK	BRISBANE	CRISTOBAL	DARWIN	DJAKARTA	HOBART	HONG KONG	HONOLULU	MANILA	MELBOURNE	NAGASAKI	OSAKA	PORT MORESBY	PUNTA ARENAS	SAIGON	SAN FRANCISCO	SEATTLE	SHANGHAI	SINGAPORE	SYDNEY	TOKYO	VALPARAISO	VANCOUVER	VLADIVOSTOCK	WELLINGTON
BALBOA	6509																										
BANGKOK	5819	10721																									
BRISBANE	1358	7680	4675																								
CRISTOBAL	6555	46	10765	7700																							
DARWIN	3399	9190	2612	2181	9236																						
DJAKARTA	4670	10642	1291	3525	10686	1530																					
HOBART	1520	7629	4735	1132	7673	3070	3520																				
HONG KONG	5060	9194	1489	4080	9238	2341	1789	5015																			
HONOLULU	3850	4684	6319	4120	4728	5122	5909	4930	4833																		
MANILA	4650	9346	1465	3550	9390	1800	1562	4464	632	4767																	
MELBOURNE	1644	7880	4604	1080	8000	3177	3390	470	4875	4940	4505																
NAGASAKI	4935	8200	2495	3925	8244	2800	2746	5069	1066	3986	1305	4850															
OSAKA	4849	7968	2784	3876	8012	2940	2746	5032	1376	3684	1567	5280	402														
PORT MORESBY	2254	8199	3551	2351	8244	1081	2485	2351	3065	3857	2499	2200	3378	3483													
PUNTA ARENAS	4650	3937	10262	5750	3983	8069	9025	5603	9708	6370	9202	5881	9522	9407	7034												
SAIGON	5122	10017	681	3977	10548	2327	927	4523	907	5542	1032	4392	2217	1929	3122	10004											
SAN FRANCISCO	5680	3246	8061	6200	3292	6991	7641	6958	6050	2091	7000	4828	5030	5992	6201	6880	7350										
SEATTLE	6170	4005	7901	6471	4051	6898	7351	7290	5768	2407	5959	4635	4705	6175	6988	6834	7004	796									
SHANGHAI	5148	8649	2251	4250	8690	2755	2523	5286	824	4336	1128	5175	462	790	3350	9768	1697	5500	4700								
SINGAPORE	5015	10504	831	3875	10548	1888	525	4000	1460	5880	1341	3950	2695	2840	2413	9482	644	7062	7350	2192							
SYDNEY	1275	7680	5072	515	7717	2453	3936	638	4480	4425	3950	582	4544	4308	1738	5150	4554	6450	6810	4636	4272						
TOKYO	4818	7699	2991	3948	7743	3033	3240	4945	1596	3415	1770	4938	695	369	3444	9271	2430	4554	4272	1048	2904	4348					
VALPARAISO	5240	2615	10857	6450	2661	8561	10190	6000	10218	5919	8400	6300	7403	9586	5146	1427	11305	5146	5899	9945	10418	5899	9298				
VANCOUVER	6200	4021	7910	6500	4067	6914	7360	7299	5777	2434	5976	7350	4544	6191	7004	7071	4566	812	126	5092	6820	6664	4280	5915			
VLADIVOSTOCK	5516	7741	3066	4591	7785	3428	3338	5740	1639	3725	1909	5640	656	730	3944	9861	2502	4800	4210	991	3002	4566	949	9606	4378		
WELLINGTON	561	6500	5986	1448	6550	3345	4755	1290	5250	4114	4750	1490	5408	5408	2440	4975	5823	5900	6433	5380	5058	1233	5185	5800	6447	5800	

Section V

Buoyage Systems

THE INTERNATIONAL ASSOCIATION OF LIGHTHOUSE AUTHORITIES (IALA) SYSTEM OF BUOYAGE

GENERAL

It is clearly desirable that the buoyage systems used throughout the world should be as consistent with one another as is possible in relation to the differing conditions in which they are used. Ideally, the shape, colour and lighting of buoys should be sufficiently uniform so that these characteristics always have the same significance to mariners wherever they may be operating.

In 1936, a "Uniform System of Buoyage" was agreed at Geneva under the auspices of the League of Nations. The United States and a number of other countries were not signatories to the agreement and the agreement itself was never ratified but, nevertheless, it formed the basis of most of the European buoyage systems although with many national variations and modifications.

In 1970, IALA began to investigate the possibility of a more effective international agreement on the unification of buoyage systems and, in cooperation with IMCO, a new system has been adopted.

The main obstacle to achieving universal agreement on a single system was that the world buoyage systems could be divided broadly into two groups:
(1) Those based on the Geneva principles whereby red buoys are left on the mariner's port hand when proceeding with the main stream of flood tide, i.e. from seaward into rivers, harbours and estuaries.
(2) Those which are based on the United States system whereby red buoys are left on the mariner's starboard hand when proceeding with the main stream of flood tide, i.e. from seaward into rivers, harbours and estuaries.

Universal agreement would require the complete reversal of one of these conventions, and IALA conceded that this was unlikely by accepting that two buoyage systems are needed at least as an interim policy.

IALA SYSTEM A

System A is a combined lateral and cardinal system of buoyage, the lateral system being based on the convention of red to port and green to starboard when navigating with a "conventional direction" of buoyage. The "conventional direction" for any area is defined arbitrarily, but it generally runs in a clockwise direction around continents and from seawards into rivers, harbours and estuaries. This system is being progressively introduced in European waters and a full description is contained in Reed's Nautical Almanac.

IALA SYSTEM B

System B is a lateral only system based on the convention of red to starboard when proceeding from seawards into rivers, harbours and estuaries. The United States system, based on the red to starboard convention, is described in the U.S. edition of Reed's Nautical Almanac and in Chapman's "Piloting Seamanship and Small Boat Handling". Similar systems are used on the Canadian coasts and in the Great Lakes and in a number of other countries.

Section W

Watchkeeping Principles

Watchkeeping Principles

INTRODUCTION

Investigations into the cases of casualties involving collisions and strandings frequently reveal that the main contributory factor has been failure to maintain an adequate navigational watch including a proper look-out.

The IMCO Council, therefore, at its twenty-fifth session decided that in the context of determining training requirements for seafarers, urgent consideration should be given to the principles relating to the keeping of a navigational watch.

The matter was considered by the Sub-Committee on Standards of Training and Watchkeeping which prepared a recommendation on basic principles and operational guidance relating to navigational watchkeeping. The Recommendation was adopted at the Eighth IMCO Assembly by Resolution A.285(VIII). Member Governments were recommended to direct the attention of shipowners, masters and watchkeeping personnel to the principles which should be observed in order to ensure that a safe navigational watch is maintained.

This publication contains an extract from the above-mentioned Recommendation and is divided into two sections:

Section I : Basic principles to be observed in keeping a navigational watch.

Section II: Operational guidance for officers in charge of a navigational watch.

IMCO RECOMMENDATIONS*

SECTION 1

BASIC PRINCIPLES TO BE OBSERVED IN KEEPING A NAVIGATIONAL WATCH

INTRODUCTION

1. The master of every ship is bound to ensure that the watchkeeping arrangements are adequate for maintaining a safe navigational watch. Under his general direction, the officers of the watch are responsible for navigating the ship safely during their periods of duty when they will be particularly concerned to avoid collision and stranding.

2. This Section includes the basic principles which shall at least be taken into account by all ships.

WATCH ARRANGEMENTS

3. The composition of the watch, including the requirement for look-out(s), shall at all times be adequate and appropriate to the prevailing circumstances and conditions.

4. When deciding the composition of the watch on the bridge the following points are among those to be taken into account:

(a) at no time shall the bridge be left unattended;

(b) the weather conditions, visibility and whether there is daylight or darkness;

(c) the proximity of navigational hazards which may make it necessary for the officer in charge to carry out additional navigational duties;

(d) the use and operational condition of navigational aids such as radar or electronic position-indicating devices and any other equipment affecting the safe navigation of the ship;

(e) whether the ship is fitted with automatic steering;

(f) any additional demands on the navigational watch that may arise as a result of special operational circumstances.

FITNESS FOR DUTY

5. The watch system shall be such that the efficiency of the watchkeeping members of the crew is not impaired by fatigue. Accordingly, the duties shall be so organized that the first watch at the commencement of a voyage and the subsequent relieving watches are sufficiently rested and otherwise fit when going on duty.

*©IMCO 1974, Reprinted by permission of the Inter-Governmental Maritime Consultative Organisation.

NAVIGATION

6. The intended voyage shall be planned in advance taking into consideration all pertinent information and any course laid down shall be checked.

7. On taking over the watch the ship's estimated or true position, intended track, course and speed shall be confirmed; any navigational hazard expected to be encountered during the watch shall be noted.

8. During the watch the course steered, position and speed shall be checked at sufficiently frequent intervals using any available navigational aids necessary to ensure that the ship follows the planned course.

9. The safety and navigational equipment with which the ship is provided and the manner of its operation shall be clearly understood; in addition its operational condition shall be fully taken into account.

10. Whoever is in charge of a navigational watch shall not be assigned or undertake any duties which would interfere with the safe navigation of the ship.

LOOK-OUT

11. Every ship shall at all times maintain a proper look-out by sight and hearing as well as by all available means appropriate in the prevailing circumstances and conditions so as to make a full appraisal of the situation and of the risk of collision, stranding and other hazards to navigation. Additionally, the duties of the look-out shall include the detection of ships or aircraft in distress, shipwrecked persons, wrecks and debris. In applying these principles the following shall be observed:

(a) whoever is keeping a look-out must be able to give full attention to that task and no duties shall be assigned or undertaken which would interfere with the keeping of a proper look-out;

(b) the duties of the person on look-out and helmsman are separate and the helmsman should not be considered the person on look-out while steering; except in small vessels where an unobstructed all round view is provided at the steering position and there is no impairment of night vision or other impediment to the keeping of a proper look-out;

(c) there may be circumstances in which the officer of the watch can safely be the sole look-out in daylight. However, this practice shall only be followed after the situation has been carefully assessed on each occasion and it has been established without doubt that it is safe to do so. Full account shall be taken of all relevant factors including but not limited to the state of weather, conditions of visibility, traffic density, proximity of navigational hazards and if navigating in or near a traffic separation scheme. Assistance must be summoned to the bridge when any change in the situation necessitates this and such assistance must be immediately available.

NAVIGATION WITH PILOT EMBARKED

12. Despite the duties and obligations of a pilot, his presence on board does not relieve the master or officer in charge of the watch from their duties and obligations for the safety of the ship. The master and the pilot shall exchange information regarding navigation procedures, local conditions and the ship's characteristics.

PROTECTION OF THE MARINE ENVIRONMENT

13. The master and officer in charge of the watch shall be aware of the serious effects of operational or accidental pollution of the marine environment and shall take all possible precautions to prevent such pollution particularly within the existing framework of existing international regulations.

SECTION II

OPERATIONAL GUIDANCE FOR OFFICERS IN CHARGE OF A NAVIGATIONAL WATCH

INTRODUCTION

1. This Section contains operational guidance of general application for officers in charge of a navigational watch, which masters are expected to supplement as appropriate. It is essential that officers of the watch appreciate that the efficient performance of their duties is necessary in the interest of safety of life and property at sea and the avoidance of pollution of the marine environment.

GENERAL

2. The officer of the watch is the master's representative and his primary responsibility at all times is the safe navigation of the vessel. He must at all times comply with the applicable regulations for preventing collisions at sea (see also paragraphs 23 and 24).

3. The officer of the watch should keep his watch on the bridge which he should in no circumstances leave until properly relieved. It is of especial importance that at all times the officer of the watch ensures that an efficient look-out is maintained. In a vessel with a separate chart room the officer of the watch may visit this, when essential, for a short period for the necessary performance of his navigational duties, but he should previously satisfy himself that it is safe to do so and ensure that an efficient look-out is maintained.

4. There may be circumstances in which the officer of the watch can safely be the sole look-out in daylight. However, this practice shall only be followed after the situation has been carefully assessed on each occasion and it has been established without doubt that it is safe to do so. Full account shall be taken of all relevant factors including but not limited to the state of weather, conditions of visibility, traffic density, proximity of navigational hazards and if navigating in or near a traffic separation scheme.

When the officer of the watch is acting as the sole look-out he must not hesitate to summon assistance to the bridge, and when for any reason he is unable to give his undivided attention to the look-out such assistance must be immediately available.

5. The officer of the watch should bear in mind that the engines are at his disposal and he should not hesitate to use them in case of need. However, timely notice of intended variations of engine speed should be given when possible. He should also keep prominently in mind the manoeuvring capabilities of his ship including its stopping distance.

6. The officer of the watch should also bear in mind that the sound signalling apparatus is at his disposal and he should not hesitate to use it in accordance with the applicable regulations for preventing collisions at sea.

7. The officer of the watch continues to be responsible for the safe navigation of the vessel despite the presence of the master on the bridge until the master informs him specifically that he has assumed responsibility and this is mutually understood.

TAKING OVER THE WATCH

8. The officer of the watch should not hand over the watch to the relieving officer if he has any reason to believe that the latter is apparently under any disability which would preclude him from carrying out his duties effectively. If in doubt, the officer of the watch should inform the master accordingly. The relieving officer of the watch should ensure that members of his watch are apparently fully capable of performing their duties and in particular the adjustment to night vision.

9. The relieving officer should not take over the watch until his vision is fully adjusted to the light conditions and he has personally satisfied himself regarding:

(a) standing orders and other special instructions of the master relating to the navigation of the vessel;

(b) the position, course, speed and draught of the vessel;

(c) prevailing and predicted tides, currents, weather, visibility and the effect of these factors upon course and speed;

(d) the navigational situation including but not limited to the following:

    (i) the operational condition of all navigational and safety equipment being used or likely to be used during the watch;

    (ii) errors of gyro and magnetic compasses;

    (iii) the presence and movement of vessels in sight or known to be in the vicinity;

    (iv) conditions and hazards likely to be encountered during his watch;

    (v) the possible effects of heel, trim, water density and squat on underkeel clearance.

10. If at the time the officer of the watch is to be relieved a manoeuvre or other action to avoid any hazard is taking place, the relief of the officer should be deferred until such action is completed.

PERIODIC CHECKS OF NAVIGATIONAL EQUIPMENT

11. The officer of the watch should make regular checks to ensure that:

(a) the helmsman or the automatic pilot is steering the correct course;

(b) the standard compass error is established at least once a watch and when possible, after any major alteration of course. The standard and the gyro compasses should be frequently compared; repeaters should be synchronized with their master compass;

(c) the automatic pilot is tested in the manual position at least once a watch;

(d) the navigation and signal lights and other navigational equipment are functioning properly.

AUTOMATIC PILOT

12. Officers of the watch should bear in mind the need to station the helmsman and to put the steering into manual control in good time to allow any potentially hazardous situation to be dealt with in a safe manner. With a vessel under automatic steering it is highly dangerous to allow a situation to develop to the point where the officer of the watch is without assistance and has to break the continuity of the look-out in order to take emergency action. The change-over from automatic to manual steering and vice versa should be made by, or under the supervision of, a responsible officer.

ELECTRONIC NAVIGATIONAL AIDS

13. The officer of the watch should be thoroughly familiar with the use of electronic navigational aids carried, including their capabilities and limitations.

ECHO-SOUNDER

14. The echo-sounder is a valuable navigational aid and should be used whenever appropriate.

NAVIGATIONAL RECORDS

15. A proper record of the movements and activities of the vessel should be kept during the watch.

RADAR

16. The officer of the watch should use the radar when appropriate and whenever restricted visibility is encountered or expected and at all times in congested waters having due regard to its limitations.

17. Whenever radar is in use, the officer of the watch should select an appropriate range scale, observe the display carefully and plot effectively.

18. The officer of the watch should ensure that range scales employed are changed at sufficiently frequent intervals so that echoes are detected as early as possible and that small or poor echoes do not escape detection.

19. The officer of the watch should ensure that plotting or systematic analysis is commenced in ample time, remembering that sufficient time can be made available by reducing speed if necessary.

20. In clear weather, whenever possible, the officer of the watch should carry out radar practice.

NAVIGATION IN COASTAL WATERS

21. The largest scale chart on board, suitable for the area and corrected with the latest available information, should be used. Fixes should be taken at frequent intervals; whenever circumstances allow, fixing should be carried out by more than one method.

22. The officer of the watch should positively identify all relevant navigation marks.

CLEAR WEATHER

23. The officer of the watch should take frequent and accurate compass bearings of approaching vessels as a means of early detection of risk of collision; such risk may sometimes exist even when an appreciable bearing change is evident, particularly when approaching a very large vessel or a tow or when approaching a vessel at close range. He should also take early and positive action in compliance with the applicable regulations for preventing collisions at sea and subsequently check that such action is having the desired effect.

RESTRICTED VISIBILITY

24. When restricted visibility is encountered or suspected, the first responsibility of the officer of the watch is to comply with the relevant rules of the applicable regulations for preventing collisions at sea, with particular regard to the soundings of fog signals, proceeding at a speed and he shall have the engines ready for immediate manoeuvres. In addition, he should:

(a) inform the master (see paragraph 25);

(b) post look-out(s) and helmsman and, in congested waters, revert to hand steering immediately;

(c) exhibit navigation lights;

(d) operate and use the radar.

It is important that the officer of the watch should have the manoeuvring capabilities including the "stopping distance" of his own vessel prominently in mind.

CALLING THE MASTER

25. The officer of the watch should notify the master immediately under the following circumstances:

(a) if restricted visibility is encountered or suspected;

(b) if the traffic conditions or the movements of other vessels are causing concern;

(c) if difficulty is experienced in maintaining course;

(d) on failure to sight land, a navigation mark or to obtain soundings by the expected time;

(e) if land or a navigation mark is sighted or a change in soundings occurs unexpectedly;

(f) on the breakdown of the engines, steering gear or any essential navigational equipment;

(g) in heavy weather if in any doubt about the possibility of weather damage;

(h) in any other emergency or situation in which he is in any doubt.

Despite the requirement to notify the master immediately in the foregoing circumstances, the officer of the watch should in addition not hesitate to take immediate action for the safety of the ship, where circumstances so require.

NAVIGATION WITH PILOT EMBARKED

26. Despite the duties and obligations of a pilot, his presence on board does not relieve the officer of the watch from his duties and obligations for the safety of the ship. He should co-operate closely with the pilot and maintain an accurate check on the vessel's positions and movements. If he is in any doubt as to the pilot's actions or intentions, he should seek clarification from the pilot and if doubt still exists he should notify the master immediately and take whatever action is necessary before the master arrives.

THE WATCHKEEPING PERSONNEL

27. The officer of the watch should give the watchkeeping personnel all appropriate instructions and information which will ensure the keeping of a safe watch including an appropriate look-out.

SHIP AT ANCHOR

28. If the master considers it necessary a continuous navigational watch should be maintained. In all circumstances, however, the officer of the watch should:

(a) determine and plot the ship's position on the appropriate chart as soon as practicable and at sufficiently frequent intervals check when circumstances permit, by taking bearings of fixed navigational marks or readily identifiable shore objects, whether the ship is remaining securely at anchor;

(b) ensure that an efficient look-out is maintained;

(c) ensure that inspection rounds of the vessel are made periodically;

(d) observe meteorological and tidal conditions and the state of the sea;

(e) notify the master and undertake all necessary measures if the vessel drags the anchor;

(f) ensure that the state of readiness of the main engines and other machinery is in accordance with the master's instructions;

(g) if visibility deteriorates notify the master and comply with the applicable regulations for preventing collisions at sea;

(h) ensure that the vessel exhibits the appropriate lights and shapes and that appropriate sound signals are made at all times;

(i) take measures to protect the environment from pollution by the ship and comply with the applicable pollution regulations.

ACKNOWLEDGEMENTS

State of Sea photographs from "Marine Observer's Handbook".

Extracts from Admiralty Tide Tables.

Diagrams showing some tracks followed by tropical revolving storms from "Meteorology for Mariners".
>> Reproduced by kind permission of H.M. Stationery Office.

>> Sea Ice Photographs.
>> Reproduced by kind permission of British Antarctic Survey,
>> Paul Popper Limited, and the Scott Polar Research Institute.

Tables for Harmonic Tidal Predictions.
>> Reproduced by kind permission of the Dutch Minister of Defence.

Extracts from "Ships' Routeing" and "Supplement".
Extracts from "Navigational Watchkeeping".
>> Reprinted by kind permission of the Inter-Governmental
>> Maritime Consultative Organisation.

We would also like to acknowledge the very kind help given to us in the production of this book by:

Dr. Terence Armstrong, Scott Polar Research Institute.

Marine Superintendent, The Meteorological Office.

Chief Inspector, H.M. Coast Guard.

Captain G. G. Watkins, City of London Polytechnic.

In addition to those mentioned above, very many people assisted with the 1st and 2nd Editions of the Ocean Navigator. Their work has often been retained, at least in part, in this 3rd Edition and their continuing contribution is gratefully acknowledged.

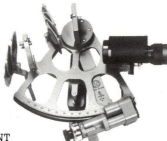

...the front cover

NP 131

CATALOGUE of ADMIRALTY CHARTS
AND OTHER HYDROGRAPHIC PUBLICATIONS

IMPORTANT

Information for the correction of Admiralty Charts and Hydrographic Publications

In the interests of navigation, mariners and others are invited to forward to Hydrographer of the Navy, address as below, any information that may come to their notice which would be useful for the correction of Admiralty Charts and other Hydrographic Publications. Early advice, with all available particulars of newly-discovered dangers, the establishment of, or changes in, any aids to navigation, is specially requested.

Copies of forms (H102 & H102a) on which to render information appear at the back of the Weekly Editions of Admiralty Notices to Mariners. Additional copies can be obtained free of charge from

Hydrographer of the Navy,
Hydrographic Department,
Ministry of Defence,
Taunton, Somerset TA1 2DN

or from any of the Admiralty Chart Agents listed on pages 2 and 3 of this catalogue.

This catalogue is corrected to the 12th September, 1976. Subsequent amendments will be found in the Admiralty Notices to Mariners. The next edition of this catalogue will be published in 1978

Price £3·65 net

TAUNTON. 1977

Published by HYDROGRAPHER OF THE NAVY.

To be obtained from the Agents for the sale of Admiralty charts.

© Crown Copyright 1977

...the back up

EVERY CHART AND PUBLICATION LISTED AND AVAILABLE IN THIS CATALOGUE MAY BE OBTAINED FROM

J.D. POTTER LIMITED

SERVING THE WORLD OF NAVIGATION SINCE 1830

145 Minories London EC3 1NH Tel: 01-709 9076 (Cables Adcharts London) Telex 887386·24 hour Telephone system